9th Conferencia Iberoamericana en Software Engineering (CIbSE 2006)

La Plata, Argentina
24 – 28 April 2006

Editors:

Jaelson Castro
Luca Cernuzzi
Silvia Gordillo

ISBN: 978-1-5108-4100-0

Printed from e-media with permission by:

Curran Associates, Inc.
57 Morehouse Lane
Red Hook, NY 12571

Some format issues inherent in the e-media version may also appear in this print version.

Printed by Curran Associates, Inc. (2017)

CIbSE - IberoAmerican Conference on Software Engineering
c/o Luca Cernuzzi
Universidad Católica "Nuestra Seóra de la Asunción",
Campus Universitario, Asunción
Barrio Santa Ana, C.C.1683, C.P. 1364
Asunción - Paraguay

Phone: +595 21 334650
Fax: +595 21 310587

lcernuzz@uca.edu.py

Additional copies of this publication are available from:

Curran Associates, Inc.
57 Morehouse Lane
Red Hook, NY 12571 USA
Phone: 845-758-0400
Fax: 845-758-2633
Email: curran@proceedings.com
Web: www.proceedings.com

Actas

IDEAS'06

9º Workshop Iberoamericano de Ingeniería de Requisitos y Ambientes de Software

24 al 28 de Abril de 2006
La Plata, Argentina

Editores

Jaelson Castro
Luca Cernuzzi
Silvia Gordillo

Actas del 9º Workshop Iberoamericano de Ingeniería de Requisitos y Ambientes de Software IDEAS'06

PRÓLOGO

El presente volumen contiene los trabajos aceptados y presentados en el IX Workshop Iberoamericano de Ingeniería de Requisitos y Ambientes de Software – IDEAS 06 celebrado en la ciudad de La Plata, Argentina, del 24 al 28 de Abril de 2006.

Muy brevemente quisiéramos mencionar los números y recordar los pasos que dimos juntos para el proceso de evaluación.
Originalmente se han postulado 107 resúmenes que finalmente han resultado en la postulación de 100 artículos. Cada articulo ha sido asignado a 3 revisores y se han discutido las eventuales discrepancias con respecto a un mismo articulo para alcanzar, donde fuera posible, un consenso. Finalmente, en la difícil decisión de aceptación/rechazo hemos adoptado el criterio de aceptar como artículos todos y solo aquellos que obtuvieron un promedio y un promedio ponderado (considerando el nivel de experiencia del evaluador) igual o superior a 4.5 sobre 7; para una sesión especial se han aceptado adicionalmente, en calidad de poster, aquellos artículos que obtuvieron un promedio y un promedio ponderado igual o superior a 4 sobre 7.
Así, el resultado final ha sido que de los 100 artículos originalmente postulados, 33 han sido aceptados para su presentación integral y otros 8 para su presentación como poster.

Consideramos que el nivel de postulación es síntoma de un creciente interés por el workshop y nos hace pensar que él mismo se está afianzando cada vez más como un foro importante de Ingeniería de Software (en términos amplios) para Ibero América. Al mismo tiempo, el porcentaje de aceptación indica un nivel de exigencia interesante para la realidad Iberoamericana que puede ayudar a posicionar mayormente el workshop para obtener un mayor reconocimiento en las calificaciones de los autores en sus respectivos países.

Evidentemente, todo esto no hubiera sido posible sin la valiosa colaboración de distintos actores a quien van nuestros más sinceros agradecimientos. Entre ellos, cabe mencionar a los autores por su esfuerzo en investigación, los revisores, ya sean miembros del comité de programa o adicionales, que han tenido que cumplir un esfuerzo particularmente intenso por la cantidad de postulaciones y el proceso adoptado, los miembros del comité organizador, los disertantes de los tutoriales, el comité de conducción de

IDEAS y todas las demás personas que de distintas formas han colaborado a que este evento pueda ser un ocasión importante para la comunidad científica en nuestra región.

Esperamos puedan disfrutar de IDEAS 06 así como de la calida acogida de La Plata.

Silvia Gordillo	**Jaelson Castro**	**LucaCernuzzi**
Presidente Conferencia	Co-Pte. Comité de Programa	Co-Pte. Comité de Programa

Comité de Programa

Presidencia de la Conferencia

Silvia Gordillo, Universidad Nacional de La Plata, Argentina

Co-Presidentes del Comité de Programa

Jaelson Castro , Universidad Federal do Pernabuco, Brasil
Luca Cernuzzi, Universidad Católica "Nuestra Señora de la Asunción", Paraguay

Miembros del Comité de Programa

Amador Duran, U. Servilla, España
Alexandre Vasconcelos, U.F. Pernambuco,Brasil
Antonio Brogi, U. de Pisa, Italia
Antonio Vallecillo, U. de Málaga, España
Carme Quer, U. P. de Catalunya, España
Cecilia Bastarrica, U. de Chile, Chile
Daniel Riesco, U. de San Luis, Argentina
Ernesto Cuadros, UNAS, Perú
Ernesto Pimentel, U. de Málaga, España
Francisco Ruiz, U. Castilla de la Mancha, España
Guilherme H. Travassos, UFRJ, Brasil
Hernán Astudillo, UTFSM, Chile
Joao Falcão e Cunha, U.do Porto, Portugal
João Araújo, U. Nova de Lisboa, Portugal
José Carlos Maldonado, U. de São Paulo, Brasil
Júlio Leite, PUC-Rio, Brasil
Luis Olsina, U. Nacional de La Pampa, Argentina
Marcelo Campo, UNICEN, Argentina
Marcelo Frias, UBA, Argentina
Mario Piattini, U. Castilla-La Mancha, España
Miguel Katrib, U. de La Habana, Cuba
Óscar Pastor, U. Politécnica de Valencia, España
Pere Botella, U. Politécnica de Catalunya, España
Raúl Monje, UTFSM, Chile
Ricardo de A. Falbo, UFES, Brasil
Tereza Kirker, UNIMEP, Brazil
Xavier Franch, U. P. de Catalunya, España

Revisores adicionales

Gabriel Infante-López - UBA, Argentina
Diego Garbervetsky – UBA, Argentina
Carlos Lopez Pombo - UBA, Argentina
Nazareno Aguirre – UBA, Argentina
Juan Pablo Galeotti – UBA, Argentina
Alejandro Vaisman – UBA, Argentina
Silvia Gordillo – U. Nacional de La Plata, Argentina
Gustavo Rossi - U. Nacional de La Plata, Argentina
Claudia Pons - U. Nacional de La Plata, Argentina
Maria de los Angeles Martín - U. Nacional de La Pampa, Argentina
Hernán Molina - U. Nacional de La Pampa, Argentina
Guillermo Covella - U. Nacional de La Pampa, Argentina
Rodrigo de Oliveira Spinola - UFRJ, Brazil
Marco Pereira Araujo - UFRJ, Brazil
Wladmir Araujo Chapetta – UFRJ, Brazil
Tayana Uchoa Conte – UFRJ, Brazil
Ana Candida Cruz Natali - UFRJ, Brazil
Jobson Massolar da Silva - UFRJ, Brazil
Paula Gomes Mian - UFRJ, Brazil
Carla Silva - UFPE, Brazil
Alex Sandro Gomes – UFPE, Brazil
Sandro Ronaldo Bezerra – UFPE, Brazil
Fernanda Ma. R. Alencar – UFPE, Brazil
Regiane Andrade Brito – UFPE, Brazil
Carlos Menezes de Albuquerque – UFPE, Brazil
Carina Alves – UFPE, Brazil
Thaizel Fuentes - U. de La Habana, Cuba
Abel Marrero - U. de La Habana, Cuba
Marcello Visconti - Universidad Técnico Federico Santa María, Chile
Horst H. von Brand - UTFSM, Chile
Benjamin Piwowarski - U. de Chile, Chile
Sara Corfini – U. de Pisa, Italy
Razvan Popescu - U. de Pisa, Italy
Massimo Cossentino - ICAR – CNR, Italy
Enrique Vargas – U. Católica "Nuestra Señora de la Asunción", Paraguay
Vicente González – U. Católica "Nuestra Señora de la Asunción", Paraguay
Magalí González – U. Católica "Nuestra Señora de la Asunción", Paraguay
Alfredo Paz-Valderrama - UNAS, Perú
Percy Pari Salas – UNAS, Perú

Alfredo Paz-Valderrama - UNAS, Perú
Raul Romero - U. de Málaga ,Spain
Nathalie Moreno - U. de Málaga ,Spain
Manuel F. Bertoa - U. de Málaga ,Spain
José Luis Pastrana - U. de Málaga, Spain
Juan Pablo Carvallo - U. Politécnica de Catalunya, Spain
Xavier Burgués - U. Politécnica de Catalunya, Spain
Enric Mayol - U. Politécnica de Catalunya, Spain
Nuria Rodríguez - U. Politécnica de Catalunya, Spain
Tomás Aluja - U. Politécnica de Catalunya, Spain
Emilio Insfrán – U. Politécnica de Valencia, Spain
Vicente Pelechano – U. Politécnica de Valencia, Spain
Hugo Estrada Esquivel - U. Politécnica de Valencia, Spain
Pedro Valderas - U. Politécnica de Valencia, Spain
Javier Muñoz - U. Politécnica de Valencia, Spain
Marta Ruiz - U. Politécnica de Valencia, Spain
Juan Sánchez Díaz - U. Politécnica de Valencia, Spain
Nelly Condori-Fernandez – U. Politécnica de Valencia, Spain
Alicia Martínez Rebollar - U. Politécnica de Valencia, Spain
Silvia Abrahão - U. Politécnica de Valencia, Spain
Victoria Torres - U. Politécnica de Valencia, Spain
Brian Matthews - CCLRC Rutherford Appleton Laboratory
Simon Lambert - CCLRC Rutherford Appleton Laboratory

Comité Organizador

Co-Presidentes del Comité Organizador

Claudia Pons, Universidad Nacional de La Plata, Argentina
Roxana Giandini, Universidad Nacional de La Plata, Argentina

Miembros

Claudia Banchoff, Universidad Nacional de La Plata, Argentina
Gabriela Pérez, Universidad Nacional de La Plata, Argentina
Ileana Carrizo, Universidad Nacional de La Plata, Argentina

Auspicios

Universidad Nacional de La Plata (UNLP)
Sociedad Argentina de Informática (SADIO)
Centro Latinoamericano de Estudios en Informática (CLEI)
Microsoft Argentina

Diseño Gráfico y Comunicación Visual

Axel Hochegger

INDICE

Gap in pagination due to unavailable papers.

Pages 1-6

Sesión 1

Ingeniería de Software 1

Towards Semi-automated Workflow-based Aggregation of Web Services

Antonio Brogi, Razvan Popescu

Computer Science Department, University of Pisa, Italy

Abstract. Service aggregation is one of the main issues in the emerging area of service-oriented computing. The aim of this paper is to contribute to the long-term objective of lifting service aggregation from manual hand-crafting to a semi-automated engineered process. We present a methodology which, given a set of service contracts, tries to construct an aggregation of such services. Service contracts include a description of the service behaviour (expressed by a YAWL workflow), as well as an (ontology-annotated) signature. The core aggregation process basically performs a control-flow and an (ontology-aware) data-flow analysis of a set of YAWL workflows to build the contract of an aggregated service.

1 Introduction

Service-oriented computing [18] is emerging as a new promising computing paradigm that centres on the notion of *service* as the fundamental element for developing software applications. In this scenario, two prominent issues involved in the development of next generation distributed software applications can be roughly synthesised as: (1) discovering available services that can be exploited to build a needed application, and (2) suitably aggregating such services to achieve the desired result. A typical example [16] of the need of aggregating services is a client wishing to make all the arrangements necessary for a trip (flights, hotel, rent-a-car, and so on). Such a client query may not be satisfied by a single service, while it could be satisfied by composing several services. Complex Web service interactions however require more than SOAP, WSDL and UDDI can offer [7], and semi-automatic aggregation frameworks based on such standards are not available yet.

The aim of this paper is to contribute to the long-term objective of lifting service aggregation from manual hand-crafting to a semi-automated engineered process. We present a methodology which, given a set of service contracts, tries to construct an aggregation of such services. Service contracts include a description of the service behaviour (expressed by a YAWL [23] workflow), as well as an (ontology-annotated) signature. The core aggregation process basically performs a control-flow and an (ontology-aware) data-flow analysis of a set of YAWL workflows to build the contract of an aggregated service. Technically, these analyses are defined by first expanding the services' workflows with dummy YAWL flow constructs, and by exploiting ontology-matching mechanisms to perform a semantics-aware data-flow analysis. It is worth noting that the aggregation process is parametric with respect to the type of semantic annotations and the matching mechanism. Namely different ontology-matching mechanisms can be plugged-in (e.g., [4,5,17]), including the "void" one for syntactic matching (matching=identity) in absence of ontological information. The result of the aggregation process is a YAWL workflow which describes the interplay among all the services considered, namely all the control-flow and data-flow relationships among them.

In this paper we will try to focus on the aggregation process, and directly consider the problem of how to aggregate a given set of service contracts. We will not describe here how service contracts can be generated from service implementations. (A thorough analysis of how to transform BPEL [3] specifications into workflows can be found in [26].) We will not describe either how the initial set of services is chosen. We may assume that it has been selected by some matchmaking algorithm in response to some client query. For instance, the composition-oriented matchmaking algorithm in [4] returns a candidate set of services which may collectively satisfy a client query. It is worth observing that the aggregation process is completely separated from the process of selecting the initial set of services. For instance, the latter can be also performed by a user browsing a (semantics-enabled) UDDI registry and selecting some services.

It is worth noting that the proposed aggregation process can accept both black-box and glass-box queries to drive the aggregation. Black-box queries simply specify the sets of inputs and outputs that the aggregated service should request and offer respectively. They are transformed into equivalent (basic) services which are then added to the registry of matched services. Glass-box queries specify instead a process behaviour (i.e., a workflow and not just inputs/outputs) and can be used to check whether it can be aggregated together with a given set of services.

The description of the proposed aggregation process can by synthesised in three main steps: (1) perform control-flow and data-flow analysis on the input services to determine their aggregation, (2) generate the contract of the aggregated service, (3) deploy the aggregated service. We will concentrate on steps (1) and (2) in this paper, and it is worth stressing the importance of separating the phase of contract generation from the deployment of the aggregated service, thus allowing multiple deployments of the latter.

2 Aggregation Framework

2.1 Service Contracts

We consider services that are described by *contracts* [13], and we argue that contracts should in general include different types of information: (a) **Ontology-annotated signatures**, (b) **Behaviour**, and (c) **Extra-functional properties**. Following [16], we argue that WSDL signatures should be enriched with ontological information (e.g., expressed with OWL [10] or WSDL-S [15]) to describe the semantics of services, necessary to automatise the process of overcoming signature mismatches as well as service discovery and composition. Still, the information provided by ontology-annotated signatures is necessary but *not* sufficient to ensure a correct inter-operation of services. Following [13], we argue that contracts should also expose a (possibly partial) description of the interaction protocols of services. Indeed, such information is necessary to ensure a correct inter-operation of services, e.g., to verify absence of locks. We argue that YAWL [23] (see below) is a good candidate to express service behaviour as it has a well-defined formal semantics and it supports a number of workflow patterns. Finally, we argue that service contracts should expose, besides annotated signatures and behaviour, also so-called extra-functional properties, such as performance, reliability, or security. (We will not however consider these properties in this work, and leave their inclusion into the aggregation framework as future work.)

We intend to build an aggregation framework capable of translating the behaviour of a service described using existing process/workflow modelling languages (e.g., BPEL, OWL-S [16], etc.) into equivalent descriptions expressed through an abstract language with a well-defined formal semantics, and vice-versa. An immediate advantage of using such an abstract language is the possibility of developing formal analyses and transformations, independently of the different languages used by providers to describe the behaviour of their services. We consider that YAWL [23] is a promising candidate to be used as an abstract workflow language for describing service behaviour. YAWL is a new proposal of a workflow/business processing system, which supports a concise and powerful workflow language and handles complex data, transformations and Web service integration. YAWL defines twenty most used workflow patterns gathered by a thorough analysis of a number of languages supported by workflow management systems. These workflow patterns are divided in six groups (basic control-flow, advanced branching and synchronisation, structural, multiple instances, state-based, and cancellation).[1] YAWL extends Petri Nets by introducing some workflow patterns (for multiple instances, complex synchronisations, and cancellation) that are not easy to express using (high-level) Petri Nets. Being built on Petri Nets, YAWL is an easy to understand and to use formalism. With respect to process algebras, YAWL features an intuitive (graphical) representation of services through workflow patterns. Furthermore, as illustrated in [22], it is likely that a simple workflow which is troublesome to model for instance in π-calculus may be instead straightforwardly modelled with YAWL. A thorough comparison of workflow modelling with Petri Nets vs. π-calculus may be found in [22]. With respect to the other workflow languages (mainly proposed by industry), YAWL relies on a well-defined formal semantics. Moreover, not being a commercial language, YAWL supporting tools (editor, engine) are freely available.

[1] Space limitations do not allow us to illustrate these patterns. A thorough description of them may be found in [24].

2.2 Aggregation Phases

As mentioned in the Introduction, a prerequisite of our framework is the set of services to be aggregated which may be obtained either by manual selection or as output of a service discovery framework.

The semi-automated aggregation framework we propose can be synthesised by the following phases:

0. **Service Translation**. This preliminary phase deals with translating real-world descriptions (e.g., BPEL + semantics, or OWL-S, etc.) of the services to be aggregated into equivalent service contracts using YAWL as an abstract workflow language for expressing behaviour, and OWL for example for expressing the semantic information. One may note that such a translation may be done off-line and hence it is not a burden for the aggregation process. (A thorough analysis of how to transform BPEL specifications into workflow patterns can be found in [26].)
1. **Core Aggregation**. During this phase YAWL processes are expanded with explicit data- and control-flow (dummy) constructs, also called Input/Output Control/Data enabler processes (or ICs/IDs/OCs/ODs for short). We then express the initial control-flow connections in terms of the newly added ICs and OCs. Next, we use data-flow dependencies (i.e., operation and message mapping among the involved parties) provided by an ontology-aware matching algorithm (e.g., [4,5,17]) to derive a data-flow mapping. We express such mapping by suitably linking IDs and ODs.
2. **Contract Generation**. Firstly, we perform a basic check to see whether the aggregated service does not have processes with unsatisfied inputs. Should this be the case, we adequately eliminate unlinked ODs and other redundant dummies introduced by the previous phase, and we cancel redundant control-flow constructs. The ontology-annotated signature and behaviour we obtain form the service contract of the aggregated service. The generated contract can be further analysed (e.g., lock analysis) and optimised.
3. **Service Deployment**. Finally, the aggregated service can be deployed as a real-world Web service (i.e., described using OWL-S, or BPEL + semantics, etc.). Clients will hence see the aggregation as another Web service that can now be discovered and further aggregated with other services. This operation is the inverse of the operation done during the Service Translation phase.

As already mentioned in the Introduction, we will describe phases (1) and (2) in the following, after introducing some definitions.

2.3 Definitions

We shall use the term "service" to denote the YAWL notion of "workflow specification", "process" to denote a YAWL "task" as well as "start" and "end" to denote YAWL "input condition" and "output condition", respectively.

We consider a set or registry of service contracts to be aggregated, where each contract corresponds to an original service implementation (e.g., described with

BPEL and OWL for semantics, etc.). A contract S consists of an ontology-annotated signature (i.e., semantic information, Sem for short) and of a behaviour description (Beh).[2]

Sem specifies the set of processes ($Procs$) as well as the name ($Sname$) and the type ($Stype$) of the service. Indeed we argue that services, processes as well as parameters (i.e., messages) should be annotated with ontological information describing their types. Such information can be used by discovery frameworks to better match services. For example, considering ontologies for services, processes and parameters, we may have for example a "stock_quote" service type, a "flight_reservation" process type, or a "notebook_computer" parameter type, and so on. $Procs$ consists of the m processes of S together with $start$ and end, which are two special dummy processes used to mark the entry end exit points, respectively, of S. A process P contains the sets of input (I) and output (O) parameters, its name ($Pname$) and type ($Ptype$). Similarly to services and processes, a parameter exposes its name ($Iname$) and type ($Itype$). Note that the matching concerns types — rather than names — of parameters, processes or services[3]. Name matching should be employed in absence of ontology-annotations. The $start$ and end dummy processes are defined similarly to the other processes P yet they do not have IOs and ontological values associated. They are named "$DummyStart\ of\ P$" and "$DummyEnd\ of\ P$", respectively.

Beh contains information about both the control-flow constructs used by processes in $Procs$ (PC), as well as information about the control-flow dependencies among such processes (PD). PC associates one join and one split construct to each process P. A join or split control construct may be one of the following: AND, OR, XOR, or EMPTY. Intuitively, the join specifies "how many" processes before P are to be terminated in order to execute P, while the split construct specifies "how many" processes following P are to be executed. The EMPTY join (split) is used when *at most one* process execution precedes (follows, respectively) the execution of P. PD defines the control-flow of S by means of a set of process pairs. A pair $< P, Q >$ specifies that P must be executed before process Q (i.e., Q may begin its execution provided P has finished its execution).

Consider the following example which will be used as a basis for presenting the applicability of our methodology, and for enhancing the description of the proposed approach. A youngster passionate about winter sports and computer science, decides to publish on her homepage a Web service providing information on the conditions of her favourite slope. Basically, she wishes that other winter sports enthusiasts like her may access her page in order to see whether the slope is practicable and the cabin is working.

[2] When necessary, indexes shall be used for disambiguation.

[3] Roughly, service matching may restrict the set of services to be considered, while process matching may help refining further the selection (e.g., matching a "computer_selling" process of an "e_shop" service) to possibly aggregate sub-services rather than whole services. Finally, parameter matching can provide the data-flow information necessary to achieve the aggregation.

One may assume that she locates the ontologically-enriched WR^4 service (see Figure 1[5]) from a (semantically anotated) UDDI registry. Next, she feeds this service as a black-box query to a discovery framework (e.g., [9] or [5]). This may lead to selecting the other two services in Figure 1.

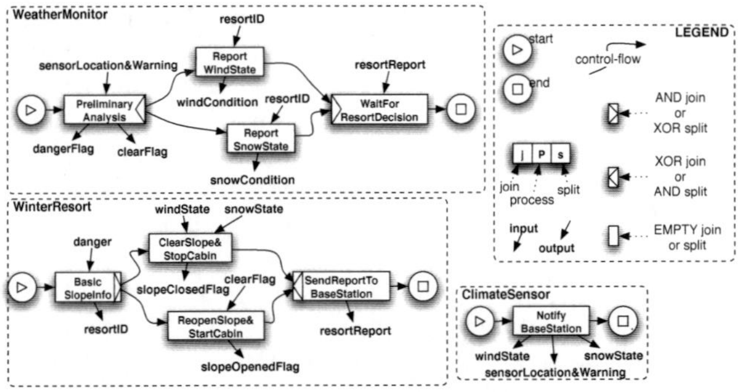

Fig. 1. Example registry with three services to be aggregated.

It is important to note that the example is not supposed to present a software masterpiece as we would like to underline the fact that different services written by different persons with different programming styles and backgrounds may present (aggregation) issues. It is likely that the selected services do not match perfectly, or that the ensemble is not optimal, and so on. Redundancies (e.g., redundant outputs) may occur as well. The three services are as follows:

CS basically gathers data from sensors located on top of the mountain. Upon invocation, it executes process NBS which outputs the sensor's location and the warning level for the slope it is monitoring sLW, as well as the snow's condition sS (e.g., indication of avalanche danger) and the wind's condition wS (e.g., strong wind leads to stopping the cabin). We may assume that CS runs periodically (e.g., every hour).

WM (or *BaseStation*) centralises data gathered from various CSs. It firstly performs a preliminary analysis (e.g., reasoning based on a history record over the past X years) through the execution of PA. On the one hand it specifies whether there is an avalanche danger by enabling dF or, on the other hand whether the slope is safe (e.g., it may be (re)opened). In the latter case cF is enabled. The AND split of PA indicates that *both* RWS and RSS are to be executed after it. RWS makes its own prediction on the wind state based on the rID input. Similarly, RSS sets the snow state based on its prediction. The AND join construct of WRD states that WRD may be executed provided *both* RWS and RSS finished execution. WRD is in charge of waiting for a report from a

[4] Due to space limitations, we shall use abbreviations throughout the paper (e.g., WR instead of $WinterResort$).

[5] In addition to the representation of YAWL tasks (i.e., processes) we graphically describe their parameters as well.

WR service (i.e., the decision of the latter on whether to close or to (re)open the slope).

WR is a service that manages access to a slope and cabin. From a workflow point of view, WR behaves differently from WM in the way that it uses a XOR split in the BSI process and a XOR join in the $SRBS$ process. The former indicates that *either* $CSSC$ *or* $RSSC$ will be activated for execution, while the latter indicates that $SRBS$ will be invoked after each execution of *either* $CSSC$ *or* $RSSC$. BSI inputs the danger flag produced by the WM and it decides either to clear the slope and stop the cabin (by executing the $CSSC$ process), or to (re)open the slope and (re)start the cabin (by executing the $RSSC$ process). Finally, $SRBS$ sends a report to the WM service with its decision.

2.4 Core Aggregation

During this phase, all processes (except *start* and *end* ones) are expanded with explicit control- and data-flow dummies. Then, a control-flow analysis expresses the initial flow dependencies in terms of the newly added dummies. Last but not least, a data-flow analysis coordinates processes of (possibly) different services by taking into account a given data-flow mapping. The three steps are detailed hereafter.

PROCESS EXPANSION

Let us consider the empty (aggregated) service A. For each process P of each service S, we generate the following five dummy processes:

- P^* corresponding to process P "stripped off" its join and split control constructs, and augmented with AND join and split constructs,
- an Input Control enabler IC_P which inherits the initial join of P,
- an Output Control enabler OC_P which inherits the initial split of P,
- an Input Data enabler ID_P which is in charge of gathering all inputs needed for the execution of P (if P has at least one input), as well as
- an Output Data enabler OD_P which "offers" all outputs of P to other processes (if P has at least one output).

With the exception of P^*, all such processes lack IOs and ontological values. Their purpose is to explicitly separate the control- and data-flow logic of P. From a control-flow point of view, IC_P and ID_P are linked as inputs of P^* while OC_P and OD_P are linked as outputs. All added dummies as well as the corresponding dependencies have to be added to Beh_A.

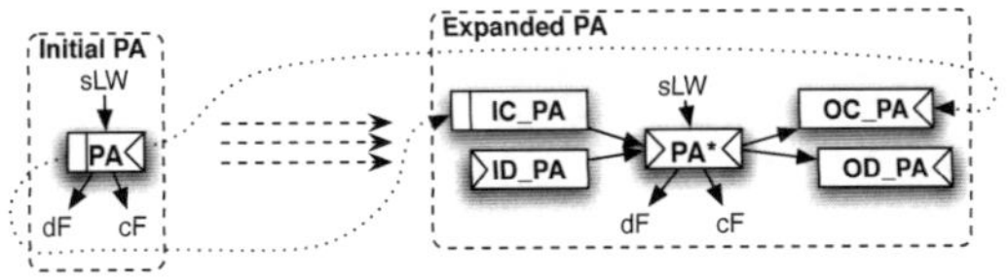

Fig. 2. Expansion of PA.

Figure 2 describes the process expansion step applied to process PA of service WM. As one may note, PA^* employs AND join and split constructs as, on the one hand, both IC_PA and ID_PA have to finish execution before executing PA^* and, on the other hand, both OC_PA and OD_PA are to be executed after PA^* terminates. From a data-flow point of view, the AND join of ID_PA indicates that all inputs of PA must be available in order to execute PA. Dually, the AND split of OD_PA specifies that after PA finishes its execution, all its outputs will be available to all processes requesting at least one of them as input.

Once all processes have been expanded, two more processes are introduced. They are IC_A and OC_A corresponding to the input and the output control enabler dummies of A. IC_A has an AND split in order to activate ICs of all services to be aggregated. Dually, OC_A has an AND join in order to wait for OCs of all services to finish execution. Links from $start\_A$ to IC_A as well as from OC_A to end_A are added to Beh_A.

Control-Flow Analysis

During this step, control-flow dependencies of each service S are specified in terms of the newly added ICs and OCs, as well as IC_A and OC_A, and then added to Beh_A. The result of applying this step on the WM service may be seen in Figure 3.[6]

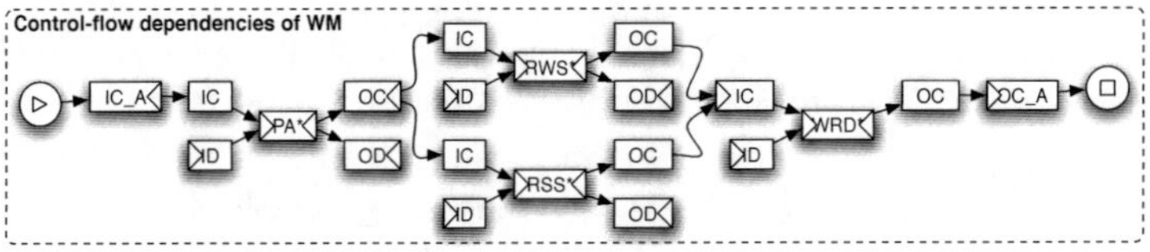

Fig. 3. Control-flow analysis for WM.

For example, the initial link between PA and RWS has been translated to a link between OC_PA and IC_RWS. Moreover, one should note that $start\_WM$ and end_WM are now connected to IC_A and OC_A respectively. That is, IC_A enables (from the control-flow point of view) IC_PA for execution. Dually, OC_WRD is connected to OC_A and hence (from the control-flow point of view) its execution is to be interpreted as the termination of WM.

Data-Flow Analysis

In order to derive data-flow information linking processes of (possibly) different services, one has to match requested inputs with offered outputs. Our flexible methodology allows for an ontology-based matching algorithm (e.g., [17,5]) to be plugged-in. "An input i of process P matches an output o of process Q if and only if $Itype_i$ is in an *exact* or *subsumes* relation with $Otype_o$". Dually, "an output o of process Q matches an input i of process P if and only if $Otype_o$ is in an *exact* or *plug-in* relation with $Itype_i$". One should note that the notion of "match" used in this paper is in line with the one defined in [17,16]. We shall call such a match a *data-flow dependency* and a set of them as *data-flow mapping*.

[6] All enabler dummies shall be abbreviated in figures from now onwards (e.g., IC instead of IC_PA, and so on).

From a data-flow point of view, a process P must have all its inputs available in order to be executable. In this paper we assume that such data-flow dependencies are provided by the matching framework. A maximal such mapping can be obtained by employing a one-to-one matching between all process parameters of the services to be aggregated. One should note that the user should be allowed to modify, cancel or add dependencies in the mapping. A data-flow mapping can be expressed in terms of IDs and ODs as follows. If input x of process P matches output(s) y of process(es) Q then we generate the following:

1. A dummy process P_x[7] with no IOs or ontological value. However, it is important to note that such a dummy employs a XOR join and an EMPTY split. This is due to the fact that values for x may be obtained from different ys, yet only one is needed. Furthermore, a link from P_x to ID_P is added to Beh_A.
2. A link from OD_Q to P_x which is added to Beh_A for every matched y.

Figure 4 illustrates the data-flow mapping for our example. Due to space issues, P_x dummy names will be abbreviated to x in figures from now onwards. One should note that the CS service is not depicted as its only process (NBS) does not have inputs.

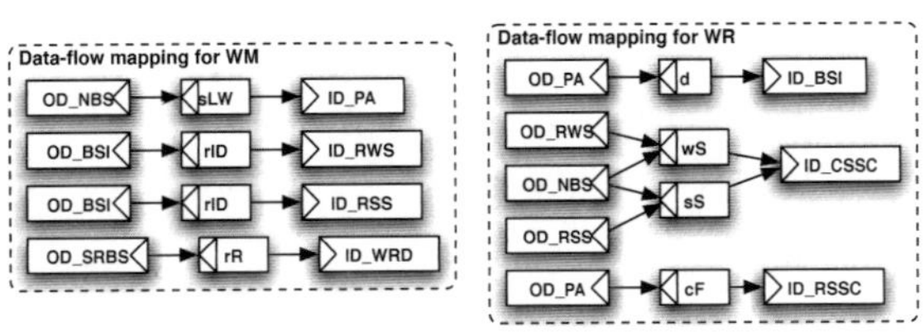

Fig. 4. Data-flow analysis for our example.

2.5 Contract Generation

During this phase, the algorithm employs an input-driven basic check and then it cleans the aggregated service A of redundant constructs.

BASIC VALIDATION

We firstly assume that all services are "well defined" in the sense that each initial process P has at least one incoming link (with the exception of "*start*") and at least one outgoing link (with the exception of "*end*"). This means that each IC has at least one incoming link, and that each OC has at least one outgoing link. At this point one may encounter two situations:

- All processes P have their inputs satisfied. In other words, every input x of P has been matched with at least one output y of a process Q. This translates to the fact that the P_x dummy process has at least one incoming

[7] For simplicity we assume here that all P_x are unique.

link. Should this be the case, we say that the aggregation is successful — in the way that there are no unsatisfied data- (and control-) flow constraints.
- At least one process P is missing some inputs. In other words there exists an input x of P which has not been matched to any output(s) y of process(es) Q. This translates to the fact that the P_x dummy process has no incoming links. Should this be the case, we say that the aggregation has not succeeded — in the way that there is at least one unsatisfied data-flow constraint. The (additional) missing inputs must be provided by other services, hence either a refined query can be launched or the needed services can be manually added to the set of services to be aggregated.

We chose to consider as valid such a "closed" workflow (i.e., without unsatisfied inputs) in order to enforce a necessary yet not sufficient condition for the execution of (all) processes. Given a valid service contract, one may use analysis tools in order to verify (dead-)lock freedom for example. As YAWL is built upon Petri Nets (PN), analysis tools for the latter can be exploited to check properties of PN translations of the former. For example WofYAWL [25] is an analysis tool for YAWL workflows. WofYAWL maps an input YAWL workflow into a PN with inhibitor arcs, and then analyses semi-positive transitions in the short-circuited net. If the net is bound, it performs a relaxed soundness check in the regular net. Finally the results are mapped back into a YAWL workflow, possibly annotating the output with warnings (e.g., in the case of unbounded nets). Figure 5 describes the aggregation contract we have obtained so far for our example.[8] One should note that all ICs (e.g., IC_PA and so on) have at least one incoming link, as well as, all OCs (e.g., OC_PA and so on) have at least one outgoing link. Moreover, all process with the exception of OD_CSSC and OD_RSSC have at least one incoming and one outgoing link. We can say that the aggregation is successful as there are no unsatisfied data- (or control-) flow constraints.

Eliminating Redundancies

As one may have noted, not all dummy constructs introduced during the **Core Aggregation** phase are necessary. Given the aggregated service is valid, we can (repeatedly) eliminate redundant items, that is, dummies and join/split constructs. One obtains at the end of this step the final service contract of A. We hereafter describe three elimination criteria.

Dummy absorption. Assume a dummy (i.e., control or data process enabler, or process added during the data-flow analysis) iD connected as input of another process P such that the pair $< join_{iD}, join_P >$ is one of the following – $\{< EMPTY, EMPTY >, < EMPTY, \alpha >, < \alpha, \alpha >\}$ –, where $\alpha \in \{AND, XOR, OR\}$. Then, we "absorb" iD into P which remains unchanged. If $< join_{iD}, join_P >$ is $< \alpha, EMPTY >$ then we absorb iD into P with the observation that P inherits the join of iD (i.e., $join_P := join_{iD}$). The scenario is dual

[8] Due to its verbosity we chose not to represent dummies introduced during the Data-Flow step – with the exception of wS and sS. Moreover, the full graphical form of the workflow (i.e., including process parameters and so on) has been omitted.

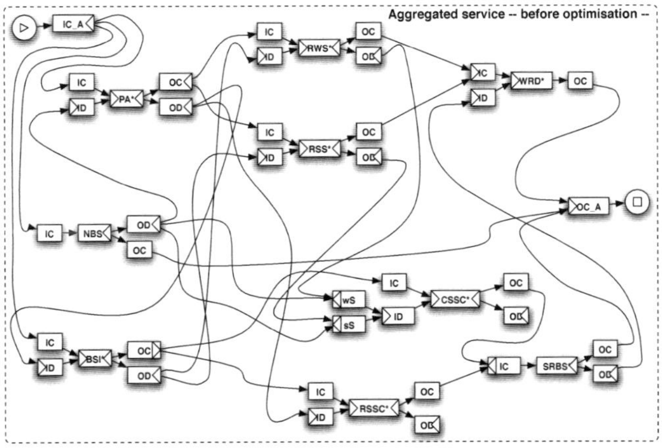

Fig. 5. Service contract A (before eliminating redundancies).

for absorbing output dummies. Absorbing means eliminating iD and updating Beh_A correspondingly.

Dummy elimination. An OD_P employing an EMPTY split construct and that does *not* have at least one outgoing link to other join of an ID_Q can be eliminated together with its corresponding link (from P to OD_P) from Beh_A. One should note that the initial AND split of OD_P should be cancelled first by the following criteria.

Join/Split elimination. A $join_P \neq$ EMPTY has to be set to EMPTY provided P has *only one* incoming link. The dual (i.e., the "reset" of $split_P$ given P has *at most one* outgoing link) is resolved in similar way.

Let us come back to our example. Figure 4 indicates that all dummies introduced during the data-flow analysis are redundant, except for wS (input of $CSSC$) and sS (input of $RSSC$). The redundant joins are cancelled first and then the respective redundant processes are absorbed into IDs and ODs. Moreover, the elimination criteria allow us to cancel almost all dummies introduced during PROCESS EXPANSION with the exception of OD_CSSC, OD_RSSC, and OC_BSI. The former two are tackled by the dummy elimination criterion. The final version of A is given in Figure 6.

3 Concluding Remarks

The aim of this paper is to contribute to the long-term objective of lifting service aggregation from manual handcrafting to a semi-automated engineered process. We have presented the kernel of a semi-automated workflow based aggregation framework of Web services. It consists of a methodology which, given a set of service contracts, tries to construct an aggregation of such services.

We have synthesised three main phases of the proposed aggregation process: (1) *Core Aggregation* – perform control- and data-flow analysis on the input services to determine their aggregation, (2) *Contract Generation* – generate the

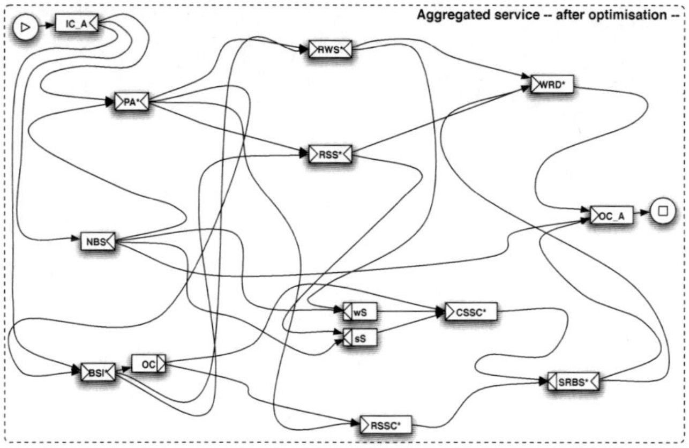

Fig. 6. Final service contract A.

contract of the aggregated service, (3) *Service Deployment* – deploy an implementation of the aggregated service. While we concentrated on steps (1) and (2) in this paper, it is worth stressing the importance of separating the phase of contract generation from the deployment of the aggregated service, which allows multiple deployments of the latter.

The main features of our approach are: (a) It can be used to aggregate services written with different description languages (e.g., BPEL + semantics, OWL-S), (b) It is (semi-)automatic – both with respect to service translation and coordination (core aggregation and contract generation), (c) It allows a seamless integration with service discovery systems (third-party matchmaking frameworks can be straightforwardly plugged in), (d) It supports both black- and glass-box queries (i.e., behaviour-less and behavioural queries), (e) It features compositional aggregation (e.g., the aggregation of A, B, and C can be computed by first aggregating A and B and then aggregating the obtained service with C), and finally (f) It supports multiple deployments of the aggregated service.

Regrettably, space limitations do not allow a thorough discussion of related work (e.g., manual [3,28], semiautomatic [9,12] or fully automatic approaches [2,11,19,20,21,27]). Surveys on Web service composition can be found in [1,6,8,14]. In manual Web service composition the requester acts as the service composer as well. She has to browse the registry, find the desired service operations and model their interactions into a flow structure. Fully automatic composition of services is very difficult to achieve as the requester has to specify all input requirements of registered service operations that make the composite service. Furthermore, processing the request is a very time consuming process. A significant number of fully automatic approaches employ planning techniques. A downside of planning is that both the goal and the status are difficult to represent. Another issue is that all services involved in the composition have to be known a priori. It is however worth observing that, while some of the previously mentioned features ((a) – (f)) are considered in some existing approaches, our approach is the first — at the best of our knowledge — that provides all of them in a single framework.

A key ingredient of our framework is the notion of service contract, which includes a description of the service's behaviour (expressed by a YAWL [23] workflow), as well as an (ontology-annotated) signature. Contracts are the basis for linking services through data-flow dependencies as well as for overcoming signature and behaviour mismatches. They also pave the way for aggregrating services written in different languages and for multiple deployments of the aggregated service.

We are currently developing a proof-of-concept implementation (in Java) of the aggregation methodology described in this paper. Further investigation will be devoted to extend the core aggregation process in order to ensure stronger formal properties of computed aggregations, and to account for the adaptation of signature and behavioural mismatches in contracts. Future work will also be devoted to the development of the semi-automated derivation of contracts from real service implementations (considering first BPEL and OWL-S, and exploiting the techniques described in [26]), and of the service deployment phase (again considering BPEL and OWL-S first).

References

1. W. Aalst, M. Dumas, and A. Hofstede. Web service composition languages: Old wine in new bottles? In *Proceedings of Euromicro '03*, pages 298–307. IEEE Computer Society, 2003.
2. D. Berardi, G. D. Giacomo, M. Lenzerini, M. Mecella, and D. Calvanese. Synthesis of underspecified composite e-services based on automated reasoning. In *ICSOC '04: Proceedings of the 2nd international conference on Service oriented computing*, pages 105–114, New York, NY, USA, 2004. ACM Press.
3. BPEL4WS Coalition. Business Process Execution Language for Web Services (BPEL4WS), 2002. http://www-106.ibm.com/developerworks/webservices/library/ws-bpel/.
4. A. Brogi, S. Corfini, and R. Popescu. Flexible Matchmaking of Web Services Using DAML-S Ontologies. In P. Traverso and S. Weerawarana, editors, *Proceedings of Second International Conference on Service Oriented Computing (ICSOC04 - short papers), IBM Research Report. NY, USA*, pages 30–45, November 15-18 2004.
5. A. Brogi, S. Corfini, and R. Popescu. Composition-oriented Service Discovery. In F. Gschwind, U. Assmann, and O. Nierstrasz, editors, *Proceedings of Software Composition '05, LNCS, vol. 3628*, pages 15–30, 2005.
6. Y. Charif and N. Sabouret. An Overview of Semantic Web Services Composition Approaches. To appear in Proceedings of the International Workshop on Context for Web Services 2005, Elsevier.
7. H.-P. Company. Web Services Concepts – a technical overview. http://www.hpmiddleware.com/downloads/pdf/web_services_tech_overview.pdf. Technical report, 2001.
8. J. Koehler and B. Srivastava. Web Service Composition: Current Solutions and Open Problems. ICAPS Workshop on Planning for Web Services, pp. 28-35, 2003.
9. Q. Liang, L. N. Chakarapani, S. Y. W. Su, R. N. Chikkamagalur, and H. Lam. A Semi-Automatic Approach to Composite Web Services Discovery, Description and Invocation. *International Journal of Web Services Research*, 1(4):64–89, 2004.

10. D. McGuiness and F. van Harmelen (Eds). OWL Web Ontology Language Overview. Web guide, February 2004. http://www.w3.org/TR/owl-features.
11. S. McIlraith and C. T. Son. Adapting Golog for composition of semantic Web services. Proceeding of 8th Conference on Knowledge Representation and Reasoning (KR'02), 2002.
12. B. Medjahed, A. Bouguettaya, and A. K. Elmagarmid. Composing Web services on the Semantic Web. *The VLDB Journal*, 12(4):333–351, 2003.
13. L. Meredith and S. Bjorg. Contracts and types. *CACM*, 46(10), 2003.
14. N. Milanovic and M. Malek. Current Solutions for Web Service Composition. *IEEE Internet Computing Online*, 8(6):51–59, Dec. 2004.
15. J. Miller, K. Verma, P. Rajasekaran, A. Sheth, R. Aggarwal, and K. Sivashanmugam. WSDL-S: Adding Semantics to WSDL - White Paper. http://lsdis.cs.uga.edu/library/download/wsdl-s.pdf.
16. OWL-S Coalition. OWL-S 1.1 release. http://www.daml.org/services/owl-s/1.1/.
17. M. Paolucci, T. Kawamura, T. Payne, and K. Sycara. Semantic Matchmaking of Web Services Capabilities. In I. Horrocks and J. Hendler, editors, *First International Semantic Web Conference on The Semantic Web, LNCS 2342*, pages 333–347. Springer-Verlag, 2002.
18. M. P. Papazoglou and D. Georgakopoulos. Service-Oriented Computing. *Commun. ACM*, 46(10):24–28, 2003.
19. R. Ponnekanti and A. Fox. SWORD: A developer toolkit for building composite Web services. Computer Science Department, StanfordUniversity, 2002. http://www2002.orgCDROM/alternate/786/.
20. S. Thakkar, A. C. Knoblock, and L. Ambite. A view integration approach to dynamic composition of Web services. Proceedings of the ICAPS '03 Workshop on Planning for Web Services, Italy, 2003.
21. P. Traverso and M. Pistore. Automated Composition of Semantic Web Services into Executable Processes. In *International Semantic Web Conference*, pages 380–394, 2004.
22. W. M. P. van der Aalst. Pi calculus versus Petri nets: Let us eat humble pie rather than further inflate the Pi hype, 2004. Available from http://tmitwww.tm.tue.nl/staff/wvdaalst/pi-hype.pdf.
23. W. M. P. van der Aalst and A. H. M. ter Hofstede. YAWL: Yet Another Workflow Language. Technical report, Queensland Univ. of Technology, FIT-TR-2003-04, 2003.
24. W. M. P. van der Aalst, A. H. M. ter Hofstede, B. Kiepuszewski, and A. P. Barros. Workflow Patterns. *Distrib. Parallel Databases*, 14(1):5–51, 2003.
25. E. Verbeek. WofYAWL Version 0.3. Technical report available online at http://home.tm.tue.nl/hverbeek/wofyawl03.pdf.
26. P. Wohed, W. M. P. van der Aalst, M. Dumas, and A. H. M. ter Hofstede. Analysis of Web Services Composition Languages: The Case of BPEL4WS. In I.-Y. Song, S. W. Liddle, T. W. Ling, and P. Scheuermann, editors, *Proceedings of the 22nd International Conference on Conceptual Modeling*, volume 2813 of *Lecture Notes in Computer Science*, pages 200–215. Springer, 2003.
27. D. Wu, E. Sirin, J. Hendler, D. Nau, and B. Parsia. Automatic Web services composition using SHOP2. Proceedings of the ICAPS '03 Workshop on Planning for Web Services (P4WS '03), 2003.
28. J. Yang and M. P. Papazoglou. Service components for managing the life-cycle of service compositions. *Information Systems*, 29(2):97–125, 2004.

Técnicas de Web Semántica para la Adaptación Dinámica de Componentes y Servicios

José L. Pastrana[1], Ernesto Pimentel[1], Miguel Katrib[2]

[1] ETSI Informática, Universidad de Málaga,Campus de teatinos s/n,
29071 Málaga, España
{pastrana, ernesto}@lcc.uma.es
[2] Facultad de Matemática y Computación, Universidad de La Habana, San Lázaro y L,
VEDADO, Ciudad de la Habana, Cuba
mkm@matcom.uh.cu

Resumen. La Web semántica es un área pujante en la confluencia de la Inteligencia Artificial y las tecnologías Web que propone introducir descripciones explícitas sobre el significado de los recursos, para permitir que las propias máquinas tengan un nivel de comprensión de la Web suficiente como para hacerse cargo de una parte, la más costosa, rutinaria, o físicamente inabarcable, del trabajo que actualmente realizan manualmente los usuarios que navegan e interactúan con la Web: seleccionar qué información es relevante al usuario y cuál no. A partir de la situación actual de la Web y sus limitaciones, en este artículo se aprovechan las técnicas y avances en este campo para ser utilizada en la adaptación de servicios de componentes distribuidos y más en concreto en el campo de componentes implementados como servicios Web. Dichas técnicas de análisis semántico aplicado a la Web pueden ser usadas para adaptar el nombre de los servicios, los parámetros de los mismos y más aun, es posible adaptar el componente que realiza el servicio.

1 Introducción

En los últimos años está de moda el uso del término Web semántica, pero ¿qué es la Web semántica? Según [1] La Web semántica es una extensión de la Web actual en la cual la información es dada con un significado bien definido, lo que permite un mejor trabajo en cooperación entre hombres y computadoras. La Web semántica propone superar las limitaciones de la Web actual mediante la introducción de descripciones explícitas del significado, la estructura interna y la estructura global de los contenidos y servicios disponibles en la WWW. Frente a la semántica implícita, el crecimiento caótico de recursos, y la ausencia de una organización clara de la Web actual, la Web semántica aboga por clasificar, dotar de estructura y anotar los recursos con semántica explícita procesable por máquinas. Según el consorcio W3C la Web semántica nos aporta un marco común que permite que los datos sean compartidos y reutilizados a través de las aplicaciones, las empresas y las personas. La Web tradicional podemos verla como un grafo (informalmente llamado tela de araña) de recursos de información enlazados entre sí. Sin embargo, dichos enlaces no aportan ninguna información ni representan relaciones entre los diferentes recursos, lo que hace que podamos tener resultados no deseados a la hora de realizar búsquedas en dicha red de recursos.

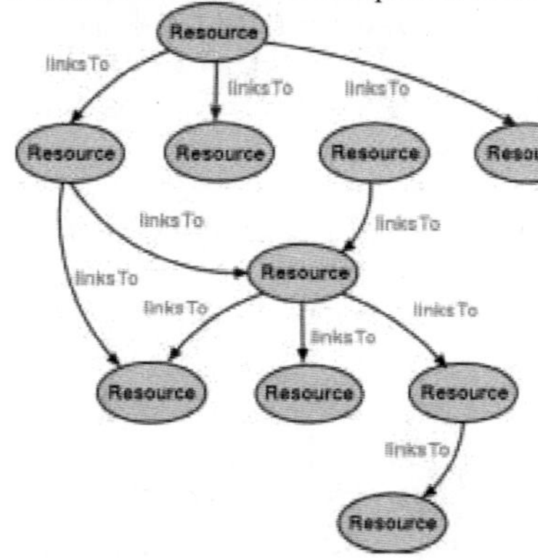

Figura 1. Esquema de Web Tradicional.

Supongamos que para ir al Workshop del IDEAS'06 deseamos buscar información en Google e introducimos en el buscador la siguiente cadena "viaje a la plata en argentina". Para empezar, obtenemos 1.160.000 resultados, lo cual para un humano es una cifra de enlaces de información difícil de procesar (al menos si desea llegar a tiempo al evento). Si nos paramos a analizar los resultados obtenidos, encontraremos que hay muchos que pueden ser interesantes para nosotros, pero que también hay gran cantidad de enlaces que no satisfacen nuestras necesidades. Por ejemplo, como podemos ver en la Figura 2, tenemos enlaces de viajes como "ARGENTINA - La Plata - Alojamientos, hoteles, información general" y otros que se refieren a hechos históricos como "Argentina: Viaje al pasado: Los Virreinatos".

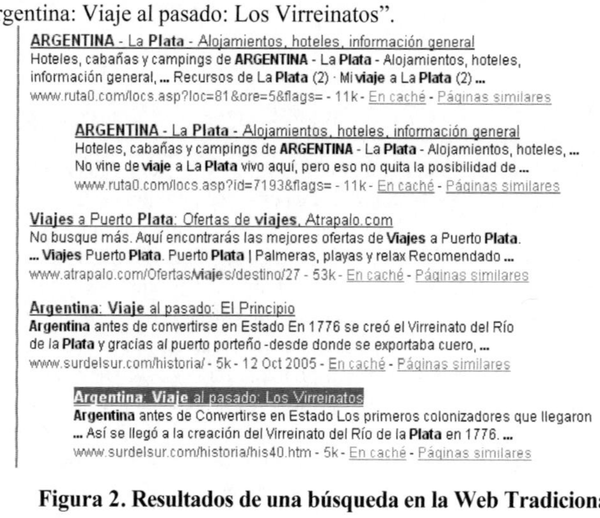

ARGENTINA - La **Plata** - Alojamientos, hoteles, información general
Hoteles, cabañas y campings de **ARGENTINA** - La **Plata** - Alojamientos, hoteles, información general, ... Recursos de La **Plata** (2) · Mi **viaje** a La **Plata** (2) ...
www.ruta0.com/locs.asp?loc=81&ore=5&flags= - 11k - En caché - Páginas similares

ARGENTINA - La **Plata** - Alojamientos, hoteles, información general
Hoteles, cabañas y campings de **ARGENTINA** - La **Plata** - Alojamientos, hoteles, ... No vine de **viaje** a La **Plata** vivo aquí, pero eso no quita la posibilidad de ...
www.ruta0.com/locs.asp?id=7193&flags= - 11k - En caché - Páginas similares

Viajes a Puerto **Plata**: Ofertas de **viajes**, Atrapalo.com
No busque más. Aquí encontrarás las mejores ofertas de **Viajes** a Puerto **Plata**. ... **Viajes** Puerto **Plata**. Puerto **Plata** | Palmeras, playas y relax Recomendado ...
www.atrapalo.com/Ofertas**Viaje**s/destino/27 - 53k - En caché - Páginas similares

Argentina: **Viaje** al pasado: El Principio
Argentina antes de convertirse en Estado En 1776 se creó el Virreinato del Río de la **Plata** y gracias al puerto porteño -desde donde se exportaba cuero, ...
www.surdelsur.com/historia/ - 5k - 12 Oct 2005 - En caché - Páginas similares

Argentina: **Viaje** al pasado: Los Virreinatos
Argentina antes de Convertirse en Estado Los primeros colonizadores que llegaron ... Así se llegó a la creación del Virreinato del Río de la **Plata** en 1776. ...
www.surdelsur.com/historia/his40.htm - 5k - En caché - Páginas similares

Figura 2. Resultados de una búsqueda en la Web Tradicional.

La solución a estos problemas es *La Web Semántica*: una Web extendida, dotada de mayor significado en la que cualquier usuario en Internet podrá encontrar respuestas a sus preguntas de forma más rápida y sencilla gracias a una información mejor definida. Al dotar a la Web de más significado y, por lo tanto, de más semántica, se pueden obtener soluciones a problemas habituales en la búsqueda de información gracias a la utilización de una infraestructura común, mediante la cual, es posible compartir, procesar y transferir información de forma sencilla. Esta Web extendida y basada en el significado, se apoya en lenguajes universales que resuelven los problemas ocasionados por una Web carente de semántica en la que, en ocasiones, el acceso a la información se convierte en una tarea difícil y frustrante.

2 Funcionamiento de la Web Semántica

Supongamos que la Web tiene la capacidad de construir una base de conocimiento sobre las preferencias de los usuarios y que, a través de una combinación entre su capacidad de conocimiento y la información disponible en Internet, sea capaz de atender de forma exacta las demandas de información por parte de los usuarios en relación, por ejemplo, a reserva de hoteles, vuelos, médicos, libros, etc.

Si esto ocurriese así en la vida real, el usuario, en su intento, por ejemplo, por encontrar información sobre su viaje a La Plata en Argentina, obtendría unos resultados exactos sobre su búsqueda. Sin embargo, como puede verse en la figura 2, la realidad es otra y la información obtenida es muy variada y se mezclan resultados deseados con resultados no deseados. El paso siguiente por parte del usuario es realizar una búsqueda manual entre esas opciones que aparecen, con la consiguiente dificultad y pérdida de tiempo. Con la incorporación de semántica a la Web los resultados de la búsqueda serían exactos. Todo ello a través de una Web en la que los datos pasan a ser información llena de significado. El resultado final sería la obtención de forma rápida y sencilla de todos los vuelos y hoteles a La Plata en Argentina.

La forma en la que se procesará esta información no sólo será en términos de entrada y salida de parámetros sino en términos de su semántica. La Web Semántica como infraestructura basada en metadatos aporta un camino para "razonar" en la Web, extendiendo así sus capacidades. No se trata de una inteligencia artificial mágica que permita a las máquinas entender las palabras de los usuarios, es sólo la habilidad de una máquina para resolver problemas bien definidos, a través de operaciones bien definidas que se llevarán a cabo sobre datos existentes bien definidos.
Para obtener esa adecuada definición de los datos [3], la Web Semántica utiliza *RDF* y *OWL*, dos estándares que ayudan a convertir la Web en una infraestructura global en la que es posible compartir, y reutilizar datos y documentos entre diferentes tipos de usuarios.

RDF proporciona información descriptiva simple sobre los recursos que se encuentran en la Web y que se utiliza, por ejemplo, en catálogos de libros, directorios, colecciones personales de música, fotos, eventos, etc.

OWL es un mecanismo para desarrollar temas o vocabularios específicos en los que asociar esos recursos. Lo que hace OWL es proporcionar un lenguaje para definir ontologías estructuradas que pueden ser utilizadas a través de diferentes sistemas. Las ontologías, que se encargan de definir los términos utilizados para describir y representar un área de conocimiento, son utilizadas por los usuarios, las bases de datos y las aplicaciones que necesitan compartir información específica, es decir, en un campo determinado como puede ser el de las finanzas, medicina, deporte, etc. Las ontologías incluyen definiciones de conceptos básicos en un campo determinado y la relación entre ellos.

3 Funcionamiento de la Web Semántica

RDF son las siglas en inglés de *Resource Description Framework* (RDF [8]), que es un lenguaje para la representación de información a cerca de los recursos disponibles en la Web. Está particularmente pensado para representar metadatos sobre recursos disponibles en la Web. Recursos tales como, por ejemplo, el título, autor, y fecha de modificación de una página Web, derechos de propiedad, disponibilidad de algún recurso compartido, etc. Sin embargo, generalizando el concepto de recurso Web, también se puede usar RDF para representar información a cerca de las cosas que pueden ser identificadas en la Web, aún cuando no puedan ser recuperadas directamente de la misma. Por ejemplo, incluir información a cerca de los productos disponibles en una tienda on-line (especificaciones, precios, disponibilidad,etc), o incluso, la descripción de las preferencias de los usuarios a la hora de solicitar información.

RDF ha sido pensado para situaciones en que esta información necesita ser procesada por aplicaciones , en vez de sólo ser mostrada al usuario. Por ello, RDF ofrece un marco común para expresar esta información de forma que pueda ser intercambiada entre diferentes aplicaciones sin pérdida de significado. Al ser un marco común, puede ser usado por los diseñadores de aplicaciones junto con las herramientas de procesamiento y análisis del mismo que se incorporan a dicho marco. Esta capacidad de intercambiar la información hace que una información pueda pasar y estar disponible de unas aplicaciones a otras para las cuales, inicialmente, no se había pensado o ni siquiera se habían creado.

RDF se basa en la idea de la definición de identificadores Web (llamados Identificadores Uniformes de recursos, *Uniform Resource Identifiers*, o *URL*), identificar las cosas a través de dichos identificadotes y describir los recursos en términos de propiedades simples y valores de las propiedades. Esto posibilita representar sentencias simples en RDF como un grafo de nodos y arcos representando los recursos, sus propiedades y valores. Además, RDF, nos ofrece una sintaxis basada en XML y llamada RDF/XML para el almacenamiento e intercambio de dicha información. Por ejemplo, en el código siguiente1, podemos ver la representación de la oración "Hay una persona identificada en http://www.lcc.uma.es/~pastrana/ cuyo nombre es José Luis Pastrana y cuya dirección de correo electrónico es pastrana@lcc.uma.es".

```
<?xml version="1.0"?>
<rdf:RDF xmlns:rdf="http://www.w3.org/1999/02/22-rdf-
syntax-ns#"xmlns:contact=
"http://www.w3.org/2000/10/swap/pim/contact#">
<contact:Person rdf:about=
"http://www.lcc.uma.es/~pastrana" >
<contact:fullName>José Luis Pastrana</contact:fullName>
<contact:mailbox rdf:resource= "mail-
to:pastrana@lcc.uma.es"/>
</contact:Person>
</rdf:RDF>
```

Al igual que HTML, RDF/XML es procesable automáticamente y al usar URL's puede enlazar porciones de información a través de la Web. Sin embargo, y al contrario con lo que ocurre con el hipertexto convencional, las URL's de RDF pueden referirse a cualquier cosa identificable, incluso cosas que no se pueden recuperar directamente en la Web (tales como la persona José Luis Pastrana). RDF también puede describir coches, negocios, personas, eventos, etc. Además, las propiedades de RDF, tienen URL's para identificar de forma precisa las relaciones existentes entre los elementos enlazados.

4 OWL: El Lenguaje de Ontologías Web del W3C

Según [9], una ontología define los términos a utilizar para describir y representar un área de conocimiento. Las ontologías son utilizadas por las personas, las bases de datos, y las aplicaciones que necesitan compartir un dominio de información (un dominio es simplemente un área de temática específica o un área de conocimiento, tales como medicina, fabricación de herramientas, bienes inmuebles, reparación automovilística, gestión financiera, etc.). Las ontologías incluyen definiciones de conceptos básicos del dominio, y las relaciones entre ellos. Básicamente, codifican el conocimiento de un dominio y también el conocimiento que extiende los dominios. En este sentido, hacen el conocimiento reutilizable.

OWL es un lenguaje de Ontologías Web (Ontology Web Language). Antes de la aparición de OWL, por lo general, se han estado utilizado lenguajes y herramientas para desarrollar ontologías destinadas a comunidades específicas (especialmente para ciencias y aplicaciones específicas de comercio electrónico), que no fueron definidos para ser compatibles con la arquitectura de la World Wide Web en general, y la Web Semántica en particular. OWL rectifica esto proporcionando un lenguaje que utiliza la conexión proporcionada por RDF para añadir las siguientes capacidades a las ontologías:

- •Capacidad de ser distribuidas a través de varios sistemas
- •Escalable a las necesidades de la Web
- •Compatible con los estándares Web de accesibilidad e internacionalización
- •Abierto y extensible

Entre los usos más comunes, hoy en día, de las ontologías en la Web caben destacar: las Reglas de categorización utilizadas para mejorar la búsqueda en los portales Web, las búsquedas basadas en contenido para medios no textuales en las colecciones multimedia, la organización taxonómica automatizada de datos y documentos para la administración de Sitios Web corporativos, la explicación de partes y la administración explícita de restricciones a la hora de la realización de la documentación de diseño, la expresión de las preferencias y/o intereses de los usuarios y el mapeo de contenidos entre sitios Web en el desarrollo de agentes inteligentes, la composición y descubrimiento de Servicios Web o la administración de derechos y control de acceso en el uso y desarrollo de servicios Web y computación ubicua.

OWL extiende RDF para permitir la expresión de relaciones complejas entre diferentes clases RDF, así como una mayor precisión en las restricciones de clases y propiedades específicas. Esto incluye:

- •Los recursos para limitar las propiedades de clases con respecto a número y tipo.
- •Los recursos para inferir qué elementos que tienen varias propiedades son miembros de una clase en particular.
- •Los recursos para determinar si todos los miembros de una clase tendrán una propiedad en particular, o si puede ser que sólo algunos la tengan.
- •Los recursos para distinguir entre relaciones uno-a-uno, varios-a-uno o uno-a-varios, permitiendo que las "claves externas" de las bases de datos puedan representarse en una ontología.
- •Los recursos para expresar relaciones entre clases definidas en diferentes documentos en la Web.
- •Los recursos para construir nuevas clases a partir de uniones, intersecciones y complementos de otras.
- •Los recursos para restringir rangos y dominios para especificar combinaciones de clases y propiedades.

OWL nos ofrece 3 sublenguajes cuyo nivel de expresión es creciente a fin de que podamos utilizar el que más se adecue a nuestras necesidades: *OWL Lite*, *OWL DL* y *OWL Full*.

- •*OWL Lite* ofrece soluciones a usuarios cuya necesidad principal es una clasificación jerárquica y simple de restricciones.
- •*OWL DL* (description logics) ofrece soluciones a usuarios que quieren la máxima expresividad que garantice que todas las conclusiones sean computables (todos los cálculos terminarán y en un tiempo finito). Incluye todas las construcciones de OWL pero sólo pueden ser usadas bajo ciertas restricciones

- *OWL Full* ofrece soluciones a usuarios que desean la máxima expresividad y la libertad sintáctica de RDF, a cambio de no ofrecernos ninguna clase de garantías computacionales.

Veamos un ejemplo de una ontología para el vino escrita en OWL.

```
<owl:Class rdf:ID="vino">
  <rdfs:subClassOf rdf:resource="&food;PotableLiquid"/>
  <rdfs:label xml:lang="es">vino</rdfs:label>
  <rdfs:label xml:lang="en">wine</rdfs:label>
  <rdfs:label xml:lang="fr">vin</rdfs:label>
  ...
</owl:Class>
```

5 Adaptación Dinámica de Componentes y Servicios con OWL

La ingeniería del Software basada en componentes (Component-Based Software Engineering o CBSE) centra sus esfuerzos en el desarrollo y construcción de aplicaciones software gracias a la integración de componentes software previamente existentes. Así, la técnica clásica de desarrollo de sistemas escribiendo código se ve complementada por el ensamblaje de componentes existentes. Por tanto, uno de los máximos objetivos perseguidos por la CBSE es la flexibilidad y facilidad de mantenimiento de los sistemas software. Algunos de esos sistemas serán tan críticos que su mantenimiento debe realizarse "al vuelo" lo que no permite parar todo el sistema, modificar y reiniciar todo el sistema.

5.1 El Problema de la Adaptación

Adaptar aplicaciones basadas en componentes se reduce a la posibilidad de adaptar uno (o más) componentes en tiempo de ejecución, o lo que es lo mismo, desconectar un componente y sustituirlo por otro nuevo (una nueva versión) [4]. Una adaptación dinámica puede ser necesaria debido a múltiples razones que podemos clasificar en 4 categorías: correctivas, adaptativas, de extensión y de perfeccionamiento.

Una adaptación *correctiva* elimina fallos de comportamiento del componente que se está ejecutando, reemplazándolo por una nueva versión que tiene la misma funcionalidad pero que funciona correctamente. Cuando lo que hacemos en una adaptación *adaptativa*, lo que se realiza es una adaptación de la aplicación en respuesta a cambios del entorno (hardware, sistema operativo, etc.). Otra clase de adaptación es la adaptación por *extensión* en la que se añaden nuevas funcionalidades al sistema mediante la adicción de nuevos componentes. Por último, las adaptaciones de *perfeccionamiento* se realizan para mejorar la aplicación aun cuando esta funciona correctamente, reemplazando un componente por otro que ha sido optimizado.

Independientemente de la razón o el motivo de la adaptación, se pueden identificar diferentes tipos de adaptación: adaptaciones de arquitectura, adaptaciones de implementación, adaptaciones de interfaces y adaptaciones de localización.

Las adaptaciones de arquitectura se producen cuando la adaptación afecta a la estructura de la aplicación y pueden ser realizadas añadiendo nuevos componentes, eliminando algunos de los ya existentes o modificando las conexiones entre ellos.

Las adaptaciones de implementación son motivadas por motivos de rendimiento, corrección o cambios del entorno que no fueron tenidos en cuenta en la implementación de un (o varios) componente(s) determinado(s). Un claro ejemplo de este tipo de adaptación se vivió en Europa con el cambio monetario al euro.

Las adaptaciones de interfaces se producen cuando se modifica la lista de servicios ofrecidos por un componente, bien sea añadiendo o eliminando funcionalidad de un componente dado.

Las adaptaciones de localización se corresponden con los cambios de migración de componentes de un lugar a otro por motivos de balanceo de carga, costos de hosting, etc. El cambio, si bien no afecta a la arquitectura, ni a las interfaces, ni a la funcionalidad de la aplicación, afecta a las comunicaciones entre los diferentes componentes del sistema.

A la hora de realizar una adaptación se deben satisfacer muchos requisitos, pero los más importantes a tener siempre en cuenta son la consistencia, el rendimiento y el grado de automatización. La consistencia concierne a la aplicación usada para adaptar la aplicación actual en tiempo de ejecución. Dicha aplicación que realice las adaptaciones debe ser altamente prioritaria. Sin embargo, eso no debe suponer que dicha aplicación de adaptación tenga todo tipo de derechos para hacer lo que quiera y cuando quiera, ya que la operación de adaptación debe preservar la consistencia de la misma. El tema del rendimiento se refiere a la duración de la adaptación y al número de componentes afectados que deben ser mínimos. Y por ultimo, el grado de automatización es un punto importante, ya que representa la capacidad de una aplicación de adaptarse a si misma; esto es posible cuando la aplicación tiene información relevante en tiempo de ejecución y es capaz de procesarla de manera que la propia aplicación se adapte a las circunstancias en tiempo de ejecución. Este es el punto de vista de nuestra propuesta y vamos a ver cómo es posible usando OWL suministrar una información processable automáticamente para adaptar peticiones de servicios en tiempo de ejecución.

5.2 Una Solución al problema de Adaptación de Servicios en Tiempo de Ejecución

Como se comentó anteriormente, la adaptación de una aplicación basada en componentes, generalmente, implica desconectar dicho componente de la aplicación y conectar a la misma una nueva versión del componente. Básicamente, podemos encontrarnos 2 tipos de aplicaciones basadas en componentes: las aplicaciones en las que todos los componentes están físicamente en la misma máquina y se enlazan juntos para formar un ejecutable y aquellas en las que los componentes están distribuidos a través de la red. En la presente propuesta supondremos que estamos trabajando con un sistema en que los componentes están distribuidos en cualquier punto y accesibles a través de la red, ya que es un caso más general y el caso de tener componentes locales puede ser simulado situando todos ellos en la misma dirección.

Cuando se realiza una modificación en un componente o se sustituye por otro, esto se hace de forma transparente al componente que requiere los servicios del modificado. El problema surge cuando, pese a ofrecer una misma funcionalidad, la interfaz del componente es diferente y la invocación del servicio no se corresponderá con la invocación original. Esto supondría que el sistema dejara de funcionar. La solución que proponemos se basa en adaptar la invocación del servicio desde el llamante mediante el uso de una ontología que permita al llamante saber cuál de los servicios ofrecidos es el que deseamos o necesitamos y cómo debemos llamarlo a partir de la información que tenemos, todo ello realizado en tiempo de ejecución.

En ese proceso de adaptación podemos encontrar 3 tipos de conflictos (no excluyentes entre sí):

- Conflicto de Nombre: ocurren cuando el nombre de un determinado servicio no coincide con el nombre que tenía anteriormente.
- Conflicto de Parámetros: ocurre cuando un determinado servicio utiliza parámetros con tipos u orden diferentes a los que utilizaba originalmente.
- Conflicto de Composición: es el más difícil de solucionar y se produce cuando un determinado servicio se transforma en la composición de varios servicios nuevos (o viceversa).

La idea de usar técnicas de Web semántica y concretamente el uso de ontologies para resolver este problema, surge de que el problema es similar: razonar y procesar el conocimiento y la información que tenemos para proporcionar al usuario aquello que realmente desea.
La gramática usada en el lenguaje natural es muy amplia y compleja, sin embargo, la gramática de la invocación de servicios es mucho más sencilla y mejor definida y su análisis nos permite distinguir entre los determinados elementos de la misma. Una invocación típica podría ser como muestra la Figura 3

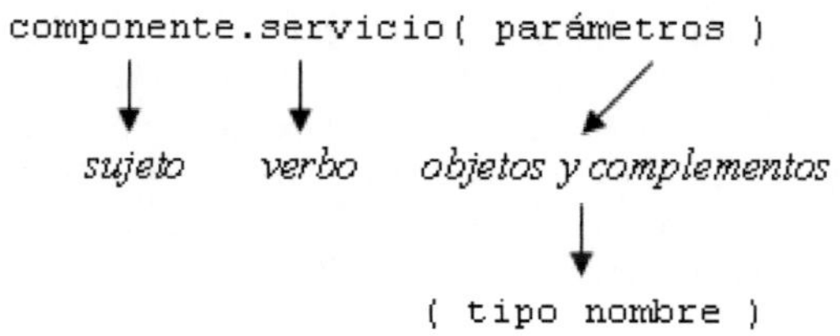

Figura 3. Gramática de la Invocación de un Servicio.

De esta manera, usando una ontología podremos saber qué servicios son equivalentes, qué complementos son equivalentes o los tipos de los mismos e incluso qué posibles sujetos (componentes que realizan un servicio) podrían ser equivalentes con la consecuencia utilidad para la tolerancia a fallos.

5.3 Uso de OWL para Implementar la Adaptación

Dentro del conjunto características que permite OWL Lite tenemos las relacionadas con equivalencias (*Equality* y *Inequality*), que nos van a permitir establecer qué conceptos son equivalentes y cuáles no. En nuestra propuesta usaremos las equivalencias de clase, propiedad y la identidad: `equivalentClass`, `equivalentProperty` y `sameAs`.

- `equivalentClass` : esta característica nos permite establecer clases de componentes que son equivalentes. Por ejemplo, la clase *coche* es equivalente a la clase *automóvil*.
- `equivalentProperty`: esta característica nos permite establecer propiedades equivalentes. Por ejemplo, *tiene un* jefe podría ser una propiedad equivalente a *tiene un* superior.
- `sameAs`: esta característica nos permite definir sinónimos de un individuo, Por ejemplo, *José* es lo mismo que *Pepe*.

Utilizando estas propiedades, estableceremos que dos servicios son sustituibles para ser adaptados si son el mismo (`sameAs`) o son una propiedad equivalente (`equivalentProperty`) y dos tipos, dos nombres o dos componentes son sustituibles para ser adaptados si son el mismo (`sameAs`) o son de una clase equivalente (`equivalentClass`).

6 Trabajos Relacionados

Analicemos las diferentes propuestas que tienen similitudes a la nuestra y las razones que nos han llevado a tomar una opción u otra:

OWL-S es una ontología para describir Servicios Web representados en OWL. OWL-S establece tres nociones de alto nivel [5]:

- *El Perfil de Servicio.* Incluye información para el anuncio y publicación de servicios y que es usado para la localización del servicio Web deseado por parte de un cliente.
- *El Modelo de Servicio.* Contiene la información relativa a la descripción de la funcionalidad de un servicio y está concebida como un proceso.
- *La Base del Servicio.* Nos da los detalles concernientes al acceso al servicio, es decir, el cómo pasar de lo abstracto a la utilización concreta de un servicio.

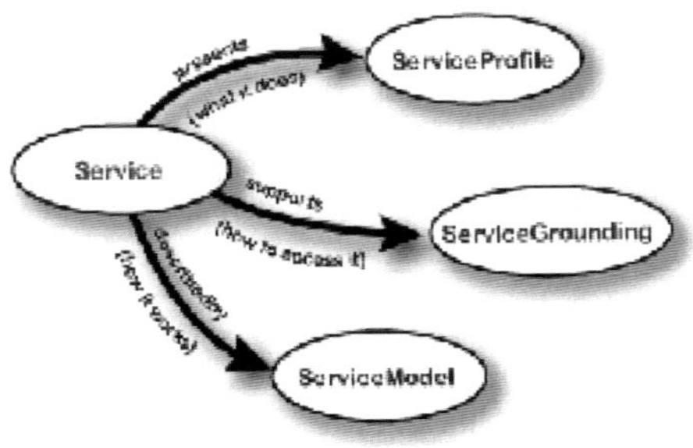

Figura 4. Nociones de Alto Nivel de OWL-S

El uso OWL-S puede ser una mejora importante en nuestra propuesta, sin embargo, en una primera versión se ha querido optar por un modelo más simple. Sin embargo, las características del perfil de servicio relativas a los parámetros pueden ser muy útiles en el proceso de adaptación. No obstante, las características que se incluyen en las tres nociones de OWL-S no son suficientes para discernir entre dos servicios para asber si son equivalentes o no.

WSMO [2] (Web Service Modeling Ontology) presenta una ontología para la descripción de servicios Web semánticos, expresados en un lenguaje nuevo (WSML) que es compatible con XML, y OWL. Propone una ontología basada en la utilización de cuatro componentes: Objetivos, Mediadores, Servicios Web y Ontologías. Debido a que la descripción de los servicios se realiza mediante una ontología que puede ser especificada en cualquier lenguaje (aunque se recomienda WSML-Core) hemos preferido no usar esta metodología aunque nuestra propuesta pudiera ser incorporada a la misma.

METEOR-S [7] centra su objetivo en la integración de tecnologías de servicios Web, tales como WSBPEL (Web Services Business Process Execution Language), WSDL (Web Service Description Language) y UDDI (Universal Description, Discovery and Integration) con tecnologías de Web semántica para poder automatizar la tarea de publicación, descubrimiento, descripción y control de flujo de los servicios Web. Sin embargo, METEOR-S carece de un modelo conceptual para la descripción de servicios y aspectos relacionados con estos, lo que nos haría complicado pode discernir entre servicios que sean equivalentes y los que no lo sean.

7 Detalles de Implementación

A la hora de realizar una implementación de la propuesta hemos asumido que nuestros componentes distribuidos serán servicios Web implementados usando el lenguaje C# bajo la plataforma *Microsoft .NET.* Microsoft .NET es un conjunto de tecnologías software desarrolladas para la conexión e intercambio de información entre personas, sistemas y dispositivos. Esto permite un nivel sin precedentes de integración de software a través del uso de Servicios Web XML, mediante el cual todo tipo de aplicaciones pueden relacionarse e interoperar a través de Internet.

Un Servicio Web no es muy diferente de una aplicación tradicional cliente-servidor. Básicamente, un cliente necesita datos o un servicio y para ello realiza invocaciones al servidor. Bajo este punto de vista, los servicios Web no ofrecen nada nuevo al mercado del software. Sin embargo, la mayor diferencia y lo que ha hecho que se convierta en una herramienta en auge viene dada del hecho de que los Servicios Web utilizan tecnologías, lenguajes y protocolos estándar como son HTTP, XML, SOAP, etc., lo que hace posible su interoperatibilidad con cualquier plataforma (propietaria o no) y con cualquier tecnología que respete los estándares antes mencionados. La plataforma *Microsoft .NET* facilita el trabajo de "fontanería" o bajo nivel a la hora de usar y desarrollar servicios Web, pero no existe ningún problema ni limitación en su uso y accesos a través de cualquier otra plataforma, lenguaje o aplicación que siga los mismos estándares.

La forma habitual de invocar un servicio proporcionado por un servicio Web es usar una clase intermediaria (*proxy*) que es generada automáticamente por la utilidad `wsdl`. Sin embargo, si queremos ser capaces de modificar nombres, parámetros, tipos, etc. de las llamadas en tiempo de ejecución necesitaremos ser capaces de construir los mensajes correspondientes para dichas invocaciones en tiempo de ejecución. Para ello lo que tendremos en un intermediario genérico que realizará las llamadas a partir de cadenas de caracteres que le pasaremos como argumentos y que serán el resultado de las adaptaciones. En el código siguiente pueden verse algunos detalles del mismo.

```
// setup the request
WebRequest webRequest=WebRequest.Create(webServiceURL);
HttpWebRequest httpWebRequest =
          (HttpWebRequest)webRequest ;
httpWebRequest.Method = "POST" ;
httpWebRequest.ContentType = "text/xml" ;
httpWebRequest.Headers.Add("SOAPAction: "+soapAction) ;
Stream sendStream = httpWebRequest.GetRequestStream();
// put Request text into the request stream
StreamWriter streamWriter = new
          StreamWriter(sendStream);
streamWriter.Write (soapEnvelope);
streamWriter.Close ();
```

```
// make the request and get the response.
WebResponse webResponse = null;
StreamReader streamReader = null ;
string result ;
try
{ webResponse = httpWebRequest.GetResponse () ;
  Stream responseStream =
        webResponse.GetResponseStream();
  streamReader = new StreamReader (responseStream) ;
  result = streamReader.ReadToEnd () ;
}
```

7.1 La Adaptación

El problema que estamos abordando se produce cuando al realizar una invocación del servicio deseado, en vez de obtener el resultado de la misma, obtenemos una excepción. Esta excepción puede deberse a que el servicio no exista en el componente remoto o a que dicho componente no está disponible. Si bien en la propuesta actual sólo nos hemos implementado una adaptación para el primero de los problemas, y supondremos que el componente remoto está disponible, la adaptación del sujeto que realiza el servicio sería sencilla y similar a lo que hemos realizado, ya que sólo habría que buscar en la red o mediante UDDI un componente que según nuestra ontología fuera el mismo (*sameAs*) o fuera de una clase equivalente (`equivalentClass`).

Centrémonos ahora en el problema que estamos abordando y supongamos que tras la solicitud de un servicio obtenemos una excepción indicando que dicho servicio no está disponible. Y tengamos en cuenta el contexto de nuestra implementación en el que los componentes remotos son servicios Web. En este caso el componente que desea el servicio ejecutará de forma automática y en tiempo de ejecución las siguientes tareas:

1. Descargar el nuevo interfaz del componente remoto (ver código 4).
2. De los servicios ofrecidos por el nuevo componente buscar aquel que, según la ontología que disponemos, sean igual (`sameAs`) o sea propiedad equivalente (`equivalentProperty`).
3. Completar la llamada usando como parámetros los que sean los mismos (`sameAs`) o son de una clase equivalente (`equivalentClass`) de entre los que tenemos de la llamada original.
4. Si el paso 3 no fuera posible ser completado se busca un nuevo servicio candidato y se repite el paso 3.

Si hubiera servicios equivalentes pero no se pudiera completar ninguno por falta de información, se completaría con valores por defecto (`null, "", 0, ''`) salvo que en la ontología haya definido algún valor equivalente al "nulo" para un tipo determinado.

8 Conclusiones y Trabajos futuros

El trabajo realizado aprovecha las técnicas y avances realizados en el campo de la Web semántica para la adaptación de servicios de componentes distribuidos y más en concreto en el campo de componentes implementados como servicios Web. Dichas técnicas de análisis semántico aplicado a la Web, como se ha podido ver, pueden ser usadas para adaptar el nombre de los servicios, los parámetros de los mismos, e incluso, el componente que realiza el servicio.

La experiencia relatada a lo largo del trabajo actual son los comienzos de un trabajo que pretende seguir con el estudio de esta vía y su inclusión en el marco de arquitectura propuesta por los autores en ediciones pasadas de IDEAS [6] para el desarrollo y coordinación de componentes software, de manera que todo esté integrado en una herramienta automática que sea capaz de generar aplicaciones software a partir de la composición de componentes previos, su coordinación y su adaptación de manera que minimice los problemas de mantenimiento y evolución a lo largo de la vida del sistema.

Referentes

1. Berners-Lee T., Hendler J., Lassila O., *The Semantic Web*, Scientific American, http://www.scientificamerican.com/article.cfm?articleID=00048144-10D2-1C70-84A9809EC588EF21&catID=2, 2001.
2. Domingue, J., Cabral, L., Hakimpour, F., Sell D., Motta, E. IRS III: A Platform and Infrastructure for Creating WSMO-based Semantic Web Services. *Proceedings of the Workshop on WSMO Implementations (WIW 2004)* Frankfurt, Germany, September 29-30, 2004
3. Hendler J.,Berners-Lee T., Miller E., *Integrating applications on the Semantic Web*, Journal IEEE Japan, 122(10):676-680, 2002.
4. Ketfi A., Noureddine B., Pierre-Yves C. *Dynamic updating of component-based applications*. SERP'02, Las Vegas, Nevada, USA, 2002.
5. Martin D., Burstein M., Hobbs J., Ora L., McDermott D., McIlraith S., Narayanan S., Paolucci M., Parsia D., Payne T., Sirin E., Srinivasan N., Sycara K., *OWL-S: Semantic Markup for Web Service.* W3C Member Submission 22 November 2004.
6. Pastrana J.,Pimentel E.,Katrib M., *Adaptación y Reutilización de Componentes Distribuidos*, en: 8° Workshop Iberoamericano de Ingeniería de Requisitos y Ambientes de Software. IDEAS?05, Universidad Técnica Federico Santa María , Valparaíso, Chile,2005
7. Verma K., Sivashanmugam K., Sheth A., Patil A., Oundhakar S., Miller J., METEOR-S WSDI: A Scalable Infrastructure of Registries for Semantic Publication and Discovery of Web Services, Journal of Information Technology and Management, Special Issue on Universal Global Integration, Vol. 6, No. 1 (2005) pp. 17-39. Kluwer Academic Publishers
8. W3C Recommendation, *RDF Primer*,http://www.w3.org/TR/2004/REC-rdf-primer-20040210
9. W3C Recommendation, *OWL Web Ontology Language. Use Cases and Requirements*, http://www.w3.org/TR/2004/REC-webont-req-20040210/.

Una Semántica de Ensamblaje y Composición de Servicios y Componentes

Camilo Rocha[2], Rafael García[1], and Rubby Casallas[1]

[1] rgarcia,rcasalla@uniandes.edu.co
Grupo de Construcción de Software
Departamento de Ingeniería de Sistemas y Computación
Universidad de los Andes, Bogotá, Colombia

[2] hrocha@escuelaing.edu.co
Centro de Estudios de Ingeniería de Software
Decanatura de Ingeniería de Sistemas
Escuela Colombiana de Ingeniería, Bogotá, Colombia

Resumen El Desarrollo de Software Basado en Componentes es una disciplina de la Ingeniería de Software que promete una mejora en la productividad de los equipos de desarrollo a partir de la reutilización de piezas de software de buena calidad. La utilización de componentes existentes reducirá costos y potenciará el trabajo a gran escala. Sin embargo, no hay una terminología ni unos conceptos unificados que faciliten el desarrollo de la disciplina. Además, las nociones de corrección sobre estos modelos son prácticamente inexistentes. Este trabajo presenta una unificación formal de la terminología y conceptos, una noción de corrección sobre un modelo y el cálculo π_{tp} (extensión tipada y poliádica del cálculo π) como formalismo de notación y derivación.

1. Introducción

En la historia del desarrollo del software el interés por la reutilización de piezas de software ha sido una constante. Las ventajas de la reutilización están asociadas a la productividad, la capacidad de mantenimiento, la portabilidad y la calidad [1,10,15]. Imaginarse un sistema de módulos es recrear un ambiente en donde piezas de software interactúan entre sí para lograr un objetivo: satisfacer una especificación. Dicha interacción obedecería a diferentes tipos de relación y una vez establecida, ésta puede usarse una y otra vez.

En general se distinguen dos tipos de módulos, los *servicios* y los *componentes*. Una relación de dependencia entre dos servicios o entre dos componentes se llama *ensamblaje*, mientras que las relaciones de un componente con su estructura interna son llamadas de *composición*. En este artículo presentamos una extensión del cálculo π, llamada π_{tp}, como formalismo para describir un sistema de servicios y/o componentes y las relaciones entre ellos. Además, con este formalismo podemos verificar la corrección de los sistemas descritos.

Este documento está organizado de la siguiente forma: la sección 2 presenta un recuento de propuestas de formalización, la sección 3 introduce un cálculo de ensamblajes como extensión del cálculo π, que sirve como base para las Semánticas de Ensamblaje y de Composición que se presentan en las secciones 4 y 5. Finalmente se presentan posibles trabajos futuros y las conclusiones.

2. Enfoques formales existentes

A pesar del auge de la Ingeniería de Software Basada en Componentes (CBSE[3]) y de la aceptación de la reutilización como su principal propuesta, hace falta un entendimiento unificado, formal y sólido de los modelos de componentes.

En [2] se propone una terminología general para los modelos de componentes que incluye componentes, conexiones, instancias, tipos y descripciones. Los *componentes* son los bloques básicos de composición en el modelo de componentes y pueden o no exhibir su estructura interna (son considerados de *caja blanca* cuando la exhiben y de *caja negra* cuando no). Las *interfaces* son elementos nombrados que agrupan métodos (entendidos como en lenguajes OO) y están asociadas a los componentes de manera unívoca. Las *conexiones* comunican interfaces con interfaces o con componentes.

Para Meyer [10], los componentes son piezas con altas exigencias de calidad llamadas *componentes confiables*[4]: un componente confiable es un elemento de software reutilizable que cuenta con propiedades de calidad específicas y garantizadas. Para Szyperski los componentes *tienen propiedades características como unidades básicas e independientes de despliegue y no tienen estado persistente* [15].

En el modelo comercial de componentes J2EE, como bloques básicos de composición, los componentes son unidades de software específicas, cuyo ciclo de vida está manejado por un contenedor, y configurables en tiempo de despliegue en el contenedor. Un contenedor es una pieza de software que suministra servicios a los componentes (v.gr. seguridad, transaccionalidad, etc.).

Pahl presenta en [12] una semántica operacional para la composición de componentes basada en una variante del cálculo π. El uso del cálculo π está motivado por la similitud entre la noción de *movilidad* del cálculo y la noción de *evolución* de los modelos de componentes. La movilidad se define como la capacidad para cambiar la conectividad de una red o de reconfigurar espacialmente la misma.

Un lenguaje de composición es cualquier lenguaje que facilite la especificación de una pieza de software en función de su composición [8, 9]. La mayoría de lenguajes de composición estudiados son de *descripción dinámica*. Estos son usados principalmente para describir aspectos dinámicos de los modelos. Ejemplos de lenguajes de descripción dinámica son las Redes de Petri, diagramas de transición de estados, álgebras de procesos y lógicas temporales. El otro grupo de lenguajes de composición, la minoría, corresponde a lenguajes de *descripción estática* que sirven para modelar las partes estáticas de los sistemas (v.gr. tipos) y operaciones de transición en términos de estados iniciales y finales. Ejemplos de lenguajes de descripción estática son la notación Z y el lenguaje B.

Las nociones de corrección para lenguajes de programación son bien conocidas. Por ejemplo, el uso de las *Hoare Logic* [6] o los *Transformadores de Predicados de Dijkstra* [5] son técnicas comunes para razonar sobre la corrección de algoritmos, tanto iterativos como recurrentes en modelos imperativos de programación. Sin embargo, este no es el caso en el dominio de la CBSE [4].

---

[3] Del inglés *Component Based Software Engineering*

[4] Del inglés *Trusted Components*

En la próxima sección presentamos nuestra propuesta para modelar el ensamblaje de servicios.

3. Un Cálculo de Ensamblaje

Gaita, un modelo de componentes desarrollado por nuestro grupo de investigación [16], diferencia entre dos tipos de *módulos*: los *componentes* que exhiben su estructura interna y los *servicios* que no la exhiben. En el modelo de servicios las instancias son nombradas y no tienen estado observable, ofrecen y requieren métodos a través de interfaces (las *facetas* son interfaces que ofrecen métodos y los *receptáculos* interfaces que requieren métodos). Las conexiones de dependencia no son jerárquicas (v.gr. no constituyen nuevos servicios) y se establecen entre facetas y receptáculos. La relación entre servicios es llamada *ensamblaje*. Un ensamblaje entre dos servicios, entre uno que ofrece y otro que requiere un método, se entiende como que el servicio que requiere el método está usando la funcionalidad ofrecida por el otro y en ningún caso se *crea* un nuevo servicio a partir de ensamblajes. A su vez la composición adquiere dos dimensiones: la primera, similar a la de ensamblaje de servicios, es llamada de *ensamblaje de componentes* y su significado es el mismo; la segunda, la de *composición de componentes*, permite la construcción jerárquica de componentes con base en otros componentes previamente construidos.

Antes de presentar la seántica de comunicación entre *procesos* que posteriormente servirá para caracterizar los servicios, en el cuadro 1 se introducen las convenciones gráficas para la descripción de servicios que sirven como referente para ilustrar las definiciones que a continuación se presentan.

Cuadro 1. Convenciones gráficas para servicios

Ícono	Interpretación
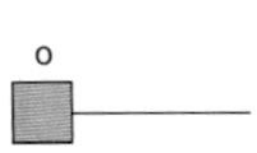	El método o es ofrecido.
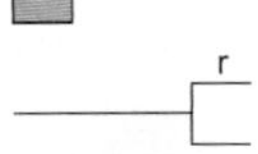	El método r es requerido.
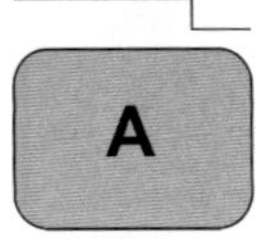	El servicio cuyo nombre es A.
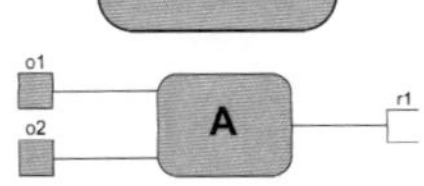	El servicio cuyo nombre es A, que ofrece métodos o_1, o_2 y requiere el método r_1.
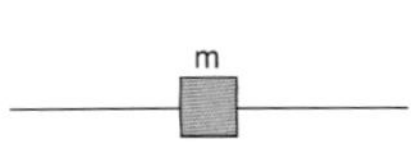	Establecimiento de una conexión para el método m
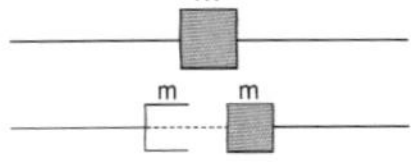	Establecimiento de una conexión para el método m

Una teoría de ensamblaje de servicios es necesaria cuando se desea analizar y razonar rigurosamente sobre el desarrollo y mantenimiento de sistemas de servicios y componentes [12]. Una vez analizadas las necesidades para calcular ensamblajes, se propone un protocolo de ensamblaje de servicios que permita definir claramente::

1. Compatibilidad y creación de conexiones entre servicios: cómo establecer conexiones entre instancias de servicios.
2. Invocación y ejecución de un método: cómo invocar y ejecutar un método a partir de instancias de servicios conectados.
3. Respuesta de una invocación: cómo enviar y recibir la respuesta a partir de la invocación y ejecución de un método.

Inspirada en la propuesta de [12], esta sección introduce el cálculo π_{tp} como extensión de π.

3.1. Sintaxis

Las acciones del cálculo π_{tp}, al igual que en el cálculo π, son los elementos básicos para describir la interacción entre procesos y están definidas como prefijos de éstos:

Definición 1 (Acciones de π_{tp}) *Las acciones α_{tp} de π_{tp} están dadas por:*

$$\alpha_{tp} \quad ::= \quad \textsc{Ptype}\ \overline{x}\langle y\rangle \mid \textsc{Ptype}\ x(y) \mid \tau$$

Las acciones se clasifican en tres tipos: las de *salida* $\overline{x}\langle y\rangle$ (el nombre y es enviado por el método x), las de *entrada* $x(y)$ (el nombre y es recibido por el método x) y la acción silenciosa y no observable τ. Más adelante se explicará el significado de las etiquetas que acompañan los dos primeros tipos de acción (v.gr. PTYPE).

Definición 2 (Prefijos de acción) *Los prefijos de acción β_{tp} de π_{tp} están dados por:*

$$\begin{array}{lll} \beta_{tp} ::= & \textsc{Req}\ \overline{m_C}\langle m_I\rangle & \textit{Petición} \\ \mid & \textsc{Pro}\ n_C(n_I) & \textit{Atención} \\ \mid & \textsc{Inv}\ \overline{m_I}\langle a_1,\ldots,a_l,m_R\rangle & \textit{Invocación} \\ \mid & \textsc{Exe}\ n_I(b_1,\ldots,b_k,n_R) & \textit{Ejecución} \\ \mid & \textsc{Rep}\ \overline{n_R}\langle c\rangle & \textit{Respuesta} \\ \mid & \textsc{Res}\ m_R(d) & \textit{Recepción} \end{array}$$

La sintaxis para la composición de expresiones en π_{tp} está dada por la *restricción* de nombres, la *composición* en paralelo, la *iteración*, la suma y el proceso **0** que no hace nada, tal como se presentan para π en [11, 14].

Definición 3 (Método) *Un método m está conformado por un puerto de contrato m_C, uno de activación m_I y uno de respuesta m_R.*

3.2. Tipos y subtipos

A diferencia de la propuesta de Pahl [12], en donde la relación de subtipo es un preorden, en π_{tp} la relación de subtipo es un orden parcial, lo cual se justifica en la medida en que los modelos pretendidos el sistema de tipos tiene antisimetría. La funcionalidad de un puerto está descrita por su tipo.

Definición 4 (Tipo de los puertos) *El tipo $\gamma_p(p)$ de un puerto p se define así:*

$$\begin{array}{ll} \gamma_p(m_C) = \text{REQ} & \gamma_p(n_C) = \text{PRO} \\ \gamma_p(m_I) = \text{INV} & \gamma_p(n_I) = \text{EXE} \\ \gamma_p(m_R) = \text{RES} & \gamma_p(n_R) = \text{REP} \end{array}$$

Las conexiones se establecen entre los puertos. Cada conexión tiene un tipo que determina el *tipo* de los elementos que puede transportar.

Definición 5 (Tipo de las conexiones) *El tipo $\gamma_c(c)$ de una conexión c se define así:*

$$\begin{aligned} \gamma_c(m_C) &= \text{CTR}(\text{SIG}(T_1,\ldots,T_k,\text{CRE}(T)),\text{PRD}(\text{PRE}),\text{PRD}(\text{POST})) \\ \gamma_c(n_C) &= \text{CTR}(\text{SIG}(T_1,\ldots,T_k,\text{CRE}(T)),\text{PRD}(\text{PRE}),\text{PRD}(\text{POST})) \\ \gamma_c(m_I) &= \text{CAC}(T_1,\ldots,T_k,\text{CRE}(T)) \\ \gamma_c(n_I) &= \text{CAC}(T_1,\ldots,T_k,\text{CRE}(T)) \\ \gamma_c(m_R) &= \text{CRE}(T) \\ \gamma_c(n_R) &= \text{CRE}(T) \end{aligned}$$

Los constructores CTR, CAC, CRE asocian tipos y su propósito es clasificar conexiones con base en la información que éstas pueden transportar. Para ello se supone que hay al menos un tipo. Los constructores SIG y PRD son constructores para la firma de los métodos y para sus precondiciones y poscondiciones respectivamente.

Se propone un sistema de tipos para controlar el correcto establecimiento de conexiones entre métodos. Los elementos de un sistema de tipos son un *contexto de tipos* con su notación e interpretaciones y unas reglas de inferencia que caracterizan su utilidad.

Definición 6 (Contexto de tipos) *Un* contexto de tipos *Γ es un conjunto finito de parejas (nombre,tipo) en donde están definidos los siguientes elementos:*

$$\begin{array}{ll} \Gamma \vdash x : T & \textit{el nombre } x \textit{ tiene tipo } T \\ \Gamma \vdash S \leq T & \textit{el tipo } S \textit{ es subtipo de } T \\ \Gamma \vdash P & \textit{la expresión } P \textit{ está bien tipada} \end{array}$$

Se define una función γ de expresiones en tipos, tal que $\Gamma \vdash P \Leftrightarrow (P, \gamma(P)) \in \Gamma$.

La relación de subtipo se da entre tipos construidos con el mismo constructor. Tres reglas estructurales contribuyen a la definición de la relación $\leq$ y la postulan como un *orden parcial*, lo cual permitirá trabajar reticularmente y traerá sus propias ventajas [3].

$$\textsc{Ref}\ \frac{\Gamma \vdash T}{T = T},\ \textsc{Anti}\ \frac{\Gamma \vdash S \leq T \qquad \Gamma \vdash T \leq S}{\Gamma \vdash S = T},\ \textsc{Trans}\ \frac{\Gamma \vdash S \leq T \qquad \Gamma \vdash T \leq V}{\Gamma \vdash S \leq V}$$

Las reglas para *subtipaje* de firmas y predicados son S-SIG y S-PRD, véase el cuadro 2 [5]. Los nombres COND, PRE, POST, SIG y sus variantes primadas son variables de tipo. Una condición es subtipo de otra si la implica[6]. Un contrato es subtipo de otro si la precondición del primero es consecuencia de la precondición del segundo y la poscondición del primero implica la poscondición del segundo (regla S-CTR). Para la activación de las conexiones se espera que la relación de subtipo para los parámetros valga, como lo establece la regla S-CAC. La regla S-CRE establece que una conexión de respuesta es subtipo de otra si los tipos de los valores que transporta forman un subtipo de los parámetros de la segunda. En [13] se presenta la consistencia de tipos del cálculo.

Cuadro 2. Reglas del sistema de tipos

$$\textsc{I-Ctr}\ \frac{\Gamma \vdash s :_c \textsc{Sig}(T_1,\ldots,T_n,\textsc{CRe}(T)) \qquad \Gamma \vdash p_1 :_c \textsc{Prd}(T) \qquad \Gamma \vdash p_2 :_c \textsc{Prd}(T)}{\Gamma \vdash \textsc{Ctr}(s,p_1,p_2) :_c \textsc{Ctr}(\textsc{Sig}(T_1,\ldots,T_n,\textsc{CRe}(T)),\textsc{Prd}(T),\textsc{Prd}(T))}$$

$$\textsc{S-Sig}\ \frac{\Gamma \vdash T_1' \leq T_1 \quad \ldots \quad \Gamma \vdash T_k' \leq T_k \qquad \Gamma \vdash \textsc{CRe}(T) \leq \textsc{CRe}(T')}{\Gamma \vdash \textsc{Sig}(T_1',\ldots,T_k',\textsc{CRe}(T')) \leq \textsc{Sig}(T_1,\ldots,T_k,\textsc{CRe}(T))}$$

$$\textsc{S-Prd}\ \frac{\textsc{cond'} \Rightarrow \textsc{cond}}{\Gamma \vdash \textsc{Prd}(\textsc{cond'}) \leq \textsc{Prd}(\textsc{cond})}$$

$$\textsc{S-Ctr}\ \frac{\Gamma \vdash \textsc{pre} \leq \textsc{pre'} \qquad \Gamma \vdash \textsc{post'} \leq \textsc{post} \qquad \Gamma \vdash \textsc{sig'} \leq \textsc{sig}}{\Gamma \vdash \textsc{Ctr}(\textsc{sig'},\textsc{pre'},\textsc{post'}) \leq \textsc{Ctr}(\textsc{sig},\textsc{pre},\textsc{post})}$$

$$\textsc{S-CAc}\ \frac{\Gamma \vdash T_1' \leq T_1 \quad \ldots \quad \Gamma \vdash T_k' \leq T_k \qquad \Gamma \vdash \textsc{CRe}(T) \leq \textsc{CRe}(T')}{\Gamma \vdash \textsc{CAc}(T_1',\ldots,T_k',\textsc{CRe}(T')) \leq \textsc{CAc}(T_1,\ldots,T_k,\textsc{CRe}(T))}$$

$$\textsc{S-CRe}\ \frac{\Gamma \vdash T' \leq T}{\Gamma \vdash \textsc{CRe}(T') \leq \textsc{CRe}(T)}$$

3.3. Compatibilidad y creación de conexiones

Usando la clasificación de arquitecturas presentada en [7], el problema que tratamos de resolver puede ser abordado usando el estilo *cliente/servidor* como patrón arquitectónico para la solución. En general, como cliente se entederá cualquier módulo que brinde funcionalidad y como servidor cualquier módulo que requiera funcionalidad.

[5] Se escriben γ_p y γ_c como $:_p$ y $:_c$ respectivamente a modo de abreviación.

[6] Desde el punto de vista lógico.

La creación de una conexión entre dos puertos de instancias de servicios debe establecerse justo antes que uno requiera invocar un método que el otro ofrece. Las acciones del cliente (que requiere el método) y del servidor (que suministra el método) se definen en el cuadro 3.

Cuadro 3. Roles de los servicios en la creación de conexiones

Rol	Definición	Descripción
Cliente	$\stackrel{def}{=}$ $\textsc{Req}\ \overline{m}\langle x\rangle.C$	El proceso *cliente* requiere el método m por el puerto x y prosigue con C.
Servidor	$\stackrel{def}{=}$ $\textsc{Pro}\ n(y).S$	El proceso *servidor* atiende el método n por el puerto y y prosigue con S.

Dos procesos pueden conectarse vía sus métodos si se satisface la relación de subtipo entre estos a nivel de contratos. La regla de inferencia LINK-S cambia la regla de acción del cálculo π que requiere que los nombres de los puertos sean los mismos. Aquí, se requiere que se cumpla la relación de subtipo entre los métodos.

$$\textsc{Link-S}\quad \frac{Cliente \xrightarrow{\overline{m}\langle x\rangle} C \qquad Servidor \xrightarrow{n(y)} S \qquad \Gamma \vdash \gamma_c(n) = \gamma_c(m)}{Cliente|Servidor \xrightarrow{\tau} C \frown S},$$

en donde

$$C \frown S \quad \stackrel{def}{=} \quad \nu z((C|S)\{x, y := z, z\}).$$

Es decir, se ha establecido una conexión común para el método m entre C y S. La compatibilidad entre los puertos está asociada a sus tipos. En el desarrollo que a continuación se hace, se supone que las expresiones están bien tipadas.

3.4. Invocación y ejecución de un método

En esta ocasión, al igual que en la anterior, los roles de cliente y servidor corresponden al servicio que invoca y al que responde respectivamente (véase tabla 4).

Se supone que una conexión entre el cliente y el servidor ha sido establecida con la regla de conexión LINK-S. Esta conexión es usada para que el cliente invoque el método n ofrecido por servidor. El cliente envía la tupla de parámetros a y el canal x al servidor como información de la invocación. Los tipos de los parámetros de la invocación deben ser compatibles.

La regla de activación ACT-S define la semántica de invocación y ejecución de un método.

$$\textsc{Act-S}\quad \frac{Cliente \xrightarrow{\overline{m}\langle a,x\rangle} C \qquad Servidor \xrightarrow{n(b,y)} S \qquad \Gamma \vdash \gamma(b) = \gamma(a) \qquad \Gamma \vdash \gamma_c(n) = \gamma_c(m)}{Cliente|Servidor \xrightarrow{\tau} C \frown S\{b, y := a, x\}}$$

Cuadro 4. Roles de los procesos en la invocación y ejecución de un método

Rol	Definición	Descripción
Cliente	$\stackrel{def}{=}$ Inv $\overline{m}\langle a, x\rangle.C$	El proceso *cliente* invoca el método m con la tupla de parámetros a y espera una respuesta por el canal x. Luego prosigue con C.
Servidor	$\stackrel{def}{=}$ Exe $n(b, y).S$	El proceso *servidor* ejecuta el método n con parámetros b y responde por el canal y. Luego prosigue con S.

3.5. Respuesta de una invocación

A diferencia de los dos planteamientos anteriores, en esta ocasión (véase tabla 5), los roles entre cliente y servidor se intercambian, ya que el servicio que antes era cliente ahora es servidor y viceversa.

Cuadro 5. Roles de los procesos en la respuesta de una invocación

Rol	Definición	Descripción
Cliente	$\stackrel{def}{=}$ Res $m(a).C$	El proceso *cliente* recibe la tupla a por el canal m y prosigue con C.
Servidor	$\stackrel{def}{=}$ Rep $\overline{n}\langle b\rangle.S$	El proceso *servidor* responde por el canal n con la tupla b y prosigue con S.

La regla de inferencia Reply-S define la semántica de una respuesta ante una invocación.

$$\text{Reply-S}\quad \frac{\begin{array}{cc} Cliente \xrightarrow{m(a)} C & Servidor \xrightarrow{\overline{n}\langle b\rangle} S \\ \Gamma \vdash \gamma(b) = \gamma(a) & \Gamma \vdash \gamma_c(m) \leq \gamma_c(n) \end{array}}{Cliente|Servidor \xrightarrow{\tau} C\{a{:=}b\} \frown S}$$

3.6. Abstracción de servicios como procesos

Los servicios hacen parte del modelo como servidores y posiblemente como clientes[7], como se pudo evidenciar anteriormente. En las definiciones se supone la coherencia de tipos de las variables, tanto para las cuantificadas como para las no cuantificadas.

Un cliente, parametrizado con una secuencia de métodos requeridos, se caracteriza de la siguiente forma:

$$C_{m_1,\ldots,m_p} \stackrel{def}{=} (|k \mid 1 \leq k \leq p \ :\ \text{Req}\ \overline{m_k^C}\langle x_k^C\rangle.!(\text{Inv}\ \overline{x_k^C}\langle a_k, y_k\rangle.\text{Res}\ y_k(b_k).\mathbf{0}))$$

El superíndice C en m_k^C y en x_k^C se debe interpretar como distintivo para identificar que el método m_k está en el cliente C.

Se caracteriza un servidor con una secuencia de métodos ofrecidos:

[7] No necesariamente requieren métodos

$$S^{n_1,\ldots,n_q} \overset{def}{=} (|k \mid 1 \leq k \leq q \; : \textsc{Pro}\; n_k^S(z_k^S).!(\textsc{Exe}\; z_k^S(b_k, w_k).\textsc{Rep}\; \overline{w_k}\langle e_k\rangle.\mathbf{0}))$$

El superíndice S en n_k^S y en y_k^S se debe interpretar como distintivo para identificar que el método n_k está en el servidor S.

Finalmente un servicio *Servicio*, parametrizado con sus métodos requeridos X y métodos ofrecidos Y, se caracteriza así:

$$Servicio_X^Y \overset{def}{=} C_X | S^Y$$

4. Semántica de Ensamblaje

Considere el siguiente ejemplo del cálculo.

Ejemplo 1 (El cálculo y nuevas convenciones) *Calcular un ensamblaje a partir de los servicios A_m^p y B_q^m.*

$$\begin{array}{l}
A_m^p | B_q^m \\
= \quad \langle \text{ Definición } \rangle \\
\textsc{Req}\; \overline{m^A}\langle P_m\rangle.\alpha_m^A | \textsc{Pro}\; p^A(P_p).\beta_p^A | \textsc{Req}\; \overline{q^B}\langle P_q\rangle.\alpha_q^B | \textsc{Pro}\; m^B(P_m).\beta_m^B \\
\equiv \quad \langle \text{ Simetría y asociatividad de } | \, \rangle \\
\textsc{Req}\; \overline{m^A}\langle P_m\rangle.\alpha_m^A | \textsc{Pro}\; m^B(P_m).\beta_m^B | \textsc{Pro}\; p^A(P_p).\beta_p^A | \textsc{Req}\; \overline{q^B}\langle P_q\rangle.\alpha_q^B \\
\rightarrow \quad \langle \text{ Link-S } \rangle \\
\alpha_m^A \frown \beta_m^B | \textsc{Pro}\; p^A(P_p).\beta_p^A | \textsc{Req}\; \overline{q^B}\langle P_q\rangle.\alpha_q^B \\
\rightarrow \quad \langle \text{ Observación } \rangle \\
\alpha_m^A \frown \beta_m^B | AB_p^q
\end{array}$$

Gráficamente, los estados inicial y final se representan como en la figura 1.

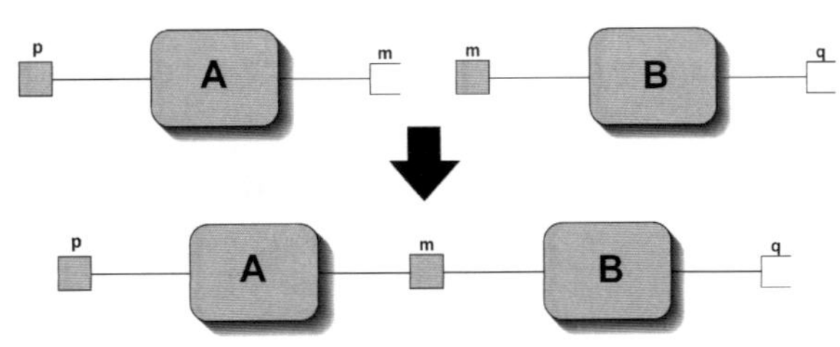

Figura 1. Estado inicial y final de un cálculo de ensamblaje

Vale la pena recalcar que existe una biyección entre la simbolización formal y la representación gráfica para el ensamblaje de servicios [13].

4.1. Noción de Corrección

Para introducir la noción de corrección son necesarias algunas definiciones y notación.

Definición 7 *Dados un ensamblaje E, un método a y un servicio S_X^Y, se define:*

1. *El conjunto asociado a un ensamblaje E, $\theta(E)$, es el conjunto de los servicios y de las conexiones en la composición de E.*
2. $a :: S_X^Y$ *denota la* invocación del método a *en el servicio* S_X^Y
3. *Un* ensamblaje es conformable *si no tiene bucles y se ofrece al menos un método*
4. $E \ltimes a :: S_X^Y$ *es un predicado que denota que la* invocación del método a *en el servicio* S_X^Y *es* satisfacible *en el* ensamblaje conformable E

Axioma 8 (Noción de corrección) *Para un método a, un servicio S_X^Y y un* ensamblaje conformable E *la invocación de a en S_X^Y es satisfacible siempre y cuando (1) a es* ofrecido *por S, (2) S* hace parte *del ensamblaje E y (3) todos los* métodos requeridos *por S están* satisfechos *por servicios correctos en E. Formalmente:*

$$E \ltimes a :: S_X^Y \equiv a \in Y \wedge S \in \theta(E) \wedge$$
$$(\forall b | b \in X : (\exists A_Z^W, \alpha_b^S \frown \beta_b^A | \alpha_b^S \frown \beta_b^A \in \theta(E) : E \ltimes b :: A_Z^W))$$

Nótese que para un servicio que no requiere métodos, la cuantificación es trivialmente cierta. Estos servicios son llamados *minimales.*

Ejemplo 2 (Satisfacibilidad) *Se desea determinar si el servicio $A_{x,y}^{z,s}$ es satisfacible en el ensamblaje $E = \alpha_x^A \frown \beta_x^B | \alpha_y^A \frown \beta_y^C | A^z | B^w | C^s$ que fue calculado a partir de los servicios $A_{x,y}^{z,s}, B^{x,w}, C^{y,s}$.*

$$
\begin{array}{ll}
 & E \ltimes A_{x,y}^{z} \\
\equiv & \langle \text{ SSAFE-S } \rangle \\
 & (\forall a | a \in \langle z, s \rangle : E \ltimes a :: A_{x,y}^{z,s}) \\
\equiv & \langle \text{ Consistencia } \rangle \\
 & (\exists a | a \in \langle z, s \rangle : E \ltimes a :: A_{x,y}^{z,s}) \\
\Leftarrow & \langle \text{ Introducción de } \exists \text{ con testigo } z \rangle \\
 & E \ltimes z :: A_{x,y}^{z,s} \\
\equiv & \langle \text{ ISAT-S } \rangle \\
 & A_{x,y}^{z,s} \in \theta(E) \wedge z \in \langle z, s \rangle \wedge (\exists D_Z^W, \alpha_x^A \frown \beta_x^D | \alpha_x^A \frown \beta_x^D \in \theta(E) : E \ltimes x :: D_Z^W) \\
 & \wedge (\exists F_Z^W, \alpha_s^A \frown \beta_s^F | \alpha_s^A \frown \beta_s^F \in \theta(E) : E \ltimes s :: F_Z^W) \\
\equiv & \langle \text{ Suposición: } A_{x,y}^{z,s} \in \theta(E) \wedge z \in \langle z, s \rangle \text{, módulo de } \wedge \rangle \\
 & (\exists D_Z^W, \alpha_x^A \frown \beta_x^D | \alpha_x^A \frown \beta_x^D \in \theta(E) : E \ltimes x :: D_Z^W) \\
 & \wedge (\exists F_Z^W, \alpha_s^A \frown \beta_s^F | \alpha_s^A \frown \beta_s^F \in \theta(E) : E \ltimes s :: F_Z^W) \\
\Leftarrow & \langle \text{ Intr. de } \exists \text{ con testigos } B^{x,w}, \alpha_x^A \frown \beta_x^B \rangle \\
 & E \ltimes x :: B^{x,w} \wedge (\exists F_Z^W, \alpha_s^A \frown \beta_s^F | \alpha_s^A \frown \beta_s^F \in \theta(E) : E \ltimes s :: F_Z^W) \\
\Leftarrow & \langle \text{ Intr. de } \exists \text{ con testigos } C^{y,s}, \alpha_y^A \frown \beta_y^C \rangle \\
 & E \ltimes x :: B^{x,w} \wedge E \ltimes y :: C^{y,s} \\
\equiv & \langle \text{ Satisfacibilidad en minimales x2, módulo de } \wedge \rangle \\
 & \mathit{true}
\end{array}
$$

Por tanto el servicio $A_{x,y}^{z,s}$ es satisfacible en E.

5. Semántica de Composición

Un componente es similar a un servicio ya que tiene un nombre, una colección de métodos ofrecidos y otra de métodos requeridos. Sin embargo, y de acuerdo con la caracterización presentada inicialmente, éstos exhiben su estructura interna que puede ser una composición de componentes.

La figura 2 muestra un componente cuyo nombre es A y cuya estructura interna es un ensamblaje de los componentes (o servicios) B, C y D.

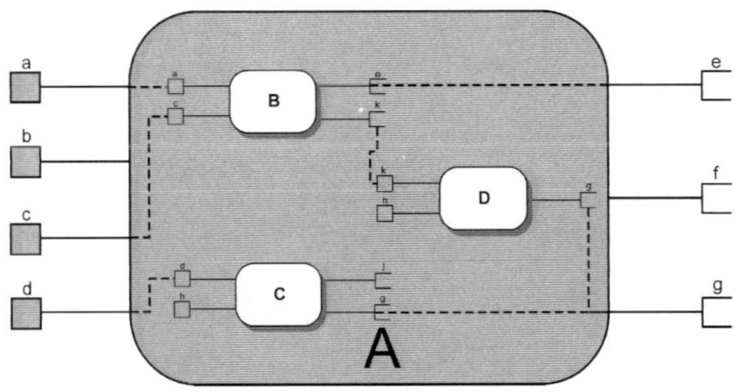

Figura 2. Representación gráfica de un componente

Definición 9 (Componente) *Se define que:*

1. *Un componente es una estructura* ${}^{Y}A^{Z}_{X} \oplus Q$ *en donde* A *es el nombre del componente,* X *la colección de métodos requeridos por el componente,* Y *y* Z *las colecciones de métodos ofrecidos por el componente, y* Q *la estructura interna del componente o su ensamblaje.*
2. *La estructura interna de un componente de nombre* A *se denota por* $\Phi(A)$.
3. *A cualquier componente que haga parte de la estructura interna de un componente de nombre* A*, se le llama subcomponente de* A.

Al igual que en el modelo de servicios, la permutación en las colecciones de métodos no es significativa. Gráficamente, usando las convenciones establecidas para servicios, un componente

$$
{}^{b}A^{a,c,d}_{e,f,g} \oplus (B|D^{h}|C^{h}_{j}|\alpha^{A}_{a} \frown \beta^{B}_{a}|\alpha^{A}_{c} \frown \beta^{B}_{c}|\alpha^{A}_{d} \frown \beta^{C}_{d}|\alpha^{B}_{k} \frown \beta^{D}_{k}|\alpha^{B}_{e} \frown \beta^{A}_{e}|\alpha^{D}_{g} \frown \beta^{A}_{g}|\alpha^{C}_{g} \frown \beta^{A}_{g})
$$

puede verse como en la figura 2.

En el modelo de componentes la semántica de composición está definida a partir de las conexiones entre los componentes del modelo. Una conexión se establece: (1) entre un método requerido y uno ofrecido, (2) entre un par de métodos ofrecidos ó (3) entre un par de métodos requeridos. La definición que se presenta a continuación, caracteriza estos tipos de conexión.

Definición 10 (Delegación y exportación) *Se distinguen tres tipos de conexiones en un componente:*

- *Las de delegación entre un método ofrecido por el componente y uno ofrecido por alguno de sus subcomponentes.*

- *Las de exportación entre un método requerido por alguno de sus subcomponentes y uno requerido por el componente.*
- *Las de ensamblaje entre un método requerido y otro ofrecido de un par de componentes.*

Se debe entender que las conexiones se establecen entre métodos compatibles, tal y como se definió para los servicios.

Por ejemplo, retomando el componente que aparece en la figura 2, las conexiones $\alpha_a^A \frown \beta_a^B$ y $\alpha_d^A \frown \beta_d^C$ son de delegación, las conexiones $\alpha_e^B \frown \beta_e^A$ y $\alpha_g^D \frown \beta_g^A$ son de exportación y la conexión $\alpha_k^B \frown \beta_k^D$ no es de ninguno de estos dos tipos.

Definición 11 (Conformado e inicial) *Un componente* ${}^X A_Z^Y \oplus Q$ *se dice*

- *bien conformado si la colección de métodos X es vacia, es decir, todos sus métodos ofrecidos han sido delegados en su estructura interna.*
- *inicial si la colección de métodos Y es vacía y en Q no ocurren conexiones de delegación o de exportación, es decir, conexiones de la forma $\alpha_a^A \frown \beta_a^B$ o $\alpha_a^B \frown \beta_a^A$ para algún B subcomponente de A.*

Un *componente* cuya *estructura interna es vacia*, es como un *servicio* o caja negra.

Los siguientes axiomas caracterizan las nociones de *delegación* y de *exportación.*

Axioma 12 (Delegación) ${}^{aX} A_Z^Y \oplus (B_W^{aT} | Q) \ \rightarrow \ {}^X A_Z^{aY} \oplus (B_W^T | Q | \alpha_a^A \frown \beta_a^B)$

Axioma 13 (Exportación) ${}^X A_{aZ}^Y \oplus (B_{aW}^T | Q) \ \rightarrow \ {}^X A_{aZ}^Y \oplus (B_W^T | Q | \alpha_a^B \frown \beta_a^A)$

Una vez se establece una delegación entre un par de métodos ninguno de ellos podrá formar parte de una nueva conexión, mientras que en la exportación el método que requiere el componente puede formar parte de nuevas conexiones. Además, un componente en cuya estructura interna no aparecen conexiones tiene una composición válida.

Definición 14 (Composición) *Una composición*[8] *es calculada a partir de un componente inicial, usando los axiomas de delegación y de exportación, y usando la regla* LINK-S *y las del cálculo* π_{tp} *en su estructura interna.*

Por ejemplo, es posible calcular una composición similar a la de la figura 2 a partir de

$$ {}^{a,b,c,d} A_{e,f,g} \oplus (B_{e,k}^{a,c} | C_{j,g}^{d,h} | D_g^{h,k}) \ , $$

y ver que el componente no está bien conformado, pues el método ofrecido b no fue delegado. La derivación se omite.

La noción de corrección que se define a continuación es similar a la de servicios, sobrecarga la notación existente y la extiende para el operador de composición. De nuevo se supondrá que la implantación de cada componente es correcta con respecto a su especificación, lo que sugiere también hablar de una noción de satisfacibilidad como noción de corrección inherente en el modelo.

[8] No confundir con la composición de procesos en el cálculo π

Axioma 15 (Noción de corrección) *Un componente* ${}^{X}A_{Z}^{Y} \oplus Q$ *es* correcto *con respecto a un* ensamblaje conformable E *siempre y cuando (1) A está* bien conformado, *(2) su* estructura interna *es* correcta *y todos los* métodos requeridos *por A están* satisfechos *por* componentes correctos *en E. Formalmente,*

$$E \ltimes^{X} A_{Z}^{Y} \oplus Q \equiv X = \lambda \wedge E \ltimes A_{Z}^{Y}$$
$$(\forall a | a \in Y : (\exists B_{W}^{T}, \alpha_{a}^{A} \frown \beta_{a}^{B} | B_{W}^{T}, \alpha_{a}^{A} \frown \beta_{a}^{B} \in \theta(Q) : Q | A^{Z} \ltimes B_{W}^{T} \oplus \Phi(B)))$$

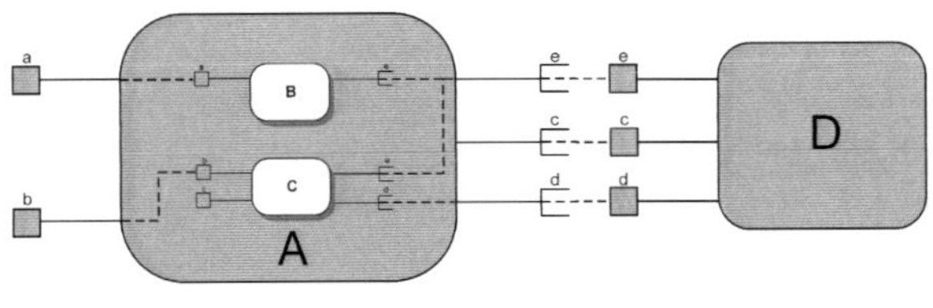

Figura 3. Representación gráfica de un componente

Ejemplo 3 *El componente A es correcto, dada su composición y ensamblaje en la figura 3.*

Claramente $X = \lambda$ *dado que todos los métodos están delegados. También* $E \ltimes A_{c,d,e}^{a,b}$ *ya que todas las dependencias de A están satisfechas por D que es minimal. El resto de la demostración no reviste mayor dificultad y se omite.*

6. Conclusiones y Trabajo Futuro

En este artículo se presentó una propuesta de una *extensión* del cálculo π como *adaptación* del cálculo de Pahl, una representación *formal* de los *conceptos y términos* de los modelos, una *semántica de ensamblaje* con una *noción de corrección* y una *semántica de composición* con una *noción de corrección.*

Por otra parte, el trabajo propuesto deja planteada la posibilidad de avanzar en varios frentes. Por ejemplo, por solo enumerar algunos, parece natural extender la semántica para tener en cuenta la *reconfiguración* en los modelos, extender la noción de corrección para *no suponer* la corrección de las implantaciones, instrumentar la ejecución de un modelo de componentes (por ejemplo Gaita) con secuencias de reducciones del cálculo π_{tp}, tal como se presentan en este documento para hacer *pruebas exhaustivas* de la implantación, resolver un *problema de decisión* asociado a la noción de corrección (dado un conjunto de servicios $\theta(E)$, un servicio $S_{X}^{Y} \in \theta(E)$ y una obligación de corrección $E \ltimes S_{X}^{Y}$, determinar si existe un ensamblaje con los servicios en $\theta(E)$ que satisfaga $E \ltimes S_{X}^{Y}$).

Referencias

1. B. Barnes and T. Bollinger. Making reuse cost-effective. *IEEE Software*, 8(1):13–24, 1991.

2. K. Bergner, A. Rausch, M. Sihling, A. Vilbig, and M. Broy. A formal model for componentware. In G. T. Leavens and M. Sitaraman, editors, *Foundations of Component-Based Systems*, chapter 9, pages 189–210. Cambridge University Press, New York, NY, 2000.
3. J. Bohórquez and C. Rocha. Towards the effective use of formal logic in the teaching of discrete mathematics. In *6th International Conference on Information Technology Based Higher Education and Training*. IEEE Computer Society, 2005.
4. Y. Chen and B. H. C. Cheng. A semantic foundation for specification matching. In G. T. Leavens and M. Sitaraman, editors, *Foundations of Component-Based Systems*, pages 91–109. Cambridge University Press, New York, NY, 2000.
5. E. W. Dijkstra. *A Discipline of Programming*, chapter 14. Prentice-Hall, Englewood Cliffs, N. J., 1976.
6. C. Hoare. An axiomatic basis for computer programming. *CACM: Communications of the ACM*, 26, 1983.
7. W. Jiao and H. Mei. Eliminating mismatching connections between components by adopting an agent-based approach. In *ICTAI '03: Proceedings of the 15th IEEE International Conference on Tools with Artificial Intelligence*, page 358, Washington, DC, USA, 2003. IEEE Computer Society.
8. M. Lumpe. *A Pi-Calculus Based Approach to Software Composition*. Ph.D. thesis, University of Bern, Institute of Computer Science and Applied Mathematics, Jan. 1999.
9. M. Lumpe, F. Achermann, and O.Ñierstrasz. A Formal Language for Composition. In G. Leavens and M. Sitaraman, editors, *Foundations of Component Based Systems*, pages 69–90. Cambridge University Press, 2000.
10. B. Meyer. The grand challenge of trusted components, Mar. 08 2003.
11. R. Milner. *Communicating and mobile systems: the π-calculus*. Cambridge University Press, 1999.
12. C. Pahl. A pi-calculus based framework for the composition and replacement of components. In *Workshop on Specification and Verification of Component-Based Systems (OOPSLA 2001)*, 2001.
13. C. Rocha. Semánticas para el ensamblaje de servicios y la composición de componentes en un modelo de servicios y componentes. Master's thesis, Universidad de los Andes, 2005.
14. D. Sangiorgi and D. Walker. *The π-calculus: a Theory of Mobile Processes*. Cambridge University Press, 2001.
15. C. Szyperski. Component software and the way ahead. In G. T. Leavens and M. Sitaraman, editors, *Foundations of Component-Based Systems*, pages 1–20. Cambridge University Press, New York, NY, 2000.
16. J. Villalobos, R. Casallas, K. Marcos, P. Barvo, and C. Rocha. Gaita-s: Model specification. Documento técnico, 2005.

Sesión 2:

Organizaciones y Aspectos

Extending UML to Support Both Agency and Organizational Architectural Features

Carla Silva[Ψ], Jaelson Castro[Ψ1], Fernanda Alencar [Ω2] and Ricardo Ramos[Ψ]

[Ψ] Centro de Informática, Universidade Federal de Pernambuco, Av. Prof. Luiz Freire s/n, Recife PE, Brazil 50732-970, +5581 21268430
{ctlls, jbc, rar2}@cin.ufpe.br
[Ω] Departamento de Eletrônica e Sistemas, Universidade Federal de Pernambuco, R. Acadêmico Hélio Ramos s/n, Recife PE, Brazil 50740-530, +5581 21268995
fmra@ufpe.br

Abstract. Proposing development methodologies is becoming a promising area in agent-oriented software engineering research. The Tropos framework offers an approach to guide the development of agent-oriented systems by using concepts based on requirements engineering. In this paper, we concentrate on the detailed design and implementation phases of the Tropos approach by proposing an extension of UML to support the specification of multi-agent systems architecture in terms of agent roles. The proposal is an improvement of previous work to describe multi-agent systems architecture in the sense that it now supports Belief-Desire-Intention (BDI) agent architecture features besides organizational architectural features. Our approach also provides some guidelines to identify the information related to the BDI agent architecture by analysing the means-ends analysis of each architectural role composing the multi-agent system. In order to validate our proposal, we apply the approach to a Content Manager System, called e-News.

1 Introduction

One of the most promising software paradigms is the agent orientation. An agent is an encapsulated computer system that is situated in some environment, and that is capable of flexible, autonomous action in that environment in order to meet its design objectives [1]. Agent orientation offers a higher level of abstraction in thinking about software systems features and behaviour. The increasing interest in software agents and multi-agent systems has recently led to the development of new approaches based on agent concepts, such as GAIA [2], AUML [3], and Tropos [4] [5]. We are working on the improvement of Tropos - a requirements-driven framework that proposes to use the same concepts at various stages during the software development lifecycle.

[1] Currently on leave of absence at ITC-IRST / University of Trento, Italy.
[2] Currently on leave of absence at FCT / Universidade Nova de Lisboa, Portugal.

Tropos supports four phases of software development: Early requirements, Late requirements, Architectural design, Detailed design.

Tropos adopts the concepts and models offered by *i** [6] framework which includes concepts such as *actor* (actors can be *agents*, *positions* or *roles*)[3], as well as social dependencies among actors including *goal*, *softgoal*, *task* and *resource* dependencies. However, to support modelling and design during the Detailed Design phase, which is the focus of this paper, Tropos also adopts extensions to UML [7], like AUML, the Agent Unified Modelling Language [3]. In fact, some languages for modelling multi-agent systems have been proposed in the last few years without considering software architecture features (e.g., ports, connectors [8]), such as AUML [3] and MAS-ML [9]. In this context, we propose a notation to capture the features of agency at the architectural level of multi-agent systems by extending the proposal for organizational architectural design [10] using UML-RT [11] introduced in [12] [13] [14]. We also provide some heuristics to identify the information related to the BDI agent architecture [15] by analysing the means-ends analysis of each agent role composing the multi-agent system architecture. We exemplify our proposal by applying the architectural role class diagram to the architectural design of an e-News system developed in the context of Tropos

This paper is organised as follows: Section 2 reviews the Tropos framework. Section 3 introduces our definition of agency metamodel and our extension of UML class diagram to support the concept of agent role. Section 4 presents our extension of the organizational architectural diagram to support the concept of agent role. Section 5 presents some heuristics to identify information of BDI agents from i* models in Tropos. Section 6 shows the application of our approach to a case study. Finally, section 6 summarises our work and points out urgent and still open issues.

2 The Tropos Approach

Tropos [4] [5] is a requirements-driven framework aimed at building software that operates within a dynamic environment. This means that both the system's environment and the system itself are modeled using the concepts offered by i* framework [6] and seen as organizations of actors, each having goals to be fulfilled and each relying on other actors to help them with goal fulfilment. The i* framework also includes the Strategic Dependency (SD) model for describing the network of relationships among actors, as well as the Strategic Rationale (SR) model for describing and supporting the reasoning that each actor goes through concerning its relationships with other actors by using a means-ends analysis.

Tropos has defined organizational architectural styles [10] for agent, cooperative, dynamic and distributed applications to guide the design of the system architecture. These architectural styles *(pyramid, joint venture, structure in 5, takeover, arm's length, vertical integration, co-optation and bidding)* are based on concepts and design alternatives coming from research on organization management. From this per-

[3] A role is an abstract actor. Concrete, physical agents such as human beings or software agents play roles. A position is a collection of roles that are typically played by a single agent.

spective, a software system is like a social organization of coordinated autonomous components that interact in order to achieve specific and possibly common goals. Fig.1 shows a MAS architecture in i* for an e-News system that applies the joint-venture style [10] at the architectural design level.

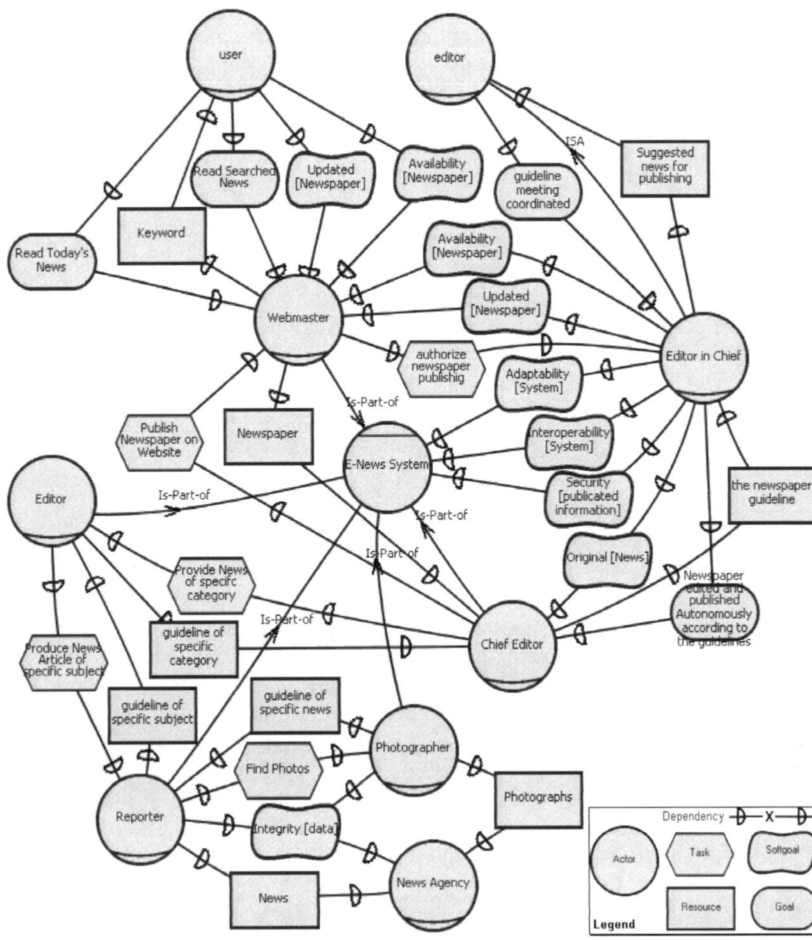

Fig. 1. An e-News Joint Venture architecture

An e-News allows users to obtain news from a newspaper web site. News related to a specific subject are extracted from different and distributed news' agencies on the Internet, translated and merged in order to provide good quality news. In a *joint venture* organisational style, a specific joint management actor (e.g. Chief Editor) coordinates tasks and manages the sharing of resources between partner actors (e.g. Editor, Webmaster, Reporter and Photographer). Each partner can manage and control itself on a local dimension and may interact directly with other partners to exchange resources, such as data and knowledge. However, the strategic operation and coordination of such system, and its actors on a global dimension, are the only responsibility of the joint management actor (i.e. Chief Editor).

When an user wishes to read news, she accesses the newspaper website maintained by a Webmaster agent which is responsible for updating the published information. The information to be published is provided and authorised by the Chief Editor agent. The Chief Editor depends on the Editor agents to have the news composed according to the newspaper guideline. Thus, it is necessary for the Chief Editor to share the newspaper guideline among the Editor agents. Each of them is responsible for bringing news about a specific subject. For example, an Editor may be responsible for political news while another one may be responsible for sports news. Each Editor selects one or many reporters/photographers which can find the news of specific subjects (e.g., basketball) to fulfill his sub-guideline (e.g., about sports news). The Chief Editor then edits the news from the Editor agents and forwards the edited news (if authorized) to the Webmaster to publish them.

As shown in Fig. 1, actors are represented as circles; dependums -- goals, softgoals, tasks and resources -- are respectively represented as ovals, clouds, hexagons and rectangles; and dependencies have the form depender⇒dependum⇒dependee. To support modelling and design during the Detailed Design phase, which is the focus of this paper, Tropos also adopts extensions to UML [7], like AUML, the Agent Unified Modelling Language [3].

3 Agent Role Class

Front to this, we have first defined a metamodel to explain our conception of agency (Fig. 2). A MAS can be conceived in terms of an *organization* which is composed by a number of roles. Each *agent* can play one or more *roles* and interacts with other agents according to protocols complied to by the roles of the involved agents. A *protocol* describes a sequence of *messages* that can be sent or received by agents. In addition, the massage must comply with an *ontology,* i.e. the vocabulary of the symbols used in the message content and their meaning (both the sender and the receiver must ascribe the same meaning to symbols for the communication to be effective).

The MAS is typically immersed in exactly one *environment* that the agents may need to interact with to accomplish their roles. *Norms* defines (i) permissions (*rights*) and (ii) responsibilities (*duties*) that an agent playing a role must obey while executing [2]. Organization norms describe a policy and constraints that must be complied to by all members, for the organization to operate harmoniously and safely [16].

We are investigating how Tropos agents can be designed using the Belief-Desire-Intention architecture [15]. Beliefs represent the information the agent has about its current environment and itself. Desires represent the possible courses of actions available to the agent. Intentions represent the state of affairs that the agent has committed to trying to bring about [1]. In Fig. 2, a *goal* is a concrete, momentary desire of an agent role [17]. A *plan* encapsulates the recipe for achieving some *goal.* An *action* determines the steps to perform a *plan.* By performing actions, agents can change de *environment*. Therefore, that change is reflected in the agent's beliefs. Agents playing a role must comply with the MAS *ontology*.

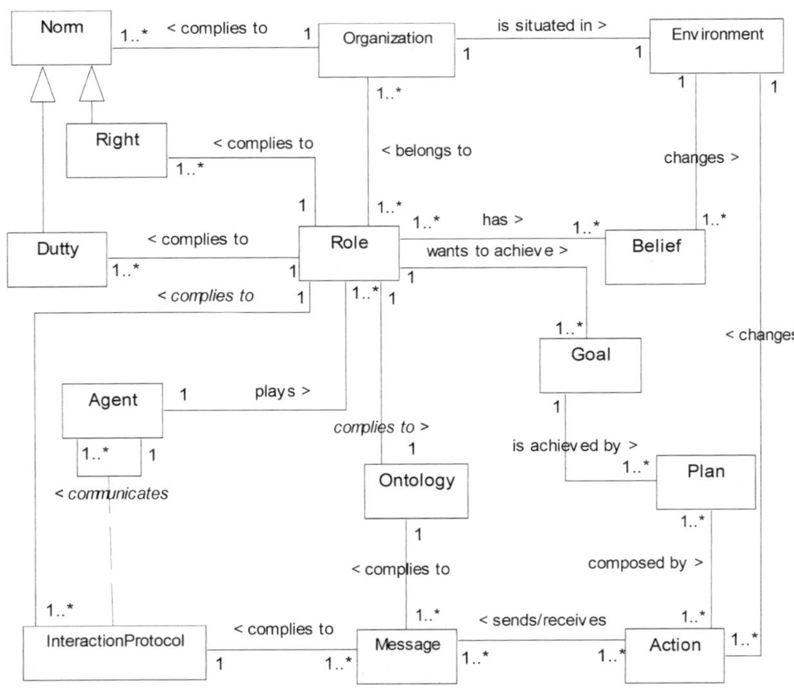

Fig. 2. Agency Metamodel

From this agency metamodel, we have created our own extension of UML to capture the features of agency using UML stereotypes [7]. In our conception, an agent role consists of the structure depicted in Fig. 3.

According to the role class depicted in Fig. 3, a role belongs to at least one organization (depicted by the stereotyped attribute <<Organization>>). Agents playing a role may have at least one belief (stereotyped attribute <<Belief>>) and one goal (stereotyped attribute <<Goal>>). Agents playing a role may exchange messages according to at least one protocol (stereotyped attribute <<Protocol>>) which complies to an ontology (stereotyped attribute <<Ontology>>). Agents playing a role must obey to at least one norm (stereotyped attribute <<Norm>>). To achieve a goal, the role must select among many plans (depicted by <<Action>> planSelecting( )). A plan (stereotyped operation <<Plan>>) is composed by a sequence of actions (stereotyped operation <<Action>>). Every role has the ability to update its beliefs and goals (depicted by <<Action>> beliefUpdating( ) and <<Action>> goalUpdating()), as the environment changes, the goals are fulfilled or messages arrive.

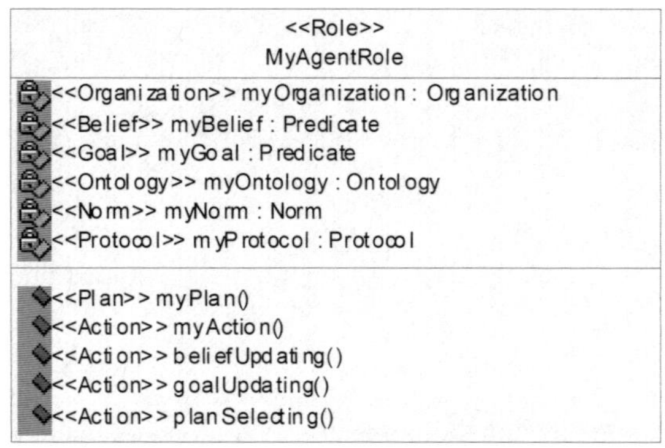

Fig. 3. Agent Role Structure

In order to use our concept of agent role in software architectural detailed design, in next section, we introduce an extended version of the structure presented in Fig. 3 to incorporate organizational architectural features.

4 Architectural Role Class

UML-RT (UML-Real Time) [11] adopts and extends UML to model real-time systems. This extension can also be used to model software architectures [8]. Some architectural modelling concepts are defined as specializations of generic UML concepts. These specializations, expressed as stereotypes, conform to the generic semantics of the corresponding UML concepts, but provide additional semantics specified by constraints [11].

In [12] [13] [14] we have presented an approach to use UML-RT as architectural description language (ADL) in Tropos. In fact, the organizational architectural styles (section 2.3.3), described initialy using the i* framework notation, now can be described using UML-RT. In particular, using UML-RT as an ADL in the Tropos methodology allow us for representing detailed information which sometimes is required in architectural design, such as set of signals that are exchanged between architectural components, which are not supported by the i* notation. Moreover, this approach encourages the use of novel organizational architectural styles in industry and other software development methodologies. In the sequel we explain how the concepts of Tropos can be accommodated within UML-RT, in order to represent organizational architectures in UML.

In Tropos actors are active entities that carry out actions to achieve goals by exercising their know-how. In UML Real-Time, capsules are specialized active classes used for modeling self contained components of a system. Hence, an actor in Tropos is mapped to a capsule in UML-RT (Fig. 4). Note that ports are physical parts of the implementation of a capsule that mediate the interaction of the capsule with the outside world.

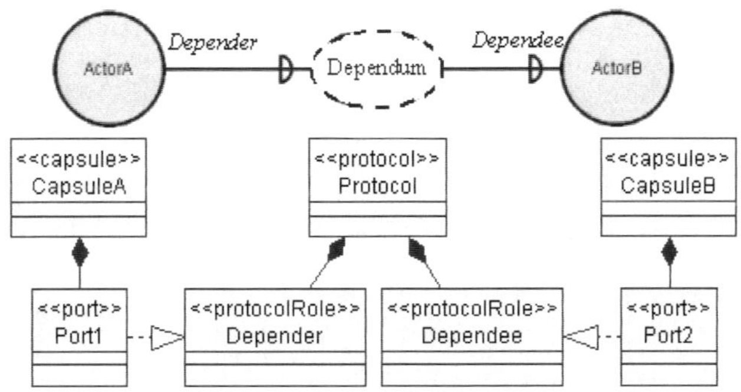

Fig. 4. Mapping a dependency between actors to UML

In Tropos a dependency describes an "agreement" (called *dependum*) between two actors playing the roles of *depender* and *dependee,* respectively. The *depender* is the depending actor, and the *dependee,* the actor who is depended upon. Dependencies have the form *depender→dependum→dependee*. In UML-RT, a protocol is an explicit specification of the contractual agreement between its participants, which play specific roles in the protocol. In other words, a protocol captures the contractual obligations that exist between capsules. Hence, a *dependum* is mapped to a protocol and the roles of *depender* and *dependee* are mapped to protocol roles that are comprised by the protocol (Fig. 4).

The type of the dependency between two actors (called *dependum*) describes the nature of the agreement. Tropos defines four types of *dependums*: goals, softgoals, tasks and resources. Each type of *dependum* will define different features in the protocol and therefore in ports that realizes its protocol roles.

Protocols are defined in terms of entities called *protocol roles*. Since *protocol roles* are abstract classes and ports play a specific role in some protocol, a *protocol role* defines the *type* of a port, which simply means that the port implements the behavior specified by that *protocol role*. Capsules are complex, physical, possibly distributed architectural objects that interact with their surroundings through ports. Note that a port is both a composite part of the structure of the capsule and a constraint on its behavior.

Goal type will be mapped to an attribute with boolean type present into the port that realizes the protocolRole *dependee*. It represents a goal that a capsule is responsible for fulfill by exchanging the signals defined in the protocolRole *dependee*.

Softgoal type is mapped to an attribute with enumerated type present into the port that realizes the protocolRole *dependee*. It represents a quality goal that a capsule is responsible for fulfill to a given extent by exchanging the signals defined in the protocolRole *dependee*.

Resource type is mapped to the return type of an abstract method placed on protocolRole *dependee* that will be realized by a port of a capsule. This return type represents a resource that a capsule is required to provide by exchanging signals defined in the protocolRole *dependee*.

Task type is mapped to an abstract method placed on protocolRole *dependee* that will be realized by a port of a capsule. It represents an activity that a capsule is required to perform by exchanging signals defined in the protocolRole *dependee*.

A more compact form for describing capsules is illustrated in Fig. 5, where the ports of a capsule are listed in a special labeled list. The protocol role (type) of a port is normally identified by a pathname since protocol role names are unique only within the scope of a given protocol. However, ports are also depicted in the collaboration diagrams (not used in this work) that describe the internal decomposition of a capsule. For further details see [11].

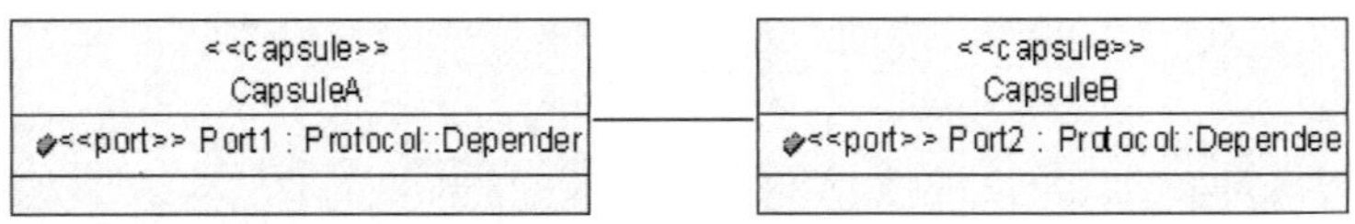

Fig. 5. A capsule class diagram

In UML-RT, each connector is typed by a protocol that specifies the *desired* behavior that can take place over that connector. A key feature of connectors is that they can only interconnect ports that play complementary roles in the protocol associated with the connector. In a class diagram, a connector is modeled by an association. Hence, a dependency (*depender→dependum→dependee*) in Tropos is mapped to a connector in UML-RT (Fig. 5).

The role class depicted in Fig. 3 need to be improved in order to support the organizational architectural features depicted in Fig. 5, besides agency features. Observe that the extended role class diagram (Fig. 6) now supports the concept of organizational architectural port [12] [13] [14] through which architectural components (i.e., agents playing some MAS architectural role) can interact with each other by playing a specific role (depender or dependee) in some protocol (depicted by the stereotyped attribute <<Port>>).

The protocol description provided in [12] [13] [14] is extended to support the FIPA performatives [18]. The performative is the communicative intention indicating what the sender intends to achieve by sending the message.

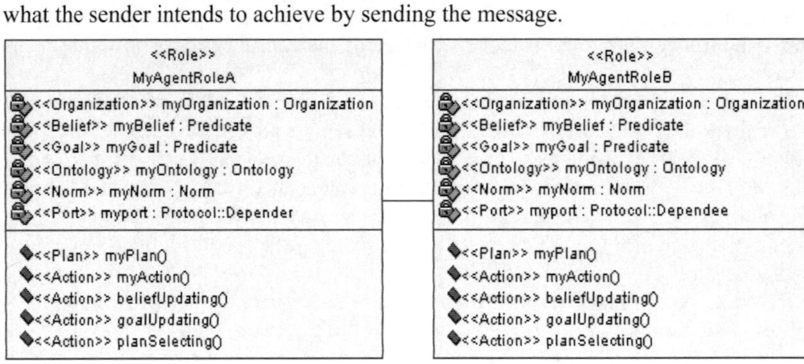

Fig. 6. Architectural role class diagram

In the specification of the protocol (Fig. 7), the <<Message>> stereotype in the <<ProtocolRole>> class indicates the FIPA performatives that an agent role performing that protocolRole may handle, i.e. the agent role communication interface. The <<incoming>> signal present in the <<ProtocolRole>> *Dependee* represents an activity that the <<Role>> |Matchmaker can be required to perform by incoming messages characterized by performatives defined in the <<ProtocolRole>> *Dependee.*

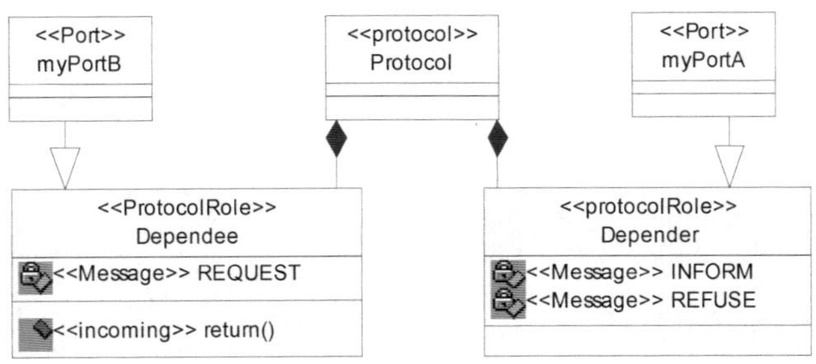

Fig. 7. Protocol Specification

5 Specifying Agents Roles

To identify the information related to the BDI agent architecture [15] it is necessary to perfom a means-ends-analysis [6] of each agent role which composes the MAS architecture. Hence, we identify the reasons associated with each role as well as goals and tasks he possesses that impel and justify each dependency he has. After this analysis, we can use the following heuristcs to guide the specification of each agent roles according to the extended role class diagrams:

i. Each dependency will create a protocol which the agent playing the Editor role, must comply to.
ii. Each resource related to the agent role becomes a belief.
iii. Each goal (or softgoal) corresponding to end-element in some means-ends relationship represents a *goal.*
iv. Each task corresponding to a means-element in some means-ends relationship represents an *plan.*
v. Each leaf task decomposed from a task corresponding to an intention represents an *action.*

In fact, many information associated to the agent roles are not addresses by these heuristics, but we are working toward solving this.

6 Case Study

First, we need to perform the means-ends analysis for each agent role composing the MAS architecture. Then, we can apply the heuristics defined by ***Specifying Agents***

Roles activity. For example, in our case study we perfom the means-ends-analysis [6] of the Editor and Chief Editor agent roles in order to detail the rationale they possess to meet its goals and dependencies. The Editor expects to obtain *specific category news edited.* To achieve this goal, the Editor has the alternative of performing the *Edit news of specific category* task. To perform this task it is necessary to perform several subtasks: *Format News Article, select uknown, recent, important and accurate news, Review Photos Quality, Review News Content, getNews* and *provide specific subject guideline* (Fig. 8).

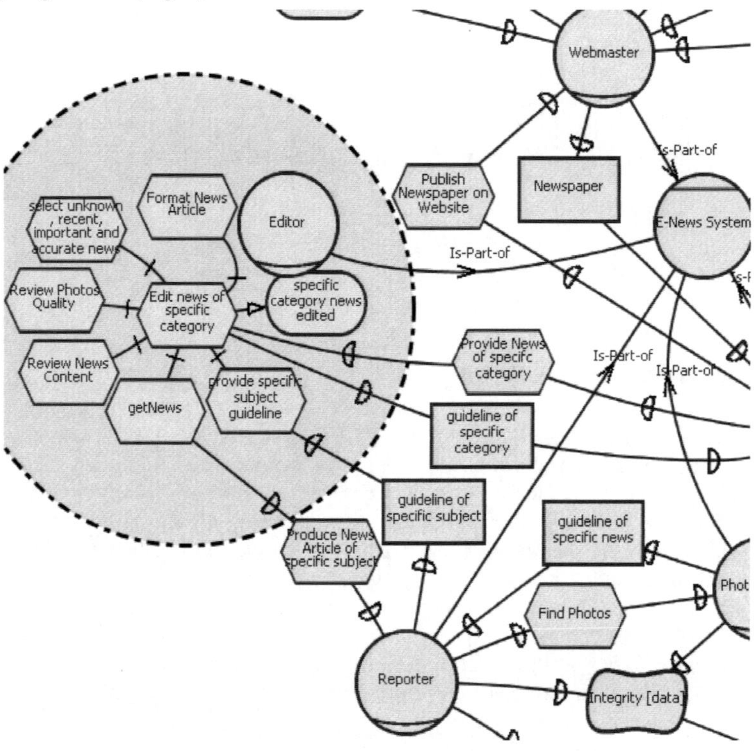

Fig. 8. Means-end analysis for Editor

The Chief Editor expects to obtain the *Newspaper edited and published according to the guideline* and to achieve this goal, he has one alternative, which is performing the *edit and publish newspaper according to guideline* task. This task is decmposed into the *Newspaper published* goal and *edit newspaper* task. The Webmaster role has the responsibilty to fulfill the *Newspaper published* goal. The *edit newspaper* task is further decomposed into three subtasks: *reviews articles content, decompose guideline by category* and *format newspaper pages* (Fig. 9).

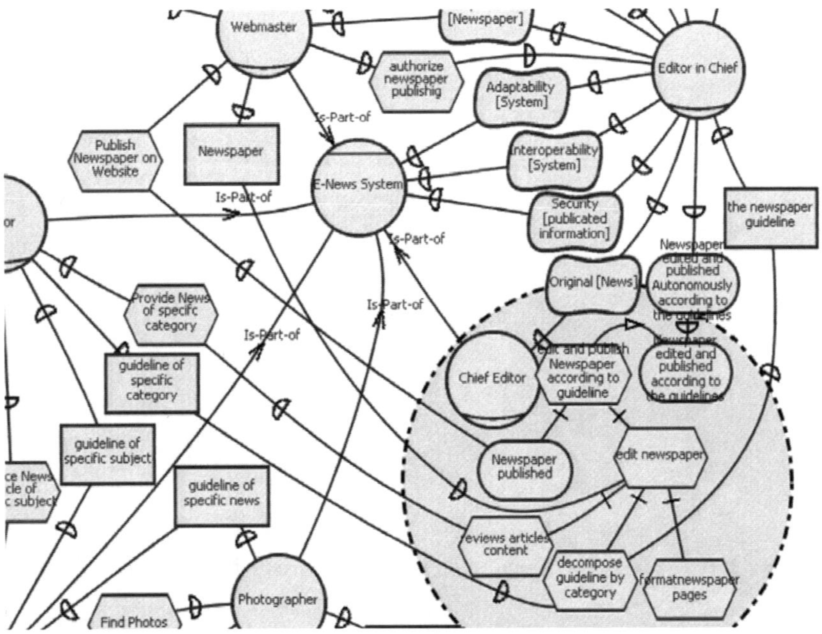

Fig. 9. Means-end analysis for Chief Editor

We have applied the heuristics provided in Section 5 to the means-end analysis of both the Editor and Chief Editor agent roles (Fig. 8 and Fig. 9), in order to identify the properties, which characterize that agent according to the extended agent role model (Fig. 6). After applying the guidelines for specifying the Editor and Chief Editor roles, we have extracted the information specified in the architectural agent role class diagram (Fig. 10) describing partially the MAS architecture.

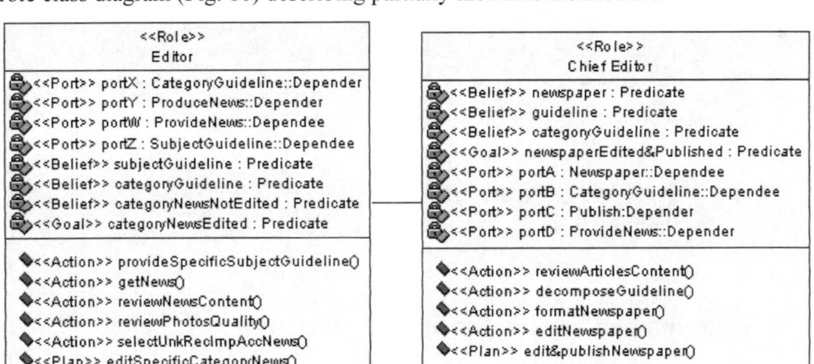

Fig. 10. Partial Agent Role Class Diagram for e-News Architecture

The communincation protocols shared by the Editor and Chief Editor roles are specified in Fig. 11 and Fig. 12. The <<Message>> stereotype in each <<Protocol-Role>> class indicates the FIPA performatives that an agent role performing that protocol may handle, i.e. the agent role communication interface. The <<incoming>> signal present in the <<ProtocolRole>> *Dependee* of Fig. 11 represents an activity that the <<Role>>, which possess the <<Port>> portW, can be required to perform by incoming messages characterized by performatives defined in the <<ProtocolRole>> *Dependee*.

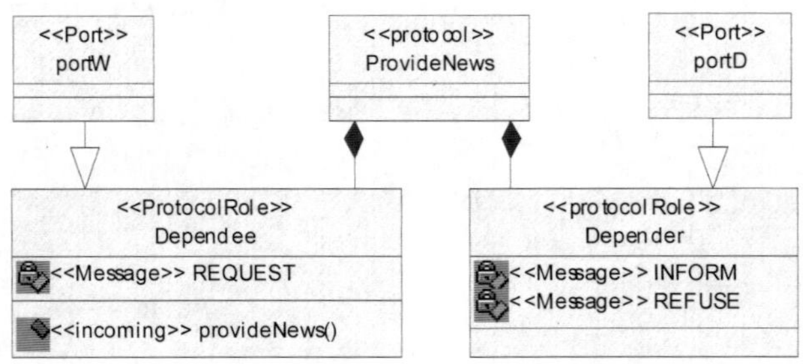

Fig. 11. ProvideNews communication protocol between Editor and Editor Chief

The <<incoming>> signal present in the <<ProtocolRole>> *Dependee* of Fig. 12 represents a resouce (information) that the <<Role>>, which possess the <<Port>> portB, can be required to provide by incoming messages characterized by performatives defined in the <<ProtocolRole>> *Dependee*.

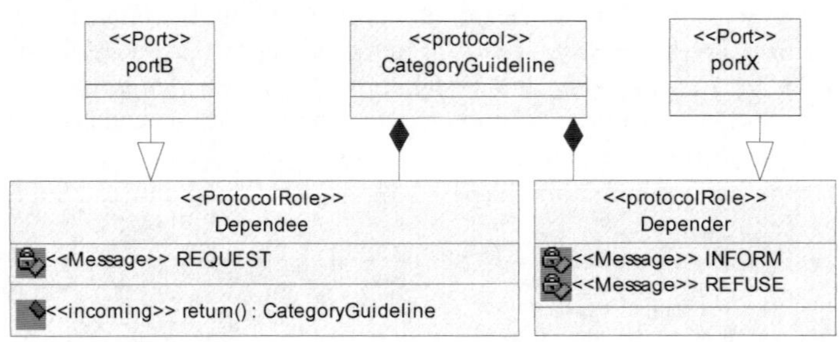

Fig. 12. CategoryGuideline communication protocol between Editor and Editor Chief

7 Conclusion and Future Work

In this work, we have defined a metamodel to explain our conception of agency. Using this metamodel, we have extended the UML class diagram to support the concept of agent role. Furthermmore, we have presented an extended description of agent role which incorporates organizational architectural features according to the proposal introduced in [12] [13] [14]. In particular, we have added to the agent role definition the concept of organizational architectural port, through which agents playing some architectural role can interact with each other according to a specific protocol. The protocol description provided in [12] [13] [14] was also extended to support the FIPA performatives [18] in order to indicate the communicative intention, i.e, what the sender intends to achieve by sending the message. Thus, the architectural role class diagram could be used in software architectural detailed design of Tropos framework.

Future work includes improving the activity for specifying agent roles by proposing a complete set of guidelines to aid the identification of agent roles'features from i* framework models is also required. We also intend to provide a complete view of the architectural design of the e-News system using the architectural role class diagram proposed in this work.

Acknowledgements

This work was supported by several research grants (CNPq Proc. 304982/2002-4, CAPES Proc. BEX 1775/2005-7, Proc. BEX 3003/05-1, Proc. BEX 3014/05-3 & CAPES/ GRICES Proc. 129/05).

References

1. Wooldridge, M.: An Introduction to Multiagent Systems. England (2002) 15-103.
2. Zambonelli, F., Jennings, N. R. and Wooldridge, M.: Developing Multiagent Systems: the Gaia Methodology, In: ACM Trans on Software Engineering and Methodology, Vol 12, Issue 3 (2003) 317-370.
3. Odell, J., Parunak, H. V. D. and Bauer, B.: Extending UML for Agents. In: Proceedings of the Agent-Oriented Information Systems at the 17th National Conference on Artificial Intelligence. iCue Publishing (2000) 3–17.
4. Castro, J., Kolp, M. and Mylopoulos, J.: Towards Requirements-Driven Information Systems Engineering: The Tropos Project. In: Information Systems News, Vol 27. Elsevier (2002) 365-89.
5. Giorgini, P., Kolp, M., Mylopoulos, J. and Castro, J.: Tropos: A Requirements-Driven Methodology for Agent-Oriented Software. Book Chapter in Agent-Oriented Methodologies. ed.: Idea Group (2005) 20-45.
6. Yu, E.: Modelling Strategic Relationships for Process Reengineering. Ph.D. thesis. Department of Computer Science. University of Toronto. Canada (1995)
7. Rumbaugh, J., Jacobson, I. and Booch, G.: The Unified Modeling Language – Reference Manual. Addison Wesley (1999)
8. Unified Modeling Language (UML) Specification: Infrastructure Version 2.0, Last access in August 2005. www.omg.org/docs/formal/05-07-04.pdf.
9. Silva, V., Lucena, C.: From a Conceptual Framework for Agents and Objects to a Multi-Agent System Modeling Language. In: Sycara, K., Wooldridge, M. (Edts.), Journal of Autonomous Agents and Multi-Agent Systems, Vol. 9, issue 1-2. Kluwer Academic Publishers, ISSN 1387-2532 (2004) 145-189.

10. Kolp, M., Giorgini, P. and Mylopoulos, J.: Information Systems Development through Social Structures. In: Proceedings of the 14th International Conference on Software Engineering and Knowledge Engineering, Ischia, Italy (2002)
11. Selic, B., Rumbaugh, J.: Using UML for Modeling Complex Real - Time Systems", Rational Whitepaper, http://www.rational.com, Last access in March 2002 (1998)
12. Silva, C.: Detailing the Architectural Design in Agent-Oriented Software Development: The Tropos Case (In Portuguese: Detalhando o projeto arquitetural no desenvolvimento de software orientado a agentes: O caso Tropos). Master Thesis. Centro de Informática, Universidade Federal de Pernambuco (2003)
13. Castro, J., Silva, C., Mylopoulos, J.: Modeling Organizational Architectural Styles In UML. In: Proceedings of the 15th Conference On Advanced Information Systems Engineering - CAISE´03, Vol. 2681. Klagenfurt/Velden: Springer Verlag (2003) 111-126.
14. Castro, J., Mylopoulos, J., Silva, C.: Agent-Driven Requirements Engineering. In: J. C. S. P. Leite, & J. H. Doorn, Perspectives on Software Requirements. 1st ed.. Boston, USA. Kluwer Academic (2004) 253-274.
15. Rao, A. S. and Georgeff, M. P.: BDI agents: from theory to practice. Technical Note 56, Australian Artificial Intelligence Institute (1995)
16. Minsky, N and Muarata, T.: On Manageability and Robustness of Open Multi-Agent Systems. In: Computer Security, Dependability, and Assurance, Carlos Lucena and Alessandro Garcia and Alexander Romanovsky and Jaelson Castro and Paulo Alencar editors; LNCS, No. 2940, Springer-Verlag (2004) 189-206.
17. Braubach, L., Pokahr, A. and Lamersdorf, W.: Jadex: A Short Overview. In: Main Conference Net.ObjectDays 2004, AgentExpo (2004)
18. FIPA. The Foundation for intelligent agents. http://www.fipa.org, Last access in March 2005.

Metamodelo para Adaptação de Processos de Software com base em Riscos

Lisandra M. Fontoura, Júlio Hartmann, Roberto Tom Price

Instituto de Informática – Universidade Federal do Rio Grande do Sul (UFRGS)
Caixa Postal 15.064 – 91.501-970 – Porto Alegre – RS – Brasil
[lisandra, jhartmann, tomprice]@inf.ufrgs.br

Resumo. Esse artigo descreve uma abordagem sistemática para gerenciar riscos em projetos de software (ASiGeR) por meio da adaptação de processos. O objetivo da abordagem é elaborar um processo definido para um projeto, visando minimizar a exposição do projeto aos riscos, identificados de acordo com o contexto. Os riscos são associados a ações preventivas, descritas por meio de padrões organizacionais e de processo. O artigo propõe um metamodelo de processo, elaborado pela integração dos metamodelos do Rational Unified Process e do Extreme Programming. O metamodelo proposto é usado para representar o processo padrão da organização, o processo definido para o projeto e os padrões. Após uma análise e uma priorização dos riscos que podem afetar o projeto, são identificados os padrões que descrevem ações preventivas aos riscos do projeto e estes são inseridos no processo da organização, dando origem ao processo definido para o projeto. A ferramenta RiskTool foi elaborada para apoiar a sistemática proposta.

1. Introdução

Processo de software pode ser definido como o conjunto de atividades que são necessárias para conceber, desenvolver, implantar e manter um software [18].

Considerando que, projetos de software apresentam diferenças quanto à tecnologia, clientes, riscos, formalismo, equipe, tamanho, etc, definir um processo único que seja utilizado em todos os projetos da organização é inviável. É necessário que, os processos de software sejam adequados ao domínio da aplicação e aos requisitos específicos de cada projeto.

O SEI, por meio do CMM-SW [27], propõe que seja definido um processo de software padrão da organização, com os elementos de processo fundamentais que são esperados em todos os projetos, e esse processo seja adaptado para cada projeto, de acordo com as características e restrições deste, dando origem ao processo de software definido para um projeto.

No entanto, adaptar o processo da organização para cada projeto é uma tarefa complexa e trabalhosa, envolvendo a seleção, elaboração e combinação de técnicas e processos, além da compreensão das características e necessidades do projeto [18]. Portanto, é desejável a pesquisa de sistemáticas e ferramentas que apóiem o projetista de processos neste trabalho.

Este artigo propõe um metamodelo de processo para representar os conceitos usados na definição de processos de software, isto é, a partir dos conceitos descritos no metamodelo são instanciados elementos de processo (atividades, papéis, artefatos, ferramentas, etc.) que são usados na construção de modelos de processo. As instâncias de elementos de processo são armazenadas em uma biblioteca. O metamodelo define a linguagem para expressar processos de software; descreve os conceitos e suas relações com a finalidade de construir e interpretar modelos de processo. ASiGeR utiliza o metamodelo proposto para representar os conceitos necessários à adaptação de processos.

Para permitir que o metamodelo seja flexível o suficiente para representar métodos ágeis, planejados e métodos que combinam características de ambos [8], o metamodelo de processo foi elaborado a partir dos metamodelos do método ágil Extreme Programming (XP) [4] e do processo planejado Rational Unified Process (RUP) [28]. É tarefa da organização definir o processo que deseja utilizar.

Considerando que, padrões organizacionais e de processo definem práticas bem-sucedidas relacionadas ao processo de software e à organização [10], as ações a serem tomadas para prevenir os riscos do projeto são descritas como padrões. Padrões são representados segundo os elementos de processo necessários à sua implantação.

Visando facilitar a atividade de definição de processos da organização e satisfazer normas e modelos de qualidade no momento da adaptação são sugeridas algumas configurações de processo. Essas configurações propõem processos simplificados, como RUP Essencial; completos, como RUP e XP; ou estendidos para satisfazer modelos de qualidade, como RUP CMM/Nível 2 e RUP/CMM Nível 3. Essas configurações são exemplos, a organização pode definir suas próprias configurações.

Um ambiente experimental de apoio à adaptação de processos foi desenvolvido. Nesse ambiente são definidas uma biblioteca de elementos de processo e uma biblioteca de padrões. De acordo com o contexto de um projeto, o processo definido para o projeto é elaborado por inserir no processo padrão da organização, os elementos de processo necessários à implantação de padrões para prevenção dos riscos identificados para o projeto.

Este artigo está organizado da seguinte maneira: a seção 2 apresenta os trabalhos relacionados. A seção 3 descreve a abordagem para gerenciar riscos. Na seção 4 é apresentado o metamodelo integrado elaborado a partir da integração dos metamodelos do RUP e do XP. A seção 5 descreve o uso de padrões para representar ações preventivas de riscos. Na seção 6 é demonstrado o ambiente experimental para apoiar a sistemática e na seção 7 são descritos as conclusões e os trabalhos futuros.

2. Trabalhos Relacionados

Em [7], é apresentada uma abordagem para a adaptação de processos de software para projetos específicos e a geração de um Ambiente de Desenvolvimento de Software Orientado à Organização para ser instanciado na estação TABA. Dentro desde mesmo projeto, é proposta uma ferramenta para gerenciar riscos chamada RiscPlan [14]. Falbo et al. [9] propõem uma abordagem para adaptação de processos baseada em gerenciamento de conhecimento e o uso de métricas coletadas em projetos passados. A ferramenta ProKnowHow apóia a abordagem proposta.

Kiper e Feather [29] e Dillon et al. [2] propõem modelos probabilísticos para gerenciar riscos, enquanto este trabalho utiliza quantificação da exposição ao risco. Modelos probabilísticos são mais complexos e difíceis de serem aplicados. Keshlaf e Hashim [25] propõem um modelo para gerenciamento de riscos e uma ferramenta, chamada SoftRisk, para apoiar o processo. Não define como os riscos são monitorados e controlados durante o projeto de software [25]. Roy [31] propõe um *framework*, chamado de ProRisk, para gerenciar riscos em projetos de software. O *framework* requer uma análise detalhada da organização e do domínio do projeto para desenvolver um conjunto de fatores de riscos e organizá-los de forma que possa refletir as diferentes perspectivas de riscos, dificultando sua utilização.

A proposta desse trabalho difere dos demais trabalhos por propor uma adaptação de processos baseada em ações preventivas para os riscos identificados, e por usar padrões organizacionais e de processo para descrever as ações preventivas e corretivas para os riscos. Um metamodelo de processo é proposto para representar os conceitos utilizados na construção de processos, e a ferramenta Risktool é elaborada para apoiar a sistemática proposta.

3. Abordagem Sistemática para Gerenciar Riscos

A abordagem sistemática para gerenciar riscos (ASiGeR) em projetos de software foi elaborada com base nas atividades descritas por Hall [19] e Boehm [6]. A Figura 1 mostra as atividades sugeridas e a seqüência de execução dessas atividades.

ASiGeR tem como vantagem a prevenção dos riscos identificados para o projeto desde o início deste, já que são inseridas ações preventivas no processo de software no momento da customização do processo da organização para um projeto específico. A seguir, uma descrição das atividades propostas por ASiGeR é apresentada.

A atividade *Identificar Riscos do Projeto* descreve como identificar os riscos que podem afetar o projeto. Para auxiliar o gerente de projeto nesta atividade, em [15] é descrita uma lista contendo os riscos mais comuns em projetos de software, elaborada a partir dos trabalhos dos autores Keil et al. [23], Addison [1], Boehm [6] e dos riscos sugeridos pelo modelo CMMI [30]. A Tabela 1 mostra essa lista de riscos classificada por tipo de risco. Riscos de cliente se originam no grau de envolvimento dos clientes com o sistema que está sendo desenvolvido; riscos de requisitos descrevem preocupações quanto ao entendimento das necessidades do cliente e a satisfação do usuário com o software desenvolvido; riscos de planejamento têm origem no planejamento inicial do projeto de software; riscos de execução descrevem situações que podem ocorrer afetando a qualidade do software e o progresso das atividades.

A lista de riscos, sugerida na Tabela 1, é utilizada pelo gerente de projeto para auxiliá-lo a identificar os riscos que podem afetar o projeto de software. O processo de identificação dos riscos não deve ficar limitado a esta lista de riscos, pode-se, por exemplo, utilizar os principais problemas que ocorreram em projetos passados da organização, como sugerido por DeMarco e Lister [13]. Essa lista de riscos é uma sugestão e deve ser constantemente avaliada e melhorada.

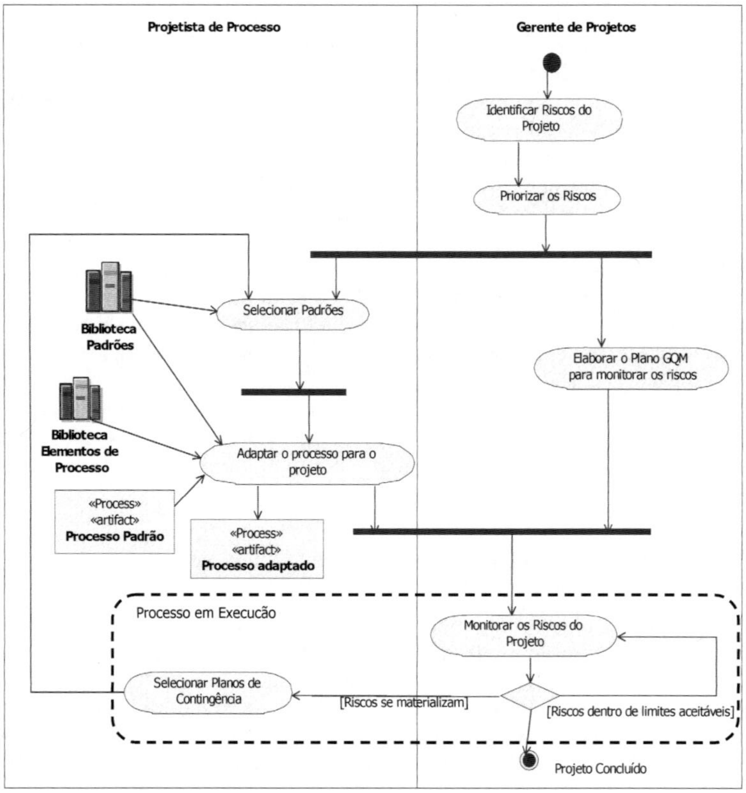

Fig. 1. Abordagem Sistemática para Gerenciar Riscos em Projetos de Software

Tabela 1. Riscos Classificados por Tipo de Risco

Cliente Falta de envolvimento dos clientes Falha em obter compromisso dos clientes Falha na gerência das expectativas dos clientes Conflito entre os departamentos do cliente	**Execução** Introdução de novas tecnologias Requisitos criados pelos desenvolvedores Desenvolvimento errado das funções ou interface Sub-contratação Uso de recursos e desempenho do sistema Projeto (desenho) inviável
Planejamento Falta de compromisso da gerência sênior Falta de conhecimento/habilidade da equipe Equipe insuficiente ou inadequada Cronograma e orçamento não-realistas Falta de uma metodologia de projeto	**Requisitos** Não-entendimento dos requisitos Escopo/objetivos do sistema não-claros Instabilidade de requisitos

Considerando que os riscos identificados para o projeto podem ser muitos, na atividade *Priorizar os Riscos* são descritas técnicas para priorizar os riscos que têm maior impacto sobre o projeto e alta ou média probabilidade de ocorrer [15].

Segundo Boehm [6], a técnica mais efetiva para a priorização dos riscos é a quantificação da exposição ao risco. A exposição ao risco (ER), algumas vezes chamada de impacto do risco ou fator de risco, é definida como o produto entre a probabilidade de um resultado não-satisfatório ocorrer e a perda associada a esse resultado não-satisfatório (impacto). Após quantificar todos os riscos, tem-se uma lista de riscos ordenada por exposição ao risco. O gerente de projeto define se todos os riscos identificados serão enfocados, ou somente os riscos com ER maior que determinado valor. Após a priorização dos riscos é necessário definir as ações preventivas para cada risco. Em [15], são sugeridas ações preventivas para mitigar os riscos mostrados na Tabela 1.

Um padrão (*pattern*) descreve a parte essencial de uma solução para um problema que é recorrente dentro de um determinado contexto [12]. Padrões organizacionais e de processos capturam práticas de sucesso no gerenciamento do desenvolvimento de software, e podem ser utilizados para formatar um novo processo de desenvolvimento para um projeto, ou então melhorar um processo já existente.

As ações preventivas podem ser vistas como padrões organizacionais e de processo, facilitando dessa forma a identificação de qual padrão adotar na customização do processo, já que existem inúmeros catálogos de padrões, tais como: [10], [11], [12], [22] entre outros. Esses padrões são armazenados em uma biblioteca de padrões e associados aos riscos que se propõem minimizar por meio de regras.

Neste trabalho, um padrão é descrito utilizando uma descrição textual, em um formato semelhante ao de James Coplien [10], que emprega os seguintes campos: *Nome*, *Classificação*, *Problema*, *Contexto*, *Forças*, *Solução*, *Relações*, *Justificativa*, e *Fonte*. Os padrões são representados a partir dos conceitos descritos no metamodelo.

No fluxo de trabalho da Figura 1, a atividade *Selecionar Padrões* define como recuperar da biblioteca de padrões, os padrões que visam prevenir os riscos identificados para um dado projeto [20]. A seleção de padrões considera as características e o contexto do projeto.

A atividade *Adaptar o Processo para o Projeto* adapta o processo padrão da organização para englobar os padrões selecionados para prevenir os riscos, gerando como resultado o processo definido para o projeto.

Durante o projeto, é necessário monitorar os riscos para garantir que estão sob controle, ou tomar ações corretivas para os riscos que estejam fora de limites aceitáveis. A atividade *Elaborar o Plano GQM para Monitorar os Riscos* define as atividades de monitoramento de riscos. Usando a abordagem Goal/Question/Metric (GQM) [17] são definidas métricas para monitorar cada risco priorizado. Com base no conjunto de métricas, é elaborado um plano de medição para o projeto, detalhando como as medidas devem ser coletadas, e com qual periodicidade. O ideal é que as medidas sejam inseridas em uma base histórica, para serem usadas em estimativas futuras e no acompanhamento do projeto, bem como servirem para extrair e comparar resultados entre projetos. As métricas auxiliam o gerente de projeto a *Monitorar os Riscos do Projeto*, dando visibilidade quanto ao progresso destes. Com o uso das métricas, o gerente de projeto obterá indicativos que o auxiliarão no controle do risco, possibilitando a identificação de riscos que ultrapassaram limites permitidos.

Neste caso, é executada a atividade *Selecionar Planos de Contingência* para resolver riscos. Os planos de contingência prevêem a seleção de padrões de resolução de riscos e a adaptação do processo ocorre com base nesses padrões de forma semelhante à adaptação baseada em padrões para prevenção de riscos.

Este artigo detalha as atividades *Selecionar Padrões* e *Adaptar o Processo para o Projeto*. Detalhes sobre as demais atividades podem ser obtidos em [15][16][20].

4. Elaboração do Metamodelo Integrado

A adaptação de processos de software pode ocorrer a partir de um processo pré-configurado ou de um metamodelo [21][26].

Um processo padrão pode ser construído de forma que se inicie com uma instância de um *framework* pré-configurado. O processo já é pré-configurado no sentido de ter um ciclo de vida e arquitetura pré-estabelecidos. Então, a customização deste processo é essencialmente uma subtração, pela qual, elementos do processo são removidos ou alterados [21]. Neste caso, os custos de adaptação do processo são baixos, uma vez que não existe o custo de construção do processo [21], porém limitado. Como exemplo de um processo pré-configurado pode-se citar o Rational Unified Process (RUP).

Outra opção é partir de um metamodelo, do qual vários processos podem ser construídos - por instanciação e montagem, isto é, são criadas instâncias de elementos do processo (metaclasses) e adicionadas regras para seqüenciamento entre essas instâncias para formar o processo [26]. O custo de criação do processo a partir do metamodelo é alto, mas tem-se um ganho em flexibilidade. Como exemplo de um metamodelo pode-se citar o *Software Process Engineering Metamodel Specification* (SPEM), elaborado pelo Object Management Group (OMG) [26].

Neste trabalho optou-se por utilizar um metamodelo para representar o processo padrão da organização, o processo definido para o projeto e os padrões. O metamodelo apresenta as seguintes vantagens: unifica os conceitos usados na representação de modelos, permite representar processos de software e combinar elementos de diferentes processos para construir novos processos. O metamodelo foi elaborado pela integração dos metamodelos do RUP e do XP. Esse metamodelo é uma sugestão e poderá ser alterado de acordo com as necessidades da organização.

O metamodelo do RUP, mostrado na Figura 2a foi extraído de [5]. Cada conceito do processo define como ele é modelado (operação ou classe) e suas associações com outros conceitos. A seguir uma breve descrição de cada elemento descrito na Figura 2a.

Ciclo de vida: do ponto de vista gerencial o ciclo de vida é composto por *fases*, e do ponto de vista técnico o ciclo de vida consiste de *disciplinas*.

Fases: são associadas a *workflow details*.

Disciplina: cada disciplina identifica um conjunto de *papéis* que participa na disciplina e define um conjunto de *workflows detail*.

Workflow Detail: especifica uma colaboração dentro de uma *disciplina*.

Atividade: representa uma atividade do processo, que um *papel* deve executar.

Artefato: são produtos gerados durante a execução das *atividades*.

Papel: representa os cargos executados por indivíduos em um projeto.

Ferramenta: representa as ferramentas de desenvolvimento usadas na organização.

Mentores de Ferramentas: é uma descrição de como executar uma *atividade* usando determinada *ferramenta*.

A partir da literatura sobre XP foi elaborado um modelo de classes, com os conceitos descritos em XP [16] (Figura 2b). O objetivo deste trabalho é elaborar um metamodelo que possibilite a representação dos elementos de processo de XP. Não é objetivo deste trabalho propor um metamodelo definitivo e exaustivo para o XP.

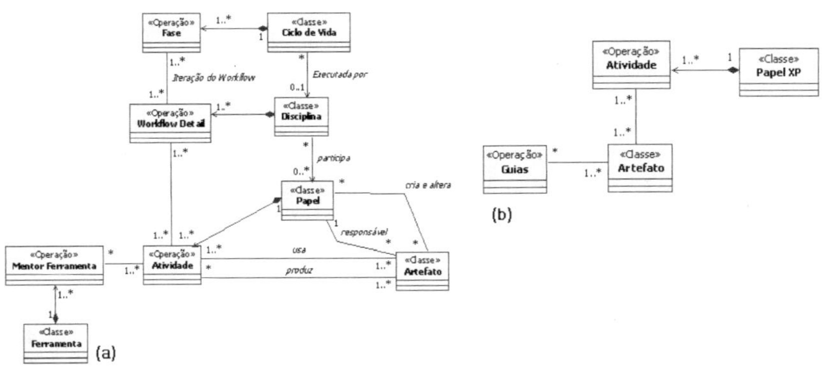

Fig. 2. (a) Elementos de processo do RUP (Extraído de [5]) e (b) Elementos de processo XP

Atividade: é executada por um *papel* XP e é associada a *artefato* e *guia*.

Artefatos: são criados ou alterados durante a execução de *atividades* por *papéis XP*.

Papeis XP: executam *atividades* e criam e alteram *artefatos*.

Guias: Contêm conselhos de como as *artefatos* podem ser elaborados. Essas indicações são geradas a partir das práticas XP, tais como: padrões de codificação, propriedade coletiva de código e semana de 40h.

Integração de visão é o processo de unir vários esquemas conceituais em um esquema conceitual global [3]. Visando elaborar um metamodelo capaz de representar elementos de processos necessários à modelagem de métodos ágeis (XP) e métodos planejados (RUP), os metamodelos do RUP e XP são integrados, usando as regras propostas por Batini [3]. A Figura 3 mostra o metamodelo resultante da integração.

Esse metamodelo descreve os elementos necessários à modelagem de processos. O objetivo é ser o mais simples possível, representando apenas os conceitos necessários à modelagem de processos para facilitar sua utilização. A tarefa de modelagem do processo da organização cabe ao projetista de processo, bem como a modelagem dos aspectos dinâmicos, como a seqüência de atividades e as colaborações.

5. Usando Padrões para Descrever Ações Preventivas

Padrões são maneiras de descrever melhores práticas e capturar experiências de uma forma que seja possível para outros reutilizarem essa experiência [22].

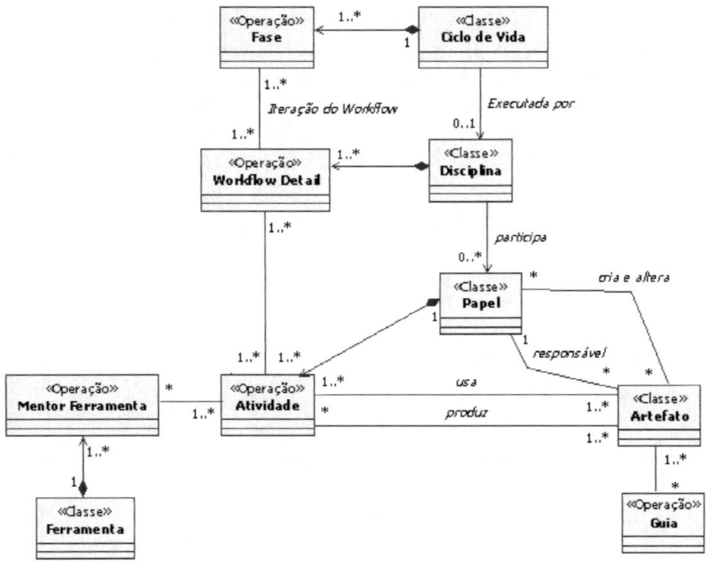

Fig. 3. Metamodelo Integrado do RUP e XP

Padrões de processo e organizacionais são usados para descrever boas-práticas no desenvolvimento de software e ações preventivas ou corretivas para situações de riscos em projetos. A Tabela 2 mostra sugestões de padrões para prevenir alguns riscos listados na Tabela 1. A associação dos riscos aos padrões foi realizada a partir da literatura [11][12][10], e é mostrada como um exemplo.

Tabela 2. Padrões Sugeridos para Prevenir Riscos

Riscos	Padrões	
	Tradicionais	Ágeis
Não-entendimento dos requisitos, falha na gerência de expectativas dos usuários e requisitos instáveis	EarlyAndRegularDelivery[10] ImpliedRequirements[11] BuildPrototype [11] ScenariosDefineProblem [11]	EarlyAndRegularDelivery [10] PlanningGame [12] OnSiteCustomer [12] SimpleDesign [12] ConstantRefactoring[12]
Projeto (desenho) inviável	ArchitectureTeam [10] LockEmUpTogether [11]	SystemMetaphor [12] SimpleDesign [12] ConstantRefactoring [12]

Para possibilitar a inserção do padrão no processo de software, os padrões precisam estar armazenados na biblioteca de padrões e definidos segundo os conceitos descritos no metamodelo integrado, isto é, para cada padrão é necessário identificar os elementos de processo necessários à sua implantação. Como exemplo, a Figura 4 mostra a representação do padrão *Planning Game*.

Isto significa que um projeto que tenha algum risco, onde seja sugerido o padrão *Planning Game* para minimizar esse risco, adaptará o processo padrão da organização inserindo neste os seguintes elementos de processo: atividades (*estimar user story, dividir user story em tarefas, definir velocidade, escrever user story, priorizar user story, definir escopo iteração, coordenar Planning Game, coletar métricas*), artefatos (*user story, tarefas, métricas*) e papéis (*desenvolvedor, cliente, medidor, treinador*).

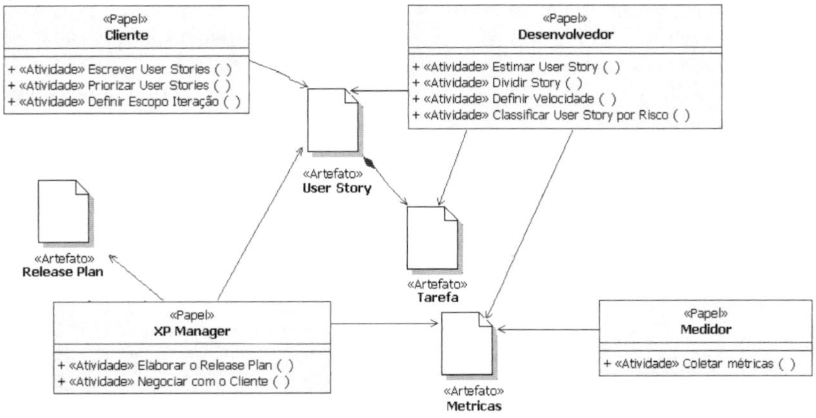

Fig. 4. Representação do Padrão Planning Game segundo o Metamodelo Integrado

Em [16], são sugeridos padrões para os riscos definidos na Tabela 1, e esses padrões são descritos segundo os elementos de processo definidos pelo metamodelo.

A próxima seção descreve RiskTool, uma ferramenta para apoiar a adaptação do processo com base nos riscos do projeto.

6. Ambiente para Adaptação de Processos com base nos Riscos

Para facilitar o uso da sistemática foi desenvolvido um ambiente composto por duas ferramentas, que são: Pattern-based Methodology Tailoring (PMT) e Risk Management Tool (RiskTool).

A ferramenta Pattern-based Methodology Tailoring (PMT) [20] é responsável pela seleção dos padrões organizacionais e de processo de um repositório de padrões como ações sugeridas ao gerente de projeto para prevenir, resolver ou minimizar cada risco identificado. Os padrões, inseridos no repositório, são associados aos riscos por meio de regras. Cada regra é aplicada a um contexto de projeto (PC) e tem um fator de eficácia (AF) [20]. O contexto do projeto é identificado usando três critérios: criticidade de defeitos, tamanho da equipe e habilidades da equipe [20]. O fator de eficácia mede o quanto o padrão ajuda na prevenção dos riscos associados. Utilizando a ferramenta PMT, o gerente de projeto cadastra o projeto de software e identifica para cada risco a probabilidade do risco ocorrer e a perda associada ao risco. A ferramenta calcula a exposição ao risco, multiplicando a probabilidade pela perda e prioriza os riscos mais importantes para o projeto. Com base no fator de priorização, informado pelo gerente, PMT seleciona os padrões que visam prevenir a ocorrência dos riscos priorizados.

RiskTool é responsável por elaborar o processo definido para um projeto por meio da adaptação do processo da organização, inserindo neste, os elementos de processo necessários para implantar os padrões, selecionados por PMT, que visam prevenir os riscos. Na biblioteca de elementos de processo estão armazenados os elementos de processo necessários para definir os processos XP, RUP e para implantar os padrões sugeridos para prevenir os riscos. Esses elementos de processo podem ser alterados ou excluídos, e novos elementos de processo podem ser adicionados.

A interface, exibida na Figura 5, possibilita associar os padrões aos elementos de processo necessários à sua definição. Como exemplo, a Figura 5 mostra a associação do padrão *Planning Game* aos elementos de processo descritos na Figura 4.

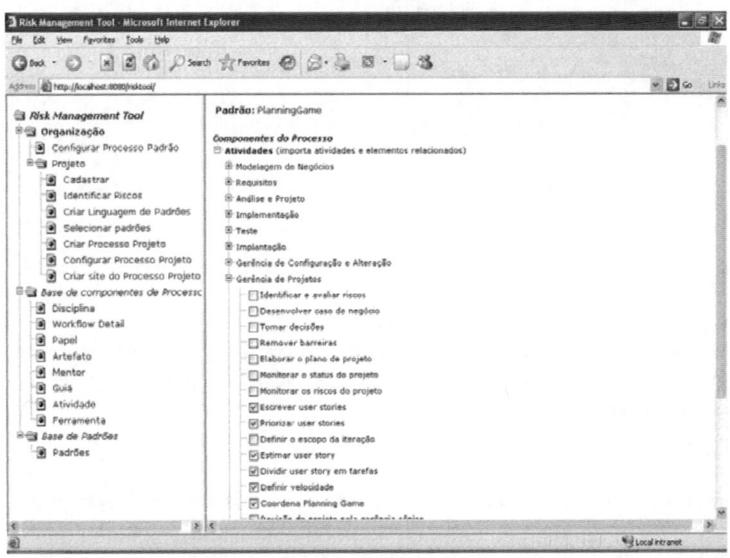

Fig. 5. Associação de Padrões a Elementos de Processo

Ao selecionar uma atividade, são selecionados automaticamente os demais elementos de processo (papéis, artefatos, guias,...) associados à atividade. Os padrões para prevenção de riscos já estão previamente associados aos elementos de processo necessários à sua implantação. O usuário pode alterar essa definição ou associar novos padrões a elementos de processo. O processo de adaptação do processo padrão da organização será descrito por meio de um estudo de caso.

6.1 Estudo de Caso

O estudo de caso foi realizado em uma universidade que possui uma equipe de seis pessoas que desenvolvem os sistemas internos da universidade, tais como: sistema acadêmico, sistema financeiro, sistema da biblioteca, sistema de almoxarifado, etc. A equipe é formada por um gerente de projeto, dois desenvolvedores, dois estagiários e o gerente do CPD, que atua como gerente sênior.

O sistema financeiro da universidade constantemente apresentava problemas, tais como: erros de execução, necessidade de ajustes, novas definições, etc. A maioria dos problemas relatados se enquadrava em: requisitos mal-definidos, instabilidade dos requisitos e falta de conhecimento da equipe do projeto. Devido às constantes manutenções, os ajustes acabavam por gerar novos "*bugs*". A equipe do projeto decidiu desenvolver um novo sistema.

Inicialmente, foi definido o processo padrão da organização. Para facilitar a definição do processo padrão da organização, em RiskTool, são sugeridas, como exemplo, algumas configurações de processo, que são:

- RUP Essencial: descreve um conjunto mínimo de elementos para utilizar RUP em um projeto [28];
- RUP Completo: inclui todas as atividades propostas por RUP [28];
- RUP/CMM 2 e RUP/CMM 3: descreve os elementos de processo necessários para implantar CMM nível 2 e nível 3, respectivamente, em um processo RUP. A definição das atividades necessárias para satisfazer as áreas-chave dos níveis 2 e 3 de CMM foi extraída de [24];
- XP: inclui todas as atividades propostas por XP [4];

Ao selecionar uma dessas configurações de processo, os elementos de processo da configuração são inseridos no processo padrão da organização. Caso o projetista não selecione uma configuração inicial, terá que selecionar todas as atividades que fazem parte do processo manualmente. Ao selecionar as atividades, são inseridos os demais elementos de processo (papéis, artefatos, guias, ferramentas, mentores) associados à atividade. É possível alterar as configurações pré-definidas ou incluir novas. O processo padrão da organização é definido uma única vez e será utilizado em todos os processos da organização. É importante salientar, que esse processo deve ser constantemente avaliado e melhorado.

No estudo de caso, foi selecionado o processo RUP essencial, por ser uma equipe de tamanho pequeno e a equipe ter experiência com RUP. O projetista, mesmo tendo selecionado uma configuração inicial, pode alterar o processo padrão da organização para incluir outras atividades que não fazem parte do RUP essencial.

A Figura 6a mostra a quantificação dos riscos para o projeto. No caso deste projeto, o fator de priorização informado foi 50%, então foram selecionados os riscos: *requisitos instáveis*, *falta de conhecimento/habilidade da equipe de projeto*, *escopo e objetivos não-claros*, *falta de compromisso da gerência sênior com o projeto*, *gold plating*, e *cronograma e orçamento não-realistas*.

Após priorizar os riscos, PMT seleciona um conjunto de padrões que pode ser utilizado para prevenir os riscos priorizados. A Figura 6b mostra a lista dos padrões selecionados automaticamente pela ferramenta. O projetista de processos seleciona os padrões que deseja incluir no processo do projeto.

O processo definido para o projeto é elaborado pela união dos elementos de processo usados para descrever o processo padrão da organização e os elementos de processo necessários para representar cada padrão selecionado. O projetista pode alterar o processo definido, para adaptá-lo a outras necessidades do projeto, que não a prevenção a riscos. Tendo concluído a adaptação do processo para o projeto, o projetista seleciona a opção de gerar *website* para o processo do projeto, como mostra a Figura 7. No *website*, cada elemento de processo é associado à sua definição. O *website* tem a finalidade de facilitar a comunicação entre os membros do projeto, e o uso do processo definido do projeto pela equipe de projeto.

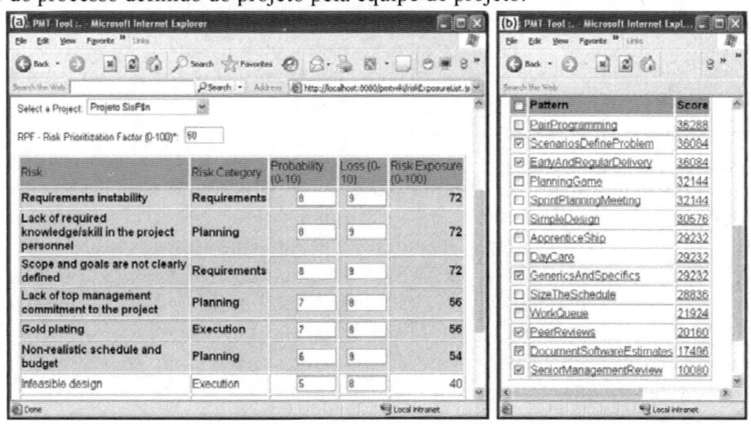

Fig. 6. Quantificação dos Riscos (a) e Padrões Selecionados para o Sistema Financeiro (b)

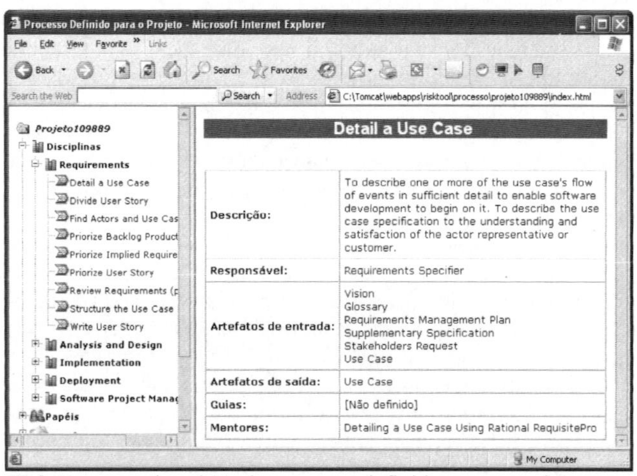

Fig. 7. *Website* com a descrição do processo definido para o projeto

7. Conclusão

Esse trabalho propõe uma sistemática para instanciar processos de desenvolvimento adaptados aos riscos de projetos de software e mostra uma ferramenta para apoiar o uso da sistemática.

A maioria das abordagens para gerência de riscos visa acompanhar os riscos e somente são tomadas ações preventivas quando o risco está próximo de se materializar [6][19]. A abordagem descrita por este trabalho é preventiva.

A adaptação de processos é um passo necessário, já que os projetos diferem em características de software, cliente, equipe, tecnologia, mercado, etc.

As associações entre padrões e riscos, e entre padrões e elementos de processo devem ser constantemente revistas e avaliadas pelo projetista, visando melhorar continuamente o processo de adaptação. Resultados de análises post-mortem de projetos podem auxiliar nessa tarefa.

O metamodelo de integração apresenta os elementos de processo conceituais usados para modelar processos e padrões. A representação de processos e padrões a partir de conceitos unificados possibilita integrá-los para gerar novos processos, adaptações e alterações de processos existentes; indiferentemente se os modelos de processos são ágeis, planejados ou híbridos.

Para demonstrar a viabilidade de se representar padrões usando o metamodelo integrado, foram selecionados padrões de catálogos de padrões [11][10][12], como sugestões para prevenção dos riscos descritos na Tabela 1. Esses padrões estão cadastrados na base de padrões de RiskTool. Cada padrão está associado aos elementos de processo necessários à sua implantação. Novos padrões e associações entre padrões e riscos podem ser inseridos na biblioteca de padrões. Novos elementos de processo, configurações pré-definidas de processos e associações entre padrões e elementos de processo podem ser inseridos na biblioteca de elementos de processo. As informações cadastradas em ambas bibliotecas podem ser alteradas e excluídas.

Trabalhos futuros incluem a definição do Plano GQM e a coleta de medidas, com base nas metas definidas no plano. Os dados coletados serão integrados e analisados de forma a medir o desempenho de cada risco, analisar os fatores de riscos, esboçar tendências e indicar quando planos de contingência de riscos devem ser acionados.

Os autores estão analisando como definir os aspectos dinâmicos e de colaboração do processo no metamodelo integrado, visando à representação da seqüência de execução das atividades.

8. References

1. Addison, T., Vallabh, S. Controlling Software Project Risks – An Empirical Study of Methods used by Experienced Project Managers. Proceedings of South African Institute of Computer Scientists & Information Technologists, September 2002, p.128-140.
2. Dillon, R. L.; Paté-Cornell, M. E.; Guikema, S. D. Optimal Use and Budget Reserves to Minimize Technical and Management Failure Risks During Complex Project Development. IEEE Transactions on Engineering Management, v. 52, n. 3, August 2005.
3. Batini, C.; Ceri, S.; Navathe, S. B. Conceptual Database Design An Entity-Relationship Approach. The Benjamin/Cummings Publications, Redwood City, 1992.
4. Beck, K. Programação Extrema (XP) Explicada: Acolha as Mudanças. Bookman, Porto Alegre, 2004.
5. Rational Software Corporation. Rational Process Workbench: Process Developer's Guide, 2002.
6. Boehm, B. Software Risk Management: Principles and Practices. IEEE Software, v.8, n.1, p. 32-41, January 1991.

7. Berger, P. Instanciação de Processos de Software em Ambientes Configurados na Estação TABA. Dissertação de Mestrado, COPPE-RJ, 2003.
8. Boehm, B; Turner, R. Using Risk to Balance Agile and Plan-Driven Methods. IEEE Computer, June 2003.
9. Falbo, R. A.; Borges, L. S. M.; Valente, F. F. R. Using Knowledge Management to Improve Software Process Performance in a CMM Level 3 Organization. Proceedings of the International Conference on Quality Software, 9., 2004. Braunschweig, Germany. IEEE Computer Society, 2004.
10. Coplien, J. Sofware Patterns. Originally published by SIGS Books and Multimedia. http://www1.bell-labs.com/user/cope/Patterns/WhitePaper/. 1996.
11. Coplien, J. A Development Process Generative Pattern Language, 2004. Disponível no endereço http://www1.bell-labs.com/user/cope/Patterns/Process/index.html.
12. Cunningham, W. Portland Pattern Repository, 2004. Disponível no endereço http://c2.com/ppr/index.html
13. DeMarco, T. Lister, T. Waltzing with Bears: Managing Risk on Software Projects. Dorset House Publishing Company, 2003.
14. Farias, L. L. Planejamento de Riscos em Ambientes de Desenvolvimento de Software Orientados à Organização. Dissertação de Mestrado, COPPE/UFRJ, 2002.
15. Fontoura, L. M.; Price, R. T. Usando GQM para Gerenciar Riscos em Projetos de Software. XVIII Simpósio Brasileiro em Engenharia de Software, 2004.
16. Fontoura, L. M. Abordagem Sistemática para Gerenciar Riscos em Projetos de Software. Proposta de Tese, UFRGS, 2005.
17. Basili, V. R, Rombach, D. The TAME Project: Towards Improvement-Oriented Software Environments. IEEE Transactions on Software Engineering, June 1988.
18. Fuggeta, A. Software Process: A Roadmap. Proceedings of the Future of Software Engineering, International Conference on Software Engineering, 22, 2000. New York: ACM Press, 2000.
19. Hall, E. M. Managing Risk. Massachusetts: Addison Wesley, 1998.
20. Hartmann, J.; Fontoura, L. M.; Price, R. T. Using Risk Analysis and Patterns to Tailor Software Processes. XIX Simpósio Brasileiro de Engenharia de Software, 2005.
21. Henderson-Sellers, B. Object-Oriented Methods and Processes, In.: Software Methods And Tools Conference (SMT'2000), Wollongong, Australia, 2000.
22. Hillside. Patterns Library. 2003. Disponível no endereço: http://hillside.net/patterns/
23. Keil, M. et al. A Framework for Identifying Software Project Risks. Communication of the ACM, v. 41, n.11, p. 76-83, November 1998.
24. Manzoni, L. V.; Price, Roberto T. Identifying Extensions Required by RUP to Comply with CMM Levels 2 and 3. IEEE Transactions on Software Engineering, February, 2003.
25. Keshlaf, A. A.; Hashim, K. A Model and Prototype Tool to Manage Software Risks. Proceedings of the 1st Asia-Pacific Conference on Quality Software, 2000.
26. Object Management Group, Inc. Software Process Engineering Metamodel Specification, Version 1.0, Technical Report formal/02-11-14, 2002.
27. Paulk, M. C. et. al. Key Practices of the Capability Maturity Model, Version 1.1, Technical Report CMU/SEI-93-TR-025, 1993.
28. Rational Software Corporation. Rational Unified Process, v. Version 2003.06.12., 2003.
29. Kiper, J. D.; Feather, M. S. A Risk-based Approach to Strategic Decision-Making for Software Development. Proceedings of the 38th Hawaii International Conference on System Sciences, Australian, 2005.
30. Software Engineering Institute, Capability Maturity Model Integration (CMMISM) , Version 1.1. Pittsburgh: Software Engineering Institute, Carnegie Mellon University, 2002.
31. Roy, G. G. A Risk Management Framework for Software Engineering Practices. Proceedings of the 2004 Australian Software Engineering Conference, 2004.

Aspects Extractor: Identificación de Aspectos en la Ingeniería de Requerimientos

Betina Haak, Miguel Díaz, Claudia Marcos, Jane Pryor

ISISTAN Instituto de Sistemas
Facultad de Ciencias Exactas, UNICEN
Paraje Arroyo Seco, B7001BBO Tandil, Argentina Tel/Fax: + 54 – 2293 – 440362 / 3
http://www.exa.unicen.edu.ar/~isistan/
E-mail: { bhaak, madiaz, cmarcos, jpryor }@exa.unicen.edu.ar

Abstract El Desarrollo de Software Orientado a Aspectos (DSOA) es un nuevo paradigma de programación cuya idea principal es proporcionar un soporte avanzado para la separación de *concerns* (características del sistema) introduciendo una nueva unidad modular, llamada aspecto. Particularmente, la ingeniería de requerimientos orientada a aspectos reduce el peligro de cambios no esperados en los productos de software a través de una identificación temprana de aspectos y resolución de conflictos. En este trabajo se presenta un enfoque automatizado para identificar aspectos en etapas tempranas del ciclo de desarrollo de software. Por medio de un conjunto de pasos los requerimientos son especificados, los aspectos son identificados automáticamente junto con los posibles conflictos entre ellos. Para el desarrollo de aplicaciones con estas características se presenta *Aspects Extractor*, una herramienta que soporta la identificación de los aspectos del sistema. Esta herramienta permite que las distintas tareas que comprende el enfoque sean realmente automatizadas.

Palabras claves: Concern, crosscutting concern no funcional, crosscutting concern funcional, aspecto candidato.

1 Introducción

La construcción de sistemas de software se está volviendo cada día más desafiante. Estos sistemas no son sólo de gran volumen, deben ser más confiables, rápidos, y fácil de usar sino que también soportan una funcionalidad cada vez más compleja. Estas características adicionales cortan transversalmente la estructura modular de los sistemas de software. Similarmente, alguna funcionalidad puede cortar transversalmente varios módulos en un sistema. Todo esto, produce que los sistemas sean más complejos de desarrollar.

Con el objetivo de facilitar el desarrollo de software con estas características se ha propuesto el Desarrollo de Software Orientado a Aspectos (DSOA) [1, 2, 3]. Las técnicas de DSOA proveen medios sistemáticos para identificación, modularización, representación y composición de *crosscutting concerns*. El término *crosscutting concern* [1, 2, 3, 4] se refiere a factores de calidad o funcionalidad del software que no puede ser efectivamente modularizada usando técnicas de desarrollo de software existentes, por ejemplo los enfoques orientados a aspectos. Es decir, un aspecto es una abstracción que modela un *crosscutting concern*. Cuando se utilizan aspectos, pueden aparecer conflictos cuando varios aspectos afectan a un mismo elemento del modelo. Una posible situación conflictiva se presentará cuando un mismo elemento del modelo se vea afectado por más de un aspecto.

Aunque se ha hecho un trabajo significativo en la Ingeniería del Software para dirigir la complejidad del desarrollo de software, se ha minimizado el tratamiento sistemático de los *crosscutting concerns*. Las técnicas de DSOA se fundamentaron en trabajos sobre técnicas y metodologías de desarrollo de software con el propósito de abordar tales *concerns* en un modo sistemático. Aunque la mayoría del trabajo inicial en DSOA se enfocó en lenguajes, frameworks y plataformas de programación orientada a aspectos (POA), un número de métodos y técnicas se han enfocado en los *crosscutting concerns* en el nivel de diseño.

El hecho de que existan *crosscutting concerns* motivó el trabajo sobre Ingeniería de Requerimientos Orientada a Aspectos. Esto se debe a que identificar *crosscutting concerns* tempranamente mejora la traceabilidad entre los requerimientos y artefactos posteriores (por ejemplo, clases en la etapa de implementación), facilita una estimación más sencilla del impacto del cambio, soporta la evolución de los requerimientos, faculta la aplicación de la orientación a aspectos desde el comienzo del ciclo de vida y previene la omisión de *crosscutting concern*.

Recientemente un número de investigadores han propuesto el uso de conceptos orientados a aspectos en etapas tempranas del desarrollo de software. A pesar de ello, se han observado ciertas limitaciones en los enfoques propuestos. En primer lugar, se carece de un modelo de *concerns* uniforme. En segundo lugar, las heurísticas utilizadas por los enfoques difieren entre sí, reduciendo la entendibilidad de los mismos y haciendo que la interpretación de los métodos sea subjetiva. Y por último, no existen herramientas de soporte estables [4].

En este trabajo se propone un enfoque automatizado en el que se trata la identificación, especificación, integración y evaluación de *concerns* en la etapa de ingeniería de requerimientos. Con el propósito de alcanzar estos objetivos, el enfoque está conformado por una serie de tareas automatizadas, que analizan la información provista por el usuario y extraen datos de interés que llevarán a la obtención de los aspectos candidatos. Por medio de la interacción con el analista, los aspectos son definidos. Con el objetivo de asistir en las etapas de identificación de aspectos candidatos se ha construido una herramienta, denominada Aspects Extractor. Aspects Extractor permite describir la funcionalidad del sistema por medio de Casos de Uso [5] e identificar automáticamente los aspectos candidatos de la aplicación. El diagrama de Casos de Uso ha sido extendido de manera tal de introducir todos los conceptos de modelamiento necesarios para las aplicaciones orientadas a aspectos en la etapa de ingeniería de requerimientos.

Este documento se organiza como sigue. En la Sección 2 se describen los objetivos principales de la Ingeniería de Requerimientos Orientada a Aspectos junto con la descripción del enfoque propuesto. En la sección 3 se describen en detalle las tareas del enfoque acompañadas de un ejemplo explicativo. La sección 4 presenta una serie de trabajos relacionados, y finalmente, en la Sección 5, se presentan las conclusiones.

2 Ingeniería de Requerimientos Orientada a Aspectos

La ingeniería de requerimientos orientada a aspectos [3, 4, 6, 7, 8, 9] reduce el peligro de cambios no esperados en los productos de software a través de una identificación temprana de aspectos y resolución de conflictos. O sea, si no se tratan los aspectos tempranamente, podrían surgir cambios en el sistema que se está desarrollando en etapas posteriores aumentando los costos de mantenimiento, desarrollo y evolución.

Actualmente, la investigación sobre el uso de aspectos en la etapa de ingeniería de requerimientos no ha sido explorada en profundidad. En este trabajo se presenta un enfoque en el contexto de ingeniería de requerimientos, que identifica, especifica, integra y evalúa aspectos en etapas tempranas del ciclo de desarrollo del software. Para lograr estos objetivos, se automatizan las tareas que conforman el modelo de ingeniería de requerimientos propuesto (Fig. 1). Esta automatización se realiza sobre la información de la funcionalidad del sistema brindada por el analista y se obtiene una lista de aspectos candidatos. El analista decide cuáles son los aspectos definitivos a partir de tal lista. Esta automatización contribuye al trabajo del analista, ya que no debe inspeccionar la especificación de casos de uso de un sistema en la búsqueda de aspectos. Además, una inspección manual sería un trabajo arduo en el cual muchos detalles interesantes podrían ser pasados por alto por falta de tiempo, fatiga o monotonía.

Un aspecto modela dos tipos de *crosscutting concerns* que afectan a otros *concerns*: *crosscutting concerns funcionales* y *crosscutting concerns no funcionales* [4]. Definimos un *crosscutting concern funcional* como aquel que permite reusar cierta funcionalidad del sistema, y que no está relacionado con los requerimientos no funcionales del mismo. Un *crosscutting concern no funcional* está mezclado en varios módulos, produciendo sistemas enmarañados que son difíciles de entender, difíciles de mantener y con una evolución costosa.

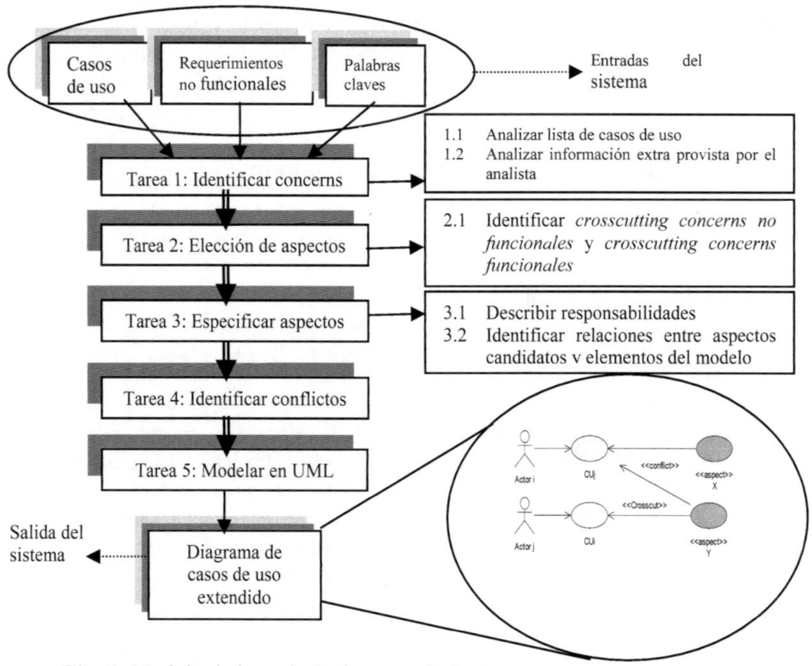

Fig. 1. Modelo de ingeniería de requerimientos

En la Fig. 1 se muestra el modelo de ingeniería de requerimientos propuesto, el cual esta conformado por cinco tareas principales: Identificar *concerns*, Elección de los aspectos candidatos, Especificar aspectos candidatos, Identificar conflictos y por último, Modelar en UML.

Tarea 1: Identificar *concerns*

Consiste en identificar a partir de los requerimientos, los posibles *concerns* de un sistema. Dicha tarea está dividida en dos sub-tareas: analizar la lista de casos de uso y analizar información extra provista por el analista. Enn la primer sub-tarea, se analizan los casos de uso y se produce automáticamente una lista de palabras relevantes que representan al caso de uso, utilizando técnicas de recuperación de información [10, 11, 12]. Por último, en la segunda sub-tarea, el analista suministrará ciertas palabras claves y requerimientos no funcionales con el propósito de enriquecer la información almacenada en el sistema para la obtención de los *concerns*.

Tarea 2: Elección de aspectos candidatos

Se subdivide en dos sub-tareas: Identificar *crosscutting concerns no funcionales* y *crosscutting concerns funcionales*, y elección de aspectos candidatos por parte del analista. En la primer sub-tarea, existen dos formas principales de identificar *crosscutting concerns no funcionales*. La primera de ellas se da cuando un *concern* corta transversalmente más de un elemento del modelo (casos de uso). La segunda forma se da cuando se identifica un caso de uso que cuenta con un requerimiento especial (no funcional) en su especificación. Para identificar *crosscutting concerns funcionales*, se debe verificar si alguno de los *concerns* se corresponde con las palabras claves que el sistema tiene almacenadas en una base de datos (Interbase). Por último, en la segunda sub-tarea, el analista seleccionará de una lista de *crosscutting concerns* (ya sean no funcionales o funcionales) presentados en la tabla, los aspectos candidatos.

Tarea 3: Especificar aspectos candidatos

Se subdivide en dos sub-tareas: identificar responsabilidades e identificar las relaciones entre aspectos para que los conflictos puedan ser detectados.

Tarea 4: Identificar conflictos

Se identifican todas las posibles situaciones conflictivas entre aspectos que están relacionados al caso de uso [13]. Si un caso de uso está afectado por más de un aspecto, entonces existe una situación conflictiva entre los aspectos involucrados [13].

Tarea 5: Modelar en UML

Basados en la información obtenida en la realización de las tareas previas, se construirá un modelo visual, el cual será una extensión de un diagrama de casos de uso [5, 14], con el agregado de los aspectos finalmente seleccionados por el analista y las posibles situaciones conflictivas entre los aspectos candidatos.

Cada una de las cinco tareas será descripta en detalle en las siguientes secciones.

3 Identificación automatizada de aspectos

En esta sección se describirán en detalle las tareas descriptas anteriormente y por medio de un ejemplo se mostrará la aplicación de las mismas.

El ejemplo es un *"Servidor de mails"*, el cual posee la funcionalidad básica de enviar y recibir mensajes, organizar los mensajes en carpetas, como así también el establecimiento de técnicas de filtrado de forma de aceptar o rechazar un determinado mail (por ejemplo, si excede un determinado tamaño). Para realizar cualquiera de estas actividades el cliente deberá estar autentificado.

3.1 Tarea 1: Identificar concerns

Esta tarea está dividida en dos sub-tareas: analizar la lista de casos de uso y analizar información extra provista por el analista.

3.1.1 Sub-Tarea 1.1: Analizar lista de casos de uso

Los casos de uso que describen la funcionalidad del sistema son utilizados para producir una lista de *concerns* candidatos, para lo cual son usadas técnicas de recuperación de información. Inicialmente son eliminadas de los casos de uso las llamadas palabras vacías, stop words [12], las cuales no aportan información, por ejemplo: pronombres, conectores, artículos, etc. Posteriormente, a las palabras representativas del caso de uso se les aplica un algoritmo de *stemming* [10, 11, 12], el cual retorna la raíz de cada una de ellas. De esta manera, al finalizar esta tarea se tiene para cada caso de uso una lista de palabras que lo representan, la cual será de gran utilidad en las siguientes tareas. Adicionalmente, se cuenta con un diccionario de sinónimos con el objetivos de uniformizar la terminología de los conceptos tratados en la aplicación.

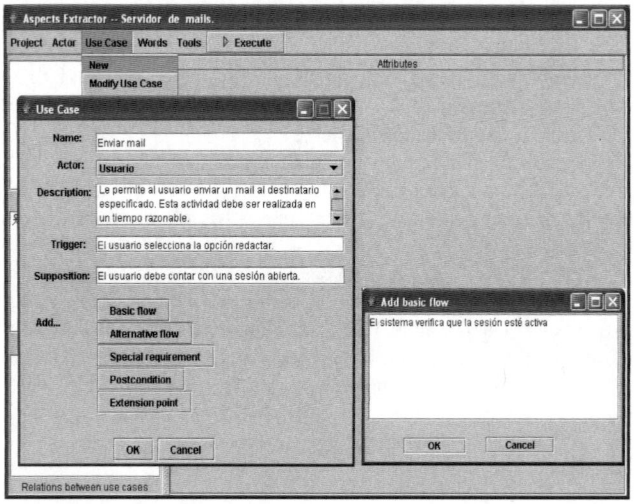

Fig. 2. Creación de casos de uso al proyecto "Enviar un mail"

En el desarrollo del ejemplo presentado, se crea el proyecto *"Servidor de mails",* especificando el idioma en el que se trabajará. Es decir, la herramienta permite trabajar en dos idiomas, inglés y español, dependiendo en aquel en que se desee realizar la especificación (en un futuro, se podría extender la funcionalidad para soportar la identificación en otros idiomas ya que el diseño de la herramienta contempla tales extensiones). En este ejemplo el idioma elegido es español. Luego se especifican los casos de uso, actores, y relaciones entre ellos. Los casos de uso especificados son:

1. Registrar.
2. Enviar un mail.
3. Abrir un mail.
4. Definir técnica de filtrado de mails.
5. Guardar un mail en una determinada carpeta.
6. Borrar un mail de una carpeta.
7. Modificar contraseña.
8. Agregar un nuevo contacto a la lista de contactos.
9. Borrar un contacto de la lista de contactos.

A fines prácticos solamente fueron cargados los tres más importantes: *enviar un mail*, *abrir un mail* y *establecer técnica de filtrado de mails*, (Fig. 2, Fig. 3).

A medida que se cargan los casos de uso, se pueden establecer las relaciones entre los mismos. Estas relaciones pueden ser *inclusión, generalización* o *extensión* [5]. En este ejemplo, no existen relaciones entre casos de uso debido a la envergadura del ejemplo presentado.

De manera similar a cómo se cargan los casos de uso, se pueden cargar los actores. En este caso el único actor presente es *usuario*, el cual ha sido cargado, como puede verse en la Fig. 3.

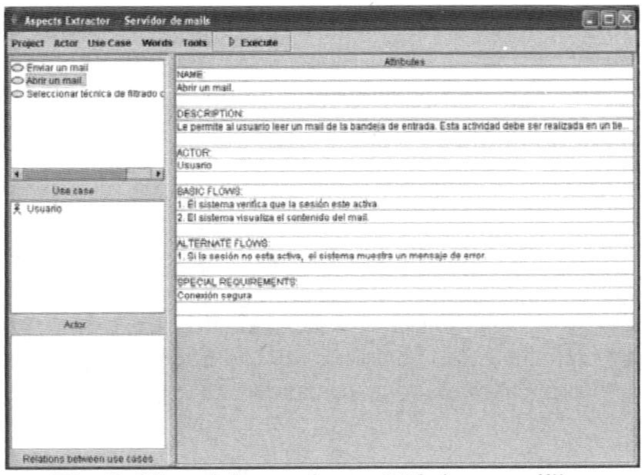

Fig. 3. Vista del caso de uso "Abrir un mail"

A pesar que la herramienta *Aspects Extractor* cuenta con medios para describir la funcionalidad del sistema con casos de uso, es posible describirlos también utilizando Rational Rose 2003. Para crearlo desde Rational Rose, lo que se hace es diseñar un diagrama de casos de uso de manera tradicional y lo luego se lo exporta a un archivo con extensión XMI. La ventaja de esta forma es que los analistas pueden estar más familiarizados con herramientas CASE al estilo Rational Rose y es más sencillo especificar sus casos de uso de esa manera, más que con la utilización de la herramienta presentada en este trabajo. Sin embargo, depende de la decisión del analista y ambas opciones son igualmente válidas. Es decir, la herramienta funciona de la misma manera de cualquiera de las dos formas. Una vez que se exportó el archivo utilizando Rational Rose, el analista puede importar el archivo con la opción del menú Project→Import XMI in Spanish (ya que en este ejemplo la especificación esta hecha en español) desde *Aspects Extractor*.

3.1.2 Sub-Tarea 1.2: Analizar información extra provista por el analista

En esta sub-tarea, el analista contará con la posibilidad de suministrar ciertas palabras claves y requerimientos no funcionales a la herramienta. Estos serán de gran utilidad, ya que contribuirán con la identificación de los *concerns*.

Ingreso de las palabras claves del sistema

Aspects Extractor cuenta con la siguiente librería de palabras claves:

- Palabras relacionadas con requerimientos no funcionales (*crosscutting concerns no funcionales*): performance, seguridad, persistencia, adaptabilidad, disponibilidad.
- Palabras relacionadas con reuso de funcionalidad (*crosscutting concern funcional*): algoritmos, técnicas, visualización. Por ejemplo, en el caso de visualización, podemos contar con visualización de datos en diagramas de torta. Si en un futuro, se quisiera otra forma de visualización, por ejemplo con diagramas de barra, dicha funcionalidad estaría claramente identificada

en un aspecto de visualización y no sería costoso cambiar a un nuevo aspecto que visualice datos de manera diferente.

En nuestro ejemplo el analista ingresa como palabras claves otros requerimientos no funcionales que se agregan a la lista anterior. Estas son: integridad y usabilidad. Sin embargo, en este ejemplo, no ingresa ninguna palabra clave relacionada con reuso de funcionalidad. El analista debe seleccionar el idioma, que en este caso es español, y el tipo de palabra clave (funcional o no funcional). Una vez que acepta, la palabra es almacenada en la base de datos.

3.2 Tarea 2: Elección de aspectos candidatos

Una vez que se tiene la totalidad de los casos de uso representados por sus palabras relevantes, es posible comenzar a identificar los aspectos candidatos, lo cual conforma el objetivo principal de esta tarea, que se subdivide en dos.

3.2.1 Sub-Tarea 2.1: Identificar crosscutting concerns no funcionales y crosscutting concerns funcionales

Para identificar *crosscutting concerns no funcionales*, se procede de dos maneras. En la primera, si alguna de las palabras que representan a un caso de uso, o un sinónimo de ella, se repite en alguno de los demás casos de uso, dicha palabra será un *crosscutting concern no funcional*, para lo cual deben comparase entre si todos los casos de uso. En el ejemplo, han sido detectados de esta manera los *concerns*: *permite, realizada, contar, verifica, contenido* y *visualizar* (Fig. 4). La segunda manera de identificar un *crosscutting concern no funcional*, es cuando alguno de los casos de uso cuenta con un requerimiento especial no funcional en su especificación. Tales requerimientos se convierten automáticamente en *crosscutting concerns no funcionales*. En el ejemplo, fue cargado en los casos de uso *enviar un mail* y *abrir un mail* el requerimiento no funcional *conexión segura* (Fig. 3), el cual se convierte en un *crosscutting concern no funcional*.

Los *crosscutting concerns funcionales* son identificados controlando si alguna de las palabras representativas del caso de uso, se corresponde con alguna de las palabras claves que el sistema tiene almacenadas. En este ejemplo fueron encontrados los *crosscutting concerns funcionales visualizar* y *técnicas*.

Una forma adicional de detección de *crosscutting concerns no funcionales* y *crosscutting concerns funcionales*, ocurre solamente si el sistema fue usado previamente y se identificaron aspectos candidatos. Dichos aspectos se almacenan en una base de datos y serán reutilizados a futuro. Entonces, se buscan concordancia de los *concerns* con los mismos. Si existe una concordancia, entonces el *concern* será candidato y su tipo dependerá del tipo del aspecto. En el ejemplo no ha sido identificado ningún *concern* de esta manera.

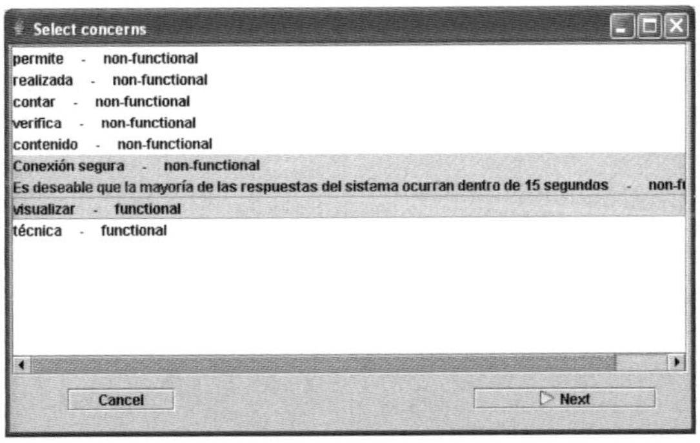

Fig. 4. *Concerns* del sistema

3.2.2 Sub-Tarea 2.2: Seleccionar aspectos candidatos

Al final de la Sub-Tarea 2.2, se tiene una lista de *concerns* (ya sean no funcionales o funcionales), la cual es presentada al analista. El analista selecciona según su intuición y experiencia los *concerns* de la aplicación.

Para el ejemplo los *crosscutting concerns* elegidos por el analista son: *conexión segura, Es deseable que la mayoría de las respuestas del sistema ocurran dentro de los 15 segundos y visualizar* (Fig. 4). Estos *concerns* se transforman a partir de este momento en aspectos candidatos. Observar que en la lista de *concerns* resultantes se agrega el tipo de *concern* (funcional o no funcional) para brindar al analista más información y una ayuda en su elección.

3.3 Tarea 3: Especificar aspectos candidatos

Se subdivide en dos sub-tareas: identificar responsabilidades e identificar las relaciones entre aspectos para que los conflictos puedan ser detectados.

3.3.1 Sub-Tarea 3.1: Describir responsabilidades

El analista debe describir la responsabilidad y la funcionalidad de todos los aspectos candidatos que ha elegido en la tarea anterior.

Por medio de la utilización de *Aspects Extractor* el analista puede especificar la responsabilidad de los aspectos y agregar los aspectos que desee si es que el sistema no los tuvo en cuenta.

Es posible renombrar los aspectos y cambiar el tipo de los mismos si es que no le parece correcto al analista el que identificó el sistema. También, puede indicar los motivos de su elección o alguna nota que pueda ser útil en las siguientes etapas del ciclo de vida de software. Por ejemplo se puede renombrar el aspecto *"Es deseable que la mayoría de las respuestas del sistema ocurran dentro de los 15 segundos"* por "*Tiempo de respuesta"* y su responsabilidad es definida como *Período de tiempo en el cual el sistema debe responder a un servicio.* De la misma forma es posible renombrar los restantes aspectos.

El analista también podría agregar un aspecto que no ha sido detectado por las tareas anteriores. Se debe ingresar un nombre de aspecto, la responsabilidad, el tipo y a qué caso de uso afecta.

Una vez que se han especificado todos los aspectos es posible visualizar los aspectos finalmente seleccionados.

3.3.2 Sub-Tarea 3.2: Identificar relaciones entre aspectos candidatos y elementos del modelo

El principal objetivo de esta Sub-Tarea es establecer la relación *crosscutting* entre cada uno de los aspectos candidatos seleccionados en la tarea anterior y los casos de uso donde fueron identificados los mismos. Esta es una tarea automatizada del sistema, para lo cual se utilizan tablas internas. A medida que se seleccionan los aspectos candidatos se guarda en una tabla los casos de uso con los que se relaciona, información que es usada en tareas posteriores.

3.4 Tarea 4: Identificar conflictos

Esta tarea consiste en identificar las posibles situaciones conflictivas que se pueden llegar a presentar en un futuro, de forma que puedan ser tratadas [13].

Una situación conflictiva es detectada cuando varios aspectos candidatos están relacionados con un mismo caso de uso. De esta manera, las tablas generadas en tareas anteriores, son utilizadas para detectar tales situaciones.

En el Servidor de mails, se producen varias situaciones conflictivas. El caso de uso *"Enviar un mail"* esta relacionado con los aspectos candidatos *"Conexión segura"* y *"Tiempo de Respuesta"*, por lo cual dichos aspectos se encuentran en una posible situación conflictiva. El caso de uso *"Abrir un mail"* esta en idéntica situación que el anterior (Fig. 5).

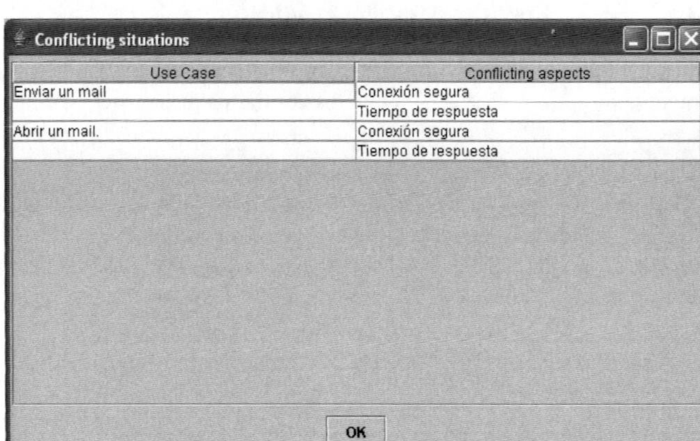

Fig. 5. Conflictos entre aspectos

3.5 Tarea 5: Modelar en UML

Basados en la información obtenida en la realización de las tareas previas, se construye un modelo visual, el cual será una extensión de un diagrama de casos de uso con el agregado de los aspectos finalmente seleccionados por el analista.

Tal modelo visual es un archivo con extensión XMI el cual debe ser importado desde la herramienta CASE Rational Rose 2003, en el que pueden observarse todas las relaciones que conforman el diagrama de casos de uso extendido. Para soportar las nuevas necesidades específicas fue necesario el agregado de estereotipos. Tales estereotipos son <<Aspecto>> y <<Crosscut>>, los cuales representan el aspecto elegido finalmente por el analista, y la relación entre este y un determinado caso de uso respectivamente.

Para el ejemplo presentado, el archivo generado ha sido denominado *"Servidor de mails.xmi"* (Fig. 6). En este podrá observarse el diagrama de casos de uso extendido, con los tres aspectos candidatos previamente seleccionados, así como también todas las relaciones entre casos de uso y aspectos y las posibles situaciones conflictivas.

En el caso de los aspectos candidatos, estos son representados con una elipse al igual que los casos de uso. Esto se debe a que los aspectos son un estereotipo para el elemento base *caso de uso.* Por cuestiones de entendibilidad del diagrama, el estereotipo <<Aspecto>> no es mostrado, en su lugar la elipse correspondiente es dibujada de un color diferente al de los casos de uso. Cabe aclara que los aspectos representados por Rational mantienen la especificación que el analista definió.

Las relaciones entre casos de uso y aspectos candidatos son representadas por flechas sin dirección color bordo, las cuales están estereotipadas con <<crosscut>>. En el caso de que la relación sea un posible conflicto, es representada de igual manera pero de color azul.

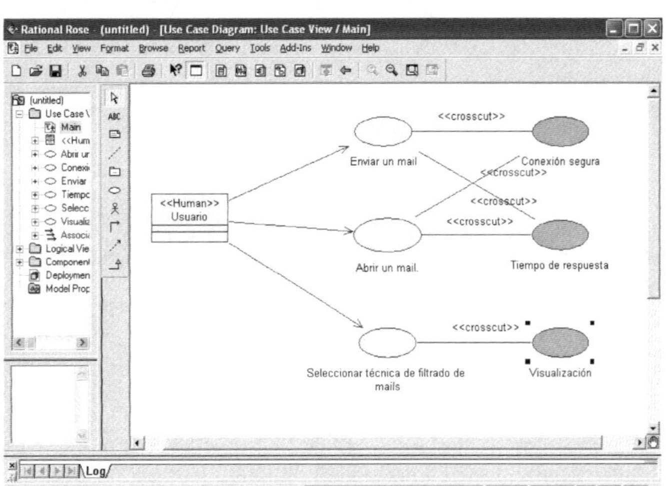

Fig.6 . Diagrama de casos de uso del el ejemplo "Servidor de mails"

En este enfoque solamente se marca la existencia de conflictos con líneas dibujadas con color azul y luego el analista deberá tratarlos de acuerdo a su conveniencia en cada uno de los casos. Según el diagrama de la Fig. 10 se pueden observar posibles conflictos. Por ejemplo, el caso de uso "*Enviar mail*", se ve afectado por el aspecto *Tiempo de respuesta* y el aspecto *Conexión segura*. Aquí no se sabe en qué orden se deben aplicar dichos aspectos o si alguno debe excluir a otro o la forma de sincronizarlos. Si un caso de uso está afectado por un solo aspecto, no existe conflicto. En la Fig. 10 se aprecia tal cuestión en la relación entre el caso de uso "*Seleccionar técnica de filtrado de mails*" y el aspecto *Visualización*. Por tal motivo la relación *crosscut* es marcada en bordo.

A partir de aquí el analista podrá seguir delimitando la funcionalidad del sistema con *Rational Rose* con los aspectos ya identificados y especificados, teniendo en cuenta las posibles situaciones conflictivas.

4 Trabajos relacionados

La investigación en las etapas tempranas del desarrollo de software orientado a aspectos (OA) está en un estado de desarrollo y se han publicado algunos resultados interesantes. A pesar de que la noción de aspecto es estable y común en el nivel de programación, la noción de aspecto en las etapas tempranas aún no está consolidada.

Rashid y otros [6] proponen soportar la separación de propiedades *crosscutting* no funcionales durante la ingeniería de requerimientos. También permite identificar las influencias de los aspectos del nivel de requerimientos sobre artefactos en etapas de desarrollo posteriores, estableciendo *trade-offs* críticos antes de que se derive la arquitectura. Se presenta un modelo AORE (Aspect-Oriented Requirements Engineering) en el cual existen varias etapas. Se comienza identificando los *concerns* del sistema y se los propone como aspectos candidatos. Luego, se definen reglas de composición y lo utiliza para componer los aspectos candidatos y los requerimientos de los desarrolladores y clientes. Utilizando una serie de tablas se identifican los aspectos y se resuelven los conflictos por prioridades. La última etapa del modelo es la identificación de las dimensiones de un aspecto.

Américo Sampaio y otros [7], proveen un enfoque orientado a la exploración de aspectos desde documentos de requerimientos. La herramienta que desarrollaron puede trabajar con cualquier clase de documento textual independientemente de su estructura y automatiza parcialmente las actividades que consumen mas tiempo, tales como identificar *concerns*, *view points* y *action words*. La herramienta permite un desarrollo acelerado porque no impone una clase de formato específico y no depende del conocimiento previo del ingeniero de requerimientos sobre los requerimientos.

Isabel Brito en [9] propone un enfoque cuyo principal objetivo es desarrollar un *framework* orientado a aspectos en el contexto de ingeniería de requerimientos. Para lograrlo, necesita desarrollar un modelo que soporte la identificación de *concerns*, desarrollar un lenguaje para especificar *concerns*, proponer un método sistemático para manejar conflictos, identificar y mapear influencias de aspectos en etapas de desarrollo posteriores para establecer *trade-*

off antes de que la arquitectura sea derivada, y por último desarrollar una herramienta simple que soporte la especificación y composición de *concerns*.

Existen tres puntos a analizar que son comunes a los enfoques descriptos anteriormente.

El primero de ellos implica la no presencia de un modelo de *concern* uniforme. Aunque la noción de *concern* parece ser el tema central de todos los enfoques, los artefactos adoptados para identificar aspectos y los modelos de *concerns* adoptados son diferentes. En el segundo punto se observa que los tipos de heurísticas utilizados por los enfoques difieren entre sí. Aunque la mayoría de ellos definen procesos explícitos, las heurísticas adoptadas están generalmente definidas implícitamente o dependen de la intuición del analista. El tercer y último punto es la no existencia de herramientas de soporte estables. Las herramientas definidas para la identificación, especificación o evaluación de aspectos tempranos no están maduras aún. No obstante hay esfuerzos extensivos para desarrollar herramientas, por ejemplo Theme/Doc [15].

5 Conclusiones

En este trabajo se presenta un enfoque automatizado para tratar con aspectos, ya sea porque corten transversalmente elementos del modelo o porque se reutilice funcionalidad durante la etapa de ingeniería de requerimientos. *Aspect Extractor* es una herramienta que soporta la construcción de este tipo de aplicaciones. Identificar y documentar aspectos tan temprano como sea posible es muy importante puesto que permite la aplicación de orientación a aspectos desde el comienzo del ciclo de vida del software, y previene las omisiones de los aspectos durante las actividades de desarrollo y mantenimiento, reduciendo de este modo los costos de desarrollo, mantenimiento y evolución.

Uno de los principales aportes que introduce el enfoque es la estandarización de entrada, mediante la especificación de casos de uso, la cual es una tarea que debe realizarse de todos modos y con la particularidad de que no se desvía la atención del analista de su fin principal (delimitar el sistema por medio de la especificación de casos de uso). Dicha funcionalidad es posible especificarla utilizando *Aspect Extractor* o por medio de una herramienta CASE que el desarrollador este familiarizado, al estilo Rational Rose. Si los requerimientos son especificados con este tipo de herramientas *Aspect Extractor* cuenta con una forma de importar los archivos XMI generados con la herramienta CASE. De manera similar cuando los aspectos y situaciones conflictivas han sido identificados, es posible exportar con *Aspect Extractor* dicha información y luego seguir trabajando con la herramienta CASE elegida.

6 Referencias

1. Kiczales, G., Lamping, J., Mendhekar, A., Maeda, C., Lopes, C., Loingtier, J., Irwin, J.. /Aspect-Oriented Programming/. In Proceedings ECOOP '97.
2. Homepage of AOSD /http://aosd.net/

3. Homepage Early Aspects: Aspect-Oriented Requirements Engineering and Architecture Design http://www.early-aspects.net/
4. Haak, B., Díaz, M., Marcos, C., Pryor, J. Un enfoque automatizado para la identificación temprana de aspectos, 2005. Workshop Chileno de Ingeniería de Software. Valparaiso Chile. Noviembre 2005.
5. Booch, G., J. Rumbaugh, and Jacobson I.. The Unified Modeling Language. User Guide. Addison-Wesley, 1999.
6. Rashid, A., Moreira, A., and Araujo, J.. Modularisation and Composition of Aspectual Requirements. In Proceedings of the 2nd International Conference on Aspect-Oriented Software Development. ACM Press, 2003.
7. Sampaio, A., Loughran, N., Rashid, A. and Rayson, P.. Mining Aspects in Requirements. March 15, 2005, Chicago, Illinois, USA.
8. Rosenhainer, L.. Identifying Crosscutting concerns in Requirements Specifications. Monday, October 25, 2004, Vancouver, Canada.
9. Brito, I., Aspect-Oriented Requirements Engineering. Trabajo de tesis de Isabel Brito, desarrollado en la Universidade Nova de Lisboa bajo la supervisión de la Doctora Ana Moreira.
10. Abu-Salem, H., Al-Omari, M., and M. W.Evens. Stemming methodologies over individual queries words for an arabian information retrieval system, 1999.
11. Figuerola, C. G.. La investigación sobre recuperación de información en español. En C. Gonzalo García and V. García Yedra, editors, Documentación, Terminología y Traducción. Síntesis, Madrid, 2000.
12. http://snowball.tartarus.org/
13. Pryor, J. and Marcos, C.. /Solving Conflicts in Aspect-Oriented Applications/. En Proceedings of the Fourth Argentine Symposium on Software Engineering (ASSE´2003), 32 JAIIO (Jornadas Argentinas de Informática e Investigación Operativa). Buenos Aires, Argentina.13 páginas. ISSN 1666-1141. Septiembre 2003.
14. Jacobson, I., Ng, Pan-Wei, Aspect-Oriented Software Develpment with Use Cases, 2005
15. E. Baniassad and S. Clarke. Theme: An approach for aspect oriented analysis and design. En International Conference on Software Engineering, 2004.

Sesión 3:

Ingeniería de Requisitos 1

Relato de um Estudo Empírico: Uma Avaliação da Metodologia de Elicitação de Requisitos de Software Baseada na Teoria da Atividade (META)

Dério Louvadino Junior[1], Luiz Eduardo Galvão Martins[1]

[1] UNIMEP, Faculdade de Ciências Exatas e da Natureza,
Piracicaba-SP, Brasil
{deriojr@terra.com.br, lgmartin@unimep.br}

Resumo
Nos últimos anos a comunidade de engenharia de software, em particular envolvendo os pesquisadores e praticantes da engenharia de requisitos, tem chamado atenção para a importância de métodos e técnicas de engenharia de requisitos que abordem aspectos sociais e antropológicos durante o processo de definição dos requisitos de software. Neste trabalho apresentamos um estudo empírico de avaliação da Metodologia de Elicitação de Requisitos Baseada na Teoria da Atividade (META), que é uma metodologia fortemente voltada à análise do contexto social em que o software se insere. O estudo empírico apresentado buscou identificar os benefícios e dificuldades da adoção desta metodologia para a elicitação de requisitos de software, baseando-se em análises do contexto socio-cultural dos agentes envolvidos. O estudo ocorreu em uma organização educacional, envolvendo a elicitação de requisitos com vistas à implementação de um pacote de gestão acadêmico-financeira para a organização. As lições aprendidas com o estudo empírico realizado ofereceram importantes orientações para uma futura revisão da metodologia adotada.

1. Introdução

Dentro da Engenharia de Requisitos existem várias abordagens para a etapa de elicitação de requisitos, por exemplo [6][10]: introspecção, observação, questionário, entrevista, JAD, cenários, prototipação, *workflow* [1], técnicas baseadas em metas etc. Cada uma destas abordagens do processo de elicitação de requisitos tem suas características próprias, com diferentes níveis de abrangência, complexidade e aplicabilidade, e a seleção de uma delas para um processo de elicitação dependerá do contexto do problema, e até mesmo da habilidade do engenheiro de requisitos em utiliza-las [4]. A *META* (***M****etodologia de* ***E****licitação de Requisitos Baseada na* ***T****eoria da* ***A****tividade*) é um paradigma inovador dentro da Engenharia de Requisitos [2][8], indo além da visão de aspectos puramente tecnológicos do sistema, incorporando no processo de elicitação de requisitos a percepção de aspectos sociológicos, psicológicos e antropológicos, que envolvem fatores humanos que estão presentes no contexto da elicitação de requisitos de muitos sistemas de software [3], e que muitas vezes são esquecidos ou relegados a um segundo plano no processo de desenvolvimento de software. O objetivo deste artigo é relatar percepções e lições aprendidas resultantes de um estudo empírico em que foi empregada a META como técnica de elicitação de requisitos de um sistema. Durante o estudo empírico pôde-se fazer uma avaliação da META com vistas a melhoria de seus procedimentos metodológicos . O estudo de caso realizado se classifica como um estudo descritivo

[11]. O restante deste artigo está organizado da seguinte forma: na seção 2 é apresentada uma visão geral da META; na seção 3 o estudo empírico é descrito com detalhes, relatando passo a passo como ocorreu o emprego da metodologia em questão e apontando pontos fortes e fracos observados em cada procedimento executado da META; a seção 4 apresenta as conclusões do artigo e aponta para trabalhos futuros.

2. Visão Geral da Metodologia Estudada (META)

A META está fundamentada nos princípios da Teoria da Atividade, que tem uma longa raiz histórica vinculada a três vertentes das ciências humanas: a filosofia clássica alemã dos séculos XVIII e XIX com Kant e Hegel, que enfatizaram o papel mental da atividade na constituição do relacionamento entre sujeito e objeto; Marx e Engels que expandiram o conceito do aspecto central da atividade que é a transformação de objetos materiais; e da Escola de Psicologia Soviética fundada por Lev S. Vygotsky durante as décadas de 1920 e 1930, com Alexei N. Leont'ev e Alexander R. Luria dando continuidade aos trabalhos de Vygotsky e introduzindo o termo atividade (que é a tradução que vem sendo utilizada para a palavra russa *deyatel'nost*) [7]. Os princípios básicos da Teoria da Atividade incluem **(1)** o princípio da unidade entre consciência e atividade, **(2)** princípio da orientação a objetos, **(3)** princípio da estrutura hierárquica da atividade, **(4)** princípio da internalização-externalização, **(5)** princípio da mediação, **(6)** e o princípio do desenvolvimento [5][9]. Cada uma das três etapas da META subdividem-se em procedimentos bem definidos, arrolados a seguir:

Etapa 1 - Divisão do problema em atividades:
- 1.1 Levantar atividades candidatas
- 1.2 Selecionar atividades
- 1.3 Descrever histórico das atividades selecionadas

Etapa 2 - Delineamento do contexto da atividade:
- 2.1 Identificar os motivos e resultados da atividade
- 2.2 Identificar os elementos no nível individual
- 2.3 Identificar os elementos no nível social
- 2.4 Modelar a atividade através do diagrama de Engeström

Etapa 3 - Descrição da estrutura hierárquica da atividade
- 1.1 Identificar as ações e operações da atividade
- 1.2 Descrever as metas das ações
- 1.3 Descrever as condições de realização das operações

A META foi organizada em torno de vários conceitos da Teoria da Atividade, que foram classificados em dois grupos [8], conforme mostrados a seguir:

- Conceitos Relativos à Estrutura Hierárquica da Atividade: gerou as definições de *atividade, motivo, ação, meta, operação e condições.*
- Conceitos Relativos aos Elementos que Formam o Contexto da Atividade: gerou as definições de *sujeito, objeto, ferramenta, comunidade, regras, divisão do trabalho e resultado.*

O contexto formado pela atividade, e seus respectivos elementos, são representados no diagrama de Engeström, Figura 1.

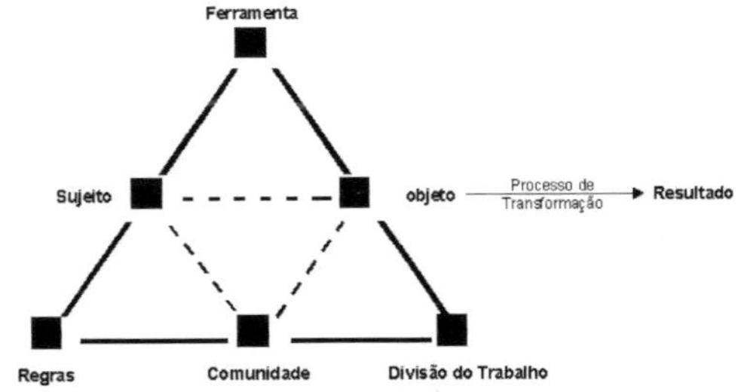

Figura 1 – Diagrama de Engeström

Uma atividade se concretiza quando um objeto (tangível ou intangível) é transformado pelo sujeito através de ações e operações subsequentes. O diagrama mostra que no contexto da atividade há um relacionamento entre sujeito (agente ou ator da atividade), objeto e comunidade (formada pelos vários sujeitos participantes da atividade no nível social). Ferramentas são artefatos de mediação da ação do sujeito sobre o objeto. Regras são normas e procedimentos estabelecidos por uma comunidade que são respeitados pelo sujeito na realização de uma atividade. A divisão do trabalho, que constitui a mediação entre a comunidade e o objeto, é o conjunto de papeis e responsabilidades que os sujeitos assumem durante a realização de uma atividade.

3. Estudo Empírico

Nesta seção apresentaremos inicialmente o contexto no qual o estudo de caso se desenvolveu. Na seqüência apresentamos uma explicação resumida do que foi feito em cada etapa do estudo de caso (que acompanhou as etapas e procedimentos presentes na META) e seus resultados, bem como as dificuldades e aspectos positivos no uso da META, e sugestões para uma futura revisão da metodologia

3.1 Contexto do Estudo

O propósito do estudo de caso foi avaliar detalhadamente o desempenho da META diante de um processo de elicitação de requisitos para um sistema informatizado de controle acadêmico, em um contexto empresarial real. O ambiente no qual foi desencadeado o processo de elicitação de requisitos pertencia à uma organização empresarial na área de educação, constituída legalmente como sociedade civil há mais de dez anos O processo de elicitação de requisitos desencadeou-se em quatro áreas funcionais, sob as quais estavam todas as atividades da empresa, sendo: Diretoria Geral; Administração Acadêmica; Administração Financeira e Controladoria. Um engenheiro de requisitos e três usuários do futuro sistema estiveram envolvidos na execução do estudo empírico realizado.

3.2 Aplicando a META

Antes do início do processo de elicitação de requisitos, fez-se necessário uma reunião com os usuários envolvidos. Tal reunião objetivou esclarecer e obter o acordo dos usuários para as seguintes questões:

- Explicar ao usuário como seria a elicitação de requisitos, a importância da participação efetiva deles neste processo, e obter deles o comprometimento com as informações elicitadas;
- Discutir com usuários as expectativas e possíveis restrições do sistema a ser implementado;
- Agendar as datas e horários, e os participantes das entrevistas de elicitação de requisitos.

3.2.1 Etapa 1. Divisão do Problema em Atividades
3.2.1.1 Levantamento das Atividades Candidatas

Desenvolvimento da etapa. Inicialmente, para a organização da execução dos trabalhos, algumas providências foram tomadas:

- Elaboração de formulários onde as informações das 3 etapas da metodologia foram registradas (vide exemplos no apêndice do artigo);
- Organização do ambiente: as sessões de elicitação de requisitos aconteceram no local de trabalho dos usuários, no horário de expediente, de acordo com a disponibilidade dos mesmos.
- Foi estabelecido um cronograma bastante flexível para a execução das sessões de elicitação de requisitos, pois não havia urgência para a implantação do sistema, e os trabalhos de elicitação deveriam priorizar a disponibilidade dos usuários. Dessa forma as sessões de elicitação iam sendo agendadas à medida que iam ocorrendo.
- Manteve-se o registro do tempo em cada sessão de elicitação de requisitos.

Na execução desta etapa da META, foi solicitado a dois usuários do futuro sistema que relatassem (individualmente) suas principais atividades durante a rotina de trabalho. Os usuários iniciaram o relato das atividades a partir da seguinte pergunta feita pelo engenheiro de requisitos: **Quais são as suas principais atividades durante a rotina diária de trabalho?**

Por exemplo, algumas das "atividades" relatadas:

A1 - conferir pagamento de alunos no programa específico;
A2 - lançar pagamentos na planilha eletrônica (de acertos) e no editor de texto (para controle visual – impresso);
A3 - fazer calendário para todas as turmas e confirmar com os professores;
A4 - providenciar certificados e históricos;
A5 - emitir mala direta.

Dificuldades encontradas. Não houve maiores dificuldades nesta primeira etapa, entretanto salientamos que muitas vezes os usuários perdiam a concentração no relato, devido ao fato do processo de elicitação estar sendo desenvolvido no local e horário de trabalho. Havia uma tendência do usuário em relatar somente atividades que, segundo o seu ponto de vista, deviam ser automatizadas pelo futuro sistema, relegando a um segundo plano as outras atividades.

Aspectos positivos. O uso de uma linguagem informal para os registros das informações levantadas facilitou a comunicação entre o engenheiro de requisitos e o usuário. Após a entrevista com dois usuários pôde-se identificar claramente, em nível social (comunidade), a divisão do trabalho estabelecida naquele contexto. Mesmo que em linhas gerais, após esta primeira fase, o engenheiro de requisitos já podia ter uma visão razoável do escopo do sistema.

Sugestões. O engenheiro de requisitos deve assumir uma postura de ouvidor, estimular o usuário a relatar suas atividades, e anotar o que é relatado, sem a preocupação de analisar se o que o usuário está relatando é atividade, ação ou operação, pois esta análise deve ser feita posteriormente. O engenheiro de requisitos deve estimular o usuário a relatar todas as suas atividades rotineiras, independentemente se elas serão ou não automatizadas pelo futuro sistema.

3.2.1.2 Selecionar as Atividades Candidatas

Desenvolvimento da etapa. Propositadamente as atividades candidatas foram transcritas exatamente nos termos empregados pelos usuários entrevistados, objetivando salientar algumas dificuldades que ocorreram neste tipo de relato. Pôde-se observar, por exemplo, que algumas das atividades candidatas relatadas pelos usuários eram pouco preenchida de significado (Atividade A3 do Quadro 1). Surgiram dúvidas como: Que tipo de calendário é este? O que será confirmado com os professores?. Outras atividades estavam incompletas e ambíguas (Atividade A5 do quadro 1). Surgiram dúvidas como: A quem se destina esta mala direta (alunos, ex-alunos, candidatos)?. Também pudemos observar mais de uma atividade distinta declaradas como única (Atividade A4 do Quadro 1). Ações cooperantes que estavam dentro do contexto de uma determinada atividade foram declaradas como atividades distintas (A1 e A2). Dessa forma, esta etapa exigiu um esforço significativo do engenheiro de requisitos, na análise e seleção das atividades a partir das definições *atividade, ação e operação* (descritas na META), e no processo de reescrever as atividades. Depois desta análise, as atividades reagrupadas e reescritas foram apresentadas aos usuários, afim de se obter o aceite e aprovação das mesmas. Por exemplo, as atividades candidatas A1, A2, A3, A4 e A5, foram reagrupadas e reescritas transformando-se em atividades selecionas, conforme apresentadas no Quadro 1.

Quadro 1 – Atividade Candidatas Selecionadas

Atividades Candidatas	**ATS (Atividades Selecionadas)**
A1 + A2	ATS1 - Controlar recebimento de mensalidades de alunos.
A3	ATS2 - Elaborar calendário escolar 2004.
A4	ATS3 - Elaborar certificados de conclusão de curso. ATS4 - Elaborar históricos escolares.
A5	ATS5 - Elaborar mala direta de endereçamento (ex-alunos).

Dificuldades encontradas. Esta etapa apresentou um alto grau de complexidade, pois a seleção de atividades não se trata apenas de um descarte de algumas atividades (o que eventualmente pode ocorrer), mas de um esforço de análise afim de avaliar a granularidade das atividades. Vale lembrar que é a partir das atividades selecionadas que todos os demais procedimentos da META se desencadeiam. Observou-se que o engenheiro de requisitos deve ter pleno domínio da metodologia na observância das definições *de atividade, ação e operação*, pois o usuário não tem a compreensão da granularidade da atividade, e frequentemente relata ações e operações como atividade. Baseando-se nas definições de *atividade, ação e operação,* o engenheiro de requisitos decidirá o que realmente deve ser entendido como atividade, e agrupar (quando necessário) ações e operações dentro da estrutura hierárquica de uma determinada atividade. Portanto, podemos indicar que, se para a execução de uma tarefa relatada pelo usuário outros tantos procedimentos devem ser executados conjuntamente (várias ações subseqüentes), tal tarefa é uma boa candidata a ser considerada uma atividade selecionada.

Aspectos positivos. Observou-se que através desta etapa foi possível elucidar aos usuários quantas são as suas atividades rotineiras, os possíveis relacionamentos entre elas, o fluxo de ações e operações dentro de uma determinada atividade, e a divisão e distribuição social das atividades. Esta etapa responde claramente ao engenheiro de requisitos por onde começar a elicitação de requisitos, pois cada atividade selecionada torna-se uma unidade de elicitação de requisitos, estabelecendo-se assim um processo de elicitação de requisitos mais organizado.

Sugestões. O engenheiro de requisitos deve fazer a seleção das atividades fora da presença do usuário. Então, num outro momento, mas antes de prosseguir para a próxima etapa, as atividades selecionadas e organizadas são apresentadas aos usuário, afim de obter uma validação das atividades selecionadas. A META não estabelece um sistema de código ou identificação para as atividades selecionadas. Sugerimos que o engenheiro de requisitos elabore um sistema de identificação, afim de manter um rastreamento/relacionamento das atividades com suas respectivas ações e operações.

3.2.1.3 Descrição do Histórico das Atividades Selecionadas

Desenvolvimento da etapa. Solicitou-se aos usuários que relatassem o histórico de cada atividade selecionada. Para auxilia-los, iniciamos o processo do relato do histórico da atividade, a partir das perguntas: **Esta atividade sempre foi realizada da forma como é feita hoje?** Em seguida, as perguntas **por quê ?, quando ?, como ?, quem ?, onde ?**, foram sendo propostas aos usuários, afim de facilitar e orientar o relato do histórico.

Dificuldades encontradas. Esta etapa foi extensa, e exigiu grande investimento de tempo e esforço, tanto dos usuários quanto do engenheiro de requisitos, pois o processo de anotação do histórico foi longo. Os usuários cansavam-se rapidamente neste procedimento, e tendiam a diminuir progressivamente o nível de detalhamento do histórico da atividade. Isto inviabilizou o processo de relatos dos históricos para várias atividades na mesma sessão de elicitação (o relato de cada atividade durou em média 25 minutos). Nesta etapa o controle do tempo, pelo engenheiro de requisitos, tornou-se fundamental.

Aspectos positivos. A descrição do histórico das atividades mostrou-nos que cada ATS (Atividade Selecionada) guarda em si uma quantidade riquíssima de informações e relacionamentos, propiciando ao engenheiro de requisitos uma boa visão das rotinas, do fluxo das informações, do uso dos recursos materiais e computacionais e das atribuições das responsabilidades dos sujeitos envolvidos. Portanto, o investimento de tempo nesta etapa é altamente recompensado pela quantidade e qualidade das informações obtidas.

Sugestões. O engenheiro de requisitos deve inicialmente ouvir atentamente o relato do histórico da atividade, anotando o máximo de informações possíveis. Mais uma vez ressaltamos que a linguagem informal auxilia muito neste processo. Solicitar ao usuário que descreva o histórico na sequência exata em que ocorrem os fatos. O engenheiro de requisitos, se desejar, poderá esboçar rapidamente um modelo da sequência dos fatos, evitando que o usuário se esqueça de algo importante. Durante o relato do histórico da atividade, o engenheiro de requisitos deve estar atento e registrar todas as informações que respondam às perguntas: O quê? Quando? Quem? Onde? Por quê? Como? Sempre que o usuário fizer referência a um formulário, arquivo, pasta ou outro material de referência, sugerimos que peça-lhe para apresentar o objeto referenciado. Estes itens serão bons candidatos a objetos e ferramentas de mediação.

3.2.2 Etapa 2. Delineando o Contexto da Atividade

3.2.2.1 Identificação dos Motivos e Resultados de Cada Atividade

Desenvolvimento da etapa. Sempre ao iniciarmos uma das etapas da META, procurávamos formular uma pergunta ao usuário, afim de auxiliar o processo de elicitação. Então, para elicitar os motivos da atividade perguntamos: **Por que razão esta atividade é realizada? Qual necessidade será suprida a partir da realização desta atividade?** Em seguida, para elicitar os resultados, perguntávamos: **O que se deseja obter com a realização da atividade?**
Para exemplificar, para a atividade ATS2 foram elicitados os seguintes motivo e resultado.
Motivo: Necessidade de organizar o desencadeamento das atividades acadêmicas, através das seqüências das disciplinas em datas e horários e períodos letivos.
Resultado: Calendário escolar estruturado, devidamente aprovado pelo Diretor e aceito pelos professores.

Dificuldades encontradas. Elicitar o motivos das atividades não foi uma tarefa trivial. Em muitos casos o usuário não tinha clareza suficiente dos motivos da atividade. Este fato exigiu do engenheiro de requisitos assumir um papel de investigação, auxiliando o usuário na busca da razão de ser da atividade e, por muitas vezes, foi necessário raciocinar junto com o usuário, afim de elicitar o real motivo da atividade.

Aspectos positivos. O fato de não ser simples determinar o motivo de uma atividade é justificável, pois durante o diálogo com os usuários vários "motivos" puderam ser elicitados, e isto aumentou a quantidade de informações acerca das atividades. Por exemplo, nos motivos elicitados na ATS2, pudemos identificar de imediato dois sujeitos envolvidos na atividade: professores e alunos. Na elicitação do resultado da atividade tem-se a informação do "produto" final obtido com a atividade.

Sugestões. O engenheiro de requisitos deve anotar primeiro os motivos, em seguida todos os resultados declarados pelo usuário. Não deve preocupar-se com a seqüência em que o usuário relata motivos e resultados, isto deve ser organizado num segundo momento.

3.2.2.1 Identificação dos Elementos no Nível Individual

Desenvolvimento da etapa. Apenas o engenheiro de requisitos trabalhou nesta etapa, baseando-se no histórico, motivos e resultados de cada atividade, e nas definições de sujeito, ferramentas e objeto (conforme apresentadas na META).

Dificuldades encontradas. Uma atenção especial precisou ser dedicada à identificação dos objetos, pois materiais como arquivos eletrônicos, dados de arquivos e formulários impressos são objetos que também podem ser transformados pelos sujeitos durante a execução da atividade.

Aspectos positivos. Esta etapa mostrou-se relevante, pois organiza a elicitação de requisitos, evidenciando os sujeitos das atividades, suas ferramentas (computadores, softwares, pastas de arquivos, etc.), com os quais os sujeitos interagem durante a realização da atividade, vinculando ao sujeito todos os seus aparatos e recursos utilizados durante a atividade. Em conseqüência da forma como esta etapa organiza a elicitação de requisitos, fica bastante claro qual é o atual grau de automatização das atividades, e quais serão os recursos do software (requisitos) necessários posteriormente.

Sugestões. Ter em mente que objeto é qualquer coisa que possa ser acessada, processada ou transformada durante a realização da atividade.

3.2.2.2 Identificação dos Elementos no Nível Social

Desenvolvimento da etapa. Como citado anteriormente, sempre procuramos propor algumas perguntas "estratégicas" ao usuário, afim de auxiliar a elicitação de requisitos. Na identificação da comunidade perguntamos: **Quais são as pessoas envolvidas com esta atividade que podem de alguma forma influenciar ou modificar o resultado da atividade?** Para identificar a divisão do trabalho perguntamos: **Qual é a responsabilidade/papel do sujeito, na realização da atividade?** Para a identificação das regras: **Há alguma norma/regra/procedimento, que direcione/priorize as ações durante a realização da atividade?**

Dificuldades encontradas. Esta etapa não apresentou dificuldades para ser realizada. **Aspectos positivos.** Esta etapa é especialmente importante para a elicitação de requisitos, pois define claramente os envolvidos em uma determinada atividade e suas respectivas responsabilidades, além de apresentar algumas informações de como deve ser executada a atividade. Por exemplo, algumas das regras da ATS2 foram: distribuir as disciplinas no calendário obedecendo a prioridade da sequência pedagógica, carga horária, disponibilidade de professor; verificar se não há conflito de horário entre os professores e turmas.

Sugestões. Sempre que o usuário citar regras/normas/procedimentos, ou formulários, pastas ou planilhas, solicitar ao usuário que seja apresentado um modelo de tais documentos, pois nestes costumam residir grande quantidade de informações que podem ficar negligenciadas.

3.2.2.3 Modelagem das Atividades Utilizando o Diagrama de Engeström

Desenvolvimento da etapa. Para a execução desta etapa, foi elaborado um quadro contendo o diagrama de Engeström, onde as informações foram distribuídas, a partir das tabelas e quadros de informações que mantinham os registros das etapas anteriores. Nesta etapa o engenheiro de requisitos trabalhou sozinho, não havendo a necessidade de entrevistar os usuários.

Dificuldades encontradas. Elaborar um quadro para os registros desta etapa não foi uma tarefa simples, pois os editores de texto são graficamente limitados e inadequados para este tipo de modelagem, e não havia disponível uma ferramenta própria para a notação deste diagrama[1].

Aspectos positivos. Embora a quantidade de informações levantada com a META tenha sido grande, como resultado dos procedimentos anteriores foi necessário pouco tempo para a modelagem das atividades no diagrama de Engeström (aproximadamente 12 minutos para cada ATS). A representação dos elementos participantes das atividade através do diagrama de Engeström apresentou bons resultados, pois a representação nos deu uma excelente visualização do contexto formado em cada atividade, possibilitando uma avaliação integrada e ampliada dos requisitos embutidos em cada atividade.

Sugestões. Esta etapa auxilia na organização geral e revisão do contexto da atividade. Entretanto, para agregar um maior potencial a esta etapa, sugerimos que se estude uma solução gráfica que agrupe os diagramas de Engeström em uma estrutura de rede de relacionamentos entre as atividades.

3.2.3 Descrição da Estrutura Hierárquica das Atividades

3.2.3.1 Identificação das Ações e Operações

---

[1] Atualmente está em desenvolvimento, dentro do programa de mestrado em Ciência da Computação da UNIMEP, uma ferramenta automatizada de apoio à META (Franceto, 2004).

Desenvolvimento da etapa. Nesta etapa o engenheiro de requisitos retomou as entrevistas com os usuários afim de elicitar as ações e operações de cada atividade. Na execução desta etapa o engenheiro de requisitos baseou-se nas definições de ação e operação descritas na META. Um modelo didático foi elaborado e apresentado aos usuários, auxiliando-os na compreensão do conceito de ação e operação, bem como a diferença entre eles.

Dificuldades encontradas. Esta etapa apresentou certo grau de complexidade, pois foi necessário um bom entendimento dos conceitos de ação e operação. Além disso não foi uma tarefa simples identificar as fronteiras entre ação e operação. Foi necessário elaborar um modelo didático que apresenta-se ao usuário um quadro contendo uma atividade e suas ações e operações (vide item III do apêndice), afim de auxilia-lo na compreensão do tipo de informação que estava sendo solicitada; além disso o registro das ações e operações também demandaram bastante tempo, pois uma atividade pode ter várias ações e cada ação pode ter várias operações.

Aspectos positivos. Este procedimento permitiu identificar no contexto da atividade "o que" e "como" as tarefas são realizadas. Em outras palavras, isto significa explicitar o detalhamento, passo a passo, da rotina de trabalho de cada usuário. Além disso, na medida em que o usuário vai compreendendo a dinâmica desta etapa, este passa a declarar as ações e operações na sequência em que elas ocorrem, o que permite ao engenheiro de requisitos esboçar um modelo de encadeamento destas ações (por exemplo, conforme o diagrama de atividades da UML).

Sugestões. A idéia de criar um modelo didático para esta etapa, e apresenta-lo ao usuário, afim de auxilia-lo no entendimento dos conceitos de ação e operação obteve êxito. Portanto sugerimos ao engenheiro de requisitos que adote esta idéia, e inclua ao lado da palavra **ação** o "o quê?", e ao lado da palavra **operação** o "como?". Este é um aspecto que deve ser revisto na META.

3.2.3.2 Descrição das Metas das Ações

Desenvolvimento da etapa. Esta etapa foi executada simultaneamente com a etapa anterior. Durante a elicitação das ações, as suas respectivas metas também foram elicitadas.

Dificuldades encontradas. A elicitação das metas nesta etapa poucas vezes apresentaram dificuldades, pois o modelo didático citado anteriormente contribui para facilitar o trabalho.

Aspectos positivos. Permite averiguar se a execução das operações levam ao alcance da meta proposta para a ação.

Sugestões. Sugerimos manter no mesmo quadro os registros das informações das etapas apresentadas em 3.2.3.1 e 3.2.3.2, pois facilita a visualização e discussão da estrutura hierárquica da atividade, e manter ao lado da palavra **meta** o "por quê?".

3.2.3.3 Descrição das Condições de Realização das Operações

Desenvolvimento da etapa. Para esta etapa foi elaborado um quadro para cada atividade, que continha o registro de suas respectivas ações e operações, em seguida foram anotadas as condições de execução de cada atividade. Como em etapas anteriores, algumas perguntas foram propostas aos usuários, para auxiliá-los na elicitação, por exemplo: **O que não pode faltar na execução desta operação? O que poderá falhar na execução desta operação?**

Dificuldades encontradas: Esta etapa não apresentou dificuldades.
Aspectos positivos. Esta etapa também teve contribuição relevante no processo de elicitação de requisitos, pois na identificação das condições de realização das operações, explicitamos o que não podia faltar ou o que poderia falhar durante a execução das operações. Dessa forma, esta etapa permitiu reunir um conjunto de informações que auxiliou o engenheiro de requisitos a prevenir problemas futuros, que alterariam a forma como são executadas as operações, colocando em risco as metas, e conseqüentemente o alcance dos resultados propostos pela atividade. O tempo investido na elaboração do quadro citado foi recompensado, pois os usuários entenderam facilmente o que se desejava identificar, e as respostas foram na maioria das vezes curtas e rápidas.

Sugestões. Fazer um esforço para reunir em um único quadro as informações obtidas nas etapas 3.2.3.1, 3.2.3.2 e 3.2.3.3, o que certamente contribui na visualização da estrutura hierárquica da atividade.

4. Conclusão

A elaboração deste trabalho se orientou na necessidade dos engenheiros de requisitos e usuários de sistemas de software em superar as dificuldades essenciais que são inerentes a qualquer processo de elicitação de requisitos. Essas dificuldades, em grande medida, estão relacionadas ao contexto social no qual o sistema em análise se insere. Com o uso da META durante a elicitação de requisitos executada (objeto de estudo do experimento realizado) pôde-se perceber, e elicitar, um grande volume de informações que estavam "escondidas" no contexto social do sistema.

O estudo de caso realizado trouxe contribuições importantes para a META, pois durante sua realização foi possível observar aspectos relevantes sobre o uso da metodologia de elicitação de requisitos, como o tempo investido em cada fase, o grau de dificuldade/facilidade de entendimento das etapas e definições propostas pela META, a quantidade e qualidade das informações elicitadas, e principalmente aspectos que envolveram os registros das informações durante a execução da metodologia. O estudo empírico trouxe indicativos factíveis sobre o potencial da META para a elicitação de requisitos, e também contribuiu apontando para aspectos da META que merecem revisões, motivando-nos para, em estudos posteriores, elaborar formalmente *guidelines*, quadros e formulários para cada etapa da META, afim de facilitar a utilização da mesma por engenheiros de requisitos.

Atualmente, estamos iniciando investigações no sentido de relacionar e posicionar a META com outras abordagens sociais na engenharia de software, tais como métodos de análise de requisitos baseados em agentes, técnicas de análise de requisitos orientadas a metas e CMD (Co-operative Method Development) [12].

Referências Bibliográficas

1. de Bortoli, L. A.; Price, A. M. A.: O uso de *workflow* para apoiar a elicitação de requisitos. Workshop de Engenharia de Requisitos, WER 2000.
2. Franceto, S.; Martins, L. E. G.: Elicitação de requisitos para o desenvolviemnto de uma ferramenta de apoio à metodologia de eleicitação de requisitos de software baseada na teoria da atividade (META). VII Workshop Iberoamericano de Ingenearia de Requisitos Y Desarrollo de Ambientes de Software – IDEAS, 2004. Peru.
3. Gregoriades, A.; Shin, J.; Sutcliffe, A.: Human-Centred requirements engineering. Requirements Engineering Conference, 12th IEEE International. RE'04, 2004.
4. Hickey, A. M.; Davis, A. M.: Elicitation Technique Selection: how do experts do it? 11th IEEE Internacional Requirements Engineering Conference (RE'03). Monterey Bay, California, USA, 2003.
5. Kaptelinin, V.: Activity Theory: Implications for human-computer interaction. In B. Nardi, (ed), Context and Consciousness: Activity theory and human-computer interaction. Cambridge, MA: MIT Press, 1996.
6. Kotonya, G.and Summerville, I.: Requirements engineering: processes and techniques. John Wiley and Sons, 1998.
7. Kuutti, K.: Activity Theory as a Potential Framework for Human-Computer Interaction. In Context and Consciousness: Activity Theory and Human-Computer Interaction, MIT Press, 1996, pp. 17-44.
8. Martins, L. E. G.: Uma Metodologia de Elicitação de Requisitos Baseada na Teoria da Atividade. Tese de Doutorado. FEEC/Unicamp, Campinas, 2001.
9. Martins, L. E.G. and Daltrini, B. M.: An Approach to Software Requirements Elicitation Using the Precepts from Activity Theory. Proceedings of the Fourteenth IEEE International Conference on Automated Software Engineering, Florida, 1999.
10. Sommerville, I. and Sawyer, P.: Requirements Engineering: A good practice guide. Wiley. 2000.
11. Yin, R. K.: Estudo de Caso: planejamento e métodos. Porto Alegre: Bookman, 2001.
12. Dittrich, Y., Rönkkö, K., Lindeberg, O., Erickson, J. and Hansson, C.: Co-operative Method Development Revisited. Proceedings of the 2005 Workshop on Human and Social Factors of Software Engineering HSSE '05, Vol. 30 Issue 4 .

APÊNDICE

I: Exemplo do formulário utilizado para os registros das informações elicitadas na Etapa 1.1.3 da META. Item 3.2.1.3, deste artigo.

META – ETAPA 1 – Formulário 02 - Descrição do Histórico das Atividades

Atividade: AT1 - Controlar recebimento de mensalidades de alunos.

Data: 31/03/04	**Horário Inicio: 8:40**	**Horário Término: 9:05**	**Página: 1/1**

Técnica Auxiliar: Entrevista; Brainstorming

Participantes da Entrevista: 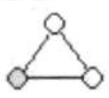	Auxiliar Administrativo	**Departamento:**	Secretaria Geral e Controladoria

Inicialmente esta atividade era registrada manualmente em relatório impresso, gerados a partir de um processador de textos. Todos os cálculos eram realizados em calculadoras manuais, e registrados no relatório impresso.
As seguintes informações constavam deste relatório: nome da turma, nome do aluno, data referente ao vencimento da mensalidade, e o valor da mensalidade a ser paga pelo aluno, e total geral das mensalidades.
Posteriormente, o controle deste relatório foi transferido para planilhas eletrônicas, uma por turma, que calculavam automaticamente o total das mensalidades pagas pelos alunos. Não havia integração entre as planilhas afim de se obter, por exemplo, o total geral de mensalidades pagas por todas as turmas. Os relatórios gerados pelo processador de texto não foram abandonados, pois o usuário continuou alimentando tais relatórios afim de obter uma "melhor visualização".
Atualmente, os relatórios citados anteriormente foram desativados, e o controle é feito via um conjunto de planilhas perfeitamente integradas entre si. Tais planilhas totalizam todas as mensalidades pagas pelos alunos, com totais parciais por parcela/turma, totais parciais turma/turma, e total geral. Nas planilhas constam as seguintes informações: nome da turma, data de início, número da parcela, data de vencimento, nome dos alunos, valor da mensalidade a ser paga pelo aluno, índice para cálculo de multas por atraso de pagamento, percentual de desconto oferecidos por aluno, observações de mensalidades pagas com atraso.
Quando novas turmas iniciam seus estudos, ou novos alunos são inseridos nas turmas que já estão em andamento, o Aux. Administrativo consulta as fichas de inscrições e os contratos de prestação de serviços educacionais, e alimenta todos os campos das respectivas planilhas.
Havendo o pagamento das mensalidades por parte dos alunos, o Aux. Administrativo lança a data de pagamento das mensalidades nas planilhas, que executam todos os cálculos automaticamente.

II: Exemplo do formulário utilizado para os registros das informações elicitadas na Etapa 2.2.3 da META. Item 3.2.2.2, deste artigo.

META – ETAPA 2 – Formulário 03 - Identificação dos elementos no nível social

Atividade: AT1 – Controlar recebimento de mensalidades de alunos.

Comunidade 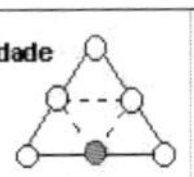	• Auxiliar Administrativo • Aluno
Divisão do Trabalho 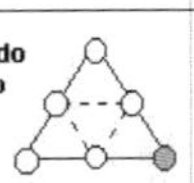	• Auxiliar Administrativo: responsável pela operação das planilhas que controlam os recebimentos de mensalidades • Aluno: responsável por efetuar (ou não efetuar) o pagamento das mensalidades nas datas estipuladas
Regras 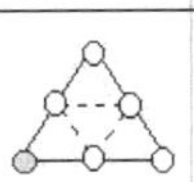	• Na planilha de controle de mensalidades de alunos os seguintes campos devem ser preenchidos: data de início do curso, número da parcela, percentual de desconto. • Os campos data de vencimento da parcela e valor da mensalidade devem ser preenchidos de acordo com as informações que constam no contrato de prestação de serviços educacionais. • A princípio o aluno efetuará o pagamento no banco. Entretanto, também poderá efetuar o pagamento diretamente com a Auxiliar Administrativo, que quitará o boleto (carimbo, data, assinatura). • Se houver extravio do boleto, a Auxiliar Administrativo gerará outro boleto.

III: Exemplo do formulário utilizado para os registros das informações elicitadas nas Etapas 3.1.1, 3.1.2, 3.1.3 da META. Itens 3.2.3.1, 3.2.3.2, 3.2.3.3, deste artigo.

META – ETAPA 3 – Formulário 01 - Descrição da estrutura hierárquica da atividade			
Atividade: AT1 - Controlar recebimento de mensalidades de alunos.			
Data:	Horário Início: 15:50	Horário Término: 15:10	Página: 1/2
Técnica Auxiliar: Entrevista			
Participantes da entrevista: 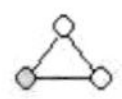	Auxiliar Administrativo	Departamento:	Secretaria Geral e Controladoria

AÇÕES	OPERAÇÕES
• Verificar os pagamentos efetuados até o dia anterior. • Meta: Extrato da conta banco atualizado à uma data específica.	• Acessar a conta banco, via Internet, com aplicativo específico fornecido pelo banco. • Condições de realização: Ter o aplicativo devidamente instalado; acesso à Internet. • Acessar no aplicativo a transferência de arquivos/retorno. • Condições de realização: Ter o aplicativo instalado e saber operá-lo. • Selecionar a linha de pagamento do dia anterior, e salvá-la. • Condições de realização: Saber operar o aplicativo
• Importar o arquivo/retorno para o aplicativo fornecido pelo banco. • Meta: Aplicativo alimentado com os dados fornecido pelo banco.	• Acessar o aplicativo fornecido pelo banco. • Condições de realização: Ter o aplicativo instalado. • Selecionar a linha da data dos dados a serem importados. • Condições de realização: Saber operar o aplicativo. • Confirmar a importação. • Condições de realização: Saber operar o aplicativo.

Uma Ontologia de Requisitos de Software

Julio Cesar Nardi, Ricardo de Almeida Falbo

Mestrado em Informática, Universidade Federal do Espírito Santo, Vitória - ES - Brasil
julionardi@yahoo.com.br, falbo@inf.ufes.br

Abstract. Tool integration in Software Development Environments (SDEs) is a complex problem. A way to improve tool integration is building them sharing a common conceptualization, given by ontologies. This paper presents a software requirements ontology developed to serve as basis for the development of tools to support the requirements engineering process in the SDE ODE (Ontology-based software Development Environment). Since in the context of ODE's Project several software engineering domain ontologies were developed, the software requirements ontology was built integrated to them, reusing conceptualizations previously established.

1 Introdução

Obter os requisitos corretos em um projeto de software é a parte mais importante e difícil do processo de software. A deficiência no tratamento de requisitos tem sido apontada como a principal causa de fracassos de projetos de software [1]. Neste contexto, o processo de Engenharia de Requisitos (ER) ganha importância, assim como o apoio automatizado a ele.

Segundo Kotonya e Sommerville [2], o processo da ER é sistemático e abrange as atividades de elicitação, análise e negociação, documentação, validação e gerência de requisitos. Para os engenheiros de requisitos, que buscam especificar requisitos dentro de prazos e orçamentos definidos, a aplicação de métodos e ferramentas é considerada crucial para se obter sucesso. Entretanto, muitas vezes, ferramentas interferem na realização das atividades da ER ao invés de apoiá-las [1]. Acreditamos que, para serem efetivas, tais ferramentas têm de ser construídas apoiadas em um entendimento de consenso acerca dos elementos envolvidos no processo de ER.

Considerando que os requisitos são o foco do processo da ER, é interessante que se tenha uma compreensão clara do que vem a ser um requisito e de como ele se relaciona com outros elementos do processo de software. Como fruto dessa compreensão, é possível construir ferramentas de apoio ao processo de ER que sejam mais amplamente utilizáveis, já que essas estão baseadas em definições compartilhadas do domínio de requisitos.

Como forma de estabelecer uma conceituação básica acerca de requisitos, desenvolvemos uma ontologia de requisitos de software a ser usada como base para a construção de ferramentas de apoio ao processo de ER no ambiente de desenvolvimento de software (ADS) ODE (*Ontology-based software Development Environment*) [3]. Como o nome indica, ODE tem sua fundamentação baseada em ontologias, partindo do pressuposto que, se as ferramentas de um ADS são construídas baseadas em ontologias, a integração das mesmas é facilitada, pois os conceitos envolvidos são bem definidos. Ontologias são usadas em ODE, dentre outros, para estruturar o ambiente e sua infra-estrutura de gerência de conhecimento e para estabelecer uma forma padrão de comunicação entre agentes (humanos e de software) no ambiente [3]. Ontologias servem a esse propósito, na medida em que elas definem um vocabulário de representação, que captura os conceitos e as relações de um domínio, e um conjunto de axiomas, que restringem a sua interpretação [4].

Este trabalho apresenta a Ontologia de Requisitos de Software desenvolvida visando à formalização do conhecimento acerca do domínio de requisitos, sobretudo, para apoiar o desenvolvimento de ferramentas para o ambiente ODE. Essa ontologia foi definida buscando seguir o critério de compromissos ontológicos mínimos, de modo que seja possível reutilizar esse conhecimento de várias formas no ambiente, tais como na comunicação entre pessoas e o ambiente, entre agentes de software atuando no ambiente, na construção e integração de ferramentas, no aprendizado de Engenharia de Requisitos dentro do ambiente etc. Além disso, uma vez que diversas ontologias já foram construídas no contexto do projeto ODE, procurou-se sempre reutilizar conceituações previamente estabelecidas, favorecendo a formação de uma rede efetiva de conceitos e relações que possa ser explorada de várias formas.

Este trabalho está organizado da seguinte forma: a seção 2 discute brevemente alguns aspectos da Engenharia de Requisitos e de ontologias, incluindo o método de construção de ontologias seguido neste trabalho; a seção 3 apresenta a Ontologia de Requisitos desenvolvida; a seção 4 trata de trabalhos correlatos; e na seção 5 são tecidas algumas considerações finais.

2 Requisitos de Software e Ontologias

A Engenharia de Requisitos (ER) é a subárea da Engenharia de Software que trata do processo de definição dos requisitos de software. Esse processo é sistemático e abrange diversas atividades, tais como elicitação, análise e negociação, documentação, validação e gerência de requisitos [2].

Requisitos de software são sentenças que expressam as necessidades dos clientes e que condicionam a qualidade do software [5], ou especificações de serviços que o sistema deve prover, restrições no sistema e conhecimentos necessários para desenvolvê-lo [2]. Uma vez capturados, requisitos de software devem ser modelados, documentados, validados e acompanhados. Nesse processo, as propriedades de um requisito e os relacionamentos com outros elementos do processo de software são definidos e alterados. Portanto, definir e entender as propriedades e relações em torno de um requisito é essencial na condução do processo de ER.

Requisitos podem ser classificados segundo alguma forma de categorização, que pode ser definida de acordo com as práticas de cada organização de software. Geralmente, eles são classificados em: funcionais (representam o que o sistema deve fazer, suas funções, podendo ser subdivididos em essenciais, desejáveis e supérfluos) e não funcionais (representam os atributos do sistema enquanto software constituído, o que inclui manutenibilidade, eficiência etc).

Acerca de um requisito é interessante saber, ainda, a sua origem, os interessados (*stakeholders*) e os responsáveis por ele. De posse desses elementos, a atividade de análise e negociação é facilitada, pois é possível identificar os envolvidos e também o ponto de partida de um requisito [2].

No centro da atividade de gerência de requisitos – além do controle de alteração e de versão de um requisito e do acompanhamento de seu estado – está a rastreabilidade, isto é, a habilidade de se acompanhar a vida de um requisito em ambas as direções do processo de software e durante todo o ciclo de vida. A rastreabilidade de requisitos só é possível se houver ligações explícitas entre requisitos e outros elementos do processo de software. Dessa forma, a identificação da composição de requisitos, das dependências entre requisitos, de requisitos conflitantes, da origem dos requisitos e de seus interessados, além da identificação de em qual artefato (documento, diagrama, etc.) produzido durante o processo de software um requisito é tratado, é de fundamental importância para que a rastreabilidade possa ser implementada [2] [6].

Os requisitos elicitados e analisados devem ser documentados. Na atividade de documentação, um Documento de Especificação de Requisitos de Software (DERS) é normalmente gerado, contendo os requisitos de software de um determinado projeto. Existem vários modelos de DERS e cada organização pode definir seu próprio modelo de acordo com suas necessidades. Qualquer que seja seu formato, o DERS é um dos artefatos mais importantes do processo de software, uma vez que é a base para praticamente todas as atividades de construção subseqüentes. Assim, é imprescindível avaliar a qualidade de um DERS. Para tal, características de qualidade devem ser apontadas e métricas devem ser estabelecidas para avaliar a qualidade do DERS.

Pela breve exposição acima, é possível notar o quanto é complexo o processo da ER. Dada essa complexidade, construir ferramentas de apoio às atividades desse processo é fundamental para a efetiva execução do mesmo. Idealmente, para serem amplamente utilizáveis, tais ferramentas devem ser construídas com base em modelos sólidos, consensuais. Neste contexto, ontologias são potencialmente úteis.

Uma ontologia define um vocabulário específico usado para descrever uma certa realidade, mais um conjunto de decisões explícitas, fixando de forma rigorosa o significado pretendido para o vocabulário. Uma ontologia envolve, então, um vocabulário de representação, que captura os conceitos, relações e suas propriedades em algum domínio, e um conjunto de axiomas, que restringem a sua interpretação [4]. Ontologias têm se tornado populares, em grande parte, pelo fato de terem como objetivo promover um entendimento comum e compartilhado sobre um domínio, que pode ser comunicado entre pessoas e sistemas de aplicação.

Como qualquer artefato de engenharia de software, ontologias têm de ser construídas seguindo métodos e técnicas adequados. Para desenvolver a ontologia de requisitos de software, foi adotado o método SABiO (*__S__ystematic __A__pproach for __B__u__i__lding __O__ntologies*) [7] [8]. SABiO define um processo para construção de ontologias, cujas principais atividades são: (i) identificação do propósito e especificação de requisitos, que visa identificar questões que a ontologia deve ser capaz de responder (questões de competência), (ii) captura da ontologia, que tem por objetivo capturar os conceitos, relações, propriedades e restrições relevantes sobre o domínio em questão; e (iii) formalização, que busca escrever os axiomas da ontologia em uma linguagem formal (neste trabalho, optou-se pela lógica de primeira ordem).

Paralelamente a todas essas atividades, ocorrem as atividades de: (iv) integração com ontologias existentes, que visa a reutilizar conceituações existentes e integrar a ontologia em desenvolvimento a uma rede de ontologias mais ampla; (v) avaliação da ontologia, que, dentre outros, trata de avaliar se a ontologia é capaz de responder às questões de competência; e (vi) documentação da ontologia, que visa a registrar o desenvolvimento da ontologia. Em sua versão mais recente [8], SABiO advoga o uso de uma extensão da UML como linguagem gráfica para representação de ontologias. Essa extensão propõe o uso de um subconjunto de elementos da UML exercendo o mesmo papel da notação de LINGO [7], a linguagem originalmente proposta. LINGO possuía primitivas para representar conceitos, relações e propriedades, e alguns tipos de relações que possuíam uma semântica bem-estabelecida, tais como relações todo-parte e sub-tipo-de, para os quais um conjunto de axiomas formais, ditos axiomas epistemológicos, era definido. Assim, apesar de se utilizar os elementos de modelo da UML, a semântica imposta é a mesma que a estabelecida para os correspondentes elementos em LINGO, conforme parcialmente mostrado na figura 1. Segundo essa extensão da UML, classes com estereótipo `<<Conceito>>` representam conceitos da ontologia. Relações são definidas como associações nomeadas. Propriedades de conceitos e relações são representadas como atributos. Relações que contêm propriedades ou que possuem aridade maior que dois são representados como classes associativas com estereótipo `<<Relação>>`. Relações de supertipo e todo-parte são representadas como relações de generalização / especialização e de agregação / composição, respectivamente. Finalmente, condicionantes entre relações são representados por restrições entre associações [9].

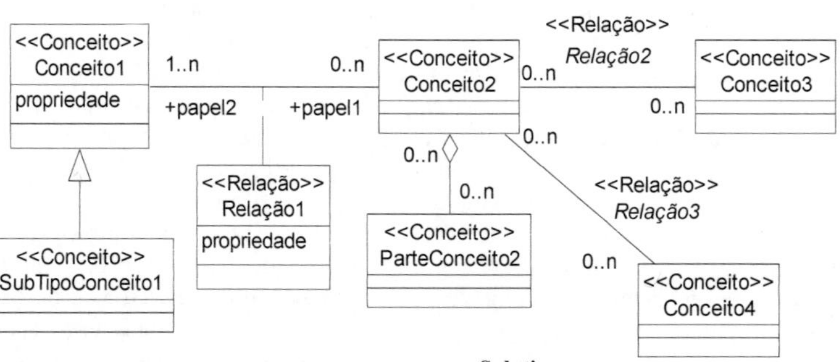

Axiomas:

Todo-Parte

(AE1) $\forall x \ \neg parte(x,x)$

(AE2) $\forall x,y \ parte(y,x) \leftrightarrow todo(x,y)$

(AE3) $\forall x,y \ parte(y,x) \rightarrow \neg \ parte(x,y)$

(AE4) $\forall x,y,z \ parte(z,y) \wedge parte(y,x) \rightarrow parte(z,x)$

(AE5) $\forall x,y \ disjunto(x,y) \rightarrow \neg\exists z \ parte(z,x) \wedge parte(z,y)$

(AE6) $\forall x \ atomico(x) \rightarrow \neg\exists y \ parte(y,x)$

Sub-tipo:

(AE7) $(\forall x,y,z)\ (subtipo(x,y) \wedge subtipo(y,z) \rightarrow supertipo(x,z))$

(AE8) $(\forall x,y)\ (subtipo(x,y) \rightarrow supertipo(y,x))$

Condicionante Ou-exclusivo:

(AE9) $(\forall a \in C2)\ ((\exists b)\ (b \in C3) \wedge R2(a,b)) \rightarrow \neg((\exists c \in C4) \wedge R3(a,c)))$

(AE10) $(\forall a \in A)((\exists c)\ (c \in C4) \wedge R3(a,c)) \rightarrow \neg((\exists b \in C3) \wedge R2(a,b)))$

Fig. 1. As principais notações da extensão da UML utilizada e os axiomas associados a ela.

3 Uma Ontologia de Requisitos de Software

Nesta seção é apresentada a Ontologia de Requisitos de Software proposta, tomando por base os artefatos definidos pelo método SABiO. Assim, começamos pela especificação de requisitos, listando as questões de competência levantadas:

QC1. O que é um requisito?
QC2. Qual a natureza de um requisito?
QC3. Quais são os requisitos de um projeto de software?
QC4. Para que módulos do sistema um requisito é alocado?
QC5. Quais os responsáveis por um requisito?
QC6. Quais os interessados (*stakeholders*) em um requisito?
QC7. Qual a origem de um requisito?
QC8. Qual o estado de um requisito?
QC9. Como um determinado requisito é decomposto em outros requisitos?
QC10. Que requisitos são dependentes de um determinado requisito?
QC11. Que requisitos são conflitantes entre si?
QC12. O que é uma especificação de requisitos de software (ERS)?
QC13. Que artefatos descrevem, modelam ou implementam um requisito?
QC14. Como gerenciar mudanças nos requisitos e nos artefatos a eles relacionados?
QC15. Como avaliar a qualidade em requisitos?

Uma vez que requisitos estão no universo da Engenharia de Software, é útil examinar outras ontologias nesse domínio. Neste trabalho foram inspecionadas as seguintes ontologias, construídas de forma integrada no âmbito do Projeto ODE:

- **Ontologia de Processo de Software:** desenvolvida em [7] e recentemente revisada em [10], essa ontologia é composta de ontologias de Atividade, Recurso e Procedimento e trata da conceituação básica acerca do domínio de processos de software, abordando conceitos de atividade, processo, projeto, artefato e recurso.
- **Ontologia de Artefatos** desenvolvida em [11], tem o intuito de prover um entendimento compartilhado acerca de alguns tipos de artefatos (documento, diagrama e código-fonte), definindo sub-ontologias para eles.
- **Ontologia de Gerência de Configuração de Software:** desenvolvida em [11], busca tratar de conceitos relacionados à gerência de configuração de software.
- **Ontologia de Qualidade de Software:** desenvolvida em [12], visa à conceituação sobre o domínio de qualidade de software, tratando de questões como avaliação da qualidade, características de qualidade e métricas.
- **Ontologia de Organizações de Software:** tem como propósito fornecer um vocabulário comum que possa ser utilizado para representar conhecimento útil sobre organizações de software, incluindo competências de seus membros.

A figura 2 mostra as ontologias integradas, destacando as dependências entre elas.

Da Ontologia de Processo, foram reutilizados os conceitos de *Projeto*, *Atividade* e *Artefato*. Requisitos são definidos no âmbito de um *Projeto* e, portanto, é importante relacionar os conceitos de *Requisito* e *Projeto*. Já o conceito de *Atividade* foi utilizado para compor o contexto no qual um requisito é originado, uma vez que um requisito pode ter origem em uma atividade do processo. Por fim, o conceito de *Artefato* é importante para a rastreabilidade, capturando em que artefatos um requisito é tratado.

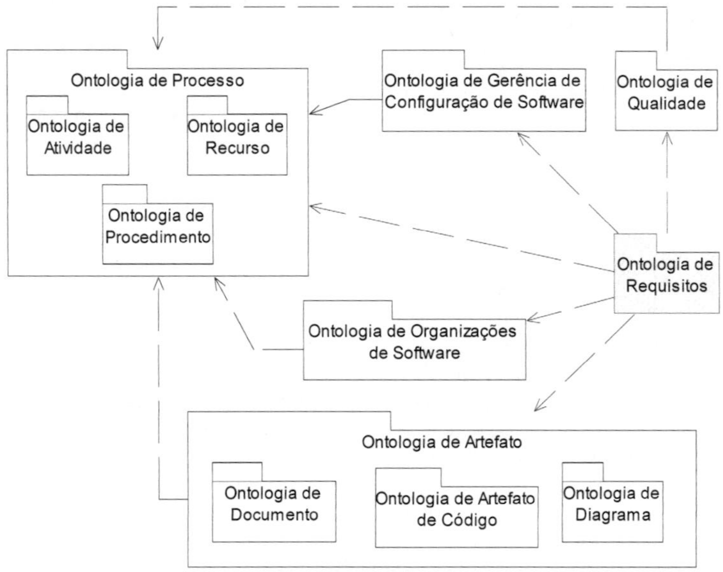

Fig. 2. A ontologia de requisitos e suas dependências com as ontologias utilizadas.

É importante ressaltar que aspectos relacionados ao processo de ER em si, tais como, atividades, sub-atividades, procedimentos etc, não foram tratados na Ontologia de Requisitos, pois já são tratados pela Ontologia de Processo. De fato, a descrição de um processo de ER pode ser feita pela instanciação da ontologia de processo.

A Ontologia de Artefato e suas sub-ontologias definem conceitos acerca de alguns tipos de artefatos e suas estruturas. Para este trabalho, foi especialmente importante a Ontologia de Documento, dado que um Documento de Especificação de Requisitos de Software (DERS) é um *Documento*. Assim, toda a conceituação usada para descrever artefatos e, mais especificamente, documentos, foi reutilizada para tratar DERSs, incluindo a definição de modelos de documento organizacionais para documentos [11].

Deve-se ressaltar que o conceito de *Artefato* é definido na Ontologia de Processo e não na Ontologia de Artefato. Isso porque a Ontologia de Artefato se propõe a conceituar alguns tipos de artefatos e não o que é um artefato. O conceito de artefato é tratado pela Ontologia de Processo, sendo definido como um produto ou insumo para atividades do processo de software [7].

Uma vez que é fundamental avaliar a qualidade em requisitos, a Ontologia de Qualidade de Software foi também utilizada, sobretudo no que se refere à qualidade de artefatos de software aplicada a DERS. Essa conceituação inclui *Características de Qualidade* diretamente e indiretamente mensuráveis, *Métricas, Medidas* etc [12].

A Ontologia de Gerência de Configuração de Software trata dos conceitos relacionados ao controle de versão e ao controle de alteração de itens de configuração, esses representando elementos do processo de software que estão sob gerência de configuração [12]. Como DERSs e requisitos devem ter sua configuração gerenciada, essa ontologia foi também integrada à ontologia de requisitos.

Da Ontologia de Organizações de Software reutilizou-se os conceitos *Pessoa e Equipe*. O primeiro representa os indivíduos de uma organização. Esse conceito é útil para se definir os interessados (*stakeholders*) e os responsáveis por um requisito. O segundo conceito, *Equipe*, define as equipes dos projetos de uma organização.

Por meio da reutilização de ontologias, associando conceitos dessas ontologias a conceitos definidos para a ontologia de requisitos, foi possível responder as questões de competência anteriormente colocadas, como veremos a seguir.

3.1 Captura e Formalização da Ontologia de Requisitos

Analisando as questões de competência anteriormente relacionadas, identificamos alguns aspectos relevantes, discutidos na seqüência:

1. Definição e Taxonomia de Requisitos (questões 1 a 4 e 12)
2. Aprovação e Interesse em Requisitos (questões 5 e 6)
3. Gerência de Requisitos (questões 7 a 11, 13 e 14)
4. Qualidade em Requisitos (questão 15)

Definição e Taxonomia de Requisitos

De maneira geral, requisitos são sentenças que descrevem serviços que um sistema deve prover, restrições que ele deve obedecer e características que ele deve possuir (*QC1*). Além disso, requisitos são definidos no âmbito de um projeto (*QC3*).

Conforme discutido na seção anterior, um DERS é um *Artefato*. Mais especificamente, um DERS é um *Documento* (*QC12*), que, segundo [11], é um artefato de software não passível de execução, constituído tipicamente de declarações textuais, normalmente associado a padrões organizacionais (roteiros e modelos de documento) que definem a forma como ele deve ser produzido.

Ainda que requisitos sejam definidos no âmbito de um projeto, é importante definir também para que módulos do projeto tal requisito é alocado (*QC4*). Para responder essa questão foram definidos os conceitos de *Escopo* e *Módulo*. Um projeto de software tem seu escopo normalmente dividido em módulos e, estabelecendo uma relação entre *Requisito* e *Módulo*, é possível acompanhar a que módulos um requisito está alocado e vice-versa.

Como podem existir vários tipos de requisito, se faz necessário criar uma taxonomia para organizá-los. Entendemos que não há um consenso acerca dos tipos de requisitos. Desse modo, optou-se por criar o conceito *Tipo de Requisito*, que admite sub-tipos, sendo que um subtipo pode ter vários supertipos e, para cada supertipo, é possível criar vários subtipos (*QC2*).

A figura 3 mostra a parte do modelo da ontologia referente às questões de competência referenciadas acima. Vale lembrar que a notação utilizada impõe implicitamente alguns axiomas. Por exemplo, os axiomas (AE1) a (AE6) da figura 1 se aplicam a todas as relações todo-parte mostradas na figura 2 (entre Escopo e Módulo, entre Módulos e entre Tipos de Requisitos), assim como os axiomas (AE7) e (AE8) da figura 1 se aplicam às relações de sub-tipo entre Artefato, Documento e Documento de Especificação de Requisitos de Software. Além desses axiomas, ditos epistemológicos, outros axiomas foram definidos, alguns deles discutidos na seqüência.

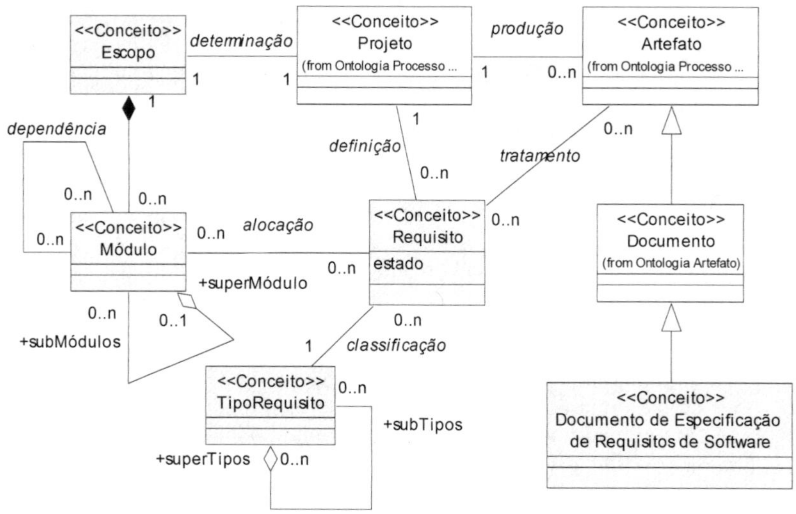

Fig. 3. Definição e Taxonomia de Requisito

Para formalizar aspectos importantes na alocação de requisitos a módulos, foram utilizados os seguintes predicados: *alocacao(r, m)*, indicando que o requisito *r* é alocado ao módulo *m*; e *submodulo(m1, m2)*, indicando que *m1* é um sub-módulo de *m2*. Esses predicados estão relacionados segundo a seguinte sentença, apontando que os requisitos alocados a um módulo estão alocados também a seus super-módulos:

$$(\forall r, m1, m2)\ (submodulo(m1,m2) \wedge alocacao(r, m1) \rightarrow alocacao(r, m2))\ (A1)$$

Além disso, é válido o axioma abaixo que define que um requisito só pode estar alocado a um módulo que esteja no escopo do projeto que definiu esse requisito. Nesse axioma o predicado *definição(r, p)* indica que o requisito *r* foi definido no projeto *p; composição(m, e)* indica que o módulo *m* compõe o escopo *e*; e *determinação(e,p)* indica que o escopo *e* foi determinado para o projeto *p*.

$$(\forall p, r, m)\ (alocação(r, m) \wedge definição(r, p) \wedge composição(m, e) \rightarrow determinação\ (e, p))\quad (AC1)$$

Deve-se ressaltar a diferença entre os axiomas (A1) e (AC1). O axioma (A1) deriva uma nova informação (e, portanto, é dito um axioma ontológico), enquanto o axioma (AC1) não deriva nova informação, mas apenas restringe o estabelecimento de relações. Axiomas desse tipo são ditos axiomas de consolidação [7].

Dada a limitação de espaço, neste artigo não apresentamos outros axiomas definidos. Apenas para registrar, a relação de dependência entre módulos é transitiva e simétrica. Além disso, há um axioma de consolidação envolvendo as relações entre Requisito, Projeto e Artefato.

Além de modelos gráficos e axiomas formais, SABiO propõe que seja elaborado um dicionário de termos com uma entrada para cada termo definido na ontologia (conceitos, relações e propriedades). Novamente por limitações de espaço, neste artigo apresentamos apenas os termos referentes aos conceitos definidos na ontologia de requisitos, mostrados na Tabela 1. Os termos em negrito nessa tabela correspondem a outros termos descritos no dicionário de termos completo.

Tabela 1. Parte do Dicionário de Termos da Ontologia de Requisitos.

Requisito	Representa especificações de serviços que o sistema deve prover, restrições do sistema e do processo de desenvolvimento e conhecimento necessário para a construção do sistema.
Documento de Especificação de Requisitos de Software	É um **documento**, portanto um **artefato** de software, formal que é utilizado para comunicação dos requisitos aos clientes, aos usuários etc, servindo de base para diversas **atividades** do **processo** de software. Sendo um documento, é normalmente associado a padrões organizacionais (**roteiros**) que definem a forma como deve ser produzido.
Tipo de Requisito	Conceito utilizado na caracterização de um requisito para retratar a dimensão que o requisito procura abordar, tal como funcional, não-funcional etc.
Módulo	É uma porção de sistema utilizada para organizar e agrupar, por exemplo, **artefatos**, **requisitos** e outros módulos que possuem certa afinidade.
Escopo	Determina os limites de um **projeto**, englobando o que faz parte do **projeto** e o que não faz. Um escopo pode ser decomposto em **módulos**.
Contexto	Caracteriza qual a situação na qual um **requisito** surgiu, procurando descrever quais as **pessoas** envolvidas, quais os **artefatos** analisados e em qual **atividade** do **processo** de software o requisito surgiu.

Aprovação e Interesse em Requisitos

O processo de Engenharia de Requisitos envolve várias pessoas de diversas áreas e com perspectivas diferentes. Dessa forma, é interessante que se saiba os interessados em cada requisito, com o intuito de facilitar a localização dos mesmos para facilitar negociações, esclarecimentos e discutir impactos de mudanças (*QC6*).

Além disso, é imprescindível que existam pessoas responsáveis por um dado requisito. Tais pessoas podem, por exemplo, aprovar um requisito antes que ele seja tratado por atividades subseqüentes do processo de desenvolvimento (*QC5*).

A figura 4 mostra a parte da ontologia de requisitos que trata dessas questões. O conceito *Requisito* se relaciona com o conceito *Pessoa*, da Ontologia de Organizações de Software, por meio das relações *interesse* e *responsabilidade*. Como os nomes sugerem, a primeira relação representa o interesse de pessoas em um requisito e a segunda representa os responsáveis por um requisito.

Dentre os axiomas definidos para essa parte da ontologia destacam-se os seguintes axiomas de consolidação:

$$(\forall\ r, p, e, pr)\ (interesse(p, r) \rightarrow participação(p, e) \land alocação\_pessoal(e, pr) \land definção(r, pr)) \quad (AC2)$$

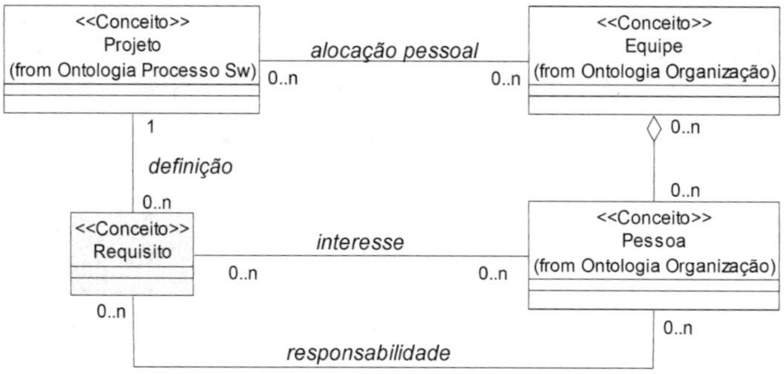

Fig. 4. Aprovação e Interesse em Requisito.

$$(\forall\ r,\ p,\ e,\ pr)\ (\mathit{reponsabilidade}(p,\ r) \rightarrow \mathit{participação}(p,\ e) \wedge \mathit{alocação\_pessoal}(e,\ pr) \wedge \mathit{definção}\ (r,\ pr)) \quad (AC3)$$

O axioma (AC2) garante que, para uma pessoa ser um interessado em um requisito, ela deve estar alocada a uma equipe do projeto no qual o requisito foi definido. Já o axioma (AC3) garante que, para uma pessoa ser responsável por um requisito, ela também deve estar alocada a uma equipe do projeto que definiu o requisito. Nesses axiomas, os seguintes predicados foram utilizados: *interesse(p, r)* indica que a pessoa *p* tem interesse no requisito *r*; *responsabilidade(p, r)* indica que a pessoa *p* é responsável pelo requisito *r*; *participação(p, e)* indica que a pessoa *p* participa da equipe *e*; e *alocação_pessoal(e, pr)* indica que a equipe *e* está alocada ao projeto *pr*.

Gerência de Requisitos

Segundo [6], a gerência de requisitos compreende controle de mudança, controle de versão, acompanhamento do estado dos requisitos e rastreabilidade.

No que tange ao controle de mudança e ao controle de versão de requisito, pode-se perceber que estamos falando de gerência da configuração de requisitos (e documentos de especificação de requisitos de software – DERS). Como destacado na seção anterior, a Ontologia de Gerência de Configuração de Software trata dessas questões. O conceito central dessa ontologia é o conceito de *Item de Configuração*, o qual representa algo que está sob gerência de configuração e, assim, só pode ser alterado segundo um procedimento de controle de alteração formalmente estabelecido e documentado. Um *Item de Configuração* possui várias *Variações*, que podem ser tanto do tipo *Variante* quanto *Versão*. Assim, para que requisitos e DERS sejam submetidos à gerência de configuração, basta relacioná-los com *Item de Configuração*, por meio da relação *derivação*, conforme definido em [11] e parcialmente mostrado na figura 5.

Ainda em relação ao controle de mudanças e envolvendo também a rastreabilidade, é necessário estabelecer uma rede de ligações com o objetivo de detectar com mais facilidade o impacto de mudanças. Essas ligações, normalmente, buscam fornecer informações acerca de dependência (*QC10*), composição (*QC9*) e conflito (*CQ11*) entre requisitos, informações sobre onde um requisito está descrito, modelado e codificado (*QC13*) e qual a origem de um requisito (*QC7*). O modelo da figura 6 procura tratar esses aspectos.

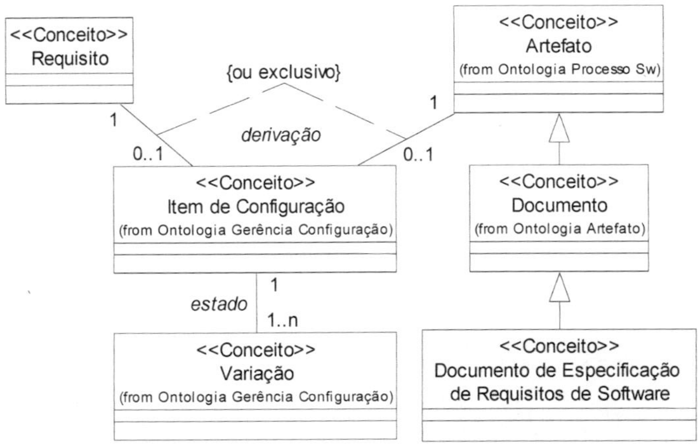

Fig. 5. Gerência de Configuração de Software aplicada a Requisitos e DERSs.

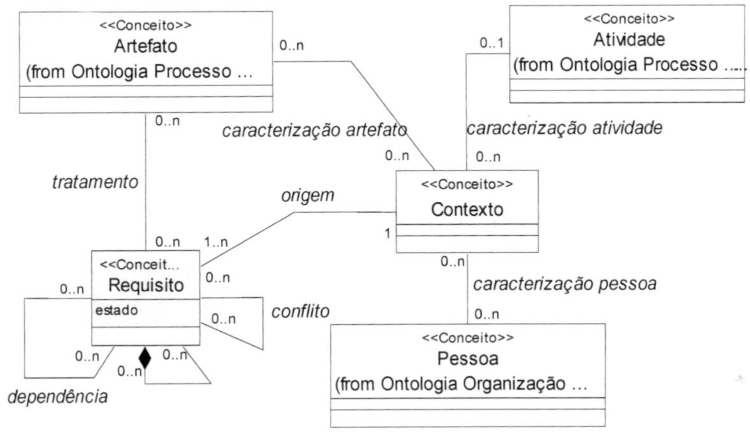

Fig. 6. Relações Importantes para a Rastreabilidade.

A relação de dependência permite estabelecer ligações de dependência entre requisitos (*QC10*), indicando que, se um requisito do qual outros requisitos dependem for alterado, é provável que os requisitos dependentes necessitem ser alterados.

No caso da composição, a situação é análoga. Por meio dessa relação, é possível tratar a decomposição de um requisito em outros (*QC9*). Se um requisito composto for alterado é provável que suas partes tenham de ser revisadas e vice-versa.

Finalmente, podem-se estabelecer relações de conflito entre requisitos (*QC11*), permitindo controlar esses conflitos, mantendo-os aceitáveis ou detectando que um conflito definitivamente não pode existir, levando à revisão dos requisitos envolvidos.

Para se ter um controle de mudanças mais efetivo, é interessante que se possa avaliar o impacto das mudanças de um requisito nos demais artefatos do processo de software. Assim, é importante saber quais artefatos (por exemplo, documento de especificação de requisitos, modelos e diagramas de análise e projeto, ou mesmo código-fonte) tratam de um requisito, para poder trilhar mudanças em um requisito para esses artefatos e vice-versa (*QC13*).

Para manter a rastreabilidade de um requisito desde a sua concepção, se faz necessário ligar o requisito à sua origem, ou seja, ligá-lo ao contexto no qual ele se originou (*QC7*). Esse contexto pode se caracterizar pela análise de artefatos, interação entre pessoas, consulta a *sites* na Internet etc. e pode, ainda, se dar no âmbito de uma atividade do processo de software.

O estado de um requisito é útil para se ter o controle, em um determinado momento, de como anda seu desenvolvimento (*QC8*). Os possíveis estados de um requisito são definidos organização a organização, e podem ser, por exemplo: *Proposto, Em Alteração, Sob Verificação, Rejeitado* etc.

Por fim, vale destacar que a questão de competência *QC14* é respondida pelo conjunto da conceituação acima discutida.

Qualidade de Requisito e de ERS

A qualidade do Documento de Especificação de Requisitos de Software (DERS) é crucial para o sucesso do projeto. De acordo com a Ontologia de Qualidade de Software [12], a qualidade de um artefato de software pode ser avaliada por meio da definição de características de qualidade e da utilização de métricas para medi-las. Assim, adotando a conceituação dessa ontologia, a questão de competência *QC15* pode ser respondida, como mostra a figura 7. Nessa ontologia, cada artefato pode ter um conjunto de Características de Qualidade de Produto relevantes para a avaliação de sua qualidade. Essas características de qualidade podem ser direta ou indiretamente mensuráveis, sendo que as diretamente mensuráveis têm correlação com métricas, enquanto as indiretamente mensuráveis podem ser medidas por meio da combinação de valores de suas sub-características.

4 Trabalhos Correlatos

Poucos trabalhos têm tratado de ontologias para requisitos. Em [13] é apresentada uma ontologia de requisitos desenvolvida para apoiar um processo genérico de gerência de requisitos no domínio de projetos de engenharia. Essa ontologia é parte de outra ontologia mais geral para capturar conhecimento de projetos de engenharia. Suas questões de competência são agrupadas nas seguintes categorias: refinamento de requisitos, rastreabilidade de requisitos, satisfação de requisito, versão e alteração, relacionamentos de requisitos com partes e estrutura de produto. Embora as categorias mencionadas e as questões de competências abordadas estejam muito próximas às deste trabalho, nossa Ontologia de Requisitos foca no domínio de requisitos de software, fazendo, portando, interação com outras ontologias do domínio de engenharia de software, enquanto a ontologia proposta em [13] reutiliza conceitos de uma ontologia de produtos.

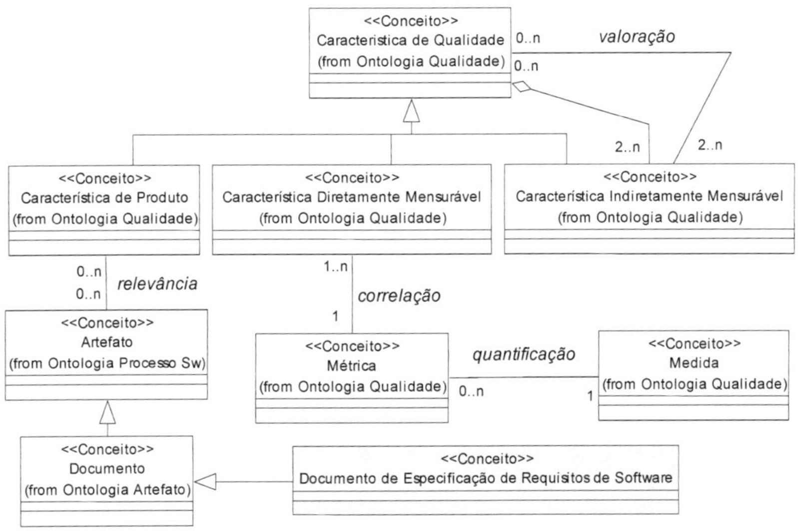

Fig. 7. Qualidade em Requisitos

No contexto de requisitos de software, Ramesh e Jarke [14] apresentam um meta-modelo que provê primitivas para categorização e descrição de modelos de rastreabilidade, permitindo tratar as seguintes questões: Que informação é representada? Quem são os interessados em desempenhar diferentes papéis no controle de objetos? Onde os objetos estão representados? Como a informação é representada? Por que um certo objeto foi criado ou modificado? Quando uma informação foi criada, capturada etc? A partir desse meta-modelo, são instanciados outros modelos de rastreabilidade que contemplam aspectos mais específicos, tais como a derivação de requisitos, a alocação de requisitos a subsistemas e a componentes, necessidades organizacionais, etc.

Ainda que o trabalho de Ramesh e Jarke não se trate de uma ontologia, claramente é correlato à Ontologia de Requisitos apresentada neste trabalho. Algumas das questões levantadas por eles foram listadas também como questões de competência neste trabalho. Contudo, aqui, procurou-se tratar o domínio de requisitos de maneira mais ampla, indo além da rastreabilidade de requisitos.

5 Considerações Finais

Neste trabalho foi apresentada uma Ontologia de Requisitos de Software objetivando definir conceitos e relações sobre o domínio de requisitos de forma facilitar a comunicação entre pessoas, entre agentes de software, construir ferramentas de apoio à Engenharia de Requisitos (ER) mais amplamente utilizáveis e auxiliar no estudo acerca de requisitos de software no contexto do Projeto ODE. Durante a construção dessa ontologia, várias outras ontologias acerca do domínio de engenharia de software foram analisadas e reutilizadas. Dessa forma buscou-se reutilizar conceituações já estabelecidas.

Como continuação deste trabalho, está-se construindo uma ferramenta de apoio à ER baseada na ontologia proposta e integrada ao ambiente ODE.

Agradecimentos

Este trabalho foi realizado com o apoio do CNPq e da CAPES, entidades do Governo Brasileiro dedicadas ao desenvolvimento científico e tecnológico, da FAPES, Fundação de Apoio à Ciência e Tecnologia do Espírito Santo, e da VixTeam Consultoria e Sistemas, empresa parceira que têm financiado o projeto e dado feedback de sua aplicação a casos reais.

Referências

1. H.F.Hofmann,F. Lehner. "Requirements Engineering as a Success Factor in Software Projects, IEEE Software, July/August 2001.
2. G. Kotonya, I. Sommerville. "Requirements Engineering: Process and Techniques". 1° Edição. Editora Wiley. 1998.
3. R.A. Falbo, et al., "Ontologias e Ambientes de Desenvolvimento de Software Semânticos", JIISIC'2004.
4. N. Guarino. "Formal Ontology in Information System". In: Proceedings of the First Int. Conference on Formal Ontology in Information Systems, Trento, Italy, June 1998. p.3-15.
5. J. C. S. P. Leite. "Gerenciando a Qualidade de Software com Base em Requisitos". In: Qualidade de Software: Teoria e Prática. 1ª. Edição. Prentice Hall. 2001. pp 238-246.
6. S. Robertson; J. Robertson. Mastering the Requirements Process. 1° Edição. Editora ACM Press, Addison Wesley. 1999.
7. R. A. Falbo. "Integração de Conhecimento em um Ambiente de Desenvolvimento de Software". Tese de Doutorado, COPPE/UFRJ, RJ, Dezembro, 1998.
8. R. A. Falbo. "Experiences in Using a Method for Building Domain Ontologies". Proc. of International Workshop on Ontology In Action, Banff, Alberta, Canada, June 2004.
9. P.G. Mian, R.A. Falbo, "Supporting Ontology Development with ODEd", Journal of the Brazilian Computer Science, vol. 9, no. 2, pp 57-76, November 2003.
10. R.A. Falbo, G. Bertollo, "Establishing a Common Vocabulary for Software Organizations Understand Software Processes", International Workshop on Vocabularies, Ontologies and Rules for the Enterprise, VORTE'2005, Enschede, The Netherlands, September 2005.
11. B. V. Nunes. "Integrando Gerência de Configuração de Software, Documentação e Gerência de Conhecimento em um Ambiente de Desenvolvimento de Software". 2005. Dissertação (Mestrado em Informática) –Universidade Federal do Espírito Santo.
12. K. C. Duarte. "Um *Framework* de Reuso no Domínio de Qualidade de Software". Dissertação de Mestrado. Departamento de Informática (DI) da Universidade Federal do Espírito Santo (UFES). Vitória-ES. Junho de 2001.
13. J. Lin, M.S. Fox, T. Bilgic. "A requirement ontology for engineering design", in: M. Sobolewski, M. Fox (Eds.), Proceedings of Advances in Concurrent Engineering (CE'96), Toronto, 1996, pp. 343-351.
14. B. Ramesh and M. Jarke, "Towards Reference Models for Requirements Traceability", IEEE Transactions on Software Engineering, Vol. 27, No. 1, 2000.

XGOOD: A Tool to Automatize the Mapping Rules between I* Framework and UML

Fernanda Alencar[1*], Flavio Pedroza[1], Jaelson Castro[2†], Carla Silva[2], Ricardo Ramos[2]

[1] Department of Eletronics and Systems, Federal University of Pernambuco
R. Acadêmico Hélio Ramos s/n, Recife/PE, Brazil, 50740-530, +1 55812126-8995
fmra@ufpe.br, flavio.pedroza@caeser.org.br
[2] Department of Computer Science, Federal University of Pernambuco
Av. Prof. Luiz Freire, s/n, Recife/PE, Brazil, 50732-970, +1 55812126-8430
{jbc, ctlls, rar2}@cin.ufpe.br

Abstract. With the popularization of the object oriented paradigm, the modeling language UML (Unified Modeling Language) has became standard for software development. However, the UML still is not enough equipped to support the modeling of the organizational requirements. The use of other modeling technique becomes necessary. The modeling technique i* covers this deficiency, being one technique used for business-oriented modeling very well spread out and accepted. The mapping between the two models is made possible through a set of guidelines that determines how the elements are mapped. In this work, we discuss a tool to support these mapping rules between the techniques i* and UML: eXtended GOOD (Goals into Object Oriented Development).

1 Introduction

Requirements capture has been acknowledged as a critical phase of software development. In fact deals not only with technical knowledge but also with organizational, managerial, economic and social issues. A requirement specification should include not only software specification but also business models and other kinds of information describing the context in which the intended system will function. However, the production of high quality specifications is not an easy task. Usually the customers do not exactly know what they want and sometimes the requirements may not reflect the real needs of the customers. It is common for requirements to be incomplete and/or inconsistent.

The model technique used depends on the type of the requirements and the phase of development. Typically, the initial phase needs a more abstract model, which supplies a general vision and an agreement of the system to be developed. The final phases of development need a more concrete model that makes possible the generation of source code. In [3, 1] was introduced the problem of using two distinct model-

* Currently on leave of absence at Universidade Nova de Lisboa, Portugal
† Currently on leave of absence at ITC-IRST, University of Trento, Italy

ing techniques for different types of requirements and phases of the development. We also proposed mapping rules that makes possible the transformation of one model into another. These rules use as base two techniques: the i-star (i *) [5, 23] and the Unified Modeling [4] (UML). Others researchers have done something similar in this same area [18, 12, 8].

The Unified Modeling Language is well suited for late-phase requirements capture. However, UML is ill equipped for early requirements capture because it can not represent how the intended system meets organizational goals, why the system is needed, what alternatives were considered, what the implication of the alternatives are for the various stakeholders, and how the stakeholders' interests and concerns might be addressed. What is required to capture such concerns is a framework that focuses on the description and evaluation of alternatives and their relationship to the organizational objectives behind the software development project. The *i** framework, is well suited for early-phase and late-phase requirements capture, since it provides for the representation of alternatives, and offers primitive modeling concepts such as those of softgoal and goal.

The purpose of this paper is to present the tool that carry through the mapping between models i * and UML automatically. We describe the mapping guidelines [2, 7] just in order to facilitate the understanding of the XGOOD [16] (eXtended Goals into Object Oriented Development) tool. The XGOOD uses the XMI [6] standard to make the persistence of the generated models. The XMI is a standard accept and approved by Object Management Group (OMG). Therefore, the XGOOD tool is compatible with various modeling CASE tools that support this standard, for example: Rational Rose [17], MagicDraw [11], Telelogic Tau [19].

The paper is divided in the following form: In section 2 we present the i* technique. In section 3 we present the rule mapping to transform early requirements into late requirements. In section 4 the XGOOD tool is presented. Finally, in section 5 we have final considerations and future works.

2 Early Requirements Capture

When developing systems, we usually need to have a broad understanding of the organizational environment and goals. The i* technique [21] provides understanding of the "why" by modeling organizational relationships that underlie systems requirements. i* offers a modeling framework that focuses on strategic actor relationships. It can be used for: (i) obtaining a better understanding of the organizational relationships among the various organizational agents; (ii) understanding the rationale of the decisions taken; and (iii) illustrating the various characteristics found in the early phases of requirements specification. The participants of the organizational setting are actors with intentional properties, such as, goals, beliefs, abilities and compromises. These actors depend upon each other in order to fulfil their objectives and have their tasks performed. The i* technique offers two models: The Strategic Dependency (SD) model, and the Strategic Rationale (SR) model. Before we describe these models, first we present our case study based on a Electronic Newspaper Domain.

When an user wishes to read news, he accesses the newspaper website maintained by a Webmaster which is responsible for updating the published information. The newspaper to be published is edited and provided to the webmaster by the Chief Editor. The Chief Editor shares the newspaper guideline among the specialized Editor agents, which are responsible for Editing news of a specific category. Each Editor contacts one or many reporters which are in charge of news of some specific subjects to fulfil its important match to be covered. From the analysis of the organizational environment of the newspaper's office we have identified the need for and automated software system in order to support the process of edition and publication of the news on the website. Thus, the E-news system comes into the picture as one actor which contributes to the fulfillment of stakeholder goals (Fig. 1).

2.1 The Strategic Dependency Model

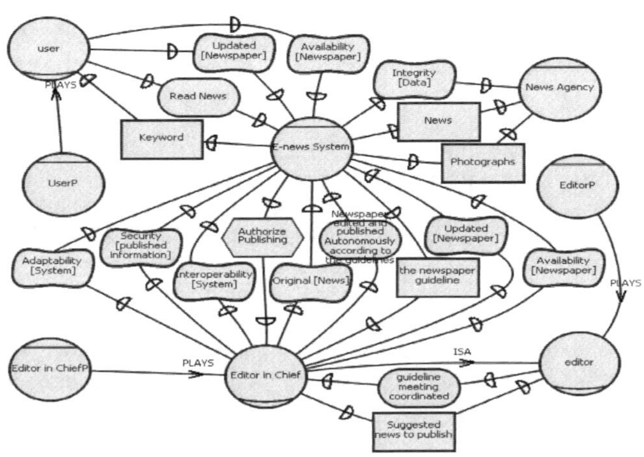

Fig. 1. E-news system SD model

The Strategic Dependency Model - SD (Fig. 1) consists of a set of nodes and links connecting them, where nodes represent actors and each link indicates a dependency between two actors. The depending actor is called depender, and the actor who is depended upon is called the dependee. Hence, an SD model consists of a network of actors, capturing the motivation and the rationale of activities. i* distinguishes four types of dependencies. Three of these are related to existing intentions – goal dependency, resource dependency and task dependency, while the fourth is associated with the notion of non-functional requirements, the so called softgoal dependency. In a goal dependency (*Read news, Newspaper edited and published autonomously according to the guidelines, Guideline meeting coordinated*), an actor depends on another to fulfil a goal, without worrying how this goal will be achieved. In a resource dependency (*News, Photography, Keyword, Newspaper Guideline, Suggested news to publish*), an actor depends on another actor to provide a physical resource or information. In a task dependency (*Authorize Publishing*), an actor depends on another to carry out a task. A softgoal dependency (*Availability[Newspaper], Updated[Newspaper], Integrity [Data], Original [News], Interoperability [System], Security [Published Information], Adaptability [System])* is similar to a goal dependency, except that a softgoal is not precisely defined. In i* we can also model different degrees of dependency commitment on the part of the relevant actors (eg. open, committed, or critical). We can also classify actors into agents, roles and positions. An agent (E-news System, UserP, News Agency, EditorP, Editor in ChiefP) is an actor with concrete physical manifestations (a person or a system). A role (user, editor, Editor in Chief) is an abstract characterization of the behaviour of a social actor within some specialized context, domain or endeavor. A position (not identified in the case study) is a set of roles typically played by one agent. Finally, i* supports the analysis of opportunities and vulnerabilities for different actors [24].

The *E-news* system allows the *user* to read specific news which is searched by providing a keyword as well as to examine news provided by the *E-news System*. Thus, an *user* depends on *E-news System* to *Read News* while the *E-news System* depends on the *user* to get a *Keyword* in order to search specific requested news. Both the user and Editor in Chief expects that E-news system to maintain the newspaper updated and available on the website. The *Editor in Chief* depends on the *E-news System* for editing and publishing newspaper according to the *newspaper guideline*. It also expects that *E-news system* to be adaptable, interoperable as well as to maintain published information secure and publish original news. The newspaper editing and publishing must be according to a guideline, which is produced by a meetting among the *Editors* and the *Editor in Chief.* Since *Editor in Chief* is a special kind of *Editor*, it can also suggest news to be included in the guideline. The *Editor in Chief* is the coordinator of the guideline meeting. Hence, the *E-news System* depends on it to get *the newspaper guideline*. To produce the newspaper it is necessary for the *E-news System* to interact with different and distributed *News Agency* on the Internet. Thus, the E-news System depends on a *News Agency* to receive *News* and *Photographs* with data integrity. When the newspaper edition is concluded, the *E-news* system depends on the Editor in Chief to have the newspaper publishing authorized.

If more details on a specific actor are required, then a detailed description or the Strategic Rationale Model can be produced.

2.2 The Strategic Rational Model

The Strategic Rationale Model (SR) (Fig. 2) provides a more detailed level of modeling by looking "inside" actors to model internal intentional relationships. It is used to: (i) describe the interests, concerns and motivations of participants process; (ii) enable the assessment of the possible alternatives in the definition of the process; and (iii) research in more detail the existing reasons behind the dependencies between the various actors. Nodes and links also compose this model. It includes the previous four types of nodes (present in the SD model, Fig. 1): goal, task, resource and soft-goal. However, three new types of relationship are incorporated: (i) means-end that suggests that there could be other means of achieving the objective (alternatives), (ii) task-decomposition that describes what should be done in order to perform a certain task and (iii) the means-end contributing for softgoals links (not identified on the Fig. 2) that will represent a partial contributions of meas (task ou softgoal) to end (softgoal).

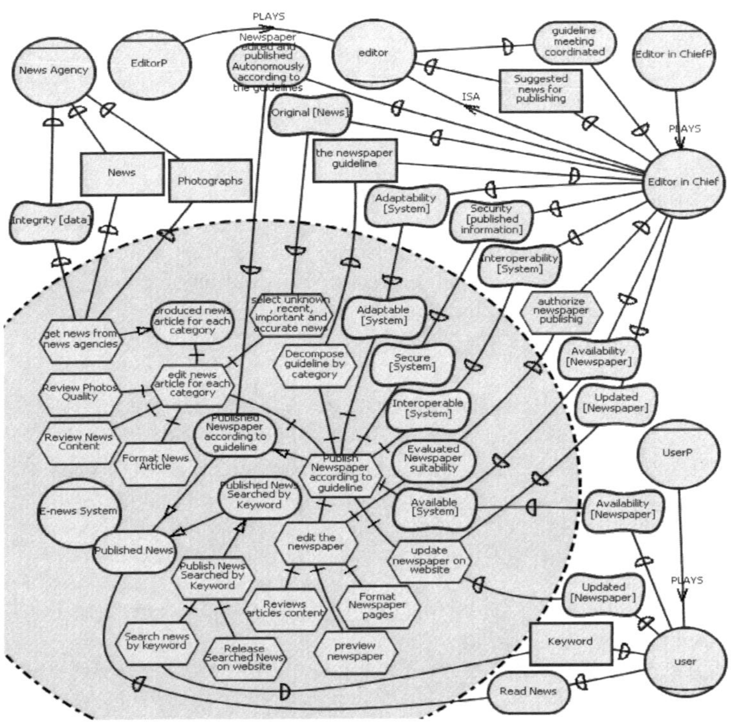

Fig. 2. E-news system SR model

The SR model (Fig. 2) focuses on one of the goal dependency identified for the *user,* namely *Read News*. To achieve that goal, the analysis postulates a goal *Published News* that can be fulfilled by means of two alternative goals: *Published News Searched by Keyword* or *Published Newspaper According to Guideline.* The former goal is fulfilledf by means of a task *Publish News Searched by Keyword*, while the latter goal is fulfilled by means of a task *Publish Newspaper According to Guideline*. Tasks are partially ordered sequences of steps intended to accomplish some (soft)goal. Tasks can be decomposed into goals and/or subtasks, whose collective fulfillment completes the task. In the (Fig. 2), *Publish News Searched by Keyword* is decomposed into tasks *Search News by Keyword* and *Release Searched News on Website* which together accomplish the top-level task. The task task *Publish Newspaper According to Guideline* is decomposed into softgoals *Available [System]*, *Interoperable [System]*, *Adaptable [System]* and *Secure [System]*, tasks *Decompose the Guideline*, *Edit News Article for each Category*, *Edit the Newspaper* and *Update Newspaper on Website*, and goal *Evaluated Newspaper Suitability* which together accomplish the top-level task. Sub-goals and subtasks can be specified more precisely through refinement. For instance, the task Edit the Newspaper is fulfilled through tasks *Review Articles Content*, *Format Newspaper Pages* and *Preview Newspaper* while the task *Edit News Article for each Category* would be collectively accomplished by goal *Produced News Article for each Category* and tasks *Select Unknown, Recent, Important and Accurate News, Review Photo Quality, Review News Content* and *Format News Article*. The goal *Produced News Article for each Category* is fulfilled by means of a task *Get News from News Agencies*.

These decompositions eventually allow us to identify actors who can accomplish a goal, carry out a task, or deliver on some needed resource for *E-news System*. Such dependencies in Fig. 1 are the resource and softgoal dependencies on *News Agency* for providing news and photos with data integrity, the resource and task dependencies on *Editor in Chief* for providing the newspaper guideline and performing authorization of newspaper publishing, and the resource dependency Keyword on *User* to perform the searching of a specific news.

3 Mapping Early Requirements into Late Requirements

The guidelines for the generation of Class Diagrams were originally proposed in [3]. Later they were extended to support the structuring elements of i* [7]. In the total there are six guidelines to generate UML class diagram (C1 to C6). Next, to facilitate the understanding of the tool we transcribe these guidelines and provide a simple example.

Guideline C1: related with the mapping of i* actors. Actors in the i* framework, can be mapped to classes in UML.

Sub-guidelines (C1.1 to C1.6) are required in order to take in account the current i* structuring mechanism which include the classification of actors into agents, roles and position.

Sub-guideline C1.1: i* agents, roles or positions can be mapped to UML classes;

Thus all agents and roles (*UserP*, *News Agency*, *EditorP*, *Editor in ChiefP ,editor*, *Editor in Chief* and *user)* will be mapped into classes with the same name (see Fig. 3).

Sub-guideline C1.2: the i* IS-PART-OF relationship between actors can be mapped as a class aggregation in UML;

In the Fig. 2 we do not have this relationship but as the system evolves it will be necessary to structure the *E-news System* actor into sub-systems.

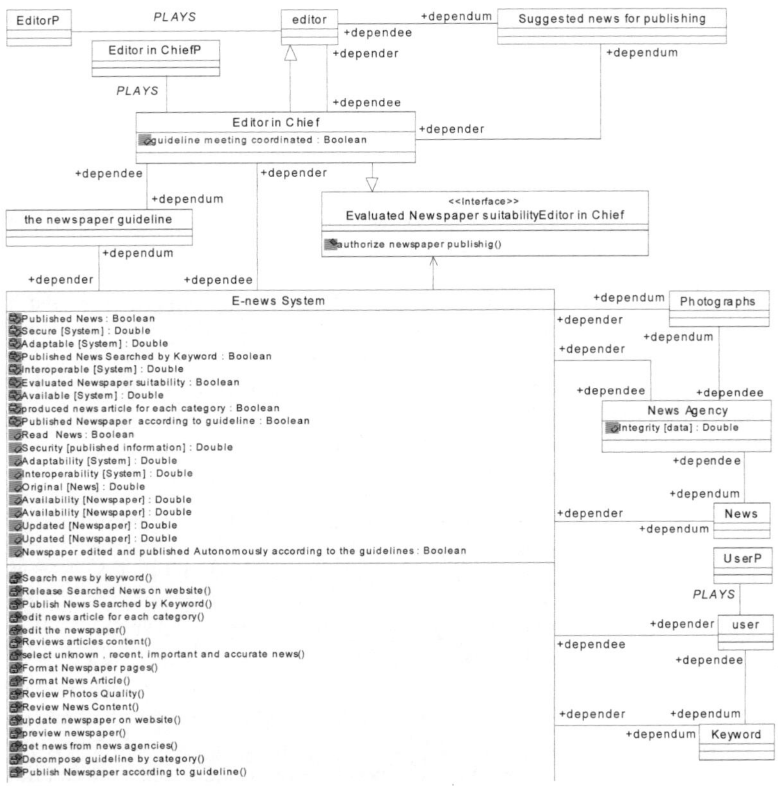

Fig. 3. Resulting E-News System Class Diagram

Sub-guideline C1.3: the i* IS-A relationship between actors can be mapped to class generalization/specialization in UML;

In the Fig. 2 we can see that *Editor in Chief* role is related *editor* role by means of a IS-A. relationship Thus, the *Editor in Chief* class is a specialization of the *editor* class.

Sub-guideline C(1.4-1.6): the i* OCCUPIES, COVERS and PLAYS relationship between can be mapped to an UML class association, labeled as OCCUPIES; COVERS and PLAY, respectivelly.

According to Fig. 2 the agent *EditorP* plays the role of an *editor.* This relationship will be mapped as a class association between the class *EditorP* and the class *editor* labeled as PLAYS (See Fig. 3).

Guideline C2: related with the mapping of i* tasks. Tasks in i*, are mapped to class operations in UML. Sub-guidelines (C2.1 and C2.2) are required.

Sub-guideline C2.1: a task defined in a SD (Strategic Dependency) model can be mapped into an operation in the interface that is realized by the class that represents the dependee.

Consider the *authorize newspaper publishing* task dependency (Fig. 1). The agent *E-news System* (depender) depends on the *Editor in Chief* position (dependee) to have the task executed. Thus, this task will appear as an operation in the *Evaluated Newspaper suitability Editor in Chief* interface.

Sub-guideline C2.2: a task defined in the SR (Strategic Rationale) model can be mapped as an operation with private visibility in the class.

In Fig. 2 we depict the internal behavior of the *E-news System* agent. Thus we can observe various tasks mapped which can be mapped as operations with private visibility in the class *E-news System*: *Seach news by keyword; Release Searched News on website; Publish News Searched by Keyword; edit news article for each category; edit the newspaper; Reviews articles content; select unknown, recent, important and accurate news; Format Newspaper pages; Format News Article; Review Photos Quality; Reviews News Content; update newspaper on website; preview newspaper; get news from news agencies; Decompose guieline by category; Publish Newspaper according to guideline.*

Guideline C3: the i* resources can be mapped to UML classes.

A resource can be mapped to a class in UML if this dependence has the characteristics of an object. It can also be transformed to an attribute. Its visibility depends on its source. It becomes a private attribute if it originated from an SR model. Otherwise, it is originated from a SD model; it is transformed into a public attribute.

All the resources present in the Fig. 2 are entities of the real world and therefore they will be mapped to UML classes.

Guideline C4: related with the mapping of i* goals/softgoals.

Goals can be mapped as boolean (goals) or numeric (softgoals) attributes with private (SR model) or public (SD model) visibility. An association is created between the depender class and the dependee class. Sub-guidelines (C4.1 and C4.2) are required.

Sub-guideline C4.1: Goals and soft goals dependencies in Strategic Dependency Models (SD) models are mapped to Boolean and enumerated public attributes, respectively, of the dependee UML class.

If we are only concerned with goals and softgoal dependences that will have to be satisfied for agent E-News System then the goals (*Newspaper edited* and *published Autonomously according to the guidelines* and *Read News)* are mapped as Boolean public attributes in the *E-news System* class. While the softgoals *(Original[News], Security[publihed information], Adaptability[System], Interoperability[System], Availability[Newspaper], Updated[Newspaper])* are mapped as enumerated public attributes in the *E-news System class* (Fig. 3).

Sub-guideline C4.2: Goals and soft goals dependencies in Strategic Rationale Models (SR), are mapped to Boolean and Enumerated local UML class attributes, respectively.

In Fig. 2, we can identify some *goals* dependencies (Published News, Published News Searched by Keyword, Evaluated Newspaper suitability, produced news article for each category and Published Newspaper according to guidelines) that can be mapped to Boolean local attribute in the E-news System class (Fig. 3). Whereas the *softgoals* (Secure[System], Adaptable[System], Interoperable[System] and Available[System]) can be mapped to enumerate local attributes in the E-news System class.

The next two guidelines are not implemented in the proposed tool because with the used versions of XML it was not possible to represent OCL. Like this, we will just be enunciating those guidelines (see [7]).

Guideline C5: related with the mapping of i* task decomposition relationship.

A task decomposition link is represented through pre and post-condition in the corresponding operation of the task that is being decomposed in OCL.

Guideline C6: related with the mapping of i* means-end relationship.

A means-end link will be represented in OCL as pre and post-conditions in the corresponding operations or as invariants of the class that will correspond to the actor in study in the SR model (Fig. 2), i..e., disjunctions (expressed in OCL) of all possible means achieving the end. Sub-guidelines (C6.1 to C6.3) are required.

Applying the above mentioned guidelines we end up with an initial organizational Class Diagram (see Fig. 3). Of course not all concepts captured in the early requirements phase will correspond to software system models. The models do not have a one-one relationship; many elements of the organisational model are not part of the software model, since not all of the organisational tasks require a software system. Likewise, many elements in the software model comprise detailed technical software solutions and constructs that are not part of the organisational model. Of course some tool support would be welcomed in order to automate the mapping process from i* descriptions into UML diagrams. Then we proposed XGOOD.

4 The XGOOD Tool

XGOOD is a tool to assist in the mapping of i* models into UML Class Diagrams. The tool was developed using the C++ language and integrated into the OME (tool used to create i* models). Through the use of the XGOOD, the user is capable to open and to visualize i* models generated by the OME tool. The user also can select how each element will be mapped. The generated class diagram is saved in XMI format [20], a standard that can be imported by various available CASE tools. The tool was tested with the MagicDraw, Rational Rose, Telelogic Tau CASE tools.

The new XGOOD provides several interesting features:

i. Option to select the mapping guidelines for each i* element. Hence, it is possible to indicate if an i* elements will be mapped or not. The XGOOD allows the user to exclude certain elements captured according to the i* technique, but that are not computational in the UML model;
ii. Inclusion of new mapping guidelines. – the XGOOD supports many guidelines and structuring elements from the i* model (role, position and agent);
iii. Adoption of an open standard to represent the generated models (such as - XML Metadata Interchange [20]) for the persistence of the generated class diagram. This facilitates the sharing of the models between various commercial tools;
iv. Integration with the OME ((Organization Modeling Environment) [15] tool.

In [2] we have just a first version of this tool. Until that moment none of those steps pointed out above was represented. The XGOOD only had been used with Rational Rose [17]. Now, Fig. 4 depicts how the XGOOD was designed in order to be used. The "*.tel" file generated by the OME containing the i* model description in the Telos syntax [13], is read by the XGOOD tool. Then, a XMI file containing the class diagram is created, allowing it to be that can be read by various UML CASE tools (for example MagicDraw [11], Rational Rose [17], Telelogic Tau [19], etc).

The tool works in the Windows operational system]. Unfortunately, the XMI standard still does not possess mechanisms to represent the restrictions in OCL (Object Constraint Language) [14], as well not all the tools of the market supports the inclusion of OCL restrictions. Hence, for the time being guidelines C5 and C6 are not supported by the XGOOD tool.

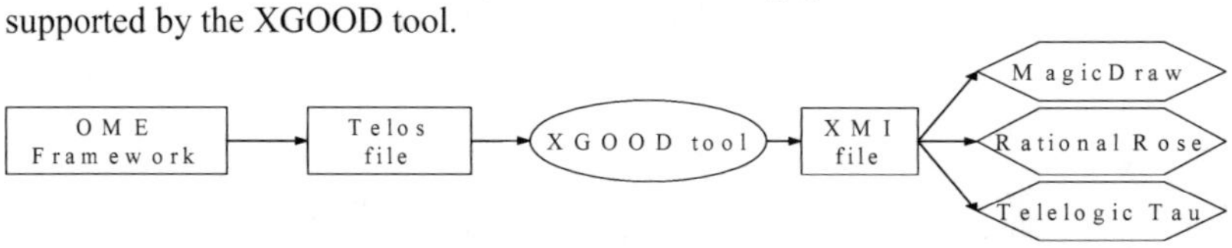

Fig. 4. XGOOD Tool.

The user interaction is made through menus and buttons, located in the toolbar. In Fig. 5 we show how the i* file (imported from the OME tool) will be depicted.

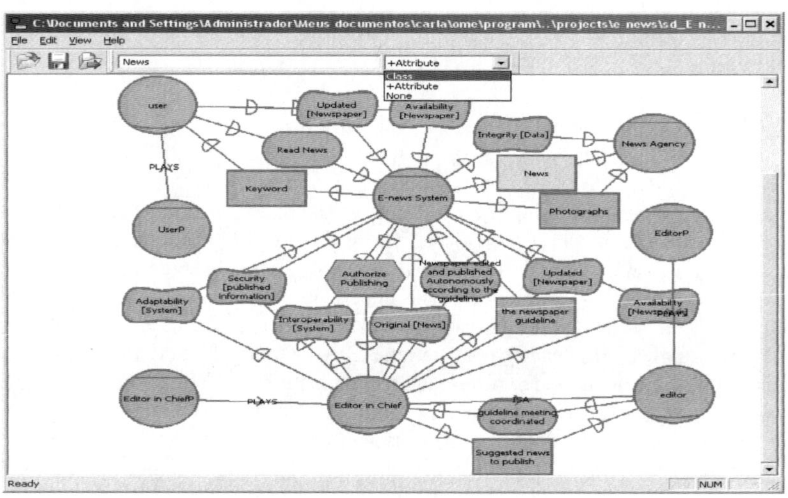

Fig. 5. XGOOD tool, latest version.

In Fig. 5 we can see the XGOOD's screen showing how the selection of the guideline is made. For example, for the *News resource* there are three available options: i) map as a public attribute; ii) map it as a class; or iii) do not map it.

At first the user must access the menu File >>Open... to select a ".tel" file. After import a ".tel" file, the i* model is shown in the main window of the tool. The user can use the mouse to interact with the model, moving and renaming the elements.

With the right mouse button, the user can access a popup menu with the mapping options of each element. He can choose if (and how) the element will be mapped. When the selection of the guidelines is concluded, the user can save the mapping options. This is possible accessing the menu File >> Save... The mapping guidelines of each element are saved in the ".tel" file itself. To generate the UML class diagram, the user access the menu File >> Export…, and a ".xml" file containing the UML class diagram, in the XMI format, is created. It is given the option to choose two different versions of XMI: version 1.0 and version 1.1.

The ".xml" file can be imported by several CASE tools [10], so the user can work and refine them. We have tested three different tools: Rational Rose [17], MagicDraw [11] e TelelogicTau [19]. In Fig. 3 we can see how the model of Fig. 5 is transformed in a class diagram and imported in the Rational Rose

It is worth noting that the OME (Organization Modeling Environment) is required for the development of i* models [15]. Hence, it would be interesting if the XGOOD tool could be integrated with the OME environment.

4.1 XGOOD integration

The OME was designed in such a way that it is possible to extend it. In fact it comes with a Java API that allows the creation of plugins to add new functionalities to the tool.

In order to integrate the XGOOD tool into the OME [15] we created a new Java class named XGOODPlugin. This class implements the OMEPlugin interface (OME interface for create plugins):

```
public class XGOODPlugin implements OMEPlugin {  ...}
```

In this XGOODPlugin class we can emphasize the method getToolbarMethods. This method is responsible for adding new buttons to the OME's toolbar. In the implementation of this method, we added a new XGOODMethod object to the OME's toolbar (see Fig. 6).

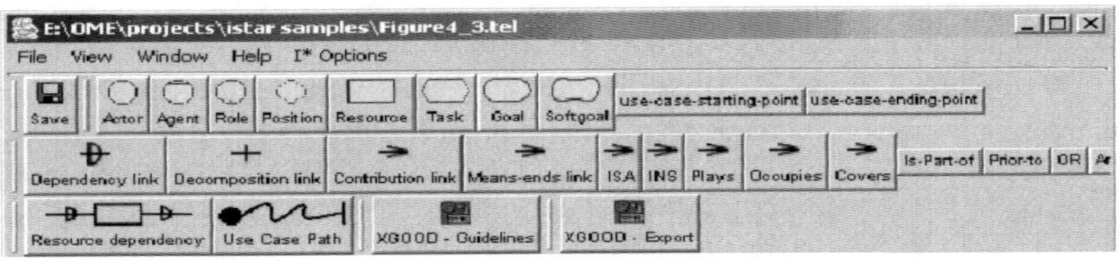

Fig. 6. XGOOD integrated into OME.

The XGOODMethod class implements a PluginMethod The main method of the XGOODMethod class is the invoke() method. This method is called every time that the button is accessed in the OME's toolbar. interface (OME interface to implement the plugins's operations).

The invoke() method opens the currently i* model that is being edited in the XGOOD tool:

```
public void invoke() {
          try { // Executes the tool
          Process p = Run-
time.getRuntime().exec(".\\XGOOD.exe \"" +
v.getSavePathname() + "\"");
          // Wait for the user to close the tool
          p.waitFor();
          }catch (Exception ex) {
                System.out.println(ex);              }
          }
```

In Fig. 6 we can see how the XGOOD was integrated into the OME. Two new buttons were added in the OME's toolbar: XGOOD - Guidelines and XGOOD – Export. We only added to the directory OME/program, two subdirectories (XM1.1 and XM1.0) and five file (XGOOD.EXE,PLUGINS\XGOODMethod.class, PLUGINS\XGOODMethod1.class, PLUGINS\XGOODPlugin.class, PLUGINS\OME\SavePlugin.class).

5 Conclusion and Future Work

For the capture of the initial requirements we have the i* modeling technique, that focus in the relationship between the actors and its intentions. With it is possible to carry through the capture of the organizational requirements that will influence in the determination of the functional requirements of the system. After the initial capture, we must refine the requirements so that they translate the functionalities of the system that will be implemented. For this we have the UML modeling technique.

We argue that the UML alone is not adjusted to deal with the different types of analyses and reasons that are necessary during the phase of requirements capture. So, the use of complementary techniques becomes necessary: i* technique, for the capture of the initial requirements and the organizational modeling; and the UML, for the capture of the late requirements, with the aid of the OCL for modeling the constraints. However, the use of two different techniques suggests the need of a tool to promote the integration of these techniques (through the proposed guidelines).

The XGOOD (eXtended Goal into Object Oriented Development) is a tool to assist in the mapping of i* models into UML class diagrams. The tool was developed using the C++ language and integrated into the OME (tool used to create i* models). Through the use of the XGOOD, the user is capable to open and to visualize i* models generated by the OME tool. The user also can select how each element will be mapped. The generated class diagram is saved in XMI format, a standard that can be imported by various available CASE tools. The tool was tested with the MagicDraw, Rational Rose, Telelogic Tau CASE tools. Also, as a case study, the tool was used to develop an optical network simulator [16].

This tool is been used in others experiments to know their effectiveness, including the development of a optical network simulator as a case study which is in use at

Fotonica's research laboratory. We motivate its usage in our research group.As we can see in Fig. 3, some attributes and class methods are duplicated since the tools do not analyze the links repetitions in the i* models. This tool helps to automate the mapping rules and this case must be revaluated.

The XGOOD tool presents some limitations which it will be better considered in the future. For example, it supports only the class diagram, does not support the OCL expressions and only works in the Microsoft Windows operational system. However, when the new version of language OCL has been approved, mechanisms will become available for the representation of its metamodel through XMI standard. Then, the mapping guidelines G6 and G7 could be incorporated into the XGOOD tool. As natural evolution of the tool, we consider a multi platform version, independent of the operational system. This version will be developed in Java [9], which will be capable to work in any operational system. Another advantage of the use of the Java language [9] is that the integration with the OME tool will be more natural and friendly, as the OME and its plugins are developed in this language.

Acknowledgments

This work was supported by several research grants (CNPq Proc. 304982/2002-4, CAPES Proc. BEX 1775/2005-7, Proc. BEX 3003/05-1, Proc. BEX 3014/05-3 & CAPES/ GRICES Proc. 129/05).

References

1. Alencar Fernanda, Castro Jaelson, Cysneiros Gilberto. Closing the Gap between Organizational Requirements and Object Oriented Modeling. Journal of the Brazilian Computer Society, v.7, n.1, (2000).
2. Alencar, F. M. R., Pedroza, F., Castro, Jaelson, Amorim, R. C. O. : New Mechanism for the Integration of Organizational Requirements and Object Oriented Modeling. In Proceedings of the VI International Workshop on Requirements Engineering - WER´03: Vol. 1, Piracicaba, Brazil, (2003) 109-123.
3. Alencar, F. M.R. de : Mapping Organizational Modeling to Precise Specification (in portuguese: Mapeando a Modelagem Organizacional em Especificação Precisa). Doctoral Thesis,. Universidade Federal de Pernambuco, Recife, Brazil. (1999).
4. Booch, G., Jacobson, I., Rumbaugh, J. : The Unified Modeling Language Reference Manual. Reading, MA: Addison-Wesley. (1999).
5. Brescian, P.; Perini, A.; Giorgini, P.; Giunchiglia, F.; Mylopoulos,J.: Tropos: An Agent-Oriented Software Development Methodology. In: Autonomous Agents and Multi-Agent System, (2004) v. 8, n.3, 203-236.
6. Brodsky, S.: XMI Opens Application Interchange. Retrieved October, 18, (2004) from http://www4.ibm.com/software/ad/standards/xmiwhite0399.pdf.
7. Castro, J., Alencar, F. M. R., Cysneiros Filho, G. A. A., Mylopoulos, J.: Integrating Organizational Requirements and Object Oriented Modeling. In Proceeding of 5th IEEE International Symposium on Requirements Engineering – RE'01: Vol. 1, Toronto, Canada: IEEE. (2001) 146-153.

8. Estrada, H., Martinez, A., Pastor, O.: Goal-based business modeling oriented towards late requirements generation. Conference on Conceptual Modeling (ER), Is International, 22nd, 2003 - October, Chicago, Illinois (EE.UU.), Il-Yeol Song, Stephen W. Liddle, Tok Wan Ling, Peter Scheuermann, Springer-Verlag, Lecture Notes in Computer Science, 3-540-20299-4, 2813, (2003) 277 - 290.
9. Java Technology. From URL http://java.sun.com/. (2005).
10. Jiang, J., Systã, T.: UML model exchange using XMI. Retrieved December, (2003), from URL http://www.cs.tut.fi/~xmlohj/linkit/XMIReport.pdf.
11. MagicDraw UML. URL http://www.magicdraw.com/.(2005).
12 Martinez, A, Castro, J. F. B., Pastor, O., Estrada, H.: Closing the gap between Organizational Modeling and Information System Modeling WER03 - VI Workshop em Engenharia de Requisitos, Piracicaba, Brasil (2003).
13. Mylopoulos, J., Borgida, A., Jarke, M., Koubarakis, M.: Telos: Representing Knowledge About Information Systems. ACM Transactions on Information Systems Vol. 8, New York, USA: ACM Press (1990) 325-362.
14. Object Constraint Language Specification. In: OMG Unified Modeling Language Specification. version 1.5. Mar. (2003) 6-1 – 6-48.
15. Organization Modeling Environment - OME. From URL http://www.cs.toronto.edu/km/ome/. (2005).
16. Pedroza, F. : Using XMI to automatize mapping i* modeling to UML modeling for implementing Optical Nets Simulator (in portuguese: Automatizando as Regras de Mapeamento entre a Modelagem i* e a Modelagem UML usando XMI para Implementação de um Simulador de Rede Ópticas). MSc. Dissertation, Universidade Federal de Pernambuco, Recife, Brazil. (2005).
17. Rational Rose. URL: http://www.ibm.com/rational/. (2005).
18. Santander, V. F. A., Castro, J. F. B.: Deriving Use Cases from Organizational Modeling. RE02 - IEEE Joint Conference on Requirements Engineering, Essen, Germany (2002).
19. Telelogic Tau. URL http://www.telelogic.com/. (2005).
20. XML Metadata Interchange Specification version 1.2. Retrieved January, (2002) From URL http://www.omg.org/technology/xml/.
21. Yu, E.: Towards Modelling and Reasoning Support for Early-Phase Requirements Engineering. In Proceedings of the IEEE International Symposium on Requirements Engineering – RE'97): IEEE. (1997) 226-235.

Sesión 4:

Ingeniería de Requisitos 2

Relating i* with Problem Frames Approach

Maria Lencastre[1], Fernanda Alencar[2*], Jaelson Castro[3†]

[1] Departamento de Sistemas Computacionais, Escola Politécnica,
Universidade de Pernambuco
Rua Benfica, 455 Madalena, 50750-410, Recife - PE – Brasil
2Departamento de Eletrônica e de Sistemas, Universidade Federal de Pernambuco,
Rua Acadêmico Hélio Ramos s/n, 50740-530, Recife – PE - Brasil
3 Departamento de Ciência da Computação, Universidade Federal de Pernambuco,
Rua Prof. Luis Freire s/n, 50740-530, Recife – PE - Brasil
{maria@dsc.upe.br, fmra@ufpe.br, jbc@cin.ufpe.br}

Abstract. In the last years many works have explored and tried to improve i*, a requirement engineering technique which aim is to model relationships among intentional agents in organizational settings and also to provide features to assist in describing processes (modelling) and directing changes (reengineering). On the other hand, Problem Frames is another software engineering approach with great impact in the scientific community. Its purpose is problem domain specification, requirements analysis and problems decomposition into sub-problems, until a recognized problem class is identified. This paper makes a relationship between these approaches and uses a small example to illustrate it. The objective is to clarify the involved concepts, describe the existing relations, and emphasize the power of each approach. As a result, we expect to use the relationships inferred for improving them and give support for the development of a new hybrid approach, which gathers the best of both.

1 Introduction

The understanding and documentation of complex social structures in the application problem domain, and their translation to technological solutions it's still an up-to-date problem in Requirements Engineering. Many new development methodologies, such as TROPOS [1] and GAIA [18], and also the AUML notation [13], have been developed in order to help this. In this paper we will investigate the i-star technique (also called i*), a conceptual and methodological approach used on two main phases of TROPOS: the Early Requirements and Late Requirements analysis.

In spite of the several works which were developed based on the i* approach in the last years, this technique still presents several issues, such as: the size, complexity and unorganized nature of the generated diagrams. The i* models get harder to understand and use as they get more complex and larger [10]. This technique also suffers

* Currently on leave of absence at FCT/UNL, Lisbon, Portugal.

† Currently on leave of absence at ITC/IRST, Trento, Italy

from other pragmatic concerns, like the learning curve and availability of efficient tools [12]. In [11], it was observed that i* could be enhanced with a catalogue of patterns, that can be used and reused together with a suitable pattern language. In [17] there is an effort to analyze and improve i*, emphasizing the importance to define a "framework" for TROPOS, which explores the complete potential of the agent technology together with hybrid solutions, e.g. Problem Frames [3, 5] and Aspects [16]. We can say that there is a lack of integration and comparisons between the existing techniques, making difficult to explore the best of them.

Problem Frames is a respected software engineering approach for requirements analysis and problem domain specifications. It groups problems by type, and call them *problem frames*; they are similar to design patterns - elements of reusable object-oriented software [2], but they are problem oriented rather than solution oriented. *Problem frames* make it easier to solve a problem, once the type of a problem is classified. This approach describes the software development as the action of building a machine to solve a problem in a given domain – an identified part of the world – to meet a requirement. The machine is a general-purpose computer specialized by software [5]. Problem Frames approach represents the real problem through several descriptions about the application domain.

In this work we investigate and make a relationship between i* and Problem Frames approach, considering their potentiality to describe problem domains. We argue that it is important to make clear what concepts have correspondence between i* and Problem Frames approach. To illustrate this, we use an example.

This paper is organized in the following way. Section 2 describes the problem to be exemplified, the i* and the Problem Frames approaches. Section 3 makes the relation between both approaches, through the analysis of the example, applying at this time Problem Frames approach, and also discusses features which must be considered in a hybrid approach. Section 4, presents some related work. Finally, Section 5 draws some conclusion and points out directions for future work.

2 Approaches for Requirement Engineering

In this section we will first detail some important concepts about i* and Problem Frames, in order to clarify and make easier the relation between them. To illustrate, we will use an adaptation of the Meeting Scheduling Problem, taken from [15]. The problem is to help a secretary to organize meetings, with the use of a scheduler system or not, and also the arrangement for the participants in meetings. In the meeting scheduling organization the appropriate dates must be found, based on an initial range of dates, and also by information provided by involved participants (preferred dates and exclusion dates). Before a suitable date can be established (final approved date), it must be agreed by all participants; and to be approved, as a final date, it must at least be approved by one of the important participants. The problem also stresses the importance of a quickly organization and less effort, facilitating in this way the arrangement of both the secretary and participants. There is also the objective to assure that participants will attend the meeting, especially important participants.

2.1 The i* Approach

When developing systems we usually need to have a broad understanding of the organizational environment and goals [15]. The i* approach can be used for: (i) obtaining a better understanding of the organizational relationships among the various organization agents; (ii) understanding the rationale of the decisions taken; and (iii) illustrating the various characteristics found in the early phases of requirements specification. The participants of the organizational setting are actors with intentional properties, such as, goals, beliefs, abilities and compromises. These actors depend upon each other in order to fulfil their objectives, and have their tasks performed. The *i* approach* offers two models: The Strategic Dependency (SD) model, and the Strategic Rationale (SR) model.

2.1.1 Strategic Dependency Model

The SD model focuses on the intentional relationships among organizational actors. It consists of a set of nodes and links connecting them, where nodes represent actors and each link represents the dependency between two actors. The depending actor is called Depender and the actor who is depended upon is called Dependee while the element of the dependence is called of Dependum.

In Fig. 1, the SD model for the Meeting Schedule example is presented. It consists of four actors: Secretary, Meeting Scheduler, Participant, and Important Participant. The Meeting Scheduler actor, represents a software system, and performs the meeting scheduling. The other two actors, the Secretary and the Participant, are responsible for providing or receiving information to the system. .

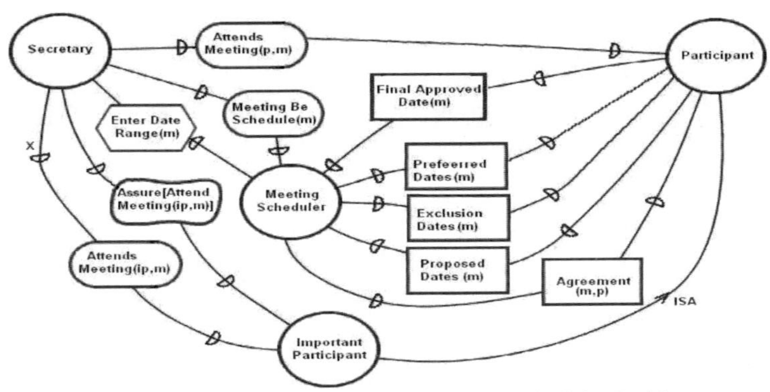

Fig. 1. Strategic Dependency Model for the Meeting Scheduler Problem

The Meeting Scheduler possesses a set of dependencies with the Participant actor. The resources dependencies, ExclusionDates(p) and PreferredDates(p), indicate that the Participant should supply information about unsuitable dates as well as some favourite dates. The Meeting Scheduler depends on these resources to continue the scheduling process, in this case it is the dependeer actor. On the other hand, the Participant depends on a proposed date (ProposedDate(m)) supplied by the Meeting Scheduler that might agree or not with the date. And finally, a FinalApprovedDate(m) will be identified by the Meeting Scheduler. The goal dependency, AttendsMeeting(p,m), considers that Participant should satisfy the goal to attend the meeting. The Agreement(m,p) dependency represents a resource that a Participant should supply to show whether one participant do not agree with the proposed date. The Assured [AttendsMeeting(ip,m)] softgoal dependency is a reference to a softgoal with a subjective evaluation.

2.1.2 Strategic Relational Model

The SR model assists in requirements engineering by allowing process elements and the rationales behind them to be expressed. During early requirement engineering, the SR model can be used to understand how systems are embedded in organizational actors routines, to generate alternatives, and to model and support actor's reasoning about the alternatives.

In Fig. 2 presents the Strategic Rationale (SR) Model of the Meeting Scheduler System, which complements the previous Strategic Dependency (SD) Model presented. Each actor internally possesses goals and routines that impel and justify each external dependency. To develop this model, we must investigate the reasons associated with each actor in relation to the dependencies with other actors. A good way to begin the decomposition is to observe how the Dependee actor can satisfy the Depender associated with the same Dependum, and then to investigate and decompose intentions and strategic organizational reasons as a whole.

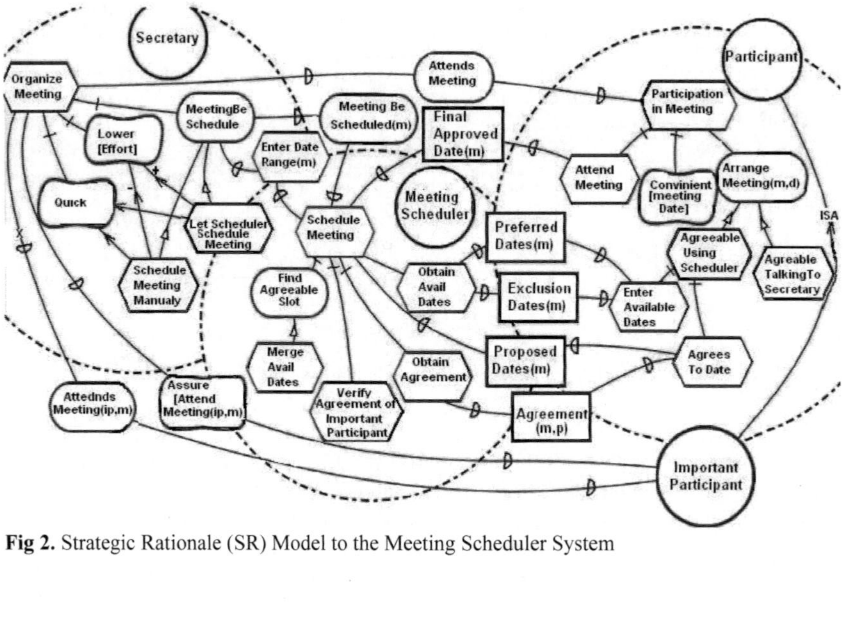

Fig 2. Strategic Rationale (SR) Model to the Meeting Scheduler System

Nodes and links also compose the SR model like in SD model. We have two new links: *means-ends* and *task-decomposition*. The means-ends link is associated to the obtaining of a certain end, which can be a goal, resource, softgoal or task. The mean to obtain the end is defined as tasks that are necessary for reach the end. The task-decomposition link is a node task, which is linked to their component tasks through a decomposition connection. It is permitted, by linking the decomposition into smaller units of a node task, to represent the way and the reasons associated with the accomplishment of the task.

In Fig. 2, the Meeting Scheduler actor possesses a Schedule Meeting task which is decomposed into other tasks using the taskdecomposition relationship: *ObtainAvail-Dates, FindAgreeableSlot, Obtain Agreement, VerifyAgreementof Important Participants*. These tasks represent the work that will be accomplished by the meeting scheduler system. In the same way, the other actors of the organizational are decomposed to represent the internal reasons that satisfy the dependencies with other actors. The Participant actor can choose the way that the goal Attends Meeting will be fulfilled: using the Scheduler Meeting or talking to the Secretary; however, the diagram does not explore the dependencies of the Secretary approach.

2.2 The Problem Frames Concepts

We can summarize Problem Frames as a software engineering technique appropriate to the description of problem domains, defining requirements and decomposing the problem into sub-problems. This technique clearly separates (a) the description of the problem without the solution, and (b) the description of the problem with the solution, that is, what is desired and planned to solve the problem. Both of the descriptions are based on domains, which are composed of phenomena and their interactions [5]. The main concepts of the approach are detailed below and are in italic format.

A *domain* is a particular part of the world that can be distinguished because it is conveniently considered as a whole, and can be considered, to some extent, separately for the other parts of the world. A *domain* can be thought as a collection of related *phenomena* (such as entities, events and states), which represent part of a physical domain in the world where the effects are observable. The only way two domains can interact is through a connection between them, which is called *interface of shared phenomena*. A domain that must be designed and built, in the form of software, to solve the *problem* is called a *machine domain*. Examples of domains and interface of shared phenomena can be seen in Fig.5, where the Meeting Scheduler is the machine domain.

A *problem* details the problem context, including explicitly the problem requirement and how the requirement is related to its domains (constraints or references the domain's phenomena), and the roles that the domains play in the problem (controlled or observed). In a *problem diagram* there are two levels of interface of shared phenomena: requirement level and specification level. An example of a problem diagram can be seen in see Fig.6. *Concerns* are aspects of a problem demanding the developer's attention. Generally, a problem has a main concern (called *frame concern*) and also other *concerns*. Example of a description of a problem main concern can be seen in Table 1.

A *problem frame* is a kind of pattern that captures and defines commonly found classes of simple sub-problems. It defines an intuitively identifiable problem class in terms of its context and characteristics of its domains, interfaces and requirements. A *problem frame* is just a generic problem, but instead of showing specific domains and requirements, it shows types of domains and types of phenomena. A *problem frame* distinguishes some broad types of domains, through *domain marks*, according to their principal characteristics. *Domain marks* are indicated as a square in the right bottom part of domains, see Fig.3.

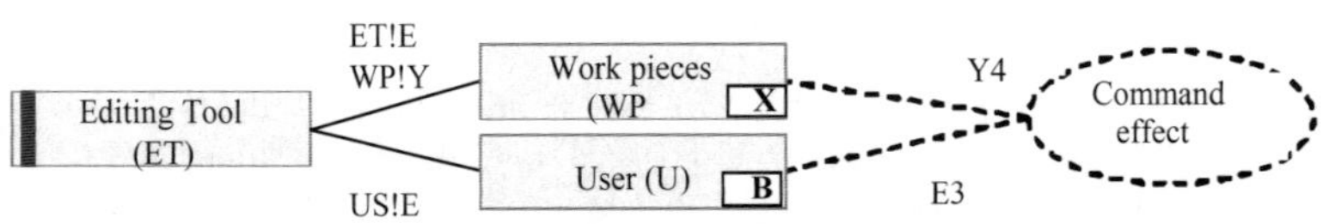

Fig. 3. Workpieces *problem frame*. It includes the machine domain Editing Tool and the problem domains User (biddable) and Workpieces (lexical). At the interface of shared phenomena we have phenomena indicating event commands (E1, E3), and other indicating symbolic phenomena (Y2 and Y4). The idea behind this *problem frame* is: "A tool is needed to allow a user to create and edit a certain class of computable processable text or graphic objects or similar structures, so that they can be used subsequently copied, printed, analysed or used in other ways. The problem is to build a machine that can act as this tool."

Domains can be classified as: (i) *Causal* (C), which properties include predictable causal relationship among its causal phenomena; (ii) *Biddable* (B), which usually consists of people; it lacks positive predictable characteristics; and (iii) *Lexical* (X), which is a physical representation of data - symbolic phenomena. *Causal phenomena* (C), are directly caused or controlled by a domain (events, roles, or states relating entities). *Symbolic phenomena* symbolize other phenomena and relationships among them (values, truths, states relating values). Commands can be represented as events (E).

Jackson supplies a repertoire of recognized problem classes - *problem frames* - with associated characteristic difficulties and solution methods. With these structures specialization the developer can emerge and reach incremental advances in software development. The repertoire includes the following *basic problem frames*: Required Behaviour, Commanded Behaviour, Information Display, Workpieces and Transformation. Fig. 3 and 4 present the Workpieces and the Transformation *problem frames*, respectively, which are further applied in our example (in section 3.2). The *frame concern* (main concern) for the each elementary *problem frame* helps understanding and describing it. For more details see [5].

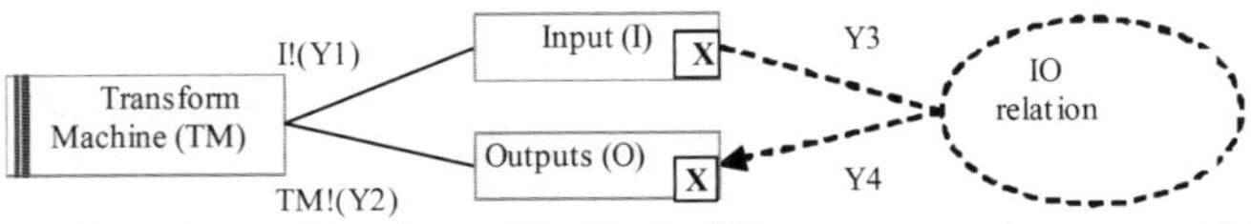

Fig. 4. Transformation *problem frame*. The idea is: "There are some given computable readable input files whose data must be transformed to give a certain required output files. The output data must be in particular format and it must be derived from the input data according to certain rules. The problem is to build a machine that will produce the required outputs ".

3 Relating Problem Frames with i* using Meeting Scheduler Example

In this section we will first illustrate the use of Problem Frames through the Meeting Scheduler example (sub-sections 3.1 to 3.4). Then, in sub-section 3.5, we will present a table describing the relationship between most important concepts of i* and Problem Frames approach, and make some considerations about it. Finally, sub-section 3.6 discusses features which must be considered in a hybrid approach.

In the application of the Problem Frames technique, we will first draw the problem context diagram, in order to determine where the problem is located, and what parts of the world it concerns. The problem requirements are identified providing a starting point for problem analysis and decomposition of problems into simpler and smaller sub-problems and simpler problem diagrams, and then look more closely at the interface between the world and the system and make the annotation of interface phenomena. The problems decomposition continues until each problem is simple enough that it can be seen to be an instance of a recognized problem frame [5]. This helps in decomposing the main problem into sub-problems, each one with its own projections (partial views) of the world and of the machine, taken from the original problem. Each identified sub-problem is presented in a specific *problem diagram*.

3.1 Building the Context Diagram

The problem of the Meeting Scheduling can be structured and analyzed by the context diagram presented in Fig.5. It includes domains which consider information from i *, such as the involved actors and also dependencies between them, and so on. The context diagram structures and delimits the problem as a number of separated domains, together with the machine to be built. It shows how these domains interact with each other and with the machine through the interface of shared phenomena.

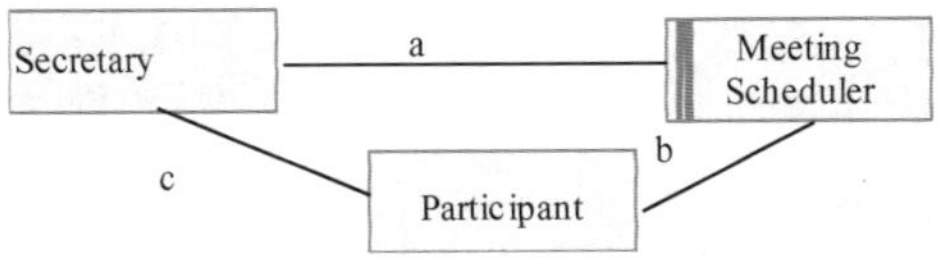

Fig.5. Meeting Scheduling context diagram. The Meeting Scheduler is the machine, software to be developed, and is represented by a rectangle with a double vertical stripe. The problem domains are the Participant (including Important Participant) and the Secretary.

In Fig.5, the connections between domains represent the interface of shared phenomena (the domains interaction), which includes the following phenomena:

- a: {EnterDateRange(m)}
- b: {ProposedDate(m), Preferred Dates, Exclusion Dates, Agreement(m,p), FinalApprovedDate (m)}
- c: {FindAgreedable Date By Talking ToSecretary}

3.2 Problem Decomposition

The Meeting Scheduling problem can be further decomposed into sub-problems. They include: (i) Organize Meeting; (ii) Schedule Meeting which, in turn, can be further split into to other sub-problems**:** Obtain Avail Dates, Find Agreeable Slot, Obtain Agreement, and Verify Agreement of Important Participant; (iii) Participate in Meeting which can further be split into to other sub-problems**:** Attend Meeting and Arrange Meeting, where the last one includes Enter Available Dates and Agree To Date. Observe that, considering the example in i*, for each actor which is exploded in a SR model a submachine in Problem Frames is created; the machine name is the name of each actor and the requirement is the major task identified. In the next subsections we will detail the Schedule Meeting Machine, illustrating the problem decomposition and *problem frames* application.

3.3 Building Sub-problems

The Meeting Scheduler sub-problem is represented by the specific *problem diagram*, see Fig. 6, which includes the problem's requirement represented by the dotted ellipse. The other rectangles are problem domains, which interact with the machine through the set of shared phenomena (interface phenomena). The *specifications phenomena* are the ones shared by the machine and these two domains, and are indicated by solid lines and letters (in the example *a* and *b,* detailed next in the text). The *requirement phenomena* are presented by dotted lines between the domains and the requirement; if the phenomena are constrained by the requirement they include an arrow, if not (only referenced) it is a simple line; they also include letters (in the example *c* and *d).* The "!" indicates the domain controlling the set of shared phenomena. We can say that a domain can be a controller domain or a controlled domain when we talk about the interface of share phenomena between domains.

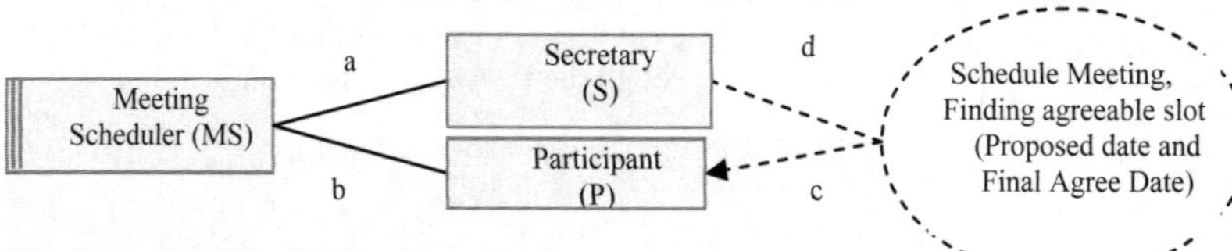

Fig. 6. Meeting Scheduler problem diagram

The Meeting Scheduler problem diagram, in Fig. 6, includes the machine domain and two other domains the Secretary and the Participant (including Important Participants). The interfaces of shared phenomena have the following phenomena, where a and b is at the specification level and c and d at requirement level:

- a: S! {LetSchedulerScheduleMeeting, EnterDateRange (m)}
- b: MS! {ObtainAvailableDates, ObtainAgreement}
  P! {EnterAvailableDate, AgreeToDate)}
- c: P! {Proposed date; Agreement (m,p); Preferred Dates; Exclusion Dates; Attendsmeeting(m,p); AssureAttendsmeeting(ip,m); FinalApprovedDate(m)}
- d: S! {EnterDateRange(m), MeetingBeScheduled(m)}

Observe that each task and resource, from the i* model, can be described as an interaction phenomenon at the interface between domains. The actors which interact with the exploded actor can be seen as domains participating in the problem domain. The dependuns are described as phenomena interactions (events, states, values, entities, etc) at the specification level. The one who is the dependee can be considered to be the controller of the shared event. The goals can be described as shared phenomena at requirements level, and the softgoals inside the problem requirements description.

As defined previously, the main *concern* of a problem is the description we must do to fit together properly in a correctness argument: the requirement, the specification and the domain description. Each description has a defined order in the problem diagram *concern* definition. In the Meeting Scheduler problem, it is required that the machine allows the Meeting Organization to quickly and with less effort schedule meeting and also help the arrangement of the participants, see Table 1.

Table 1. Main Concern description for Meeting Scheduler problem diagram

Ordered Description	Kind of description
1. When the Secretary issues the command **Let Scheduler Schedule Meeting**	*domain description*
2. The Meeting Scheduler asks she to **Enter Date Range(m)**	*machine specification*
3. Resulting in the satisfaction of the task **Enter Date Range(m)**	*requirement*
4. The Meeting Scheduler starts the event **Obtain Available Date**	*machine specification*
5. Participant then **Enter Available Dates (s)**	*domain description*
6. Resulting in the **Preferred Dates** and **Excluded Dates** of the participant to be obtained	*requirement*
7. Based on these dates the machine invoke the operation **Merge Available Dates** to satisfy the goal **Finding Agreeable Slot**	*machine specification*
8. Which in turn results in the **Proposed Date(s)** being obtained	*requirement*
9. The Meeting Scheduler emits the command **Obtain Agreement** for the Participant(s)	*machine specification*
10. The Participants emits the **Agree to Date**	*domain description*
11. Resulting in obtaining the **Agreement (m,p),** that is, if they agree or not with the proposed date for the meeting	*requirement*
12. Then the Verify Agreement of Important Participant occurs, identifying if at least one important participant agrees with the **Meeting be Schedule**	*machine specification*
13. Then the **Final Approved Date** is obtained	*requirement*
14. Which can result in satisfying the goal of the participant	*requirement*

Attend Meeting or not	

To establish the argument we propose the following argumentation of requirements, specification and domain proprieties described in Table 1, which is organized in the following way: the first column represents the order of the whole description, that is the argumentation, and the second column classifies the description of the respective line, that is, if it is part of: a domain description, the requirement, or machine specification.

3.4 Identifying Elementary *Problem Frames*

A *problem frames* is the familiar sub-problem classes that an application to be developed could rely on, and basic problem frames are elementary ones identified in [5]. As described before, the Meeting Scheduler can be split into to other sub-problems: *ObtainAvailDates, FindAgreeableSlot, ObtainAgreement, and Verify AgreementofImportantParticipant.*

The *ObtainAvaiableDate* and *ObtainAgreement* subproblems, can be classified as a class of problem which applies the elementary Workpieces *problem frame*, presented in Fig 3. In the case of *ObtainAvaiableDate*, the user domain can be seen as the Participant, which enters information about available dates. These dates will be stored in a symbolic form, through the lexical domain AvailableDates, and this information will be later recovered by the system for a specific purpose. The interface of shared phenomena of Fig.7, includes commands started by the Participant, internal operation to available dates (i.g. store available dates), and will result in available dates (such as PreferredDates and ExclusionDates) to be stored. The required effects are the syntactically correct user commands (ex: null dates are ignored, etc). More details can be seen in [5].

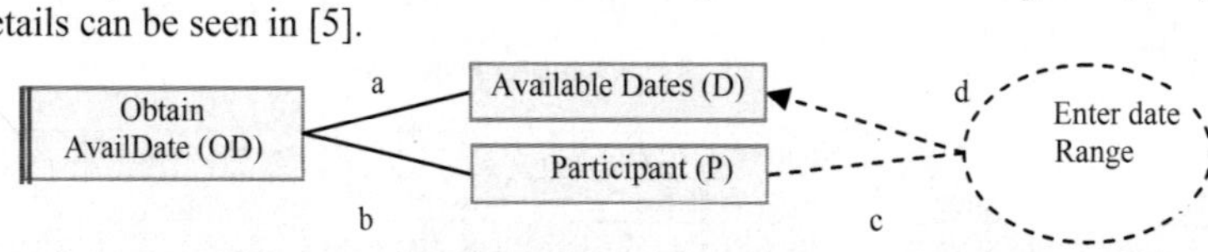

Fig. 7. Obtain Avail Date problem diagram, applying the Workpieces problem frame

In Fig.7, the connections between domains represent the interface of shared phenomena (the domains interaction), which includes the following phenomena:

- a: OD!{StoreDate (m)}
- b: P!{EntryDates(m)}
- c: P! {Available commands}
- d: D!{ParicipantsDate Stored }

Other elementary *problem frame*, the *Transformation,* can be applied to the subproblems *FindAgreeableSlot* and *VerifyAgreementofImportantParticipant.* It includes two lexical domains and a machine which makes some transformation in the involved data (see Fig 4 for details).

3.5 Relations among both Approaches

In order to help the understanding what concepts can have equivalence or not between both approaches, we have selected a group of them that is shown in Table 2. In the horizontal direction the i* concepts are presented and, in the same way, vertical direction presents the Problem Frames concepts. Our purpose is to make a parallel between the involved approaches. Previously, during the study of both examples, we have emphasized the description of relevant concepts (such as *problem frames* and *frame concern,* from Problem Frames), even if they do not have a correspondence in the other approach and vice-versa. However, Table 2 only shows the concepts that have correspondence; the considerations between the other ones, with no relation, are done later in the text (section 4). In spite of our first illustration has started with i*, our objective here is not to make a transformation between diagrams (from i* to Problem Frames), but to be a step to do so in future work.

The *actors* in i*, which represent the participants of the organization, are related to *domains*. Each represents a scope of the problem, that's, a particular part of the world that can be distinguished because it is conveniently considered as a whole. An actor, which represents the system to be built, can be seen as a *machine domain.* Table 2 distinguishes system actors and external actors in i* technique (horizontal line), in order to help our correlation. In fact this distinction does not exist explicitly in i*.

Table 2. Realting i* concepts with Problem Frames

i*concepts x Problem Frame	Actor		Dependum				Dependee	Depender
	System	External	Resource	Task	Goal	SoftGoal		
Domain								
Machine Domain								
Problem Requirement				Actor´s Main task (SR)				
Specification Phenomena Interface								
Requirement Phenomena Interface								
Control Domain								
Controlled Domain								
Requirement Description								

In i* technique, the *actors* depend upon each other in order to fulfil their objectives and have their tasks performed. They achieve this through the definition of dependency between them. This dependency has its correspondence, in Problem Frames, with the *interface of shared phenomena*, which represent the interaction between the domains. In Table 2, this interface is described levels (in horizontal line) the *specification phenomena interface* and the *requirement phenomena interface*.

The *dependee* is represented by the *control domain*, the *depender* by the *controlled domain* and the *dependum* by the *interface of shared phenomena*. However, depending on the kind of *dependun* it is transformed in different way: the i* *task* and *resource* are presented at the level of the *specification phenomena interface* and the goals are transformed to *requirements* level. The *tasks* can also be at the *problem requirement* description (especially if they are main tasks), as well as resources, goals and Softgoals.

Some concepts from Problem Frames approach, such as *problem frame* (a problem defined pattern), and *frame concern* (main concern), have no relation in the i *. As described before, in the introduction section of this paper, both were issues identified in the literature about i*. The *frame concern* description not only gives an order to the existing i* *tasks* (considered at domain specification), which is an identified problem in i*, but it also suggests an integrate argumentation with the problem domain description, requirements description and machine specification. On the other hand, some concepts of i*, such as *is-A*, *means-end*, and *influence*, have no explicit correspondence in Problem Frames. These represent existing limitations of Problem Frames, which can be considered in future works to improve this approach. Also, in spite of the decomposition of sub-problems, the task decomposition is not fully represented in Problem Frames; it only represents problems composition through the interaction of machines with the same domain.

3.6 Discussion

Considering Problem Frames perspective, we can identify several positive points. The context diagram represents a diagram in a higher level of abstraction, delimiting the world by domains and their interaction, and excluding details such as directions between domain interactions (i* dependencies). This is an advantage when we compare to i* strategic model, which can be large and complex to understand, not giving a simple overview of what is going on. Also, the classification proposed in Problem Frames, for elements and their relationship's (such as entity, event, truth, state, role, etc), seems to be a promising way for exploring the power of aspects techniques, and also to improve system traceability and models organization. The existence of previous defined classes of problems (*problem frames*) and their application helps in the solution of complex problems. The concept of domain is rich, since we can decompose it, and also use it together with the related functionality in problem diagrams. Furthermore the frame concern description gives more details in a problem solution through a specific argumentation.

On the other hand i* is more strong in dealing with goals perspective, it considers positive and negative influences between model elements, and also supports softgoals. This technique allows also representing, in a clear way, the task decomposition and the means-end (alternatives) perspective not present in the Problem Frames approach. All these considerations suggest that the identified points take part of the best of both approaches and that must be present in an hybrid approach, supporting together: a powerful way of representing goals, ways of supporting traceability, task decomposition, patterns identification, models more precisely defined, etc.

4 Related Works

There have been several threads of work on exploring i* power together with other approaches. These include Alencar et al [11], Donzelli [6], and Martinez [7] though their work uses the OO Method instead of UML. However, we did not find in the literature any work which try to compare or even relate both approaches: the i* and Problem Frames. On the other hand, in spite of Problem Frames power for domain description, it is not an easier or intuitive approach. Efforts to help using and understanding it are presented in the literature. In [4] Problem Frames is places within the framework of Requirements Engineering and its subsequent formalization in a Reference Model is described in [12]. A formalization of Jackson's concept of Problem Frames and elementary problem frames are illustrate in [14]. Other works also use Problem Frames, such as [4, 8]. In [9] a meta-model for Problem Frames Approach is presented with the aim to improve its understanding and give support for the development of a specific tool and mapping between other techniques.

5 Conclusion

In this work, we have discussed different aspects that motivate the use of i* and Problem Frames approaches. Our contribution was to make the relationship between them, using an example to illustrate it. This work can be considered a preliminary study for the definition of a hybrid approach, which aim is to take the benefit of each of them. The advantage of having an hybrid approach is that it will not only incorporate the common characteristics, but also be enriched with many other important features such as: reduction of the initial underling complexity in some i* diagrams, through the use of a simpler diagram which presents an overview of the system; the support for the development of more organized models, which have enough information to implement good levels of traceability; include task decomposition, goals, softgoals and influences; reduce system inconsistency and improve its comprehension, through the use of a less informal and more rigorous way of naming model elements; as well as identify classes of problems to be further applied to more complex ones.

We can consider several subtasks for achieving a new hybrid methodology and also ontology. To do so, we can point some intermediary/parallel works that must be directions to future works. One of them is the definition of a process for applying i*, on its own. Other has to due with the refinement of the proposed relations, among the two considered techniques, through the realization of more complex examples. Another proposed work is a detailed mapping, describing step by step how to transform a model to another and vice-versa. These will facilitate the achievement of a new degree of comprehension and knowledge for defining a hybrid approach, which can also be further enriched by concepts taken from early aspects approach [16]. We can also consider that each technique can be individually improved with these studies.

Acknowledgements

This work was supported by several research grants (CNPq Proc. 304982/2002-4, CAPES Proc. BEX 1775/2005-7, Proc. BEX 3003/05-1 & CAPES/ GRICES Proc. 129/05).

References

1. Bresciani, P. et al.: Tropos: An Agent-Oriented Software Development Methodology. Autonomous Agents and Multi-Agent System, vol. 8, n.3 (2004) 203-236
2. Gamma, E., Helm, R., Johnson, R., Vlissides J.: Design Patterns: Elements of Reusable Object- Oriented Software. Addison-Wesley, Massachesetts (1995)
3. Hall, J., Rapanotti, L., Jackson, M.: Problem Frames Semantics for Software Development. Lecture Notes in Software Systems Model, vol.4 (2005) 189-198
4. Bray, I., Cox, K.: The Simulator: Another Elementary Problem Frame? Proceedings of the 9th Int. Workshop on Requirements Engineering – REFSQ (2003)
5. Jackson, M.: Problem Frames: Analysing and Structuring Software Development Problems. Addison-Wesley (2001)
6. Donzelli, P., Bresciani P.: Goal-Oriented Requirements Engineering: A Case Study in E-government. 15th Int'l Conference, CAISE'03, Proceedings. LNCS 2681 (Springer) Australia, (2003) 601-616
7. Martinez, A., Castro, J., Pastor, O., Estrada, H.: Closing the Gap Between Organizational Modeling and Information System Modeling. Proc. of the 6th Int. Workshop on Requirements Engineering, WER'03. Piracicaba (2003).
8. Lencastre, M. et al.: Problem Frames Application on FEM Simulators. 6th Iberoamerican Workshop on Requirements. Engineering and SW Environments, IDEAS, Paraguay (2003)
9. Lencastre, M. et al.: A Meta-model for the Problem Frames Approach. WiSME: 4th Workshop in Software Model Engineering, Jamaica (2005)
10. Results of 2nd i* Workshop, London. Available at: http://istar.rwthaachen.de/tiki_index.php?page_ret_id=16 Accessed on: 15/11/2005
11. Alencar, F., Cysneiro, G., Castro, J.: Support for Structuring Mechanisms in the integration of Organizational Requirements and Object Oriented Modeling. Proc. of the 5th WER, Valencia (2002)
12. Cysneiros, L., Werneck, V., Amaral, J., Yu, E.: Agent/goal Orientation versus Object Orientation for Requirements Engineering: A Practical Evaluation Using an Exemplar. Proc. 8th WER, Portugal (2005)
13. Odell, J., Parunak, H., Bauer, B.: Representing Agent Interaction Protocols in UML. Agent-Oriented Software Engineering-AOSE Workshop, Paolo Ciancarini and Michael Wooldridge eds., Springer-Verlag, Berlin (2001)
14. Castro, J., Kolp, M., Mylopoulos, J.: Towards Requirements Driven Information Systems Engineering:The Tropos Project. Journal Information Systems, Holanda, vl.27, n.6 (2002)
15. Yu, E.: Modelling Strategic Relationships for Processing Reengineering. PhD Thesis in Informatics. Department of Computer Science, University of Toronto, Toronto (1995)
16. Moreira, A., Araújo, J.: Handling Unanticipated Requirements Change with Aspects, Software Engineering and Knowledge Engineering Conference (SEKE'04), Canada (2004)
17. Castro, J. et al.: Integração de Técnicas de Requisitos com Aspectos: O Caso TROPOS, Projeto CGCI/CAPES/MEC N.129/05, Programs of International Cooperation Brazil/ Portugal (2005).
18. Zambonelli, F., Jennings, N., Wooldridge, M.: Developing Multiagent Systems: the Gaia Methodology. ACM Trans on Software Engineering and Methodology vol. 12, n.3, (2003)

Uma Ontologia para Engenharia de Requisitos

Raul A. Medeiros Jr., Pedro Porfírio M. Farias, Arnaldo Dias Belchior

Universidade de Fortaleza, Curso de Mestrado em Informática Aplicada,
Fortaleza, Brasil, 60.811-905
raul.medeiros@serpro.gov.br, porfirio, belchior{@unifor.br}

Resumo. Um dos principais objetivos da engenharia de requisitos é construir requisitos de software de fácil entendimento e que sejam consistentes tanto para os clientes, quanto para os desenvolvedores. Para auxiliar no entendimento desses requisitos pelas partes envolvidas, este trabalho apresenta uma ontologia para a engenharia de requisitos de software, com o objetivo de facilitar a compreensão de seus conceitos e propiciar a melhoria da comunicação entre desenvolvedores e clientes, contribuindo, assim, para reduzir a incidência de problemas posteriores ao longo do ciclo de vida do software.

1 Introdução

Apesar de atualmente se desenvolver mais produtos de software e cada vez mais sofisticados, é também verdade que alguns problemas surgidos durante o processo de desenvolvimento ainda continuam trazendo enormes prejuízos para os envolvidos. Uma questão central, comum a alguns problemas decorrentes de falhas no processo de produção ou de manutenção de software, está na precariedade dos processos de produção empregados, principalmente devido à não-observância de princípios da engenharia de requisitos.

A engenharia de software associa a palavra "requisitos" desde o início da produção de software. Um produto de software deverá ser construído de acordo com seus requisitos. Experiências reais e pesquisas comprovam que um precário entendimento dos requisitos tem levado a inúmeros problemas no processo de desenvolvimento de software [1].

Portanto, constitui uma boa prática a realização de investimentos em engenharia de requisitos, como forma de evitar problemas futuros ou mudanças ao longo do processo de desenvolvimento. Uma farta quantidade de pesquisas estatísticas tem revelado que corrigir um erro no início do processo de desenvolvimento sai bem mais barato do que corrigir esse mesmo erro somente no seu final. Os números variam de 1 para 20 e até de 1 para 200, dependendo do tipo de produto considerado e da etapa do processo de desenvolvimento onde o problema foi detectado. Há também várias pesquisas relatando que uma grande quantidade dos erros de desenvolvimento se deve ao insuficiente entendimento dos requisitos. Naturalmente, um dos principais objetivos da engenharia de requisitos é a construção de requisitos de fácil entendimento, tanto para quem os solicitou, quanto para os seus desenvolvedores [1].

Para auxiliar no entendimento dos requisitos entre as duas principais partes envolvidas (clientes e desenvolvedores), este trabalho propõe a utilização de uma ontologia para o processo de engenharia de requisitos.

As ontologias são úteis para apoiar a especificação e a implementação de qualquer sistema de computação complexo. Elas podem ajudar os envolvidos a compreender melhor determinadas áreas de conhecimento, e apoiá-los a alcançar um consenso no entendimento sobre tais áreas.

Este trabalho compõe-se de cinco seções. Na seção 2, evidenciamos a relevância da área de engenharia de requisitos. Na seção 3, conceituamos ontologia e discorremos sobre padrões e metodologia de construção de ontologia. Na seção 4, propomos uma ontologia para engenharia de requisitos. Na seção 5, apresentamos a conclusão do trabalho.

2 Engenharia de Requisitos de Software

A engenharia de requisitos de software é uma área recente; contudo, tem-se desenvolvido muito rapidamente. Em 1993, no primeiro Simpósio Internacional de Requisitos promovido pelo IEEE, foram delimitadas as fronteiras entre a engenharia de requisitos e as demais atividades de engenharia de software. A comunidade científica visualizou a engenharia de requisitos, em particular, como um tópico de pesquisa, a exemplo da modelagem e da análise [1].

Atualmente, várias abordagens que tratam da qualidade de processos de software enfatizam o gerenciamento de requisitos como etapa importante do processo de construção de software. O CMMI [2], por exemplo, define duas áreas de processo para requisitos. Uma área de processo é um conjunto de práticas relacionadas entre si que, quando executadas coletivamente, satisfazem um conjunto de objetivos tidos como importantes para sua operacionalização.

A primeira área de processo, que pertence ao nível "2" de maturidade (abordagem por estágio), é a Gerência dos Requisitos, que tem por finalidade controlar os requisitos do projeto e do produto de software, além de identificar inconsistências entre requisitos e planos de projeto. A segunda área, pertencente ao nível "3" de maturidade, é o Desenvolvimento de Requisitos, que objetiva produzir e analisar requisitos do cliente, do produto e dos componentes do produto.

A ISO 9001:2000 [3] recomenda que se deve assegurar que os requisitos do cliente sejam determinados e atendidos com o propósito de aumentar a sua satisfação. Para facilitar o gerenciamento eficaz dos requisitos, é essencial que quaisquer mudanças acordadas nesses requisitos sejam comunicadas a todos os seus envolvidos.

Um importante conceito na engenharia de requisitos é a rastreabilidade, que consiste na habilidade de seguir relacionamentos ou conexões. Segundo Gotel e Finkelstein [4], rastreabilidade de requisitos é a habilidade de descrever e seguir a vida de um requisito, em duas direções: para frente e para trás.

A rastreabilidade é essencial para o processo de desenvolvimento, pois muitas informações são usadas e produzidas e devem permanecer conectadas. Quando se desenvolvem sistemas de grande porte, torna-se difícil lembrar-se de todos os relacionamentos entre as informações. Para sistemas de equipes multidisciplinares, mormente as geograficamente dispersas, é impossível conhecer todas as conexões entre suas informações [5].

3 Ontologia

A palavra *ontologia* vem do grego *ontos* (ser) + *logos* (palavra), e procura distinguir o estudo do ser do estudo dos vários tipos de seres na ciência natural. Como uma disciplina da filosofia, uma ontologia construída tem a preocupação de prover categorias de sistemas que agreguem uma certa visão do mundo [6].

Uma ontologia é uma especificação de uma conceituação [6], isto é, uma descrição de conceitos e relações que existem em um domínio de interesse. Basicamente, uma ontologia consiste desses conceitos e relações, e de suas definições, propriedades e restrições, descritas na forma de axiomas.

Segundo Gruber [7], uma ontologia é uma especificação formal e explícita para um conceito compartilhado. Nesse contexto, padrões de conceituação para um modelo abstrato são meios explícitos em que os elementos são claramente definidos e também meios formais que podem ser processados por máquinas.

Grunninger [8] relata, entre outras questões, a possibilidade do uso de ontologias para comunicação entre homens e sistemas computacionais, para inferência computacional e para o reuso e a organização de conhecimento.

Na ciência da computação, ontologias têm sido desenvolvidas, por exemplo, na inteligência artificial, para facilitar o compartilhamento de conhecimento e seu reuso. Atualmente, a utilização de ontologias tem-se expandido em outras áreas, como a integração inteligente de informação, sistemas cooperativos, produtos de software baseados em agentes, e no comércio eletrônico [9].

Diversas linguagens foram propostas para a descrição de ontologias. A partir dessas experiências, a linguagem OWL (*Ontology Web Language*) [10] foi elaborada como um padrão a ser utilizado na Web pela W3C (*World Wide Web Consortium*).

Uma ontologia escrita em OWL deve incluir as descrições de classes, propriedades e suas instâncias. As classes podem ser relacionadas através de equivalência, disjunção e enumeração. Classes podem ser especializadas por subclasses, podem ser definidas como expressões *booleanas* de classes, etc. As propriedades em Owl podem ser propriedades de objetos (*ObjectProperties*) e propriedades de tipos de dados (*DatatypeProperties*). Podem ter domínio, intervalo de valoração, podem sofrer restrições de cardinalidade, etc. Propriedades podem ser transitivas, simétricas, funcionais e ser invertidas. As declarações utilizadas para construir uma ontologia implicitamente formalizam seus axiomas. A semântica formal da OWL permite realizar inferências automaticamente.

O desenvolvimento de ontologias parece ser mais uma arte do que uma ciência [11]. Até agora, grupos de pesquisadores estão tentando resolver esse problema, desenvolvendo metodologias específicas. Gruninger e Fox [12] propuseram a metodologia TOVE (Toronto Virtual Enterprise). Essa metodologia foi derivada da experiência dos autores no *Enterprise Integration Laboratory* para o desenvolvimento e a evolução de ontologias integradas. Foram utilizados cenários de motivação para descrever problemas ou exemplos que não eram adequadamente referenciados por ontologias existentes. Os cenários de motivação fornecem um conjunto intuitivo de possíveis soluções para os problemas encontrados, fornecendo uma idéia inicial da semântica pretendida para objetos e seus relacionamentos, que comporão a ontologia.

Segundo Noy e McGuinness [13], o desenvolvimento de ontologias observa alguns regras que parecem dogmas e que, em muitos casos, podem subsidiar as decisões:

- *Não há uma única maneira correta de modelar um domínio – há sempre formas viáveis e alternativas. A melhor solução depende da aplicação que o autor tem em mente e das extensões que o antecederam.*
- *O desenvolvimento de ontologia é um processo iterativo.*
- *Os conceitos devem ser fechados nos objetos (físicos ou lógicos), e as relações, no seu domínio de interesse. Os conceitos devem ser nomes (objetos) ou verbos (relacionamentos) nas sentenças que descrevem o seu domínio.*

Noy e McGuiness [13] propõem um processo interativo para o desenvolvimento de ontologias, a partir de um guia elaborado com suas experiências na ferramenta Protégé-2000 [14]. Inicialmente, a ontologia é desenvolvida de forma tosca, sendo revisada e refinada progressivamente em seus detalhes. Ao longo da definição da ontologia, são discutidas decisões de modelagem que o autor precisará tomar, sendo então apresentados os prós e os contras e as implicações de possíveis soluções. Esse processo compreende as seguintes etapas:

- *Determinar o domínio e o escopo da ontologia;*
- *Reusar ontologias acaso existentes;*
- *Enumerar importantes termos na ontologia;*
- *Definir classes e hierarquia entre elas;*
- *Definir as propriedades das classes; e*
- *Criar instâncias das classes.*

4 Ontologia para Engenharia de Requisitos de Software

A ontologia para engenharia de requisitos que está sendo apresentada foi desenvolvida a partir da metodologia proposta por Noy e McGuiness [13], seguindo as etapas sugeridas. Primeiramente, determinamos o escopo da ontologia (item 4.1). Como insumo desta atividade, utilizamos referências bibliográficas na área e uma pesquisa de campo junto a especialistas de requisitos.

Em uma segunda etapa (item 4.2), procuramos identificar ontologias que se adequassem ao nosso escopo, com a finalidade de reutilização e de tornar a nossa ontologia mais genérica e que pudesse se integrar com outras ontologias. Na etapa seguinte (item 4.3), definimos os termos relevantes para nossa ontologia. A quarta etapa (item 4.4) foi a definição das classes, sua hierarquia, propriedades e restrições. Para tanto, adotamos a linguagem OWL. Utilizamos a ferramenta Protege-2000 e o plug-in ezOWL [15] para exibir graficamente o modelo. Finalmente, instanciamos essa ontologia aplicando-a a três sistemas de uma empresa certificada CMM2, que trabalha com construção e manutenção de software. Um dos projetos foi parcialmente descrito no item 4.5 para exemplificar os conceitos apresentados.

4.1 Escopo e Domínio da Ontologia

A ontologia proposta tem como objetivo dar suporte à engenharia de requisitos no que se refere ao levantamento, à documentação, às métricas e à qualidade de requisitos de software, procurando melhorar a comunicação entre os envolvidos no processo de desenvolvimento de software.

Ela deverá ser capaz de responder às seguintes questões de competência para requisitos de software:

- *O que é um requisito?*
- *Quais os tipos de requisito?*
- *Como levantar requisitos adequadamente?*
- *Como rastrear os requisitos?*
- *Que critérios de qualidade são desejáveis para requisitos?*
- *Quais métricas estão associadas a quais requisitos?*

4.2 Reuso de Ontologias

Na literatura pesquisada, identificamos algumas ontologias que podem ser parcialmente reutilizadas na construção da ontologia proposta, como se vê a seguir:

- *Ontologia de Qualidade de Software* [16]: A ontologia proposta neste trabalho objetiva elucidar a terminologia da área de Qualidade de Software, de modo a facilitar o entendimento e uniformizar os conceitos utilizados. As questões de competência enfocadas dizem respeito à natureza, à relevância e às métricas utilizadas para quantificar características de qualidade. A ontologia gerada foi utilizada para construção de um *framework* de objetos, o qual foi utilizado para construção de duas ferramentas.
- *Ontologia para Métricas e Indicadores para Sistemas Web* [17]: são apresentados e especificados os principais conceitos e relações de uma ontologia para métricas e indicadores de software, baseada principalmente em conceitos da ISO, entre outros padrões. Pode ser útil no suporte a diferentes processos de qualidade, métodos e ferramentas que fundamentam diversos indicadores e métricas.

4.3 Termos Relevantes na Ontologia

Na ontologia proposta, temos um conjunto de termos considerados relevantes, destacados a seguir:

- **Componente**: parte do produto de software entregue ao contratante [2].
- **Cliente**: pessoa ou grupo de pessoas que irão utilizar o produto de software.
- **Critérios de qualidade**: características que avaliam a qualidade de um requisito de software. Esses critérios foram baseados em Beaufond [18]:
  - *Avaliabilidade*: capacidade de o requisito poder ser avaliado com relação à forma e conteúdo.
  - *Completitude*: o requisito deve garantir que os aspectos nele abordados foram totalmente cobertos.
  - *Consistência*: o requisito deve está isento de contradições entre os aspectos especificados para ele.
  - *Não-ambigüidade*: o requisito deve abordar apenas aspectos considerados imprescindíveis ao seu entendimento, evitando-se, assim, descrições desnecessárias e irrelevantes.

  - *Não-redundância*: o requisito não deve abordar aspectos tratados em outro requisito, evitando-se, assim, que uma mesma questão seja tratada em mais de um lugar.
  - *Rastreabilidade*: o requisito deve ser rastreável, identificando-se a agregação de detalhes de dados específicos, desde sua visão mais global, até a mais detalhada, e vice-versa.
- **Especificação de componente**: documentação de um componente de software.
- **Funcionalidade**: requisito descrito em um nível de negócio mais alto do que o descrito pela técnica de documentação de requisitos. São características que um software deve possuir para atender às necessidades dos clientes.
- **Informações ambientais**: representam as regras de negócio relacionadas com o contexto político, econômico e padrões que podem afetar a organização [19].
- **Informações organizacionais**: representam as regras da organização. As regras de aquisição e o uso dos sistemas computacionais originam-se dessas informações [19].
- **Métricas**: parâmetros utilizados para quantificação de alguma característica dos requisitos de software.
- **Necessidade**: o problema (oportunidade) operacional ou de negócios, que deve ser resolvido para justificar a aquisição ou o uso do software.
- **Regras de negócio**: declaração da política ou condição que deve ser satisfeita dentro do negócio.
- **Requisito**: descreve uma condição ou capacidade com a qual um sistema deve estar de acordo, seja ela diretamente derivada de necessidades dos usuários ou declarada em um contrato, um padrão, uma especificação ou outro documento afim [20].
- **Requisito funcional**: especifica ações que um sistema deve ser capaz de executar, a partir do comportamento de entradas e saídas desse sistema, sem considerar suas restrições físicas.
- **Requisito não funcional**: descreve condições em geral relacionadas ao ambiente do sistema. Diz respeito a questões como usabilidade, eficiência, confiabilidade e restrições.
- **Técnicas de documentação**: utilizadas para extrair e documentar requisitos de sistema.

4.4 Modelo Proposto

O modelo ora proposto foi elaborado a partir da OWL [10], utilizando-se os conceitos de classe e propriedade.

Inicialmente, construímos a classe Cliente. Essa classe está relacionada com a classe `Necessidade`, através da propriedade `temNecessidade`, cuja cardinalidade é maior que um, já que não faz sentido construir um sistema sem necessidades. Na classe `Necessidade`, teremos documentadas todas as necessidades (propriedade `descricao`) do cliente. A propriedade `atendidaPorFuncionalidade` da classe `Necessidade` informa como essas necessidades estão sendo atendidas (Figura 1).

A partir da classe `Funcionalidade`, entramos nos requisitos, ou seja, nas classes derivadas da classe `Requisito`. Deste ponto em diante, começamos a controlar características como métrica e qualidade. Essas características estão descritas nas propriedades da classe `Requisito`: `temMétrica` e `temQualidade` (Figura 1). A propriedade `temQualidade` é do tipo da classe `Qualidade`, descrita nos termos relevantes (item 4.3) com critérios de qualidade. Ela contém os critérios de qualidade. Há vários atributos de `Qualidade` para um requisito, e todos são importantes; contudo, a utilização de todos eles oneraria muito o processo de desenvolvimento. Por isso, optamos por utilizar os "considerados" mais importantes segundo consulta feita a especialistas, por meio de questionário. O atributo `temMétrica` é uma instância da classe `Métrica`. Essa classe é utilizada para mensurar os requisitos.

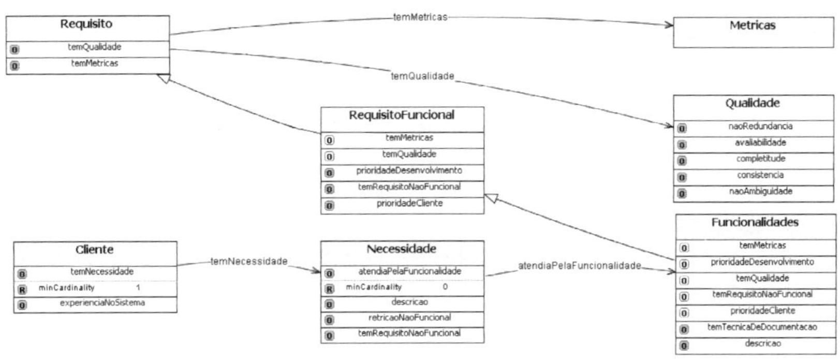

Figura 1. Modelo para requisitos do cliente

As classes `RequisitoFuncional` e `RequisitoNaoFuncional` são subclasses da classe `Requisito`, que por sua vez é composta da união das duas. Começando pela classe `RequisitoNaoFuncional`, modelamos algumas características não funcionais como subclasses dela (Figura 2). Essas características são as utilizadas nas empresas pesquisadas como requisitos não-funcionais dos seus projetos de software.

Os objetivos desta decisão, já que elas são praticamente idênticas, são a herança da propriedade `atendidaEmRequisito`, a facilidade de sua referência em outras classes e um refinamento na rastreabilidade. O rastreamento dos requisitos não-funcionais nem sempre é simples; um requisito não-funcional como desempenho deve ser atendido em vários requisitos funcionais, podendo inclusive ser atendido por outro requisito não-funcional, como, por exemplo, uma restrição física (classe `RestricaoFisica`) na qual especificaria uma configuração de uma máquina onde o sistema seria executado.

A classe `RequisitoFuncional` possui uma propriedade `temRequisitoNaoFuncional` (Figura 2). Isto se deve ao fato de um requisito funcional ou de sua hierarquia poder possuir um requisito não-funcional específico dele. Por exemplo, um requisito específico pode ter um tempo de resposta máximo que se aplica apenas a ele. As classes `Funcionalidades`, `TecnicaDeDocumentacao` e `EspecificacaoComponente` refinam cada vez mais um requisito; ou seja, uma funcionalidade é mais bem detalhada em uma ou várias técnicas de documentação, que por sua vez é mais bem detalhada em uma ou várias especificações de componente.

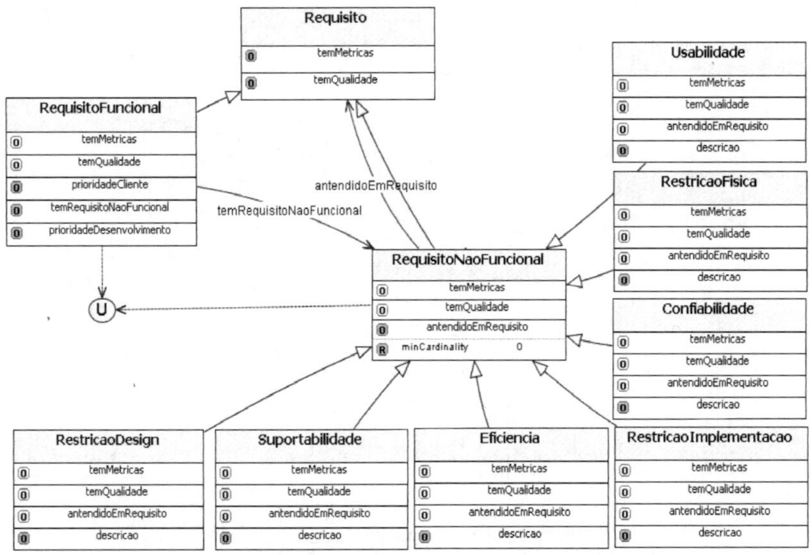

Figura 2. Modelo para requisitos funcionais e requisitos não-funcionais

A classe `TecnicaDeDocumentacao` refina as funcionalidades. Ela possui uma propriedade chamada `temRegraDeNegocio`, que é uma instância da classe `RegraDeNegocio`. Nas empresas pesquisadas, derivamos uma classe `CasoDeUso` da classe `TécnicaDeDocumentação`, por ser essa técnica utilizada nas organizações. A `RegraDeNegocio`, além de descrever as regras de negócio, é subdividida em `InformaçãoAmbiental` e `InformaçãoOrganizacional`, como forma de melhor organizá-las.

Por último, a classe `EspecificacaoComponente`, na qual está descrito, de forma mais refinada, cada componente gerado no processo de desenvolvimento, possui a propriedade `temComponente`, que a liga ao componente por ela especificado.

O modelo completo da ontologia para engenharia de requisitos de software está representado na Figura 3, em que o modelo de requisito não-funcional (Figura 2) foi compactado com a finalidade de possibilitar melhor visualização.

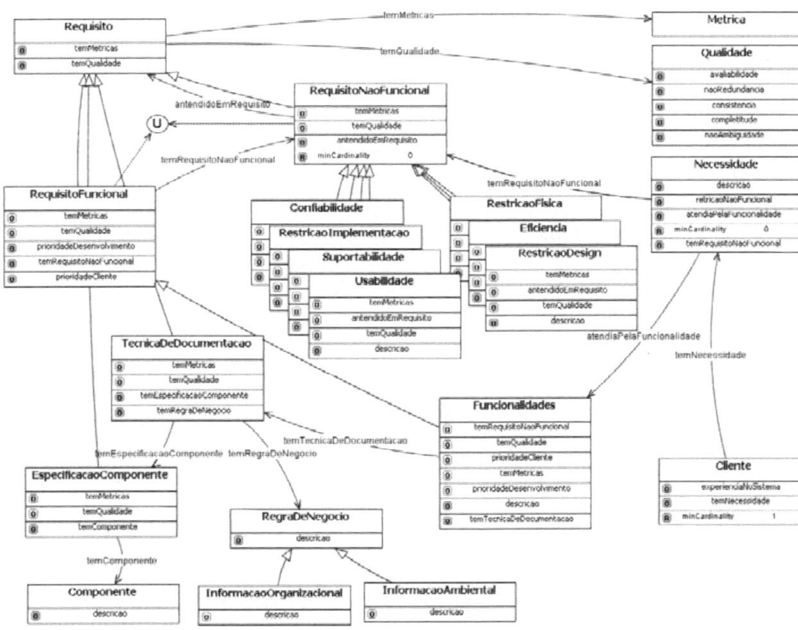

Figura 3. Modelo gráfico da ontologia de engenharia de requisitos

4.5 Aplicação da Ontologia

Para exemplificar os conceitos aqui apresentados, utilizaremos um sistema de uma empresa pública brasileira desenvolvido para controlar treinamentos internos. Não temos a intenção de descrever todos os requisitos do sistema, nem todas as rastreabilidades correspondentes, mas apenas exemplificar a utilização da ontologia. Com o propósito de facilitar a leitura, deixamos de descrever alguns atributos das classes. As cinco tabelas elaboradas foram geradas a partir de instâncias das classes da ontologia. Para facilitar o entendimento da rastreabilidade do sistema, utilizaremos a coluna “código” inexistente no modelo.

A classe Cliente, descrita na Tabela 1, especifica a experiência do cliente. A experiência no sistema foi discretizada com valores de 1 a 5, em que 5 representaria uma maior experiência no sistema. Na Tabela 2, apresentamos a classe Necessidades. Na Tabela 3, apresentamos a classe Técnica de Documentação instanciada como Casos de Uso. Na Tabela 4, apresentamos a classe Funcionalidades. A prioridade no desenvolvimento e a prioridade do cliente foram discretizadas com valores de 1 a 5, em que 5 representa uma maior prioridade. Na Tabela 5, apresentamos a classe Requisito Não-Funcional.

Tabela 1. Classe Cliente

Cód.	Cliente	Experiência no sistema	Tem Necessidade
C1	Gestor de Programa de Treinamento	5	N1, N3
C2	Coordenador de Treinamento	5	N1, N2, N3
C3	Instrutor Interno	3	N3
C4	Participante de Treinamento	1	N3
C5	Chefia Imediata	2	N3
C6	Gerência Sênior	2	N1, N3
C7	Líder de Projeto	3	N1, N3
C8	Setor de Recursos Humanos	2	N4

Tabela 2. Classe Necessidades

Cód.	Necessidade	Descrição	Requisito Não-Funcional	Atendida pela Funcionalidade
N1	Viabilizar treinamento	Realizar operações necessárias para que um treinamento seja implementado.	RNF1	F1, F2, F3, F4
N2	Acompanhar treinamento	Tratar todas as atividades de acompanhamento dos treinamentos.	RNF1	F5, F6, F7, F8
N3	Disponibilizar consultas	Possibilitar a realização de consultas.	RNF1	F9
N4	Gerar relatórios	Gerar e disponibilizar relatórios periódicos do sistema.	RNF1	F10

Tabela 3. Classe Técnica de Documentação instanciada como Casos de Uso

Código	Técnica de Documentação
T1	Caso de Uso: Incluir/Excluir/Alterar Treinamento
T2	Caso de Uso: Incluir/Excluir/Alterar Turma
T3	Caso de Uso: Incluir/Excluir/Alterar Ementa
T4	Caso de Uso: Incluir/Excluir/Alterar Participante
T5	Caso de Uso: Consultar Agenda
T6	Caso de Uso: Encerrar Treinamento
T7	Caso de Uso: Gerar Indicador
T8	Caso de Uso: Incluir/Excluir/Alterar Indicador
T9	Caso de Uso: Incluir/Excluir/Alterar Avaliação
T10	Caso de Uso: Controlar Presença

Tabela 4. Classe Funcionalidades

Cód.	Funcionalidade	Descrição	Prioridade de Desenvol-vimento	Prioridade Cliente	Técnica de Docu-mentação
F1	Manter treinamento	Possibilita ao usuário criar, cancelar, alterar e excluir treinamentos (cursos ou eventos) no sistema.	5	5	T1, T2
F2	Manter ementa	Possibilita ao usuário criar, excluir e alterar ementas de treinamentos no sistema.	2	1	T2, T3
F3	Manter lista de participantes	Possibilita ao usuário incluir, excluir e alterar participantes de treinamentos	1	3	T4
F4	Manter turmas	Possibilita ao usuário criar, excluir ou alterar turmas de treinamentos.	3	5	T2
F5	Gerar registro de notas da avaliação de aprendizado	Possibilita ao usuário gerar registro de notas da avaliação de aprendizado, para impressão.	3	4	T2
F6	Manter presenças	Possibilita ao usuário cadastrar e alterar presenças em cursos e eventos.	1	2	T10
F7	Manter notas da avaliação de aprendizado	Possibilita ao usuário cadastrar e alterar notas da avaliação de aprendizado dos participantes.	2	5	T9
F8	Encerrar treinamento	Possibilita ao usuário dar o treinamento por concluído.	4	2	T6
F9	Consultar agenda de treinamentos	Possibilita ao usuário visualizar a agenda de treinamentos por pólo, equipe e pessoa.	2	2	T5
F10	Gerar indicadores de resultado	Possibilita ao usuário a geração de indicadores de resultados dos treinamentos, com base nas informações cadastradas pelos coordenadores de treinamento.	4	1	T7

Tabela 5. Classe Requisito Não-Funcional

Código	Tipo de Requisito Não-Funcional	Requisito Não-Funcional	Técnica de Documentação
RNF1	Usabilidade	O sistema deve conter ajudas em todas as telas.	T1, T2, T3, T4, T5, T6, T7, T8, T9, T10
RNF2	Eficiência	O sistema deve estar disponível nos cinco dias úteis da semana, funcionando 12 horas por dia, com início às 8h e término às 20h.	
RNF3	Restrição física	O sistema deve estar disponível na *Intranet*.	

5 Resultados Obtidos

Aplicamos a ontologia aqui proposta em dois sistemas de domínio de aplicação governamental, identificados na Tabela 6 como Sistema 1 e Sistema 2. Aplicamo-la também em um de domínio comercial, identificado por Sistema 3. O Sistema 1 é um sistema legado; o Sistema 2 era um novo sistema; e o Sistema 3 era um sistema que vinha sofrendo freqüentes modificações.

Tabela 6. Características dos Sistemas em que a Ontologia foi Aplicada

Classe	Quantidade		
	Sistema 1	Sistema 2	Sistema 3
Necessidades	08	05	06
Funcionalidades	26	15	30
Casos de Uso	94	30	86
Informações Ambientais	10	05	04
Informações Organizacionais	05	07	03
Regra de Negócio	30	12	35
Componentes	172	85	226

Com a aplicação do modelo, pode ser demonstrado, para os clientes e os desenvolvedores, como os requisitos são mapeados nas funcionalidades, e como as funcionalidades são mapeadas nas especificações de componente durante o ciclo de desenvolvimento de software. A aplicação do modelo facilitou o processo de aceite dos requisitos[1] pelo cliente.

Quando ocorre uma mudança de requisitos, podemos facilmente percorrer o modelo e identificar os requisitos e componentes impactados e suas respectivas métricas, para replanejamento do projeto de software. Ou seja, o sistema pesquisado tem uma regra de negócio de informação ambiental, em alguns cálculos. Caso essa regra de negócio seja alterada, iremos percorrer o modelo procurando os casos de uso que a utilizam. Em seguida, procuramos os componentes associados a esses casos de

[1] Aceite dos requisitos: documento utilizado na empresa, no qual o cliente atesta estar ciente do seu pedido e do que deverá ser-lhe entregue no final do processo de desenvolvimento.

uso e suas métricas (ponto por função). Agindo desta forma, poderemos mensurar o tempo necessário para a adequação do sistema à nova lei.

Podemos apontar também uma elevação da qualidade dos requisitos. Todos os requisitos possuem atributo de qualidade explicitamente mostrado. Os atributos são alimentados em todo o processo de software e revisados em cada etapa do processo.

Em resumo, podemos destacar:

- *melhor entendimento dos requisitos como um todo, tanto pelo cliente quanto pelos desenvolvedores*;
- *maior clareza das transformações do requisito no processo de construção do software*;
- *rastreabilidade mais apurada*;
- *acompanhamento facilitado das métricas e atributos de qualidade, estes últimos utilizados nas revisões por pares*.

6 Conclusão

Apresentamos a primeira versão de uma ontologia para engenharia de requisitos de software. A ontologia apresentada foi validada através de consultas a especialistas na área, objetivando obter um consenso sobre os conceitos utilizados. Tal consenso foi obtido após reuniões destinadas a dirimir os pontos de conflito, e após a eliminação de visões particulares. Por exemplo, os conceitos relacionados com Casos de Uso, Atores e métricas como Pontos de Função foram suprimidos da ontologia, por se tratar de instâncias de conceitos apresentados. Foram observados os modelos de dados utilizados em ferramentas como RequisitePro [21] e CaliberRM [22]. Ainda objetivando validar a ontologia, instanciamos os requisitos levantados para dois sistemas, de acordo com a proposta.

Como resultados no processo de validação dessa ontologia, podemos destacar: (*i*) melhor entendimento dos requisitos do sistema por parte dos envolvidos; (*ii*) maior clareza das transformações do requisito ao longo do desenvolvimento do sistema; e (*iii*) rastreabilidade mais apurada dos requisitos.

No sentido de aprofundar ainda mais o estudo, recomenda-se a realização de um trabalho futuro voltado para especificação formal da rastreabilidade, por meio de consultas à ontologia apresentada, com utilização de linguagens apropriadas. A linguagem *Sparql* objetiva fazer consultas a documentos RDF. Até o momento, não foi padronizada uma linguagem de consulta a ontologias escritas em OWL. Entretanto, a linguagem OWL-QL, uma evolução da linguagem DQL (DAML *Query Language*) emerge como uma candidata para este fim.

Referências Bibliográficas

1 LEITE, Júlio C. S. P.; DOORN, Jorge H. Perspectives on software requirements: an introduction. In: Perspectives on software requirements. Kluwer Academic Press, 2003. Cap. 1. ISBN 1-4020-7625-8.

2 CAPABILITY Maturity Model Integration, version 1.1. Pittsburgh: Software Engineering Institute, Carnegie Mellon, 2002.

3 ASSOCIAÇÃO BRASILEIRA DE NORMAS TÉCNICAS. NBR ISO 9001: sistemas de gestão de qualidade: requisitos. Rio de Janeiro, 2000.

4 GOTEL, Orlena C. Z.; FINKELSTEIN, Anthony C. W. An analysis of the requirements traceability problem. In: INTERNATIONAL CONFERENCE ON REQUIREMENTS ENGINEERING, 1., 1994, Colorado Springs. CS Press, 1994.

5 PINHEIRO, Francisco A. C. Requirements traceability. In: Perspectives on software requirements. Kluwer Academic Press, 2003. Cap. 5. ISBN 1-4020-7625-8.

6 GRUBER, Thomas R. Towards principles for the design of ontologies used for knowledge sharing. In: Int. J. human-computer studies. 1995. v. 43, p. 5-6.

7 GRUBER, Thomas R. A translation approach to portable ontology specifications. In: Knowledge Acquisiton. 1993. v.5, p. 199-200.

8 GRUNINGER, Michael; LEE, Jintae. Ontology application and design. Communication ACM, Feb. 2002.

9 BREITMAN, Karin K.; LEITE, Júlio C. S. P. Ontology as a requirements engineering product. In: International Requirements Engineering Conference, 11., 2003.

10 W3C. Ontology web language. Disponível em: <http://www.w3c.org/TR/2004/REC-owl-features-20040210>. Acesso em: mar. 2004.

11 USHOLD, Mike; GRUNINGER, Michael. Ontologies: principles, methods and applications. Knowledge Engineering Review, v. 11, n. 2, p. 93-136, 1996.

12 GRUNINGER, Michael, FOX, Mark S. Methodology for design and evaluation of ontologies. In: WORKSHOP ON BASIC ONTOLOGICAL ISSUES IN KNOWLEDGE SHARING, 1995.

13 NOY, Natalya F.; McGUINNESS, Deborah L. Ontology devepment 1001: a guide to creating your first ontology. KSL Technical Report, Stanford, 2001.

14 NOY, Natalya. F. et al. Creating semantic web contents with Protege-2000. In: IEEE INTELLIGENT SYSTEMS, 2001, p. 60-71.

15 EzOWL. Editor visual para OWL no Protege-2000. Disponível em: <http://iweb.etri.re.kr/ezOWL/>. Acesso em: maio 2004.

16 DUARTE, Kátia C.; FALBO, Ricardo A. Uma ontologia de qualidade de software. In: WORKSHOP DE QUALIDADE DE SOFTWARE, 7., SIMPÓSIO BRASILEIRO DE ENGENHARIA DE SOFTWARE, 14., 2000, João Pessoa.

17 MARTIN, Maria A.; OLSINA, Luís. Towards an ontology for software metrics and indicators as the Foundation for a Cataloging Web System. In: FIRST LATIN AMERICAN WEB CONGRESS, 2003.

18 BEAUFOND, Clifton E. C. Avaliação da qualidade de especificações orientadas a objetos. 1997. Tese (Doutorado em 1997) – Coordenação dos Programas de Pós-graduação em Engenharia, Universidade Federal do Rio de Janeiro, Rio de Janeiro.

19 TORANZO, Marco; CASTRO, Jaelson F. B.; MELLO, Elton. Uma proposta para melhorar o rastreamento de requisitos. WER, 2002.

20 RUP – Rational Unified Process, version 2002.05.00.

21 Rational Requisite Pro, version 2003.06.15.

22 Borland CaliberRM, version 2005 release 2.

Proceso de Elicitación de Requerimientos para Software Empaquetado y Software a Medida

[1]Natalia Andriano, [2]Mónica Balzarini
[1] GSG Argentina natalia.andriano@motorola.com
[2] Estadistica. Universidad Nacional de Córdoba-CONICET.

Resumen. Actualmente en la Argentina existe una creciente demanda de exportación de productos de Software. Este hecho inusual representa una gran oportunidad y a la vez un desafío, debido a que nuestro país posee grandes capacidades para desarrollar software a medida, pero carece de estas capacidades para el desarrollo de software empaquetado. Esta necesidad de desarrollo de software empaquetado fue expresada durante la 33 JAIIO en la Ciudad de Córdoba, Septiembre de 2004. Para lograr conseguir y asegurar mercados internacionales, es necesario desarrollar productos de calidad, es decir, desarrollar el producto que el cliente/mercado desea, dentro del cronograma establecido y con los costos de desarrollo definidos. Para conseguir esto, el primer paso es lograr un excelente Proceso de Elicitación de Requerimientos. Este trabajo tiene como objetivo la comparación del proceso de Elicitación de Requerimientos en el desarrollo de software a medida y software empaquetado.

1. Introducción

El primer paso para lograr desarrollar un producto de software de calidad es la etapa de desarrollo de Requerimientos. Como es sabido, la etapa de desarrollo de requerimientos más allá de la administración de los mismos, de todo proyecto de software es muy importante, tan importante que si se realizara de manera errónea se podría estar desarrollando el software incorrecto [1]. Dicha importancia queda justificada en la siguiente razón: cuanto más tarde en el ciclo de vida se detecta un error, más cuesta repararlo, debido al incremento en el costo de reparación a medida que se avanza en el ciclo de vida del proyecto [1]. El impacto de los errores en la etapa de Requerimientos es un punto muy importante a tener en cuenta, ya que: el software resultante puede no satisfacer a los usuarios; las interpretaciones múltiples de los requerimientos pueden causar desacuerdos entre clientes y desarrolladores; puede gastarse tiempo y dinero construyendo el sistema incorrecto [26]. Entre todos los problemas pertenecientes a la ingeniería de software, los requerimientos son la causa de la mayor cantidad de problemas. Cada problema en los requerimientos es extremadamente costoso de resolver, porque representa un alto porcentaje del entendimiento del problema a ser resuelto por el software. Los problemas en los requerimientos son descubiertos probablemente en el desarrollo del sistema [1].
Actualmente en la Argentina existe una creciente demanda de exportación de productos de Software. Este hecho inusual representa una gran oportunidad y a la vez un desafío, debido a que nuestro país posee grandes capacidades para desarrollar software a medida, pero carece de estas capacidades para el desarrollo de software empaquetado. Esta necesidad de desarrollo de software empaquetado fue expresada durante la 33 JAIIO en la Ciudad de Córdoba, Septiembre de 2004.

2. Marco Teórico

En la Ingeniería de Requerimientos se trata de descubrir cuales son las metas, necesidades y expectativas de los *stakeholders*, ajustar las expectativas de los mismos y comunicarlas a los desarrolladores [2]. La Ingeniería de Requerimientos está formada por una serie de procesos bien diferenciados. A continuación se muestra en la figura 1 los distintos procesos que la componen:

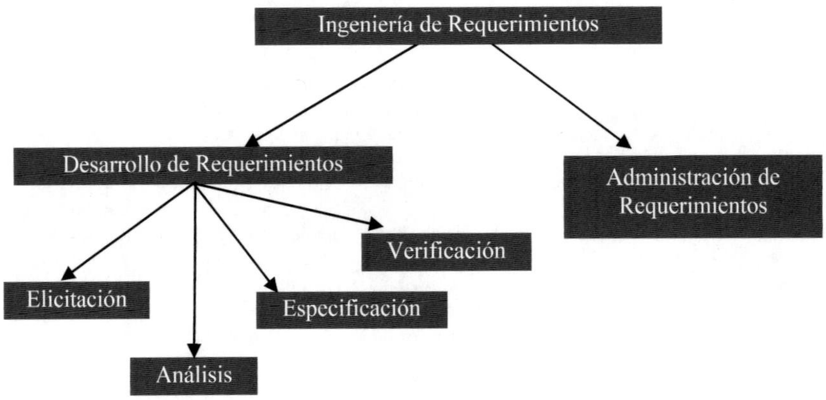

Figura 1: Procesos de la Ingeniería de Requerimientos [9]

2.1 Proceso de Análisis de Requerimientos

En el proceso de análisis de Requerimientos se trata de analizar, precisamente, la información recibida desde los usuarios, para distinguir las necesidades de tareas, de los requerimientos funcionales, reglas de negocio, atributos de calidad, soluciones sugeridas, e información extraña [9].

2.2 Proceso de Especificación de Requerimientos

Es el proceso de grabado o el registro de los requerimientos en una o más formas, incluyendo el lenguaje natural y formal, representaciones simbólicas o gráficas [11].

2.3 Proceso de Validación de Requerimientos

Es el proceso de confirmación con el cliente o usuario del software que los requerimientos son válidos, correctos y completos. La validación es crítica para resaltar las disparidades entre las perspectivas de los *stakeholders* y para descubrir las supuestos subyacentes [10].

2.4 Proceso de Administración de Requerimientos

No es suficiente para las organizaciones simplemente recolectar requerimientos de múltiples *stakeholders* y luego plasmarlos dentro de un solo sistema. Alguien o algún equipo debe ser responsable de administrar esos requerimientos a lo largo del ciclo de vida de manera tal de mantener la visibilidad y control del proceso de entrega del software [10].

2.5 Proceso de Elicitación de Requerimientos

La Elicitación de Requerimientos es el primer y más crítico paso dentro de la Ingeniería de Requerimientos [1]. Realizado de manera errónea nos llevará a productos con calidad pobre, fechas de entregas tardías y costos fuera del presupuesto. El propósito de la Elicitación es recolectar información de los clientes como ser problemas y necesidades; y capturar esa información como requerimientos candidatos (tanto técnicos como no técnicos) junto con la justificación que da soporte a dicho requerimiento [12]. Es el proceso de descubrir los requerimientos para un sistema a través de la comunicación con los clientes, usuarios del sistema y otras personas que tengan algún tipo de interés en el desarrollo del sistema [13]. Existen diferentes elementos a elicitar [2]: límites del sistema, *stakeholders*, metas, tareas, factibilidad, riegos, etc.

3. Técnicas de Elicitación de Requerimientos

Para los propósitos de comparación del proceso de elicitación de requerimientos tanto para software empaquetado como para software a medida, se tomaron en cuenta 8 de las técnicas utilizadas que a continuación se detallan brevemente (encuestas, entrevistas, prototipación, observación, RAD, JAD, Win Win):

3.1 Entrevistas

Las entrevistas elicitan información detallada de un individuo. Para su correcta aplicación requieren habilidades sociales generales, capacidad para escuchar y conocimiento de tácticas de entrevistas. Se definen cuatro fases para la realización de entrevistas [11]: 1) Identificación de candidatos: se deben seleccionar cuidadosamente los candidatos a ser entrevistados, ya que un candidato mal seleccionado podría resultar en una pérdida de tiempo o en la elicitación de datos incorrectos. 2) Preparación: es la etapa previa a la entrevista propiamente dicha. El entrevistador deberá hacer arreglos con respecto al cronograma de entrevistas, se deberán planear cada una de las entrevistas teniendo en cuenta el tiempo en el que llevará la entrevista y un tiempo adicional para destinarle al entrevistado en el caso que quiera hacer algún comentario extra y para la realización de un resumen de dicha entrevista. 3) Desarrollo de la entrevista: en el momento que comience la entrevista el entrevistador deberá introducirse y deberá explicar el objetivo de la entrevista y cuáles son las metas de la misma, las preguntas se deberán realizar teniendo en cuenta el orden especificado y tratando de que la conversación no se salga de curso. A medida que el entrevistado va respondiendo las preguntas se deberá ir explorando las respuestas a través de la resumen, re-expresión y obtención de confirmación de las mismas. 4) Continuación: antes de comenzar con la siguiente entrevista se deberá realizar un resumen, además se deberá enviar una copia al entrevistado y pedir confirmación del resumen realizado.

3.2 Encuestas

Las encuestas son una técnica simple que permite obtener mucha información de una gran cantidad de personas de una manera rápida y eficiente [14]. Según [15] las encuestas elicitan el punto de vista del cliente del área de negocio, sus metas, procesos, problemas, mejoras sugeridas, estructura lógica, entre otros. Una de las ventajas que provee esta técnica es que las encuestas pueden ser reutilizadas en nuevos proyectos. Una encuesta podría ser tabulada completamente y ser re-expresado en una serie de diferentes diagramas. Las tablas y los diagramas deben ser validados por el cliente. Como resultado se obtiene una manera rápida y efectiva de obtener una caracterización detallada de la perspectiva del cliente del sistema actual [15]. Como una buena práctica a tener en cuenta es que las encuestas deben ser prototipadas y verificadas antes de ser distribuidas.

3.3 Tormenta de Ideas

La tormenta de ideas es una técnica simple para la generación de ideas. Las personas que asisten a este tipo de reuniones sugieren y exploran sus ideas libremente. Generalmente las reuniones se realizan con 4 a 10 personas; una de ellas deberá actuar como líder para comenzar pero no para restringir. Algunas de las ventajas son: genera una amplia variedad de puntos de vistas, estimula el pensamiento creativo, se logra construir una imagen más completa del problema, provee un ambiente social mucho mas confortable y además es fácil de aprender [11]. Involucra tanto a la idea de generación como a la de reducción. Las ideas mas creativas, e innovadoras generalmente surgen de la combinación de ideas no relacionadas. La tormenta de ideas presenta algunas reglas [13]: no está permitida la crítica y el debate; dejar que la imaginación vuele; generar la mayor cantidad de ideas posibles; cambiar y combinar las ideas; reducción de ideas; eliminación de las ideas que no valen la pena mayor discusión; agrupación de las ideas similares; priorización de las ideas restantes.

3.4 RAD (Rapid Application Design)

RAD (Diseño Rápido de Aplicaciones) es un proceso de desarrollo de software que permite la construcción de sistemas útiles en menos de 90 días [16]. Es una metodología para comprimir el análisis, el diseño, la construcción, y las fases de prueba en una serie de ciclos de desarrollo cortos e iterativos. Esto tiene un número de ventajas distintas sobre el modelo secuencial tradicional del desarrollo [17]. RAD utiliza generalmente la metodología de programación orientada al objeto, que intrínsecamente fomenta la reutilización del software [18].

3.5 JAD (Joint Application Design)

Según [20] JAD define una serie de actividades *pre-workshop* a llevar a cabo, entre las que podemos mencionar: Identificación de los objetivos y limitaciones del proyecto, Identificación de los factores críticos de éxito, Definición de los entregables del proyecto, Definición el cronograma de las actividades del *workshop*, Selección de los participantes, Preparación del material del *workshop*, Organización de las actividades y ejercicios, Preparar, informar y educar a los participantes, Coordinar la logística del *workshop*.

3.6 Prototipación

La prototipación es el proceso de creación de un sistema que ilustra las características relevantes del mismo. Comienza por el estudio preliminar de los requerimientos del usuario y concluye con una serie de requerimientos formulados y un prototipo desechable. Es un proceso iterativo el cual permite la definición del comportamiento del sistema, y en particular la apariencia del mismo. Esta técnica es realmente útil cuando el prototipo puede ser construido sustancialmente rápido [11].

3.7 Win Win

Es una técnica de elicitación de requerimientos que utiliza un enfoque para la recolección de los mismos a través de una herramienta de soporte. Esta técnica da resultados positivos tanto al desarrollador como al usuario y ayuda en la determinación de prioridades [11]. Establece objetivos y procedimientos para los equipos integrados de productos - qué es lo que deben tratar de hacer los participantes? Cómo deberían proceder? Cómo sabrán cuando hayan terminado? La condición fundamental de éxito de esta técnica es, que el proyecto será exitoso si y solo si se crean "ganadores" con cada uno de los *stakeholders* [1].

3.8 Observación

La técnica de observación posee un enfoque en el cual la base es que el mundo social está ordenado. Este orden social puede no ser obvio, no describible por el sentido común. No puede asumirse que el orden social posee una estructura a priori. El orden social es logrado sobre una base de momento a momento a través de acciones colectivas de los participantes (en vez de a través de cualquier estructura preexistente); por ejemplo el orden social será solo observable en el caso que el observador se sumerja en él. La observación debe realizarse en un ambiente natural [21].

4. Alternativas de Productos de Software

El software empaquetado es una parte significativa del mercado del software. El desarrollo de un software empaquetado es diferente del desarrollo de un software a medida. Las diferencias se encuentran en los modelos del ciclo de vida, las fases de ingeniería de requerimientos y de arquitectura [22].

4.1 Software Empaquetado

Muchas veces son la solución ideal. Hay muchos sistemas, en los que no tiene sentido el desarrollo de un software a medida ya que por mucho menos se puede comprar uno empaquetado que cubrirá todas las expectativas. En otras ocasiones, encontramos software empaquetado que fue diseñado justo para nuestro tipo de negocio. Económico y rápido. Si fue comprado a una empresa importante, podremos solicitar que alguien lo modifique y el costo será para recordar toda la vida. Esto sin contar las innumerables ocasiones en las que tendremos que modificar nuestra forma de trabajo para que el sistema sirva [23]. El software empaquetado es mejor para funciones que cambian lentamente y que no son estratégicas para la empresa. El mejor ejemplo es la contabilidad. No existe negocio que tenga problemas para encontrar una solución para comprar que satisfaga todas sus necesidades, a excepción por las organizaciones que son institucionalmente diferentes con respecto a sus prácticas de contabilidad. Sin embargo, si se piensa que una función es estratégica o que el modelo de negocio es único, hay que tener cuidado con las soluciones empaquetadas. Muchas compañías sufren al tratar de hacer que software empaquetado encuadren con sus operaciones [24].

4.2 Software a Medida

Es un sistema que está hecho exclusivamente para quien lo necesita abarcando cualquier situación prevista y adaptándose lo mejor posible a la forma de trabajo particular de cada negocio [23]. Se puede personalizar lo que sea necesario, incluyendo la forma de cargar los datos o los colores de las pantallas. Si hay cualquier cambio en cualquier situación que implique un cambio en el programa, usted contará con la gente que lo diseñó para eso [23]. El sistema será totalmente flexible a sus necesidades. La desventaja de este tipo de software es que el costo puede fácilmente duplicar al de un empaquetado y hay una demora importante entre el desarrollo y la depuración de errores [23]. Aunque de todas formas, el resultado final será muchísimo más satisfactorio que el que pueda dar un sistema empaquetado. Otra ventaja que ofrece el software a medida, es que en muchas oportunidades una empresa necesita una determinada aplicación que cumpla con una pequeña tarea que haría ganar mucho tiempo a sus empleados. Estas situaciones pueden ser de lo más variadas y no hay software empaquetado que las cumpla. En estas ocasiones, una aplicación a medida es la gran solución, ya que haría exactamente lo que se necesita que haga [23].

5. Materiales y Métodos

Para lograr un claro entendimiento del estado del arte con respecto al proceso de Elicitación de requerimientos en Córdoba – Argentina, se realizaron dos encuestas, uno destinado a desarrolladores de software y otro destinado a usuarios de software. Las encuestas fueron subidas a una página de Internet, de manera tal que cualquier persona pudo tener acceso directo a las mismas. Esto además permitió el amplio alcance que la misma tuvo. Ambas direcciones web fueron enviadas a distintas empresas del medio, distintos cursos de grados en distintas universidades (Universidad Tecnológica Nacional, Universidad Blas Pascal, Universidad Católica de Córdoba), distintos cursos de post grado (Universidad Blas Pascal.
Para los objetivos de este trabajo, solo se tomará en cuenta la encuesta realizada a desarrolladores de software.

6. Principales Resultados Obtenidos con respecto a la totalidad de los proyectos desarrollados (tanto a medida como empaquetado)

Un total de 55 desarrolladores respondieron la encuesta, de los cuales solo el 16% de los mismos desarrollaron en algún momento de sus vidas un software empaquetado y un 84% desarrollaron o desarrollan software a medida (ver Fig. 2); esta es una clara evidencia de la falta de desarrollo de software empaquetado que existe hoy en día en nuestro país.

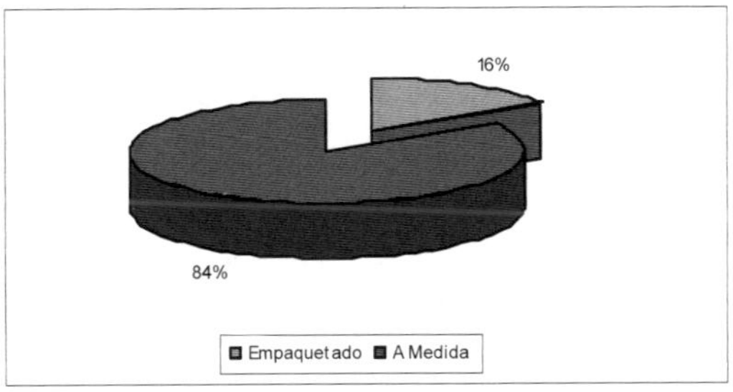

Figura 2: Tipos de Software

Teniendo en cuenta la totalidad de los proyectos desarrollados (tanto a medida como empaquetado) vemos que sólo el 24% de los mismos no presentó desviaciones en las estimaciones de tiempo y el tiempo real de desarrollo. Lo que concluye que el 76% de los proyecto que se desarrollan actualmente, poseen una cierta desviación en el tiempo planificado de desarrollo y el tiempo real de desarrollo (ver Fig. 3).

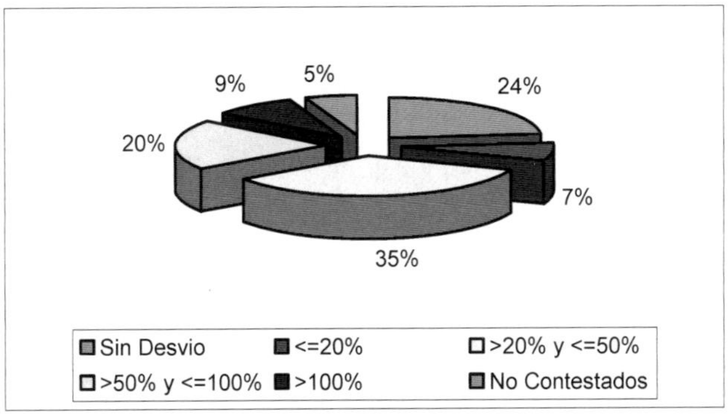

Figura 3: Tiempo estimado de desarrollo vs. Tiempo real de desarrollo

En la Fig. 4 se muestran las distintas causas que fueron identificadas como posible responsables del desvío entre estos tiempos (Tiempo estimado de desarrollo vs tiempo real de desarrollo). Las causas de desvío señaladas con un cuadrado rojo (■) son aquellas propias de la etapa de requerimientos. Los resultados sugieren que las causas con mayor frecuencia son las pertenecientes a esta etapa, es decir, 2 - Los requerimientos relevados no eran claros y 9 - Cambios en los requerimientos; además más de una causa referida a requerimientos pueden presentarse, confirmando la importancia que la literatura revisada cita sobre la elicitación de requerimientos.

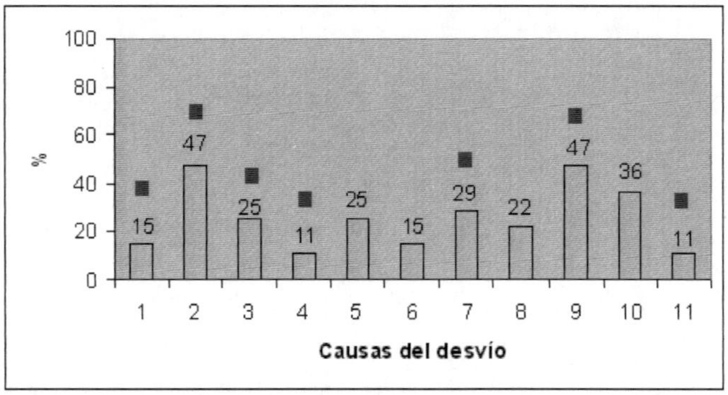

Figura 4: Causas del desvío. Referencias: 1 - No se relevaron los requerimientos, 2 - Los requerimientos relevados no eran claros, 3 - Los requerimientos relevados eran ambiguos, 4 - Los requerimientos relevados eran inconsistentes entre si, 5 – Hubo muchos cambios en el negocio del usuario y no se manejaron bien esos cambios, 6 – No se realizó diseño, 7 - No se entendieron los requerimientos del usuario, 8 – El equipo desarrollador no tenía experiencia en la tecnología utilizada, 9 - Cambios en los requerimientos, 10 – No se diseñaron casos de test, 11 - Los requerimientos no eran verificables

La Fig. 5 muestra que el 11% de los desarrolladores consideran que el grado de satisfacción del cliente respecto del software entregado es muy alto, el 56% de los encuestados respondió que es alto, y sólo el 2% de los mismos consideraron que el grado de satisfacción fue muy bajo).

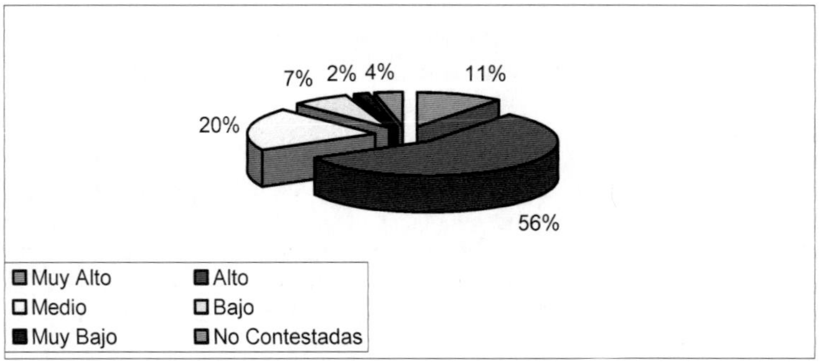

Figura 5: Grado de Satisfacción del cliente respecto del software desarrollado

Dentro del ciclo de vida tradicional de desarrollo (Requerimientos, Análisis, Diseño, Codificación, Testing) vemos que más del 84% de los encuestados planifica y realiza la etapa de requerimientos (ver Fig 6).

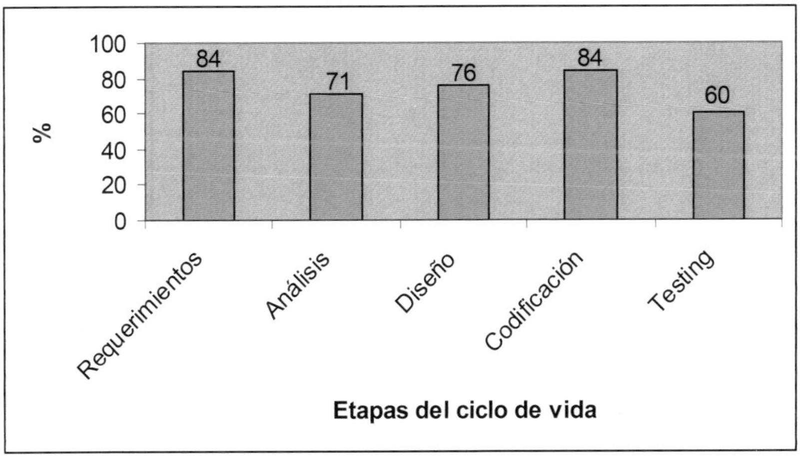

Figura 6: Etapas del ciclo de vida del software tenidas en cuenta a la hora del desarrollo

La Fig. 7 muestra la importancia de la etapa de requerimientos según la percepción de los desarrolladores, el 86% de los encuestados respondió que la misma es Muy Importante; el 5% respondió que era Importante y ninguno de los encuestados respondió que era Poco Importante o que No tiene sentido realizarla pero un 9% no contestó la pregunta.

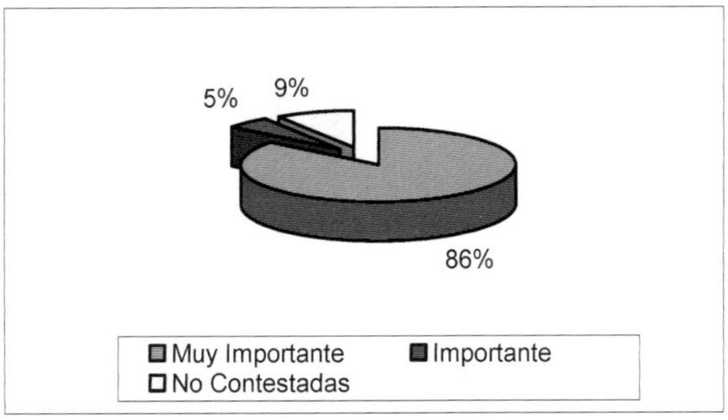

Figura 7: Importancia de la etapa de requerimientos según la percepción de los desarrolladores

En la Fig. 8 se observa que las técnicas menos utilizadas por los desarrolladores de nuestro medio son JAD, RAD, y Win Win , y a la misma vez las técnicas más utilizadas y conocidas por los encuestados son: Encuestas , Entrevistas, Prototipación, Tormenta de Ideas y Observación; sin embargo también existe un alto porcentaje de los encuestados que no conocen o no utilizan estas técnicas (Encuestas: 50%, Entrevistas: 62%, Prototipación: 35%, Tormenta de Ideas: 31%, Observación: 34%).

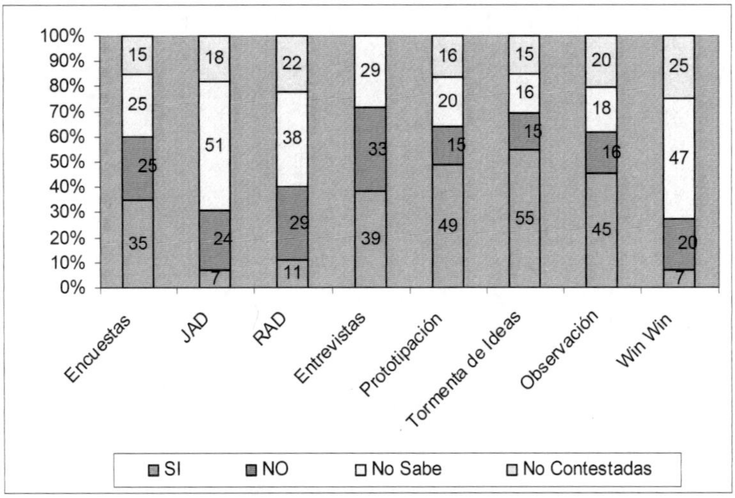

Figure 8: Técnicas de Elicitación de requerimientos utilizadas.

Dentro del ciclo de vida del proyecto, se realizan una serie de actividades para lograr que el desarrollo de un producto sea de calidad (ver Fig. 6). Durante la realización de estas actividades es recomendable la inclusión de los usuarios, de manera de garantizar que el producto entregado sea correctamente desarrollado y sea producto correcto. Sin embargo solo el 20% de los encuestados respondió que no tuvo problemas para que el cliente entienda las actividades que se estaban realizando y el 47% respondió afirmativamente. Es decir, que los usuarios no estuvieron bien informados de las actividades necesarias a desarrollar para lograr un producto de calidad, y por lo tanto no estuvieron lo suficientemente incluidos dentro del proceso.

7. Comparación del Proceso de Elicitación de Requerimientos para desarrollo de Software a Medida y Software Empaquetado

La Fig 9 muestra la evaluación de la asociación entre el tipo de software y las siguientes prácticas recomendadas para el desarrollo de software [1]. Se muestra a continuación la comparación del desarrollo de SW a medida y empaquetado, de acuerdo a la frecuencia de utilización de estas prácticas durante el proceso de elicitación de requerimientos.

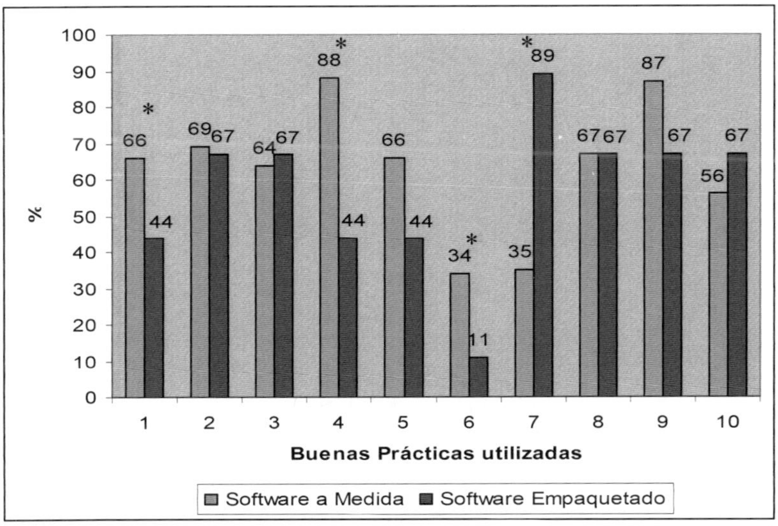

Figure 9: Comparación de la utilización de buenas prácticas para la elicitación de requerimientos entre software a medida y empaquetado. Referencias: 1) Evaluar la factibilidad del sistema; 2) Tener en cuenta consideraciones políticas y organizacionales; 3) Registrar el origen de los requerimientos; 4) Tener en cuenta restricciones del ambiente; 5) Registrar la razón o importancia de los requerimientos; 6) Recolectar requerimientos desde múltiples puntos de vista; 7) Reutilizar requerimientos; 8) Identificar todas las clases de usuarios; 9) Planificar las actividades; 10) Realizar un resumen de cada una de las actividades realizadas

El asterisco (*) indica que existe una diferencia estadísticamente significativas entre ambos tipos de software en cuanto a la frecuencia de utilización de la práctica asociada ($p<0,05$). Los resultados sugieren que la evaluación de la factibilidad del sistema, la consideración de restricciones del ambiente; la recolección de requerimientos desde múltiples puntos de vista y la reutilización de requerimientos; son prácticas que están estadísticamente asociadas a la variable. La presencia de las diferencias encontradas corrobora la hipótesis de que el tipo de alternativa de software condiciona la utilización o no de las buenas prácticas sugeridas por la ingeniería de desarrollo. Las diferencias en frecuencias observadas para las restantes actividades no fueron estadísticamente significativas.

El siguiente (Fig. 10) es un gráfico que muestra en comparación las técnicas utilizadas para la elicitación de requerimiento en las diferentes alternativas de software.

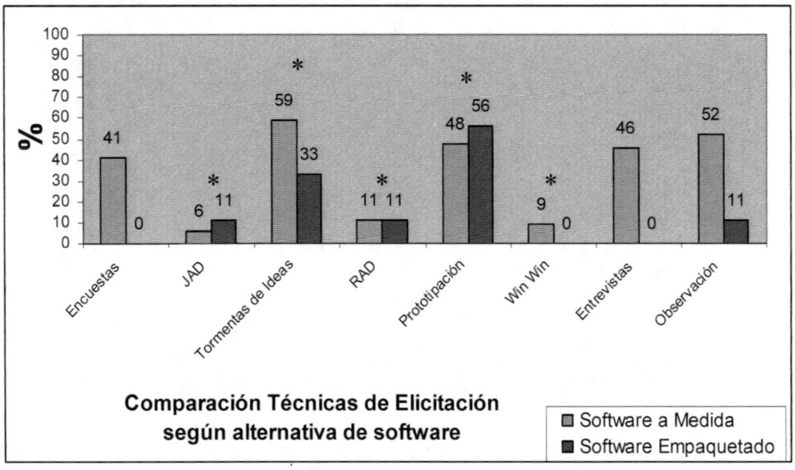

Figure 10: Comparación Técnicas de Elicitación utilizadas para Sw a Medida y Empaquetado

En la Fig 10 se observa que se encontraron diferencias estadísticamente significativas ($p<0,05$) respecto a las técnicas más utilizadas para la elicitación de requerimientos cuando se comparan aquellas más usadas en el software a medida respecto al empaquetado. Mientras que la tormenta de ideas y la prototipación se identificaron como técnicas comunes de elicitación independientemente del tipo de software, las Entrevistas, las Encuestas y la Observación se utilizan casi exclusivamente para elicitar el conocimiento del usuario solo en el caso del software desarrollado a medida.

8. Conclusiones

De acuerdo al estudio anteriormente desarrollado se puede concluir que nuestro país carece del desarrollo de software empaquetado, ya que solo el 16% de los encuestados respondieron que alguna vez tuvo la oportunidad de desarrollar uno. Esto puede ser tomado como un llamado de atención y una oportunidad de mejora para la industria del software nacional, en el sentido de promocionar el desarrollo y la industria de este tipo de software.

También vemos que el 76% de los proyectos de desarrollo de software que se realizan poseen una cierta desviación, y que esa desviación tiene como causa principal al proceso de requerimientos (65%), esto quiere decir, que las empresas deben hacer foco en este proceso lo antes posible de manera tal de minimizar las posibilidades de desvío en la fecha de entrega, costos, funcionalidad, etc. de los productos desarrollados.

Teniendo en cuenta las prácticas adoptadas para la elicitación de requerimientos tanto de software empaquetado como software a medida, vemos que los resultados sugieren que la evaluación de la factibilidad del sistema, la consideración de restricciones del ambiente; la recolección de requerimientos desde múltiples puntos de vista y la reutilización de requerimientos; son prácticas que están estadísticamente asociadas a

la variable (alternativa de software), mientras que las demás buenas prácticas estudiadas no sugirieron una asociación estadísticamente significativa.
Analizando las técnicas de elicitación seleccionadas (entrevistas, encuestas, prototipación, win win, RAD, JAD, observación y tormenta de ideas) se puede deducir que las técnicas comunes de elicitación de requerimientos para ambas alternativas de software son la tormenta de ideas y la prototipación. Por otro lado, se identificó como técnicas propias de la elicitación de software a medida a las entrevistas, las encuestas y a la observación. Se puede concluir sobre esta asociación, que para el desarrollo de un software a medida el desarrollador tiene la oportunidad de tener un mayor contacto con el usuario, y de esta manera poder elicitar mejor los requerimientos.
Aunque en este trabajo solo se tuvo en cuenta la encuesta realizada a los desarrolladores de software, y no a los usuarios, observamos que el proceso requerimientos, y más específicamente el proceso de elicitación de requerimientos es un factor clave para el éxito de los proyectos de desarrollo de software, tanto a medida como empaquetado.
Será interesante asociar la perspectiva de los desarrolladores con las de los usuarios, tarea que estamos actualmente desarrollando, para caracterizar mejor nuestro mercado y obtener información estadística que permita ganar oportunidades a través de un accionar especifico y oportuno determinado a partir de los requerimientos.

9. Referencias

[1] Bohem, Barry R. 1981. Software engineering economics. Englewood Cliffs, N.J.: Prentice – Hall

[2] Bashar Nuseibeh & Steve Easterbrook. "Requirements Engineering: A Roadmap". Department of Computing. Imperial College of Science, Technology & Medicine. London SW7 2BZ, UK

[3] Software Engineering methodology. Chapter 4.0 Requirements Definition Stage. DOE

[4] IEEE Std. 610.12, 1990

[5] G. Kotonya and I. Sommerville, Requirements Engineering: Processes and Techniques, John Wiley & Sons, 2000.

[6] Software Engineering: Principles and Practice. Second Edition. Hans van Vliet. John Wiley & Sons.

[7] Guide to the Software Engineering Body of Knowledge 2004 Version SWEBOK IEEE – 2004 Version

[8] Ian Sommerville and Pete Sawyer. Requirements Engineering: A good practice guide. Lancaster University. 1997

[9] Wiegers K. E. 1999. Software Requirements. Microsoft Press.

[10] MITIGATING RISK WITH EFFECTIVE REQUIREMENTS ENGINEERING How to improve decision-making and opportunity through effective requirements engineering. Part two in a series about understanding and managing risk. April 2005

[11] Angela Tuffley CIT3190 IT Project Course. Requirements Elicitation & Management

[12] Avionics Software Engineering. Requirements Management Guidebook. Software Engineering Management Working Group. 1998

[13] Michael Madigan StorageTek Manager, PAL Engineering. Requirements Elicitation

[14] Eliciting requirements Overview Theoretical framework Engine.mht.

[15] Eliciting Stakeholders' Knowledge of Goals and Processes to derive IT Support. Stewart Green. The University of the West of England

[16] http://csweb.cs.bgsu.edu/maner/domains/RAD.htm

[17] http://www.credata.com/research/methodology.html

[18] http://www.selectbs.com

[19] http://www.umsl.edu/~sauter/analysis/JAD.html

[20] http://www.bee.net/bluebird/jaddoc.htm

[21] Steve Easterbrook 2000-2004. Department of Computer Science.University of Toronto. Lecture 4: Requirements Elicitation. 04-Elicitation-techniques.pdf

[22] IJsbrand Oudshoorn. Vrije Universiteit Amsterdam student number: 1275208 Development of Packaged Software. April 2004.

[23] http://www.braindesarrollos.com.ar/

[24] http://techrepublic.com.com/5100-10878-1058616.html

[25] http://www.umsl.edu/~sauter/analysis/JAD.html

[26] *Standish94, http://www.standishgroup.com/chaos/toc.php*

Sesión 5:

Requisitos y Desarrollo de Software

Aumentando a Compreensão de Requisitos em Desenvolvimento de Software com Equipes Distribuídas

Regiane Andrade Brito[1, 2], Alexandre Marcos Lins de Vasconcelos[1]

[1] Centro de Informática – Universidade Federal de Pernambuco (UFPE)
Caixa Postal 7851, 50732-970, Recife – PE – Brasil

[2] Serviço Federal de Processamento de Dados (SERPRO)
Av. Perimetral da Ciência, 2010, 66077-530, Belém – PA – Brasil

{rab3, amlv}@cin.ufpe.br

Resumo. Esse artigo apresenta uma proposta para melhorar a compreensão de requisitos entre equipes distribuídas. É apresentado um processo colaborativo para engenharia de requisitos e um modelo de rastreamento originado a partir desse processo, o qual auxilia desenvolvedores de aplicações colaborativas. A validação do modelo foi realizada através da construção de uma aplicação integrada a um *groupware* e um estudo de caso simulando a execução de um projeto *open source* real. Uma análise de vinte e quatro ferramentas de gerenciamento de requisitos avaliou o suporte fornecido por ferramentas comerciais, *open source* e *free*, servindo também de base para definição de requisitos e viabilidade da proposta.

1 Introdução

O desenvolvimento de software com equipes geograficamente distribuídas é uma realidade e várias empresas já utilizam esse estilo de desenvolvimento, denominado Desenvolvimento Distribuído de Software (DDS). Em um outro está o desenvolvimento de software livre, onde um grupo de pessoas colabora para o aprimoramento contínuo de produtos de software cujo código fonte e demais artefatos relacionados encontram-se disponíveis através da internet. Vale ressaltar que o desenvolvimento de software já é uma atividade complexa quando realizada localmente, com equipes distribuídas essa complexidade é ainda maior.

Em ambos os cenários é necessário vencer as barreiras impostas pela distância geográfica. Estudos indicam que equipes distribuídas enfrentam problemas como: falta de coordenação, comunicação ineficiente, diferenças de fusos horários, diferenças culturais e perda do espírito de equipe.

Nesse contexto, a disciplina de engenharia de requisitos merece maior atenção [1], por ser considerada a maior responsável pela qualidade do sistema final [2] e por ser uma atividade complexa que requer muita interação entre pessoas com conhecimentos e culturas diferentes, o que tende a ser ampliado nessas situações de distribuição.

Segundo [3], a engenharia de requisitos distribuída precisa de um novo processo. Ainda, pesquisas apontam que algumas empresas que realizam desenvolvimento distribuído de software não realizam o rastreamento de requisitos [4]. Um dos motivos deve ser a dificuldade em controlar as informações provenientes de várias localidades. Além disso, o entendimento de requisitos entre equipes distribuídas já é uma atividade por si só bastante complexa.

Um modelo adequado para rastreamento de requisitos auxilia as atividades de engenharia de requisitos com equipes distribuídas, uma vez que fica mais fácil entender o *rationale* e tomar decisões sobre mudanças em requisitos. Em especial, o pré-rastreamento [5] deve utilizar as inúmeras interações que ocorrem em ferramentas de colaboração para auxiliar o processo de engenharia de requisitos. Portanto, novos modelos de rastreamento devem tratar questões específicas de desenvolvimento distribuído e a utilização de tecnologias de colaboração deve ser considerada.

Neste trabalho é proposto um processo e um modelo de rastreamento que vincula diferentes tipos de informação, provenientes de ferramentas de *groupware* e gerenciamento de requisitos e que auxiliam a compreensão do *rationale*. Esse modelo foi utilizado na construção de um protótipo de uma aplicação de gerenciamento de requisitos integrado a um *groupware open source* bem conhecido (o *eGroupware*). Um estudo de caso é apresentado para validar a proposta.

A seção 2 apresenta uma discussão sobre engenharia de requisitos com equipes distribuídas. A seção 3 avalia ferramentas de gerenciamento de requisitos quanto o suporte necessário para equipes distribuídas. A seção 4 discute o processo de engenharia de requisitos proposto. A seção 5 apresenta um modelo de rastreamento para engenharia de requisitos. A seção 6 apresenta a ferramenta Codipse-Req construída para validar o modelo proposto. A seção 7 apresenta um estudo de caso e a seção 8, as referências.

2 Engenharia de Requisitos com equipes distribuídas

Engenharia de requisitos (ER) é o processo de descoberta de funcionalidades e restrições de um sistema, identificando stakeholders e suas necessidades, bem como documentando essas descobertas de uma forma que possibilite a análise, comunicação e implementação futura [2].

No desenvolvimento com equipes co-localizadas, a coleta de requisitos ocorre em reuniões face a face, considerada a forma mais efetiva de comunicação [6]. Esses encontros tornam mais fáceis também as atividades de negociação e resolução de conflitos.Em DDS essas atividades tendem a ser dificultadas por problemas inerentes da distribuição geográfica, além dos problemas já conhecidos como dificuldade de comunicação entre os *stakeholders* [7]. Alguns estudos de caso relatam experiências na área de engenharia de requisitos distribuída, apresentando as lições aprendidas [4][8].

Existem algumas propostas na literatura que também fornecem suporte ao trabalho colaborativo em engenharia de requisitos, como o ambiente CRETA [9] que é baseado na web e permite a integração com um processo de engenharia de requisitos e o Teamwave instanciado para engenharia de requisitos [6]. No entanto, esses ambientes não tratam diretamente sobre desenvolvimento com equipes distribuídas e não mencionam como o rastreamento de requisitos deve ser tratado.

3 Análise Qualitativa de Ferramentas de Gerenciamento de Requisitos

Essa seção avalia ferramentas de gerenciamento de requisitos *open source, free* e comerciais, quanto ao suporte oferecido para colaboração. O resultado dessa avaliação serve para validar a importância do protótipo desenvolvido, servindo também para definição dos requisitos da proposta.

Esse avaliação é denominada *feature analysis* [10]. Nesse tipo de avaliação identifica-se um conjunto de requisitos necessários para que usuários realizem determinada atividade. Então, essa avaliação pode ser realizada por uma única pessoa que verifica se estes requisitos estão presentes nos objetos de avaliação.

3.1 Requisitos para suporte à colaboração

Para realizar a avaliação, primeiramente é necessário identificar os critérios. Para isso, foi definido um conjunto de requisitos desejáveis em ferramentas de gerenciamento de requisitos. Esse levantamento foi feito através de estudos relacionados a ferramentas cooperativas [9] [11] [6] e engenharia de requisitos distribuída [12].

Aspectos de suporte a grupos costumam ser utilizados na literatura como forma de especificar as funcionalidades das ferramentas cooperativas em geral [13]. Por isso, os requisitos identificados foram mapeados para *features* (F1 a F13), as quais foram agrupadas de acordo com estes aspectos [13].

➢ **Comunicação – conectividade e ligação:** O primeiro obstáculo à cooperação é vencer o isolamento e a distância entre cada membro de uma equipe de trabalho, ou seja, estabelecer comunicação e a conectividade entre as partes [13].

F1 – Manutenção de requisitos através de interface *web*: Deve ser possível a manutenção de requisitos através da *web,* para facilitar o uso pela equipe distribuída. Além disso, a visualização através da *web permite* resolver problemas de interoperabilidade, bem como a validação por clientes remotos.

F2 – Autoria Cooperativa: Deve possibilitar o acesso de múltiplos usuários, na edição (síncrona ou assíncrona) de requisitos, identificando através de um mecanismo adequado os usuários que realizaram modificações.

F3 – Troca de Mensagens: Deve ser possível comunicar com os demais participantes, através de fóruns e mensagens instantâneas, por exemplo. Essa funcionalidade também deve estar presente de forma não vinculada a requisitos, pois nas fases iniciais os requisitos não foram definidos.

F4 – Registro de comentários: Suporte a inserção de comentários, dúvidas, e anotações vinculadas a um determinado requisito.

➢ **Coordenação – acompanhamento e produção:** Esse conceito está relacionado ao acompanhamento de atividades. Especificar como a interação se dará, definir restrições e controlar a execução das tarefas são questões que precisam estar presentes para garantir a produtividade e o sucesso do grupo [13].

F5 – Suporte a execução do processo: A ferramenta deve possibilitar algum tipo de suporte à execução do processo, por exemplo, através de definição de listas de itens a fazer, registro de *templates*, registro e *follow-up* de reuniões.

F6 – Controle de Acesso: Deve permitir a criação de permissões para alteração/visualização de requisitos, de forma individual ou para um grupo ou perfil.
F7 – Baseline e controle de versões: deve ser possível criar *baselines* para controlar requisitos. Além disso, deve ser possível comparar diferentes versões de *baselines*.
F8 – Automação na geração de artefatos: Apesar dessa *feature* apresentar relação com a F5, a geração adequada dos artefatos é imprescindível em uma ferramenta de gerenciamento de requisitos e por isso é tratada como um *feature* diferente.

- **Memória de Grupo – registro e histórico de interações:** O suporte a memória de grupo compreende mecanismos que identifiquem as razões por detrás de decisões. Para isso, é necessário capturar as informações e organizá-las de maneira associativa, que englobe não só os produtos gerados (conhecimento formal), como também a experiência e o conhecimento para esta solução (conhecimento informal) [13].

F9 – Base de Conhecimento*:* A ferramenta deve possuir uma base de conhecimento sobre o projeto, onde estão disponíveis informações sobre o domínio do problema, auxiliando os desenvolvedores na definição e entendimento de requisitos.
F10 – Manutenção de *rationale:* A ferramenta deve apresentar um mecanismo para manutenção do *rationale* de requisitos, por exemplo, através da vinculação com arquivos e discussões de origem.
F11 – Histórico de alteração: Permitir registrar quem, porque, quando e como uma determinada alteração foi realizada ou apenas solicitada. Além disso, alguns desses registros devem ser automáticos.

- **Percepção – contexto e localização:** O conceito de percepção busca prover recursos para que todos tenham a noção do contexto de suas atividades dentro do contexto geral do processo, para compreender como o resultado gerado pelas atividades alheias podem interferir nas suas atividades [13].

F12 – Status do requisito: Consultar o progresso de um requisito (proposto, aceito, entre outros) através de um mecanismo adequado durante o ciclo de vida do projeto.
F13 – Pesquisas *ad hoc*: Consultar requisitos de acordo alguns critérios importantes, tais como: data, responsável, entre outros.

3.2 Quadro comparativo

As ferramentas analisadas estão presentes em uma lista abrangente de ferramentas para gerenciamento de requisitos, construída a partir de um *survey* realizado pelo *International Council On Systems Engineering* [14]. Foi acrescentado a esta lista, ferramentas *open source* que já haviam disponibilizado *releases* nos *sites* pesquisados (*sourceforge* e *tigris*). O protótipo desenvolvido nesse trabalho (Codipse-Req) também foi adicionado.

As ferramentas foram classificadas em: (C) – Comercial, (F) – *Free,* e (O) – *Open Source*. Uma ferramenta é considerada *free* se for disponibilizada por uma licença que permite a sua utilização de forma gratuita, mas não necessariamente disponibiliza seu código fonte. Uma ferramenta *open source,* é disponibilizada sob uma licença que torna disponível seu código fonte, entretanto não é necessariamente gratuita. As ferramentas *open source* presentes nessa comparação, são também *free*. Em relação à presença de determinada *feature*, será utilizada a seguinte legenda: (✓) – Quando a funcionalidade estiver presente, (×) – Quando a funcionalidade não estiver presente e (⦸) – Quando a funcionalidade estiver presente parcialmente.

Tabela 1 Comparação de Ferramentas de Gerenciamento de Requisitos

			Comunicação				Coordenação				Mém. Grupo			Percepção	
No.	Ferramenta	Ti	F1	F2	F3	F4	F5	F6	F7	F8	F9	F10	F11	F12	F13
1	Accept Planner	C	✓	✓	✓	×	✓	✓	✓	✓	✓	✓	✓	✓	✓
2	Analyst Pro	C	×	✓	×	×	⃠	✓	⃠	✓	×	✓	⃠	✓	✓
3	CaliberRM	C	✓	✓	✓	✓	×	✓	✓	✓	×	×	✓	✓	✓
4	CARE 3.2	C	⃠	✓	×	✓	×	✓	⃠	⃠	×	⃠	✓	✓	✓
5	Catalyze	C	⃠	✓	×	✓	×	✓	✓	✓	×	⃠	✓	✓	✓
6	CORE 5.1	C	⃠	✓	×	✓	×	✓	⃠	✓	×	⃠	✓	✓	✓
7	Cradle 5.2	C	×	✓	×	✓	×	×	⃠	✓	×	⃠	✓	✓	×
8	Doors	C	✓	✓	×	✓	⃠	✓	✓	✓	×	⃠	✓	✓	✓
9	DRES	O	✓	✓	×	✓	×	×	×	×	×	×	⃠	✓	×
10	Envision VIP	C	×	✓	×	✓	✓	✓	×	✓	×	×	✓	✓	✓
11	GatherSpace	F	✓	×	×	×	×	×	×	×	×	×	⃠	×	×
12	Rational RequisitePro	C	⃠	✓	⃠	✓	×	⃠	✓	⃠	×	⃠	✓	✓	✓
13	IRqA 3.0	C	✓	✓	✓	✓	×	✓	✓	✓	×	✓	×	✓	✓
14	Jeremia	O	×	✓	×	✓	×	×	×	×	×	×	✓	×	×
15	Kollabnet Editor	C	×	✓	×	×	×	⃠	⃠	⃠	⃠	⃠	✓	⃠	×
16	PACE	C	✓	✓	✓	✓	⃠	✓	⃠	✓	×	⃠	✓	✓	✓
17	RaQuest 2.1	C	×	✓	×	✓	×	✓	✓	×	⃠	×	✓	✓	✓
18	RDT 3.0.2	C	×	✓	×	×	×	✓	✓	✓	×	×	✓	✓	×
19	RMTrak	C	×	×	×	×	×	⃠	⃠	✓	×	×	✓	✓	✓
20	SoftREQ	F	✓	×	×	×	×	×	⃠	⃠	×	×	×	✓	✓
21	SpeeDEV Rel 4.0	C	✓	✓	✓	✓	⃠	✓	✓	✓	×	⃠	✓	✓	✓
22	TrueReq Product Desktop	C	⃠	✓	⃠	✓	⃠	✓	⃠	✓	×	⃠	✓	✓	✓
23	XTie-RT	C	×	✓	×	×	×	×	×	×	×	×	✓	✓	✓
24	Codipse-Req	O	✓	✓	✓	×	✓	✓	×	✓	✓	✓	×	✓	✓

Apesar do processo de avaliação ter sido bastante detalhado, ele foi baseado principalmente em documentos disponíveis nos sites das ferramentas. Uma análise mais detalhada, utilizando versões de avaliação deve ser realizada para validar as informações.

Pode-se perceber que a maioria das ferramentas estudadas se preocupa com automação, e não fornecem a mesma importância em comunicação e colaboração, o que dificulta sua adoção por equipes distribuídas.

Outra constatação interessante é que não existe atualmente uma ferramenta de gerenciamento de requisitos *free* ou *open source* que possua as funcionalidades necessárias para o gerenciamento de requisitos em si (com exceção do protótipo desenvolvido neste trabalho, todas não permitem nem ao menos a exportação dos dados cadastrados).

4 Processo para Engenharia de Requisitos Distribuída

Esse processo foi definido com base em dois outros processos existentes: o primeiro descreve um processo para *web* baseado no RUP [15] e o segundo descreve um processo de engenharia de requisitos para desenvolvimento distribuído [1]. Apesar do trabalho de [1] também apresentar um processo para Engenharia de Requisitos Distribuída, ele não está ligado a utilização de tecnologias de colaboração, ou seja, apesar de considerar a importância da utilização, não explica como esta deve ser dada. Além disso, houve a preocupação em seguir o processo genérico descrito em [7].

Nessa proposta, os participantes estão totalmente distribuídos conforme mostrado na figura 1 e usam um ambiente adequado para trabalhar cooperativamente, que satisfaça as características exigidas pelo processo.

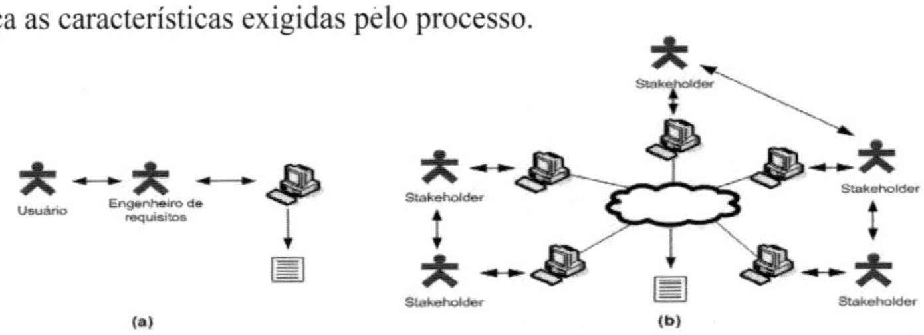

Fig. 1. a) um processo mediado por um desenvolvedor (b) um processo totalmente cooperativo, adaptado de [16]

4.3 Visão geral do processo

O processo de engenharia de requisitos proposto considera a interação com três bases: (1) base de conhecimentos formais contendo informações sobre o processo em execução, clientes e usuários, (2) base de conhecimentos informais contendo informações e dicas sobre a execução do processo e informações sobre cultura, idioma e histórico de interações com os clientes e (3) base de informações de negócio que agrupa informações sobre o projeto atual, tais como documentos e artefatos gerados. Essas bases juntas auxiliam o fornecimento de informações contextuais.

O processo é considerado distribuído porque insere aspectos (em especial, a construção das bases citadas anteriormente) que permitem a sua execução de forma colaborativa pela equipe distribuída. Dessa forma, a distribuição não está no processo em si, mas em como ele é executado.

4.4 Fases do processo

É importante ressaltar que embora exista uma distinção clara entre as fases, algumas delas comumente ocorrem em paralelo [7].

(a) Planejar atividades: Nesta fase ocorrem os planejamentos de como será a comunicação e gerência de requisitos durante a execução do projeto. Utilizando a base de conhecimentos formais e informais de projetos passados, é possível decidir quais as formas de interação mais adequadas às características do cliente. Os artefatos esperados são o plano de comunicação e o plano de gerência de requisitos.

(b) Organizar conhecimento: Durante essa fase, todo o conhecimento obtido em pesquisas e interações e armazenado nas bases de conhecimento formal e informal deve ser refinado para que apenas o que estiver relacionado com o projeto seja mantido. Dessa forma, deve-se construir uma base de informações de negócio, que deve ser disponibilizada e atualizada por todos os stakeholders durante o projeto. Nessa fase também deve ser construída a primeira versão do documento de visão do sistema, onde objetivos gerais e restrições podem ser identificados.
(c) Elicitar requisitos: O objetivo dessa fase é definir os requisitos do sistema, através dos *stakeholders* envolvidos. Através da base de conhecimento informal é possível ver quais técnicas de elicitação foram mais bem sucedidas em experiências passadas, além de outras informações úteis. Através da base de informações de negócio é possível visualizar todas as informações coletadas sobre o projeto. Os artefatos esperados são atas de reuniões (registradas como *logs* das interações realizadas), documento de visão atualizado, modelo de casos de uso e glossário.
(d) Analisar e Negociar Requisitos: Assim que os requisitos forem elicitados e antes dos mesmos serem documentados, é necessário verificar se estes foram especificados corretamente. A análise de requisitos tem por objetivo avaliar os requisitos identificados, podendo fornecer mais informações sobre estes ou descobrir conflitos. Se conflitos surgirem, então a atividade de resolução de conflitos deve tentar resolvê-los e formalizar um compromisso no qual todos os envolvidos estejam de acordo. As alterações em requisitos devem ser documentadas para o entendimento do *rationale.*
(e) Documentar Requisitos: Durante essa fase os requisitos são documentados de forma adequada e são disponibilizados para clientes e desenvolvedores através da base de informações de negócio. Os artefatos esperados nessa fase são o documento de requisitos e especificações de casos de uso.
(f) Validar requisitos: O objetivo dessa fase é checar se os documentos estão em conformidade com padrões e se estão especificados corretamente (quanto a conflitos, consistência, completude). A validação pode ser realizada através de reunião síncrona entre todos os participantes ou de uma revisão assíncrona dos clientes e usuários sobre os artefatos, onde estes devem deixar seus comentários. A atividade de pré-revisão dos artefatos deve ser realizada antes das reuniões para verificar se os mesmos possuem erros de ortografia e se estão em conformidade com padrões especificados [7] e anotações devem ser realizadas. Se uma reunião síncrona for realizada para revisão, um relatório contendo as atividades a serem realizadas deve ser gerado.
(g) Gerenciar requisitos: Depois de especificados, os requisitos devem ser controlados quanto à alteração, pois estes servirão de base na construção do sistema. A atividade de gerenciar dependências deve ser realizada durante todo o ciclo de vida do processo atualizando a matriz de rastreamento, pois a partir dela é possível rastrear os requisitos com outros requisitos e artefatos relacionados, sendo muito importante para analisar impacto de alterações futuras. Além disso, se uma proposta de alteração tiver sido submetida, é necessário analisar os impactos que serão causados pela alteração e estas devem ser comunicadas e aprovadas antes de serem realizadas.
(h) Gerenciar informações e conhecimento: O objetivo dessa fase é assegurar que as bases de informações de negócio e as de conhecimento formal e informal sejam regularmente atualizadas. Dessa forma, novas informações são submetidas e incorporadas a sua respectiva base e se necessário atualizações na matriz de rastreamento devem ser realizadas.

5 Modelo de Rastreamento de Requisitos

Essa seção apresenta um modelo para auxiliar a engenharia de requisitos distribuída. De forma geral, esse modelo visa orientar o desenvolvimento de aplicações colaborativas para engenharia de requisitos distribuída.

Toranzo [17] identificou associações para auxiliar na construção de modelos de rastreamento. A associação satisfação <sat> deve ser usada para expressar que algo deverá ser realizado nas instâncias da classe destino para satisfazer as instâncias da classe origem a qual ela está associada. A associação recurso <rec> indica que a instância da classe origem tem uma dependência de um recurso em relação à classe destino. A associação responsável <resp> visa capturar a participação, responsabilidade e ação das pessoas sobre artefatos ou elementos do processo. Essas associações foram utilizadas na construção do modelo mostrado na figura 2.

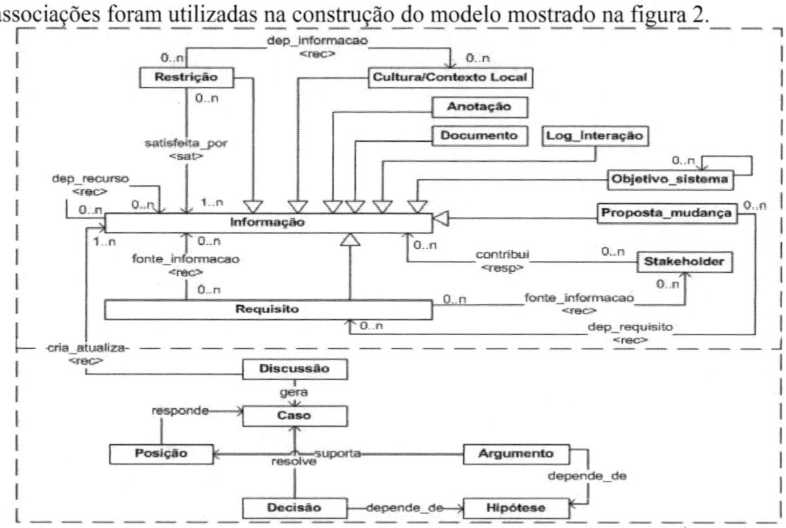

Figura 2 – Modelo intermediário de rastreamento de requisitos

A parte inferior da figura 2 apresenta um modelo proposto em [18] e baseado no *framework* IBIS (*Issue-Based Information Systems*). A parte superior apresenta as informações que devem ser rastreadas. A classe principal é "Informação" e é utilizada pra representar requisitos, restrições, informações sobre cultura e contextos das equipes em cada localidade, qualquer tipo de anotação, interações, documentos, objetivos do sistema e propostas de mudanças em requisitos.

A associação "dep_recurso" (em informação) indica que uma informação é originada a partir de uma ou várias informações. Restrições podem estar associadas a determinadas localidades e são expressas pela associação "dep_informacao". Estas restrições devem ser satisfeitas em informações futuras (um documento, por exemplo). A participação de *stakeholders* no fornecimento de informações está representada por 'contribui' e como recursos na geração de requisitos, como mostrado em 'fonte_informacao'. Por fim, requisitos são originados de diferentes fontes de informação e propostas de mudança estão relacionadas a um ou vários requisitos.

6 A ferramenta CODIPSE-Req

A ferramenta foi construída como parte do projeto CODIPSE (*COoperative and DIstributed Process Suport Environment)* (disponível em http://codipse.tigris.org). O projeto CODIPSE é um projeto de software livre cujo objetivo é a idealização de um ADS (Ambiente de Desenvolvimento de Software) que forneça suporte ao trabalho cooperativo em equipes distribuídas. Dentro do contexto do ambiente CODIPSE, a ferramenta Codipse-Req está relacionado à fase de engenharia de requisitos, onde diferentes *stakeholders* podem se comunicar e colaborar.

Nessa primeira versão, a ferramenta foi desenvolvida como uma aplicação para o ambiente *eGroupware.* Através dela é possível realizar o gerenciamento de requisitos para vários projetos, apresentando funcionalidades para manter usuários, requisitos funcionais e não funcionais, casos de uso e glossário. Além disso, é possível a manutenção do *rationale,* relacionando requisitos entre si e entre casos de uso, fóruns, listas a fazer, entradas na agenda de eventos e com arquivos anexados. O status atual das *features* implementadas pode ser visto no quadro comparativo da seção 3.2.

6.5 Modelagem usando a notação i*

O *framework* i* [19] foi construído para facilitar a modelagem e compreensão dos ambientes organizacionais e seus sistemas de informação. É composto pelos modelos de dependência estratégica e razão estratégica. O modelo de dependência estratégica é usado para descrever as relações de dependência entre os vários atores. O modelo de razão estratégica é usado para descrever os interesses e anseios dos *stakeholders* e como eles devem ser atingidos pelo sistema [19].

Na figura 3 está representado o modelo de dependência estratégica. Neste modelo estão identificados os atores da aplicação, que são: Engenheiro de Requisitos, Gerente de Projetos, Cliente, Administrador do sistema, Sistema para Colaboração, Sistema de Gerenciamento de Requisitos e qualquer outro *Stakeholder* não citado.

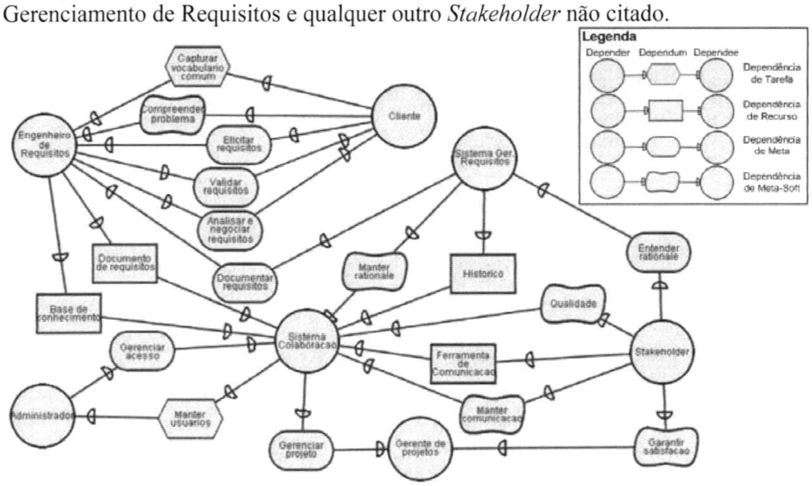

Fig. 3. Modelo de Dependência Estratégica

O Cliente precisa que o Engenheiro de Requisitos capture o vocabulário comum, compreenda o problema e realize a elicitação dos requisitos. Por outro lado, o Engenheiro de Requisitos depende do cliente para validar os requisitos identificados e durante a análise e negociação de requisitos.

O Engenheiro de Requisitos realiza ainda a tarefa de documentar requisitos e elabora o documento de requisitos que deve ser mantido pelo sistema de colaboração. Durante a realização de suas atividades, ele utiliza as informações disponíveis na base de conhecimento disponibilizada pelo sistema de colaboração.

O administrador do sistema depende do sistema de colaboração para gerenciar o acesso dos grupos de usuários e usuários e manter os dados cadastrais destes.

O *rationale* dos requisitos é mantido através da integração com o sistema de colaboração, através de diversos dados históricos.

Qualquer *stakeholder* precisa do sistema de gerenciamento de requisitos para entender o *rationale* do que já foi identificado. A qualidade do processo depende em parte da boa comunicação entre os envolvidos e de ferramentas de comunicação eficientes, além de um gerenciamento eficaz.

6.6 Visão Geral da Arquitetura

A arquitetura da solução apresenta os aplicativos do *egroupware* através de componentes individuais, apresentada em visão macro na figura 4. Os principais componentes relacionados a aplicação desenvolvida (requisitos) são fórum, agenda, *infolog* (controle de itens a fazer) e o componente phpgwapi, que contem funcoes utilitárias a todo o *eGroupware.*

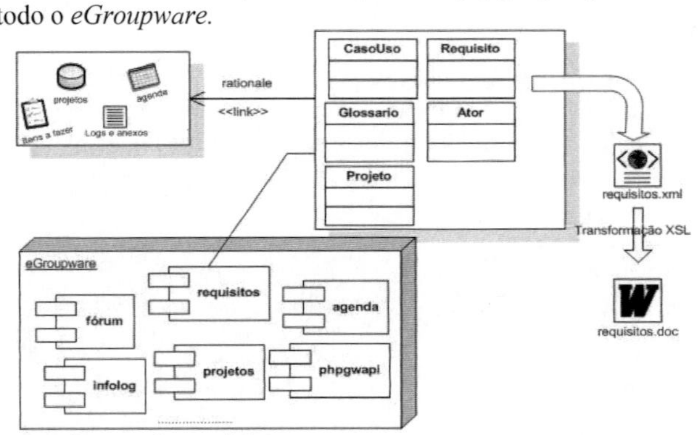

Fig. 4. Macro arquitetura do protótipo

A aplicação desenvolvida agrupa classes relacionadas a glossário, casos de uso, requisitos funcionais e não-funcionais, atores e o projeto em si. Além disso, permite manter links a nível de projeto, requisitos e caso de uso com outras aplicações da plataforma (como projetos, agenda, itens a fazer) e permite anexar arquivos.

Através do módulo de exportação, é possível a exportação para o padrão XML do Microsoft Word, através da representação das informações em XML e aplicação de uma transformação XSL, como demonstrado na figura.

7 Estudo de Caso

O objetivo deste estudo de caso é coletar todas as interações de um projeto *open source* maduro. O desenvolvimento no estilo *open source* é baseado em colaboração e na maioria dos casos as equipes estão distribuídas, formando o cenário ideal. Para demonstrar a aplicabilidade e benefícios, todas as interações disponíveis foram inseridas no protótipo e um documento de requisitos foi construído para o projeto com base nessas inúmeras informações espalhadas.

O projeto escolhido foi o XPlanner, que além de ser um projeto maduro, trata sobre ambientes de desenvolvimento de software, que é um dos temas de interesse desse trabalho. O XPlanner tem como objetivo fornecer suporte a equipes que utilizam processos ágeis, tais como XP (eXtremme Programming) e Scrum. Para isso, disponibiliza mecanismos que possibilitam que as premissas desses processos possam ser realizadas através do sistema, facilitando a distribuição entre os participantes.

O processo de Engenharia de Requisitos é essencialmente colaborativo e depende da qualidade das interações realizadas, além da experiência dos envolvidos. Se essas interações forem realizadas de forma distribuída, o ambiente deve apresentar diferentes formas de comunicação. As aplicações do eGroupware utilizadas foram: fórum, agenda de eventos, ferramenta de solicitação de mudança e controle de tarefas.

Participam do desenvolvimento do projeto XPlanner cerca de cinco desenvolvedores (cadastrados no *sourceforge*). Foram atribuídos papéis a cada um deles, após análise dos tipos e intensidade de contribuições. Essa atribuição era necessária para facilitar o entendimento. Raquel (engenheiro de requisitos) e Mateus (engenheiro de processo) foram acrescentados devido à inexistência de gerenciamento de requisitos e execução de processo (de forma explícita) anteriormente. Dessa forma, os participantes do processo foram os seguintes: Gerente de Projetos (Jacques Morel), Engenheiro de Requisitos (Raquel), Engenheiro de Processo (Mateus), Desenvolvedor (Matteo Regazzi, Ole Sandum, Kelly Mower, Stephen Bate) e Cliente (Comunidade de Software Livre).

Através da aplicação para gestão de conhecimento do eGroupware, o Engenheiro de Processo criou três pastas (Conhecimento Formal, Conhecimento Informal e Informações de Negocio) para disseminar as informações necessárias a todos.

Documentos referentes ao domínio do problema, como artigos sobre eXtreme Programming, e questionamentos sobre metodologias de desenvolvimento de software eram constantemente inseridos na pasta de conhecimento informal. Um documento descrevendo o processo com mais detalhes e os *templates* disponíveis para utilização foram adicionados na pasta de conhecimento formal.

O gerente de projetos então construiu o "Plano de Gerência de Requisitos" e "Plano de Comunicação" (fase a) e disponibilizou na pasta de Informações de Negócio. Ficou decidido que a comunicação seria realizada através do ambiente eGroupware, e-mails individuais e ferramenta para mensagem instantânea MSN Messenger. Através do eGroupware, a comunidade de software livre (cliente) poderia sugerir novas funcionalidades e participar das discussões correntes. No entanto, apenas os participantes do projeto teriam poder para decidir o que seria incluído. Ficou estabelecido que os requisitos identificados fossem mantidos através da ferramenta para gerenciamento de requisitos Codipse-Req.

Utilizando as informações disponíveis na pasta de conhecimento formal e informal, reuniões realizadas e discussões em fóruns relacionados, o engenheiro de requisitos descreveu a visão geral e restrições do sistema e identificou os usuários na ferramenta Codipse-Req, criando *links* para as informações que a originaram. Após isso, disponibilizou esse documento de visão na pasta de informações de negócio (fase b).

Durante a elicitação de requisitos (fase c), foram marcadas reuniões na agenda de eventos. Após a realização das mesmas, o *log* da ferramenta MSN Messenger era anexado e eram inseridos registros sobre o que foi decidido ou discutido. O Engenheiro de Requisitos então, cadastrou os rascunhos iniciais dos requisitos e termos utilizados na ferramenta Codipse-Req. As atas de reuniões correspondem as anotações feitas na agenda de eventos e ao *log*.

Em paralelo a elicitação de requisitos, ocorreu a Analise e Negociação de Requisitos (fase d). Nessa fase, ocorreram reuniões para discutir duvidas e inconsistências. Para manter o *rationale,* foram mantidos os *links* dos requisitos iniciais com qualquer interação que tenha levado a sua alteração.

A documentação de requisitos (fase e) vinha ocorrendo desde a elicitação, com a versão rascunho dos requisitos. No entanto, durante a documentação os requisitos se transformaram em versões finais, prontos para serem implementados após validação.

A validação (fase f) ocorreu através de reuniões síncronas (onde novamente o *log* das discussões deve ser mantido), ou através do aceite dos responsáveis (nesse projeto, o gerente de projeto tem a palavra final, pois não há um cliente formal).

Para gerenciamento de requisitos (g), foi utilizado o protótipo desenvolvido. A responsável pela engenharia de requisitos (Raquel), cadastrou as informações e gerou os artefatos esperados. A tela 5 demonstra os requisitos cadastrados.

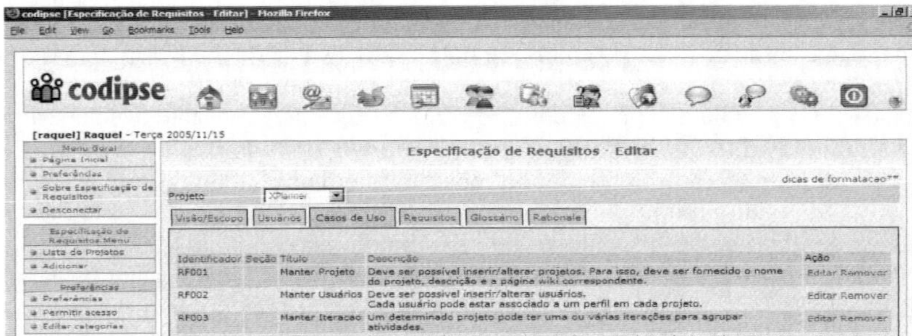

Fig. 5. Tela Principal do Protótipo

Por fim, novos conhecimentos e informações (fase h) são constantemente inseridos e alimentam o projeto em si, que depende dessas informações e interações. De forma conceitual estão controladas na ferramenta de gestão de conhecimento, mas também estão espalhadas em fóruns e *logs*. Para permitir o *rationale* de requisitos, foram criados *links* para as informações de origem. Um exemplo de como esses *links* eram mantidos é mostrado na figura 6.

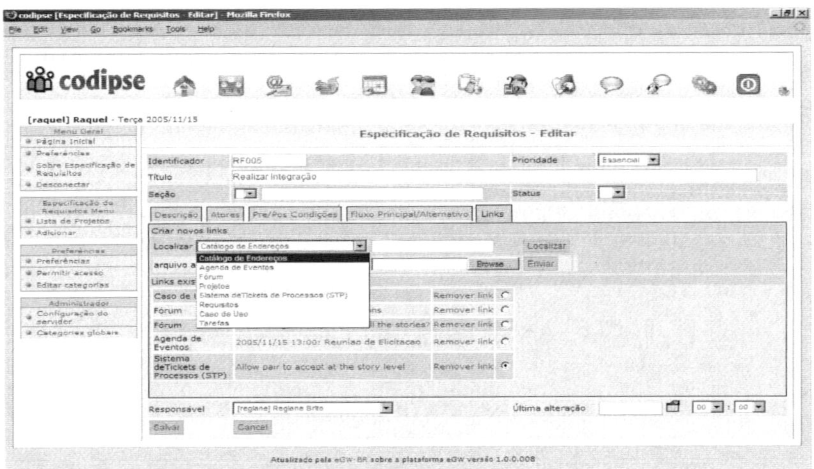

Fig. 6. Tela de edição de caso de uso

8 Considerações Finais e Trabalhos Futuros

A utilização de tecnologias de colaboração tem sido apontada como um dos principais fatores para auxiliar a engenharia de requisitos distribuída [20] [4] [8]. Pode-se perceber que o processo, embora não seja tão rigoroso, possui a maioria das características definidas em processos como RUP. A diferença esta no fato de que as pessoas não estão fisicamente próximas e por isso, devem usar soluções alternativas para comunicação e isto deve ser tratado no processo.

A *feature analysis* das ferramentas de gerenciamento de requisitos constatou que a maioria das ferramentas de gerenciamento de requisitos não fornece suporte adequado às equipes distribuídas e identificou a inexistência de ferramentas *open source* ou *free* que forneça a automação necessária para um gerenciamento eficiente.

Esse artigo apresentou uma proposta para melhorar o entendimento dos *stakeholders* durante a etapa de requisitos. Para isso, foi definido um processo colaborativo de software para engenharia de requisitos distribuída, o qual assume algumas interações entre os envolvidos. Ao analisar essas interações é possível prover informações úteis para os participantes iniciantes e antigos. Além disso, um modelo de rastreamento e um protótipo de gerenciamento de requisitos foram definidos e validados.

No entanto, ainda é necessária a validação do trabalho em um número maior de estudos de caso e/ou realização de experimentos controlados, não realizados devido à falta de tempo hábil.

Como trabalhos futuros, estão previstas melhorias no protótipo desenvolvido através da integração com a área de Inteligência Artificial. Com isso será possível, por exemplo, auxiliar o engenheiro de requisitos a extrair requisitos dos *logs* de reuniões realizadas e gerar automaticamente o *log* dessas reuniões.

9 Referências

1. Lopes, L. T. "Um Modelo de Processo de Engenharia de Requisitos para Ambientes de Desenvolvimento Distribuído de Software". Pontifícia Universidade Católica do Rio Grande do Sul, Faculdade de Informática, 2004
2. Nuseibeh, B. e Easterbrook, S. "Requirements Engineering: A Roadmap". The Future of Software Engineering, Anthony Finkelstein, pp.37-46, ACM Press, 2000
3. Zowghi, D. "Does Global Software Development need a Different Requirements Engineering Process?". Proceedings of International Workshop on Global Software Development, 2002
4. Damian, D. e Zowghi, D. "Requirements Engineering challenges in multi-site software development organizations". Requirements Engineering Journal, 8, pp.149-160, 2003
5. Gotel, O. e Finkelstein, A. "Contribution Structures". Technical Report, Department of Computing, Imperial College of Science, Technology and Medicine, London, U.K., 1994
6. Herlea, D. E. e Greenberg, S. "Using a Groupware Space for Distributed Requirements Engineering". Proceedings of WET ICE,California, USA, 1998
7. Kotonya, G. e Sommerville, I. "Requirements Engineering: Processes and Techniques". John Wiley & Sons Ltda, ISBN: 0-471-97208-8, 1998
8. Prikladnicki, R., Audy, J. L. N., e Evaristo, R. "Requirements Management in Global Software Development: Preliminary Findings from a Case Study in a SW-CMM context". International Workshop on Global Software Development, 2003
9. Togneri, D., Falbo, R., e Menezes, C. "Supporting Cooperative Requirements Engineering with an Automated Tool". Anais do V WER, 2002
10. Kitchenham, B. A. "Evaluating Software Engineering Methods and Tool. Part 1: The Evaluation Context and Evaluation Methos". ACM Sigsoft.Software Engineering Notes vol 21 no 1, 1996
11. Machado, M., Santos, F., Werner, C. M. L. et al. "Uma infra-estrutura de apoio à aquisição cooperativa de conhecimento em engenharia de domínio". Anais do XIII Simpósio Brasileiro de Engenharia de Software, 1999
12. Damian, D. e Zowghi, D. "The impact of stakeholders' geographical distribution on managing requirements in a multi-site organization". Proceeding of the IEEE Joint International Conference on Requirements Engineering, 2002
13. Araújo, R. M. "Ampliando a cultura de processos de software – um enfoque baseado em groupware e workflow". Tese de doutorado. UFRJ - COOPE, 2000
14. INCOSE Tools Database Working Group (DBWG). "Requirements Management Tools Survey". http://www.paper-review.com/tools/rms/read.php, 2005
15. Didier, A. C. V. B. "WRE-Process: Um Processo de Engenharia de Requisitos Baseado no RUP". Dissertação de Mestrado da Universidade Federal de Pernambuco, Centro de Informática, 2003
16. Ambriola, V. e Gervasi, V. "The Case for Cooperative Requirement Writing". ECOOP Workshop on Automating the OO Software Development Process, 1998
17. Toranzo, M., Castro, J. F. B., e Mello, E. "Uma Proposta para Melhorar o Rastreamento de Requisitos". Anais do V Workshop em Engenharia de Requisitos, 2002
18. Ramesh, B. e Jarke, M. "Towards Reference Models for Requirements Traceability". Technical Report, Georgia State University, 1999
19. Yu, E. "Towards Modelling and Reasoning Support for Early Phase Requirements Engineering". 3rd IEEE International Symposium on Requirements Engineering, Washington D.C., USA., 1997
20. Lloyd, W. J., Rosson, M. B., e Arthur, J. D. "Effectiveness of Elicitation Techniques in Distributed Requirements Engineering". ICRE Proceedings, 2002

Formalizando el Rol del Analista de Excepciones en un Proceso de Desarrollo de Software basado en Herramientas CASE

Catherine Bidart F. y Jorge Jiménez C.

Área de Investigación y Desarrollo, Empresas TUXPAN, Chile
cbidart@tuxpan.com, jota@tuxpan.com

Abstract

Mientras más tarde se detecte un error en un sistema, más caro resulta su corrección. De acuerdo a la afirmación anterior, es durante el análisis de requerimientos donde se debe colocar el mayor esfuerzo en la detección temprana de defectos, los que más adelante puedan resultar en fallas de las aplicaciones. Por otra parte, muchos de los errores que provocan fallas en los sistemas se producen por casos de negocio no manejados, específicamente por que no se consideraron las excepciones en los procesos del negocio que se están automatizando. En este trabajo se presenta un método basado en la inclusión de un nuevo rol para un proceso de desarrollo de software iterativo e incremental, el que permite detectar tempranamente posibles fallas de las aplicaciones, a causa de las excepciones de negocio no manejadas. Se propone además, algunas técnicas que automatizan el trabajo de este nuevo participante en el equipo de desarrollo y que incluso pueden aportar en la generación automática de código y documentación a partir de los resultados de su trabajo.

Introducción

Este trabajo se realiza en el contexto de una empresa de desarrollo de software, que ha alcanzado el nivel 3 del modelo de madurez CMMI, gracias a la normalización y ejecución exitosa de una metodología de desarrollo de sistemas de información, basada en herramientas CASE construidas a medida para la fábrica. La metodología que acá se presenta como base para la inclusión del nuevo rol propuesto se basa en iteraciones sobre artefactos UML2 que incrementalmente producen nuevos artefactos y generan el código final de las aplicaciones.

Identificación del Problema

El desarrollo de un sistema de información administrativo se basa en la automatización de un proceso de negocio, el que puede ser existente (manual o antes automatizado con otra tecnología) o provenir desde un rediseño. En cualquier caso, el método de desarrollo que se usa como base en este trabajo, asume que el proceso de negocio que se automatiza está ya definido, y que la primera etapa es un análisis de requerimientos sobre este proceso de negocio que determina los casos de uso que se implementarán en el sistema.

Para el desarrollo de sistemas medianos y grandes, el trabajo inicial se divide en equipos de trabajo, cada uno liderado por un analista de requerimientos que se encarga de algunos procesos relacionados del negocio. El trabajo del analista de requerimientos, es seguir las diferentes rutas del proceso de negocio e ir proponiendo casos de uso que automaticen o apoyen las decisiones en las actividades que en él se definan. Ocurre normalmente que los procesos de negocios son modelados por especialistas en el negocio o profesionales de áreas de administración y no por especialistas en sistemas de información. Debido a esto, es muy probable que un modelo de procesos de negocio no incluya todas las posibilidades o casos que en la práctica se deben resolver en forma manual, y que muchas veces ni siquiera están documentados. El analista de requerimientos no debiera suponer que el modelo de negocios es el negocio en sí y menos que contiene todas las posibilidades y decisiones que en la operación del negocio podrían llegar a ocurrir. Desgraciadamente la cantidad de trabajo del analista, los plazos y los costos del proyecto suelen terminar con un análisis de requerimientos sobre los modelos y no se contrastan o validan con el detalle necesario contra el negocio real.

El problema recién mencionado se puede resumir como: El analista de requerimientos basa la identificación de los casos de uso en un modelo de procesos de negocio que no incluye todas las posibilidades (bifurcaciones) y decisiones de la operación que excepcionalmente ocurren en el negocio real.

La detección de una excepción de negocio que más tarde se presenta como un error o falla del sistema en producción o en etapas tardías del desarrollo, presenta muchas ventajas respecto al costo y la calidad de los sistemas entregados. Entre estas ventajas destacan:

- Algunos estudios han encontrado que el esfuerzo en retrabajo producto de la corrección de errores, es alrededor del 50% del costo total de un proyecto [JONES-86]
- Por otra parte, hasta un 60% de los errores pueden provenir por fallas en el análisis de requerimientos [GILB-88] (antes de comenzar el diseño).
- El costo producto del retrabajo para corregir un error una vez que el sistema está en producción es entre 50 y 200 veces mayor que el haberlo resuelto durante la etapa de requerimientos [BOPA-88]

El trabajo normal del analista de requerimientos es seguir los flujos (físicos o de lógica de control) del modelo de procesos de negocio e identificar los casos de uso que mejor automatizan cada actividad dentro de él. Esto corresponde a un pensamiento de tipo convergente respecto a los modelos estudiados y a los expertos entrevistados, el que puede representarse con la pregunta "¿qué pasa si ...?". Los conceptos de pensamiento convergente y divergente se usan acá de acuerdo a lo planteado por Thomas Kuhn en [KUHN-77]. Usar el pensamiento convergente como base para realizar un análisis de requerimientos es quizá la forma más rápida y productiva en términos de cantidad y profundidad de los casos de uso identificados por unidad de tiempo; sin embargo, implícitamente se están dejando fuera muchas posibilidades de ejecución del proceso y no se consideran casos de uso o cursos alternativos de ejecución de los casos de uso para las excepciones del negocio.

Se propone acá incluir como parte del proceso formal de análisis de requerimientos el pensamiento divergente durante la identificación y profundización de los casos de uso. Este pensamiento divergente se puede representar por la pregunta "¿qué pasa si no ...?".

Se reconoce que para un analista trabajando mediante pensamiento convergente puede ser muy complicado usar al mismo tiempo el pensamiento divergente para completar sus casos de uso, incluso la práctica ha demostrado que los perfiles de analistas varían entre aquellos que deben usar un tipo de pensamiento y el otro. Por ello, en la metodología de desarrollo que se propone en este trabajo, se separan ambos roles y se propone que sean ejecutados por diferentes participantes del equipo de desarrollo.

Manifestación del Problema

Las metodologías de desarrollo de software modernas se basan en iteraciones sobre diferentes elementos que se modelan desde los negocios que se estudian, para producir otros elementos que pueden corresponder a otros artefactos de modelos, documentación o código de las aplicaciones.

Los principios básicos de la metodología que será referenciada son:

- Metodología Iterativa: Se propone el uso de una metodología que, luego de una primera etapa de análisis de requerimientos y definiciones iniciales, comience a iterar sobre elementos funcionales (Casos de Uso de UML) que sirven como base para el análisis, el diseño, la construcción y las pruebas. Al subproceso completo de construcción de un caso de uso se le llama Ciclo de Desarrollo.
- Metodología Incremental: A medida que los ciclos de desarrollo se van ejecutando, los productos y subproductos van completando en forma incremental. Cada ciclo de desarrollo aporta en la completitud de los diferentes Modelos y productos finales.

Esta metodología, comienza con iteraciones sobre procesos de negocio para obtener casos de uso que representen las funcionalidades requeridas para el desarrollo de un nuevo sistema. A esta etapa se le denomina análisis de requerimientos.

Las entradas para poder completar la etapa de análisis de requerimientos son modelos de procesos de negocios, los que comúnmente se entregan en la forma de diagramas de actividades (UML2). Iterando sobre cada uno de los procesos que se automatiza y estudiándolos en profundidad, los analistas de requerimientos producen casos de uso de un nuevo sistema que automatizará los procesos estudiados.

Para ilustrar en forma más clara el problema, se propone el siguiente ejemplo: Una empresa comercial decide rediseñar y automatizar su proceso de órdenes de compras, de tal forma que las órdenes puedan ser colocadas directamente por los clientes vía Internet y la aprobación comercial (capacidad de crédito del cliente) y la operacional (disponibilidad de los artículos solicitados) se puedan realizar en paralelo, disminuyendo los tiempos de aprobación total de estas órdenes. El diagrama de procesos rediseñados entregado por la compañía podría ser el mostrado en la figura 1.

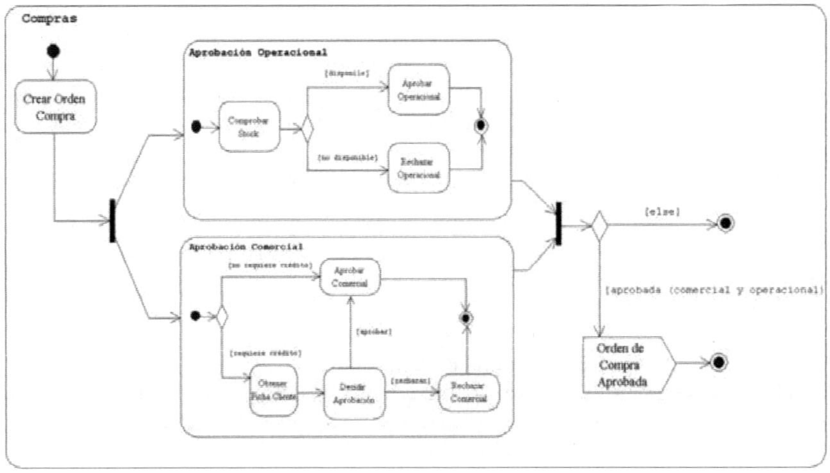

Fig. 1. Diagrama de Procesos de ejemplo

Si la orden de compra es aprobada comercial y operacionalmente, se emite una señal que es capturada por un orquestador para generar facturas, guías de despachos y los movimientos contables asociados a la transacción.

El proceso de análisis de requerimientos comienza con la identificación de los casos de uso que implementan el proceso descrito.

A partir de la información del proceso y de las entrevistas con los conocedores del negocio, el analista de requerimientos debe plantear una propuesta de solución en base a casos de uso. Para el ejemplo mencionado un posible diagrama de casos de uso que representa una automatización del proceso, sería el mostrado en la figura 2.

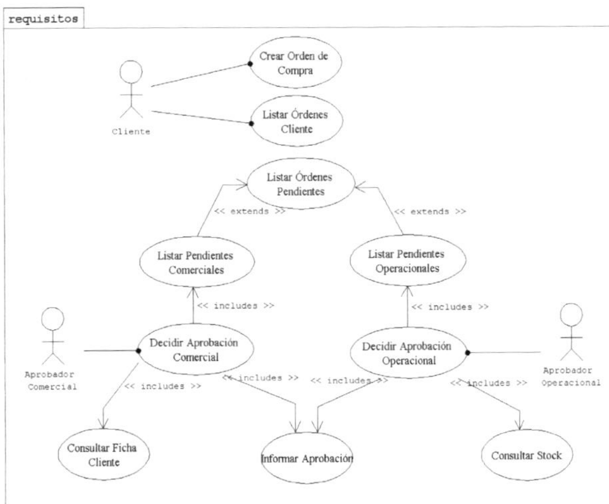

Fig. 2. Diagrama inicial de Casos de Uso de ejemplo

El diagrama de casos de uso, junto con sus descripciones y prototipos son mostrados a los clientes y finalmente aprobados.

Dependiendo de la metodología que se utilice, los casos de uso pueden contener diferente tipo de información. En el caso de la metodología base usada acá, las plantillas de casos de uso contienen las siguientes áreas de documentación.

1. Propósito
2. Descripción de eventos e interacción con el usuario.
3. Precondiciones y Postcondiciones (contrato)
4. Cursos Alternativos

El segundo punto de la documentación puede ser apoyado por un prototipo evolutivo, el que será tomado por el desarrollador y programará el comportamiento descrito en las interfaces de usuario. El tercer punto es usado por los desarrolladores para programar los servicios de lógica del negocio y de acceso a datos.

Al mismo tiempo que el analista de requerimientos especifica los casos de uso, él va identificando algunas clases del negocio (modelo conceptual). De acuerdo a la metodología usada como base en este trabajo, no se hace una diferencia entre modelo conceptual y de diseño en las clases del sistema, sino que es el mismo modelo el que evoluciona dependiendo de la etapa del proyecto.

Usando el patrón de diseño del Value Object o Transfer Object [SUN-05] el analista de requerimientos puede obtener una primera versión de las clases persistentes del sistema como se muestra en la figura 3.

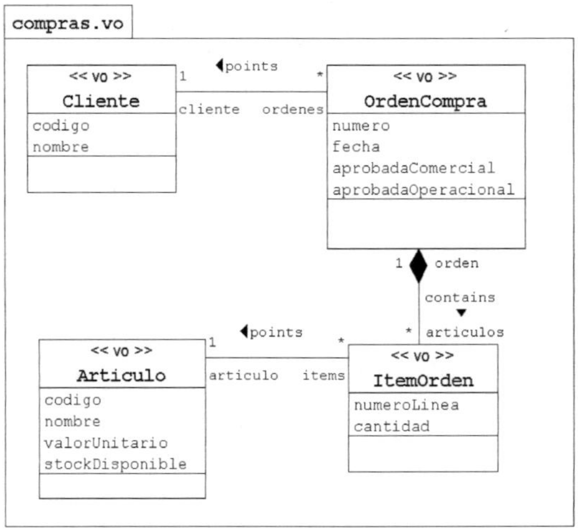

Fig. 3. Modelo de clases inicial.

De acuerdo al modelo de procesos que se presentó, los diagramas propuestos de casos de uso y de clases persistentes soportan su automatización mediante el desarrollo de un sistema de información que se ejecute en un servidor de aplicaciones, y disponible para los clientes a través de Internet.

Al iniciarse la puesta en marcha del sistema podrían aparecer algunos problemas que requieran de mantenciones y que son detectados la primera vez que ocurre algún caso no contemplado por el analista de requerimientos ni los encargados del rediseño del proceso.

Ejemplo de Excepción de negocio no detectada

Un cliente coloca una orden de compra para un artículo no disponible en stock. El usuario encargado de dar la aprobación operacional es informado por el sistema de la no disponibilidad de stock suficiente para ese artículo y decide rechazar la solicitud. El cliente consulta el estado de la orden de compra que colocó y aparece como pendiente, ya que ésta está aún esperando la aprobación comercial, a pesar que ya se conoce el resultado final de la aprobación (rechazado debido a que requiere ambas aprobaciones).

El funcionamiento correcto del sistema debiera ser que al producirse cualquier rechazo, ya sea operacional o comercial, la orden es automáticamente rechazada y no se requiere esperar por el otro tipo de aprobación.

Al detectarse esa falla (la responsabilidad de la falla; es decir si es del cliente o el desarrollador, se deja explícitamente fuera del contexto de este trabajo) se debe planificar una mantención al sistema. El cambio requerido es en los servicios que marcan la orden como rechazada comercial y operacionalmente. En estos servicios se debe agregar la lógica necesaria para que automáticamente invoquen al otro tipo de rechazo y se marque el responsable como automático.

Los cambios producto de la mantención involucran casos de uso, diagramas de clase, casos de pruebas funcionales y unitarios, documentación de sistema y usuarios, y código de la aplicación. Además de los esfuerzos requeridos para efectuar estos cambios, se debe considerar los tiempos necesarios para la ejecución de las pruebas del sistema, nueva instalación y posibles capacitaciones a los usuarios.

Claramente el costo de haber detectado la falla luego de haber puesto en producción el sistema es mayor a la detección temprana, mientras se realiza el análisis de requerimientos. El caso ideal es que se detecte y documente mientras se rediseña el proceso de negocio, sin embargo, los analistas de procesos comúnmente no tienen la visión del software que automatizará los procesos que modelan y pueden cometer estas omisiones que aparecen luego en la implantación de los sistemas.

Solución Propuesta

Se propone la creación de un rol responsable de detectar estas excepciones de negocio durante la etapa de análisis de requerimientos. A continuación, se detallan las tareas específicas que este rol debe ejecutar durante el proceso de desarrollo de software propuesto, se explica el aporte de cada una de estas tareas, y se propone una forma para aprovechar la información capturada por él para la generación automática de código usando un herramienta CASE.

Durante la confección de los casos de uso, el analista de excepciones es responsable de la documentación de algunas secciones del caso de uso. Específicamente:

- Precondiciones: Debe establecer para cada dato usado sus valores límite y las posibles relaciones que entre ellos deban satisfacerse.
- Postcondiciones: Debe verificar objetos o cambios de estado dependientes de los directamente referenciados en el caso de uso. Debe además especificar posibles dependencias temporales este estos objetos.
- Cursos Alternativos: Debe especificar claramente las respuestas del sistema en los casos de excepción, particularmente cuando algunas de las precondiciones no es satisfecha. Debe acordar durante la etapa de análisis de requerimientos los

mensajes de error que el usuario esperaría como respuesta a la insatisfacción de cada una de las precondiciones.

Una de las formas de apoyar el trabajo de los diferentes roles dentro de un proceso de desarrollo es el uso de checklists, las que corresponden a una serie de preguntas o ítems dentro una lista y que el responsable debe verificar para dar por completada su tarea. Este método, además de facilitar el trabajo del analista de excepciones, permite fácilmente agregar la experiencia de proyectos terminados al proceso de desarrollo, facilitando su evolución [SFIG-93].

El checklist propuesto para el analista de excepciones es el siguiente:

1. Para cada Caso de Uso liberado por el analista de requerimientos
   a. Para cada uno de los objetos (value objects) usados en el caso de uso
      i. Para cada uno de los atributos editados en el caso de uso
         - □ Existe precondición para valor mínimo
         - □ Existe precondición para valor máximo
         - □ Existen reglas internas del atributo: Dígito verificador, formato fechas
         - □ Existen cursos alternativos para valores fuera de rango. Escribir mensaje de error esperado.
         - □ Existen cursos alternativos para cada regla insatisfecha. Escribir mensaje de error esperado.
         - □ Existen dependencias entre atributos editados: Rangos de fechas, valores numéricos. Escribir mensaje esperado.
         - □ Existen reglas respecto a atributos de objetos relacionados: Rangos de fechas, valores numéricos. Escribir mensaje de error esperado.
      ii. Existen precondiciones respecto a objetos relacionados(existencia, no existencia o estado). Escribir mensaje de error esperado.
      iii. Existen postcondiciones para objetos relacionados. Especificarlas para los desarrolladores.
   b. Para cada parámetro de la operación editado en el caso de uso
      i. Existe precondición para valor mínimo
      ii. Existe precondición para valor máximo
      iii. Existen reglas internas del atributo: Dígito verificador, formato fechas
      iv. Existen cursos alternativos para valores fuera de rango. Escribir mensaje de error esperado.
      v. Existen cursos alternativos para cada regla insatisfecha. Escribir mensaje de error esperado.
      vi. Existen dependencias entre atributos y parámetros editados: Rangos de fechas, valores numéricos. Escribir mensaje esperado.
2. Existen restricciones de seguridad para la ejecución del caso de uso. Escribir mensaje de error esperado.
3. Existen precondiciones de temporalidad para el caso de uso. Debe este caso de uso ser ejecutado después de otro. Escribir mensaje de error esperado.
4. Existe la lista de negaciones de negocio para cada una de las precondiciones.

En el último punto del checklist se menciona la lista de negaciones de negocio. Esta lista, corresponde a otra herramienta propuesta y su objetivo es entregar a los encargados de aprobar los requerimientos del sistema una visión de las condiciones en que no será posible ejecutar el caso de uso. Esta lista corresponde a la negación de las precondiciones, escritas de la forma: "No se podrá ejecutar la acción ... si no se cumple que ...". De esta forma, se espera que el usuario lea explícitamente qué casos de negocio quedarán fuera de la solución que se implementa antes de comenzar su desarrollo y no la primera vez que éstos ocurran después de implantado el nuevo sistema.

Las precondiciones de un caso de uso se pueden representar en términos de lógica como:

Sean p1, p2, ..., pn las precondiciones del caso de uso.
Sea q la sentencia: "Puede ejecutar la operación" **(1)**

Se satisface que (p1 ^ p2 ^ ... ^ pn) => q

Es responsabilidad del analista de excepciones el detectar aquellas precondiciones críticas y que pueden ser reconocidas por la contraparte una vez implantado el sistema, y presentarlas en su forma de negación, de la forma:

Sea pi una precondición crítica:
NOT(pi) => NOT(q) **(2)**

De esta forma, el encargado de aprobar los requerimientos del sistema antes de comenzar su construcción, será notificado explícitamente de aquellos casos en que ciertas operaciones no podrán ser realizadas, y se disminuye considerablemente la posibilidad de que aparezcan ese tipo de mantenciones una vez construidas las funcionalidades.

En el ejemplo dado anteriormente, el caso de uso "Decidir Aprobación Operacional" debiera contener la siguiente precondición:

"La orden de compra se puede aprobar sólo si el stock es suficiente para todos los artículos solicitados". Esta se obtendría desde el chequeo de objetos asociados (objeto Stock) de acuerdo al checklist mostrado.

La lista de negaciones para ese caso de uso deberá contener entonces una línea del tipo:
"La orden de compra no se podrá aprobar si al menos uno de los artículos solicitados no tiene stock disponible". Colocando tanto la forma positiva como negativa de la precondición se maximiza la posibilidad de entendimiento por parte de los usuarios aprobadores de los requerimientos del nuevo sistema.

Como se observa en el checklist de apoyo a las funciones del analista de excepciones, muchas de las tareas que debe realizar tienen que ver con las precondiciones y la definición de los cursos alternativos, muchos de los cuales existen como alternativas a la insatisfacción de alguna de las precondiciones. Por otra parte, existen tipos de precondiciones que son comunes y se repiten constantemente en variados sistemas de información, especialmente aquellas relativas a validaciones de valores y formatos de atributos.

El proceso de desarrollo usado acá como base, y para el que se ha formalizado este nuevo rol, está apoyado fuertemente por el uso de una herramienta CASE llamada Z4Bees, la que apoya desde las etapas de modelamiento de procesos hasta la generación de código, testing funcional y unitario e implantación de los sistemas. Como parte del trabajo de formalización del rol del analista se han agregado a Z4Bees funciones que facilitan la captura de la información para este nuevo usuario de la herramienta y se aprovecha esta información en la generación de código de la forma que a continuación se detalla.

Para aprovechar al máximo las capacidades de generación de código a partir de la información capturada por el analista de excepciones, es necesario ya contar con las primeras versiones de modelos de clases (Value Objects o Clases Persistentes en la metodología base) con sus atributos. Dentro de una metodología incremental e iterativa como la usada, esto no es un problema, ya que estos modelos apoyan la confección de los casos de uso y son incrementales por lo que serán refinados y usados durante el resto del desarrollo ara la generación del código de las clases y los modelos de datos, entre otras cosas.

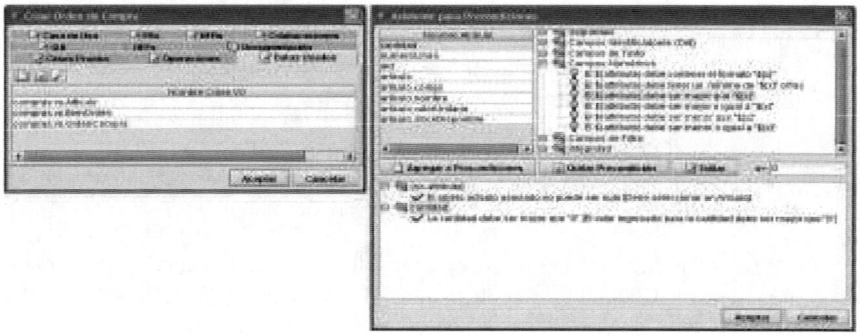

Fig. 4. Asistente de precondiciones para un objeto dentro de un caso de uso

El analista de excepciones debe asociar al caso de uso las clases de objetos persistentes que utilizará.

Para el ejemplo antes mencionado, en el caso de uso “Crear Orden de Compra”, los objetos persistentes usados en la operación principal son la Orden de Compra, los Items de la Orden de Compra y los Artículos, tal como se muestra en la figura 4.

Seleccionando una de las clases asociadas al caso de uso, es posible iniciar el asistente para precondiciones. Este asistente es usado por al analista de excepciones para escribir las precondiciones seleccionándolas desde una biblioteca existente, parametrizándolas y asociándolas a los atributos o relaciones de la clase de objetos seleccionada. Cada precondición que se puede seleccionar desde la biblioteca actúa sobre un atributo o relación de la clase seleccionada y puede contener un parámetro (x) el que se usa como parte de su definición. Por ejemplo, una precondición puede corresponder a "El nombre del cliente debe contener al menos ${x} caracteres".

Además del parámetro X que se puede configurar para cada precondición aplicada al caso de uso, la precondición tiene asociada la información que se muestra en la figura 5:

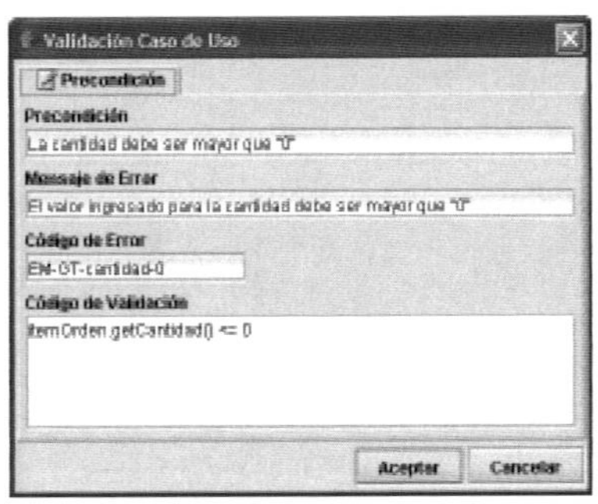

Fig. 5. Información estructurada de una precondición

El atributo "precondición" corresponde al texto que aparecerá en la documentación del caso de uso, mientras que el mensaje de error aparecerá en la aplicación generada por la herramienta CASE en caso de no satisfacerse la condición de validación expresada en el "código de Validación" (código java en este caso). El código del error se exportará por la herramienta CASE al diseño de la vista (patrón de diseño del MVC) asociado al idioma del sistema operativo en donde se ejecuta la herramienta y luego, usando la misma herramienta, podrán ser agregados otros idiomas al mismo código de error. El aporte a la generación de código y documentación de cada uno de estos campos se explica con más detalle a continuación.

Usando el valor de "precondición" la herramienta permite generar automáticamente la documentación de precondiciones del caso de uso. Para el ejemplo mostrado en la figura 5, se genera el siguiente texto:

Precondiciones sobre ItemOrden
□ La cantidad debe ser mayor que "0"

La precondición y el mensaje de error esperado son usados para generar automáticamente parte de los cursos alternativos. La solución generada luego en código Java (J2EE para aplicaciones web) por la herramienta, relee la misma página manteniendo los valores ingresados por los usuarios y mostrando al inicio de ésta y resaltado, el mensaje de error asociado a la precondición. Esto se genera además en la documentación del caso de uso, en la sección de cursos alternativos de la forma:

Para ItemOrden □ Si no se cumple que : La cantidad debe ser mayor que "0", se mantiene activa la misma página y al inicio se muestra el mensaje: "El valor ingresado para la cantidad debe ser mayor que "0"

El framework J2EE para el que genera código la herramienta CASE hace uso extensivo del patrón de diseño MVC. Asociados al diseño de las vistas quedan los mensajes de error (o cualquier texto que pueda depender del diseño y del idioma) identificados por un código. Los códigos de error y el texto de los mensajes son exportados desde las precondiciones del caso de uso automáticamente al diseño de las vistas para ser disparados de acuerdo a la condición de validación.

El código de validación se genera en la clase controladora (MVC) asociada a la vista que captura los atributos de los objetos, justo antes de invocar al servicio que implementa las reglas de negocio y modifica el estado persistente de los objetos. Si este código de validación debe generarse en la clase controladora (capa de presentación) o al inicio de los servicios de clases de negocio (patrón de los Business Objects) puede ser tema de discusión, pero queda fuera del alcance de este trabajo. Se decidió usar la clase controladora en la capa de presentación sólo por efectos de escalabilidad en sistemas de alta demanda, ya que (incluso comercialmente) puede ser más barato escalar la capa de presentación (que puede estar basada en OpenSource) que la capa del dominio (en donde muchos clientes no aceptan OpenSource y prefieren respaldo de marcas).

En la clase controladora asociada a la vista que captura cada ítem de la orden de compra se genera un servicio para las validaciones antes de ejecutar la operación final. Usando la información de la biblioteca de precondiciones, en este servicio se genera el siguiente código:

```
compras.vo.ItemOrden itemOrden =
(compras.vo.ItemOrden)getVO();

if (itemOrden.getCantidad() <= 0) {

  errorMessages.add(transformText("${EM-GT-cantidad-
0}"));}
```

Conclusiones y Trabajo Futuro

En el momento en que se realiza este trabajo aún no hay ningún proyecto completado en que se haya utilizado esta propuesta. Sin embargo, usando datos de un proyecto anterior se podrían determinar las ventajas del uso del nuevo rol. Como ejemplo, se usará un proyecto de tamaño medio con complejidad media alta. Los datos del proyecto son:

- Esfuerzo total: 4,100 horas hombre
- Costo real del orden de los US$ 80,000
- Número total de defectos (fallas y errores): 997

Si se consideran las estadísticas nombradas en [GILB-88], se puede asumir que alrededor de 600 defectos tienen su origen en el análisis de requerimientos. Si suponemos que sólo la tercera parte de ellos podrían haber sido detectados usando el checklist y la lista de negaciones, la cantidad de errores habría disminuido en 200.

Si usamos las estimaciones en [JONES-86] entonces podemos asumir que de los US$ 80,000 de costo toal del proyecto, el 50% se dedicó a retrabajo producto de errores, por lo que US$ 40,000 se invirtieron en corregir aproximadamente 1000 errores, lo que resulta en un costo de $40 por error.

Usando las estimaciones anteriores, el costo total del proyecto sin 200 errores habría disminuido en $US 8,000; es decir en un 10%, lo que habría justificado, por sí solo, la inclusión de este rol dentro del proyecto. Además de las ventajas económicas recién nombradas, la calidad del producto entregado ante el cliente habría aumentado; sin importar la responsabilidad del origen de los defectos.

Como trabajo futuro queda la retroalimentación del proceso producto de las estadísticas de nuevos proyectos que vayan finalizando, y su inclusión como mejoras en las tareas asignadas al nuevo rol. Debido al crecimiento de los esfuerzos de corrección de una falla a medida que el proyecto avanza, cada nueva mejora en los cheklists y en los métodos de detección temprana de posibilidades de falla, es un aporte considerable al resultado final del proyecto; tanto en su rentabilidad como en la calidad del software producido.

Referencias bibliográficas

1 Jones, Capers, ed. *Tt orial: Programming Productivity: Issues for the Eighties, 2nd Ed.* (Los Angeles: IEE Computer Society Press), 1986. [JONES-86]

2 Gilb, Tom. *P rinciples of Software Engineering Management* (Wokingham, England: Addison-Wesley), 1988. [GILB-88]

3 Boehm, Barry W. and Philip N. Papaccio. "Understanding and Controlling Software Costs," *IEEE Transactions on Software Engineering,* v. 14, no. 10, October 1988, pp. 1462-1477. [BOPA-88]

4 "Office of Safety and Mission Assurance Software Formal Inspections Guidebook" NASA - National Aeronautics and Space Administration - Agosto 1993 [SFIG-93]

5 Tomas S. Jun. "La Tensión Esencial" . Editorial Fondo de Cultura Económica, ISBN: 968-16-1100-4 [KUHN-77]

6 Paul Solomon, "Using CMMI® to Improve Earned Value Management" Technical Note, CMU/SEI-2002-TN-016 [SEI-05] http://www.sei.cmu.edu/pub/documents/02.reports/pdf/02tn016.pdf (noviembre 2005)

7 Sun Microsystems, "J2EE Patterns Catalog" [SUN-05] http://java.sun.com/blueprints/patterns/catalog.html (noviembre 2005)

Método Semiautomático para la Identificación de Operaciones a partir de Grafos Conceptuales

Carlos Mario Zapata J.[1] – Aldrin Fredy Jaramillo[2] – Fernando Arango I.[1]

[1] Grupo UN-INFO, Escuela de Sistemas, Universidad Nacional de Colombia, Sede Medellín
{cmzapata, farango}@unalmed.edu.co
[2] Departamento de Ingeniería de Sistemas, Universidad de Antioquia
afjara@udea.edu.co

Resumen

Desde sus inicios, las herramientas CASE han asistido a los analistas en el trazado y edición de diferentes tipos de diagramas. Actualmente existe una tendencia para asistir a los analistas en la concepción de algunos diagramas UML, como el diagrama de clases. En los trabajos correspondientes a esta tendencia, el reconocimiento de las operaciones del diagrama de clases sigue siendo un problema abierto. En este artículo se presenta un método para la identificación de las operaciones del diagrama de clases partiendo de Grafos Conceptuales y empleando para ello un enfoque lingüístico.

Palabras clave: Diagrama de Clases UML, Operaciones, Grafos Conceptuales, Estructuras Léxicas Conceptuales.

Abstract

From introduction of CASE tools, they have been supported analysts in diagram drawing and editing. Currently, there's a trend for supporting analysts in UML diagram conception, mainly Class Diagram. In this trend, works on class diagram have failed in operations recognition, which is even an open problem. In this paper we present a method for class diagram operation identification from Conceptual Graphs and with a linguistic approach.

Keywords: UML Class diagram, Operations, Conceptual Graphs, Lexical Conceptual Structures.

1. Introducción:

El estado del arte en Herramientas CASE (Computer-Aided Software Engineering) muestra estas herramientas en la actualidad como versátiles asistentes en el trazado y edición de diagramas, e incluso con capacidades de generación automática de partes del código fuente de las diferentes aplicaciones [1]. Sin embargo, la concepción misma de los diagramas ha constituido un trabajo casi exclusivo del analista, quien debe interpretar la documentación del proceso de elicitación de requisitos para elaborar dichos diagramas [2].

Como una respuesta, promediando la década de los noventa se comenzó a gestar una tendencia que procura la asistencia a los analistas en las etapas previas al trazado de los diagramas. En especial, algunos trabajos se han concentrado en el diagrama de Clases de UML [3], [4] y [5], el cual representa los aspectos estructurales del dominio de un problema [6]. En estos trabajos se reconocen algunos elementos del diagrama de clases, como las clases, los atributos y las asociaciones, pero en ninguno de ellos se reconocen las operaciones del diagrama de clases.

En este artículo se presenta un método semiautomático que permite la identificación de las operaciones del diagrama de clases, partiendo de una representación intermedia del problema (cercana al discurso), que está constituida por los Grafos Conceptuales [7], y empleando un conjunto de elementos lingüísticos.

El artículo está organizado de la siguiente manera: en la sección 2 se muestran algunos trabajos para la obtención de diagramas de clases a partir de lenguaje natural; en la sección 3 se resumen los conceptos fundamentales sobre los que se apoya la propuesta; en la sección 4 se presenta la propuesta de solución; en la sección 5 se presenta un caso de estudio para mostrar los resultados de aplicación. Las conclusiones y trabajos futuros se incluyen en las secciones 6 y 7 respectivamente.

2. Trabajos Previos en obtención de elementos del diagrama de Clases a partir de Lenguaje Natural:

Desde Coad y Yourdon, quienes presentaron algunas reglas para identificar elementos del diagrama de clases, en la orientación por objetos [8], ha existido la intención de automatización de este proceso. Sin embargo, sólo hasta mediados de la década de los noventa comenzaron a surgir proyectos que materializaban esta idea. Algunos de los trabajos más destacados en este campo han sido:

- NL-OOPS: Propone algunas reglas heurísticas para la generación del diagrama de clases [3]. Esas heurísticas parecen "sugerencias" y no tanto reglas que tengan aplicación o validez universal. Además, se genera un diagrama de clases muy incompleto.
- CM-BUILDER Propone un diagrama de clases mucho más completo que NL-OOPS, tomando como base un recurso computacional similar a una ontología general del mundo, donde se requiere que los diferentes elementos hayan sido preclasificados en una taxonomía de objetos, eventos y atributos [4]. En ausencia de esta taxonomía, CM-BUILDER no posee herramientas de reconocimiento de los diferentes elementos del diagrama de clases.
- NIBA: Propone la elaboración de diferentes diagramas UML (especialmente clases y actividades, aunque establecen que podrían obtener otros como secuencias y comunicación), con un enfoque lingüístico bastante sólido que incluye NTMS (siglas en alemán de Morfosintaxis Teórica del Lenguaje Natural) [5]. En este proyecto se obtiene un diagrama de clases con muchos elementos identificados, pero aún así siguen haciendo falta algunos de ellos.

De forma particular, los trabajos presentados fallan sistemáticamente en la identificación de las operaciones del diagrama de clases, lo cual permite un punto de partida para el trabajo que se presenta en este artículo.

3. Conceptos Fundamentales.

3.1. Grafos Conceptuales

Son un grafos bipartitos [7] con dos diferentes clases de nodos: Conceptos y relaciones. Los Conceptos representan entidades, acciones y atributos, y poseen dos atributos: el tipo y el referente. El tipo indica la clase de elemento representado por el concepto. El referente indica la instancia específica de la clase referida por el nodo. Las Relaciones muestran la interrelación entre los nodos de conceptos. Los nodos de relaciones tienen a su vez dos atributos: uno para la valencia y otro para el tipo. La valencia indica el número de conceptos involucrados en la relación, mientras que el tipo expresa su rol temático de acuerdo con la gramática de casos [9].

3.2. Clasificación de los verbos por su aspecto léxico (Aktionsart)

Muchos lingüistas y filósofos han observado que los verbos representan situaciones (eventos o estados) con diferentes propiedades de aspecto léxico, a lo cual se ha denominado Aktionsart. Este término fue introducido por W. Streitberg en 1891 con la intención de crear un vocablo técnico para el aspecto léxico. En la actualidad la Aktionsart (o modo de acción) es también denominada aspecto inherente o carácter aspectual. Una de las principales clasificaciones que reconoce el aspecto léxico de los verbos es realizada por Vendler [10] quien discrimina los verbos aspectualmente en cuatro tipos: Estados, realizaciones, actividades y logros. En la Tabla 1 se presentan las características asociadas con cada tipo, tomando en consideración la presencia (+) o ausencia (-) de telicidad (capacidad de dirigirse hacia un objetivo), dinamismo (propiedad de los verbos que realizan acciones) y durabilidad (duración en el tiempo; cuando el verbo es instantáneo, la durabilidad tiende a cero).

Tabla 1. Características de los tipos de verbos definidos por Vendler.

Tipo de verbo	Telicidad	Dinamismo	Durabilidad	Ejemplos
Estado	-	-	+	Conocer, tener
Actividad	-	+	+	Marchar, pintar
Realización	+	+	+	Destruir
Logro	+	+	-	Notar, ganar

En algunas de las propuestas analizadas en la sección anterior, se emplea una representación intermedia que facilita la transición hacia los diferentes diagramas; para esas representaciones intermedias, se emplean redes semánticas y grafos conceptuales. En esta propuesta se define un nuevo tipo de representación intermedia que se denomina "Esquema Preconceptual".

El dinamismo establece la diferencia entre eventos ([+Dynamic]) y estados ([-Dynamic]). La durabilidad denota situaciones que toman tiempo (estados, actividades y realizaciones). Los verbos télicos denotan situaciones con un fin u objetivo inherente; la presencia de telicidad se denota [+telic] y su ausencia se denota [-telic]. Los verbos marcados [+telic] en un lexicón (diccionario computacional donde aparecen las palabras con sus respectivos aspectos sintácticos y semánticos asociados de acuerdo con los criterios definidos para la composición del mismo) son uniformemente interpretados como tales, independientemente de otros constituyentes o contextos pragmáticos, mientras que los verbos marcados como [-telic] no tienen una interpretación homogénea, es decir, su telicidad dependerá del contexto [11]. Esto significa, por ejemplo, que a pesar de que un verbo haya sido clasificado como de actividad los demás constituyentes de la frase podrían determinar que la sentencia completa sea télica.

De la propuesta de Vendler, en relación con la identificación de los elementos de un diagrama de clases, se puede concluir:

- Los verbos de estado son candidatos a asociaciones.
- Los logros no son candidatos a operaciones puesto que no poseen durabilidad.
- Las actividades no son candidatas a operaciones puesto que carecen de telicidad, es decir, no se dirigen a un punto final (objetivo).
- Las realizaciones, por sus características aspectuales (dinamicidad, durabilidad y telicidad), son candidatas a operaciones.
- En ocasiones el verbo solo no es un indicador de pertenencia a una categoría. Se requiere información adicional de la frase. Por ejemplo: Los verbos correr y escribir aparecen en las categorías actividad y realización. Por lo tanto cuando el verbo corresponde a la categoría actividad, debe verificarse la telicidad de la frase. Si la frase es télica, el verbo es candidato a una operación.

3.3. Estructuras Léxicas Conceptuales (ELC)

Los aspectos léxicos hacen referencia al tipo de situación denotada por el verbo, solo o en combinación con otros constituyentes. De acuerdo con Dorr y Olsen [12] es posible representar los aspectos léxicos de los verbos, solos o en la frase, usando representaciones de Estructuras Léxicas Conceptuales (ELC), de manera que tales resultados estén disponibles en un lexicón para diferentes aplicaciones de Procesamiento del Lenguaje Natural (un lexicón con información de las ELC de verbos del español puede encontrarse en [13]). Así mismo, Dorr y Olsen han establecido patrones de ELC asociados a las categorías verbales propuestas por Vendler (véase Tabla 2) y un algoritmo para la determinación de las características aspectuales de los verbos que hacen parte del lexicón:

Tabla 2. Patrones de ELC asociados a las categorías verbales

Tipo de verbo	Patrón	ELC
3.2.1. Estado	1	be ident/perc/loc (thing 2) …
3.2.2. Actividad	1	act loc/perc (thing 1) …
	2	act loc/perc (thing 1) (with instr …
	3	act loc/perc (thing 1) (on loc/perc (thing 2)) …
	4	act loc/perc (thing 1) (on loc/perc (thing 2)) (with instr …
3.2.3. Realización	1	cause/let (thing 1) (go loc (thing 2) (toward/away_from …))…
	2	cause/let (thing 1) (go/be ident (thing 2) …
	3	cause/let (thing 1) (go loc (thing 2) …
	4	cause/let (thing 1) (go exist (thing 2) …
3.2.4. Logro	1	go loc (thing 2) (toward/away_from …)…
	2	go loc (thing 2) …
	3	go exist (thing 2) …
	4	go ident (thing 2) …

Algoritmo para la determinación de características aspectuales:

// L = Estructura Léxica Conceptual a ser evaluada.

// Nodo inicial = Primer nodo de la ELC por ejemplo:

// Dada la ELC: cause/let (thing 1) (go loc (thing 2) (toward/away_from …))…

// El nodo inicial es: cause/let. De manera similar el nodo interno corresponde a:

// (toward/away_from …)

1. Inicialice: T(L) = [∅T], D(L) = [∅D], R(L) = [∅R]
2. Si el nodo inicial de L ∈ {CAUSE, LET, GO} entonces T(L) = [+T]

Si el nodo inicial de L ∈ {CAUSE, LET} entonces D(L) = [+D], R(L) = [+R]

Si el nodo inicial de L ∈ {GO} entonces D(L) = [+D]

3. Si el nodo inicial de L ∈ {ACT, BE, STAY} entonces

Si el nodo interno de L ∈ {TO, TOWARD, FORTemp} entonces T(L) = [+T]

Si el nodo inicial de L ∈ {BE, STAY} entonces R(L) = [+R]

Si el nodo inicial de L ∈ {ACT} entonces D(L) = [+D], R(L) = [+R]

4. Regrese T(L), D(L), R(L)

De acuerdo con lo anterior, una posible operación ocurre cuando:

1. El nodo inicial de la ELC corresponde a las primitivas CAUSE o LET.
2. El nodo inicial de la ELC corresponde a la primitiva ACT y el nodo interno corresponde a TO, TOWARD o FORTemp. En este caso, el verbo correspondiente podría ser atélico pero la actividad completa podría ser télica

En la siguiente sección se presenta la propuesta

4. La Propuesta de Solución:

En la sección 2 se encontró que uno de los principales problemas, que aún subsiste para el trazado automático del diagrama de clases de UML, es la identificación de las operaciones asociadas con cada clase. Con base en los conceptos fundamentales enunciados en la sección 3, es posible enunciar un método que busque la solución de estas limitaciones. En este método se deben realizar las siguientes actividades:

1. A partir de un Modelo Verbal en Lenguaje Natural, el analista debe generar los grafos conceptuales correspondientes a cada oración.
2. Para cada grafo obtenido en el paso anterior, se establece el sentido de utilización del verbo. El sentido de un verbo no es único; por ejemplo, el verbo adquirir puede tener el sentido de aprender (si lo que se adquiere es información) o comprar (si lo que se adquiere es un bien). En un lexicón pueden encontrarse los posibles sentidos de un verbo y las ELC asociadas a cada uno de estos sentidos. Este proceso se realiza apareando los roles temáticos de los grafos conceptuales con los roles temáticos presentes en cada uno de los sentidos de los verbos del lexicón. Como resultado se obtiene un subconjunto de sentidos, el cual es presentado al usuario en un orden determinado con base en el grado de coincidencia obtenido en el apareamiento. Finalmente, de este subconjunto de sentidos el analista elegirá el que más se acomode a la oración, según su criterio. La realización en forma automática de este proceso no es un asunto trivial y su discusión está fuera del alcance de este artículo. Esta tarea se hará de forma asistida por el usuario con base en los roles temáticos.
3. Una vez establecido el sentido del verbo se determina la categoría del mismo mediante la utilización de las ELC asociadas al verbo en el lexicón. De acuerdo con lo planteado en la sección anterior serán candidatos a operaciones aquellos verbos cuyas ELC cumplan las siguientes condiciones:

- El nodo inicial de L $\in$ {CAUSE, LET} ó
- El nodo inicial de L $\in$ {ACT} y el nodo interno de L $\in$ {TO, TOWARD, FORTemp} (Actividad télica).

Para apoyar la realización de este proceso, se desarrolló la herramienta GSC Mapper [14], que es una herramienta computacional que permite el paso de los requerimientos de un sistema, representados mediante Grafos Conceptuales al Diagrama de Clases de UML. Para llevar a cabo la transformación, se requiere el ingreso al GSC Mapper de los Grafos Conceptuales correspondientes al problema en estudio en formato XML (eXtensible Markup Language). GSC Mapper se encarga de obtener los elementos del diagrama de clases, siguiendo las heurísticas de mapeo descritas en esta propuesta, y apoyado en un lexicón de verbos, obtenido a partir de una adaptación del lexicón de la Universidad de Maryland [13]. Al final se obtienen dichos elementos, permitiendo la posibilidad de guardarlos en un archivo estándar de intercambio de documentos UML (XMI - Xml Metadata Interchange), el cual puede ser visualizado y editado en cualquier herramienta CASE que soporte el estándar XMI.

GSC Mapper se apoya en dos herramientas para la generación de los resultados intermedios y finales del mapeo:

- La herramienta CharGer®, del profesor Harry Delugach, que permite la creación y edición de grafos conceptuales y su conversión al formato XML.
- La herramienta CASE Poseidón®, que recibe el código XMI generado por el GSC Mapper y permite la graficación del Diagrama de Clases de UML.

En relación con los recursos internos del GSC Mapper, se tiene lo siguiente:

- GSC Mapper simplifica el lexicón de verbos de la Universidad de Maryland. Dentro de los elementos más relevantes del lexicón se encuentran:
  - Sentido: Es la forma como es usado el verbo en la oración. Para cada verbo se tienen en el lexicón varias entradas diferenciadas con la palabra inglesa correspondiente al sentido del verbo.
  - Roles theta: También conocidos como roles temáticos o casos semánticos. Es el nombre de los roles participantes en asociaciones con predicados. Los predicados pueden ser verbos, sustantivos, adjetivos o preposiciones. Dentro de los roles más importantes se cuentan: agente, paciente, tema, instrumento, experimentador, locación, objetivo y percibido.
  - LCS (Lexical Conceptual Structure): Es un grafo dirigido con una raíz; representa la estructura de un verbo en una oración, con sus respectivos roles y sentidos.
- Las heurísticas de mapeo son las reglas utilizadas para reconocer elementos del Grafo Conceptual, que hacen parte del Diagrama de Clases de UML. Para realizar el trazado completo del diagrama, además de las heurísticas correspondientes a las operaciones, debieron emplearse otras para identificar clases, atributos y asociaciones, así:
  - Los conceptos que están asociados con el verbo mediante un rol agente o experimentador son candidatos a clases.
  - Vendler ha realizado una de las principales clasificaciones de los verbos. Estos se clasifican en: estados, realizaciones, actividades y logros. A partir de esta clasificación se determina que los verbos clasificados como realizaciones, pasan a ser candidatos a operaciones. También los verbos clasificados como actividades télicas (situaciones con un fin u objetivo inherente) pasarán a ser candidatas a operaciones.
  - Los verbos que son clasificados como estados, pasarán a ser candidatos a asociaciones, siempre y cuando se haya mapeado como clase candidata al menos un concepto vinculado a la asociación.
  - Los conceptos vinculados en las asociaciones, que no han sido mapeados como clases candidatas, pasarán a ser atributos del otro concepto que ya ha sido mapeado como clase.

En la siguiente sección, se emplearán los recursos desarrollados para ejemplificar con un caso de estudio la obtención semiautomática de operaciones del Diagrama de Clases de UML a partir de Grafos Conceptuales.

5. Aplicación de las reglas mediante un caso de estudio:

Para demostrar la aplicabilidad del método propuesto, se seleccionó un escenario de un Modelo Verbal que describe el dominio de una librería, que fue tomado de Harmain y Gaizauskas [4]. El texto completo es el siguiente:

1) Una biblioteca presta ítemes a sus clientes.
2) Cada cliente es un miembro.
3) Cada cliente posee una tarjeta de membresía.
4) Cada tarjeta de membresía tiene un número único.
5) Cada cliente tiene número de miembro, nombre, dirección y fecha de nacimiento.
6) La biblioteca tiene secciones de temas.
7) Cada sección tiene una marca de clasificación.
8) Un código de barras identifica únicamente a un préstamo.
9) Hay 2 tipos de ítemes de préstamo, cintas de idiomas y libros.
10) Una cinta de idioma tiene un titulo del idioma (Ej. Francés), y nivel (Ej. principiante).
11) Un libro tiene un título y autor(es).
12) Un cliente puede prestar hasta 8 ítemes.
13) Un ítem puede ser prestado, reservado o renovado para extender un préstamo actual.
14) Un ítem es entregado al cliente.
15) El número de membresía del cliente es escaneado por
un lector de código de barras.
16) El número de membresía del cliente es ingresado manualmente.
17) La biblioteca valida el número de membresía.
18) La biblioteca valida el número de ítemes a prestar.
19) El ítem es sellado.
20) El ítem es entregado al cliente.
21) La biblioteca busca ítemes
22) La biblioteca actualiza registros de ítemes.

Los Grafos Conceptuales correspondientes al dominio enunciado se elaboran en la herramienta CharGer®, y se pueden observar en la Figura 1. Esta herramienta permite la opción de guardar el texto en un archivo XML, que luego se carga en GSC Mapper para iniciar el proceso de obtención del diagrama de clases, tal como se muestra en la Figura 2. Posteriormente, al presionar la opción "Mapear" en el GSC Mapper, con la ayuda del analista se eligen los sentidos de los diferentes verbos presentes en el escenario para arrojar luego el inventario de elementos que se muestra en la Figura 3. El diagrama de clases resultante se almacena en un archivo XMI que se carga posteriormente en la herramienta Poseidón®, como se aprecia en la Figura 4.

En comparación con las propuestas discutidas en la sección 2, GSC Mapper identifica un conjunto de operaciones para las clases, empleando el método semiautomático de esta propuesta. En consecuencia, sus resultados no son comparables con dichas propuestas.

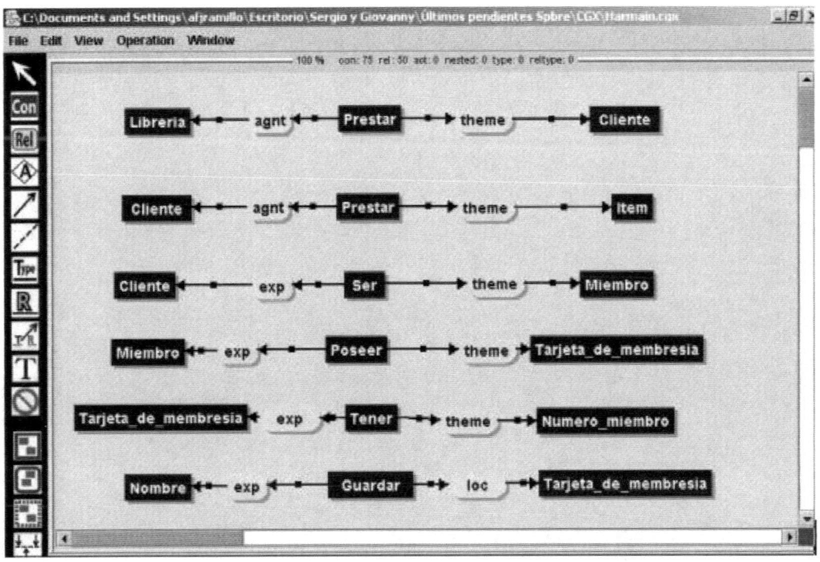

Figura 1. Grafos Conceptuales del ejemplo elaborados en la herramienta CharGer®.

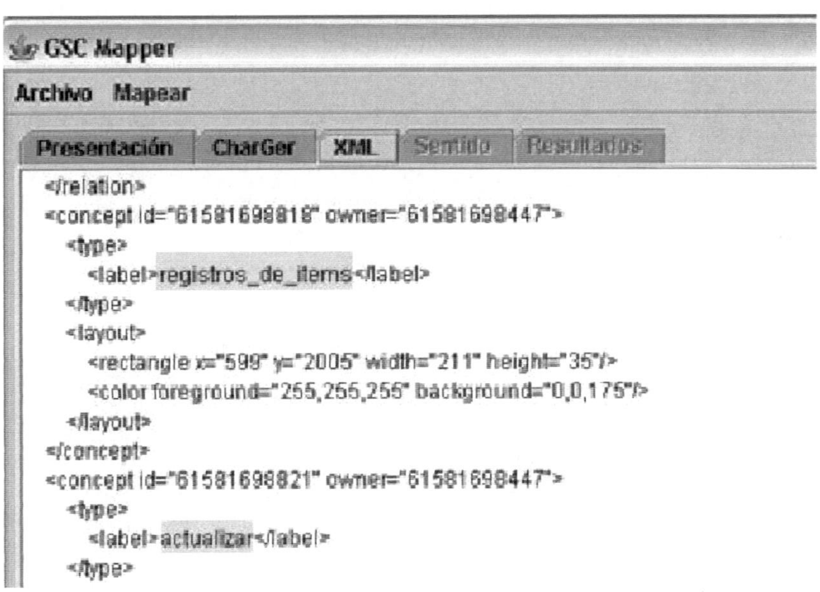

Figura 2. Archivo en XML cargado por GSC Mapper para iniciar el proceso de Mapeo.

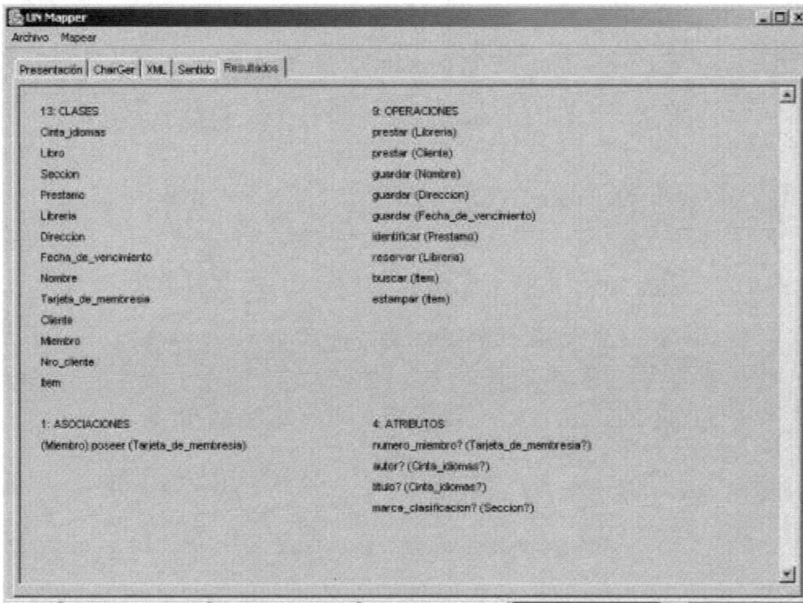

Figura 3. Inventario de elementos identificados por GSC Mapper para el escenario del ejemplo.

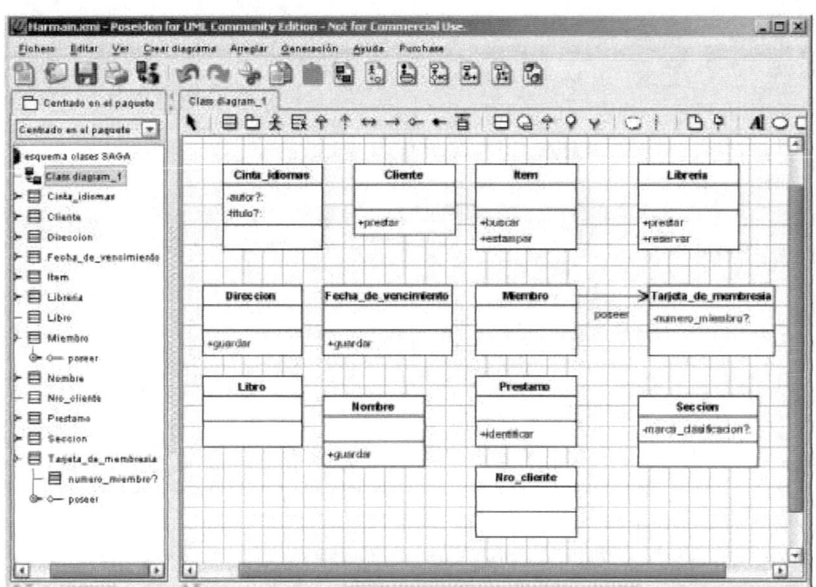

Figura 4. Diagrama de clases resultante cargado por la herramienta Poseidón®.

Para corroborar la validez del método propuesto, se debió recurrir a una prueba experimental en la cual se recopilaron siete escenarios diferentes, provenientes de las diferentes fuentes bibliográficas sobre el tema (se incluye el escenario planteado en esta sección) y se envió una encuesta a 18 expertos en el tema, profesores de Ingeniería de Software y de Análisis y Diseño Orientado por Objetos, de diversas Universidades de la ciudad de Medellín. El objetivo de la encuesta era que estos expertos identificaran las operaciones de cada uno de los escenarios, con el fin de tener un punto de comparación con los resultados que pudiese arrojar este método.

Al recibir y tabular los resultados de la encuesta, se encontró que aún entre los expertos no existía un consenso sobre lo que podía ser considerado como una operación del diagrama de clases. Por ello, se decidió adoptar un criterio de mayoría de votación en el cual, si más del 50% de los expertos identificaban un verbo como operación, se asumía que efectivamente lo era.

A partir de la identificación de las operaciones realizada por los expertos, se calcularon dos métricas para determinar la validez del método propuesto. Esas métricas fueron descritas por Harmain y Gaizauskas [4] y se denominan Recall (Medida de completitud de los resultados) y Precisión (Medida de calidad de los resultados). Las fórmulas para el cálculo de esas métricas son las siguientes:

Recall = Ncorrect / Nkey
Precisión = Ncorrect / (Ncorrect + Nincorrect)

Donde: Ncorrect es el número de operaciones correctamente identificadas por el método propuesto, Nkey es el número total de operaciones correctas (Las identificadas por los expertos) y Nincorrect es el número de operaciones identificadas incorrectamente (que no coinciden con los resultados de los expertos). En la tabla 3 se resumen los resultados obtenidos para evaluar la validez del método propuesto.

Tabla 3. Resumen total de completitud y precisión del método propuesto

	Ncorrect	Nkey	Nincorrect
Escenario 1	3	4	2
Escenario 2	1	1	0
Escenario 3	1	1	0
Escenario 4	6	7	0
Escenario 5	3	5	3
Escenario 6	3	6	5
Escenario 7	2	2	1
Total	19	26	11
Recall total	19/26 = 73.07%		
Precisión	19/(19 + 11) = 63.33%		

6. Conclusiones:

Se presentó en este artículo un método semiautomático para la identificación de operaciones a partir de Grafos Conceptuales, se ejemplificó con un caso de estudio y se midió la validez de los resultados mediante el cálculo de dos indicadores basados en criterio experto.

Sobre los trabajos previos, se muestra un progreso en la identificación de las operaciones del diagrama de clases, incorporando además heurísticas que permiten el reconocimiento de otros elementos del diagrama. La realización del prototipo de la herramienta GSC Mapper, basada en el método aquí descrito, y que interactúa con otras herramientas como el CharGer® (para la edición de Grafos Conceptuales) y Poseidon® (para la edición de los diagramas de clases), es otro de los logros de este trabajo.

Se muestra adicionalmente que un enfoque lingüístico puede aportar en la solución a problemas de la Ingeniería del Software y el modelamiento. Además, la validación que se realizó del método reafirma el hecho de que es un asunto en el cual los expertos aún no tienen un consenso, resaltando aún más el hecho de que se requieren métodos que aborden la problemática de manera mucho más automática.

7. Trabajos Futuros:

Quedan, sin embargo, asuntos por resolver, tales como:

- La alta participación que aún tiene el analista en el proceso de identificación de las operaciones del diagrama de clases a partir de los Grafos Conceptuales. Entre más automático sea el proceso, menor posibilidad de errores humanos en el mismo.
- La incorporación de heurísticas que posibiliten la identificación de otros elementos del diagrama de clases o inclusive de otros diagramas.
- La elaboración de un método que permita la construcción de los Grafos Conceptuales a partir de lenguaje natural

Referencias:

1. Pressman, R. Ingeniería del Software: Un enfoque práctico. McGraw–Hill, Madrid, 2002.
2. Zapata, C. M. y Arango, F. Los Modelos Verbales en Lenguaje Natural y su utilización en la elaboración de esquemas conceptuales para el desarrollo de software: Una revisión crítica. Revista Universidad EAFIT, Vol. 41, No. 137, 2005.
3. Mich L. NL-OOPS: From Natural Natural Language to Object Oriented Requirements using the Natural Language Processing System LOLITA. Journal of Natural Language Engineering, Cambridge University Press, Vol. 2, No. 2, 1996.
4. Harmain, H. y Gaizauskas, R. CM-Builder: An Automated NL-based CASE Tool. En: Proceedings of the fifteenth IEEE International Conference on Automated Software Engineering (ASE'00), Grenoble, 2000.
5. NIBA Project. Linguistically Based Requirements Engineering - The NIBA Project. Proceedings 4th Int. Conference NLDB'99 Applications of Natural Language to Information Systems, Klagenfurt, 1999.
6. OMG. OMG Unified Modeling Language Specification. Object Management Group. Disponible en: http://www.omg.org/UML/
7. Sowa, J. F. Conceptual Structures: Information Processing in Mind and Machine. Addison-Wesley, Reading, MA, 1984.
8. Coad, P. y Yourdon, E. Object – Oriented Analysis. Yourdon Press, New Jersey, 1990.
9. Fillmore, Ch. The Case for Case. Universals in Linguistics Theory. E. Bach. R. Harms eds. Holt, Rinehart and Winston Publishing Company, 1968.
10. Vendler, Z. Verbs and Times. Linguistics in Philosophy. Ithaca. New York, CUP, 1957.
11. Olsen, M. The semantics and pragmatics of lexical aspect features. Studies in the Linguistic Sciences. Vol. 24. N. 2, 1994.
12. Dorr, B. Olsen, M. Aspectual modifications to a LCS database for NLP applications. Laboratory for Language and Media Processing. Department of Computer Science and Institute for Advanced Computer Studies. University of Maryland, 1997.
13. Dorr, Bonnie J. : Computational Lexicon. Copyright (c) University of Maryland. 2001. Disponible en: http://www.umiacs.umd.edu/~bonnie/publications.html
14. Jiménez, S., Villegas G., Jaramillo, A. F., Zapata, C. M., Arango, F. GSC Mapper: Mapeador de grafos de Sowa a diagramas de clases. Encuentro de Tecnologías de Información Aplicadas a la solución de problemas EITI2005, 2005.

Sesión 6:

Bases de Datos y Sistemas Pervasivos

Una Aproximación Dirigida por Modelos para el Diseño de Bases de Datos XML Seguras

Belén Vela[1], Eduardo Fernández-Medina[2], Esperanza Marcos[1] y Mario Piattini[2]

(1) Grupo Kybele. Departamento de Lenguajes y Sistemas Informáticos
Universidad Rey Juan Carlos
C/ Tulipán, s/n - 28933 Móstoles, Madrid, España
{Belen.Vela, Esperanza.Marcos}@urjc.es
(2) Grupo Alarcos. Departamento de Tecnologías y Sistemas de Información
Centro Mixto de Investigación y Desarrollo de Software UCLM-Soluziona
Universidad de Castilla-La Mancha
Paseo de la Universidad, 4 – 13071 Ciudad Real, España
{Eduardo.FdezMedina, Mario.Piattini}@uclm.es

Resumen. En este artículo se propone una aproximación metodológica para el desarrollo dirigido por modelos de bases de datos (BD) XML seguras. Esta propuesta se enmarca dentro de MIDAS, una metodología dirigida por modelos para el desarrollo de Sistemas de Información Web (SIW) basada en la arquitectura MDA (*Model Driven Architecture*) propuesta por el OMG (*Object Management Group*). El proceso de desarrollo de una BD XML en MIDAS propone usar como modelo independiente de plataforma (PIM, *Platform Independent Model*) el modelo conceptual de datos y como modelo específico de plataforma (PSM – *Platform Specific Model*) el modelo de esquemas XML, ambos representados en UML. En este trabajo se modifican dichos modelos para poder añadir aspectos de seguridad para el caso de que la información almacenada se considere crítica. Se propone, por un lado, el uso de la extensión de UML para incorporar los aspectos de seguridad a nivel de PIM y, por otro lado, se modificará el perfil para esquemas XML previamente definido, con el fin de incorporar los aspectos de la seguridad en todas las etapas del desarrollo de una BD XML. También se definirán los *mappings* para pasar del PIM Seguro al PSM para BD XML Seguras. El proceso de desarrollo de la BD XML Segura se mostrará mediante un caso de estudio: un SIW para la gestión de información hospitalaria en una BD XML.

Palabras clave: Desarrollo de bases de datos XML Seguras, Seguridad en bases de datos, XML, MDA, UML, OCL.

1 Introducción

XML es el estándar actual para el intercambio de información y el transporte de datos entre aplicaciones heterogéneas. Tradicionalmente la información de los documentos XML se almacenaba en ficheros o en Sistemas de Gestión de Bases de Datos (SGBD) convencionales, o bien haciendo la correspondiente transformación a una base de datos (BD), generalmente relacional, o utilizando campos de tipo fichero, por ejemplo, de tipo CLOB (*Character Large OBject*). Sin embargo, la aparición de las BD XML proporciona una alternativa mejor y más directa para almacenar y gestionar los documentos XML. En la actualidad, existen diferentes soluciones para el almacenamiento de documentos XML que según [22], se pueden clasificar en dos grupos: las BD XML nativas como Tamino [20], eXcelon XIS [6], eXist [3] o ToX [1]; y las extensiones de BD XML, que permiten el almacenamiento de documentos XML en SGBD convencionales, habitualmente relacionales u objeto-relaciones (OR). Por ejemplo, Oracle [19] incluye desde la versión 9*i* release 2 nuevos aspectos para el almacenamiento de XML (XML DB de Oracle). También otros productos como IBM DB2 XML Extender [13] o Microsoft SQLXML [17] incluyen extensiones para el almacenamiento de XML. En [22] se realiza un estudio de las principales soluciones de BD XML.

Para la mayoría de las organizaciones la gestión, seguridad y confidencialidad de la información resulta ser un tema crítico [5]. Además, algunos autores remarcan que la seguridad en BD debe ser tenida muy en cuenta, no como un aspecto relegado al final de su desarrollo, sino incluido en todas las etapas de su ciclo de vida [4,10,12]. Incluso la Fundación para el Control y Auditoría de Sistemas de Información insiste en que los gestores han de asegurar que la seguridad se considera de manera integral y explícita en todas las etapas del desarrollo de los sistemas de información [14]. También en el caso de las BD XML es la seguridad un punto clave que debe ser considerado explícitamente y que tiene que tenerse en cuenta de forma ortogonal a todo el proceso de desarrollo de este tipo de BD [11].

Aunque existen diferentes ideas para integrar la seguridad en el proceso de desarrollo de sistemas de información, en el ámbito de las BD la seguridad se suele considerar sólo a nivel de criptografía. Recientemente, hemos propuesto una metodología para diseñar BD relacionales teniendo en cuenta los aspectos de seguridad de la información en todas las etapas del proceso de desarrollo [8]. Pero, sin embargo, no existen trabajos que traten el tema de la seguridad a la hora de desarrollar una BD XML.

En este artículo vamos a integrar el aspecto de seguridad en la aproximación metodológica para el desarrollo de BD XML [21] que se enmarca en MIDAS [15], una metodología dirigida por modelos para el desarrollo de Sistemas de Información Web (SIW). MIDAS propone el uso de estándares a lo largo de todo el proceso de desarrollo, así como el uso de UML para el modelado del SIW independientemente del nivel de abstracción o del aspecto del sistema a modelar. Dado que UML no permite representar directamente todos los modelos necesarios, MIDAS incorpora algunas extensiones de UML existentes y define, o adapta, otras nuevas, siempre que es necesario [7,16].

MIDAS propone una arquitectura dirigida por modelos, basada en MDA (*Model Driven Architecture*) propuesta por el *Object Management Group* (OMG) [18] y considera a la hora de modelar el sistema los aspectos de contenido, hipertexto y comportamiento. Todos estos aspectos se consideran a nivel de Modelos Independientes de Computación (CIM - *Computation Independent Model*), Modelos Independientes de Plataforma (PIM - *Platform Independent Model*) y Modelos Específicos de Plataforma (PSM - *Platform Specific Model*) [2]. La Fig. 1 muestra de forma resumida la arquitectura dirigida por modelos de MIDAS simplificada, donde se proponen los CIM, comunes a todo el sistema, así como los diferentes PIM y PSM para representar los aspectos de contenido, hipertexto y comportamiento.

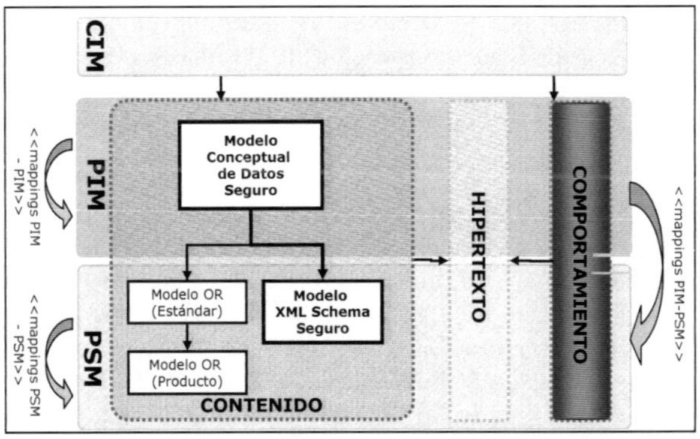

Fig. 1. Arquitectura de MIDAS simplificada

Se contempla una tercera dimensión que incluye otros aspectos a tener en cuenta en el desarrollo de un SIW, como son la arquitectura del sistema o la seguridad, que son ortogonales a los presentados en la Fig. 1. La Fig. 2 muestra la arquitectura de MIDAS con las tres dimensiones mencionadas.

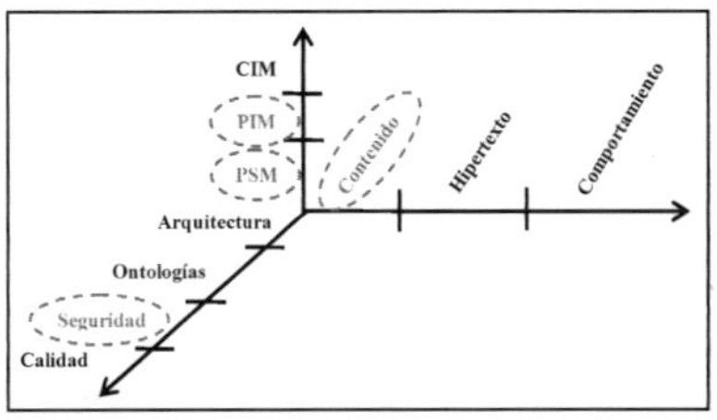

Fig. 2. Dimensiones a considerar en un desarrollo de un SIW

Este trabajo se centra en el aspecto del ***contenido,*** que se corresponde con el concepto tradicional de una BD, y el aspecto ortogonal de la ***seguridad*** para los niveles de ***PIM*** y ***PSM*** (ver Fig. 2). En la siguiente sección 2 veremos el desarrollo de BD XML Seguras en el marco de MIDAS. Como PIM de datos se usa el modelo conceptual de datos que se representará mediante un diagrama de clases extendido, usando la extensión a UML propuesta en [7,9] para incorporar los aspectos de seguridad a este nivel. El perfil para PIM de datos seguros se resumirá en la sección 2.1. Como PSM en MIDAS se propone usar el modelo OR o el modelo de esquemas XML, dependiendo de la tecnología que se necesite utilizar. En este artículo se muestra la parte relativa al diseño de BD XML Seguras y por lo tanto, como PSM se usará el modelo de esquemas XML, usando el perfil para BD XML previamente definido en [21]. En el apartado 2.2 de este artículo presentaremos una adaptación del mismo para incorporar los aspectos de la seguridad específicos para este tipo de BD XML. También se mostrarán en el apartado 2.3 las reglas de transformación para pasar del PIM de datos seguro al PSM de datos, que será el esquema de la BD XML Segura. Estas reglas están basadas en las definidas en [21], donde se describen unos *mappings* para obtener el PSM de datos, pero sin considerar los aspectos de seguridad. En este artículo adaptaremos dichas reglas para obtener el esquema de la BD XML Segura incluyendo las restricciones necesarias para la seguridad.

En la sección 3 de este trabajo se presenta también un caso de estudio de un SIW para la gestión y el análisis de información de hospitales, mediante el que se ha definido y validado la propuesta para el desarrollo de una BD XML Segura.

Finalmente, en la sección 4 se muestran las principales conclusiones obtenidas y se plantean futuros trabajos.

2 Desarrollo de Bases de Datos XML Seguras en MIDAS

Como ya se ha dicho en el apartado anterior, en este trabajo nos centramos en el aspecto de **contenido** de MIDAS, que se corresponde con el concepto tradicional de una BD. El desarrollo de una BD depende de varios aspectos: en primer lugar, de si ya existe una BD en la organización y, por otro lado, de la tecnología que se desea utilizar, es decir, si se desea utilizar una BD OR [16] o una BD XML [21]. Además es necesario tener en cuenta si la BD que se desea desarrollar incluye información que sea necesario proteger y que, por lo tanto, sea necesario recoger aspectos de seguridad desde las etapas más tempranas del desarrollo de la BD.

Vamos a pasar a describir en detalle el proceso de desarrollo de una BD XML Segura partiendo de cero, así como las técnicas y los modelos necesarios:

- A nivel de **PIM** se realiza el diseño conceptual de datos. Para ello se utiliza el modelo conceptual de datos, sin tener en cuenta la tecnología seleccionada, ya que se trata de un modelo independiente de la plataforma. Este PIM de datos se representa mediante un diagrama de clases UML. En el caso de nuestra propuesta se usará, como ya se ha dicho anteriormente, el diagrama de clases UML extendido, para poder representar los aspectos de seguridad junto con un conjunto de restricciones de seguridad que han sido expresadas a través del lenguaje OSCL [9], como veremos en el subapartado siguiente (2.1).
- A nivel de **PSM** se lleva a cabo el diseño lógico de datos. En este punto sí que es necesario tener en cuenta la tecnología seleccionada, que en nuestro caso será una BD XML. Se parte del PIM de datos seguro obtenido en el nivel anterior y se aplican las reglas de transformación que se resumen en el subapartado 2.3. El PSM de datos seguro se representará mediante un esquema XML en UML extendido (ver subapartado 2.2). En este caso, el esquema de la BD XML será el esquema XML obtenido, que considerará los aspectos de seguridad necesarios.

La tabla 1 resume las tareas, técnicas y notaciones que se deben llevar a cabo a la hora de desarrollar una BD XML Segura

Tabla 1. Proceso de desarrollo de una BD XML Segura

	MIDAS: Desarrollo de BD XML Seguras		
Nivel	Tareas	Modelos	Notación
PIM	Diseño Conceptual de Datos con Seguridad	Modelo Conceptual de Datos Seguro	Diagrama de Clases (UML Extendido)
PSM	Diseño Lógico de Datos con Seguridad	Modelo Lógico de Datos Seguro	Esquemas XML (MIDAS-UML)

Ahora vamos a pasar a ver en primer lugar el PIM de datos seguro, resumiendo el perfil de UML que se ha desarrollado para modelar BD seguras a nivel de PIM (subapartado 2.1), después se verá el PSM de datos seguro, resumiendo el perfil de UML para esquemas XML adaptado para BD XML Seguras (subapartado 2.2), y finalmente, se resumen las reglas para transformar el PIM de datos seguro en el PSM de datos para incluir en el esquema XML los aspectos de seguridad que se han definido en el PIM de datos (subapartado 2.3).

2.1 PIM de Datos Seguro

Para desarrollar un PIM de datos seguro se ha desarrollado un perfil de UML (más detalles pueden ser encontrados en [9]). El perfil de UML definido permite clasificar tanto a datos como a usuarios bajo varios criterios de clasificación, con el objeto de poder llevar a cabo un control de acceso obligatorio. Los criterios son los siguientes:

- **Niveles de seguridad:** Permiten definir una jerarquía de niveles, como los tradicionales en entornos militares: sin clasificar, confidencial, secreto y alto secreto.
- **Roles de usuarios:** Permiten definir un conjunto jerárquico de roles de usuarios que representan las funciones jerárquicas dentro de una empresa.
- **Categorías de usuarios:** Permiten definir una organización o clasificación horizontal (no jerárquica) de grupos de usuarios.

Además de esta información de clasificación, este perfil permite definir tres tipos de restricciones:

- **Reglas de clasificación dinámica de datos:** Permiten definir los datos de clasificación de distintas instancias dependiendo del valor de uno o varios atributos de las instancias.
- **Reglas de autorización:** Permiten definir qué usuarios podrán acceder a qué datos y realizar qué acciones, dependiendo de una condición expresada en OCL.
- **Reglas de auditoría:** Permiten especificar situaciones en las que nos interesa registrar un rastro de auditoría para analizar qué usuarios acceden a la información. Para ello se definen condiciones expresadas con OCL.

Para la definición de todos estos elementos, consideramos el perfil UML, llamado *Conceptual Secure DB* (extensión de UML y OCL para diseñar BD seguras), que está compuesto de un conjunto de tipos de datos, valores etiquetados y estereotipos, además de la definición de un conjunto de reglas bien formadas.

El paquete que contiene todos los estereotipos que han sido definidos en este perfil de UML puede ser analizado en la Fig. 3. Estos estereotipos se pueden clasificar en las siguientes tres categorías:

- Los necesarios para representar la información de seguridad en los *elementos del modelo* (el propio modelo, las clases, atributos, asociaciones e instancias).
- Los necesarios para modelar las *restricciones de seguridad* para a) definir la clasificación dinámica de cualquier elemento del modelo, b) definir reglas de autorización, y c) definir reglas de auditoría dependiendo de tipos de acceso quizás de alguna condición expresada en OCL.
- El estereotipo *UserProfile*, que es necesario para especificar restricciones dependiendo de alguna propiedad de un usuario o de un grupo de usuarios, por ejemplo, dependiendo de la ciudadanía, edad, etc.

Una descripción en detalle de todos estos estereotipos, así como de todos los valores etiquetados que han sido definidos para estos estereotipos puede ser analizada en [9].

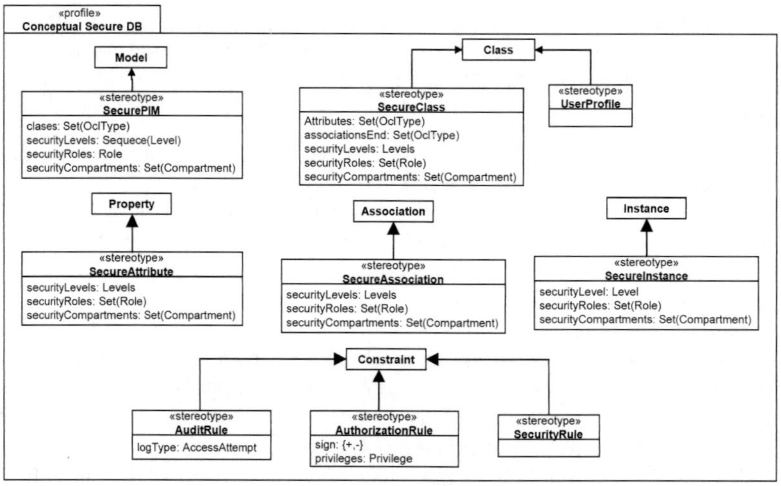

Fig. 3. Perfil para BD Seguras: *Conceptual Secure DB*

2.2 PSM de Datos Seguro

En MIDAS se propone usar como PSM de datos el modelo de esquemas XML, representado en UML extendido, utilizando el perfil definido en [21]. Para incluir los aspectos de seguridad en este modelo, en este artículo, hemos adaptado dicho perfil añadiendo los elementos necesarios para poder recoger la seguridad.

En la Fig. 4 se muestra los elementos que se han añadido con el fin de adaptar el perfil para poder representar esquemas XML seguros mediante un diagrama de clases UML. La extensión define un conjunto de estereotipos nuevos para permitir recoger en notación gráfica en UML todos los componentes de un esquema XML seguro, manteniendo las asociaciones, el orden y el anidamiento entre los distintos elementos.

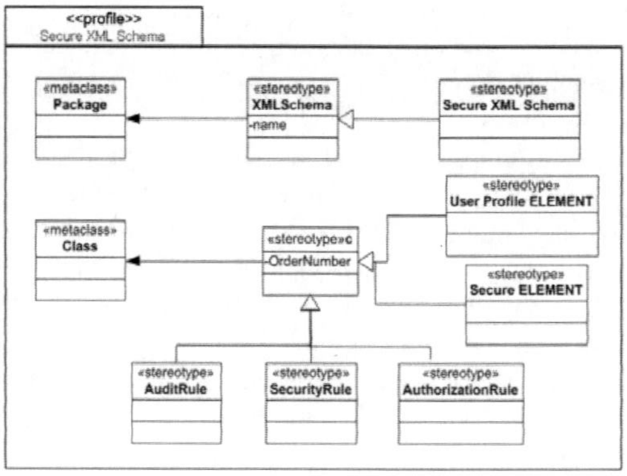

Fig. 4. Perfil para esquemas XML seguros: *Secure XML Schema*

2.3 Reglas de Transformación para pasar del PIM al PSM de Datos Seguro

De forma similar a como las metodologías para BD relacionales u objeto-relacionales proponen algunas reglas para la transformación de un esquema conceptual en un esquema lógico estándar, en MIDAS se proponen reglas de transformación para pasar del nivel de PIM al de PSM de datos. En este trabajo, se han definidos las reglas necesarias para obtener un PSM de datos seguro partiendo del PIM de datos seguro. A continuación, mostraremos estas reglas para recoger las características propias de la seguridad, basándonos en el trabajo de [21], donde se definieron los *mappings* para obtener un esquema de una BD XML.

- **Transformación del PIM de datos seguro**
  El modelo conceptual de datos, es decir, el *PIM de datos seguro,* se transforma, a nivel de PSM, en un esquema XML denominado *'Secure Data PSM'*. Este se representará con un paquete UML estereotipado con <<Secure XML SCHEMA>> que incluye todos los componentes del PSM de datos seguro. Además también contendrá los atributos de seguridad (*securityLevel, securityRoles* y *securityCompartments)* del PIM de datos seguro. Estos se definirán dentro del esquema XML como elementos globales. Estos atributos de seguridad se podrían haber incluido como atributos del esquema, sin embargo, si se representasen de este modo, no se considerarían elementos de primer orden, ni se podría recoger que pueden tener una cardinalidad máxima múltiple.
- **Transformación de la clase *User Profile***
  Esta clase incluye la información que se desee restringir sobre uno o varios usuarios. Se transformará incluyendo un elemento global estereotipado con <<User Profile ELEMENT>>, que contendrá un *complexType* de tipo secuencia con todos los atributos de la clase representados como subelementos.
- **Transformación de clases seguras**
  De forma genérica una clase UML se transforma en un elemento del esquema XML con el mismo nombre que la clase de la que procede [21]. Para transformar las clases UML *seguras*, estereotipadas con <<SecureClass>> hay que incluir además las características seguras que tengan las mismas. Las clases seguras pueden tener tres atributos específicos: *securityLevel*, *securityRoles* y *securityCompartments*. Las clases seguras se transformarán en elementos seguros estereotipados con <<Secure ELEMENT>>. Cada elemento seguro contendrá un tipo complejo de tipo secuencia, que contendrá como subelementos, entre otros, los atributos seguros, indicando con el atributo de los subelementos *maxOccurs* el número de posibles instancias de los atributos de seguridad.
- **Transformación de atributos seguros**
  Dado que los atributos de una clase, según la propuesta de [21], se transforman como subelementos del elemento que representa la clase UML a la que pertenecen los atributos, si un atributo tiene sus propios atributos de seguridad asociados, estos se representarán como subelementos del elemento que representa el atributo correspondiente. Así, los atributos de seguridad definidos sobre un atributo se transformarán en subelementos <<Secure ELEMENT>>.
- **Transformación de asociaciones seguras**
  En el caso de la transformación de asociaciones, en [21] se hizo un estudio detallado de la forma más apropiada para mapear las mismas al nivel de PSM. Las asociaciones entre dos clases se transforman, de forma genérica, incluyendo

un subelemento en uno de los elementos, correspondiente a una de las clases implicada en la relación, con una o varias referencias al otro elemento implicado en la asociación. En el caso de ser una asociación con seguridad, este subelemento tendría a su vez subelementos para representar a los atributos de seguridad correspondientes (*securityLevel*, *securityRoles*, *securityCompartment*) estereotipados como <<Secure ELEMENT>>.

- **Transformación de restricciones de seguridad**
  A la hora de realizar la transformación de las restricciones de seguridad que se hayan definido a nivel de PIM de datos seguro, estas se pueden definir para cualquier elemento (modelo o clase), aunque lo normal suele ser definirlo a nivel de clase. Si se definen a nivel de modelo, se crearán elementos globales dentro del esquema para recogerlo, en los demás casos se crearán subelementos del elemento del que dependan. Existen diferentes restricciones de seguridad:

  a) las reglas de auditoría (***AuditRule***): Se transformarán creando un subelemento estereotipado con <<AuditRule>> con nombre "AuditRule_" más el número de la regla. Este elemento será de tipo *complexType* y contendrá una secuencia de dos elementos: un elemento *AuditRuleType* de tipo simpleType de tipo base *string* con una restricción de tipo *enumeration* con los valores: *all*, *frustatedAttempt*, *successfullAccess*; y otro elemento *AuditRuleCondition* que será un elemento de tipo *string*, que contendrá la expresión XPATH asociada a la expresión en OCL.

```
<complexType>
    <sequence>
       <element name= "AuditRuleType">
          <simpleType>
                <restriction base= "string">
                   <enumeration value= "all"/>
                   <enumeration value= "frustatedAttempt"/>
                   <enumeration value= "successfullAccess"/>
                </restriction>
          </simpleType>
       </element>
       <element name= "AuditRuleCondition" type="string"/>
    </sequence>
</complexType>
```

  b) las reglas de autorización (***AuthorizationRule***): Se transformarán creando un subelemento estereotipado con <<AuthorizationRule>> con nombre "AuthorizationRule_" más el número de la regla. Este elemento será de tipo complexType y contendrá una secuencia con tres elementos: un elemento *AuthorizationRuleSign* de tipo simpleType de tipo base *string* con una restricción de tipo *enumeration* con los valores: + o - ; otro elemento *AuthorizationRulePrivileges* de tipo simpleType de tipo base *string* con una restricción de tipo *enumeration* con los valores: *read*, *insert*, *delete*, *update* y *all*; y otro elemento *AuthorizationRuleCondition* que será de tipo *string* y contendrá la expresión XPATH asociada a la expresión en OCL.

```
<complexType>
    <sequence>
       <element name= "AuthorizationRuleSign">
             <simpleType>
                   <restriction base="string">
                      <enumeration value="+/> <enumeration value="-"/>
                   </restriction>
             </simpleType>
       </element>
```

```
<element name= "AuthorizationRulePrivileges">
      <simpleType>
            <restriction base="string">
               <enumeration value="read"/>
               <enumeration value="insert"/>
               <enumeration value="delete"/>
               <enumeration value="update"/>
               <enumeration value="all"/>
            </restriction>
      </simpleType>
   </element>
   <element name= "AuthorizationRuleCondition" type="string"/>
  </sequence>
 </complexType>
```

c) la clasificación dinámica de cualquier elemento del PIM (***SecurityRule***) se transforma creando un subelemento estereotipado con <<SecurityRule>>, con nombre "SecurityRule_" más el número de la regla. Este elemento será de tipo complexType y contendrá una secuencia con un elemento de tipo *string* con la expresión XPATH asociada a la expresión en OCL.

```
<complexType>
     <sequence>
        <element name= "SecurityRuleCondition" type="string"/>
     </sequence>
</complexType>
```

En la Tabla 2 se resumen las reglas de transformación para pasar del PIM de datos al correspondiente PSM utilizando tecnología de BD XML. En [21] aparecen las reglas de forma detallada, sin incluir el aspecto de la seguridad.

Tabla 2. Reglas de transformación para pasar del PIM al PSM de datos seguro

PIM de datos	**PSM de datos**
PIM de datos seguro	**Esquema XML con seguridad <<Secure Data PSM>>**
Atrib. securityLevels	Elemento global del esquema (maxOccurs=unbounded)
Atrib. securityRoles	Elemento global del esquema
Atrib. securityCompartments	Elemento global del esquema (maxOccurs=unbounded)
Clase Segura	**Elemento XML con seguridad <<Secure Element>>**
Atrib. securityLevels	Subelemento (maxOccurs=unbounded)
Atrib. securityRoles	Sublemento
Atrib. securityCompartments	Sublemento (maxOccurs=unbounded)
Clase Segura User Profile	**Elemento XML global <<User Profile Element>>**
Atributo	**Subelemento**
Atrib.securityLevels	Subelemento (maxOccurs=unbounded)
Atrib. securityRoles	Sublemento
Atrib. securityCompartments	Sublemento (maxOccurs=unbounded)
Asociación	
Atrib. securityLevels	Subelemento del elemento de la asociación (maxOccurs=unbounded)
Atrib. securityRoles	Subelemento del elemento de la asociación
Atrib. securityCompartments	Sublemento de elemento de la asociación (maxOccurs=unbounded)
Restricción	Subelemento con complexType de tipo secuencia con subelementos
AuditRule	- AuditRuleType de simpleType con restricción enumeration - AuditRuleCondition de tipo string, que contendrá la expresión XPATH asociada a la expresión en OCL
AuthorizationRule	- AuthorizationRuleSign de simpleType con restricción enumeration - Privileges de simpleType con restricción enumeration - AuthorizationRuleCondition de tipo string, que contendrá la expresión XPATH asociada a la expresión en OCL
SecurityRule	- Subelemento de tipo string con expresión XPATH

3 Caso de Estudio

En esta sección aplicamos nuestra extensión de UML para desarrollar el PIM de datos seguro de un caso de estudio en el contexto de sistemas de información hospitalarios. A continuación, a través de las reglas de transformación que hemos definido en la sección 2.3, construimos una BD XML Segura utilizando la otra extensión de UML para PSM de datos seguros.

Para este ejemplo se ha definido una jerarquía de usuarios simplificada (ver Fig. 5 izquierda), compuesta de un rol genérico "Empleado de Hospital", que se separa en los roles "Personal Sanitario" y "Personal no Sanitario". El primero de estos roles se divide en "Doctor" y en "Enfermero", mientras que el segundo se especializa en "Mantenimiento" y en "Administrativo". Adicionalmente, para este caso de estudio se ha considerado tres niveles de seguridad, "Sin Clasificar", "Secreto" y "Alto Secreto" (ver Fig. 5 derecha). Para este ejemplo, por simplicidad no hemos definido categorías de usuarios, pero podrían haberse considerado categorías regionales (Región España, Región Argentina, etc.), criterios profesionales (Pediatría, Cirugía, etc.).

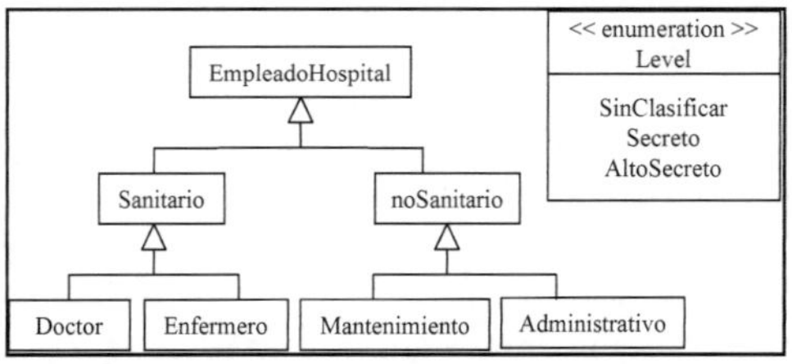

Fig. 5. Jerarquía de Roles de Usuarios y Niveles de Seguridad

La Fig. 6 muestra el PIM de datos seguro, representado con un diagrama de clases que contiene muchos detalles, pero nosotros explicaremos tan sólo algunas clases para poder enfocar nuestra atención en los aspectos de seguridad. Las clases del diagrama que mencionaremos son (el resto son obvias y no profundizaremos en ellas) *UserProfile, Paciente* y *Admisión*. La clase *UserProfile* contiene los distintos campos de información que son registrados para todos los usuarios que tendrán acceso a la BD. La clase *Paciente* contiene información de todos los pacientes del hospital, y puede ser accedida por los usuarios que tengan al menos el nivel de seguridad secreto y realicen roles administrativos o sanitarios. La clase *Admisión* contiene la información de todas las admisiones del hospital, y puede ser accedido por usuarios que realizan tareas sanitarias o de administración, y que además tengan un nivel de seguridad secreto. Ponemos en esta clase, que los atributos *diagnóstico*, *resultado* y *medicinas* sólo podrán ser accedidos por personal sanitario (y no administrativo), y que el atributo *coste* puede ser visto por administrativos, pero no por personal sanitario. Existe una asociación entre las clases *Paciente* y *Admisión*, y además, podemos apreciar que existen numerosas restricciones de seguridad asociadas a estas clases.

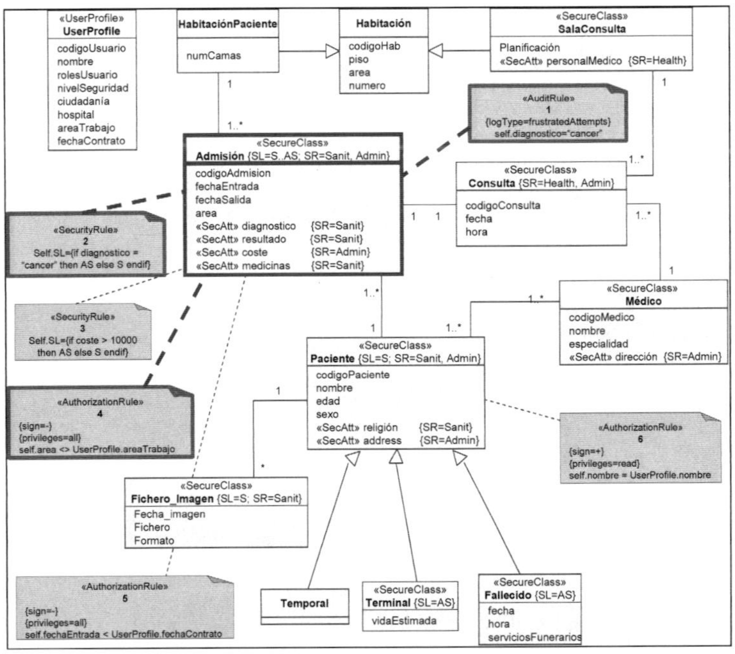

Fig. 6. PIM de datos con Restricciones de Seguridad

Hemos identificado cada una de las restricciones de seguridad con un número. El detalle de cada una es como sigue:

1. Se trata de una restricción estereotipada que representa una regla de auditoría. Esta regla especifica que todos los accesos que sean denegados por el mecanismo de control de acceso (valor etiquetado logType igual a frustratedAttempts), correspondientes a instancias de la clase *Admisión* cuyos diagnóstico sea cáncer (expresión OCL self.diagnostico='cancer'), deberían ser registrados para futura auditoría. Esta regla de auditoría nos ayudará a identificar posibles atacantes que traten de acceder a información confidencial sin tener los permisos necesarios.
2. Esta restricción define una regla de seguridad dinámica que especifica el nivel de seguridad de cada instancia de la clase *Admisión*. Si el valor del atributo diagnóstico es 'cancer', entonces el nivel de seguridad de la admisión será alto secreto, y de lo contrario sólo será secreto.
3. Esta es otra regla de seguridad dinámica para la clase *Admisión*. En este caso, el nivel de seguridad dependerá del valor del atributo *coste*, que indica el precio del servicio hospitalario.
4. El concepto que modela la cuarta restricción es una regla de autorización. Podríamos denegar el acceso (signo = -) a la información de admisiones a usuarios cuya área de trabajo sea diferente que el área sanitaria de una admisión particular (self.area <> UserProfile.areaTrabajo).
5. Por motivos de confidencialidad, podríamos denegar el acceso (signo = -) a la información de admisiones a todos los doctores cuya fecha de contrato en el hospital sea posterior a la fecha de entrada en el hospital de los pacientes

(self.fechaEntrada < UserProfile.fechaContrato). Esta restricción especifica esa regla de autorización.

6. Finalmente, podemos considerar a los pacientes como usuarios especiales del sistema en el sentido de que podrían tener acceso solamente a sus propios datos personales. En ese caso, es necesario especificar una regla de autorización positiva (signo = +) indicando como condición que el nombre del usuario sea igual al nombre del paciente (self.name = UserProfile.nombre).

Podemos observar que utilizando la extensión de UML, es posible especificar un amplio abanico de restricciones de confidencialidad en el PIM de datos seguro.

A la hora de transformar el PIM de datos seguro de la Fig. 6 aplicaremos las reglas definidas en el apartado 2.3 y obtendremos el PSM de datos. En la Fig. 7 podemos ver parte del PSM de datos seguro que hemos obtenido.

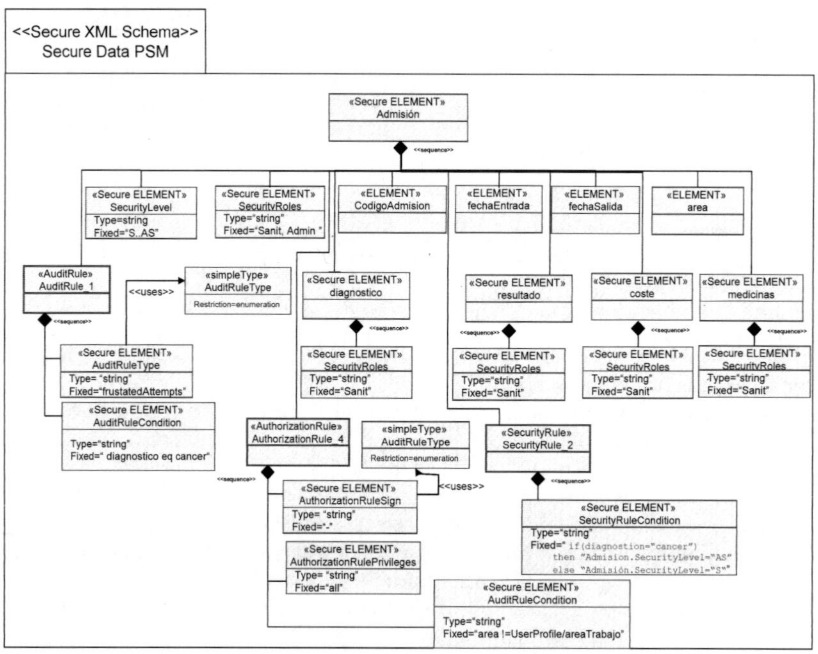

Fig. 7. Parte de PSM de datos con Seguridad

En primer lugar, hemos creado un paquete UML estereotipado con <<Secure XML Schema>> denominado *Secure Data PSM*, que incluirá todos los elementos obtenidos al transformar el PIM de datos seguro. En nuestro caso, por motivos de espacio, nos hemos centrado en la transformación de la clase ***Admisión*** y en la transformación de algunas de las restricciones, concretamente, las reglas ***AuditRule1***, ***AuthorizationRule4*** y ***SecurityRule2***, siguiendo los pasos indicados en la sección 2.3.

A la hora de transformar la clase segura *Admisión* se creará en primer lugar un elemento estereotipado con <<Secure ELEMENT>> que contendrá un complexType con los subelementos que representan a los atributos propios de la clase (codigoAdmisión, fechaEntrada, fechaSalida, area). Además contendrá los subelementos correspondientes a los atributos de seguridad (*Security Level* y *Security Roles*) y estereotipados con <<Secure ELEMENT>>. El valor de estos atributos se recogerá con el atributo *fixed* de estos elementos.

Los atributos *diagnostico*, *resultado*, *coste* y *medicinas* de dicha clase son atributos seguros y por lo tanto, se representarán como elementos seguros <<Secure ELEMENT>> y por lo tanto, tienen sus propios subelementos que representan los atributos seguros.

4 Conclusiones y Trabajos Futuros

Hoy en día existen diversas soluciones para el almacenamiento de datos XML, pero aún no existe una metodología para el diseño sistemático de BD XML que incorpore la seguridad en todo el proceso de desarrollo, si la información a almacenar se considera crítica.

En este trabajo se ha integrado el aspecto de seguridad en la aproximación metodológica para el desarrollo de BD XML en el marco de MIDAS que es una metodología dirigida por modelos para el desarrollo de SIW basada en MDA. Según el proceso especificado para el desarrollo de BD XML Seguras, para el PIM de datos seguro se usa la extensión a UML para incorporar los aspectos de seguridad a nivel conceptual y para el PSM de datos seguro se ha modificado el perfil para BD XML previamente definido, con el fin de incorporar los aspectos de la seguridad. Además, se han definido las reglas de transformación para pasar del PIM de datos seguro al PSM de datos seguro, que será el esquema de la BD XML Segura. Se ha desarrollado el caso de estudio para la gestión de información hospitalaria para validar nuestra propuesta; en este artículo se muestra una parte del mismo, en el que se define el esquema de la BD XML Segura para una parte del PIM de datos seguro desarrollado.

Existen diferentes direcciones en las que vamos a seguir trabajando para extender la propuesta de este artículo. Una de las líneas, en la que hemos empezado a trabajar es en la automatización de las transformaciones de las restricciones expresadas en OCL a nivel de PIM para convertirlas al lenguaje XPATH. Además se pretende realizar la implementación de diferentes casos de estudios, para detectar nuevas necesidades, así como analizar las facilidades para incorporar los aspectos de seguridad que proporcionan los diferentes gestores de BD XML, tanto los nativos como las extensiones para XML que tienen los SGBD. Por otro lado, también vamos a incluir el aspecto de la seguridad en el módulo para el desarrollo semi-automático de BD XML de la herramienta CASE (MIDAS-CASE) que estamos desarrollando.

Agradecimientos

Esta investigación se ha llevado a cabo en el marco de los siguientes proyectos: GOLD financiado por el Ministerio de Educación y Ciencia (TIN2005-00010/), DIMENSIONS (PBC-05-012-2) financiado por FEDER y por la Consejería de Ciencia y Tecnología de la Junta de Comunidades de Castilla-La Mancha, RETISTIC (TIC2002-12487-E) y CALIPO (TIC2003-07804-CO5-03), de la Dirección General de Investigación del Ministerio de Ciencia y Tecnología.

Referencias

1. Barbosa, D., Barta, A., Mendelzon, A., Mihaila, G., Rizzolo, F. y Rodriguez-Gianolli, P. *ToX - The Toronto XML Engine*, International Workshop on Information Integration on the Web, Rio de Janeiro, 2001.

2. Cáceres, P., Marcos, E. y Vela, B. *A MDA-Based Approach for Web Information System Development.* Workshop in Software Model Engineering in UML Conference. San Francisco, USA, octubre, 2003.
3. Chaudhri, A.B., Rashid, A. y Zicari, R. (Eds.). *XML Data Management. Native XML and XML-Enabled Database Systems.* Addison Wesley, 2003.
4. Devanbu, P. y Stubblebine, S. *Software engineering for security: a roadmap*, in: A. Finkelstein (Ed.), The Future of Software Engineering, ACM Press, 2000, pp. 227-239.
5. Dhillon, G. y Backhouse, J. *Information System Security Management in the new Millennium.* Communications of the ACM. 43, 7. pp.: 125-128, 2000.
6. eXcelon Corporation. *Managing DXE. System Documentation Release 3.5.* eXcelon Corporation. Burlington. Recuperado de: www.excelon.corp.com, 2003.
7. Fernández-Medina, E. y Piattini, M. *UML for the Design of Secure Databases.* Proceedings to the The 1st International Workshop on Security in Information Systems (SIS 2002) (Into the 4th International Conference on Enterprise Information Systems), pp. 25-38. Abril, 2002. Ciudad Real (España), 2002.
8. Fernández-Medina, E. y Piattini M. *Designing secure databases.* Information & Software Technology 47(7): 463-477. 2005
9. Fernández-Medina, E. y Piattini, M. Extending OCL for Secure Database Design. in International Conference on the Unified Modeling Language (UML 2004). 2004. Lisboa, Portugal. Springer-Verlag, LNCS 3273. pp. 380-394. 2004.
10. Ferrari E. y Thuraisingham B., *Secure Database Systems*, in: M. Piattini, O. Díaz (Ed.), Advanced Databases: Technology Design. Artech House, 2000.
11. Ferrari, E. *Secure DataBase Systems.* Segunda Reunión RETISBD. Murcia (España), junio 2001.
12. Ghosh, A., Howell C., Whittaker J., *Building software securely from the ground up*, IEEE Software 19 (1) (2002) 14-17.
13. IBM Corportation. *IBM DB2 Universal Database -XML Extender Administration and Programming, Product Documentation Version 7.* IBM Corporation, 2000.
14. ISACF, Information Security Governance. Guidance for Boards of Directors and Executive Management, Information Systems Audit and Control Foundation, USA, 2001.
15. Marcos, E., Vela, B., Cáceres, P. y Cavero, J.M. *MIDAS/DB: a Methodological Framework for Web Database Design.* DASWIS 2001. Yokohama (Japan), noviembre, 2001. Springer-Verlag, LNCS 2465, pp. 227-238, septiembre, 2002.
16. Marcos, E., Vela, B. y Cavero J.M. *Methodological Approach for Object-Relational Database Design using UML.* Journal on Software and Systems Modeling (SoSyM). Springer-Verlag. Ed.: R. France y B. Rumpe. Vol. SoSyM 2, pp.59-72, 2003.
17. Microsoft Corporation. *Microsoft SQL Server - SQLXML 2.0*, System Documentation. Microsoft Corporation, 2000.
18. OMG. *MDA Guide Version 1.0.* Document number omg/2003-05-01. Ed.: Miller, J. y Mukerji, J. Recuperado de: http://www.omg.com/mda, 2003.
19. Oracle Corporation. *Oracle XML DB. Technical White Paper.* Recuperado de: www.otn.com, enero, 2003.
20. Software AG. *Tamino X-Query. System Documentation Version 3.1.1.* Software AG, Darmstadt, Alemania. Recuperado de: www.softwareag.com, 2001.
21. Vela, B., Acuña, C. y Marcos, E. *A Model Driven Approach for XML Database Development*, 23rd. International Conference on Conceptual Modelling (ER2004). Springer Verlag, LNCS 3288, pp. 780-794. 2004.
22. Westermann, U. y Klas W. *An Analysis of XML Database Solutions for the Management of MPEG-7 Media Descriptions.* ACM Computing Surveys, Vol. 35 (4), pp. 331-373, diciembre, 2003.

Transforming Ternary Relationships to Database Schemas

Rafael Camps[1], Dolores Cuadra[2]
[1] Universitat Politècnica de Catalunya (Barcelona-Spain)
rcampsy@yahoo.com
[2] Universidad Carlos-III (Madrid-Spain)
dcuadra@inf.uc3m.es

Abstract. There are fourteen different possible patterns of functional dependencies in ternary UML associations or relationships. We present the transformation from all these patterns to normalized relational database schemas, including their specific constraint enforcement. SQL implementations are proposed. Not all the ternary patterns can be transformed to relational schemas using keys and inclusions (key or non-key based); more complex restrictions are needed.

1 Introduction

The so-called Entity-Relationship model (ER) introduced by Chen [5] is about to be 30 years old. Although a really standard ER model does not exist, it becomes the most popular approach for conceptual modeling of databases. One of the ER elements that have been traditionally a source of confusion is the relationship with degree greater than two, the *n*-ary relationship or *n*-ary association in UML terms [16]. During the last few years several researchers have fully analyzed the *n*-ary relationships, trying to clarify their use and the meaning of cardinalities. Jones-Song [11,12] McAllister [13,14] Génova [9] and Hartmann [10] are very good examples of such a task. The set of cardinalities of a relationship, draw a pattern of functional dependencies. The purpose of this paper is to present the transformation of all the fourteen different ternary patterns to relational database schemas.

Section 2 presents the two major approaches for the cardinality, using examples. In sections 3 and 4, functional dependency patterns and embedded cardinalities are analyzed. Section 5 presents the transformation from the fourteen functional dependency ternary patterns to normalized tables, including all the needed SQL constraints. In section 6 we discuss about minimum cardinality values. And in section 7 we summarize some conclusions.

2 UML and Merise Approaches

There are two main approaches to the cardinality concept [13]. The approach adopted by UML [16] (usually known as Chen approach or Look-Across approach) was previously adopted by Teorey [17], Ullman-Widom [19], Jones-Song [11], McAllister [13], etc. Another approach was proposed in the Merise method [15] (also known as Look-Here approach) and adopted by Batini-Ceri [1], Yourdon-Method [20], etc.

If *R* is a ternary relationship between entities *A, B,* and *C*, and we are using the UML approach for cardinalities, a ***1*** in the leg of *A* means that each pair of instances *b,c* (*b* from *B* and *c* from *C*) cannot be associated to more than one instance *a* (from *A*). However, in the Merise approach the meaning of the ***1*** in the leg of *A* is that each instance *a* cannot be associated to more than one pair of instances *b,c*. Because the semantics of both approaches is useful, some authors suggest the use of both approaches (e.g.: Génova [9], Elmasri-Navathe [8]). Other authors propose a generalized cardinality constraint having both approaches as particular cases (Thalheim [18], Hartmann [10]).

In this paper, we assume all the *n*-ary relationships follow the UML approach, but comments about Merise approach will be made when useful. In both approaches, two values can be used for the cardinality: the minimum and the maximum values. We consider ***0*** or ***1*** for the minimum cardinality value and ***1*** or ***** for the maximum cardinality value (the meaning of ***** is "no limit"). So we only use functional cardinalities. Until section 6, we will assume that the minimum value is zero. The minimum value zero in the leg of *A* will be interpreted, according to UML [9], as "it is not mandatory that every potential pair of instances *b,c* has to be associated to some instance *a*". In section 6 we will discuss the case of minimum value equal to 1.

Before analyzing all the ternary patterns and their transformation to relational database schemas, we will show the importance of the differences between the two approaches, UML and Merise, using an example. Seeing the Fig. 1., we will interpret the diagram of a ternary relationship according to both approaches. The key attributes (identifiers) of the entities are signaled with <<*K*>>.

The entities are *Product* (identified by *Pro-id*), *State* (identified by *Sta-id*), and *Dealer* (identified by *Dea-id*). The relationship is named *Concession*. Each instance of the *Concession* relationship represents a concession to a dealer for the distribution of a product into a state and has a date of concession (*Con-date*).

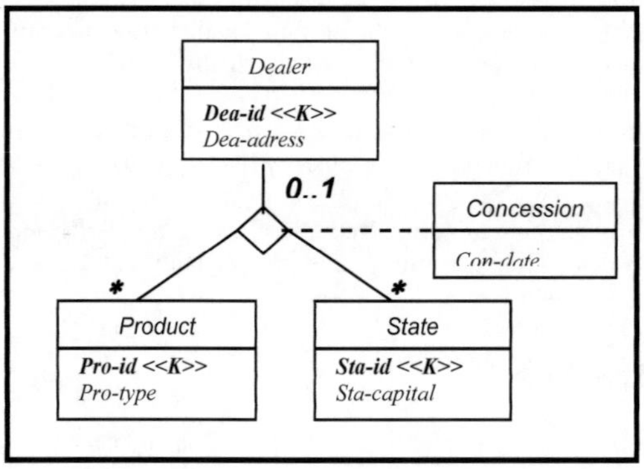

Fig.1: An example of ***1 * **** relationship

According to the UML approach, the semantics of Fig. 1 is as follows: a) each pair of one dealer and one state can be associated to many products, b) each pair of one product and one dealer can be associated to many states, and c) because of the ***1*** in the *Dealer* leg, in each state a product cannot be distributed by more than one dealer. Note that a dealer can distribute several products and a product can be distributed by several dealers. Also, a dealer can have concessions in several states and several dealers can have concessions in a state. Note that the minimum cardinality is 0. Therefore, we accept that a potential pair *product-state* doesn't have any concession. If we would have needed to represent information about *product-state* pairs that have no concession, they should not be part of the *Concession* relationship. A new relationship (binary relationship) could be defined and a restriction could be added to exclude these pairs from the *Concession* relationship.

Let us interpret the Fig.1 according to the Merise approach. The meaning of ***1*** as a maximum cardinality in the *Dealer* leg is: a dealer cannot participate in more than one instance of *Concession*, so it cannot be associated to more than one pair *product-state*. In other terms, each dealer cannot distribute more than one product and only in one state. The * in the *Product* leg means that a product can be associated to many pairs *state-dealer*.

If by error we input the diagram of Fig.1, to an automatic tool that interprets it as being UML ternary association, but should be interpreted as Merise (or *vice versa*), it would make completely erroneous assumptions, and the resulting relational schema would be wrong.

It is important to note that it is not possible to represent the semantics of the Merise interpretation of this example (Fig. 1 and pattern *#6* in Fig.5) by simply a UML ternary association diagram. If we use the UML notation but we need to express Merise cardinality restrictions, we will need to supplement the UML diagram with additional restrictions. And the semantics of the UML interpretation (pattern *#3*, Fig.5) cannot be represented using the Merise notation approach, although we supplement the diagram with additional restrictions.

3 Cardinality and FDs

In a UML association diagram (relationship diagram using ER terms) between three entities *X, Y,* and *Z,* there are three cardinalities, one in each leg. A symbol ***1*** in the leg of *Z* represents a functional dependency (FD) of the type $(X,Y) \rightarrow Z$. But between three entities, we can think at three types of FDs that we can label depending on their shape, as:

UML ternary FD	if it is	$(X,Y) \rightarrow Z$
Merise ternary FD	" " "	$X \rightarrow (Y, Z)$
Simple FD	" " "	$X \rightarrow Y$

We do not need to use the Merise ternary FD type because according to the *decomposition* rule (one of the Armstrong rules [8]) a Merise ternary FD is equivalent to two simple FDs; $X \rightarrow (Y,Z) \Leftrightarrow X \rightarrow Y$ and $X \rightarrow Z$

In order to describe all the FD constraints between three related entities, so to fully describe all the structural constraints in a ternary relationship, we should define nine different cardinalities:

- The three UML ternary cardinalities (one for each pair of entities) to describe the maximum number of *Z*s associated to each pair *XY*, where a ***1*** means a UML ternary FD, $(X,Y) \rightarrow Z$
- Six binary cardinalities (two for each pair of entities) to describe the maximum number of *Y*s associated to each *X*, where a ***1*** means a simple FD, $X \rightarrow Y$

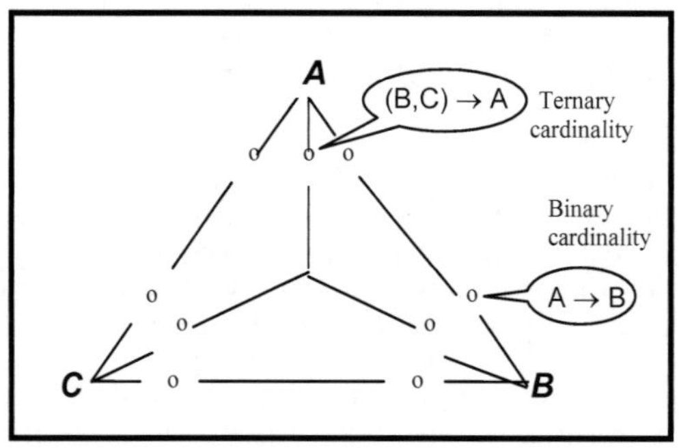

Fig.2: FD pattern schema

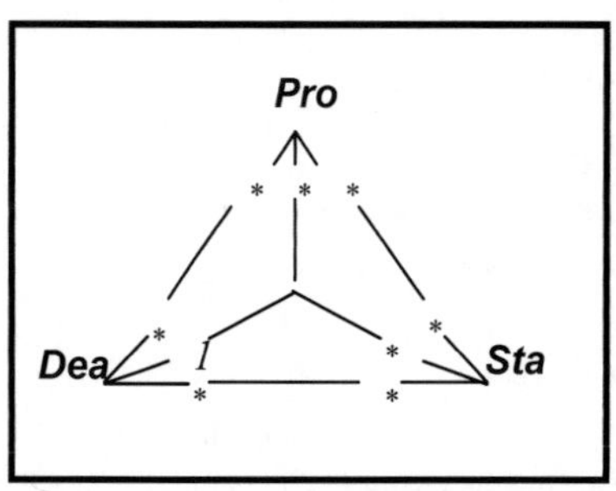

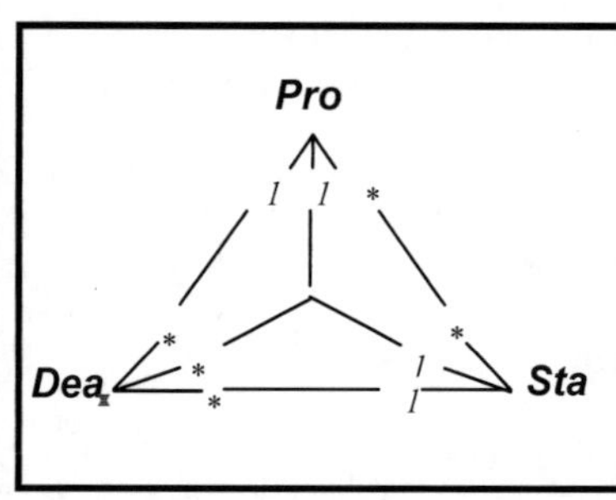

Fig.3: FD pattern for Fig1 as being UML   Fig.4: FD pattern for Fig1 as being Merise

Fig. 2 is a representation of FD patterns and it shows graphically the nine possible cardinalities. This graphical pattern was proposed in [2] and an improved approach is proposed by Demetrovics et al [6]. The external lines, the ternary triangle sides, are to describe the simple dependencies and can be viewed as if they were binary relationships being an integral part of the ternary relationship. Each ***1*** is a FD. In order to maintain a uniform notation, the simple FDs will be always noted with a ***1*** in the side of the dependent entity. The purpose of this FD pattern schema is only to be a pedagogical artifact, not a proposal for UML diagrams.

In Fig. 3 and 4, we represent the FD pattern for the *Concession* example of Fig.1, interpreted for each one of the two approaches: UML and Merise

4 Implied and Imposed Cardinalities

In practice, during the preliminary steps of the database design, relationships are often not strictly used. But, when the ER diagram is to be translated to a relational schema, perhaps using an automatic tool, it should be complete with true *n*-ary relationships used properly, expressing the full set of actual FDs from the modeled domain.

There are some implication rules between FDs, the Armstrong rules [8]. We have already seen the *decomposition* rule. The *augmentation* rule states that

$$X \rightarrow Y \quad \Rightarrow \quad (X, Z) \rightarrow Y$$

So, each ***1*** corresponding to a binary cardinality implies a ***1*** in a ternary cardinality. For example, in Fig.4 the ***1*** for the simple dependency *Dealer* → *State,* produces an implied ***1*** in the ternary cardinality for *State,* because the UML ternary FD (*Dealer, Product*) → *State*. Symmetrically, the ***1*** corresponding to the simple dependency *Dealer* → *Product* produces an implied ***1*** for (*Dealer, Sate*) → *Product.*

A third type of FD implication is due to the *transitivity* rule (as in pattern *#9* in Fig. 5): $X \rightarrow Y \text{ and } Y \rightarrow Z \quad \Rightarrow \quad X \rightarrow Z$

Each ***1*** corresponding to a UML ternary FD does not imply any simple FD. So, for a UML ternary association diagram (without additional restrictions) the implied binary cardinalities in the FD pattern are always **** ****. For example, in Fig.3, the UML ternary FD (*Product,State*) → *Dealer* does not produce any simple dependency. The semantics of this Fig. 3 is mainly expressed by this ternary FD. The meaning is the following restriction; "A product in a state cannot have more than one dealer". Now let us assume that we add the following constraint to the concession relationship; "Each dealer cannot distribute more than one product" that is the simple FD: *Dealer* → *Product.* This new simple FD is an imposed restriction, still taking part of the relationship because each concession (each instance of this ternary relationship) must relate one product, one state and one dealer. This imposed simple FD, produces a derived UML ternary FD (*Dealer, State*) → *Product.* See Dullea [7] and Jones-Song [12] for an analysis of the permitted impositions.

Note that this new FD pattern (equivalent to the FD pattern #12 in Fig 5) cannot be represented by UML ternary notation, or by Merise's, because they don't allow us to explicitly express binary cardinalities into a ternary relationship. The simultaneous use of both approaches doesn't allow us to express all the possible FD patterns either.

According to the definition of the instances of an *n*-ary relationship *R,* each instance informs about the association of *n* entity instances. Therefore, the ternary relationship cannot have any instance informing about an association between *b* and *c*, without having one *a* involved in the association. If we want to have such binary independent instances of the ternary relationship, then we should have a separated binary relationship. For example, perhaps we need to include the degree of knowledge that people of a state have about a product, independently of the fact that the product is distributed in this state or not.

5 Transformation to Relational Tables

5.1 FD Patterns and Relational Tables

As we have seen, it is possible to think about nine cardinalities inside a ternary relationship and each one of the cardinalities can have two values, ***1*** or *******,. So combining all the cardinality values in the ternary relationship, we obtain 2^9 possibilities. However, because of Armstrong rules, not all the combinations are valid. Moreover, some combinations are redundant because they are equivalent by permutation of elements, so by isomorphism. After eliminating all the impossible and the redundant patterns, only 14 unique FD patterns are obtained. The FD patterns are closed sets of FDs, so they are equivalent to closure operations [4]. And it is known that over a 3-element set there are (up to automorphism) 14 closure operations.

In Fig. 5 we display the following details for each one of the fourteen ternary patterns: a) FDs graphical pattern b) Minimal set of FDs and derived FDs c) UML ternary association diagram with additional FDs if necessary. The entity identifiers are signaled with <<*K*>> d) Normalized relational schema with -if necessary- additional restrictions expressed in SQL.

All the relational schemas have four tables (Fig. 5): one table for each entity A, B, C and the table R to represent the attribute r and its determinants. But, obviously, other normalized schemas are possible. The candidate keys are underlined. The label *"nac"* means "null accepted", and *"nn"* means "not null". We assume the "not null" restriction for all the candidate keys, except when *"nac"* is indicated. Each foreign key attribute, denoted by an arrow above it, references an attribute with same name situated in the table pointed out by the arrow.

The set of ***1***s in each FD pattern of Fig. 5 is a closed set of FDs. The set of bold ***1***s correspond to a minimal set of FDs from which all the non-bold ***1***s are derived. So, this set is a *minimal cover* [8] of the FD pattern. The *r*'s attributes of a ternary relationship are functionally dependent on *(A-id, B-id, C-id)*. But applying the Armstrong rules to the FD patterns of Fig. 5, the dependency of *r* can be simplified as follows:

Patterns	Dependencies of *r*
#0	$(A\text{-}id, B\text{-}id, C\text{-}id) \rightarrow r$
#1	$(A\text{-}id, B\text{-}id) \rightarrow r$ and $(B\text{-}id, C\text{-}id) \rightarrow r$ and $(A\text{-}id, C\text{-}id) \rightarrow r$
#2	$(A\text{-}id, B\text{-}id) \rightarrow r$ and $(B\text{-}id, C\text{-}id) \rightarrow r$
#3	$(A\text{-}id, B\text{-}id) \rightarrow r$
#4	$A\text{-}id \rightarrow r$ and $B\text{-}id \rightarrow r$ and $C\text{-}id \rightarrow r$
#5	$A\text{-}id \rightarrow r$ and $C\text{-}id \rightarrow r$
#6,10	$C\text{-}id \rightarrow r$
#7,11,12	$(A\text{-}id, C\text{-}id) \rightarrow r$
#8	$(A\text{-}id, C\text{-}id) \rightarrow r$ or $(B\text{-}id, C\text{-}id) \rightarrow r$
#9	$A\text{-}id \rightarrow r$
#13	$A\text{-}id \rightarrow r$ and $(B\text{-}id, C\text{-}id) \rightarrow r$

These dependencies of *r* determine the candidate keys of table R.

Observe in Fig. 5 that only four patterns (*#0 to #3*) can be represented by a UML ternary association without additional restrictions. It is possible to represent the ternary patterns, using UML binary associations except for patterns *#1 #2 #9 #11* and *#12* where additional restrictions must be added.

Now we will comment about some particularities of the ternary patterns.

5.2 Patterns *#0* to *#3* - Traditional UML Patterns

The pattern *#0* is the most popular case. It is the case where no FDs exist between the keys *A-id, B-id,* and *C-id.* So, its semantics is the same if the cardinalities interpretation is UML as well as if it's Merise. The patterns *#1 #2* and *#3* are characterized by having at least one UML ternary FD, but no simple FD*s*. These four patterns can be represented by a UML ternary association without additional restrictions. All the other ten patterns can also be represented as one UML ternary association but adding imposed simple dependencies. None of these three UML *n*-ary associations (*#1* to *#3*) can be represented using Merise approach. Observe that in pattern *#1* all the ternary cardinalities are ***1***, but all the implied binary cardinalities are still *******. The table R for the four patterns, *#0* to *#3*, has one, two or three multicolumn keys. For example, in table R for pattern #1 we underlined three overlapped candidate keys, corresponding to the three UML ternary FDs:

(A-id, B-id) $\rightarrow$ *C-id*
(B-id, C-id) $\rightarrow$ *A-id*
(A-id, C-id) $\rightarrow$ *B-id*

For these four UML traditional patterns (*#0* to *#3*) non-key based inclusions are not needed. The case in Fig. 1 with UML interpretation is one example of pattern *#3*.

5.3 Patterns *#4* to *#13* - Patterns with Imposed Simple FDs

The patterns *#4* to *#13* have some imposed simple FDs. The simple dependencies are to be an integral part of the ternary relationship, so in our relational schema we must represent these FDs as inclusion restrictions. Except for patterns *#12* and *#13,* all the UML ternary FDs are implied by the simple FDs.

The three patterns *#4 #5* and *#6* can be characterized by having only simple FD pairs of the form $X \rightarrow Y$ and $X \rightarrow Z$. They could be named Merise patterns, because each pair of simple FDs can be considered implied by a Merise ternary FD: $X \rightarrow (YZ)$. Each pair $X \rightarrow Y$ and $X \rightarrow Z$ is represented in table R by declaring *X* as a key. For example; pattern *#4* contains three pairs of simple FDs and they imply the three UML ternary FDs. So, all the nine cardinalities are set to ***1***. All the FDs are included in the table R as a set of three single-column keys. An example of pattern *#6* is the case represented in Fig.4. It is the example of Fig.1 but interpreting the cardinalities as Merise: *Dealer* $\rightarrow$*(Product , State).*

For patterns *#7* to *#11* some inclusions are non-key based, so they cannot be expressed by SQL foreign key restrictions. All the schemas for the patterns *#7* to *#12* have restrictions involving existence loops, so the transactions that maintain the tables need to enforce the constraints at *commit time* (*DEFERRED,* in SQL terms). Observe that for patterns *#11* and *#12*, it is not possible to obtain an equivalent set of normalized tables using only keys and inclusion dependencies (key or non-key based). We need to use more powerful restrictions. For all the additional restrictions we use SQL assertions. A detailed analysis of the case *#11* can be found in [3].

Pattern *#13* is the only one among the fourteen possible cases that produces a table R with a mix of multiple-attribute and single-attribute keys. An example of pattern *#13* could be the case of Fig.1 but overlapping both interpretations, UML and Merise. The FDs are: *(Product State)→Dealer, Dealer→Product* and *Dealer→State.* So the semantics of this example is: "in a State a product cannot be distributed by more than one dealer" and moreover "each dealer cannot distribute more than one product and only in one state". So if Coke is distributed in Spain by DISSA company, no other company can distribute Coke in Spain. And DISSA cannot have any other distribution.

6 Participation and Minimum Cardinality

We assumed in all previous sections that the minimum cardinality value is zero. Now we will analyze the translation of cardinalities with minimum value equal to 1. The UML interpretation of such cardinality value in the leg of entity A, is that each possible combination of an instance of B with an instance of C, must have associated at least one instance of A. But an instance of A can exist without being associated to B and C instances (see other interpretations in Génova[9]). In practice, this is an extremely unusual restriction. To enforce this semantic we can utilize an inclusion involving a Cartesian product: B•B-id x C•C-id $\subseteq$ $\pi_{\text{B-id,C-id}}$ R

This restriction can be expressed in SQL using the following assertion:

CHECK ((*SELECT COUNT(*) FROM* R) =
(*SELECT COUNT(*) FROM* B) *
(*SELECT COUNT(*) FROM* C))

Therefore, the minimum value equal to 1 in a ternary cardinality (UML approach) is no equivalent to the classical mandatory participation restriction. If we need to express the mandatory participation restriction for an entity A, we need that each instance of A has to be associated at least to one instance of R. That is a non-key based inclusion: A•A-id $\subseteq$ R•A-id that can be expressed in SQL as the following assertion:

CHECK (*NOT EXISTS*
((*SELECT* A-id *FROM* A)
EXCEPT
(*SELECT* A-id *FROM* R)))

Note that the classical mandatory participation restriction is exactly the meaning of a 1 in a minimum cardinality if we are using the Merise interpretation.

In patterns *#4 #5 #6* and *#13* there is al least one entity *X* being the left hand of a Merise ternary FD *X→(YZ)*. If a mandatory participation restriction occurs in such entity *X,* table X can be collapsed with table R. For example in the pattern *#4*, if all the three entities are mandatory, the four tables could be collapsed to a single one:

R (<u>A-id</u>, a, <u>B-id</u>, b, <u>C-id</u>, c, r)

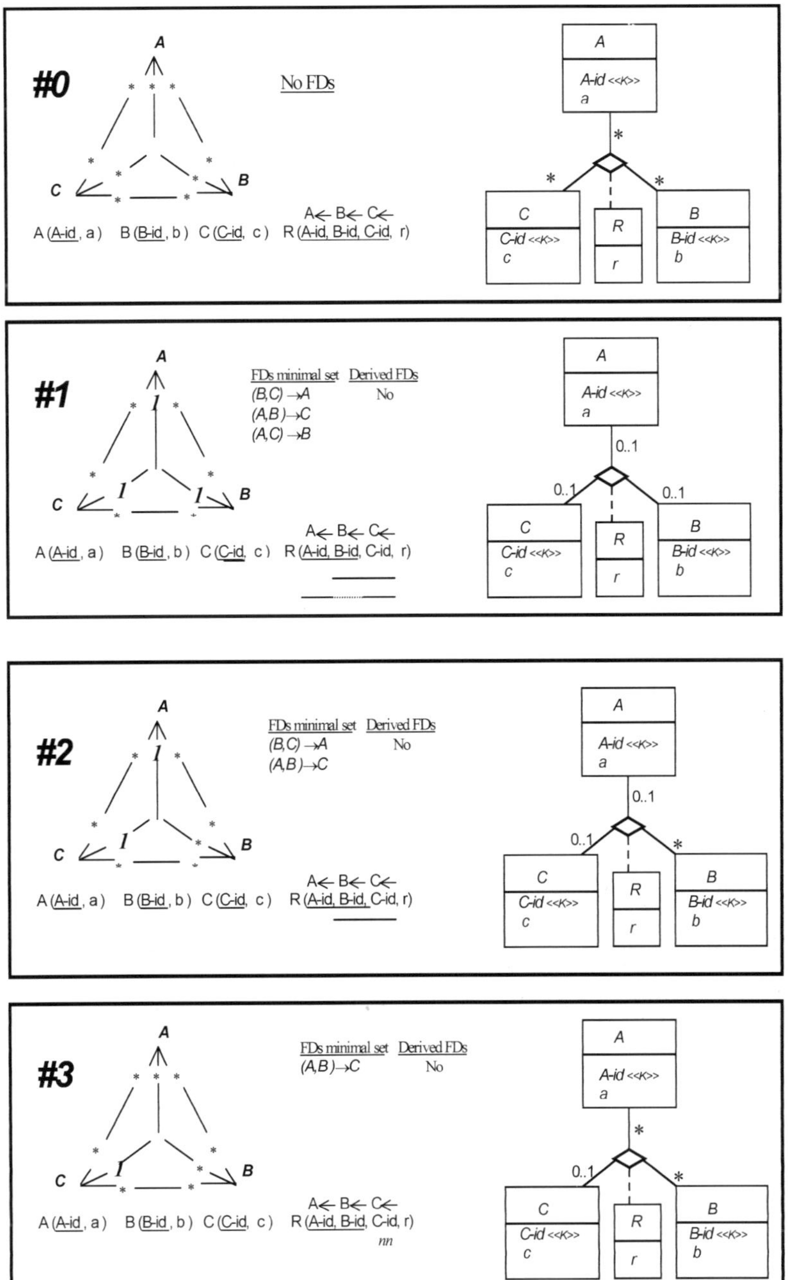

Fig.5 (1) : FD patterns, relational schemas and ternary UML diagrams

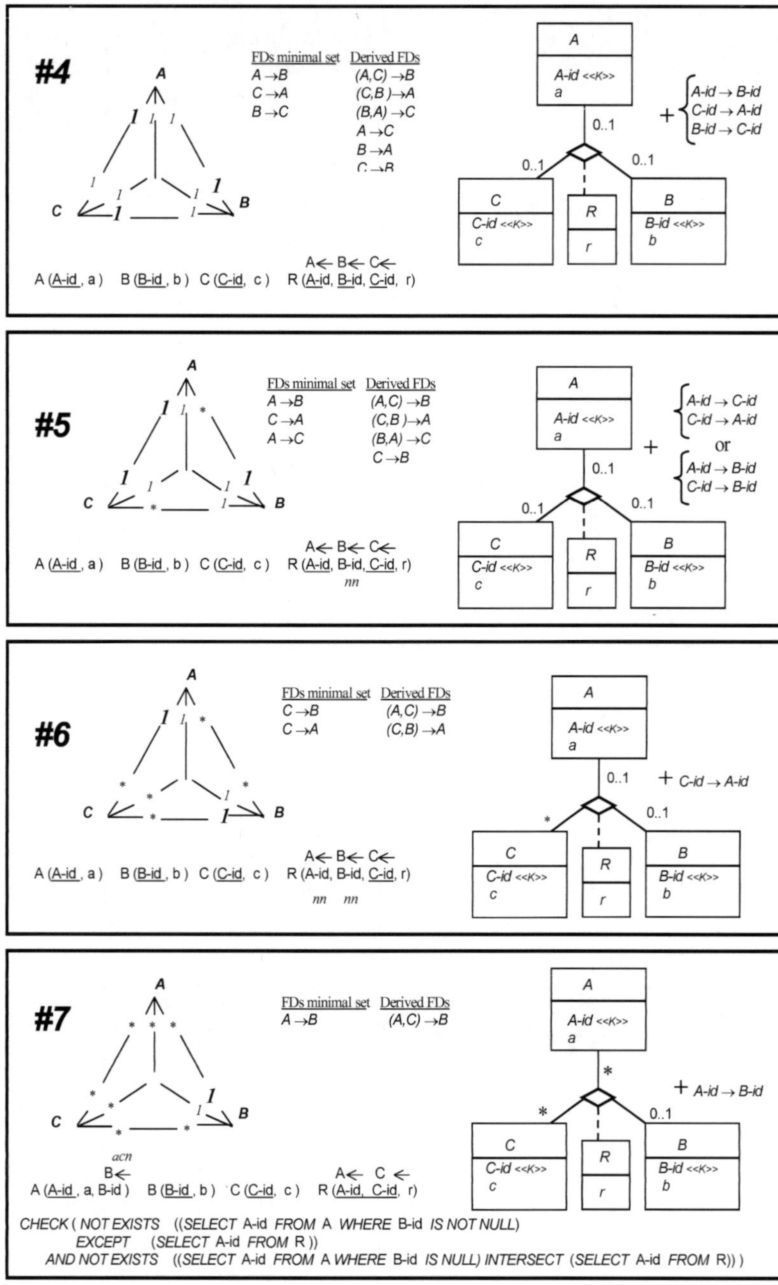

Fig.5 (2) : FD patterns, relational schemas and ternary UML diagrams

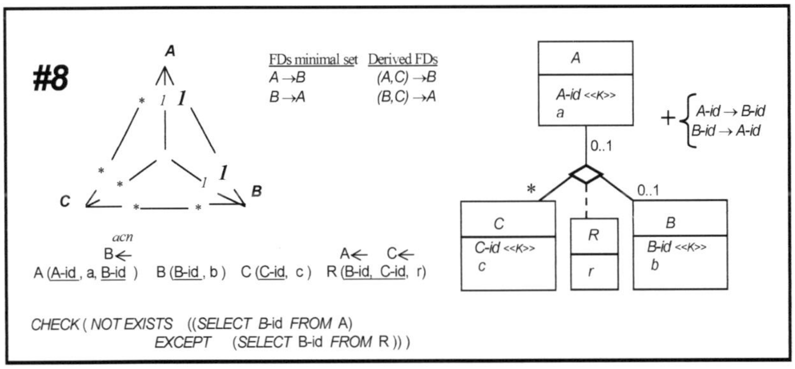

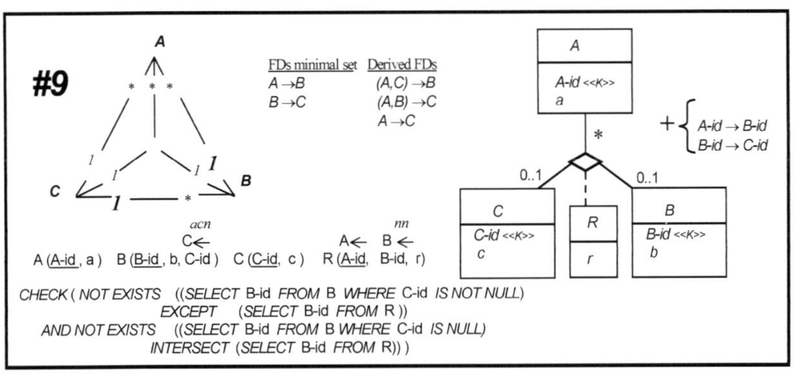

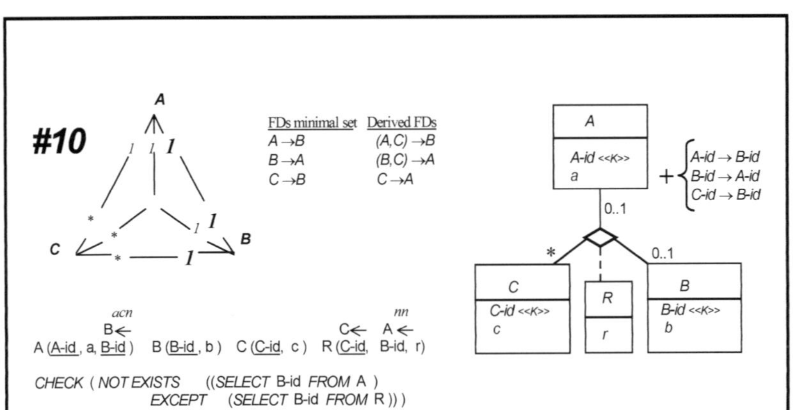

Fig.5 (3) : FD patterns, relational schemas and ternary UML diagrams

#11

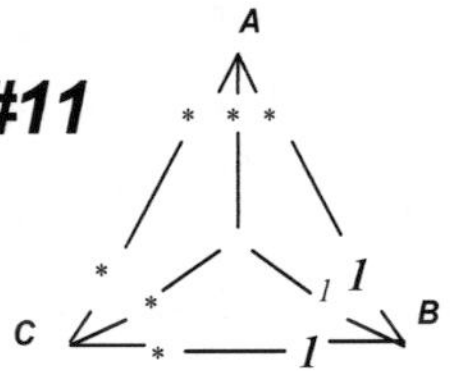

FDs minimal set	Derived FDs
$A \rightarrow B$	$(A,C) \rightarrow B$
$C \rightarrow B$	

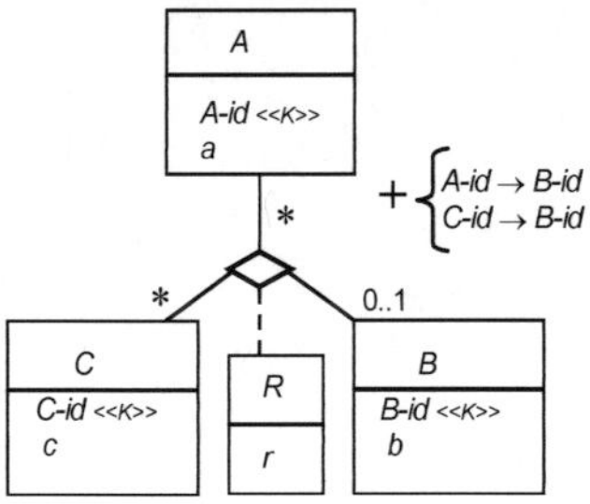

A (<u>A-id</u>, a, B-id) [B-id: acn, B←] B (<u>B-id</u>, b) C (<u>C-id</u>, B-id, c) [B-id: acn, B←] R (<u>A-id, C-id</u>, r)

```
CHECK  ( NOT EXISTS  ((SELECT A-id, C-id FROM R)
                 EXCEPT    (SELECT A-id, C-id FROM (A NATURAL JOIN C )))
      AND NOT EXISTS   ((SELECT A-id FROM A WHERE B-id IS NOT NULL)
                 EXCEPT    (SELECT A-id FROM R))
      AND NOT EXISTS   ((SELECT C-id FROM C WHERE B-id IS NOT NULL)
                 EXCEPT    (SELECT C-id FROM R)) )
```

#12

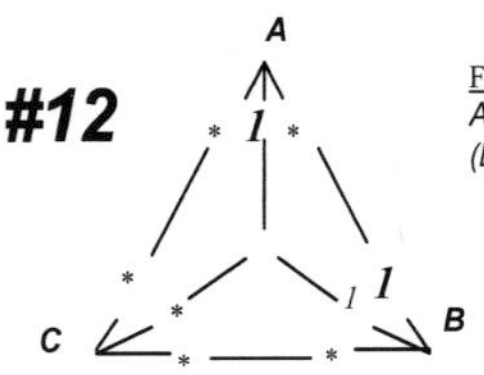

FDs minimal set	Derived FDs
$A \rightarrow B$	$(A,C) \rightarrow B$
$(B,C) \rightarrow A$	

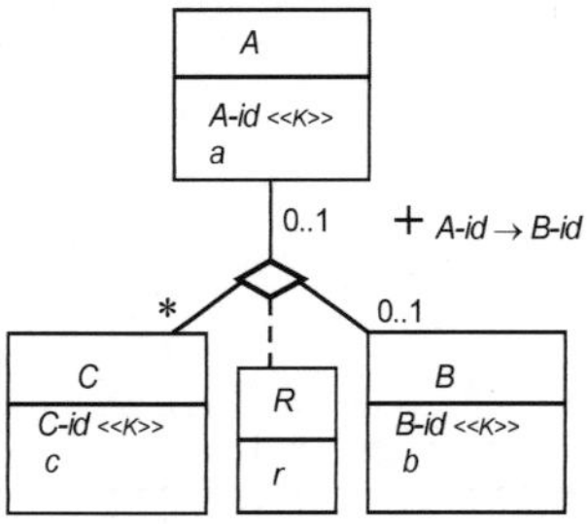

A (<u>A-id</u>, a, B-id,) [B-id: acn, B←] B (<u>B-id</u>, b) C (<u>C-id</u>, c) R (<u>A-id, C-id</u>, r) [A←, C←]

```
CHECK  ( UNIQUE   (SELECT B-id, C-id FROM (A NATURAL JOIN R)) )
```

#13

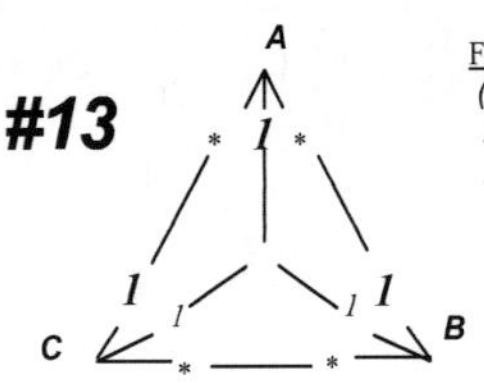

FDs minimal set	Derived FDs
$(B,C) \rightarrow A$	$(A,C) \rightarrow B$
$A \rightarrow B$	$(A,B) \rightarrow C$
$A \rightarrow C$	

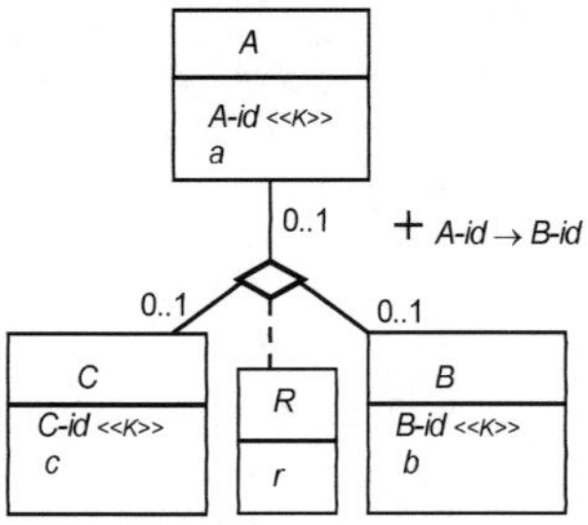

A (<u>A-id</u>, a) B (<u>B-id</u>, b) C (<u>C-id</u>, c) R (<u>A-id</u>, <u>B-id, C-id</u>, r) [A←, B←, C←]

Fig.5 (4) : FD patterns, relational schemas and ternary UML diagrams

7 Conclusions

All the fourteen FD ternary patterns can be expressed using the UML approach, using one UML ternary association plus, in some cases, some additional imposed simple FDs. This would not be true for Merise approach. So, the fourteen patterns could be expressed graphically with UML class diagrams if we had a graphical notation to specify imposed simple FDs.

The transformation from ternary relationships to a relational schema is not always a simple subject. Many cases of *n*-ary patterns are not translatable to relational schemas using keys and key based inclusions (foreign keys) alone: non-key based inclusions are to be declared. Two ternary patterns (*#11* and *#12*) cannot be translated even with such inclusions; more complex restrictions are needed.

N.B. Acknowledgements

We are in debt to all the people that helped us with their ideas, mainly to; G.Génova, S.Hartmann and B.Thalheim.

This paper is partially supported by the Spanish research project CICYT-TIN2004/07083.

References

1. C.Batini, S.Ceri, S.B.Navathe: Database Design: An Entity-Relationship Approach, Prentice-Hall (1991)
2. R.Camps: Transforming N-ary Relationships to Database Schemas: An Old and Forgotten Problem, Research Report LSI-02.5.R, Universitat Politecnica de Catalunya, Spain (2002)
3. R.Camps: From Ternary Relationship to Relational Tables: A Case Against Common Beliefs, ACM/SIGMOD-Record , 31 (2) (2002) 46-49
4. N.Caspard, B.Monjardet: The lattices of closure systems, closure operators and implicational systems on a finite set: a survey, Discrete Applied Mathematics, 127 (2003)
5. P.P.S.Chen: The entity relationship model: toward a unified view of data, ACM Transactions on Database Systems, 1 (1) (1976) 9-36
6. J.Demetrovics, A.Molnár, B.Thalheim: Graphical Reasoning for Sets of Functional Dependencies, ER-2004, (2004) 166-179
7. J.Dullea, I.Y.Song: An Analysis of Structural Validity of Ternary Relationships in Entity-Relationship Modeling, Proc. 7th Intl. Conf. on Information and Knowledge Management (1998) 331-339
8. R.Elmasri, S.B.Navathe: Fundamentals of Database Systems, Addison-Wesley, (2000)
9. G.Génova et al.: Semantics of the Minimum Multiplicity in Ternary Associations in UML, Proceed. 4th Intl. Conf. on UML (2001)
10. S.Hartmann: Reasoning about participation constraints and Chen's constraints, 14th Australian Database Conference (2003)
11. T.Jones, I.Y.Song: Analysis of binary/ternary cardinality combinations in entity relationship modeling, Data & Knowledge Engineering, 19 (1), (1996) 39-64

12. T.Jones, I.Y.Song: Binary Equivalents of Ternary Relationships in Entity-Relationship Modeling: a Logical Decomposition Approach, Journal of Database Management, April-June 2000, (2000) 12-19
13. A.J.McAllister: Complete rules for n-ary relationship cardinality constraints, Data & Knowledge Engineering, (1998) 255-288
14. A.J.McAllister, D.Sharpe: An Approach for Decomposing N-ary Data Relationships Software Practice & Experience, 28(2), (1998) 125-154
15. Rochfeld, H.Tardieu: Merise: An information system design and development methodology, Information & Management, 6, (1983) 143-159
16. J.Rumbaugh, I.Jacobson, G.Booch: The Unified Modeling Language Reference Manual, Addison-Wesley (1999)
17. T.J.Teorey, D.Yang, J.P.Fry: A Logical Design Methodology for Relational Databases Using the Extended Entity-Relationship Model, ACM Computing Surveys, 18(2), (1986) 197-222
18. B.Thalheim: Entity-Relationship Modelling, Springer Verlag (2000)
19. J.D.Ullman, J.Widom: A First Course in Database Systems, Prentice-Hall (1997)
20. Yourdon, Inc.: Yourdon Method, Prentice-Hall (1993)

Un Framework basado en OSGi para el Desarrollo de Sistemas Pervasivos *

Javier Muñoz, Carlos Cetina, Estefanía Serral, Vicente Pelechano

Departamento de Sistemas Informáticos y Computación
Universidad Politécnica de Valencia
Camí de Vera s/n, E-46022, Spain
{jmunoz, ccetina, eserral, pele}@dsic.upv.es

Resumen Actualmente está creciendo el número y la complejidad de los sistemas pervasivos. Este tipo de sistemas integran dispositivos y sistemas software para proporcionar servicios a los usuarios de un entorno físico. Este trabajo presenta un framework, implementado utilizando la tecnología OSGi, que tiene como objetivo facilitar el desarrollo de sistemas pervasivos. El framework ha sido desarrollado en el contexto de un método de producción automática de sistemas pervasivos basado en los enfoques del desarrollo dirigido por modelos y las factorías software. En el artículo se presenta tanto la arquitectura que sigue el framework y su diseño interno, como el modo de utilizarlos para el desarrollo de un sistema pervasivo en concreto.

1. Introduccion

Los sistemas pervasivos tratan de construir entornos donde los elementos de computación desaparezcan a ojos de los usuarios pero su funcionalidad continúe proporcionándose. Esta visión fue descrita inicialmente por Weiser [13] en los inicios de los años 90. Actualmente podemos encontrar sistemas pervasivos en entornos como los automóviles, oficinas, edificios públicos y, por supuesto, en nuestros hogares. Los requisitos que deben satisfacer este tipo de sistemas abarcan una gran cantidad servicios en áreas como la multimedia, las comunicaciones o la automatización.

Con el objetivo de aumentar tanto la productividad en el desarrollo como la calidad de los sistemas desarrollados, los autores han propuesto un método para el desarrollo de sistemas pervasivos [9] basado en las últimas tendencias de la ingeniería del software, como son la Model Driven Architecture (MDA) [11] y el enfoque de las Factorías de Software [3]. Siguiendo las guías propuestas por las Factorías de Software, se ha definido una línea de producto para el tipo de sistema pervasivo que deseamos desarrollar. Uno de los resultados de esta línea de producto es un framework para el desarrollo de sistemas pervasivos. Un framework es "*una aplicación semi-completa que puede ser especializada para*

* This work has been developed with the support of MEC under the project DESTINO TIN2004-03534 and cofinanced by FEDER.

producir aplicaciones concretas" [5]. El framework que se presenta en este artículo, implementado utilizando la tecnología OSGi [7], encapsula la estructura y funcionalidad compartida por los sistemas que produce el método. Es importante destacar, que aunque el framework ha sido desarrollado dentro de un método en concreto puede utilizarse de manera independiente.

Este trabajo contribuye al área del desarrollo de sistemas pervasivos, ya que propone una arquitectura para este tipo de sistemas y presenta un framework que la implementa y da soporte. La estructura del artículo es la siguiente: en la Sección 2 se describe brevemente el método en el contexto del cual se ha desarrollado el framework y que ha marcado fuertemente sus características principales. La Sección 3 presenta la arquitectura de los sistemas que son objeto de desarrollo del framework y la estrategia general de ejecución de estos sistemas. La Sección 4 describe el diseño interno y detallado del framework. En la Sección 5 se mostrará un ejemplo de cómo se debe utilizar el framework para implementar un sistema pervasivo. Finalmente, en la Sección 6 se incluyen algunas conclusiones del trabajo, se compara el framework con otros que tiene el mismo objetivo y se presentan los trabajos futuros.

2. Descripción General del Método

El desarrollo de un sistema pervasivo supone el uso de diversas tecnologías para satisfacer los requisitos de los usuarios. Habitualmente estas tecnologías proporcionan a los desarrolladores constructores de bajo nivel de abstracción. MDA [11] y las Factorías de Software [3] proporcionan estrategias para aumentar el nivel de abstracción y la productividad en el desarrollo de sistemas complejos.

Para salvar el salto de abstracción entre los lenguajes de modelado y las tecnologías de implementación, el enfoque de las Factorías de Software propone la construcción de frameworks, tal y como se muestra en la Figura 1 (A). Aplicando principios de la ingeniería de dominios, se desarrolla un framework que aumenta el nivel de abstracción de la tecnología. De esta manera se reduce la cantidad de código que debe ser generada a partir de los modelos de alto nivel de abstracción.

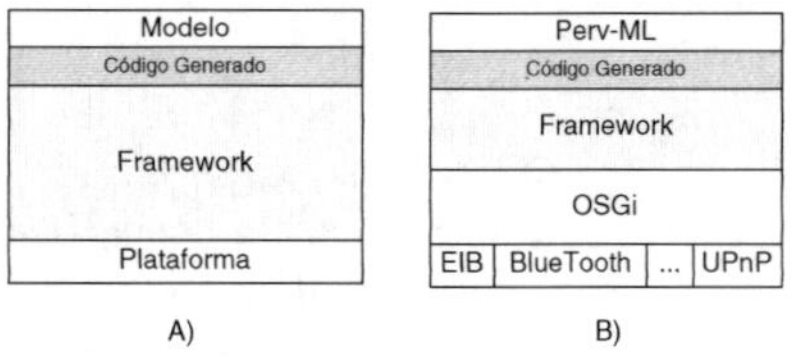

Figura 1. Estrategia propuesta por las Factorías Software y nuestra aplicación.

Siguiendo esta estrategia, nuestro enfoque metodológico para el desarrollo de sistemas pervasivos, que fue presentado en [9], está basado en:

- La construcción de un lenguaje de dominio específico para el desarrollo de sistemas pervasivo.
- La construcción de un framework que aumente el nivel de abstracción y proporcione constructores similares a los que define el lenguaje de dominio específico.
- La definición de transformaciones que conviertan los modelos construidos utilizando el lenguaje de dominio específico en código fuente que extienda el framework construido.

Aplicando este enfoque, en primer lugar hemos definido PervML (Pervasive Modeling Language), un lenguaje de dominio específico para describir sistema pervasivos de un modo independiente de tecnología [10]. PervML promueve la separación de roles, de modo que los desarrolladores pueden categorizarse en analistas y arquitectos.

Los **Analistas del Sistema** capturan los requisitos y describen el sistema pervasivo a alto nivel de abstracción utilizando la metáfora **servicio** como la principal primitiva conceptual para abstraer la funcionalidad que requiere el usuario. Los analistas construyen tres modelos gráficos que constituyen lo que llamamos la *Vista del Analista.* En estos modelos el analista describe (1) los tipos de servicios (mediante sus interfaces, las relaciones entre ellos y un diagrama de transición de estados para describir su comportamiento), (2) los distintos componentes que van a proporcionar los servicios del sistema y (3) como estos componentes interactúan entre sí.

Por otra parte, los **Arquitectos del Sistema** especifican qué dispositivos y/o sistemas software externos implementarán los servicios. Denominamos proveedor de enlace (*binding provider*) a aquellos elementos que son responsables de enlazar el sistema pervasivo con su entorno físico o lógico. Por ejemplo, un sensor de luminosidad se encarga de medir una característica física del entorno, mientras que un servidor de correo electrónico permite enviar información a agente que están fuera del ámbito del sistema. Los arquitectos construyen otros tres modelos que constituyen lo que llamamos la *Vista del Arquitecto.* En ellos el arquitecto describe (1) cada tipo de proveedor de enlace (mediante su interfaz), (2) los proveedores de enlace que se utilizan en cada componente, y (3) las acciones que deben llevarse a cabo cuando se invoca cada operación de cada componente.

El proceso de desarrollo siguiendo el método que proponemos se inicia realizando la especificación del sistema utilizando PervML. Entonces, esta descripción es transformada automáticamente en el código que extiende y completa el framework de implementación que se describe en este artículo. Actualmente ya existe una versión de este compilador de PervML realizada utilizando las extensiones para modelado de la plataforma Eclipse[1].

[1] http://www.eclipse.org/emf

3. Arquitectura del Framework

El framework para sistemas pervasivos que se presenta en este artículo ha sido diseñado con la intención de servir de soporte a los sistemas especificados utilizando el lenguaje de modelado PervML. Por lo tanto, un objetivo crítico ha sido proporcionar primitivas similares a aquellas utilizadas por el lenguaje. Este requisito ha hecho que la arquitectura de los sistemas generados por el framework siga una estructura y estrategia de ejecución análoga a la propuesta por el lenguaje de modelado para especificar los sistemas. A continuación se describe tanto la estructura como la estrategia global de ejecución.

3.1. Estructuración del Framework

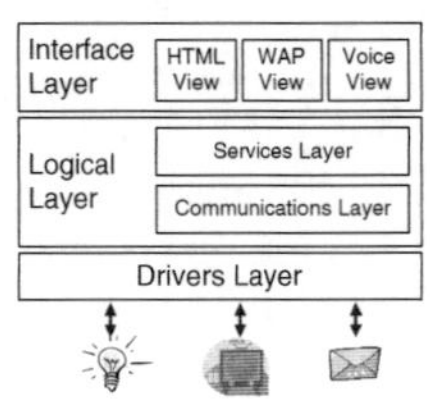

Figura 2. Estructura de la arquitectura del framework

La estructura de los sistemas desarrollados con el framework para sistemas pervasivos que se propone en este trabajo sigue los patrones arquitectónicos *Layers* y *Model-View-Controller* [1]. Mediante el patrón *Layers* organizamos los elementos del sistema en capas con unas responsabilidades bien definidas. Por otra parte, mediante el patrón *Model-View-Controller* proporcionamos soporte a la existencia de varias interfaces de usuario para interactuar con el sistema. En los sistemas pervasivos es habitual encontrarse con esta situación, donde los usuarios del sistema pueden interactuar simultáneamente utilizando distintos tipos de interfaz: web, PDA, comandos de voz, etc. La Figura 2 muestra de forma esquemática la arquitectura del sistema. A continuación se describen más detalladamente cada una de las capas.

La **Capa de Drivers** se encarga de gestionar la comunicación directa con los dispositivos o sistemas software externos que conforman el sistema. Los drivers deben desarrollarse completamente de manera manual, ya que han de tratar con cuestiones específicas de la tecnología y del fabricante.

Con el objetivo de poder ser tratados de manera homogénea por las capas superiores, los drivers que proporcionen acceso al mismo tipo de dispositivo o sistema software deben proporcionar una la misma interfaz. Por ejemplo, los drivers que permitan manejar una bombilla implementarán la misma interfaz (con operaciones para encender, apagar y consultar el estado), independientemente de si la bombilla se controla mediante una red EIB o utilizando la tecnología X10. Algo similar ocurrirá con los drivers que proporcionen acceso a redes de mensajería instantánea como Messenger, Jabber o ICQ.

La **Capa de Comunicaciones** proporciona una representación de los proveedores de enlace (*binding providers*) que son usados en capas superiores. Esta capa contiene los aspectos de la comunicación con los dispositivos y sistemas software que son independientes de tecnología y fabricante. Por ejemplo, se encarga de registrar los acceso al proveedor de enlace, de notificar los cambios en el driver a todos los elementos de capas superiores que requieran esa información, etc. Por todo ello, existe una relación una a uno entre los elementos de la capa de drivers y los elementos de esta capa. Por ejemplo, si el sistema contiene un sensor de temperatura de la tecnología LonWoks, existirá un driver para tratar con las cuestiones específicas de esa tecnología y un proveedor de enlace con funcionalidad común a todos los sensores de temperatura.

La **Capa de Servicios** se encarga de abstraer la funcionalidad que implementan las capas inferiores para ofrecerla tal y como la esperan los usuarios del sistema. Cada uno de los elementos de esta capa, a los que llamamos **componentes**, proporcionan un tipo de servicio. Para hacer uso de la funcionalidad proporcionada por un tipo de servicio se establece un contrato (definido mediante pre y post condiciones de las operaciones) y un protocolo, que establece las operaciones que pueden invocarse en un momento dado. Para implementar su funcionalidad, un componente puede hacer uso de proveedores de enlace (dispositivos y sistemas software externos) o de otros componentes.

Finalmente, en este capa también se pueden implementar interacciones entre componentes. En este ámbito entendemos una interacción como una secuencia de comunicaciones entre componentes, conceptualmente no relacionados a priori, para proporcionar una funcionalidad requerida por el usuario. Por ejemplo, el usuario puede requerir que se atenúe la iluminación de una sala al iniciarse la reproducción de un objeto multimedia. Conceptualmente, los servicios de iluminación y de reproducción de objetos multimedia no están relacionados entre sí pero, en un sistema en concreto, el usuario puede desear establecer una interacción entre ellos.

Por último, la **Capa de Interfaz** se encarga de proporcionar el acceso al sistema por parte de cualquier tipo de usuario (tanto personas como otros sistemas software). En un contexto pervasivo es habitual proporcionar distintos tipos de interfaces para acceder al mismo sistema. Por ejemplo, una interfaz web para acceder remotamente, una PDA o un teléfono móvil para acceder con movilidad, o una interfaz a través de TV para gestionar de manera centralizada un hogar. Por ello, se ha considerado adecuado aplicar el patrón *Model-View-Controller* en el framework. Siguiendo este patrón, sobre la capa de servicios se sitúa un elemento controlador. Las distintas interfaces (vistas) del sistema se comunican con este controlador para interactuar con el sistema. En la sección 4.2 se ofrecen más detalles de ese elemento.

Con el objetivo de ilustrar la arquitectura descrita, la Figura 3 muestra de manera esquemática una pequeña parte de un sistema desarrollado utilizando el

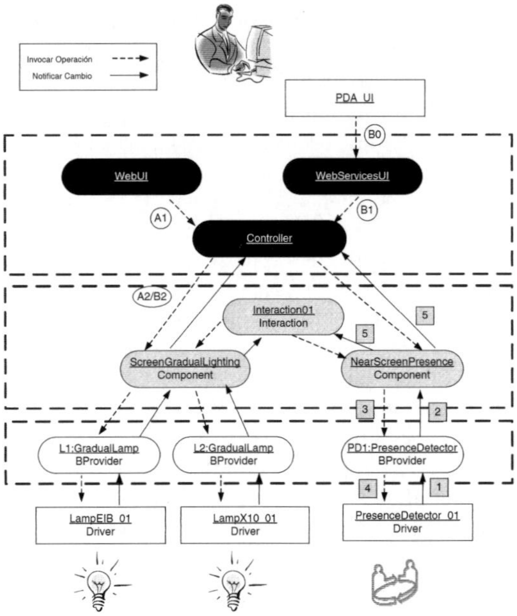

Figura 3. Esquema de una porción de un sistema desarrollado con el framework.

framework. En concreto la figura muestra dos componentes, uno de los cuales implementa un servicio de iluminación gradual y el otro un servicio de detección de presencia. El primero de ellos utiliza dos lámparas para implementar el servicio, mientras que el segundo utiliza un detector de presencia. Existe en el sistema una interacción para disminuir la intensidad del servicio de iluminación cuando se detecta presencia. En la figura también se representan el controlador, dos interfaces de usuario (mediante páginas web y mediante servicios web) y las relaciones entre todos los elementos del sistema.

3.2. Estrategia Global de Ejecución

Una vez presentada la estructura de los sistemas desarrollados utilizando el framework, es necesario describir su estrategia de ejecución; es decir, las reglas que definen las secuencias de acciones que suceden en el sistema cuando este se encuentra en funcionamiento. Existen dos tipos de eventos que pueden iniciar una secuencia de acciones:

1. Un driver detecta una cambio en el entorno (físico o lógico) del sistema.
2. Desde una interfaz de usuario, se solicita interaccionar con algún servicio; es decir, se solicita la ejecución de alguna operación.

La secuencia de acciones que se llevan a cabo en **el primer caso** se muestra en los cuadros numerados de la Figura 3. La detección de cambio es notificada desde la capa de drivers hacia arriba, a la capa de comunicaciones. En esta capa, el proveedor de enlace distribuye la notificación de cambio a todos los componentes que hacen uso de él.

Es importante hacer notar que en esta notificación no se informa del contenido de la modificación; es responsabilidad del componente consultar a sus proveedores de enlace para averiguar cual ha sido el cambio. Existe la posibilidad de que no haya ocurrido ningún cambio en el componente. Por ejemplo, supongamos que el detector de presencia de nuestro ejemplo devuelve la probabilidad de que haya alguien en su radio de acción, pero el servicio que proporciona el componente debe devolver un valor binario: hay presencia o no lo hay. El componente puede fijar en un 80 % la probabilidad para considerar que sí existe presencia. En una situación como esa, aunque el driver notifique un cambio del 20 % al 30 %, en el componente no habrá ocurrido una modificación, ya que continúa indicando que no detecta presencia.

Por lo tanto, es necesario que el componente confirme que realmente existe una modificación desde su punto de vista. En caso de que así se produzca, este cambio puede hacer que se cumpla la condición de algún disparador o de alguna interacción. Esto hace necesario que el componente notifique de la existencia de un cambio a todos los elementos que están suscritos a él. Como resultado de este proceso, es posible que se invoque alguna operación de un componente o que se inicie una interacción.

En **el segundo caso**, que se muestra en los círculos numerados de la Figura 3, el inicio de las acciones se realiza en alguna interfaz de usuario. La interfaz de usuario transmitirá una solicitud al controlador. El controlador se encargará de buscar al componente y realizará la invocación de la operación.

4. Diseño e Implementación del Framework

En este apartado se describe el diseño e implementación del framework para sistemas pervasivos, cuya arquitectura se ha presentado de manera general en la sección anterior. En la primera subsección se realiza una breve introducción a OSGi, la tecnología utilizada para realizar la implementación. A continuación se describe el diseño de las distintas capas del framework.

4.1. OSGi

La Open Service Gateway Initiative (OSGi) es una asociación de empresas creada con el objetivo de definir un estándar abierto para el desarrollo de pasarelas residenciales. El estándar define un entorno para la ejecución de servicios y una serie de servicios básicos, como registro (*Logging*), servidor web, búsqueda de servicios, etc. Además, OSGi [7] dispone de pasarelas a muchas de las tecnologías utilizadas actualmente en los sistemas pervasivos, por lo que se ha seleccionado como tecnología sobre la que implementar el framework.

Para poder entender la implementación de framework es necesario conocer algunos conceptos básicos de OSGi:

- **Bundle**: Un bundle es un archivo JAR de Java en cuyo manifiesto se utilizarán algunas etiquetas definidas por OSGi. Es el mecanismo utilizado para distribuir e instalar aplicaciones y servicios en la plataforma.
- **Service**: Dentro del la plataforma OSGi, se considera que un servicio es un objeto registrado como proveedor de una determinada interfaz.
- **Activator**: En OSGi, un activador es la clase que se encargar de gestionar el ciclo de vida de un Bundle. Esta clase tiene unos métodos *start* y *stop* que son invocados cuando el Bundle se arranca y detiene, respectivamente.
- **Wire**: Un *wire* es un canal de comunicación entre dos servicios siguiendo una estrategia productor/consumidor.

4.2. Diseño del Framework

El framework se puede estructurar en dos partes bien diferenciadas:

- el soporte a los elementos de la **Capa Lógica** (proveedores de enlace, componente e interacciones)
- el soporte a las **Interfaces de Usuario**.

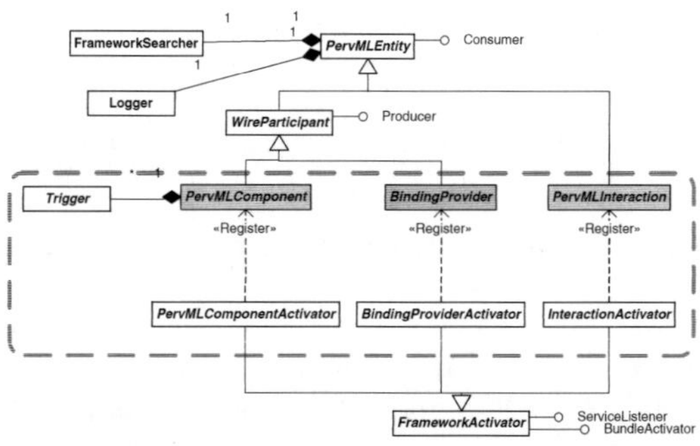

Figura 4. Estructura de clases para soportar las capas de Comunicaciones y Servicios

La Figura 4 muestra la estructura de clases que proporcionan soporte a la **Capa Lógica**. Los elementos sombreados dan soporte a los elementos de la capa intermedia de la Figura 3. Los elementos dentro del recuadro punteado serán los utilizados finalmente para extender del framework y generar el sistema final, tal y como se describirá en la Sección 5.

Las clases *PervMLEntity* y *WireParticipant* se encargan de implementar las interfaces que permiten utilizar el mecanismos de *Wire* de OSGi, así como de facilitar acceso a objetos de las clases *FrameworkSearcher* y *Logger*. El resto de clases de esa jerarquía (en el recuadro) contienen los puntos de extensión del framework. En ellas se definen los atributos que deben inicializarse al instanciar el framework, y se implementan, utilizando el patrón de diseño *Template Method* [2], las estrategias de ejecución de cada uno de los elementos.

La otra jerarquía de clases mostrada en la figura contiene los elementos de soporte a la creación de los activadores. *FrameworkActivator* es la clase más abstracta y se encarga de definir la estrategia general de los activadores y los puntos de extensión. También implementa algunas operaciones que se encargan de realizar funcionalidad atómica, como registrar en OSGi un objeto bajo una interfaz o crear un *Wire* entre dos servicios. El resto de activadores más específicos implementan algunos de los puntos de extensión, dejando otros abstractos para que sean escritos al instanciar el framework.

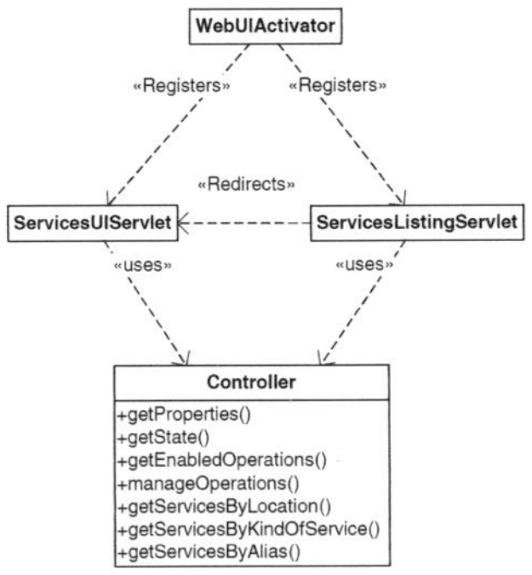

Figura 5. Estructura de clases para soportar la capa de Interfaz

La Figura 5 muestra el diagrama de clases que proporcionan soporte a la **Capa de la Interfaz**. Como ya se ha comentado al describir la arquitectura, se ha aplicado el patrón MVC. En nuestros sistemas, los elementos que forman parte del *Modelo* son los *Component*; mientras que la capa de interfaz contiene el *Controlador* y las distintas *Vistas*.

Al realizar el diseño del *Controlador* se ha considerado que el usuario realizará dos tareas a la hora de interactuar con el sistema:

1. **Seleccionar el servicio con el que desea interactuar** de entre todos los disponibles en el sistema. Para ello será necesario proporcionar mecanismos de estructuración, acceso y búsqueda de los componentes.
2. **Interactuar con un servicio en concreto**. En esta interacción el usuario recibirá información del servicio y podrá solicitar la ejecución de alguna funcionalidad que este ofrece.

Siguiendo esta filosofía, el controlador tiene **dos grupos de métodos** para soportar estas tareas:

- El primero de los grupos está formado por los métodos *getServicesByLocation*, *getServicesByKindOfService* y *getServicesByAlias*. Estos métodos devuelven una lista con información sobre los servicios del sistema, filtrándolos por distintos criterios.
- El segundo de los grupos está formado por los métodos *getProperties*, *getState*, *getEnabledOperations* y *manageOperation*. Las tres primeras operaciones son invocadas a la hora de crear la interfaz de usuario, ya que devuelven información de un componente específico. En concreto, la primera de ellas devuelve las propiedades invariables de un servicio (el tipo de servicio, su ubicación, etc.), la segunda devuelve el estado del servicio (por ejemplo, si se encuentra encendido o apagado, o si está detectando presencia) y, finalmente, la tercera devuelve las operaciones que el componente puede ejecutar en ese instante. Por último, *manageOperation* se encarga de invocar una operación en un *Component* utilizando las capacidades de reflexión de Java.

En la Figura 5 también se muestran las clases que proporcionan la vista a través de páginas web. Se trata de dos *servlets* de Java, cada uno de los cuales se utiliza para soportar una de las dos tareas descritas anteriormente. Los *servlets* realizan invocaciones a las operaciones del controlador para generar las páginas web que serán mostradas a los usuarios.

Es importante hacer notar que todas las clases de esta capa son concretas; es decir, no necesitan extenderse ya que son válidas para todos los sistemas. Esto se ha conseguido gracias a que (1) todos los componentes implementan una interfaz que puede ser utilizada por el controlador y (2) se han utilizado las capacidades de reflexión de Java a la hora de ejecutar las operaciones específicas de los componentes.

5. Uso del Framework

En esta sección se describe cómo instanciar el framework para implementar un sistema persvasivo. En cada subsección se proporciona una breve visión para cada una de los elementos del sistema.

5.1. Creación de los Proveedores de Enlace

Como puede observar en la Figura 6 tanto los drivers como los proveedores de enlace con los que se relacionan implementan una misma interfaz. Por ejemplo, los dos drivers para acceder a lámparas que proporcionan iluminación gradual y su proveedor de enlace implementan la interfaz *GradualLamp*.

Sólo existe un proveedor de enlace por cada tipo. Será en el activador donde se creen dos instancias, las cuales recibirán como parámetros de su constructor su propio identificador y el identificador del driver con el que están emparejados. A continuación se muestra el código contenido en el punto de extensión del activador (método *specificStart*), donde los identificadores de los drivers son *LampEIB_01* y *LampX10_01*.

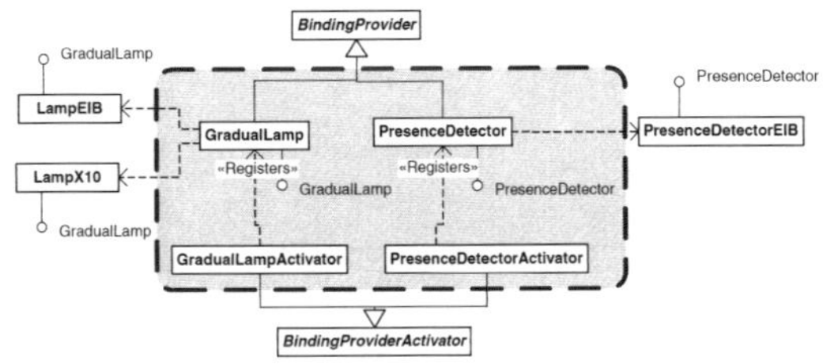

Figura 6. Estructura de clases para implementar los proveedores de enlace

```
public void specificStart(){
    registerBProviders("LampEIB_01","L1",new BProvider("L1",this.context));
    registerBProviders("LampX10_01","L2",new BProvider("L2",this.context));
}
```

La implementación de las operaciones del proveedor de enlace se limita realizar la invocación en el driver. Para ello, se hace uso de un método llamado *runMethod* que realiza la invocación utilizando las capacidades de reflexión de Java. A continuación se muestra el código de la operación *On()* del proveedor de enlace que representa una lámpara gradual.

```
public void On(){
    runMethod("On",new Object[0]);
}
```

5.2. Creación de los Componentes e Interacciones

La Figura 7 muestra **la estructura de clases para implementar los componentes** del sistema. Como puede observarse cada componente está implementado en dos clases (por ejemplo, *GradualLighting* y *ScreenGradualLighting*), atendiendo al siguiente criterio:

- La clase más abstracta (*GradualLighting* en el ejemplo) implementa aquella funcionalidad que es común para todos los componentes que proporcionan un mismo servicio. Esto incluye métodos para calcular las operaciones que pueden ser invocadas en un momento dado, las pre y post condiciones de las operaciones y la estrategia general de ejecución de las operaciones del servicio.
- La clase más específica (*ScreenGradualLighting* en el ejemplo) implementa las acciones de las operaciones. Hay que tener en cuenta que en el sistema podría existir otro componente que proporcionase el servicio de iluminación gradual, el cual utilizase otro tipo de dispositivos (por ejemplo, lámparas que permiten indicar un porcentaje de luminosidad o lámparas que sólo permiten 4 posiciones de intensidad) y, en ese caso, las acciones a llevar cabo cuando se ejecutasen las operaciones serían necesariamente distintas aunque el servicio proporcionado fuese el mismo.

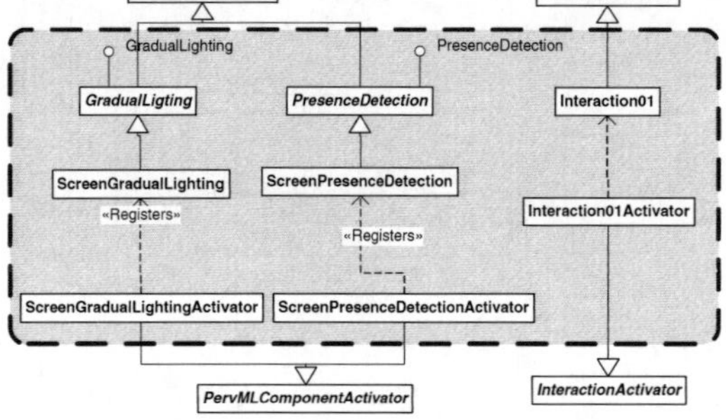

Figura 7. Estructura de clases para implementar los componentes y las interacciones

A continuación se muestra la implementación del método para fijar la intensidad del componente que proporciona el servicio *GradualLighting*. La estrategia que se sigue consiste en dividir la intensidad entre las dos lámparas, de manera que el primer 50 % lo proporciona la lámpara *L1* y el segundo 50 % *L2*.

```
public void setIntensityImplementation(int intensity){
     org.oomethod.interfacesBProviders.gradualLamp.Interface L1, L2;

     L1 =(org.oomethod.interfacesBProviders.gradualLamp.Interface)
            frameworkSearcher.getBProvider("L1");
     L2 =(org.oomethod.interfacesBProviders.gradualLamp.Interface)
           frameworkSearcher.getBProvider("L2");

     if ( intensity >= 50) {
           L1.on();
           L2.set( (intensity - 50)*2 );
      } else {
            L1.set( intensity *2 );
            L2.off();
      }
}
```

Por otra parte, el activador del componente es el encargado de inicializar alguna variables específicas y de crear los canales de comunicación (Wires) con los proveedores de enlace. Para ello implementa las operaciones que forman los puntos de extensión proporcionados por el framework.

```
package org.oomethod.components.screenGradualLighting;

public class Activator extends ComponentActivator {
    protected void initialize(){
       componentPID="ScreenGradualLighting";
       implLocation="/Dept/Floor1/Lab103";
       componentInstance=new Component(this.context,componentPID);
    }

    protected  void createAllWires(WireAdmin wa){
       this.createWire(wa,"L1",componentPID);
       this.createWire(wa,"L2",componentPID);
    }
}
```

En la Figura 7 también aparecen las **clases para implementar la Interacción** del ejemplo. Una interacción deberá implementar los puntos de extensión definidos por el framework:

- el método *checkCondition* evalua la condición de inicio de la interacción.
- el método *doAction* realiza las invocaciones sobre los distintos componentes que participan en la interacción.

A modo de ejemplo, a continuación se muestra el código del método que evalua la condición de la interacción.

```
public boolean checkCondition(){
     ScreenPresenceDetection = frameworkSearcher.getComponent("NearScreenPresenceDetector");
     ScreenGradualLighting = frameworkSearcher.getComponent("ScreenGradualLighting");

     boolean returnValue;

     returnValue = ScreenPresenceDetection.presenceDetected() &&
                        (! ScreenGradualLighting.isLighitng() );

     return returnValue;
}
```

6. Trabajos Relacionados y Conclusiones

Se han propuesta otras arquitecturas y frameworks para sistemas pervasivos. **one.world**, propuesta por Grimm [4], se basa en *tuplas* como modelo de datos, *entornos* como el mecanismo de estructuración para construir aplicaciones pervasivas, y *eventos* como el mecanismo de comunicación. Además, proporciona varios servicios básicos (como un motor de consultas, chekpoints y migración) para soportar la construcción de aplicaciones. **MediaBroker** [8] es un framework para sistemas distribuidos. Los principales componentes de MediaBroker son los clientes (que producen o consumen algún tipo de datos). Esta arquitectura ha sido implementada utilizando el lenguaje de programación C. Kirby [6] propone un arquitectura activa que está ideada principalmente para proporcionar soporte al desarrollo de aplicaciones sensibles al contexto. Describe un servicio de eventos globales utilizando una arquitectura P2P para difundir la información de contexto. Las aplicaciones pervasivas pueden activar su funcionalidad como respuesta a estos eventos. Rossi [12] también propone un framework centrado en el soporte al desarrollo de aplicaciones sensibles al contexto. El framework aplica patrones de diseño con el objetivo de extender aplicaciones OO «tradicionales» para proporcionarles funcionalidad sensible al contexto. En concreto, se proporciona soporte para tratar con información relativa a la ubicación.

Nuestro framework da soporte al desarrollo de aplicaciones siguiendo el método descrito en la Sección 2. En nuestro caso, la información relativa al contexto es descrita como un servicio más que permite consultar información del entorno físico mediante el uso de los proveedores de enlace adecuados (por ejemplo, para tratar con información de ubicación se podrían utilizar sensores de presencia, chips RFID o receptores GPS, entre otros). Además, nuestro framework ha sido implementado utilizando tecnología que está siendo utilizada actualmente por la industria, por lo que es de aplicación directa. Por otra parte, el uso del concepto de driver y las características de OSGi nos permiten integrar toda la funcionalidad proporcionada por otras tecnologías actuales que pueden ser aplicadas en este área, como EIB, LonWorks, UPnP, X10, Bluetooth, etc. Finalmente, remarcar que nuestro framework proporciona soporte a todos los niveles de la aplicación, desde la relación con los dispositivos hasta la interfaz de usuario.

Nuestra líneas de trabajo futuro se centran en varias tareas: (1) continuar implementando casos de estudio utilizando el framework y el método propuesto, (2) extender el método y el framework con nuevas características, como adaptación automática a nuevos servicios, *end-user development* y seguridad, y (3) proporcionar nuevos tipos de interfaces de usuario.

Referencias

1. Frank Buschmann, Regine Meunier, Hans Rohnert, Peter Sommerlad, and Michael Stal. *Pattern-Oriented Software Architecture*, volume 1: A System of Patterns. Wiley, 1996.
2. Erich Gamma, Richard Helm, Ralph Johnson, and John Vlissides. *Design Patterns*. Addison-Wesley, 1994.
3. Jack Greenfield, Keith Short, Steve Cook, and Stuart Kent. *Software Factories*. Wiley Publising Inc., 2004.
4. Robert Grimm, Janet Davis, Eric Lemar, Adam MacBeth, Steven Swanson, Thomas Anderson, Brian Bershad, Gaetano Borriello, Steven Gribble, and David Wetherall. System Support for Pervasive Applications. *ACM Transactions on Computer Systems*, 22(4):421–486, November 2004.
5. Ralph Johnson and Brian Foote. Designing Reusable Classes. *Journal of Object-Oriented Programming*, 1(5):22–35, June/July 1988.
6. Graham Kirby, Alan Dearle, Ron Morrison, Mark Dunlop, Richard Connor, and Paddy Nixon. Active architecture for pervasive contextual services. In *International Workshop on Middleware for Pervasive and Ad-hoc Computing*, 2003.
7. Dave Marples and Peter Kriens. The Open Services Gateway Initiative: An Introductory Overview. *IEEE Communications Magazine*, 39(12):110–114, 2001.
8. Martin Modahl, Ilya Bagrak, Matthew Wolenetz, Phillip Hutto, and Umakishore Ramachandran. MediaBroker: An Architecture for Pervasive Computing. In *Second IEEE International Conference on Pervasive Computing and Communications (PerCom'04)*, page 253, 2004.
9. Javier Muñoz and Vicente Pelechano. Building a Software Factory for Pervasive Systems Development. In *17th Advanced Information Systems Engineering (CAiSE)*, volume 3520 of *LNCS*, pages 329–343. Springer-Verlag, May 2005.
10. Javier Muñoz, Vicente Pelechano, and Joan Fons. Model Driven Development of Pervasive Systems. In *I International Workshop on Model-Based Methodologies for Pervasive and Embedded Software (MOMPES)*, pages 3 - 14, June 2004.
11. Object Management Group. Model Driven Architecture Guide, 2003.
12. Gustavo Rossi, Silvia Gordillo, and Andrés Fortier. Seamless Engineering of Location-Aware Services. In *OTM Workshops*, volume 3762 / 2005 of *LNCS*, page p. 176. Springer-Verlag, 2005.
13. Mark Weiser. The Computer for the 21st Century. *Scientific American*, 265(3):94–104, Sept. 1991.

Sesión 7:

MDA y Componentes

Aplicando MDA al Diseño Conceptual de Almacenes de Datos

Leopoldo Zepeda, Matilde Celma

Departamento de Sistemas Informáticos y Computación
Universidad politécnica de Valencia
Valencia, España
leopoldo@correo.ccs.net.mx, mcelma@dsic.upv.es

Resumen. Un Almacén de Datos (AD), es una base de datos diseñada para dar apoyo al proceso de toma de decisiones en una organización. A pesar de la difusión que ha tenido la tecnología relacionada con los ADs, sentimos que aún hacen falta métodos que guíen el diseño conceptual del AD. Este artículo, se concierne con el diseño conceptual de ADs. El método que proponemos se basa en tres fases. La primera fase, extrae un conjunto de esquemas multidimensionales a partir del esquema conceptual de la base de datos operacional. Esto se logra por medio de un conjunto de reglas de transformación definidas en el marco de Model Driven Architecture (MDA). La segunda fase, consiente en identifica y elegir los requisitos de usuario. Por último, los requisitos de usuario son usados para seleccionar y refinar los esquemas multidimensionales.

1. Introducción

En la actualidad, los ADs, se han convertido en una tecnología de gran utilidad para el análisis de los datos y la planificación estratégica. Una característica importante en los ADs, es que mantienen información histórica procedente de diferentes bases de datos operacionales.

La organización de los datos de un AD, llamada esquema multidimensional [1], es muy simple: los datos a ser analizados o hechos, constituyen el centro del esquema y alrededor del centro, otros datos describen las dimensiones sobre las cuales el análisis de los datos puede ser realizado.

En algunas ocasiones, el AD extrae su contenido directamente de las bases de datos operacionales, en situaciones mas complejas, la arquitectura del AD puede ser multinivel, y el contenido del AD puede ser cargado de repositorios intermedios.

A pesar de la existencia de números métodos y herramientas dirigidos a solucionar problemas relacionados con la implementación física del AD o a la manipulación estática de sus datos, se ha puesto poca atención al diseño conceptual de este tipo de sistemas, probablemente asumiendo que es una tarea trivial.

Este artículo, se refiere al diseño conceptual de ADs, iniciando en la descripción conceptual (esquema ER) de la base de datos operacional. El principio de esta propuesta, se basa también en el supuesto de que el diseño de un AD, debe ser conducido por los requisitos de usuario.

El método propuesto en este artículo consiste de tres fases: 1) Obtención de un conjunto de esquemas multidimensionales candidatos a partir del esquema ER. 2) Definición de los requisitos de usuario. 3) Selección y refinamiento del esquema multidimensional.

Este método, toma ventaja de dos perspectivas de diseño de ADs complementarias. La fase 2, enfatiza los requisitos de usuario, mientras que en la fase 1, el análisis del esquema ER muestra la semántica de la base de datos operacional existente. La fase final, integra los dos puntos de vistas y genera una solución que refleja los requisitos de usuario y es soportada por las bases de datos operacionales.

La primera fase del método que proponemos esta dedicada a examinar el modelo conceptual de la base de datos operacional, generando los esquemas multidimensionales candidatos para el AD. La solución a esta fase, se ha abordado en el contexto de MDA, para esto, hemos definido un conjunto de reglas de transformación entre el metamodelo ER y el metamodelo OLAP. Aunque esta fase puede generar un gran número de esquemas multidimensionales candidatos, este análisis se puede realizar de manera automática.

En la segunda fase, los requisitos de usuario son recogidos por medio de entrevistas. El propósito de las entrevistas es obtener información acerca de las necesidades de análisis de la compañía. Como base para esta fase, adaptamos un método de elicitación de requisitos basado en metas.

La tercera fase, contrasta la información obtenida en la segunda fase, con los esquemas multidimensional candidatos generados en la primera fase, posteriormente, es responsabilidad del diseñador refinar manualmente el esquema multidimensional seleccionado.

El resto del artículo se organiza como sigue: en la sección 2, se hace una revisión del estado del arte. En la sección 3, se muestran los conceptos básicos de MDA. En la sección 4, se presenta la metodología de diseño propuesta y por último en la sección 5, se presentan las conclusiones y trabajos futuros previstos.

2. Estado del Arte

En esta sección, presentamos las contribuciones relacionadas con el diseño conceptual de AD que son más cercanas a nuestra metodología.

Cabibbo & Torlone [2] proponen un método para derivar esquemas multidimensionales a partir del esquema conceptual de la base de datos operacional, y realizar su implementación basada en tablas relacionales y vectores multidimensionales. La derivación del esquema multidimensional (MD) se realiza en los siguientes pasos: (1) identificación de hechos y dimensiones, (2) reestructuración del esquema ER, (3) derivación del grafo de dimensiones, y (4) traslado al modelo multidimensional. Los esquemas multidimensionales se basan en grafos formados por F-Tables (tablas que sirven como implementación abstracta de la base de datos relacional y vectores multidimensionales). El método de diseño que proponen construye un esquema MD a partir de la base de datos operacional, donde un esquema MD consiste de un conjunto finito de dimensiones, un conjunto finito de F-Tables, y un conjunto finito de niveles.

Golfarelly M. & Dario M [3], proponen un método para la transformación de diagramas Entidad Relación (ER) a una estructura de árbol. Este método representa la tabla de hechos como la raíz del árbol y los atributos de dimensiones como el árbol descendente. Los elementos del árbol son los hechos, atributos, dimensiones y jerarquías; otros elementos que también son representados son la aditividad de los atributos de hechos con las dimensiones. La metodología de diseño consiste de 5 pasos: (1) análisis del sistema de información, (2) diseño conceptual, (3) validación del esquema, (4) diseño lógico, (5) diseño físico.

Estas dos propuestas, se relacionan con el diseño conceptual de ADs a partir de la descripción del esquema conceptual de la base de datos operacional. Sin embargo, aun no integran en su fase de diseño los requisitos de usuario. La contribución más importante de estas propuestas consiste en la incorporación de notaciones gráficas que representan en el esquema aspectos multidimensionales.

Los principales inconvenientes que presentan estas propuestas son: (a) No utilizan una notación estándar para el modelado conceptual. (b) El uso de una notación propia convierte a estas metodologías en soluciones particulares y aisladas. (c) No consideran en su fase de diseño conceptual los requisitos de usuario.

3. Conceptos Básicos de MDA

Model Driven Architecture (MDA) consiste en un conjunto de estándares que permiten la creación, implementación, evolución y desarrollo de sistemas dirigidos por modelos. MDA introduce algunos conceptos importantes: modelo independiente de la plataforma (PIM), modelo específico de la plataforma (PSM), lenguaje de transformación y reglas de transformación. Cada elemento de la Figura 1, desempeña un papel importante en MDA. MOF es el metamodelo usado para definir modelos. PIM modela la funcionalidad, la estructura y la conducta del sistema. PSM está orientado a la implementación [4].

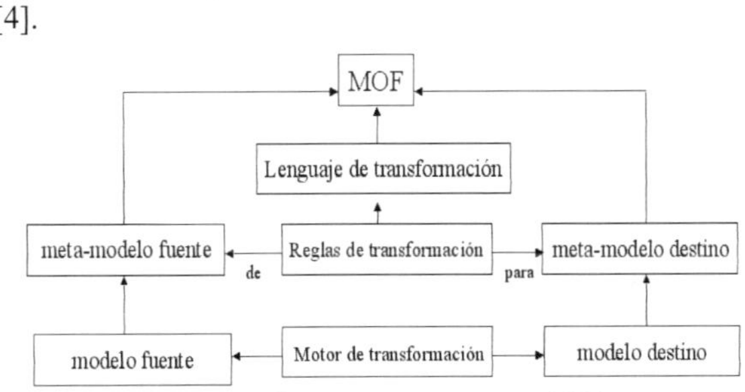

Figura 1. Elementos que componen a MDA

Las reglas de transformación establecen las correspondencias entre un metamodelo fuente y un metamodelo destino y permiten la transformación de esquemas. El motor de transformación aplica las reglas de transformación al esquema fuente y devuelve el esquema destino. La especificación de las reglas de transformación se realiza en un lenguaje que permite definir patrones de transformación sobre los metamodelos. Un patrón de transformación captura las propiedades comunes para una familia de transformaciones a nivel modelo.

Una transformación se especifica por su signatura, la cual se forma por el nombre de la transformación, el nombre de los elementos del metamodelo fuente y el nombre de los nuevos elementos del metamodelo destino. Por ejemplo, la signatura de la transformación *EntXCub* es:

```
(Cube)[name="C"+en,Med=M,CDA=CDH]←EntXCub(Entity)[name=en,Col=Atr,Relship=F]
```

La expresión se interpreta de la siguiente forma: al aplicar la regla de transformación **EntXcub** sobre la clase tipo *Entity*, se obtiene una clase tipo *Cube* y dos relaciones (*Med* y *CDA)*. La secuencia de reglas de transformación que producen un esquema destino a partir de un esquema fuente es llamada historia del proceso de transformación [6].

Common Warehouse metamodel (CWM). CWM es un lenguaje creado específicamente para modelar aplicaciones de bases de datos [7]. Este metamodelo tiene meta clases específicas para el modelado de cualquier base de datos relacional, OLAP, XML, ER, etc. A continuación se presenta el metamodelo OLAP [8] y el metamodelo ER [9] ya que van a utilizarse en este trabajo.

El metamodelo OLAP (Figura 2), consiste en un esquema de clases que representa los conceptos del modelo OLAP (modelo multidimensional): dimensión, cubo de datos, medida, jerarquía, etc. En el metamodelo OLAP, un cubo de datos (hecho) se asocia a un conjunto de dimensiones y contiene un conjunto de medidas; una dimensión se compone de niveles relacionados entre si en jerarquías.

El metamodelo ER (Figura 3) representa todos los conceptos del modelo ER: entidad, atributo, relación, etc. Una relación representa una asociación entre dos o más instancias de entidad. Cada extremo de una relación (RelationShipEnd), puede tener de manera opcional nombre y multiplicidad.

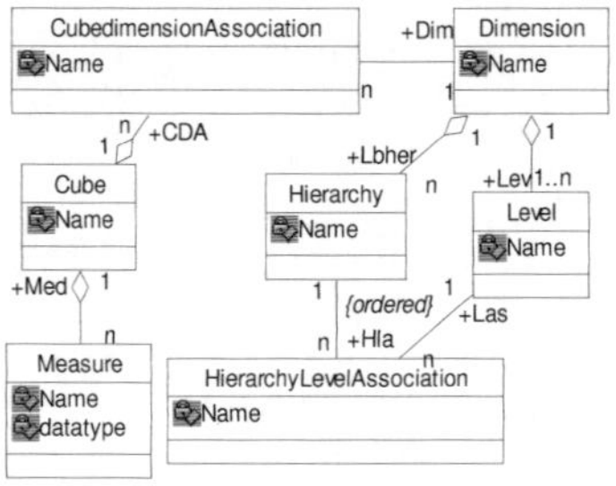

Figura 2. Metamodelo OLAP

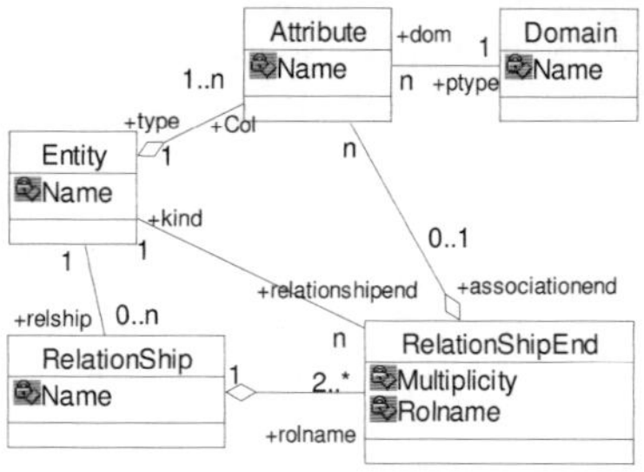

Figura 3. Metamodelo ER

4. Metodología de Diseño

Como ya se ha comentado en la introducción, la metodología que se propone consta de tres fases:

4.1. Fase 1. Obtención de un Conjunto de Esquemas Multidimensionales Candidatos a partir del Esquema ER

Para explicar el proceso de transformación entre un modelo ER y un modelo OLAP, primeramente describimos la correspondencia entre los conceptos de cada metamodelo. Posteriormente, mostramos las reglas de transformación.

4.1.1. Correspondencias semánticas entre un metamodelo OLAP y un metamodelo ER

Las correspondencias, son especificaciones definidas entre los conceptos de ambos modelos. Estas especificaciones, se realizan a nivel metamodelo, estableciendo una relación semántica. Nosotros identificamos dos tipos de correspondencias entre el metamodelo ER y el metamodelo OLAP.

Correspondencias simples: estas correspondencias, definen una relación entre dos conceptos que pertenecen a distintos metamodelos, por ejemplo, entre una entidad y un cubo, o entre un atributo y una medida. Las correspondencias simples que se identificaron son:

- Una entidad de cubo candidata es una entidad *ej* € ER tal que *ej* hace referencia a otra entidad, pero no es referenciada por ninguna otra. Cada entidad de cubo candidata, se corresponde con un cubo de datos del modelo mutidimensional.
- Cada relación (Relationship), de una entidad de cubo candidata e_j a una entidad e_i, con cardinalidad muchos a muchos o muchos a uno se corresponde con una dimensión y con una clase CubedimensionAssociation.
- Cada atributo de tipo numérico, de una entidad de cubo candidata se corresponde con una medida del modelo multidimensional..
- Cada entidad relacionada con una entidad de cubo candidata se corresponde con un nivel.

Correspondencias complejas: estas correspondencias, definen una relación entre dos o más elementos del metamodelo ER que representan un solo concepto en el metamodelo OLAP. Las correspondencias complejas identificadas son:

- Para definir una jerarquía, es necesario identificar todas las rutas disponibles a partir de la entidad de cubo candidata y las relaciones muchos a muchos o muchos a uno. Una jerarquía es formada, cuando no se encuentran mas relaciones.
- Una clase HierarchyLevelAssociation, se crea empleando una secuencia de entidades que pertenecen a la misma jerarquía.

4.1.2. Reglas de transformación

En esta sección se describen las reglas de transformación[1] usando el lenguaje Model Transformation Lenguaje (MTL) [10]. El proceso de transformación entre el metamodelo ER y el metamodelo OLAP inicia con la regla de transformación **EntXCub**. Esta regla transforma cada entidad de cubo candidata en un cubo de datos, con el mismo nombre de la entidad candidata pero con el prefijo "C". Esta regla, se compone de las reglas **AtrXMed** y **RSEXCDA**.

```
Relation EntXCub { Domain(Entity)[name=en,Col=A,Relship=R]
Domain(Cube)[name="C"+en, Med=M,CDH=CDA]
When(A ForAll(a|AtrXMed(a,M.tochoice()) and
R ForAll(r|RSEXCDA(r,CDA.tochoice()))
Where (Self. oppositeAssociationEnd → NotEmpty()
Implies Self.OppositeAssociationEnd.Multiplicity.is Not (*))}
```

Todos los atributos numéricos de la entidad de cubo candidata, se transforman directamente en medidas del cubo por medio de la regla de transformación **AtrXMed**.

```
Relation AtrXMed {
Domain (Attribute) [Name=attN, Type=(Domain) [Name=type]]
Domain (Measure) [Name=attN, datatype=type]
Where (type="Integer" or type="Double")}
```

Cada relación de la entidad de cubo candidata, toma dos significados durante el proceso de transformación. Los cuales son definidos por las reglas **RSEXCDA** y **RSEXDim**. La regla de transformación **RSEXCDA**, transforma cada relación con multiplicidad *..1 ó *..* (*self.Association.Multiplicity.is("*")*), en una clase de asociación *CubeDimensionAssociation*.

```
Relation RSEXCDA{
Domain(RelationShip)[Name=NRship] Domain(CubeDimensionAssociation)
      [Name="CDA"+NRship, Dim=d]
When (RSEXDim(RelationShip,d))
Where(self.Association.Multiplicity.is("*")}
```

La regla **RSEXDim**, convierte cada relación en una dimensión. En la representación textual de esta regla, se muestra que el nombre de la dimensión se forma con el nombre de la clase *RelationShip* y el caracter "D". También se muestra que esta regla se compone de las reglas de transformación **SecEXHer** y **EntXLev.**

```
Relation RSEXDim (
Domain (RelationShip) [Name=NRship]
Domain(Dimension)[Name="D"+NRship,Lbher=h,Lev=l]
When ((EntXLev(RelationShip, l.tochoice()) and
HierarchyAux (For All (haux | SecEXHer (haux, h.tochoice()))
```

Las entidades relacionadas directamente con una entidad de cubo candidatas, son consideradas niveles de dimensión raíz. Dado un nivel de dimensión raíz, cada una de las entidades que se relacionan directamente con él con una multiplicidad *..1 o con multiplicidad *..*, son niveles de dimensión de jerarquías distintas. De manera recursiva, se van identificando las entidades que se relacionan con cardinalidad *..1 con un

[1] Por razones de espacio se omiten detalles de implementación de las reglas.

nivel de dimensión ya identificado, obteniendo las jerarquías. El proceso acaba cuando a partir de una entidad ya no se encuentran relaciones *..1 o *..*, con otras clases que no hayan sido procesados anteriormente. La regla de transformación **EntXLev**, inicia el proceso de transformación a partir de cada relación de la entidad de cubo candidata. En la línea (1) la regla de transformación se encarga de seleccionar la entidades relacionada directamente con la entidad de cubo candidata, esta entidad representa el nivel raíz de la jerarquía. En la línea (2), la expresión: *Secuence (Object EntityAux {Name:= Nivel}),* crea una secuencia de Niveles, que pertenecen a la misma jerarquía. La línea (3) identifica las relaciones del nivel raíz y de manera recursiva identifica los demás niveles de dimensión (línea 6). Cuando no existen más relaciones (línea 4), se crea una jerarquía (línea 5). Por último en la línea (7), se crean los niveles. La secuencia **EntityAux**, que se creó en la línea (2), contiene una colección de entidades que en el metamodelo destino representan Niveles (Levels). La secuencia **HierarchyAux**, almacena la secuencia **EntityAux**, en donde cada secuencia representa una jerarquía de dimensión.

```
Relation EntXLev {
Domain (ReletionShip ) [Name=NRship]
Where(
(1)Nivel:=NRship.opposite.resolveone(#Entity). Name;
(2) Secuence (Object EntityAux  {Name:= Nivel})
(3) Var rship:= Nivel.RelationShip;
(4) If rship = null {
(5) Secuence (Object HierarchyAux {Dato := EntityAux})}
(6) rship ForAll (rs |EntXLev (rs,__));)
(7) Domain (Level) [Name=Nivel, Lev=Las]
(8) When (Las→select(l|l.ocliskindof(Level))

Intermediate class OLAP::HierarchyAux {Dato:Secuence}
Intermediate class OLAP:: EntityAux {Name :String}
```

Al finalizar la regla **EntXLev**, el flujo del proceso de transformación vuelve a la regla **RSEXDim**. Esta regla extrae cada elemento de la secuencia **HierarchyAux** (extrae una secuencia **EntityAux**) y lo envía a la regla **SecEXHer**, la cual crea una clase de jerarquía por cada secuencia que recibe.

```
Relation SecEXHer {
Domain(EntityAux)[Secuence SecE]
Domain(Hierarchy)[Name="Her"+SecE.name,Hla=La]
When(SecE ForAll (e| SecEXHLA(e,La.tochoice())}
```

Por cada entidad de la secuencia EntityAux, se hace un llamado a la regla **SecEXHla**. La cual crea una clase de asociación (HierarchyLevelAssociation).

```
Relation SecEXHLA {
Domain (Entity) [Name=En]
Domain (HierarchyLevelAssociation) [Name=En]}
```

4.1.3. Caso de estudio

A continuación, mostraremos la metodología por medio de un ejemplo. El esquema de la Figura 4, corresponde a una instancia del metamodelo ER. Este esquema se refiere a las ventas de una cadena de tiendas. Al aplicar la regla de transformación

EntXCub, se identifican dos entidades candidatas a ser cubos de datos en el esquema OLAP: *Línea* y *Pronósticos*.

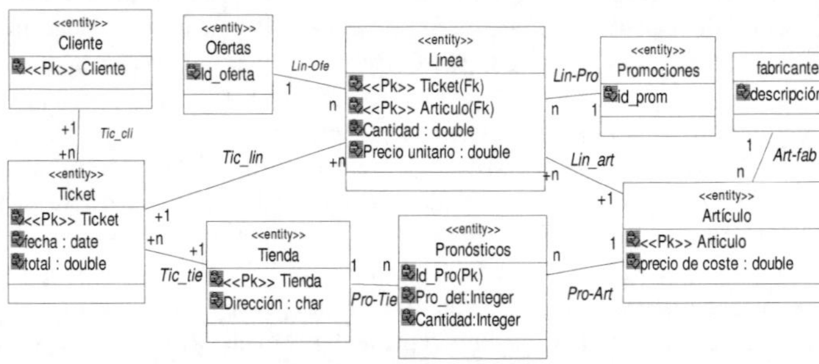

Figura 4. Modelo Entidad Relación Ventas

Empleando la notación de signatura, la siguiente historia describe la transformación de la entidad *Línea* en cubo de datos y la de sus columnas numéricas en medidas (por limitaciones de espacio se omite el proceso de derivación de la entidad *Pronósticos*).

T1:(Cube) [Name = "C"+ "Línea", Med = AtrXMed(A), CDA = RSEXCDA(R)] ← **EntXCub** (Entity) ["Línea" = en, Col = A, Relship = R]

T2:(Measure)[Name="Cantidad",datatype=double]←**AtrXMed** (Attribute)["Cantidad"=Name, ptype=(Domain)["double"=Name]

T3:(Measure) [Name = "Precio unitario",datatype=double]←**AtrXMed** (Attribute) ["Precio unitario"=Name,ptype=(Domain)["double"=Name]

Por cada relación de la entidad *Línea*, se deben realizar las reglas de transformación **RSEXCDA** y **RSEXDim**. Debido a que la relación *Línea*, tiene cuatro relaciones, las reglas se realizan cuatro veces creando, cuatro clases de asociación (CubeDimensionAssociation) y cuatro clases de dimensión:

T4:(CubeDimensionAssociation)[Name="CDA"+"Lin-Ofe",Dim=*RSEXDim*(RelationShip)] ← **RSEXCDA** (RelationShip) ["Lin-Ofe"= Rname]

T6:(CubeDimensionAssociation) [Name="CDA"+"Lin-Pro", Dim = RSEXDim (RelationShip)] ← **RSEXCDA** (RelationShip) ["Lin-Pro" = Rname]

T7: (CubeDimensionAssociation) [Name="CDA"+"Lin-art", Dim = RSEXDim (RelationShip)] ← **RSEXCDA** (RelationShip) ["Lin-art"= Rname]

T8:(CubeDimensionAssociation)[Name="CDA"+"Tic-lin", Dim = RSEXDim (RelationShip)] ← **RSEXCDA** (RelationShip) ["Tic-lin" = Rname]

A continuación se muestra la historia para derivar la dimensión *DTic-lin* a partir de la relación *Tic_Lin*. El mismo procedimiento se debe seguir para transformar las relaciones *Lin_ofe, Lin_pro y Lin_art*.

T9:(Dimension) [Name="D"+"Tic-lin",Lbhe=SecEXHer (EntityAux), Lev=EntXLev (ReltationShip)] ← **RSEXDim** (RelationShip) ["Tic-lin" = Rname]
T10:(Level) [Name="L"+"Ticket"] ← EntXLev (Entity) ["Ticket"=En]
T11:(Level)[Name="L"+"Cliente"]←EntXLev (Entity) ["Cliente"=En]
T12:(Level) [Name="L"+"Ticket"] ← EntXLev (Entity) ["Ticket"=En]
T13:(Level)[Name="L"+"Tienda"] ← **EntXLev**(Entity) ["Tienda"=En]

La secuencia **Hierarchyaux** que se formo mientras se efectuaba la regla de transformación **EntXLev**, tiene los siguientes datos: *{{Ticket, Cliente}, {Ticket, Tienda}}*. Los datos representan los niveles que pertenecen a la misma jerarquía. Cada elemento de la secuencia se extrae en la regla de transformación **RSEXDim** y se envía a la regla **SecEXHer**. Esta regla crea una clase de jerarquía por cada dato que recibe y además crea una clase *HierarchyLevelAssociation*.

T14: (Hierarchy) [Name="Her"+sName, Hla=SecEXHla (e)] ← **SecEXHer** (EntityAux) [" Cliente"=sName, EntityAux (Name e))]
T15:(HierarchyLevelAssociation) [Name="HLA"+"Ticket",] ← **SecEXHla** (Entity) ["Ticket"= En]
T16:(HierarchyLevelAssociation) [Name="HLA"+"Cliente",] ← SecEXHla (Entity) ["Cliente"= En]
T17: (Hierarchy) [Name="Her"+sName,Hla=SecEXHla (e)] ← **SecEXHer** (EntityAux)[" Tienda"=sName, EntityAux (Name e)]
T18:(HierarchyLevelAssociation)[Name="HLA"+"Ticket",]← **SecEXHla** (Entity) ["Ticket"= En]
T19:(HierarchyLevelAssociation)[Name="HLA"+"Tienda",]← **SecEXHla** (Entity) ["Tienda"= En]

Del esquema de punto de venta, es posible obtener dos esquemas multidimensionales candidatos: *CLínea y CPronósticos* (Figura 6 y 7). De los cuales, se elegirá y depurara aquel que cumpla con los requisitos de usuario.

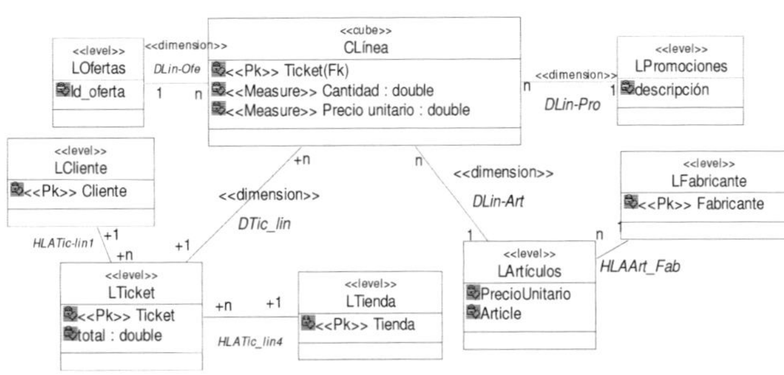

Figura 7. Esquema candidato CLínea.

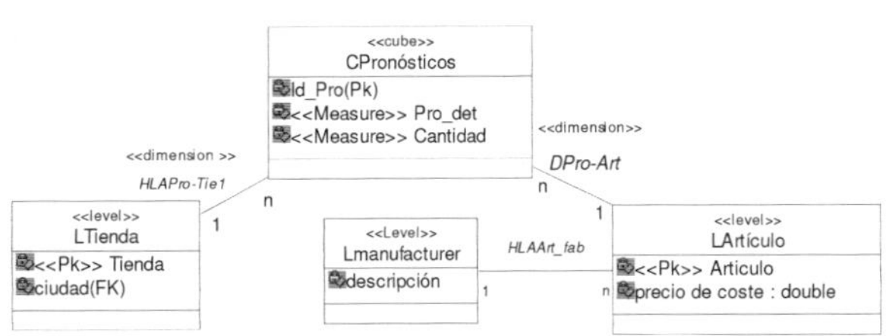

Figura 8. Esquema candidato CPronósticos.

4.2. Fase 2. Requisitos de Usuario

La segunda fase de la metodología consiste en capturar los requisitos de los usuarios del AD. (Por razones de espacio se mostrará una versión resumida de esta fase). A diferencia de otras metodologías de diseño de ADs existentes, este conjunto de requisitos no se considera el punto de partida para el diseño conceptual del AD. El modelo de requisitos será utilizado para seleccionar y refinar los esquemas que se generan a partir del proceso de transformación realizado en la fase 1. Como base para la elicitación de requisitos, adaptamos un método basado en metas [12]. Seleccionamos este método, ya que permite identificar los requisitos de usuario relacionados con los procesos de negocio que se pretenden analizar de una manera natural [13]. Esta fase se divide en dos etapas: obtención de los requisitos de usuario del AD, análisis de los requisitos.

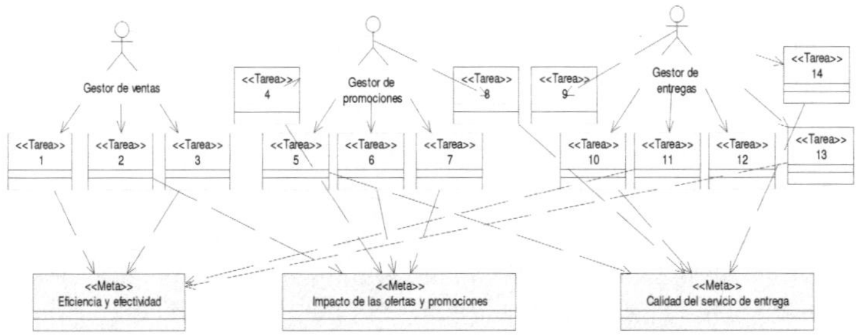

Figura 7. Relación entre tareas, usuarios y metas

4.2.1. Requisitos de usuario del AD

Para obtener los requisitos de usuario, es necesario aplicar técnicas tradicionales de la ingeniería de software: entrevistas, lluvia de ideas, etc. De esta etapa se debe obtener una descripción no técnica del AD que refleje los objetivos que se persiguen con el desarrollo del proyecto. El primer paso consiste en identificar y definir los procesos de negocio que se desea analizar. El siguiente paso consiste en identificar las tareas que forman al proceso de negocio. Una vez definidas las tareas, se analizan las analogías entre cada una de ellas y se integran en una meta en común. Esto se realiza con el fin de reducir el número de tareas a una cantidad más fácil de manejar.

Ejemplo (continuación): En nuestro caso de estudio, entrevistamos cerca de 10 personas organizadas en 3 grupos operando en niveles distintos. En la Figura 7, se muestra la relación entre los usuarios entrevistados (cada grupo es representado por un administrador: *Gestor de entregas, Gestor de promociones y Gestor de ventas*) y las tareas que cada uno de ellos realiza. Inicialmente, se le pidió a cada uno de los participantes que explicara las actividades que realizan diariamente. Finalmente, empleando la técnica "*lluvia de ideas*", se obtuvo la definición inicial de las tareas. Una formulación precisa de las tareas es fundamental para propósito del diseño del AD. Para apreciar este punto mostraremos la definición de las tareas 2, 4 y 8.

T2. Analizar el comportamiento de los clientes ante los distintos medio de promoción (ferias, muestras, regalos, concursos, cupones, etc.).

T4. Analizar el servicio de entregas de mercancías, con el fin de hacer un seguimiento del promedio de tiempo de entregas.

T8. Analizar las ventas, con el fin de estudiar el desempeño, en relación al número de órdenes de ventas generadas a partir de las ofertas.

En nuestro ejemplo, las tres tareas se aplican al mismo contexto (*Ventas).* La diferencia entre ellas es el objeto de estudio. En la tarea cuatro (T4), el estudio se refiere a las *entregas*. En la tarea ocho (T8) y dos (T2), el estudio se enfoca en las *promociones*. La tarea T8 puede integrarse con la tarea T2, ya que las dos se relacionan con el mismo proceso: *promociones*. Al realizar la integración de las tareas en metas, en nuestro caso de estudio, se identificaron tres metas, representadas como Meta 1, Meta 2 y Meta 3 las cuales, resumen las tareas del proceso de negocio:

Meta 1. Eficiencia y efectividad de ventas. Conocer cada detalle del proceso de ventas, con el fin de mejorar la eficiencia y efectividad del área. El análisis de las ventas permitirá controlar los indicadores clave de desempeño para poder detectar tendencias, patrones y visualizar de manera inmediata cambios relevantes en el proceso de ventas.

Meta 2. Impacto de las ofertas y promociones. Conocer con profundidad el comportamiento de los clientes ante las ofertas y promociones. Lo cual permitirá a la empresa controlar y disminuir el desgaste de las relaciones con los clientes más valiosos, optimizar su rentabilidad e identificar las oportunidades de venta apropiadas.

Meta 3. Calidad del servicio de entrega. Conocer la forma como se entregan las mercaderías a los clientes, monitoreando los procesos de entrega por región, producto y punto de entrega entre otros. También se interesan en conocer todas las actividades relacionadas con el cumplimiento de las operaciones de entrega, permitiendo al usuario medir la calidad del servicio de entrega.

4.2.2. Análisis de los requisitos

La definición y clasificación de las metas realizada es insuficiente para seleccionar un esquema candidato. Es necesario analizar cada meta con mas detalle, por esta razón es necesario recabar información adicional acerca del proceso de negocio. Especialmente, es necesario definir, entender y documentar las medidas (simples y compuestas), las dimensiones y los niveles que responden a las preguntas que el usuario tiene acerca del proceso de negocio. Las Tablas 1 y 2 contienen la definición parcial de las metas M1, M2 y M3, la cual será utilizada para seleccionar y refinar un esquema multidimensional candidato. Una vez que las medidas y dimensiones han sido definidas, es necesario clasificarlas como aditiva, semi-aditiva o no aditiva. Siguiendo la clasificación propuesta por Horner [14], la medida *Numctes* es considerada no-aditiva sobre la dimensión *Lin_art* (semi-aditiva) y *Gross margin profit* como no aditiva.

Tabla1. descripción de medidas

Measure	Formula
Qtysold	Sum (qty)
Numctes	Count ()
Sales	Sum (qty*price)
Margin Profit	Sales-Sum(cantidad*Article.priceU)
GrossMargin Profit	Margin Profit/Sales

Tabla 2. Descripción de dimensiones

Dimension
Tiempo
Cliente
Artículo
Promoción
Tienda

4.3. Fase 3: Selección y Refinamiento del Esquema Multidimensional Seleccionado

Para seleccionar un esquema multidimensional, es necesario contrastar la estructura de los esquemas multidimensionales candidatos con la información recabada durante la Fase 2. La evaluación se base en el número de elementos del esquema multidimensional candidato. El objetivo es seleccionar el esquema multidimensional que mejor satisfaga los requisitos de usuario. Esta fase se lleva a cabo en dos pasos: comparación y refinamiento manual.

4.3.1 Comparación. Es necesario hacer una comparación entre los elementos de los esquemas candidatos y los datos obtenidos de los requisitos de usuarios. Las métricas para decidir sí un esquema multidimensional candidato los contempla son:

Correspondencia de atributos. Se deben identificar los atributos de la clase de cubo que tengan una correspondencia directa (**D**) o indirecta (**I**) con los datos identificados en los requisitos de usuario. La comparación es directa, cuando los datos de los requisitos de usuario están disponibles de manera inmediata en el esquema candidato. La comparación es indirecta, cuando es necesario realizar una función sobre ciertos elementos del esquema candidato para derivar algunos conceptos relacionados con los requisitos de usuario.

Correspondencia de dimensiones. Es necesario identificar las dimensiones de cada esquema candidato que se relacionan con las dimensiones obtenidas de los requisitos de usuario. De esta fase se obtiene una tabla de correspondencias la cual permitirá seleccionar y modificar los esquemas multidimensionales candidatos.

Tabla 3. Correspondencia de atributos

Med\Esquema	CLínea	CPronostico
QtySold	D	×
Numctes	D	×
Sales	I	×
Margin Profit	I	×
GrossMarginProf	I	×

Tabla 4. Correspondencia de dimensiones

Dim\Esquema	CLínea	CPronostico
Tiempo	×	×
Tienda	√	√
Artículo	√	√
Promoción	√	×
Cliente	√	×

Ejemplo (Continuación). Las correspondencias para los atributos y las dimensiones se muestran en las tablas 3 y 4 respectivamente. De esta información podemos seleccionar el esquema **CLínea**, ya que este esquema captura mejor los requisitos de usuario y es soportado por las bases de datos operacionales.

Refinamiento manual. Una vez seleccionado el esquema, este debe ser modificado manualmente. Los cambios deben realizarse a partir de la información obtenida en la fase 2. Las modificaciones que pueden realizarse sobre el esquema son: **a)** *Eliminar atributos innecesarios***.** b) *Agregar medidas.*

c) *Agregar restricciones de aditividad.* Por omisión, consideramos que las medidas son aditivas sobre todas las dimensiones. Una medida semi-aditiva se representa en el esquema con el estereotipo <SA> y una medida no-aditiva con el estereotipo <NA>.

d) *Agregar la dimensión tiempo*. La dimensión tiempo, siempre debe formar parte del esquema multidimensional final.

e) *Eliminar niveles innecesarios*. Posiblemente, no todos los niveles del esquema multidimensional, sean de interés. De ser así, el nivel debe eliminarse, pero sus descendientes deben conservarse (en caso de que se requiera). Si el nivel eliminado tiene descendientes, se incrementara el número de dimensiones del esquema.

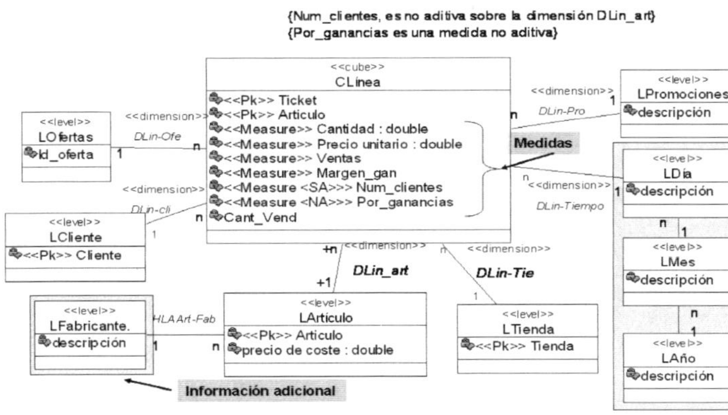

Figure 8. Esquema multidimensional Final

Ejemplo (Continuación). En la Figure 8, se muestra el esquema multidimensional final (modelado con el perfil presentado en [15]). En el esquema se muestra que existe información adicional a la solicitada por el usuario (p.e. *LFabricante*). Esta información, puede ser o no ser de interés para el usuario, pero esta disponible en la base de datos operacional.Los cambios que se efectuaron al esquema **Clínea** son: a) se agrego la dimensión tiempo. b) Se agregaron las medidas *QtySold*, *Numctes*, *Grossmargin-Profit*, *Sales* y *MarginProfit*. C) Se añadieron dos restricciones de aditividad para las medidas: *Numctes* y *Grossmarginprofit. d)* Se eliminó el nivel raíz Ticket *(*ya que la información que contiene se puede obtener de la clase de cubo *Cline*), con lo que se obtuvieron dos nuevas dimensiones: *DLin_Cli, DLin_Sto*.

5. Conclusiones y Trabajos Futuros

En este trabajo, se presenta una metodología semiautomática para el diseño conceptual de ADs. La cual esta formada por tres fases. La segunda fase, se refiere a la consolidación de los requisitos de usuarios, esta actividad es por naturaleza un proceso difícil e interpersonal, donde la información es seccionada y refinada gradualmente a partir de fuentes de información informales y algunas veces incoherentes. La interacción con los usuarios del AD se ha llevado a cabo usando entrevistas y lluvias de ideas. En contraste, la segunda y tercera fases parten de la descripción de información estructurada y formal (p.e. el esquema) y por consecuencia, pueden ser automatizadas. La selección de MDA como método que guía la primera fase, se justifica por la necesidad de analizar el esquema ER empleando medios estandarizados. Las ventajas de emplear MDA para el diseño conceptual del AD son varias: a) es posible verificar la correctitud de las reglas de transformación, debido a que son especificadas de manera precisa e independiente de cualquier plataforma. b) El uso de un medio estandarizado y uniforme para el diseño conceptual de AD. c) Las transformaciones permiten lograr la evolución de modelos (correctiva y perfectiva).

En conclusión, la experiencia que hemos obtenido al aplicar el método propuesto en nuestro caso de estudio es satisfactoria. La combinación de la primera y segunda fase ha contribuido de manera coherente a evaluar los requisitos de usuario y la disponibilidad de los datos. El método propuesto fue esencial al dirigir al diseñador a encontrar una solución posible de implementar y que sea consistente con los requisitos de usuario. El trabajo demuestra que las ideas de MDA son perfectamente válidas para el diseño de ADs. Las reglas de transformación se han implementado en el lenguaje de transformación Atlas [16] y se ha logrado generar los esquemas multidimensionales de manera correcta. Los trabajos futuros, incluyen extender esta propuesta con la intención de incrementar los criterios de selección de esquemas candidatos (fase 3).

Referencias

[1] Kimball R., Ross M. The Data Warehouse Toolkit, second edition, John Wiley & Sons. 2002

[2] Cabibbo, L. and Torlone. A logical approach to multidimensional databases. In Proceedings of the International Conference on Extending Data Base Technology (EDBT '98,Valencia, Spain, Mar.). 183–197. 1998

[3] Golfarelli, M., Maio, D., and Rizzi, S.. Conceptual design of data warehouses from E/R schemes. In Proceedings of the 31st Hawaii International Conference on System Sciences (HICSS '98, Kona, Hawai). 1998.

[4] OMG, Model Driven Architecture, document number ormsc/2001-07-01, Architecture Board ORMSC1, 2001.

[5] Kleppe A., Warmer J., Bast W. MDA Explained. The Practice and Promise of The Model Driven Architecture. Addison Wesley. 2003.

[6] Hainaut, J.. Specification Preservation in Schema Transformations. Applications to Semantics and Statics, Data & Knowledge Engineering, Vol 9. Elsevier, 1996

[7] John P, Dan Chang, S. Tolbert and David M. "Common Warehouse Metamodel Developer´s Guide", Wiley Publishing, Indiana, 2003.

[8] Object Management Group (OMG), Common Warehouse Metamodel (CWM) specification 1.0.1. http://www.omg.org/cgi-bin/doc?formal/03-03-02

[9] OMG, Common Warehouse Metamodel specification (Extensions). http://www.omg.org/cgi-bin/doc?ad/2001-02-02

[10] OMG 2nd Revised Submission: MOF 2.0 Query/Views/Transformations. http://www.omg.org/cgi-bin/doc?ad/05-03-02

[11] M. R. Jensen, T. H. Moller, and T. B. Pedersen: Specifying OLAP Cubes On XML Data. JIIS 17(2-3): 255-280, 2001.

[12] Annie A., "Goal Based Requirements Analysis", in Proceedings Second International Conference on Requirements Engineering. ICRE '96, pp. 136-144, April 1996.

[13] Estrada H., Martinez A., Using Goal-Refinement Tree to obtain and refine organization requirements. ICCSA 2004. PP. 506-513

[14] Horner, J., Song, I.Y., and Chen, P. "An Analysis of Additivity in OLAP Systems". DOLAP'04, November 12–13, 2004, Washington, DC, USA.

[15] Zepeda, L. Celma M.. An UML Profile for Data warehouse Design in Proceedings of Institute Polytechnic National, México. 2003.

[16] The Atlas Transformation Language , http://www.sciences.univ-nantes.fr/lina/atl/

MDA Approach for Collaborative Business Processes: Generating Technological Solutions based on Web Services Composition

Pablo David Villarreal[1], Enrique Salomone[1,2], Omar Chiotti[1,2]

[1]CIDISI, Universidad Tecnológica Nacional - Facultad Regional Santa Fe, Lavaise 610, 3000, Santa Fe, Argentina
(pvillarr@frsf.utn.edu.ar)
[2]INGAR-CONICET, Avellaneda 3657, 3000, Santa Fe, Argentina
({salomone,chiotti}@ceride.gov.ar)

Abstract. In order to establish B2B Collaborations with their partners, enterprises have to focus on the modeling and specification of collaborative business processes and partners' interfaces that compose the B2B information system. Currently, standards for web services composition are having more and more interest to specify and implement these processes and interfaces. In this paper, we propose a MDA approach to support the modeling of collaborative processes and the automatic generation of technological solutions based on web services composition. Particularly, we discuss the generation of specifications based on the BPEL standard, from collaborative process models defined with the language UP-ColBPIP. This language supports the conceptual modeling of technology-independent collaborative processes as interaction protocols. The rules to transform UP-ColBPIP models into BPEL specifications are defined.

1. Introduction

Currently, enterprises are focusing on the setting up of Business-to-Business (B2B) Collaborations with their partners. Two abstraction levels have to be considered in these B2B collaborations: a business level and a technological level [15,18].

In the business level, partners have to focus on the definition of *collaborative business processes*, which describe the explicit behavior of the collaboration along with the partners' responsibilities. Through the definition of these processes, partners undertake to jointly carry out decisions to achieve common goals, coordinate their actions and exchange information. In this level, collaborative processes have to be defined in an independent way of the implementation technology, because business analysts and system designers do not want to deal with the technical details.

In the technological level, enterprises have to focus on the implementation of the B2B information system that supports the collaborative processes. This system is made up of autonomous, heterogeneous and distributed components owned by enterprises to support the joint execution of collaborative processes. Interoperability between these components can be achieved by using B2B protocols [5] [6]. Two important interoperability aspects are supported by these protocols: the specification of the collaborative processes in an executable language and the specification of the partners' interfaces that compose the B2B information system. Currently, there are two main technologies proposed for the specification of B2B protocols [5]: standards based on Web Services Composition, such as BPEL (Business Process Execution Language) [4] and WS-CDL (Web Services Choreography Description Language) [10]; and standards based on Business Transactions, such as ebXML [14].

Hence, collaborative processes must be defined first in a business level using a technology-independent language and then in a technological level using a B2B standard. However, the development of these B2B solutions is complex and costly [1]. In addition, both definitions must have a mutual correspondence [5].

The Model-Driven Architecture (MDA) Initiative [12] has been identified as a key enabler to support the development of collaborative processes [18]. In this way, we proposed a method for collaborative processes [15] based on the principles of MDA. This MDA approach supports: the design of collaborative processes independent of the idiosyncrasies of particular B2B standards; and the automatic generation of specifications based on a B2B standard from conceptual collaborative process models. The main benefits of this approach are: (1) increase of the abstraction level because the main artifacts of the development are the technology-independent collaborative process models; (2) reduction of development time and costs because solutions are generated automatically from conceptual models of collaborative processes; (3) the generated technological solutions are consistent with the processes defined in the business level; (4) independence of the collaborative process models from the B2B standards, which increases the reuse of these models.

In previous work, we described the generation of technological solutions based on ebXML [18] using a MDA approach. However, web services are having more and more interest to implement B2B information systems. In addition, currently vendor support is stronger for web services than ebXML.

In this paper, we focus on the application of a MDA approach for the generation of technological solutions based on web services composition to implement collaborative processes. In particular, we use the BPEL standard. BPEL supports the specification of collaborative processes only from the point of view of one partner. However, an important requirement in the collaborative process modeling and specification is the representation of the global view of the interactions between the partners [18]. Hence, to generate solutions based on BPEL, a BPEL process for each partner has to be specified. Moreover, BPEL processes have to be consistent to each other to represent the semantics of a collaborative process. In this paper, we show how this consistence can be achieved through the use of a MDA approach. It allows BPEL processes of each partner can be automatically derived from the common collaborative process models defined using the language UP-ColBPIP [15,17,18].

This paper is organized as follows. Section 2 describes the MDA approach we propose for collaborative processes. Section 3 briefly describes the modeling language UP-ColBPIP used to model technology-independent collaborative processes. Section 4 gives an overview of BPEL and describes the transformation of UP-ColBPIP models into BPEL and WSDL specifications. Section 5 discusses related work. Section 6 presents conclusions and outlines future research directions.

2. An MDA Approach for Collaborative Business Processes

The MDA initiative [12] proposes a conceptual framework along with a set of standards (UML, MOF, XMI, etc.) to build model-driven development methods. One principle of MDA is the building of systems can be organized around a set of models by imposing series of transformations between models, organized into an architectural framework of layers and transformations. In MDA, a system can refer to: software, an enterprise, a set of enterprises, and so on. In the domain of collaborative processes, the system to be built includes the specifications of: the collaborative processes in an executable language and the partners' interfaces of the B2B information system.

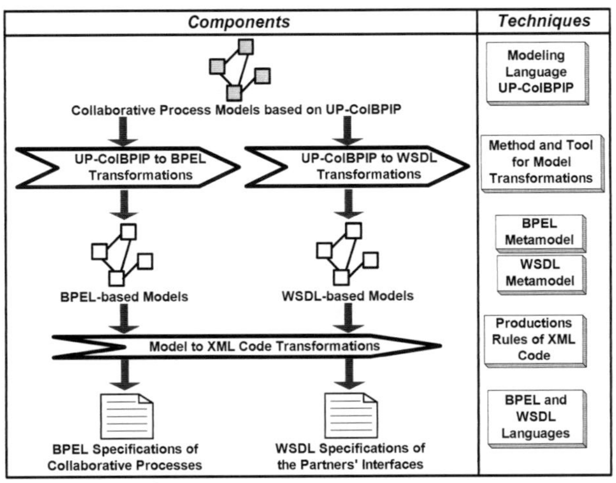

Fig 1. MDA Approach for Collaborative Processes

Figure 1 shows the corresponding components of the MDA approach we are proposing along with the techniques we provide to build the components:

- **Collaborative Business Process Models based on UP-ColBPIP**. They are the technology-independent process models and are built through the modeling language *UML Profile for Collaborative Business Processes based on Interaction Protocols (UP-ColBPIP)* [15,17,18]. This UML Profile is based on UML 2.
- **BPEL and WSDL models**. BPEL models represent the technology-dependent collaborative process models. Web services composition standards are based on the Web Service Description Language (WSDL), which is used to define web services of the partners. WSDL models represent the technology-dependent partners' interfaces. To build these models we define their corresponding metamodels, which can be derived from the XML schemas provided by these B2B standards. Thus, a model corresponds to a XML document. Although the XML code may be directly generated from UP-ColBPIP models, this intermediate representation allows the transformation be more modular and maintainable.
- **Transformations of UP-ColBPIP models to BPEL and WSDL models**. These transformations define a set of transformation rules to allow the generation of

BPEL process models from UP-ColBPIP models. They define the correspondence between the UP-ColBPIP concepts and the BPEL and WSDL concepts. Then, these transformation rules are implemented through a method and a tool for model transformations, which support the definition and automatic execution of the rules.

- **BPEL and WSDL Specifications**. The final outputs of the transformations are the XML documents of the BPEL process specifications and the WSDL partners' interfaces specifications. The transformation of technology-dependent models into the corresponding specifications is almost direct. This can be supported through XML production rules that convert a UML object model into a XML document.

In this work, we focus on UP-ColBPIP models and the definition, in a conceptual way, of the transformations of UP-ColBPIP to BPEL and WSDL. The other techniques and components are out of scope of this paper. They can be found in [15].

3. The Modeling Language UP-ColBPIP

UP-ColBPIP is a modeling language to design technology-independent collaborative processes [15,17,18]. It encourages a top-down approach and provides the conceptual elements to support the modeling of four views for collaborative processes:

- *B2B Collaboration View*, which defines the partners, the roles they fulfill, their relationships, the collaborative agreement parameters and the hierarchy of common business goals to be fulfilled by the partners in a B2B collaboration.
- *Collaborative Processes View*, which defines the processes partners have to perform. They are defined informally extending the semantics of use cases.
- *Interaction Protocols View*, which defines the interaction protocols that realize the collaborative processes.
- *Business Interfaces View*, which defines the business services and interfaces required by partners to support the message exchange of the interaction protocols.

The first and second views correspond to the analysis stage, in which the requirements of collaborative processes are defined. The last views correspond to the design stage of collaborative processes. From these views, technological solutions can be generated. Following we describe the Interaction Protocols View.

3.1. The Interaction Protocols View

This view focuses on the design of interaction protocols to realize the behavior of the collaborative processes. In the domain of B2B collaborations, an interaction protocol describes a high-level communication pattern through a choreography of business messages between partners playing different roles [16]. The main objective of modeling collaborative processes through interaction protocols is to fulfill the requirements of B2B collaborations [15,16]: enterprise autonomy, decentralization, peer-to-peer interactions, global view of the collaboration and support for negotiations.

In contrast to activity-oriented process models, process models based on interaction protocols focus on the message exchange between enterprises. Activities each partner performs for processing the information to be received, or producing the information to be sent, are not defined in the interaction protocols.

Modeling interaction protocols, the focus is on the representation of the global view of the interactions between the partners. The message choreography describes the peer-to-peer interactions and partners' responsibilities of the roles they fulfill.

In addition, B2B interactions cannot be restricted to mere information transfer [8]. Instead, it is necessary to represent the communication and the creation of commitments between the partners. These communicative aspects can be represented through interaction protocols, because they are based on the use of speech acts [13]. In an interaction protocol, a business message has a speech act associated, which represents the intention that a partner has with respect to an exchanged business document through the message. In this way, designers of a collaborative process focus on the semantics of each message selecting the most appropriate speech act. Furthermore, decisions and commitments done by the partners can be known from the speech acts. This enables the definition of negotiations in collaborative processes.

UP-ColBPIP extends the semantics of UML2 Interactions to model interaction protocols. Hence, they are defined using UML2 Sequence Diagrams. Following we describe the main conceptual elements used to define interaction protocols. As example we describe the interaction protocol *Demand Forecast Request*, which supports a simplified collaborative demand forecast process between two partners.

3.2.1. Interaction Protocol. Figure 2 shows the sequence diagram of the *Demand Forecast Request* protocol. It is stereotyped <<protocol>>.

3.2.2. Role and Partner. The partners and their roles they fulfill in an interaction protocol are represented through the lifelines. In the protocol of Figure 2, the partner "A" play the role supplier, and the partner "B" play the role customer.

3.2.3. Business Message. It defines an interaction between two roles, a sender and a receiver. A business message contains a speech act and a business document. The semantics of a business message is defined by its speech act associated. A business message expresses the sender has done an action, which generates the communication of a speech act representing the sender's intention with respect to the exchanged business document. Also, the message indicates the sender's expectative the receptor then acts according to the semantics of the speech act. As example, for the message *request(DemandForecast)*, the associated speech act indicates the supplier's intention of requesting to the customer a demand forecast. The speech act request also implies the customer cannot respond with any speech act but a suitable speech act, such as agree, or refuse. The suitable speech acts depend on the speech act library used to define the messages of the protocol and on the semantics of the speech acts.

A business message is a one-way asynchronous communication. This feature is essential in B2B interactions because the sender's internal control must not be subordinated to the receptor's response. A business message is managed by the receptor just as a signal to be interpreted for activating its internal behaviors.

3.2.4. Control Flow Segment. It represents complex message sequences in the choreography of an interaction protocol. It contains a control flow operator and one or more interaction paths. An *interaction path* (*interaction operand* in UML2) can contain any protocol element, such as: messages, terminations, interaction occurrences, and nested control flow segments. The stereotype *control flow segment* extends the semantics of the *combined fragment* of UML2 to provide suitable control flow operators for defining collaborative processes. It is represented as a box with a rounded-rectangle in the upper-left corner that contains a control flow operator.

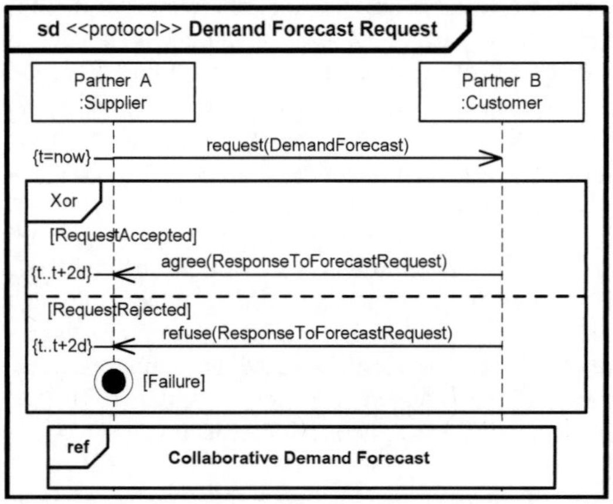

Fig. 2. An Example of an Interaction Protocol

The semantics of a control flow segment depends on the operator used: Xor, Or, And, If, Loop, Transaction, Exception, Stop and Cancel. The *And* operator represents the execution of parallel interaction paths in any order. The *Xor* operator represents that only one path, of a set of alternative paths, can be executed in case its condition is evaluated to true. The *Or* operator represents the selection of several paths from several alternatives. Each path is executed in case its condition is evaluated to true. The *If* operator represents a path that is executed when its condition is true, or nothing is executed. This can also have an *else* path, which is executed when the condition of the first path is false. The *Loop* operator represents a path that can be executed while its condition is satisfied. Two types of *Loop* segments can be defined: a loop "For" with the condition "(1,n)", where its path must be executed at least one time; and a loop "While" with the condition "(0,n)", where its path can be executed zero or *n* times. The *Transaction* operator indicates messages and paths of the segment have to be done atomically, and messages cannot be interleaved with messages of other paths. The *Exception* operator represents a path to be followed if an exception occurs according to the path's condition. The *Stop* operator represents paths that manage exceptions and require the abrupt termination of the protocol. The *Cancel* operator represents paths to be followed to manage exceptions. Different to *Stop* and *Exception* operators, the exception to be managed can occur in any point of the interaction protocol. A segment with this operator has to be defined at the end of the protocol.

The protocol of Figure 2 has a control flow segment with the operator *Xor* and two paths. Each path has a condition. This segments indicates the *customer* can respond of two different way: it accepts the supplier's request and commits to carry out the demand forecast in the future (message *agree(ResponseToForecastRequest)*); or it rejects the supplier's request. In this case the protocol ends.

3.2.5. Conditions and Time Constraints. Conditions represent logical expressions that constraint the execution of a message or a path into a control flow segment. They can be defined in natural language or using OCL expressions. Time constraints are used to define duration or deadlines on messages or protocols. A time constraint can be defined using relative or absolute dates. In the protocol of Figure 2, the messages of the control flow segment have a relative time constraint, which indicates these messages have to be sent before two days, then of the occurrence of the first message.

3.2.6. Interaction Occurrence. It represents the invocation of another interaction protocol, which is referred as the nested protocol. In Figure 2, if the *customer* agrees on the *supplier's* request, the protocol continues with the invocation of the nested protocol *Collaborative Demand Forecast*.

3.2.6. Termination. It represents an explicit end of a protocol. Two termination types can be defined: *success* and *failure*. *Success* implies the protocol has ended in a successful way. *Failure* indicates the protocol has not ended as it was expected. This only indicates the protocol did not follow the expected business logic. In Figure 2, if the customer rejects the supplier request, the protocol ends with a failure. Else, then of invocating to the nested protocol, the protocol finishes in an implicit way.

4. Generating BPEL specifications from UP-ColBPIP Models

In this section we discuss how models of collaborative processes defined with UP-ColBPIP can be used to generate BPEL specifications that enable the execution of these processes. First, we describe the transformations of UP-ColBPIP concepts into WSDL concepts. Then, we give an overview of the BPEL standard. Finally, we describe the transformations of UP-ColBPIP concepts into BPEL concepts.

4.2. Transformation of UP-ColBPIP to WSDL

In UP-ColBPIP, a role has a public business interface, which contains its required and provided business interfaces. These interfaces contain the business services that support the sending and receiving of business messages. These elements define the Business Interfaces View of a UP-ColBPIP model [15].

Hence, a WSDL model is generated for each role defined in a UP-ColBPIP model, because WSDL interfaces of the partners are derived in a direct way from the roles' provided business interfaces. The number of UP-ColBPIP to WSDL transformations to be done is equal to the number of partners defined in the UP-ColBPIP model.

Table 1 shows the correspondence between the concepts. Due to in UP-ColBPIP the business messages are asynchronous, WSDL operations are defined in an asynchronous way with an input message. Request/response operations are not generated. A business document is transformed into a message in WSDL.

Next code shows a fragment of the WSDL document that contains the interface of the role *customer*. As example, operation *request_ForecastDemand* was defined on the customer's port type to support the reception of the first message of the protocol.

```
<wsdl:definitions ...>
<message name="Msg:DemandForecast"/>
<message name="Msg:ResponseToForecastRequest"/>
<portType name="PT:Customer_InterfaceWithSupplier">
   <operation name="agree_DemandForecast ">
        <input message="Msg:DemandForecast"/>
   </operation>
</portType>
```

Table 1. Transformation of UP-ColBPIP concepts into WSDL concepts

UP-ColBPIP Concept	WSDL Concept
Role	Service
PublicBusinessInterface	PortType
BusinessService (from the Provided Interface)	Operation
BusinessDocument	Message

4.1. Overview of BPEL

The Business Process Execution Language (BPEL) [4] is an XML-based language intended to specify business processes in terms of a control flow that involves operations provided by one or several web services. It supports the definition of abstract and executable processes. An abstract process defines a business protocol, also known as conversation protocol [2]. This type of protocol defines the order in which a partner sends messages to and receives messages from its partners to achieve a business goal. An executable process defines the service business logic that supports the behavior of a partner in the interaction with other partners. This internal logic involves the manipulation of the partner's private data, the rules that determines the alternative paths, and the invocations to operations of private web services.

An activity in a BPEL process is either primitive or structured. Primitive activities are: invoke, to invoke a web service operation; *receive*, to wait for the reception of a message; *reply*, to reply to a message; *wait*, to remain idle for a given time period; *throw*, to raise exception errors; *assign*, to copy data from one variable to another; and *empty*, to do nothing. Structured activities are defined using the following control flow constructs: *sequence*, to define a sequential order between activities; *pick*, for non-deterministic alternatives based on events, such as message reception or time alarm; *switch*, to represent conditional routing; *flow*, to represent parallel execution routing and it is also used to define dependences between activities through the use of *control links*, in which the target activity of a control link may only start when the source activity has ended; *while*, to represent iterations; and *scope*, to group activities to be treated by the same fault-handler and within a given transactional context.

The above BPEL concepts are used to define both executable and abstract processes. An executable process can be considered as a refinement of an abstract process and it contains a mix of private and public aspects of a partner.

4.3. Transformation of UP-ColBPIP to BPEL

An important feature of BPEL is both abstract and executable processes are defined from the point of view of one partner. Figure 3 represents the correspondence between the process concepts we proposed in the business level and those proposed by BPEL in the technological level. The semantics of a collaborative process based on interaction protocol is represented by means of BPEL abstract processes, one by each partner involved in the protocol. This means that a BPEL abstract process represents the behavior of the role fulfilled by one partner in a collaborative process.

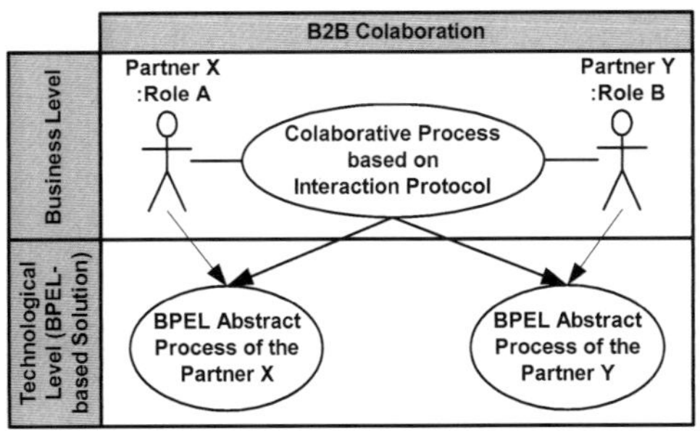

Fig. 3. Correspondence between a UP-ColBPIP process and BPEL processes

Several BPEL models have to be generated from a UP-ColBPIP model. On one hand, a BPEL model specifies just one process, whereas a UP-ColBPIP model can have a number of interaction protocols. On the other hand, an abstract process models have to be generated for each role involved in an interaction protocol. Therefore, the number BPEL abstract process to be generated from a UP-ColBPIP model is defined as follow: $AP = \sum_{ip=1}^{NoIP} R_{ip}$. *NoIP* is the number of interaction protocols of the UP-ColBPIP model and R_{ip} is the number of roles involved in each *ip* protocol.

In BPEL is necessary to indicate what WSDL interfaces of the other partners will be used in the process. This is done defining the *partnerLinkType* before the definition of the BPEL processes. As example, next code shows the partner link types.

```
<partnerLinkType name="PLT:CustomerSupplier">
  <role name="Customer">
    <portType name="PT:Customer_InterfaceWithSupplier"/>
  </role>
  <role name="Supplier">
    <portType name="PT:Supplier InterfaceWithCustomer"/>
  </role>
</partnerLinkType>
```

4.3.1. Transformation of Interaction Protocols. As we discussed above, for each role involved in an interaction protocol, a BPEL abstract process is generated. Therefore, a BPEL abstract process can be considered as the implementation of the lifeline of the role fulfilled by a partner in an interaction protocol.

The partner with its role represented by an abstract process is referred as the process owner. At the beginning of a process, *partner links* have to be defined to indicate the relationship between the process owner and its partners. A *parternLink* indicates the *partnerLinkType*, the role of the process owner (attribute *myRole*), and the roles of the partners (attribute *partnerRole*).

As example, the next code shows the BPEL abstract process of the role *customer* fulfilled by a partner in the interaction protocol *Demand Forecast Request*. Also, it shows the partner links defined in this process. Due to space limitations we do not detail the peer process corresponding to the role *supplier*.

```
<process name="DemandForecastRequest Customer" ....  abstractProcess="yes">
  <partnerLinks>
   <partnerLink name="LinkToSupplier"
       partnerLinkType="PLT:CustomerSupplier"
       myRole="Customer" partnerRole="Supplier"/>
  </partnerLinks>
```

4.3.2. Transformation of Business Messages. They can be transformed into three types of activities: *receive* or *pick*, and *invoke*. When a business message is sent by the process owner, an activity *invoke* is generated with the corresponding operation defined in the port type of the role that receives the message.

When a business message is received by the process owner and it has not an associated time constraint, it is transformed in an activity *receive*. This activity contains the operation through the process owner receives information. The operation is part of the port type of the process owner.

When a business message is received by the process owner and does not have an associated time constraint, it is transformed in an activity *pick*. This activity is defined with two events: *onMessage*, which indicates the reception of the message through the corresponding operation of the process owner port type; and *onAlarm*, which is used to represent the time constraint. Only one of these events can occur. So, if the message is received, the *onMessage* event occurs. Else, if the message is not received within the deadline defined in the *onAlarm* event, this event occurs and the actions defined in it are executed. If the time exception occurs in a process, it has to be informed to the partner. To do that, in the port types of the partner, an operation *timeException* is defined. It is invocated to inform the exception. The invocation is done through an activity *invoke* defined in the event *onAlarm*.

As example, the next code shows the activities generated in the supplier's process, from the *request* and *agree* messages of the protocol *Demand Forecast Request*.

```
<invoke partnerLink="LinkToCustomer"
     portType="PT:Customer_InterfaceWithSupplier"
     operation="request_DemandForecast"  inputVariable="DemandForecast"/>
....
<pick>
  <onMessage partnerLink="LinkToCustomer"
     portType="PT:Supplier_InterfaceWithCustomer"
     operation="agree_ResponseToForecastReceipt"
          variable="ResponseToForecastReceipt"/>
  <onAlarm for="t..t+2"
     portType="PT:Customer_InterfaceWithSupplier"  operation="timeException">
     <terminate/>
  </onAlarm>
</pick>
```

4.3.3. Synchronizing the Start of a BPEL Process. A BPEL process starts with an activity *receive* or *pick*, with its attribute *createInstance* settled to "yes". The process starts when the operation defined in this activity is invoked. However, it is necessary to synchronize the beginning of BPEL processes representing an interaction protocol. This is due to in BPEL there is not way to correlate instances of different processes.

To represent this synchronization, a "start" operation is added for each collaborative process in the port type of each partner. In the example, we generate the operation *start_DemandForecastRequest* in the port types of the customer and supplier. Then, it is necessary to identify the initiator of the protocol. In the BPEL process of the initiator, we add an activity *receive* with the operation *start_ DemandForecastRequest*. This operation will be invocated by the initiator from an internal application, when it requires starting the collaborative process. In addition, an activity *invoke* is added, which contains the "start" operation defined in the port type of the other partner. This activity enables the instantiation of the process of the other partner. Therefore, in the process of this partner, an activity *receive* with the corresponding "start" operation is added.

Next code shows the start of the *supplier's* process (the initiator of the protocol).

```
<receive partnerLink="LinkToSupplier"
    portType="PT:Supplier_InterfaceWithCustomer"
    operation="start_DemandForecastRequest"
        inputVariable="ProtocolInstanceNumber"/>
<invoke partnerLink="LinkToCustomer"
    portType="PT:Customer_InterfaceWithSupplier"
    operation="start_DemandForecastRequest"
        inputVariable="ProtocolInstanceNumber"/>
```

The next code shows the start of the *customer*'s process.

```
<receive partnerLink="LinkToSupplier"
    portType="PT:Customer_InterfaceWithSupplier"
    operation="start_DemandForecastRequest"
        inputVariable="ProtocolInstanceNumber"/>
```

4.3.4. Transformation of Control Flow Segments. They are transformed into structured activities, according to the operator used (Summarized in Table 2).

BPEL does not support distributed transactions among several processes. Hence, a segment with the operator *Transaction* cannot be represented in BPEL. This problem is recognized in BPEL and the *WS-Transaction* language is proposed for the definition of these transactions [4]. Also, a segment with the *Cancel* operator does not have a counterpart in BPEL, although it could be implemented through *fault handlers* that have to be synchronized with the *fault handlers* of the partners' processes.

The next code shows the transformation of the control flow segment of the interaction protocol *Demand Forecast Request* into the *customer's* process.

```
<switch>
  <case condition="bpws:getVariableData('RequestAccepted')=TRUE">
      <sequence>
        <!— Code of the first interaction path --!>
      </sequence>
  </case>
  <case condition="bpws:getVariableData('RequestRejected')=TRUE">
      <sequence>
        <!— Code of the second interaction path --!>
      </sequence>
  </case>
</switch>
```

4.3.5. Transformation of Terminations. The implicit and explicit termination of a protocol has also to be represented taking into account the synchronization of the BPEL processes of the partners, in a similar way to the synchronization of the start of these processes. Therefore, in the port type of the partners the operation *end_DemandForecastRequest* is added. Then, in each BPEL process, an event handler is added indicating the possible reception of a message through the "end" operation.

Table 2. Transformation of Control Flow Segment into BPEL Structured Activities

Control Flow Segment	BPEL Structured Activity
Xor	Switch (One *case* for each interaction path)
Or	Flow (Activity dependencies using *links* with transition and join conditions, and activities *empty*)
And	Flow
Loop (0,n); Loop (1,n)	While (BPEL does not differentiate types of loop)
If	Switch (One *case* and optionally an *otherwise*)
Exception	Switch
Stop	Switch, followed by activities defining the process termination.

Next code shows the failure termination of the protocol Demand Forecast Request in the customer's process. It has an activity invoke that informs to the supplier's process the termination. Then, the activity *terminate* ends the customer's process.

```
<invoke partnerLink="LinkToSupplier"
    portType="PT:Supplier_InterfaceWithSupplier"
    operation="end_DemandForecastRequest"
        inputVariable="ProtocolInstanceNumber"/>
<terminate/>
```

Next code denotes the counterpart required in the supplier's process that finishes it.

```
<eventHandlers>
   <onMessage partnerLink="LinkToCustomer"
         portType="Supplier_InterfaceWithCustomer"
         operation="end_BlanketPurchaseOrder">
      <terminate/>
   </onMessage>
   ...
</eventHnadlers>
```

5. Related Work

MDD approaches have been proposed to generate technological solutions based on web services composition [2, 7, 11]. They focus on the modeling and automatic code generation of business or conversation protocols. Therefore, they support the modeling and specification of the behavior of collaborative processes but only from the point of view of one partner. As a result: they do not support a global view in the modeling of collaborative processes; and they do not intend to support the synchronization and the progress of the process instances of each partner.

Moreover, some MDD approaches are not based on a standard conceptual framework, such as MDA [2]. Other approaches do not consider all the components required in a MDA approach. In [7], a UML Profile is provided for the modeling of technology-dependent models, but it does not support technology-independent process models. As a result, this approach influences the adoption of one standard.

In [9], the transformation of collaborative processes defined with the UN/CEFACT Modeling Methodology (UMM) to BPEL specifications has been proposed. This approach does not consider the application of a MDA approach to support the development of collaborative processes. This is the main difference with our approach. In addition, although from a UMM business collaboration, two or more BPEL processes are generated, this approach does not generate the extra XML code necessary for the synchronization of the BPEL processes' instances of each partner.

Finally, in the context of web services composition standards, the specification of the global view of the interactions between the partners is only supported by the WS-CDL language [10]. However, WS-CDL is not an executable language and it is expected to be used in conjunction with BPEL. In this approach, partners use WS-CDL to agree on the choreography of messages to achieve common goals. This choreography then is used to generate BPEL abstract processes for each partner. However, there are two important limitations of the above approach. On one hand, WS-CDL is a technology-specific language and it does not provide a graphical notation to define services choreographies. As it is highlighted in [3], global service choreographies are more a design than an implementation artifact, and hence, a graphical modeling language is more useful than a XML syntax. In addition, collaborative processes should be defined independent of the technology [18]. On the other hand, it remains open how WS-CDL specifications can be mapped into BEPL and hence, it is not clear if all WS-CDL concepts can be mapped into BPEL [3].

In contrast to above approaches, through the modeling of interaction protocols, we focus on a whole view of the choreography of messages exchanged between partners. Also, BPEL abstract processes are derived from interaction protocols. This ensures BPEL processes of each partner, which implement an interaction protocol, are consistent between them and can be synchronized in run-time by partners' systems.

6. Conclusions and Future Work

In this work, we have proposed a MDA approach for the conceptual modeling of collaborative business processes and the generation of technological solutions based on web services composition. In particular, we have described how it is possible to implement collaborative processes using the BPEL standard. The main contribution of this approach is the generated solutions based on web services composition are consistent with the UP-ColBPIP models defined in the business level. Thus, it allows decreasing the complexity, time and costs in the generation of this solutions.

In this MDA approach, we use the UP-ColBPIP language for the conceptual modeling of collaborative processes. The use of interaction protocols supports several important aspects of the B2B collaborations: enterprise autonomy, decentralization, peer-to-peer interactions and negotiations. Mainly, interaction protocols allow describing the commonly agreed global view of the interactions between the partners.

BPEL supports the definition of collaborative processes from the point of view of one partner. Therefore, the semantics of a collaborative process based on interaction protocol have to be represented in the technological level through several BPEL abstract processes, one by each partner. This adds an extra complexity to the generation of solutions based on web services composition, because BPEL processes representing an interaction protocol have to be consistent to each other. Through the proposed MDA approach, this consistence is achieved due to BPEL processes are generated from the common view defined in the interaction protocols.

In addition, as part of this MDA approach we have defined the transformations of UP-ColBPIP models into BPEL specifications. They define the correspondence between the concepts of both languages. As result of these transformations, on one hand, most of the UP-ColBPIP concepts can be represented in BPEL. On the other hand, BPEL does not provide concepts to define the synchronization of two different abstract processes. Therefore, extra code, which does not belong to the process logic, has to be added to support the synchronization of the processes' instances representing an interaction protocol instance.

Our ongoing work is about the implementation of these transformations through a method and a tool that we have developed for model transformations. The objective of this implementation is the execution and generation in an automatic way of the BPEL and WSDL specifications from UP-ColBPIP models.

References

1. Baghdadi, Y.: ABBA: An architecture for deploying business-to-business electronic commerce applications. Electronic Commerce Research and Applications. 3(2004) 190-212
2. Baïna, K, Benatallah, B., Cassati, F., Toumani, F.: Model-Driven Web Service Development. CaiSE'04, Springer (2004) 290-306.
3. Barros, A., Dumas, M., Oaks, P.: A Critical Overview of the Web Service Choreography Description Language (WS-CDL). BPTrends Newsletter 3 (2005).
4. BEA, IBM, Microsoft, SAP, Siebel: Business Process Execution Language for Web Services. http://www-106.ibm.com/developerworks/library/ws-bpel/, 2003.
5. Bernauer, M., Kappel, G., Kramler, G.: Comparing WSDL-based and ebXML-based Approaches for B2B Protocol Specification. Proceedings of ISOC'03 (2003).
6. Bussler, C.: The Role of B2B Engines in B2B Integration Architectures. ACM SIGMOD Record, Special Issue on Data Management Issues in E-Commerce, 31(1) (2002)
7. Gardner, T.: UML Modelling of Automated Business Processes with a Mapping to BPEL4WS, 17th ECOOP, Darmstadt, Germany (2003).
8. Goldkuhl, G., Lind,M.: Developing E-Interactions – a Framework for Business Capabilities and Exchanges. Proceedings of the ECIS-2004, Finland, 2004.
9. Hofreiter, B., Huemer, C.: Transforming UMM Business Collaboration Models to BPEL. International Workshop on Modeling Inter-Organizational Systems (MIOS), 2004.
10. Kavantzas, N., Burdett, D., Ritzinger, G., Fletcher, T., Lafon, Y.: Web Services Choreography Description Language Version 1.0. W3C Working Draft (2004), W3C.
11. Koehler, J., Hauser, R., Kaporr, S., Wu, F., Kurmaran, S.: A Model-Driven Transformation Method. 7th International Enterprise Distributed Object Computing, 2003.
12. Object Management Group: MDA Guide V1.0.1, 2003. http://www.omg.org/mda
13. Searle, J.R.: Speech Acts, an Essay in the Philosophy of Language, Cambridge Univ., 1969.
14. UN/CEFACT and OASIS: ebXML Business Specification Schema Version 1.10, http://www.untmg.org/downloads/General/approved/ebBPSS-v1pt10.zip (2001)
15. Villarreal, P.: Method for the Modeling and Specification of Collaborative Business Processes. PhD Thesis. Universidad Tecnológica Nacional, Santa Fe, Argentina (2005).
16. Villarreal, P., Salomone, H.E. and Chiotti, O.: B2B Relationships: Defining Public Business Processes using Interaction Protocols. Journal of the Chilean Society of Computer Science, Special issue on the Best Papers of the JCC 2003, Vol. 4(1) (2003).
17. Villarreal, P., Salomone, H.E. and Chiotti, O.: A UML Profile for Modeling Collaborative Business Processes based on Interaction Protocols. Argentine Symposium on Information Systems (ASIS 2004), Proc. of the 33 JAIIO, Córdoba, Argentina (2004).
18. Villarreal, P., Salomone, H.E. and Chiotti, O.: Applying Model-Driven Development to Collaborative Business Processes. 8th Ibero-American Workshop of Requirements Engineering and Software Environments, Chile, 2005.

Una Plataforma de componentes heterogéneos para Entornos de Diseño con soporte J2EE

Emilio G. Ormeño [1], Sergio F. Ochoa [2]

[1] Universidad Nacional de San Juan, Facultad de Ciencias Exactas, Físicas y Naturales, Av. José I. de la Roza y Meglioli, edificio Islas Malvinas, San Juan, Argentina
eormeno@iinfo.unsj.edu.ar
[2] Departamento de Ciencias de la Computación, Universidad de Chile, Blanco Encalada 2120, Santiago, Chile
sochoa@dcc.uchile.cl

Abstract. Dentro de los desarrollos de software empresarial, uno de los principales actores continúan siendo las aplicaciones cliente/servidor construidas sobre J2EE. La fortaleza y robustez de esta tecnología brinda ventajas que han sido ampliamente discutidas por la comunidad científica del área. Sin embargo, la implementación de aplicaciones cliente/servidor altamente interactivas, como los entornos de diseño, continúa siendo un desafío cuando se usa J2EE. Esto se debe a la carga de transacciones que requiere para mantener coordinados cliente y servidor, lo cual afecta la performance y la capacidad de procesamiento de transacciones. Para paliar esta problemática, éste artículo presenta una plataforma llamada EBCDS (Enterprise Business Component Development System), la cual está compuesta por componentes Java, que permiten construir aplicaciones J2EE que combinan una alta interactividad con el usuario, sin dejar de lado los aspectos de escalabilidad, seguridad y buen soporte para transacciones.

1. Introducción

En la actualidad es indiscutible el rol que juega la plataforma J2EE (Java 2 Enterprise Edition) [12] en el desarrollo de aplicaciones empresariales. Esta plataforma propone patrones de diseño que se adaptan a la gran mayoría de los sistemas de información que una moderna organización requiere, facilitando así el desarrollo de muchas de las aplicaciones empresariales. Estas aplicaciones usualmente involucran componentes distribuidos, seguros, escalables y capaces de soportar una carga de transacciones importante. Aunque este soporte es ampliamente reconocido, la implementación de aplicaciones cliente/servidor altamente interactivas continúa siendo una limitación para J2EE. La implementación de ese tipo de aplicaciones, tales como un entorno de diseño gráfico, requiere que cada interacción con el usuario esté asociada a una o más interacciones entre las aplicaciones cliente y servidor. Esto es operativamente poco viable, debido a la sobrecarga de transacciones que esto implica y al ancho de banda que requiere. Aunque las empresas que promueven y apoyan el desarrollo de la plataforma J2EE son conscientes de esta limitación, las implementaciones tanto comerciales como open source continúan si mostrar avance en este tópico. Tal es el caso de productos como IBM Websphere [21], JBoss [5], Oracle Application Server [6] y su entorno de desarrollo JDeveloper [7], entre otras. Por ese motivo, se puede decir que las aplicaciones empresariales altamente interactivas han quedado fuera de ésta plataforma. Por lo tanto, el equipo de desarrollo es quien debe proveer sus propios mecanismos de soporte.

Por otra parte, distintos tipos de las aplicaciones Web que hacen de front-end de servidores J2EE, también podrían ser utilizadas para implementar aplicaciones cliente altamente interactivas. Si bien el tipo y la calidad de los recursos que hoy pueden ser utilizados con este objetivo se han ido enriqueciendo con cada vez más tecnologías, tales como Applets [4], módulos Flash [10], Javascript [9], etc., éstos aun no son suficientes como para soportar escenarios de interacción de alto rendimiento.

Para reducir el impacto de esta problemática, presentamos en este paper una plataforma llamada EBCDS (Enterprise Business Component Development System), la cual está compuesta por componentes Java que permiten construir aplicaciones clientes J2EE que combinan una alta interactividad con el usuario, sin dejar de lado los aspectos de performance, escalabilidad, seguridad y buen soporte para transacciones. También provee la capacidad de distribuir sus componentes, al proveer adaptadores en los que es posible conectar mecanismos de persistencia tales como EJB (Enterprise Java Beans) [8], o simplemente un sistema de archivos, en función de las necesidades de la organización.

En la siguiente sección se presenta el concepto de clientes pesados (o altamente interactivos) y su relevancia en determinados tipos de sistemas de información. En la sección 3 se explica la plataforma EBCDS, su concepto, arquitectura, y sus componentes principales. En la sección 4 se describen los trabajos relacionados, y finalmente, en la sección 5 se presentan las conclusiones y el trabajo a futuro.

2. J2EE y los Clientes Pesados

En este artículo se le llamará cliente pesado a aquellos módulos cliente, que demandan una alta tasa de interacciones con componentes del servidor. En la actualidad a la hora de desarrollar aplicaciones empresariales, es decir, aquellas que están compuestas por componentes escalables, seguros, capaces de operar usando transacciones, y que permiten el acceso a ellos en forma distribuida, las organizaciones usualmente optan por soportar sus aplicaciones sobre la plataforma J2EE, debido a los beneficios que ésta les aporta:

- Simplifica la compleja tarea de escribir código confiable, distribuido, escalable y con manejo de seguridad, al proveer un conjunto estándar de componentes de software reutilizables y adaptables [14].
- Provee una API estándar, la cual al ser utilizada por diferentes vendedores de software para mantener la compatibilidad entre ellos.
- Provee una clara separación entre la lógica de negocio, la persistencia de datos y despliegue de la aplicación. Esto promueve la modularización de las aplicaciones [13], la separación de intereses y la distribución de componentes.

- Promueve la separación en capas de la aplicación [15], lo cual mejora la reutilización y el desarrollo de diferentes partes de la aplicación, por parte de diferentes equipos de trabajo (diseñadores gráficos, arquitectos de software, programadores, administradores de base de datos, etc).

La Fig. 1 muestra las diferentes capas involucradas en una aplicación J2EE y las tecnologías por ésta provista. En dicha figura se puede observar que el los clientes livianos (thin clients) acceden al servidor de aplicaciones y a los datos sólo a través un servidor Web.

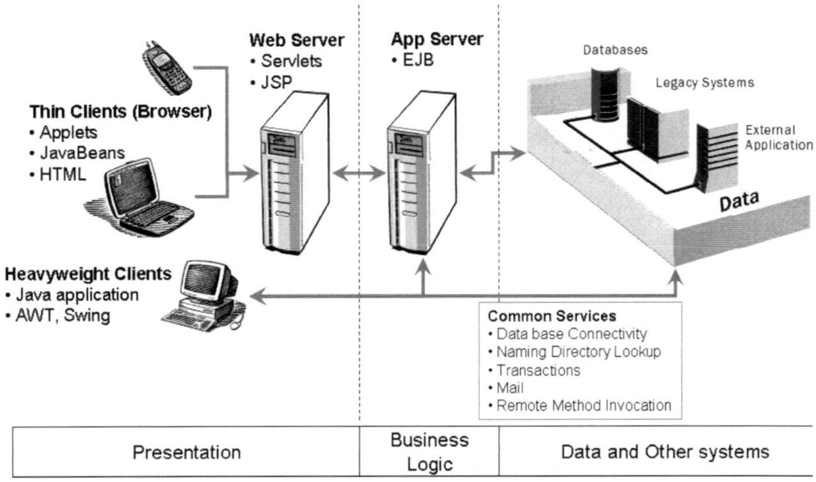

Fig. 1. Arquitectura de n-capas de la plataforma J2EE

Por otra parte, los clientes pesados (heavyweight clients) o aplicaciones Java comunes pueden acceder directamente al servidor de aplicaciones o a la base de datos, a través de las APIs provistas por la plataforma J2EE. En la medida que se reduzca la granularidad de las operaciones que viajan entre el cliente y el servidor, la sobrecarga de todos los elementos involucrados (incluyendo la red) aumentará en consecuencia.

Con el fin de proveer soluciones reutilizables a este problema de interacción, se han desarrollado una serie de patrones de diseño [1], entre los cuales se destaca el patrón Transfer Object [11, 16]. Este patrón propone la inclusión de un objeto de transferencia (transfer object) entre el cliente y el servidor, como una forma de disminuir la cantidad de transacciones entre éstos. Dicho objeto funciona como un capacitor, que agrupa transacciones del cliente y las replica al servidor en forma de bloque.

Al iniciar la interacción entre un cliente y un servidor de aplicaciones, uno o más objetos de transferencia son creados y alojados en la máquina donde ejecuta la aplicación cliente. Típicamente, esto objetos son copias de uno o más objetos del servidor que viajan hasta el cliente y sobre los cuales se realizan las transacciones, que luego retornan al servidor para actualizar los objetos reales.

Con el fin de ejemplificar este proceso, la Fig. 2 muestra un esquema típico en donde la aplicación cliente realiza invocaciones directas al servidor. Por otra parte, la Fig. 3 muestra el mismo cliente realizando transacciones contra un servidor, pero utilizando un objeto de transferencia como intermediario. Debido a que el objeto de transferencia está alojado en el cliente, las interacciones entre éste y la aplicación cliente no utilizan la red, por lo tanto no sobrecargan el medio de comunicación y ayudan a mantener la performance del sistema. Además, este esquema de trabajo, hace a las aplicaciones más escalables debido a que se puede jugar con la granularidad de los bloques de transacciones que cada objeto de transferencia replica al servidor. De esta manera, el número de invocaciones al servidor se podría reducir significativamente.

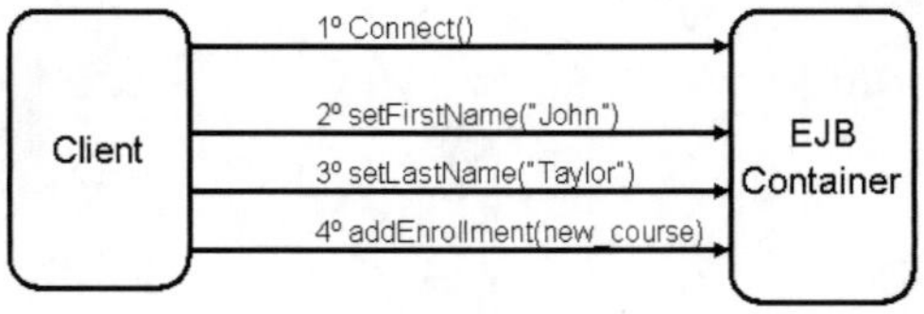

Fig. 2. Invocaciones directas entre el cliente y el servidor

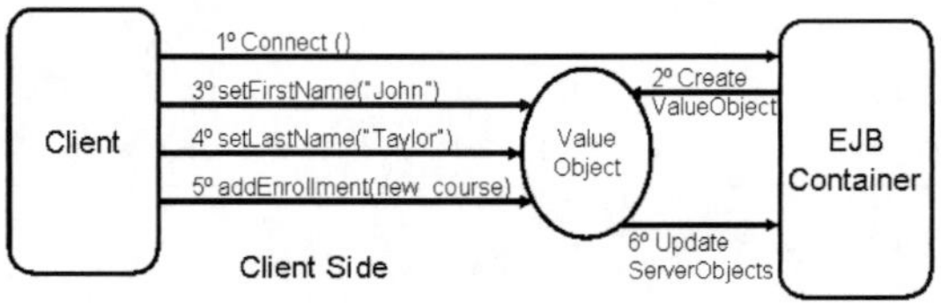

Fig. 3. Introducción de un objeto de transferencia

La plataforma EBCDS implementa el patrón Transfer Object y brinda además un manejo de transacciones transparente para el desarrollador. Esta plataforma ha sido implementada como una extensión de J2EE, como el objetivo de ayudar a superar las limitaciones antes mencionadas. La siguiente sección muestra en mayor detalle los diferentes componentes de EBCDS.

3. Plataforma EBCDS

Un Componente EBCDS es un componente Java orientado exclusivamente al manejo de un formato específico de información de naturaleza persistente la cual posee al menos una entidad raíz a la cual está vinculado. Este componente se encuentra contenido por un Cliente EBCDS con quien se comunica a través de interfaces. Las dos principales responsabilidades del cliente son:

1. Brindar acceso a la interfaz gráfica de los componentes, a su funcionalidad a través de componentes gráficos tales como ventanas, menús, barras de herramientas, menú contextual, etc.
2. Comunicarse con el manejador de persistencia.

Las siguientes características son aplicables a los componentes EBCDS:

- Son componentes de software.
- Sirven para actualizar datos con una estructura preestablecida.
- Dado que a priori el componente no posee información respecto al mecanismo de persistencia que será utilizado para sus instancias, tiene definido un modelo con la estructura de los datos.
- Poseen una alta cohesión y un acoplamiento bajo o nulo con otros componentes que no estén dentro de su mismo paquete (en caso de existir).
- Tienen definidas interfaces gráficas para representar y actualizar los datos.
- Las interfaces gráficas (las cuales pueden ser Web) a la que denomina Vistas, proveen mecanismos estándar para publicar su funcionalidad de forma tal que el ebcds_client pueda accederla.
- Tienen significado solo dentro de un ebcds_client, el cual realiza la persistencia de sus instancias.

3.1. Dominio de aplicación

La plataforma EBCDS está orientada a un tipo específico de aplicaciones que poseen las siguientes características:

- Están formadas por componentes heterogéneos, es decir que agrupados en la aplicación tienen una semántica coherente, pero en particular tienen significado propio y pueden existir por si solos.
- Dichos componentes fueron desarrollados para actualizar un formato específico de datos, es decir, con una estructura conocida.
- El usuario de la aplicación, en función de un perfil, puede instalar o desinstalar componentes y paquetes de componentes.
- Los componentes tienen una alta cohesión y un acoplamiento muy bajo o nulo respecto a otros componentes instalados en la aplicación, a menos que pertenezcan a un mismo paquete.
- La interfaz de la aplicación o sus componentes pueden ser Web.
- Cualquier componente tiene medios para acceder a la interfaz de la aplicación.
- Las instancias de un determinado tipo de componente pueden ser distribuídas a otras aplicaciones que poseen ese mismo tipo de componente.

Debido a esas características, el campo de aplicación se reduce a entornos de desarrollo de alto nivel o diseño en los que los componentes se pueden instalar o desinstalar sin que se vea afectada la aplicación.

3.2. Arquitectura de EBCDS

La plataforma EBCDS (Enterprise Business Components Development System) motiva al equipo de desarrollo a mantener una clara separación funcional, a través de clases de Modelo, Vista y Servicio (transacciones). Esto facilita la separación de intereses en productos de software y ayuda a modularizar las aplicaciones.

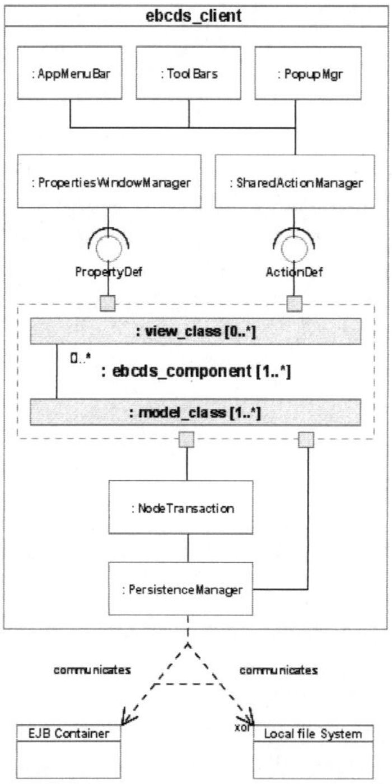

Fig. 4. Arquitectura de EBCDS

Cabe hacer notar que los componentes de la plataforma ejecutan (y embeben la lógica de negocio) del lado del cliente, lo cual les permite especializarse para diversos tipos de aplicaciones empresariales. Especialmente, aquellas con interfaces gráficas altamente interactivas, tales como aplicaciones colaborativas sincrónicas y sistemas distribuidos.

La Fig. 4 muestra la arquitectura de la versión actual de EBCDS. Allí cada componente que ejecuta del lado del cliente y está soportado por un conjunto de clases y archivos de configuración que conforman los llamados Componentes EBCDS. Del otro lado operan los componentes que manejan la persistencia de datos y aquellos que sirven a los componentes EBCDS que residen en los clientes. Estos componentes que ejecutan en el servidor poseen una interfaz, que independiza a los clientes de las implementaciones particulares de los módulos de servicio. A continuación se detallan los elementos más importantes de la plataforma.

3.3. Clases de Modelo

Las clases de modelo de EBCDS realizan una representación abstracta de las entidades persistentes pero del lado del cliente. Encapsulan y proveer la funcionalidad básica para el acceso a los atributos y definición de métodos del negocio. La Fig. 5 muestra un diagrama simplificado de clases que corresponden al componente de modelo ofrecido por EBCDS. A fin de aclarar cómo se trabaja con estos componentes, se presentará como ejemplo una solución EBCDS a un problema simple. El problema consiste en poder actualizar dos entidades que están directamente vinculadas. Estas entidades son Employee y Task (Fig. 6), donde cada empleado puede tener asociadas cero o más tareas.

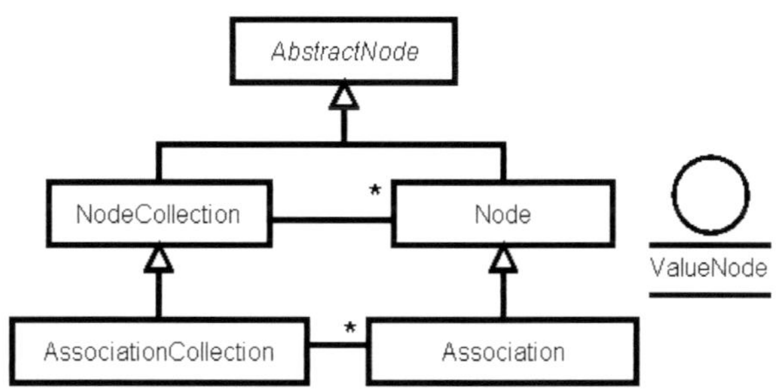

Fig. 5. Diagrama de clases de modelo de EBCDS

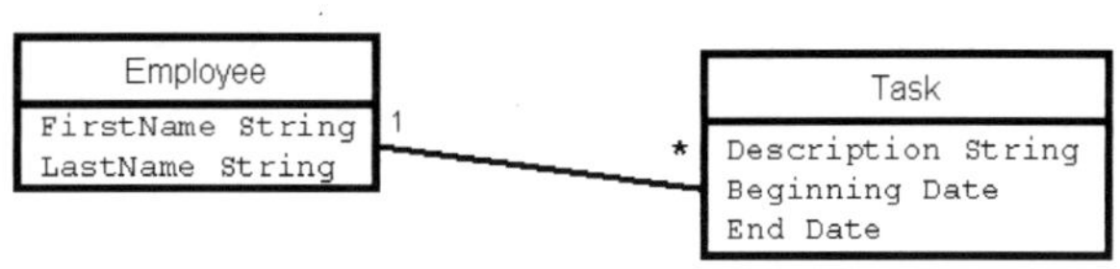

Fig. 6. Entidades a ser modeladas con EBCDS

La Fig. 6, muestra el problema planteado, mientras que la Fig. 7 muestra un diagrama con una posible solución para implementar la lógica del negocio de estas dos entidades. Esto puede hacerse a través de extensiones a la clase Node, que es la clase raíz de toda entidad, incluida la relación entre ellas a través de una clase NodeCollection, la cual es la raíz de las colecciones.

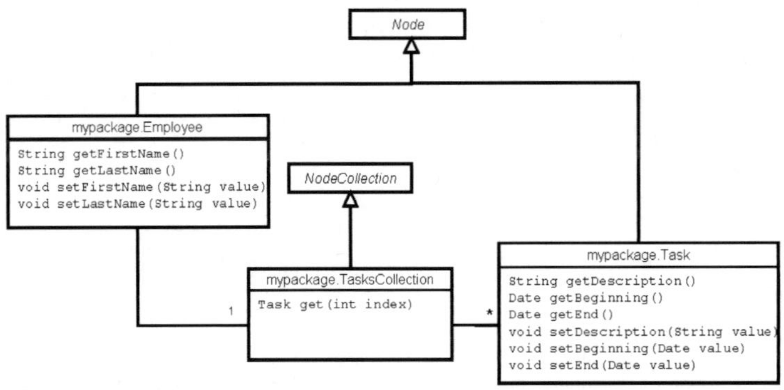

Fig. 7. Implementación del problema utilizando las clases de modelo de EBCDS

Las clases de modelo interactúan con el manejador de persistencia, a través del cliente a fin de lograr dos funciones básicas: acceso a transacciones y acceso a los datos (persistencia) el cual se presenta en la secciónn 3.4.

Las clases de servicio modifican las clases de entidad, las cuales residen en el servidor. Cada modificación realizada a una clase de entidad es capturada por el servicio de transacciones y son enviadas al manejador de persistencia (que se explica en la sección 3.3) cuando desde el entorno se invoca el método commit().

3.4. Componente de Manejo de Persistencia

El componente manejador de persistencia es el encargado de asegurar la persistencia de las entidades y de sus actualizaciones en algún medio físico o de red. Este componente provee además una interfaz común para facilitar la implementación de diferentes mecanismos de persistencia, tales como: EJB, sistema de archivos y colas de mensajes.

Continuando con el ejemplo de empleados y tareas introducido previamente, la Fig. 8 muestra cómo la interfaz de usuario accede al conjunto de entidades de empleado, al realizar una solicitud (commit) al servicio de persistencia. El último nivel del diagrama de secuencia corresponde a la interfaz de acceso a datos, la cual implementa el patrón Fachada (Facade) [1].

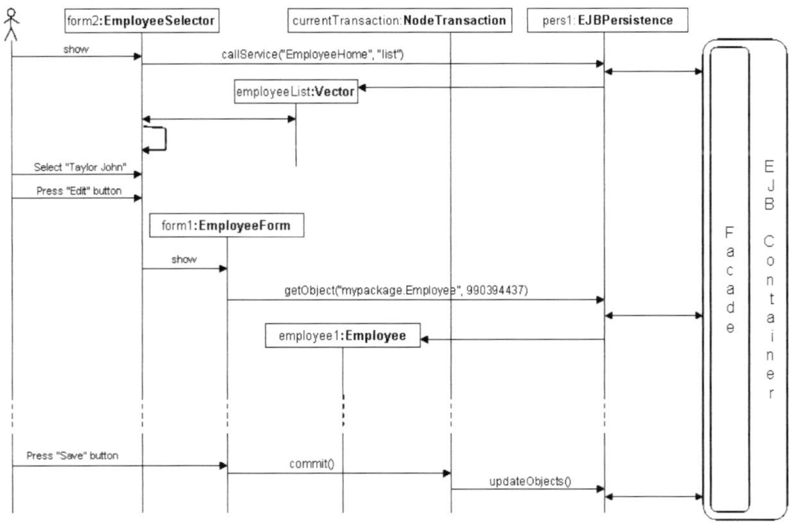

Fig. 8. Diagrama de secuencia para la obtención del conjunto de empleados utilizando el servicio de persistencia de EBCDS

3.4. Componentes de Vista

Los componentes de vista de la plataforma EBCDS, están representados a través de un framework llamado Wwing [3], el cual agrupa y relaciona un conjunto de componentes Web visuales [2]. Wwing posee una API que simplifica la construcción de la capa de presentación Web de aplicaciones J2EE. De esa manera motiva al desarrollador a programar sus clases bajo la forma de una típica interfaz orientada a eventos; o sea, a través del ensamblaje de componentes visuales dentro de un contenedor y programando las acciones a realizar ante los eventos producidos por el usuario. Todo ello, sin tener que lidiar con las complejidades de HTML, JavaScript o con los problemas relacionados al estilo de presentación. Si bien esta API es una parte muy importante de EBCDS, su inclusión excede el alcance de este artículo, debido a que constituye en sí mismo otra plataforma y otro conjunto de especificaciones relacionadas.

Como muestra de la utilidad de EBCDS se desarrolló un ambiente de diseño, construcción y distribución de courseware sobre la base de EBCDS. Este ambiente llamado CDS (Course Development System) [19, 20], sigue un paradigma de construcción en base a componentes didácticos reutilizables (texto, imágenes, video, foros de discusión, chats, y actividades personales y grupales). Los courseware creados utilizando CDS se emplean para apoyar el proceso de enseñanza-aprendizaje en el Departamento de Ciencias de la Computación de la Universidad de Chile. Dichos courseware implementan todos sus componentes didácticos utilizando

EBCDS, debido a que existe una elevada interacción entre los usuarios (profesores, ayudantes y alumnos), tanto durante la etapa de construcción como durante su puesta en producción.

4. Trabajos Relacionados

Entre las plataformas estudiadas y que guardan relación con la presente propuesta, quizás la que más se acerca al concepto de soporte para la interactividad de aplicaciones cliente, es Oracle ADF (Application Development Framework) [17]. Este framework de componentes multicapa facilita el desarrollo de aplicaciones J2EE, además de la conectividad con diversas tecnologías de persistencia. La Fig. 9 muestra la arquitectura general de este producto.

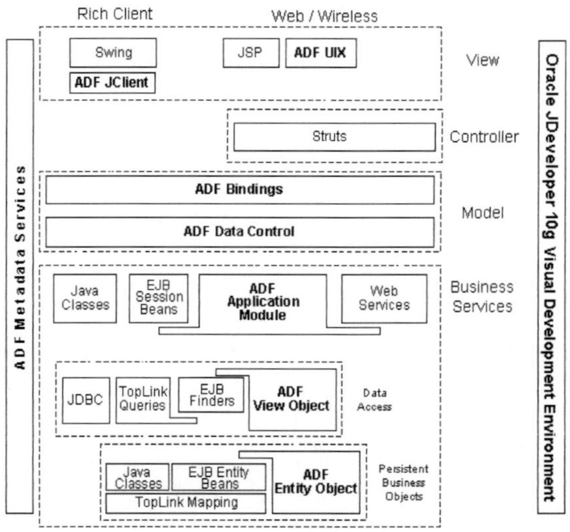

Fig. 9. Arquitectura de Oracle ADF

La construcción de aplicaciones con esta plataforma requiere del entorno de desarrollo JDeveloper [7], el cual automatiza la mayoría de las tareas involucradas en una compleja arquitectura, como la de ADF. Como se puede apreciar en la figura 11, la arquitectura del producto incluye clientes pesados (rich clients), los cuales se desarrollan sobre JClient [18]. Este componente de ADF consiste en un conjunto de APIs que facilitan el acceso a las capas inferiores de la arquitectura.

Si bien ADF es una excelente herramienta de desarrollo que facilita en gran medida la implementación del patrón Transfer Object, no se adapta a nuestras necesidades dado que nuestro interés radica en un limitado espectro de clientes pesados, en donde la interacción con el usuario es muy alta. Tal es el caso de un diseñador gráfico, un procesador de texto, un sistema colaborativo o una herramienta de e-learning como CDS (Course Development System) [19, 20]. Por otro lado, todo el entorno JDeveloper está orientado a lograr interfaces de usuario estándares, que si bien están muy bien representadas para la gran mayoría de las situaciones, no se adaptan al tipo de aplicaciones antes mencionadas.

5. Conclusiones y Trabajo Futuro

La plataforma EBCDS es un principio de solución para los problemas que presentan determinados sistemas de información empresariales, en los que la interacción con el usuario es muy elevada. Si bien este tipo de sistemas encajan dentro de una muy estrecha franja de aplicaciones, existe un mercado importante. Muchas organizaciones han optado por la plataforma J2EE debido a las ventajas que esta les provee, razón por la cual EBCDS no representa mas que una extensión, que permite extender dichas ventajas a escenarios que no están considerados en forma nativa en la plataforma J2EE.

El hecho de que EBCDS implemente el patrón Transfer Object, hace que la plataforma herede también la principal problemática que este patrón posee: la concurrencia. Debido a que la interacción entre el cliente y el modelo se realiza con una copia local de uno o más componentes alojados en el servidor, es altamente probable que un acceso concurrente pueda producir versiones incompatibles. Para solucionar este problema un requisito en el que se está trabajando actualmente es en la posibilidad de bloquear componentes que pueden ser accedidos en forma simultánea.

Otra de las tareas en la que se está trabajando en pos de mejorar la plataforma, es en la medición de la satisfacción de los desarrolladores que emplean EBCDS. Para ello se están utilizando cuestionarios confiables [22], con alumnos de la Universidad Nacional de San Juan y del curso de CC51A-Ingeniería de Software de la Universidad de Chile.

6. Agradecimientos

Este trabajo ha sido parcialmente financiado por las iniciativas Programa Incentivos, Ministerio de Educación de la Nación/Universidad Nacional de San Juan, Nro. 21/E345 (Argentina), Fondecyt No. 1030959 (Chile) y por el Chile-Korea IT Cooperation Center (Chile).

7. Referencias

1. Gamma, E., Helm, R., Johnson, R., Vlissides, J. Design Patterns: Elements of Reusable Object Oriented Software. Addison-Wesley. (1994).
2. Rosenfeld L., Morville P. Information Architecture for the World Wide Web. O'Reilly & Associates, (1998).

3. Ormeño, E., Ochoa, S., Zapata, S. Swing: Una Plataforma de Componentes Visuales Reutilizables para Aplicaciones Web. IV Workshop Chileno en Ingeniería de Software. Arica, Chile. (2004).
4. Sun Microsystems. JavaSoft, Applets, http://java.sun.com/applets/. Last visit: June, 2005.
5. Jboss Inc. http://www.jboss.org. Last visit: June, 2005.
6. Oracle Corp. Oracle Application Server 10g, http://www.oracle.com/technology/products/ias. Last visit: June, 2005.
7. Oracle Corp. Oracle JDeveloper 10g, http://www.oracle.com/technology/products/jdev. Last visit: June, 2005.
8. Sun Microsystem. Enterprise JavaBeans Specification, Version 2.0. Pág. 34.
9. Netscape. Netscape Deveage: Core JavaScript 1.5, http://devedge.netscape.com/library/manuals/2000/javascript/1.5/guide. Last visit: July, 2005.
10. Macromedia. Flash MX 2004, http://www.macromedia.com/software/flash/. Last visit: August, 2005.
11. Oracle Corp. Core J2EE Patterns: Best Practices and Design Strategies, http://www.oracle.com/technology/products/jdev/collateral/papers/10g/adftoystore/readme.html#core-patterns. Last visit: June, 2005.
12. Sun Microsystems. Java 2 Platform Enterprise Edition http://www.javasoft.com/j2ee. Last visit: July, 2005.
13. Johnson, R., Roberts, D. Frameworks = (Components + Patterns). Communications of the ACM, Vol. 40, No. 10, October, (1997) 39-42.
14. Roberts, D., Johnson, R. Evolve Frameworks into Domain-Specific Languages. Proceedings of the 3rd Patterns Languages of Programming Conference, PloP'96. Illinois, EEUU, September, (1996).
15. Estublier, J., Favre, J. Component Models and Component Technology. Book Chapter in Building Reliable Component-Based Systems, I. Crnkovic, M. Larsson editors. Archtech House Publishers, (2002).
16. Crawford, W., Kaplan, J. J2EE Design Pattern. O'Reilly & Associates. (2003).
17. Oracle Corp. Oracle Application Development Framework: ADF, http://www.oracle.com/technology/products/jdev/htdocs/905/adffaq_otn.html. Last visit: June, 2005.
18. Oracle Corp. ADF JClient Facilities. http://www.oracle.com/technology/products/jdev/collateral/papers/9.0.5.0/jclient10g.pdf. Last visit: June, 2005.
19. Ormeño, E., Ochoa, S. CDS (Courseware Development System): Un Ambiente de Desarrollo de Courseware. Memorias del VII Congreso Argentino de Ciencias de la Computación (CACIC 2001). El Calafate, Santa Cruz, Argentina. Oct. 16-20, 2001.
20. Ochoa, S., Ormeño, E., Pino, J. Reusing Courseware Components. Proceedings of the XIV International Conference on Software Engineering and Knowledge Engineering (SEKE'02). ACM Press. Ischia, Italy. July 15-19, (2002). 549-556.
21. IBM. Websphere Journal. http://websphere.sys-con.com. Last visit: July, 2005.
22. Zapata, S., Lund, M., Ochoa, S. Una Herramienta para la Medición Continua de la Satisfacción de Usuarios de Software. II Workshop en Ingeniería de Software,

realizado en el marco de la Jornadas Chilenas de Computación (JCC 2002). Copiapó, Chile, 2002.

Sesión 8:

Medición y Evaluación 1

Medición y Evaluación de Calidad en Uso: Un Caso de Estudio para una Aplicación E-Learning

Guillermo Covella, Luis Olsina

GIDIS_Web, Departamento de Sistemas,
Facultad de Ingeniería, Universidad Nacional de La Pampa,
Calle 9 y 110, (6360) General Pico, La Pampa, Argentina.
{covellag , olsinal}@ing.unlpam.edu.ar

Abstract. En el artículo se propone un enfoque cuantitativo para medir y evaluar calidad en uso, o sea la calidad percibida por los usuarios en contextos reales de uso, para aplicaciones software/Web. La propuesta metodológica está guiada por un marco de medición y evaluación, que a su vez se basa en una ontología de métricas e indicadores. Se ilustra la propuesta con un caso de estudio de evaluación de calidad en uso para una aplicación e-Learning. Se analizan los datos obtenidos y se arrojan conclusiones finales.

1. Introducción

El empleo masivo de aplicaciones de software, y últimamente de aplicaciones Web, prácticamente en todos los ámbitos del desempeño humano, han convertido a los usuarios en potenciales referentes para evaluar la calidad de dichos productos. Sin embargo, las cuestiones relacionadas a la calidad –especialmente a la calidad que perciben los usuarios reales- han sido postergadas o con frecuencia ignoradas, ya sea por las urgencias en entregar los productos rápido al mercado, eventuales ahorros de costo o falta de recursos humanos capacitados, entre otros factores. Justamente esta cuestión, más una cierta falta de precisión en la definición de términos clave empleados para medir y evaluar alguna de las perspectivas de la calidad de producto software (en particular de aplicaciones Web), constituyen un motivación importante para los estudios, discusiones y aportes incluidos en este trabajo.

Sin negar el aporte de los métodos heurísticos [14], es posible considerar que enfoques basado en modelos, con procesos de evaluación sustentados en metodologías de inspección, eminentemente objetivos antes que subjetivos y cuantitativos más que cualitativos, pueden resultar una contribución valiosa. Se propone para ello una visión ingenieril para evaluar calidad en uso, que se sostiene en tres fundamentos:

a) un *modelo conceptual* de calidad en uso;

b) un *marco de medición y evaluación* de referencia [20] para la adopción, diseño y cálculo de las métricas e indicadores necesarios para medir y evaluar calidad en uso; y

c) una *metodología* de referencia [17] para llevar adelante completamente el proceso de evaluación.

Para ilustrar la propuesta se diseñó y ejecutó un caso de estudio con la participación de usuarios reales en un contexto real de uso, sobre un tipo particular de producto software: una aplicación Web para el dominio de e-Learning. El interés sobre el dominio de e-Learning está dado por la importancia que está adquiriendo la Web como soporte a procesos de entrenamiento y enseñanza/aprendizaje, en el ámbito empresarial y educativo respectivamente, y en este último caso con mucho énfasis a nivel universitario [13].

Dado que medir y evaluar la calidad en uso de un producto software permite determinar el grado en que un producto satisface las necesidades y expectativas de un usuario final realizando tareas concretas y en un contexto de uso particular, a continuación se presenta una propuesta que contribuye a la medición y evaluación sistemática y disciplinada de calidad en uso de productos Web.

El artículo se organiza de la siguiente manera. En la sección 2 se discuten los conceptos de calidad, calidad en uso, usabilidad y criterios para evaluación de calidad en uso; luego, en la sección 3 se presenta un marco de medición y evaluación y una metodología adaptada para calidad en uso para realizar el estudio. En la sección 4 se ilustra un caso de estudio sobre una aplicación de e-Learning, es decir, se detallan aspectos de diseño e implementación de medición y evaluación para un modelo de calidad en uso. Finalmente, se analizan los datos obtenidos y se arrojan conclusiones finales.

2. Discusión y Trabajos Relacionados

El concepto de calidad en uso ha evolucionado en los últimos veinte años acompañando a la industria del software. En la opinión de Bevan [3], el cambio fundamental es la atención cada vez mayor que merecen tanto los usuarios como el contexto considerados, cuando se evalúa el desempeño de un producto software en uso. Las normas ISO recientes reflejan la importancia de tener en cuenta el punto de vista de los usuarios y la última versión del estándar 9126-1 [11] confirma una apertura conceptual en las definiciones, ya que se especifica a la calidad en uso como un modelo diferente, complementario al modelo de calidad interna y externa de producto de software.

2.1 Calidad y Calidad en Uso

El término calidad es empleado frecuentemente en la literatura y en la práctica de las organizaciones, básicamente agregando valor o realzando propiedades de un producto o servicio; no obstante, existen distintos enfoques acerca de su significado en determinados contextos. Considérense por ejemplo las definiciones dadas en algunas normas ISO en general. En el estándar ISO 9000 [7] se define calidad como el "*grado en el que un conjunto de características inherentes [al producto] cumple con los requerimientos*" aclarándose que inherente significa que existe algo especial como característica o propiedad permanente.

Por otra parte, en ISO 14598-1 [9] ya no considera a la calidad disociada de las necesidades de los usuarios sino que calidad en uso puede ser evaluada de acuerdo a la eficacia, productividad y satisfacción con las que una clase de usuario específico puede alcanzar metas específicas en un ambiente particular de trabajo.

La versión actual del estándar ISO 9126-1 [11] tiene un enfoque integrado de calidad, propiciando la inclusión de requerimientos de calidad en uso ya en la especificación de requerimientos del producto. Es posible decir también que el modelo de calidad en uso del estándar ISO 9126-1 es una ampliación (o adaptación) del modelo ISO 9241-11 [8], específicamente para software, considerando que la calidad en uso puede ser medida y evaluada teniendo en cuenta el grado en que el software o aplicación Web cumple con las necesidades de usuarios reales, en un contexto específico de uso.

2.2 Usabilidad y Calidad en Uso

Los términos usabilidad y calidad en uso han estado empleándose como sinónimos en la comunidad de Ingeniería de Software y Web por un largo período. En una encuesta donde se repasa el uso del término usabilidad bajo distintos enfoques Folmer *et al* [6] afirman, citando a Bevan *et al* [2], que el término usabilidad tiene su origen en el concepto de "*user friendly*", pero que esta frase fue adquiriendo un sentido vago y subjetivo, sugiriéndose el término usabilidad para reemplazarla. Luego usabilidad fue definida como una característica principal de la calidad de un producto de software en el estándar 9126 [10] y fue ampliada también en el estándar 9126-1, esta vez con calidad en uso, que ofrece una idea más amplia y completa de calidad que usabilidad.

Un experto reconocido en usabilidad, J. Nielsen [15], no elabora una definición precisa de usabilidad, sino que a través de una serie de heurísticas ofrece criterios cualitativos para evaluar usabilidad. Según el autor, *usabilidad* se constituye en base a cinco atributos: *Facilidad de Aprendizaje*, *Eficiencia*, *Facilidad de Memorización*, *Baja Tasa de Errores* y *Satisfacción*.

Por otro lado, el estándar 9241-11 propone una definición más concreta de usabilidad, pero curiosamente en los trabajos [3, 6], en donde el estándar es reseñado se emplean los términos calidad en uso y usabilidad respectivamente. En el primer caso se enfatiza el carácter más amplio del concepto de calidad en uso respecto de usabilidad. En el segundo caso, se emplea el término usabilidad literalmente, pero se remarca que mantiene una sintonía con la definición dada para calidad en uso del estándar 9126-1, es decir una idea de usabilidad que representa el objetivo del diseño o la meta final del producto.

2.3 Definición de Calidad en Uso para Producto Software

El estándar ISO 9126-1 define calidad en uso como "*la capacidad de un producto de software de facilitar a usuarios específicos alcanzar metas específicas con eficacia, productividad, seguridad y satisfacción en un contexto específico de uso*". Añade que "*...es medida sobre los resultados de usar el software en el ambiente, antes que sobre las propiedades del software en sí mismo*". Las características de calidad en uso están definidas tal como se muestran en la tabla 1.

Característica	Definición
Eficacia	*La capacidad del producto de software para facilitar a los usuarios alcanzar metas específicas con exactitud y completitud en un contexto específico de uso.*
Productividad	*La capacidad del producto de software para invertir la cantidad apropiada de recursos en relación a la eficacia alcanzada en un contexto específico de uso.*
Seguridad	*La capacidad del producto de software para alcanzar niveles aceptables de riesgo de dañar a las personas, el negocio, el software, la propiedad o el ambiente en un contexto específico de uso.*
Satisfacción	*La capacidad del producto de software para satisfacer a los usuarios en un contexto específico de uso.* *Nota [del estándar ISO]: Satisfacción es la respuesta del usuario a la interacción con el producto, e incluye la actitud hacia el uso del producto.*

Tabla 1. Definición de características de Calidad en Uso en el estándar ISO/IEC 9126-1.

Según este estándar existe, entre las tres perspectivas de calidad de software (interna, externa y en uso), una relación que puede sintetizarse así: medir y evaluar la calidad en uso por medio de métricas e indicadores puede ayudar a validar la calidad externa del software; calidad en uso evalúa el grado de excelencia de un producto y puede ser usada para validar el grado en que el software o aplicación Web cumple con necesidades específicas de los usuarios. A su vez, medir y evaluar la calidad externa puede ayudar a validar la calidad interna.

2.4 Criterios para Medir y Evaluar Calidad en Uso

Si se considera que la evaluación de calidad en uso se realiza sobre un producto software o Web operativo, es necesario emplear un contexto real de trabajo, definir y seleccionar el perfil de usuario, el equipamiento y las tareas a realizar. Se trata de una evaluación que se orienta a objetivos de tareas, ya que es necesario evaluar cuan eficaces, productivos, seguros y satisfechos resultan los usuarios empleando un producto, en un contexto específico. Se revisan a continuación algunos métodos y técnicas pertinentes a la evaluación de calidad en uso de un producto software; específicamente aquellos que han sido adaptados para la evaluación de calidad en uso de aplicaciones Web.

2.4.1 Métodos y Técnicas para Evaluar Calidad en Uso

El borrador del estándar 9126-4 [12] indica genéricamente "*las métricas de calidad en uso miden el grado en que un producto satisface las necesidades de un usuario específico, para lograr metas específicas con eficacia, productividad, seguridad y satisfacción*", pero no prescribe qué método o técnica aplicar.

En la técnica de testing con usuarios, se puede observar la reacción de los usuarios llevando a cabo tareas reales con el software y también es factible una evaluación rápida y eficaz a partir del seguimiento sobre la interfase del producto. Pero no siempre es factible replicar un medio ambiente representativo o encontrar usuarios con las mismas características de los usuarios reales, llevando a cabo el estudio a un costo razonable.

Los métodos de inspección, en cambio, abaratan costos en los estudios, simplificándolos y prescindiendo de parte del equipamiento e instalaciones usado en el testing con usuarios, ya que es suficiente con la labor de los expertos. La confiabilidad de los resultados está relacionada al nivel de conocimiento de los evaluadores. Particularmente para la Web la primer metodología en emplear inspección de características y atributos fue WebQEM (*Web Quality Evaluation Methodology*) [17]; que adaptada para evaluar calidad en uso, se emplea en el presente caso de estudio (ver sección 4).

La evaluación guiada por heurísticas se realiza a partir de un checklist y principios de usabilidad ya establecidos. Por ejemplo, se pueden consultar los aportes de Nielsen [14] donde el checklist puede ser utilizado también como base de un cuestionario que deben responder los usuarios y no sólo como una lista de control del nivel de cumplimiento de objetivos o guías de usabilidad. Una contra de esta técnica es que distintos grupos de expertos, realizando una evaluación sobre el mismo producto, suelen partir de heurísticas diferentes y, con frecuencia, la opinión de los expertos suele diferir.

Cuando se diseñan y documentan procesos de medición y evaluación de calidad en uso es necesaria, al menos, la siguiente información [19]:

a) Descripción de los componentes del contexto de uso incluyendo el tipo de usuario, equipamiento, medio ambiente, y tareas a realizar con el producto;
b) Especificación de las métricas e indicadores de calidad en uso de acuerdo al propósito deseado y la necesidad de información.

Para este trabajo se empleó el modelo de calidad en uso reseñado en la sección 2.3, basado en un conjunto de métricas e indicadores, integrados a partir de un marco de medición y evaluación con base ontológica [18]. Para llevar adelante el proceso de medición y evaluación se emplearán métodos de inspección y testing, como se verá en la sección 4.

3. Panorama del Marco Conceptual de Medición y Evaluación.

Un marco de medición y evaluación robusto y consistente debe estar construido sobre una base conceptual claramente especificada. Para el marco de medición y evaluación adoptado (INCAMI [20]), la base ontológica permite explicitar formalmente los principales conceptos del dominio de métricas e indicadores, como así también sus propiedades, relaciones y axiomas [18]. Además, se basa en la suposición que para que una organización pueda medir y evaluar con un propósito definido, debe primero especificar los requerimientos no funcionales, comenzando por las necesidades de información, luego debe definir un conjunto de métricas útiles para el propósito de la medición y, finalmente, interpretar las métricas por medio de indicadores contextuales, con el objetivo de evaluar o estimar el grado de cumplimiento de los requerimientos especificados.

Los componentes principales del marco de medición y evaluación son: a) La definición y especificación de los requerimientos no funcionales, b) El diseño y ejecución de la medición, c) El diseño y ejecución de la evaluación, d) La gestión de las recomendaciones, y e) La definición del proyecto en sí mismo. A continuación se ilustran las definiciones de los conceptos clave con un ejemplo concreto para cada uno de ellos, orientado a medir y evaluar calidad en uso (ver más detalles en [20]).

3.1 Necesidad de Información, Modelo de Concepto y Atributos

La *Necesidad de Información* se define como la visión y el conocimiento necesario para administrar objetivos, metas, riesgos y problemas. Básicamente remite a dos puntos de partida: metas que la organización desea alcanzar o bien riesgos y/o problemas que impiden alcanzar las metas deseadas. Una relación que se visualiza en la Fig. 1 para la clase Necesidad de Información es con la clase Concepto Calculable.

Un *Concepto Calculable* es una relación abstracta entre atributos de entidades y una Necesidad de Información; por ejemplo, calidad y calidad en uso son instancias de concepto calculable. Un Concepto Calculable puede estar compuesto por otros subconceptos, y podría así ser representado por un *Modelo de Concepto* (por ej., el modelo de calidad en uso).

Por otra parte, una *Entidad* es un objeto, que puede ser caracterizado por un conjunto de atributos mensurables. La entidad evaluada es una aplicación Web del dominio de e-Learning.

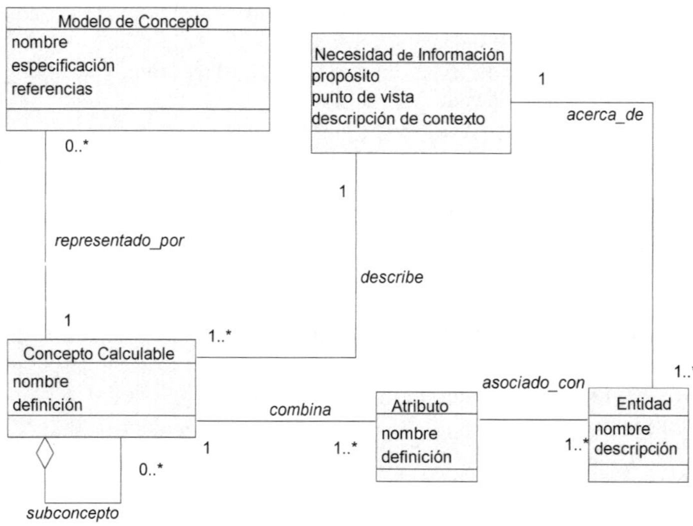

Fig. 1 Modelo conceptual básico para requerimientos no-funcionales centrado en modelos.

Un *Atributo* es una propiedad mensurable de una entidad, y se debe emplear un subconjunto que sea útil para el concepto calculable especificado, conforme a la necesidad de información. En la Fig. 3 se muestra el árbol de requerimientos para nuestro caso de estudio, en donde se observa conceptos, sub-conceptos y atributos.

Cada atributo puede ser cuantificado por una o más métricas, pero para un proyecto en particular sólo se debe seleccionar una métrica.

3.2 Métricas y Medición

Por su parte, una *Métrica* contiene la definición de un método de medición o un método de cálculo y la escala asociada, tal como se aprecia en la Fig. 2. El *Método de Medición* es la secuencia particular de operaciones y posibles heurísticas, especificada para permitir la realización de la descripción de una métrica por una actividad de medición. Por otro lado, la *Escala* se define como un conjunto de valores con propiedades definidas. La propiedad más importante de una escala es su tipo, considerando que puede ser *Categórica* o *Numérica*. A su vez, dependiendo de la naturaleza de la relación entre los componentes de la escala, pueden clasificarse en: nominal, ordinal, intervalo, proporción o absoluta.

Las métricas pueden ser directas, sobre las que puede aplicarse un método de medición (objetivo o subjetivo); o indirectas, que son aquellas definidas en función de otras métricas y se calculan en base al método de cálculo asociado, es decir en base a una fórmula. Luego, para cada métrica definida es necesario llevar a cabo el proceso de medición, o sea la actividad que, empleando la definición de la métrica, permite obtener valores de medidas (en la sección 4.6 ilustraremos una métrica para nuestro caso de estudio). Sin embargo, el valor de una métrica no representará por sí mismo el nivel de satisfacción de un requerimiento elemental, por ello es necesario definir una nueva correspondencia (Indicador Elemental).

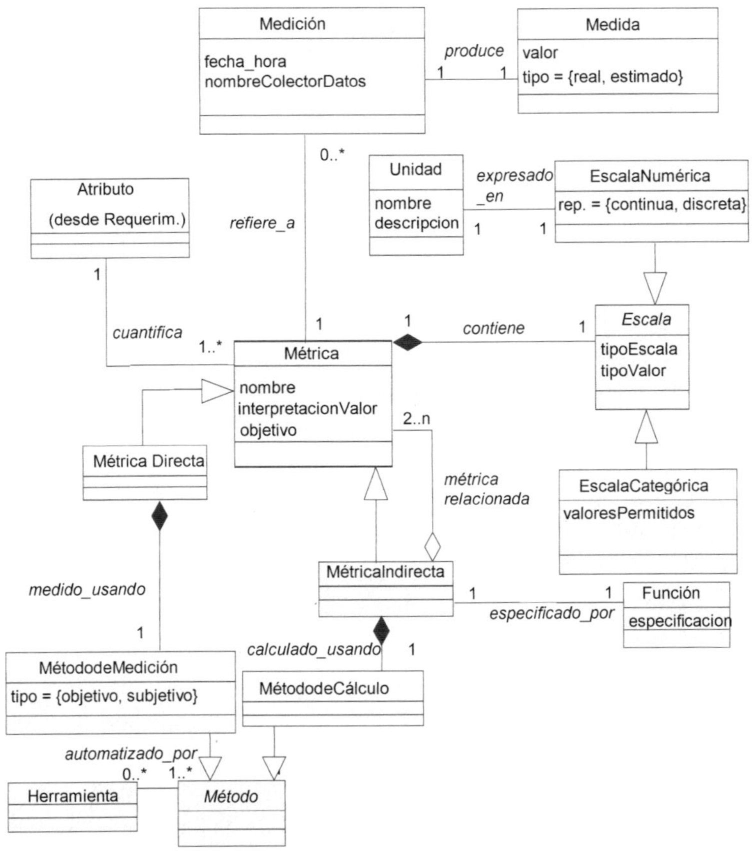

Fig. 2 Modelo conceptual básico de medición centrado en métricas.

3.3 Indicadores y Evaluación

El término *Indicador* está definido como el método de cálculo y la escala que, junto al modelo y criterios de decisión, permiten obtener una estimación o evaluación de un concepto calculable con respecto a una necesidad de información definida. Un indicador elemental es aquel que no depende de otros indicadores para evaluar o estimar un concepto a un nivel de abstracción bajo. Un indicador parcial o global está definido como aquel que, derivado de otros indicadores, permite evaluar o estimar un concepto a un nivel de abstracción más alto. Los indicadores también tienen una escala y un método de cálculo.

Para poder establecer el mapeo o correspondencia entre una métrica y un indicador es necesario considerar, teniendo en cuenta la necesidad de información de un usuario, un *Modelo Elemental* más ciertos *Criterios de Decisión* (ver más detalles en [18]).

3.4 Adaptando WebQEM para Calidad en Uso

La metodología WebQEM [17] corresponde a un método cuantitativo de inspección de características y atributos (a partir de un modelo de concepto como calidad) y está centrada en evaluadores expertos. Utiliza un modelo de calidad jerárquico basado en [11] y adaptado a necesidades (sub-características) propias de la Web. WebQEM ha sido empleada en varios casos de estudio [5, 16, 19] y en proyectos de evaluación de sitios de empresas.

Resultó un desafío en el presente caso de estudio, articular la interacción entre evaluadores expertos y usuarios finales. A las actividades propuestas en el primer paso de WebQEM "*Definición de las metas de evaluación y selección del perfil de usuario*" se agregó, como labor para los expertos, el diseño de las tareas que debían realizar los usuarios y la especificación del contexto en el que se llevarían a cabo las tareas. Por otra parte, otra cuestión sobre la que se hizo hincapié respecto de la adaptación fue en integrar aspectos de evaluación subjetiva, dado que era imprescindible evaluar la satisfacción de los usuarios –eminentemente subjetiva- con respecto a la aplicación Web evaluada.

Finalmente, es necesario resaltar que hay una correspondencia entre las fases de WebQEM y los componentes del marco de medición y evaluación mencionado en la sección 3. Para el diseño de las métricas se implementó una instancia de dicho modelo. Esta instanciación permitió adoptar y adaptar algunas métricas sugeridas en el estándar [12] y diseñar un nuevo conjunto de métricas. Para el caso de estudio se seleccionó el modelo de calidad en uso de ISO del que se han considerado sólo tres de las cuatro características, a saber: *Eficiencia*, *Productividad* y *Satisfacción*.

4. Caso de Estudio sobre una Aplicación E-Learning

El caso de estudio se llevó a cabo en abril de 2004, sobre una aplicación Web denominada "*QPlus Campus Virtual*", empleada desde fines de 2002 por la Facultad de Ingeniería de la UNLPam para un curso de nivelación de ingresantes. Las tareas propuestas a los usuarios fueron diseñadas en relación a un conjunto de tareas típicas para el perfil de usuario al que pertenecen los alumnos, teniéndose también en cuenta la funcionalidad y servicios de la aplicación Web a evaluar.

4.1 Objetivos del Caso de Estudio

Los objetivos del caso de estudio fueron: a) validar un modelo de calidad en uso para evaluación de aplicaciones Web; y b) conocer la percepción de la calidad en uso que tienen, como usuarios finales, los alumnos ingresantes a la Facultad respecto de la aplicación Web "*Qplus Campus Virtual*". La hipótesis para el caso de estudio en cuanto al segundo objetivo es que, al menos a nivel de características, el sitio está por encima de un umbral de satisfacción aceptable (70% en nuestro caso).

4.2 Perfil de la Audiencia

Con el objetivo de completar un conjunto predefinido de tareas, fue convocado un grupo de usuarios (perfil de visitante intencional), que tuvo a disposición por medio de la citada aplicación Web, un curso de introducción a la Matemática. Empleando un mecanismo al azar se seleccionaron seis alumnos voluntarios que usaron la aplicación durante el período diciembre-2003/febrero-2004. Para definir la cantidad de usuarios participantes se tuvo en cuenta la opinión de Nielsen [14] quien afirma que pueden obtenerse resultados significativos con la participación de un número pequeño de usuarios si es factible repetir la prueba. Otros usuarios que pueden considerarse para estudios semejantes dentro del mismo perfil, tal como se propone en [1] son: profesores y tutores.

4.3 Tareas para Evaluar Calidad en Uso

Para el diseño de las tareas, y teniendo en cuenta las consideraciones en [1], se propusieron a los usuarios las siguientes: distribuir información, proveer material de aprendizaje, ofrecer diversos mecanismos de comunicación sincrónica y asincrónica y gestionar un aula virtual. También se tuvieron en cuenta las particularidades del producto a evaluar y la cantidad de tareas a llevar a cabo por cada usuario, que debe ser limitada. De este análisis surgieron las siguientes tareas específicas:

Tarea 1. Navegar contenidos disponibles para la asignatura, en base a una pregunta sobre el material de estudio ya utilizado.

Tarea 2. Realizar una consulta a un profesor, empleando el mecanismo de comunicación asincrónico apropiado.

Tarea 3. Participar en un foro de opinión, debiéndose tipear un mensaje en la sección pertinente al tema de la opinión.

Tarea 4. Organizar el material de estudio. Aquí los alumnos debían transferir contenido entre distintas carpetas, creadas por los propios usuarios.

4.4 Descripción del Contexto

La importancia del contexto radica en que no es factible obtener conclusiones válidas al evaluar un mismo producto en contextos distintos o bien en un contexto que no está correctamente especificado. Los aspectos relevantes que se deben especificar son: la descripción del producto, los requerimientos de hardware y software e instalaciones, y el perfil de usuario detallado en la sección anterior.

El caso de estudio se llevó a cabo en el laboratorio del grupo *GIDIS_Web*, que fue levemente adaptado para simular un ambiente de estudio para los usuarios. Los participantes trabajaron individualmente sin ser interrumpidos. Fueron video-filmados y seguidos a través de una sesión de pantalla remota; a su vez cada sesión fue registrada y grabada en disco. Para registrar la actividad de los usuarios se empleó una variedad de herramientas y equipamiento. La completitud y la duración de las tareas fueron verificadas mediante un seguimiento realizado a partir de la reproducción de las secuencias de pantalla y los videos correspondientes.

Para la evaluación de satisfacción se empleó un cuestionario de diez ítems adaptado del cuestionario SUE (*Systematic Usability Evaluation*) [4]. Este instrumento tiene a su favor:

a) ser sencillo de completar y calcular;
b) estar estadísticamente validado; y
c) haber sido empleado con anterioridad para evaluar aplicaciones de software.

4.5 Definición y Especificación de los Requerimientos de Calidad en Uso

En esta fase se deben establecer conceptos y atributos que, agrupados jerárquicamente, representen el modelo de calidad en uso instanciado para el perfil de usuario citado, tal como se detalla en la Fig. 3.

1. Calidad en Uso
   1.1. Eficacia
      1.1.1. *Completitud de Tareas*
      1.1.2. *Eficacia de Tarea*
   1.2. Productividad
      1.2.1. *Eficiencia en relación a Completitud de Tareas*
      1.2.2. *Eficiencia en relación a Eficacia*
   1.3. Satisfacción

Fig. 3 Árbol de requerimientos para el caso de estudio de calidad en uso.

Para poder llevar a cabo el proceso de medición será necesario, en la siguiente fase, determinar las métricas y criterios elementales de evaluación para los atributos seleccionados.

4.6 Diseño de la Evaluación Elemental

La propuesta de las métricas informadas en ISO 9126-4 fue analizada detalladamente con el fin de adoptar y/o adaptar alguna para ser empleadas en este caso de estudio. Cada métrica tiene un método de medición (o de cálculo) debidamente especificado y la recolección fue obtenida luego de un proceso de observación a través de distintos medios visuales (video-filmación, secuencias de pantalla) o, para la característica satisfacción, empleando un cuestionario. El tipo de escala es proporción o intervalo y las mediciones fueron verificadas dos veces. Cada métrica se presenta en base a una plantilla que resume los metadatos principales de acuerdo a la ontología de métricas e indicadores. Como ejemplo, se presenta una de las métricas para calidad en uso (de igual modo se procedió con las métricas de todos los atributos de la Fig. 3).

Concepto Calculable (Característica): *Eficacia.*

Atributo**:** *Completitud de Tareas*.

Definición: proporción de las tareas completadas por los usuarios respecto de las tareas propuestas.

Objetivo: permite conocer en qué medida las tareas propuestas han sido completadas por los usuarios. A diferencia del atributo *Eficacia de Tarea*, aquí se toma en cuenta sólo las tareas que han sido completadas correctamente en su totalidad.

Nombre de la Métrica: *Promedio de la Proporción de Tareas Completadas sobre Tareas Propuestas para Todos los Usuarios* (o sea para n usuarios realizando m tareas), P_CT.

Interpretación: $0 \leq P\_CT \leq 1$, cuanto más próximo a 1 mejor.

Objetivo: calcular, para todos los usuarios de un perfil, el promedio de la proporción de tareas completadas en relación a las tareas propuestas.

Método de Cálculo (Fórmula): $P\_CT = \sum CT / n$, donde n es la *cantidad de usuarios* y CT, *completitud de tareas*.

Escala: numérica; Tipo de Escala: proporción. Unidad (descripción): proporción de tareas completadas sobre tareas propuestas.

Como indicado previamente, con los valores de las métricas no es posible estimar o evaluar un concepto calculable. Es necesario contar con los indicadores que permitan la evaluación, a partir de los criterios de decisión asociados. Para cada métrica asociada a un atributo del árbol de requerimientos, se diseñó un indicador elemental. En todos los casos, un puntaje en el rango *no satisfactorio* indica la urgencia de poner en práctica acciones de mejora. La plantilla siguiente ejemplifica el indicador asociado a la métrica P_CT.

Concepto Calculable Relacionado: *Eficacia*

Nombre: *Grado de Cumplimiento Respecto a Proporción de Tareas Completadas sobre Tareas Propuestas*, %P_CT_P.

Modelo Elemental:%P_CT_P= P_CT x 100, P_CT: *Promedio de la Proporción de Tareas Completadas sobre Tareas Propuestas para Todos los Usuarios*.

Criterio de Decisión: Rango (niveles de aceptabilidad): 0≤ %P_CT_P ≤ 45: *no satisfactorio*, 45< %P_CT_P ≤70: *marginal (regular)* 70<%P_CT_P≤100: *satisfactorio*.

Escala: numérica. Tipo de Escala: proporción. Unidad: porcentaje.

4.7 Definición de la Evaluación Global

Para poder finalizar la evaluación es necesario definir un indicador global por medio de un modelo de agregación, que permita evaluar o estimar globalmente el concepto calculable *calidad en uso*. En relación al modelo de agregación se consideró apropiado un modelo lógico multi-criterio que permite modelizar relaciones de simultaneidad, reemplazabilidad y neutralidad entre atributos (ver [17] para más detalles). Se empleó la herramienta WebQEM_Tool para el cálculo del indicador global de calidad en uso.

5. Resultados del Caso de Estudio

5.1 Implementación de la Evaluación Elemental

Implementar la evaluación elemental significa básicamente ejecutar el proceso de recolección de datos, computar las métricas e indicadores elementales y documentar los resultados encontrados.

5.1.1 Cómputo de las Métricas

Para cada métrica directa, la recolección de datos fue guiada por la secuencia de pasos que indican los métodos de medición. Una vez obtenidos los datos que permiten conocer los valores de las métricas directas, fue factible computar las métricas indirectas, a partir de los respectivos métodos de cálculo.

A seguir se ilustra para el atributo *Completitud de Tareas* (ver Sección 4.6) la métrica que lo cuantifica. Para el cálculo de la métrica *Promedio de la Proporción de Tareas Completadas sobre Tareas Propuestas para Todos los Usuarios* (*P_CT*) se calcularon primero las métricas directas e indirectas necesarias (ver tabla 2).

En el último paso se obtuvo el valor de *P_CT* como el cociente entre la sumatoria de los resultados obtenidos para la métrica *Proporción de Tareas Completadas sobre Tareas Propuestas* y el número de usuarios. El resultado obtenido fue 0,542.

Usuario	# Tareas Completadas	# Tareas Completadas / # Tareas Propuestas
U1	2	0,5
U2	1	0,25
U3	1	0,25
U4	1	0,25
U5	4	1
U6	4	1

Tabla 2. Resultados para la métrica *Proporción de Tareas Completadas* (Correctamente) *sobre Tareas Propuestas*. Las tareas propuestas fueron 4 (ver sección 4.3) y participaron 6 usuarios.

La interpretación de la métrica *P_CT* dice que el resultado debe ser entre 0 y 1 y que es mejor cuanto más próximo a uno se encuentre. Del mismo modo se procedió con las otras métricas, no incluidas aquí por razones de espacio.

5.1.2 Cómputo de los Indicadores Elementales

En este paso, una vez especificados los criterios y un modelo elemental para pasar de valores de métricas a indicadores, se realizó el cálculo correspondiente a los indicadores elementales. Esto permite realizar una interpretación inicial de las métricas al nivel más bajo (atributos) del árbol de requerimientos. Para el cálculo de los indicadores elementales es necesario estandarizar las unidades en que están expresados. En este caso, los métodos de cálculo para los distintos indicadores permiten obtener valores como porcentaje de modo que se puedan contrastar los resultados versus los rangos de aceptabilidad establecidos en el diseño. Para el indicador elemental ejemplificado en la sección 4.6, %P_CT_P, el valor se obtiene como el producto entre el valor de la métrica *P_CT* (0,542) y 100.

5.2 Implementación de la Evaluación Global

El objetivo principal de la evaluación global es obtener el valor del indicador global de calidad en uso. Los resultados de los indicadores parciales y del global de calidad en uso, luego de ejecutar el modelo de agregación, se presentan en la tabla 3.

Código	Concepto Calculable	Característica	Atributo/Indicador Elemental	Valor [%]
1	Nivel de Calidad en Uso			**57,45**
1.1		Nivel de Eficacia		59,70
1.1.1			Grado de Cumplimiento Respecto a Proporción de Eficiencia de Tareas Completadas	54,20
1.1.2			Grado de Cumplimiento Respecto de Eficiencia de Tareas Considerando Eficacia	65,60
1.2		Nivel de Productividad		51,89
1.2.1			Grado de Cumplimiento Respecto a Proporción de Eficiencia de Tareas Completadas	49,80
1.2.2			Grado de Cumplimiento Respecto de Eficiencia de Tareas Considerando Eficacia	54,04
1.3		Nivel de Satisfacción		87,08
1.3.1			Grado de Cumplimiento respecto a Satisfacción de Usuarios	87,08

Tabla 3. Resultados de los indicadores elementales, parciales y global de Calidad en Uso.

5.3 Análisis de Resultados

Considerando los resultados obtenidos, se observa que el valor del indicador global de calidad en uso resultó por debajo del valor mínimo de aceptabilidad (70 % en este caso), arrojando un 57,45%. Además, teniendo en cuenta el puntaje a nivel de características, esto es: Eficacia (59,70) y Productividad (51,89) no se cumple con la hipótesis de que "*al menos a nivel de características, el sitio está por encima de un umbral de satisfacción aceptable*". Sólo la característica Satisfacción (87,08%) superó el umbral mínimo de aceptabilidad. Esto permite inferir que la percepción subjetiva que tienen los usuarios del producto es muy favorable, a pesar de que no resultaron productivos ni altamente eficaces en la realización de las tareas propuestas.

6. Conclusiones

Las conclusiones se consideran desde dos perspectivas: por un lado respecto de los resultados del caso de estudio en sí y, por otro lado, en relación a los metadados obtenidos para las métricas e indicadores de calidad en uso.

Respecto a los resultados del estudio, una vez realizado el análisis, sólo queda por sintetizar que una posible causa por la que el producto evaluado no resultó eficaz y productivo en la medida de lo esperado para el perfil de usuario intencional, fue la falta de un mínimo entrenamiento en este tipo de aplicación de e-Learning por parte de los alumnos ingresantes; otra causa, podría ser un débil diseño del producto en sí, en consideración de requerimientos no-funcionales. Por otro lado, en relación a la percepción subjetiva y según los resultados obtenidos, los usuarios se sintieron satisfechos empleando el producto, por encima del nivel esperado. Se debe ser consciente que se debería repetir el caso de estudio para poder obtener conclusiones con mayores evidencias respecto a las debilidades de calidad en uso de la aplicación "QPlus Campus Virtual"; de hecho, hemos planificado repetir el estudio en Marzo/Abril del 2006.

El caso de estudio permitió además validar una propuesta de evaluación sistemática de calidad en uso para aplicaciones Web. Se puede afirmar en este sentido, que la metodología y el marco de medición empleados resultaron suficientemente robustos y a la vez flexibles, como para evaluar calidad en uso en forma metódica y sistemática. Resultaron robustos porque habiéndose probado anteriormente en casos de estudio de calidad interna y externa de producto, cada fase y las actividades dentro de cada fase, tienen también sentido y resultan apropiadas para diseñar la evaluación de calidad en uso. Son flexibles porque permitieron la integración de actividades propias de la evaluación de calidad en uso, tales como la definición de tareas y la especificación del contexto, y el uso de un modelo específico de calidad en uso -distinto al de calidad interna y externa de producto-, en la fase de definición y especificación de los requerimientos de calidad.

En relación a la segunda perspectiva de estas conclusiones, se puede afirmar que los metadatos obtenidos, o sea la definición exhaustiva de atributos, métricas e indicadores (e información ontológica relacionada a estos conceptos), pueden ser empleados para otros proyectos de medición y evaluación de calidad en uso favoreciendo la reusabilidad y, por otra parte, la consistencia en ulteriores análisis de datos. Contar con valores medidos de métricas directas y valores calculados de métricas indirectas e indicadores, sin el recaudo de contar con todos los metadatos asociados, puede llevar a obtener conclusiones erróneas a partir de análisis de datos no comparables.

Finalmente, se debe tener en cuenta que no es posible generalizar los resultados de una evaluación de calidad en uso para el mismo producto en otros contextos. La validez externa de un estudio de calidad en uso está por lo tanto fuertemente restringida por el contexto.

Referencias

1. Avgeriou, P.; Papasalouros, A.; Retalis S., Skordlakis; (2003) "Towards a Pattern Language for Learning Management Systems" ISSN: 1436-4522.
2. Bevan N.; Kirakowski, J., Maissel J.; (1991) "What is Usability". Proceedings of the 4th International Conference on HCI, Stuttgart.
3. Bevan, N.; (1995) "Usability is Quality in Use", 6th International Conference on Human Computer Interaction, Yokohama, Anzai & Ogawa (Eds.), Elsevier.
4. Brooke, J.; "SUS –A 'quick and dirty' usability scale". Digital Equipment Co Ltd., Reading, UK. http://www.usability.serco.com/trump/documents/Suschapt.doc.
5. Covella, G.; Olsina L.; (2002) "Specifying Quality Attributes for Sites with E-Learning Functionality". ICWE'02, Santa Fe, Argentina, pp. 154-167, ISSN 1666-6526.
6. Folmer, E.; Bosch, J.; (2004) "Architecting for Usability: a Survey", Journal of Systems and Software, 70(1/2) pp. 61-78.
7. ISO 9000 Norma Int'l. (2000) Sistemas de Gestión de la Calidad- Conceptos y Vocabulario.
8. ISO 9241-11 (1998) "Ergonomic requirements for office work with visual display terminals (VDT) - Part 11 Guidance on Usability".
9. ISO/IEC 14598-1. Information Technology-Software Product Evaluation-Part 1: General overview, 1999.
10. ISO/IEC 9126 (1991) "Information technology - Software product evaluation - Quality characteristics and guidelines for their use.
11. ISO/IEC 9126-1:2001. Software Engineering— Software Product Quality—Part 1: Quality Model, Int'l Org. for Standardization, Geneva.
12. ISO/IEC DTR 9126-4. Software Engineering –Product Quality - Part 4: Quality in Use Metrics.
13. Milutinovic, V.; Skundric N.; (2003) "Will Distance Learning Create a Global University?" IEEE Computer, 36(3).
14. Nielsen, J.; (1995-2006) The Alertbox column, http://www.useit.com/alertbox/
15. Nielsen J., Molich R., Snyder C., Farrell S.; (2001) E-Commerce User Experience. NN Group.
16. Olsina, L.; Lafuente, G.; Rossi, G. ; (2000) "E-commerce Site Evaluation: a Case Study" LNCS 1875 of Springer, 1st International Conference on Electronic Commerce and Web Technologies, EC-Web 2000. London, UK, pp. 239-252.
17. Olsina, L.; Rossi, G.; (2002) "Measuring Web Application Quality with WebQEM". IEEE Multimedia, 9(4), pp. 20-29.
18. Olsina, L.; Martín M.; (2004) "Ontology for Software Metrics and Indicators". Journal of Web Engineering, Rinton Press, US, Vol 2 Nº 4, pp. 262-281, ISSN 1540-9589.
19. Olsina, L.; Covella, G.; Rossi, G.; (2005) "Web Quality". Capítulo del Libro "Web Engineering: Theory and Practice of Metrics and Measurement for Web Development". Emilia Mendes y Nile Mosley Editores, Spinger Verlag. ISBN: 3-540-28196-7.
20. Olsina, L.; Papa, F.; Molina H.; (2005) "Organization-oriented Measurement and Evaluation Framework for Software and Web Engineering Projects". In LNCS Vol. 3579, ICWE 2005, Sydney, Australia, pp. 42-52, ISBN: 3-540-27996-2.

Evaluación de la Usabilidad en un Entorno de Arquitecturas Orientadas a Modelos[1]

Sergio España, Inés Pederiva, José Ignacio Panach, Silvia Abrahão, Óscar Pastor

Departamento de Sistemas Informáticos y Computación
Universidad Politécnica de Valencia
Camino de Vera s/n, 46071 Valencia, España
{sergio.espana,ipederiva,jpanach,sabrahao,opastor}@dsic.upv.es
+34 96 387 7000

Resumen. Con el creciente interés en el paradigma de las arquitecturas orientadas a modelos (Model-Driven Architecture), los modelos conceptuales son la columna vertebral del proceso de desarrollo de software. En este trabajo se presenta un marco de evaluación de usabilidad en el contexto de la tecnología OlivaNova Model Execution, la implementación industrial del método de producción automática de software OO-Method. Presentamos un modelo de usabilidad que es la base para el marco de evaluación y una clasificación de problemas de usabilidad obtenida como resultado del proceso de evaluación. En consecuencia, la usabilidad de un sistema software es evaluada y mejorada en la fase de modelado conceptual basándose en las correspondencias entre la definición abstracta de la interfaz de usuario y sus implementaciones software.

1 Introducción

Con el desarrollo de aplicaciones generadas automáticamente a partir de modelos conceptuales se presenta un desafío poco explorado: la evaluación temprana de la usabilidad en productos software. Determinar cualidades de usabilidad en la etapa de análisis garantiza la calidad del producto y se adelanta a resolver problemas de interacción del usuario. La propuesta *Model Driven Architecture (MDA)* [12] es propicia para este tipo de desarrollo de aplicaciones ya que promueve el uso de modelos durante el proceso de desarrollo y permite que éstos puedan ser transformados hasta la obtención del código fuente del software final.

A pesar del crecimiento de la propuesta MDA, poco se ha considerado respecto a la evaluación temprana de usabilidad; no hay propuestas sistemáticas que descompongan el concepto de usabilidad en atributos medibles y determinen la relación de estos atributos con los patrones de interfaz. Así mismo, no se encuentran clasificaciones de las relaciones entre componentes abstractos de un modelo de interfaz, con componentes de la aplicación final.

Usando la tecnología OlivaNova™ Model Execution [4](ONME), en este trabajo mostraremos que las interfaces de usuario generadas automáticamente a partir del mé-

---

[1] Este trabajo está subvencionado por los proyectos DESTINO con ref. TIN2004-03534 y MAUSE *(Towards the Maturation of IT Usability Evaluation)* financiado por la COST European Action n°294.

todo de producción automático de software OO-Method [20] satisfacen un cierto nivel de usabilidad. Este nivel es alcanzado por construcción, a diferencia de la usabilidad de interfaces de usuario obtenida por métodos artesanales tradicionalmente usados.

Para realizar la evaluación de usabilidad definimos un modelo de usabilidad en base a la ISO/IEC 9126-1 [11]. Para lograr esto, sostenemos que un modelo de usabilidad debe incluir atributos de rendimiento y atributos de percepción. Ejemplo de atributos de rendimiento son la operabilidad y facilidad en el aprendizaje, mientras que los atributos de percepción, como el grado de atracción, son más subjetivos. Además, el modelo de usabilidad debería incluir: (1) el tipo de atributo de usabilidad: mediante una clasificación explícita; (2) la ponderación de los atributos de usabilidad en función del dominio de la aplicación; (3) la relación entre atributos: para detectar cómo un atributo incide positiva o negativamente en otro atributo; y (4) usabilidad vs. tipos de usuarios: para ponderar atributos según los perfiles de usuarios.

Este artículo está organizado como sigue. La sección 2 presenta los patrones conceptuales que provee el modelo de presentación ONME a partir de los cuales genera el código de las interfaces para las distintas plataformas. La sección 3 presenta el marco de usabilidad general, el modelo de usabilidad propuesto y su relación con la arquitectura MDA [12]. La sección 4 muestra la aplicación del modelo propuesto sobre un caso práctico. En la sección 5 se compara el modelo propuesto con los trabajos existentes. Finalmente, la sección 6 presenta las conclusiones y trabajos futuros.

2 Desarrollo de Interfaces de Usuario con ONME

ONME es la implementación realizada por CARE Technologies [4] del método de producción automático de software OO-Method [20]. OO-Method se basa en la separación del espacio del problema y del espacio de la solución siguiendo las directrices de MDA [12][14]. OO-Method comprende básicamente de los siguientes modelos:

El *Modelo Conceptual* que está dividido en cuatro vistas complementarias: (1) Modelo de Objetos que describe las propiedades estáticas del sistema en términos de clases y sus relaciones; (2) Modelo Dinámico que describe los aspectos relacionados con el control, las vidas válidas y la interacción entre objetos; (3) Modelo Funcional que describe la semántica asociada a los cambios de estado de los objetos provocados por la ejecución de eventos; y finalmente, el (4) Modelo de Presentación, que permite la especificación abstracta de los requisitos de interfaz de usuario.

Mediante una *Compilación de Modelos* se establecen las reglas de transformación de un Modelo Conceptual a su representación software correspondiente en una plataforma tecnológica concreta. Nos centraremos en el Modelo de Presentación, a partir del cual se genera la interfaz de usuario que determina la usabilidad de una aplicación.

2.1 El Modelo de Presentación

El Modelo de Presentación [15] permite la especificación abstracta de las interfaces de usuario por medio de un lenguaje de patrones conceptuales denominado Just-UI [16]. El modelo se estructura en tres niveles o capas de especificación.

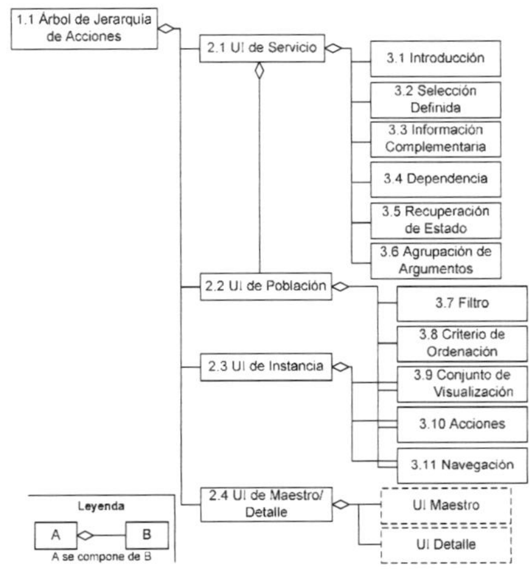

Fig. 1. Patrones de presentación en el espacio del problema

- **Nivel 1. Árbol de jerarquía de acciones (AJA):** Expresa cómo la funcionalidad será presentada al usuario.
- **Nivel 2. Unidades de interacción (UIs):** Modela abstracciones de interfaz con laque el usuario interactuará. Existen cuatro unidades: (1)*UI de servicio:* modela la presentación de un diálogo para que un usuario lance un servicio;(2)*UI de instancia:* modela la presentación de los datos o estado de una instancia. Se define sobre una clase y se le proporciona un conjunto de visualización (qué información ha de ser mostrada), otro de acciones (qué funcionalidad debe ofertarse sobre el objeto) y por último un conjunto de navegación (qué información relacionada puede ser accedida); (3)*UI de población:* permite mostrar un conjunto de instancias de una clase. Se pueden establecer mecanismos de filtrado y ordenación para facilitar la selección y consulta de objetos; (4)*UI de maestro/detalle:* modela unidades de interacción construidas a partir de UIs más sencillas.
- **Nivel 3. Patrones elementales (PEs):** Permiten restringir y precisar el comportamiento de las diferentes unidades de interacción. La *selección definida* permite al analista proporcionar por enumeración los elementos válidos para un argumento de un servicio y el *patrón de información complementaria* permite especificar una información adicional que será mostrada al usuario.

3 Un marco de Usabilidad adecuado a MDA

La Figura 2 presenta las correspondencias entre los modelos propuestos por el paradigma MDA y los modelos que se manejan en un proceso de desarrollo con la tecnología ONME. El análisis del sistema produce el Modelo Conceptual, incluyendo el Modelo de Presentación que contiene la definición abstracta del interfaz del sistema. El Modelo Conceptual es asimilable al PIM (*Platform-Independent Model*) de MDA puesto que describe todos los aspectos funcionales de la aplicación, independientemente de la plataforma software en la que vaya a implementarse y ejecutarse [14]. En una segunda fase, la compilación de modelos convierte el Modelo Conceptual en un Modelo de Aplicación que se corresponde con el PSM (*Platform-Specific Model*) de MDA. Automáticamente se vuelve a transformar el Modelo de Aplicación en el Código Fuente de la aplicación final, correspondiente al *Code Model* de MDA, en un paso que resulta transparente al analista desarrollador.

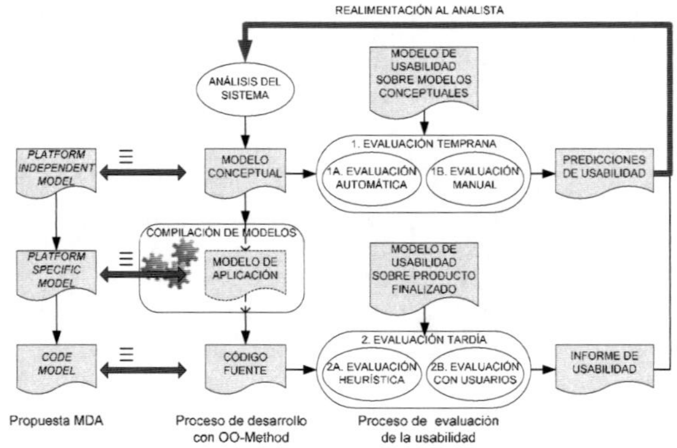

Fig. 2. Correspondencia entre MDA y OO-Method, y evaluación temprana de la usabilidad.

Habitualmente, la evaluación de la usabilidad se viene realizando sobre la aplicación ya desarrollada (sobre el *Code Model*), mediante técnicas heurísticas, testings con usuarios, etc. Esta estrategia supone una realimentación completamente fiable para el analista y el diseñador y es la más frecuentemente usada.

La aportación de este trabajo consiste en adelantar la evaluación a la fase de análisis (modelado conceptual), de manera que, como información de entrada, se toma el PIM y se obtiene como salida un informe de predicciones de usabilidad que realimentará el análisis del sistema, en particular el Modelo de Presentación. Así se asegura la *usabilidad independiente de plataforma*, como un aspecto de la calidad interna, que puede ser evaluada automática (1A) o manualmente (1B). Por otro lado el modelo propuesto también soporta la evaluación de la calidad externa (usado como pautas o *guidelines*, 2A). Estas técnicas complementan la habitual evaluación de la calidad en uso (frecuente en la Interacción Persona-Ordenador, 2B).

3.1 Usabilidad independiente de plataforma

El objetivo del marco propuesto es evaluar la usabilidad sobre un modelo independiente de plataforma y proporcionar al analista una realimentación que sugiera cambios sobre el Modelo de Presentación, con el fin de prevenir la aparición de errores y problemas de usabilidad en la aplicación que se generará. Este es un proceso iterativo que se repite hasta que el Modelo Conceptual tenga el nivel de usabilidad requerido.

El primer paso en la definición del marco fue definir un modelo de usabilidad basado en el estándar ISO/IEC 9126-1[11]. Se fue aumentando la granularidad de las subcaracterísticas de la usabilidad en una descomposición jerárquica, hasta llegar a definir atributos medibles. Para obtener estos atributos se analizaron varias taxonomías de criterios de usabilidad propuestas en la literatura [8][9][21], entre las que destaca la de Bastien y Scapin [3] y sus criterios ergonómicos validados empíricamente.

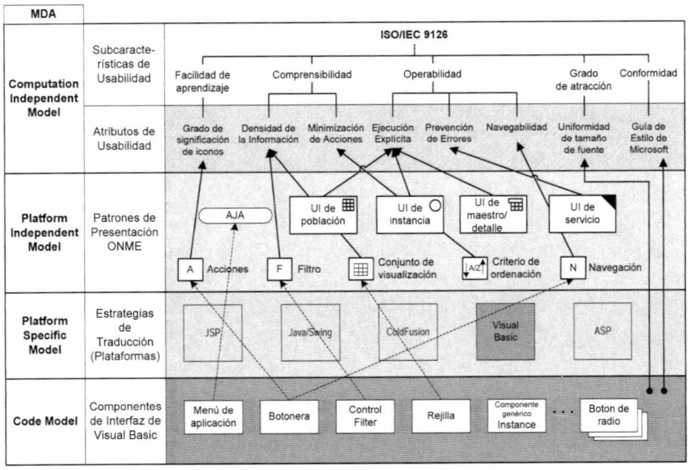

Fig. 3. Modelo de Usabilidad propuesto.

El modelo fue presentado en [19][1], y ha sido revisado y actualizado hasta convertirse en el árbol que presentamos en este trabajo. Los atributos de usabilidad, situados en las hojas del árbol se relacionan con los patrones de presentación, las abstracciones de la interfaz pertenecientes al PIM. En la Figura 3 se ilustra algunas de estas relaciones. La finalidad es determinar qué patrones de presentación contribuyen a la satisfacción de determinados atributos de usabilidad provenientes de la ergonomía de interfaces de usuario. Cabe destacar que las subcaracterísticas grado de atracción y conformidad no pueden ser evaluadas de manera objetiva en la fase de modelado conceptual y, por lo tanto, se definen relaciones con componentes del *Code Model*; solo podrán ser evaluadas tras la generación de la aplicación final.

3.2 Usabilidad dependiente de plataforma

ONME oculta el PSM al desarrollador al definir una estrategia de compilación que directamente obtiene el código fuente de la aplicación final a partir del Modelo Conceptual. En este espacio intermedio se encuentran las distintas estrategias de generación de código existentes que dan soporte a la generación automática de aplicaciones de tres capas (interfaz, lógica de negocio y base de datos) para diversas plataformas (Visual Basic, Java/Swing, ColdFusion, JSP, ASP y PocketPC). En función del generador de código seleccionado, los patrones de presentación abstractos son instanciados en la arquitectura software correspondiente, en un proceso denominado *reificación*.

Existen subcaracterísticas de la usabilidad que deben ser evaluadas sobre la concreción de los patrones de presentación para una plataforma determinada; por lo tanto se establecen relaciones entre estas subcaracterísticas y los componentes software que conforman la interfaz gráfica resultante.

Es el caso de la subcaracterística grado de atracción, en la que hemos diferenciado aspectos sintácticos (p.e. uniformidad del color y el estilo de la fuente) y semánticos (p.e. atracción subjetiva). En este caso, los atributos sintácticos están garantizados por la estrategia de traducción que implementa la tecnología ONME. La evaluación de los atributos semánticos escapa a la evaluación temprana que aquí presentamos, puesto que debe realizarse con usuarios.

3.3 Modelo de Usabilidad

El árbol de atributos de nuestro modelo (ver Tabla 1) constituye una taxonomía de los aspectos que componen la usabilidad de una aplicación. Para desarrollar el modelo de usabilidad se realizaron las siguientes actividades: definición de los objetivos de calidad perseguidos, especificación de las características y atributos de usabilidad, especificación de relaciones y confección del modelo dotándolo de potenciales métricas.

Tabla 1. Árbol de aributos de usabilidad

1. **Facilidad de aprendizaje**
1.1. Facilidades de Ayuda
1.1.1. Completitud de Documentación
1.1.2. Documentación Multiusuario
1.1.2.1. Distinción por Capacitación
1.1.2.2. Distinción por Rol
1.2. Predecibilidad
1.2.1. Grado de Significación de Iconos
1.2.2. Título de Iconos o Enlaces
1.2.3. Determinación de la Acción
1.3. Realimentación Informativa
1.4. Facilidad de Memorización
2. **Comprensibilidad**
2.1. Legibilidad
2.1.1. Tamaño de Fuente
2.1.2. Contraste
2.1.3. Disposición
2.2. Facilidad de Lectura
2.2.1. Agrupación Cohesiva de la Información
2.2.1.1. Agrupación por Disposición
2.2.1.2. Agrupación por Formato
2.2.2. Densidad de la Información
2.3. Familiaridad de conceptos
2.3.1. Significación del Etiquetado
2.3.2. Internacionalización
2.4. Reducción de la Carga de Trabajo
2.4.1. Brevedad
2.4.1.1. Inicialización de Valores
2.4.1.1.1. Completitud de Valores Iniciales
2.4.1.1.2. Modificabilidad de Valores Iniciales
2.4.1.2. Minimización de acciones
2.4.2. Autodescripción
2.3. Orientación al usuario
2.3.1. Calidad de los Mensajes
2.3.2. Navegabilidad
3. **Operabilidad**
3.1. Capacidades de Instalación
3.1.1. Facilidad de Instalación
3.1.2. Multiplicidad de Instalación
3.1.3. Capacidad de Actualización
3.1.4. Transparencia de Actualización
3.2. Validación de datos
3.3. Capacidad de Control
3.3.1. Aplazamiento de Edición
3.3.2. Soporte de Cancelación
3.3.3. Ejecución Explícita
3.3.4. Soporte de Interrupción
3.3.5. Soporte de Deshacimiento
3.3.6. Soporte de Rehacimiento
3.4. Capacidad de Adaptación
3.4.1. Adaptabilidad
3.4.2. Adaptatividad
3.5. Consistencia
3.5.1. Comportamiento Constante de Controles
3.5.2. Permanencia de Controles
3.5.3. Estabilidad de los Controles
3.5.4. Consistencia de Orden
3.5.5. Consistencia de Etiquetado
3.6. Gestión de Errores
3.6.1. Prevención de Errores
3.6.2. Recuperación de Errores
3.7. Monitorización del Estado del Sistema
4. **Grado de atracción**
4.1. Metáfora
4.2. Uniformidad del Color del Fondo
4.3. Uniformidad del Color de la Fuente
4.4. Uniformidad del Estilo de la Fuente
4.5. Uniformidad del Tamaño de la Fuente
4.6. Uniformidad en Disposición de Elementos
4.7. Atracción Subjetiva
5. **Conformidad**
5.1. Cumplimiento con ISO/IEC 9126 (partes 1 y 3)
5.2. Cumplimiento con ISO 9241-10
5.3. Cumplimiento con Guía de Estilo de Microsoft
5.4. Cumplimiento con Guía de Estilo de Java

El objetivo de nuestro modelo de usabilidad es analizar el Modelo de Presentación con el propósito de evaluar su usabilidad desde la perspectiva del investigador y en el contexto de la iniciativa MDA instanciada sobre ONME. Considerando las subcaracterísticas como una forma de agrupar aspectos de la usabilidad con relación entre sí, estructuramos jerárquicamente los atributos de usabilidad basándonos en ISO/IIEC 9126-1 [11]. La descomposición es necesaria para poder aplicar métodos de inspección de la usabilidad y para identificar y arreglar los problemas de usabilidad detectados.

3.3.1 Facilidad de Aprendizaje

La facilidad de aprendizaje referencia a los atributos que dotan a un producto software de permitir al usuario aprender su manejo. Esta subcaracterística consiste en **facilidades de ayuda** (ayuda en línea y documentación, en sus aspectos de completitud y adaptación a distintos perfiles de usuario), así como la **predecibilidad**, que se refiere a la facilidad con que un usuario puede determinar el resultado de sus acciones futuras (p.e. grado de significación de los iconos y determinación de la acción), la **realimentación informativa** en respuesta a sus acciones y la **facilidad de memorización**.

3.3.2 Comprensibilidad

La comprensibilidad se refiere a atributos que facilitan entender si el software resulta adecuado y cómo puede usarse. Descomponemos esta subcaracterística para diferenciar la propia **legibilidad** óptica de los textos e imágenes de la **facilidad de lectura,** que a su vez consta de la **agrupación cohesiva de información** presentada y **densidad de la información**. La **familiaridad de conceptos** es un aspecto relativo al contexto social, cultural y laboral del usuario. La **brevedad** está principalmente relacionada con patrones que reducen el esfuerzo cognitivo del usuario (dotar de valores iniciales a los campos de los formularios, evitar interacciones innecesarias). Respecto a la **orientación al usuario,** pasa por asegurar la **calidad de los mensajes** y **navegabilidad**. La navegabilidad está relacionada con guiar al usuario proveyendo mecanismos para informar de la ruta y la posición actual. En nuestro modelo, la navegabilidad puede ser medida en términos de la ausencia de navegaciones cíclicas entre Unidades de Interacción abstractas (UIs).

3.3.3 Operabilidad

La operabilidad se refiere a los atributos que facilitan el control del usuario y la operación. Esta subcaracterística referencia a la capacidad del sistema para proporcionar **capacidades de instalación** (facilidad de instalación, transparencia de actualización, etc), realizar **validación de datos** y ofrecer **capacidad de control** del usuario en la ejecución de servicios. Sobre la **capacidad de adaptación** de la interfaz de usuario hacemos una diferenciación entre *adaptabilidad*, capacidad del software de ser adaptado por el usuario, y *adaptatividad*, capacidad del software de adaptarse a las necesidades del usuario (la diferencia está en el agente de la adaptación) [18]. La **consistencia** operacional en la ejecución de servicios y controles es otra subcaracterística de la operabilidad, al igual que la **gestión de errores** y la **capacidad de monitorizar el estado del sistema** por la cual el sistema comunica información al usuario sin ser el resultado de una interacción con éste.

3.3.4 Grado de Atracción

Algunos aspectos del grado de atracción relacionados con el diseño estético pueden ser cuantificados desde una perspectiva sintáctica midiendo la **uniformidad de la interfaz** en términos del tamaño y estilo de la fuente utilizada, del uso que se hace del color y de la disposición de los elementos en la pantalla. Estas uniformidades son garantizadas por las estrategias de generación de código de ONME. Otros aspectos son de carácter semántico y proponemos evaluarlos subjetivamente: un adecuado uso de la **metáfora** y el grado de **atracción subjetiva**, medible mediante cuestionarios.

3.3.5 Conformidad

Conformidad se mide evaluando la concordancia del PIM con los siguientes estándares: ISO/IEC 9126-1 y -3 e ISO 9241-10 y la concordancia del *Code Model* con las guía de estilo de Microsoft [13] y de Java [22]. Las dos primeras valoraciones se centran en el espacio del problema y las dos últimas en el espacio de la solución, pues analizan el cumplimiento de la guía de estilo de Microsoft y del *look and feel* de Java por parte de los componentes software empleados en las diferentes estrategias de generación automática de código.

Para cada atributo se ha estudiado cómo afecta positiva o negativamente a otros y se ha definido explícitamente las diferencias con otros atributos con los cuales parecía solaparse. Además, se han definido relaciones entre los atributos de usabilidad y los patrones de interfaz del PIM y sus propiedades, estableciendo correspondencias entre los niveles CIM y el PIM. La estrategia de traducción automática proyecta estas correspondencias hasta el CM (*Code Model*), logrando que el modelo de usabilidad tenga efecto en todas las capas del paradigma MDA.

Igualmente importante es definir métricas para cuantificar cada atributo. Dada la correspondencia entre los atributos de usabilidad y los componentes del PIM, las métricas se calcularán sobre este modelo con la salvedad de las métricas semánticas, cuya valoración se realizará contra la interfaz final.

La siguiente tabla muestra las relaciones establecidas entre algunos atributos de usabilidad y los patrones de interfaz del PIM. En la tercera columna se explica la razón fundamental de esta relación, mientras que en la última se proponen métricas.

Tabla 2. Subcaracterísticas, atributos, patrones de presentación y métricas.

Subcaract. / Atributo	Elementos del PIM afectados	Razón fundamental	Métricas
Facilidad de Aprendizaje / Completitud de Documentación	HAT, UI de Instancia, UI de Población, UI de Servicio	La existencia de una ayuda en línea facilita al usuario el aprendizaje de la herramienta; por lo tanto hay que comprobar que el analista ha definido mensajes de ayuda en los patrones de interfaz.	Proporción de acciones de una UI que tienen definidas mensajes de ayuda. Índice de completitud de mensajes de ayuda definidos para una UI. Índice de completitud de mensajes de ayuda para el modelo.
Comprensibilidad / Densidad de la Información	Acciones, Conjunto de visualización, UI de Servicio (argumentos), Filtro	La densidad de la información afecta a la facilidad de lectura de la interfaz, por lo tanto debe evitarse presentar al usuario información innecesaria para la tarea que está realizando.	Proporción de acciones invocables en una UI de Servicio. Proporción de UIs de Población en las que se definen filtros.
Comprensibili-	Introducción,	Los valores por defecto redu-	Proporción de patrones de Introduc-

Subcaract. / Atributo	Elementos del PIM afectados	Razón fundamental	Métricas
dad / Completitud de Valores Iniciales	Selección Definida	cen la carga de trabajo del usuario y facilitan la comprensión.	ción y Selección Definida que definen un valor inicial.
Operabilidad / Consistencia de Etiquetado	UI de Servicio, UI de Instancia, UI de Población, Navegación	Las etiquetas relativas a argumentos, campos y navegaciones deben ser consistentes a lo largo de las UIs para facilitar su reconocimiento.	Proporción de campos relativos al mismo dato con etiquetas consistentes a lo largo de UIs relacionadas. Proporción de navegaciones iguales con etiquetas consistentes a lo largo de UIs relacionadas.
Operabilidad / Significación del Etiquetado	Alias en los patrones: Introducción, Información Complementaria, Selección Definida, Filtros, Navegación, Agrupación de Argumentos y Acciones	Una etiqueta es significativa para los usuarios cuando hay una fuerte relación semántica entre aquellas etiquetas y los ítems o acciones a los que se refiere.	Proporción de elementos con un alias definido explícitamente por el analista Proporción de elementos con nombres significativos para cada patrón (propiedad). Proporción total de elementos con nombres significativos.

En algunos casos es posible y conveniente definir métricas con distinta granularidad. Por ejemplo, para el atributo **completitud de documentación**, podríamos verificar la existencia de mensajes de ayuda definidos para todos y cada uno de los elementos de una UI de Población determinada: campos del conjunto de visualización, acciones ofertadas, filtros, navegaciones, etc. Por ejemplo <proporción de acciones de una UI que tienen definidas mensajes de ayuda>. Ahora bien, a la hora de computar una métrica genérica para la UI (un índice de completitud), podemos realizar una media ponderada de las métricas anteriores, pues no es igual de relevante el mensaje de ayuda en los campos de un filtro como lo es en las acciones ofertadas al usuario. Los índices particulares de cada UI se pueden combinar en un único índice de completitud de documentación relativo al modelo PIM valorado.

Se puede observar que el atributo **significación del etiquetado** está relacionado con prácticamente todos los patrones, pues la propiedad de *alias* (la etiqueta que se presenta al usuario) se puede definir para todas las abstracciones de la interfaz. Por ejemplo, en la UI de Servicio cada argumento tiene una etiqueta, lo mismo ocurre con los campos de las UIs de Instancia y de Población. Respecto a las métricas, podemos diferenciar las de carácter sintáctico, verificables sobre el PIM en una evaluación temprana, y las de carácter semántico, que se calcularán sobre el *Code Model*. Entre las métricas sintácticas se propone obtener la <proporción de elementos con un alias definido explícitamente por el analista>, lo cual es más relativo a la completitud porque no asegura la significación de la etiqueta escogida por el analista y su evaluación puede ser automatizada.

Entre las métricas semánticas hay algunas que, si bien requieren intervención humana, pueden todavía evaluarse sobre el PIM porque se corresponden con propiedades de patrones de interfaz: <proporción de elementos con nombres significativos para cada patrón>. Por último, hay otras métricas que implican necesariamente una evaluación con usuario, sobre el *Code Model*. Es el caso de <proporción de elementos cuyo nombre considera significativo el usuario>. El leitmotiv del marco propuesto es precisamente que la evaluación temprana sobre el PIM minimice la aparición de problemas de usabilidad en las evaluaciones tardías sobre el CM.

4 Caso de estudio

Hemos tomado un caso práctico de gestión de campings generado con OlivaNova para ilustrar el uso del modelo de usabilidad propuesto para la evaluación de la calidad externa (ver Figura 2, 2A). El negocio principal del camping es el alquiler de *Bungalows* o *Parcelas*. Los usuarios pueden también utilizar las instalaciones deportivas (*ServiciosUsados*) sin recargo o por una cierta cantidad de dinero. También pueden concertar *ServiciosExtra* como excursiones, etc. Al final de la *Estancia* del cliente se emite una *Factura*. Además, las principales funciones que el sistema debe proporcionar son: control de la ocupación de las parcelas y bungalows, seguimiento del cliente y facturación. A continuación se muestra el Modelo de Objetos del caso de estudio, a partir del cual se especifica el Modelo de Presentación.

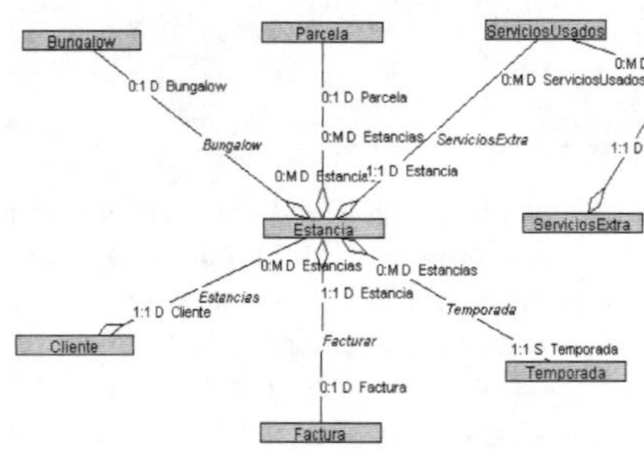

Fig. 4. Modelo de Objetos

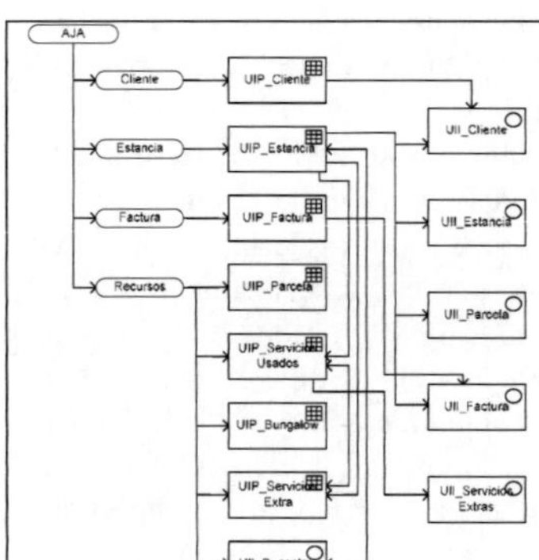

UI de servicio:
Nombre:UIS_Crear
Argumentos: Estancia, Total, ModoPago, NumFactura, FechaPago, Pagada, FechaEmision
UI de instancia:
Nombre: UII_Temporada
Conjunto de visualización: Descripción, FechaFin, FechaInicio, Id, Nombre, Recargo
UI de población:
Nombre: UIP_Factura
Conjunto de visualización: FechaEmision, FechaPago, ModoPago, Nímero, Pagada, Total
Acciones: Pagar, Crear, Cambiar, Destruir
Navegación: Estancia, Cliente, Factura
Criterio de ordenación: <Número, Asc>
Filtro: Estancia.Cliente = VCliente

Fig. 5. Modelo de Presentación

La Figura 5 muestra en la primera columna el árbol de jerarquía de acciones para la aplicación estudiada. En la segunda columna se muestra una descripción detallada de cada uno de los patrones con los que se generan las interfaces que utilizaremos para detectar problemas de usabilidad.

Para registrar cada uno de los problemas de usabilidad, nos hemos basado en el método de clasificación CUP [23] (*Classification of Usability Problems*). En cualquier caso, hemos extendido esta plantilla para reflejar a qué **patrón del Modelo de Presentación** afecta cada uno de los problemas detectados y qué **atributo de usabilidad** se ve implicado. A continuación, presentamos dos problemas de usabilidad a modo de ejemplo.

Identificador: 1

Descripción: la aplicación no facilita la entrada del dato *Modo Pago*. Debería aparecer una lista desplegable para que los valores introducidos sean homogéneos, ya que el conjunto de valores posibles es pequeño. Además, podría aparecer por defecto la forma de pago más utilizada comúnmente.

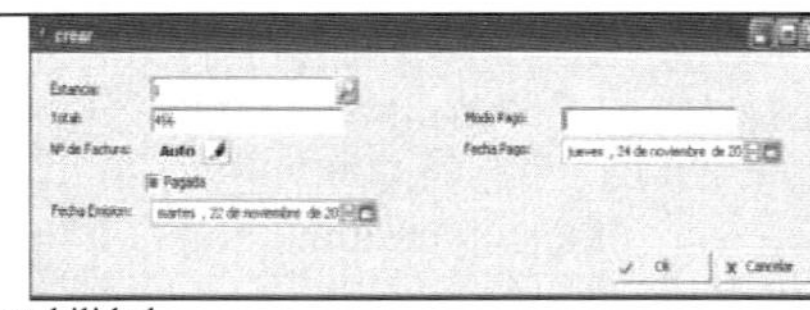

Actividad en la que se encontró el defecto: evaluación usabilidad
Detonante: al crear una *Factura*
Impacto: moderado
Fase en la que se debe reparar: diseño de la presentación
Clasificación del error: mejoras
Causa: Personal
Atributo de usabilidad afectado: minimización de acciones y valores por defecto
Patrón de presentación afectado: ausencia de *Selección Definida*, dentro de la *UI de Servicio*
Prevención del error: identificar aquellos argumentos que tengan pocos valores posibles
Solución: introducir una lista desplegable mediante el patrón de *Selección Definida* y establecer como valor por defecto el modo de pago más utilizado.

Identificador: 2

Descripción: al listar las facturas solo aparece un filtro por cliente, pero no existe un filtro para ver por fecha de pago o ver solo los que estén sin pagar. Esta ventana va a presentar mucha información y hay que facilitarle la búsqueda al usuario.

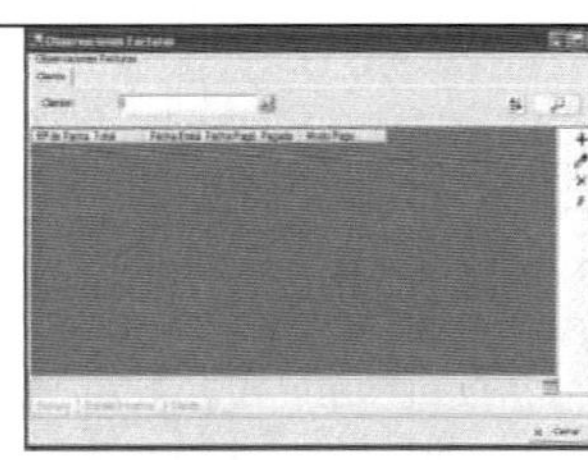

Actividad en la que se encontró el defecto: evaluación usabilidad
Detonante: al listar todas las instancias de la clase *Factura*
Impacto: moderado
Fase en la que se debe reparar: diseño de la presentación
Clasificación del error: mejoras
Causa: Personal
Atributo de usabilidad afectado: densidad de la información
Patrón de presentación afectado: afecta a *Filtro* dentro de *Unidad de Interacción de Población*
Prevención del error: utilizar distintos filtros para una interfaz que muestre gran cantidad de información
Solución: introducir un filtro por *fecha de pago* y otro por el atributo *pagado*.

5 Comparación con trabajos relacionados

En los últimos años varios modelos de calidad han sido propuestos en la literatura. Estos modelos fueron definidos basándose en estándares existentes como la ISO/IEC 9241-11 [10] y la ISO/IEC 9126-1 [11] o partiendo desde cero. La ISO/IEC 9126-1 es un modelo de calidad genérico de propósito general. La ISO 9241-11 es un estándar que define la usabilidad como la medida en la que un producto pueden usarlo determinados usuarios para conseguir objetivos específicos con efectividad, eficiencia y satisfacción en un contexto de uso especificado. Aunque estos modelos son útiles, deben ser adaptados para su utilización.

Dromey et al. [6], Dix et al. [5], y Nielsen [17] proponen modelos propios para descomponer la usabilidad. La propuesta de Dromey se basa en definir propiedades de *comportamientos* y *usos*. El *comportamiento* es algo que el software presenta cuando se ejecuta bajo la influencia de un conjunto de entradas. El *uso* es algo que diferentes usuarios hacen con o para el software. Las propiedades que plantea Dromey, son un subconjunto de los atributos que incluimos en nuestro modelo. Por ejemplo: la propiedad *transparencia*, que indica la facilidad de comprensión y de recordar la funcionalidad, se podría incluir en nuestra subcaracterística *comprensibilidad y facilidad de memorización*.

Dix et al. [5] proponen un modelo de usabilidad centrado en tres categorías principales: *facilidad de aprendizaje*, *flexibilidad* y *robustez*. Cada una de estas categorías se subdivide en principios más específicos que la soportan. Este modelo es similar a nuestra propuesta. Nosotros partimos de subcaracterísticas de usabilidad para llegar a atributos medibles y Dix parte de categorías parar llega hasta principios específicos. Los principios propuestos por Dix están recogidos en uno o más de nuestros atributos. Por ejemplo, la *capacidad de personalizar* que propone Dix, está reflejada en los atributos *adaptatividad* y *adaptabilidad*.

Nielsen [17] modela la usabilidad como parte de un modelo más amplio que parte de la *aceptación del sistema*. Dentro de la *aceptación del sistema* está la *aceptación práctica* que incluye la *utilidad* y, dentro de esta última, la usabilidad. Nielsen descompone la usabilidad en los siguientes atributos: *facilidad de aprendizaje*, *eficiencia*, *capacidad de memorizar*, *errores* y *satisfacción*. Hay ciertos atributos existentes en nuestro modelo que no aparecen modelados en la propuesta de Nielsen, como por ejemplo la *compresibilidad* y la *operabilidad*. También plantea algunos componentes, como por ejemplo la *satisfacción*, que engloban a atributos de nuestro modelo, el *grado de atracción* en este caso.

Por otro lado, otros trabajos se basan en la extensión o composición de estándares existentes. Este es el caso de las propuestas de Van Welie et al.[24], Fitzpatrick et al. [7], Abran et al.[2], y Shneiderman [21].

Van Welie et al. [24]. proponen un modelo con tres capas y relaciones entre ellas. La capa superior es la de *Usabilidad* (ISO/IEC 9241) y está dividida en tres aspectos: *eficiencia*, *efectividad* y *satisfacción*. La siguiente capa contiene un número de *indicadores de uso* que son índices del nivel de usabilidad que se puede observar en la práctica, cuando los usuarios están trabajando. Cada uno de estos *indicadores* contribuye a ciertos aspectos abstractos de la capa superior. La capa inferior se conoce como *significados*, usados como heurísticas para mejorar los indicadores de uso. Van Welie se centra más en aspectos medibles a través de pruebas de usuario dejando de lado aquellos aspectos que proponemos que sean medidos en la fase de modelado conceptual, como por ejemplo la *operabilidad*.

Fitzpatrick et al. [7] proponen tres ramas a examinar para identificar los atributos de un producto software usable. La primera rama es la de *calidad del software*, es decir, el grado en el que el software posee una combinación de atributos deseada. La segunda rama son las *obligaciones legales*. Son las obligaciones relacionadas con los mínimos requisitos de salud y seguridad que debe tener un equipo. La última rama es la *interacción persona ordenador*, que se describe como el estudio de las personas, la tecnología de los ordenadores y la forma en que unos influyen en los otros. Fitzpatrick considera como factores de calidad solo aquellos que dan soporte al usuario final. Distingue entre factores de calidad externos e internos. En los internos incluye ciertos atributos como la *facilidad en el mantenimiento, la reusabilidad y la portabilidad*.

Abran et al. [2] propusieron un modelo apoyándose en la ISO 9126 y sobre todo en la 9241-11, tomándola como base. Además, incluye las subcaracterísticas *facilidad de aprendizaje* y *seguridad*. El modelo propuesto por Abran es similar a nuestra propuesta. Una de las subcaracterísticas contempladas en el modelo propuesto y que no aparece en el de Abran, es la *operabilidad*, al igual que en la propuesta de Van Welie.

Shneiderman [21] propone que objetivos medibles y precisos guíen al diseñador, al evaluador, al comprador y al administrador. Esto se debe hacer para cada usuario y cada tarea. Shneiderman propone cinco factores humanos que son centrales para la evaluación de usabilidad: *tiempo de aprendizaje, rendimiento, tasa de errores por usuario, mantenimiento del conocimiento adquirido de la aplicación* y *satisfacción subjetiva*. En nuestro modelo aparecen ciertas subcaracterísticas de la usabilidad, como por ejemplo la *comprensibilidad* y la *operabilidad*, que no aparecen reflejados en los objetivos de diseño de la interfaz de usuario que propone Shneiderman.

6 Conclusiones

En este trabajo se ha presentado una estrategia de evaluación de usabilidad en la fase de modelado conceptual de un método de producción automática de software que sigue los principios de MDA. Esta estrategia de evaluación ha sido llevada a cabo a través de la definición de un modelo que descompone el concepto de usabilidad en atributos medibles y que clarifica las relaciones existentes entre estos atributos y los elementos del modelo independiente y dependiente de plataforma. Como consecuencia, la usabilidad de un sistema software puede ser evaluada y mejorada en el espacio del problema. Al mejorar la calidad interna, parece sensato suponer que se reducirá el número de defectos de usabilidad que aparecerán durante las evaluaciones de calidad externa y calidad en uso. Pretendemos demostrar esto empíricamente en trabajos futuros.

El modelo de usabilidad propuesto ha sido aplicado en la evaluación de varios casos de estudio reales desarrollados con la tecnología ONME, aunque este modelo puede ser usado para evaluar cualquier aplicación desarrollada siguiendo las directrices de MDA.

Como trabajo futuro se plantea definir métricas para el Modelo de Presentación que nos permitan automatizar la evaluación de la usabilidad. También tenemos previsto realizar pruebas con usuarios para comprobar empíricamente la mejora de la usabilidad a nivel conceptual y medir las subcaracterísticas subjetivas.

Referencias

[1] Abrahão, S., Ó. Pastor and L. Olsina (2005). A Quality Model for Early Usability Evaluation. INTERACT05 International COST 294 Workshop on User Interface Quality Models (UIQM), Rome, Italy.

[2] Abran A., Khelifi A., Suryn W., Seffah A. (2003) Usability Meanings and Interpretations in ISO Standards, Software Quality Journal, 11 (4) pp. 325-338.

[3] Bastien, J. M. C., & Scapin, D. L. (1993). Ergonomic criteria for the evaluation of human-computer interfaces (Report No. 156). Rocquencourt, France: Institut National de Recherche en Informatique et en Automatique..
[4] Care Technologies: http://www.care-t.com Última visita: Nov-2005
[5] Dix, A., Abowd, G., Beale, R. and Finlay, J. (1998), Human-Computer Interaction, Prentice Hall Europe.
[6] Dromey R.G. (1998) Software Product Quality: theory, Model and Practice, Technical report, Software Quality Institute, Griffith University, Nathan, Brisbane, Australia.
[7] Fitzpatrick, R. and C. Higgins (1998). Usable Software and Its Attributes: A Synthesis of Software Quality, European Community Law and Human-Computer Interaction Proceedings of HCI on People and Computers XIII.Springer-Verlag: 3-21.
[8] Folmer E., Bosch J. (2004) Architecting for usability: A Survey, Journal of Systems and Software, 70(1) 61-78.
[9] Hix, Deborah and H. Rex Hartson (1993), Developing User Interfaces: Ensuring Usability Through Product & Process. New York, NY: John Wiley & Sons.
[10] ISO 9241-11 (1998) Ergonomic requirements for office work with visual display terminals - Part 11: Guidance on Usability.
[11] ISO/IEC 9126-1 (2001), Software engineering - Product quality - 1: Quality model.
[12] MDA: http://www.omg.org/mda Última visita: Nov-2005
[13] Microsoft, "Guía de Estilo para el diseño de aplicaciones .NET". 2004. http://www.microsoft.com/spanish/msdn/arquitectura/DesignGuidelines/DesignGuidelines.asp Última visita: Nov-2005
[14] Molina J.C., Pastor O. "MDA, OO-Method y la tecnología OlivaNova Model Execution". I Taller sobre desarrollos dirigidos por modelos, MDA y aplicaciones. Málaga, 2004.
[15] Molina P., Especificación de interfaz de usuario: De los requisitos a la generación automática, PhD Thesis, DSIC, Universidad Politécnica de Valencia, Marzo de 2003.
[16] Molina, P. J. Meliá, S. and Pastor, O. (2002), Just-UI: A User Interface Specification Model. In Ch. Kolski and J. Vanderdonckt (Eds.), Computer-Aided Design of User Interfaces III, Kluwer Academics Publisher, 63–74.
[17] Nielsen, J. (1993). Usability Engineering. Morgan Kaufmann Publishers Inc.
[18] Oppermann R., Rossen R., Kinshuk, "Adaptability and Adaptivity in Learning Systems", Knowledge Transfer (Volume II). A. Behrooz (Ed), Pace, London, UK, 1997, pp. 173-179.
[19] Ortiz, J. C., Condori-Fernandez, N., Abrahão S., A (2005) Un Marco de Usabilidad para las Aplicaciones Generadas con la Tecnología OlivaNova Model Execution, VI Congreso Español de Interacción Persona Ordenador (Interacción 2005), Granada, España,.
[20] Pastor, O., Gómez, J., Insfrán, E. Pelechano, V. (2001) The OO-Method Approach for Information Systems Modelling: From Object-Oriented Conceptual Modeling to Automated Programming. Information Systems, 26(7) 507–534.
[21] Shneiderman, B. (1998), Designing the User Interface: Strategies for Effective Human-Computer Interaction, Addison-Wesley, Reading, Massachusetts, USA.
[22] Sun Microsystems. "Java Look and Feel Design Guidelines", 2001. http://java.sun.com/products/jlf/ Última visita: Nov-2005
[23] Hvannberg, E. T. and L.-C. Law (2003). Classification of Usability Problems (CUP) Scheme. M. Rauterberg, M. Menozzi and J. Wesson, Human-Computer Interaction INTERACT 2003, Zurich, Switzerland, pp. 655-662.
[24] Welie, M. v., G. C. v. d. Veer and A. Eliëns (1999). Breaking Down Usability. NTERACT 99, Edinburgh. IOS Press, pp. 613-620

Análisis Comparativo de Propuestas de Establecimiento de Requisitos de Seguridad para el Desarrollo de Sistemas de Información Seguros

Daniel Mellado[1], Eduardo Fernández-Medina[2] y Mario Piattini[2]

[1] Ministerio de Trabajo y Asuntos Sociales; Gerencia de Informática de la Seguridad Social; Madrid, España
Daniel.Mellado@alu.uclm.es
[2] Grupo ALARCOS, Dpto. de Tecnologías y Sistemas de Información, Centro Mixto de Investigación y Desarrollo de Software UCLM-Soluziona; Universidad de Castilla-La Mancha. Ciudad Real, España, Paseo de la Universidad 4, 13071.
(Eduardo.Fdez-Medina, Mario.Piattini)@uclm.es

Abstract. Las soluciones de seguridad actuales están principalmente centradas en proporcionar defensas de seguridad, en vez de resolver una de las principales causas de los problemas de seguridad, un diseño apropiado de los Sistemas de Información (SI). En este artículo se hace un análisis comparativo de nueve propuestas técnicas relevantes que dan importancia al establecimiento de requisitos de seguridad en el desarrollo de SI. Las propuestas analizadas aportan aspectos muy importantes relativos a la seguridad que pueden ser usados como base para nuevas metodologías o extensiones de las existentes. Sin embargo, satisfacen parcialmente los criterios necesarios para el establecimiento de requisitos de seguridad, con garantías e integración en el desarrollo de SI. Por tanto concluimos que no son lo suficientemente específicas para el tratamiento sistemático e intuitivo de requisitos de seguridad en las primeras fases de desarrollo software, aunque partes de éstas propuestas empleadas complementariamente pueden ser usadas para dicho propósito.

1 Introducción

Hoy en día los sistemas de información son vulnerables a multitud de amenazas. Además, cuanto más se incrementa la complejidad de las aplicaciones y servicios, más aumenta la potencialidad de sufrir brechas de seguridad [28]. Y en la actual Sociedad de la Información, que depende de multitud de sistemas software cuya misión es crítica. Resulta crucial que los SI sean asegurados apropiadamente desde el principio [3, 21], debido a las potenciales pérdidas a las que se enfrentan las organizaciones que confían en todos estos SI.

Como sabemos, es ampliamente aceptado el principio que establece que la construcción de la seguridad en las etapas tempranas del proceso de desarrollo es más eficaz respecto a los costes y tiene como resultado diseños más robustos [18]. Sin embargo, el gran problema es que en la mayoría de los proyectos software la seguridad se trata una vez el sistema ha sido diseñado e implementado. Debido en muchos casos, a una gestión inapropiada de la especificación de los requisitos de seguridad del nuevo sistema, ya que la denominada fase de especificación de requisitos suele realizarse con unas cuantas descripciones o la especificación de objetivos plasmados en unos pocos folios [11]. Además, habitualmente los requisitos de seguridad no son bien entendidos en sí. De forma que, incluso cuando se intenta especificar los requisitos de seguridad, muchos desarrolladores tienden a describir soluciones de diseño en términos de mecanismos de protección en lugar de realizar proposiciones declarativas sobre el grado de protección requerido [11]. Otro motivo por el que se infravaloran los requisitos de seguridad puede tener su origen en que muchas veces son percibidos como un obstáculo para alcanzar los hitos de los proyectos y suponen un gasto extra de recursos para el proyecto, como así lo demuestra la controversia que rodea al asunto del Retorno de la Inversión en la Seguridad o ROSI [9].

Una parte muy importante en el proceso de desarrollo software para conseguir sistemas software seguros es la denominada Ingeniería de Requisitos de Seguridad. La cual proporciona técnicas, métodos y normas para abordar esta tarea en el ciclo de desarrollo de los SI. Y debería implicar, como afirman Kotonya y Sommerville en [19], el uso de procedimientos repetibles y sistemáticos para asegurar que el conjunto de requisitos obtenidos es completo, consistente y fácilmente comprensible y analizable por parte de los diferentes actores implicados en el desarrollo del sistema. Un buen documento de requisitos debe incluir tanto requisitos funcionales (relativos a los servicios que el software o sistema debe proporcionar) y los no-funcionales (relativos a las denominadas características de calidad, como rendimiento, portabilidad, seguridad etc.) [11]. Por su parte, los requisitos de seguridad deben ser descritos de forma concreta antes de que se diseñe la arquitectura del sistema [2], en consonancia con [22], en el sentido de que la seguridad debe ser considerada durante todo el proceso de desarrollo y debería ser definida conjuntamente con la especificación de requisitos.

Actualmente, las soluciones de seguridad están principalmente centradas en proporcionar defensas de seguridad en vez de resolver una de las principales razones de los problemas de seguridad, que se refieren a un diseño apropiado de los sistemas de información. En este artículo se estudian 9 propuestas técnicas relevantes que dan importancia a la elicitación de requisitos de seguridad en de desarrollo de Sistemas de Información (Brescianiet et al. 2004; Breu et al. 2004 y Breu y Innerhofer-Oberperfler 2005; Firesmith 2003 y 2004; Jennex 2005; Myanmar, Lee, y Yurcik, 2005; Toval et al. 2001 y Gutierrez et al. 2005; Peeters 2005; Poopp et al. 2003; Yu 1997). Estas propuestas serán expuestas brevemente y comparadas en este artículo, sirviendo una primera aproximación al estado del arte actual de los requisitos de seguridad en el desarrollo de Sistemas de Información.

El resto del artículo esta organizado de la siguiente forma: en la sección 2, describiremos cada una de las propuestas que incorporan la elicitación de requisitos de seguridad en las primeras fases del desarrollo del SI. A continuación, en la sección 3, mostraremos el marco de comparación que hemos usado para realizar el análisis comparativo de cada una de estas propuestas, y ofrecemos una comparación de las mismas. Finalmente en la sección 4 expondremos nuestras conclusiones.

2 Propuestas Técnicas que Incorporan Requisitos de Seguridad

Las propuestas que serán analizadas en nuestra comparación se mencionan a continuación:

- Bresciani, et al. 2004: "Requisitos de seguridad en Tropos" [6].
- Breu, et al. 2004 y Breu & Innerhofer–Oberperfler, 2005: "Hacia un desarrollo sistemático de sistemas seguros" [7] y "Análisis de seguridad de SI dirigido por el modelo de negocio" [8].
- Firesmith, 2003 y 2004: "Casos de uso de seguridad" [12] y "Requisitos de seguridad en Open Process Framework" [13].
- Jennex 2005: "Modelando requisitos de seguridad para el desarrollo de SI" [16].
- Myagmar, Lee, y Yurcik, 2005: "Modelado de amenazas como base para los requisitos de seguridad" [23].
- Toval et al. 2001: "Requisitos de seguridad en SIREN" [27] y Gutiérrez, et al. 2005: "Requisitos de seguridad para servicios web basados en SIREN" [14].
- Peeters 2005: "Ingeniería ágil de requisitos de seguridad" [24].
- Popp et al. 2003: "Desarrollo de sistemas con seguridad crítica mediante extensión de los casos de uso" [25].
- Yu 1997: "Requisitos de seguridad basado en el marco de trabajo i*" [29].

Hemos elegido estas propuestas porque la mayoría de ellas tratan de resolver el problema de la seguridad en las primeras fases del desarrollo de SI y hacen énfasis en los requisitos de seguridad para el desarrollo de sistemas de información seguros. A continuación se describen brevemente cada una de las propuestas.

2.1 Requisitos de Seguridad en Tropos (propuesta de Bresciani et al. 2004) [6]

Tropos es una metodología dirigida por los requisitos, orientada a agentes y metas que emplea las nociones básicas tomadas de este tipo de metodologías (meta, tarea, dependencia social, etc.) como elemento central a través de todo el ciclo de desarrollo. Y se considera un método de desarrollo conducido por los requisitos ya que son los artefactos desarrollados durante la etapa de análisis de los requisitos los que marcan el resto de etapas (arquitectura y diseño a bajo nivel) del marco de trabajo. Por tanto, Tropos es un método de desarrollo de sistemas software que se compone de las siguientes etapas fundamentales:

1. Análisis de Requisitos.
   - Análisis de los Requisitos en las Etapas Iniciales: análisis organizacional que define los actores y sus metas.
   - Análisis de los Requisitos en las Etapas Finales: requisitos funcionales y no funcionales (la seguridad entre ellos) refinados.
2. Diseño a Alto Nivel o Diseño Arquitectónico, en el que se define el sistema a partir de sus subsistemas principales y del conjunto de relaciones de control y de información presentes entre ellos.
3. Diseño a Bajo Nivel, en el que se realiza un refinamiento de los subsistemas hasta obtener sus componentes atómicos y sus relaciones..

2.2 Hacia un Desarrollo Sistemático de Sistemas Seguros y Análisis de Seguridad de SI Dirigido por el Modelo de Negocio (propuestas de Breu et al. 2004 [7] y Breu & Innerhofer–Oberperfler, 2005 [8])

Los autores proponen un nuevo modelo de procesos para la ingeniería de seguridad. Este modelo de procesos extiende el desarrollo de software dirigido por casos de uso y orientado a objetos a través de un tratamiento sistemático de los temas relacionados con la seguridad. También introducen la noción de aspectos de seguridad describiendo los más relevantes requisitos de seguridad y las contramedidas en su nivel adecuado de abstracción. Además definen un micro-proceso para el análisis de seguridad que apoya el desarrollo sistemático de componentes seguros dentro del desarrollo iterativo de sistemas.

El proceso central está basado en una aproximación general que puede ser fácilmente mapeado a cualquiera de los modelos de procesos establecidos. En cuanto a los artefactos, éstos esenciales son el Modelo de Negocio (que describe los procesos de trabajo), el Sistema de Requisitos (que describe los casos de uso del sistema), la Arquitectura de Aplicación (que describe los componentes lógicos del sistema y los flujos principales de mensajes), y la Arquitectura Software (que describe la estructura técnica). Basándose en el concepto de construcción iterativa de software, introducen un micro-proceso para el análisis de seguridad, que consta de 5 pasos: elicitación de requisitos de seguridad, análisis de amenazas y riesgos, toma de medidas y comprobar la corrección de las medidas relacionadas y los requisitos. De forma que estos 5 pasos son repetidamente realizados en cada nivel de abstracción durante el desarrollo incremental.

Por último, los autores concluyen que la seguridad de la información es una cuestión del negocio, y por esta razón su gestión debe ser dirigida por el negocio. Además, piensan que una vinculación con los estándares más relevantes y un soporte en la valoración de la conformidad con los mismos, debería ser parte integral de su metodología de gestión de la información de seguridad. Lo cual iría junto con proporcionar una función de la documentación que registre la toma de decisiones.

2.3 Casos de uso de seguridad y requisitos de seguridad en Open Process Framework (propuesta de Firesmith, 2003 [12] y 2004[13])

Donald Firesmith en [13] ofrece unos pasos que permiten definir requisitos de seguridad a partir de plantillas reutilizables. Su análisis de los requisitos de seguridad se basa en dos principios básicos obtenidos de OCTAVE (Operationally Critical Threat, Asset, and Vulnerability Evaluation) [1] basado en los recursos y dirigido por el riesgo. Los pasos en su proceso para la identificación y análisis de los requisitos de seguridad son: identificación de los activos; identificar los tipos de atacantes más probables; identificar las posibles amenazas sobre los activos; determinar los impactos negativos, para cada recurso vulnerable; estimar y priorizar los riesgos de la seguridad en relación con los recursos vulnerables y en base a las amenazas más relevantes y a su impacto potencialmente negativo; seleccionar los subfactores de seguridad, para limitar el riesgo a un nivel aceptable; seleccionar las plantillas relevantes, para cada subfactor y riesgo de la seguridad; identificar los requisitos funcionales relevantes; determinar el criterio de seguridad; determinar la métrica de seguridad y determinar el nivel mínimo aceptable; especificar el requisito.

Adicionalmente, en [12], el autor propone que estos requisitos de seguridad deberían basarse en el análisis de activos y servicios que tienen que ser protegidos y en las amenazas de seguridad de las que estos activos y servicios tienen que ser protegidos. Para ello propone los casos de uso de seguridad, que deben de ser usados para especificar los requisitos de seguridad que la aplicación tiene que cumplir para protegerse satisfactoriamente de las amenazas de seguridad más relevantes [12]. A diferencia de los casos de mal uso, que son un tipo especializado de casos de uso, usados para analizar y especificar amenazas de seguridad

Por último, dado que los sistemas suelen poseer requisitos de seguridad similares el autor sugiere el uso de plantillas para especificar los requisitos de seguridad de forma que sean fácilmente reutilizables entre sistemas.

2.4 Modelando requisitos de seguridad para el desarrollo de SI (propuesta de Jennex, 2005) [16]

Jennex plantea, usando análisis de barreras y el concepto de defensa en profundidad, modificar el paradigma de diseño integrado de Siponen y Baskerville [26] en una metodología más gráfica y fácil de entender.

El análisis de barreras, se trata de un método para identificar las amenazas o peligros y determinar la efectividad de los factores de mitigación actualmente existentes. Es también usado en el momento en que una barrera falla para determinar la causa y corregir el problema determinando la futura acción preventiva. La ventaja de este método es que ayuda a identificar los factores fortuitos/ocasionales y las acciones necesarias para corregir los problemas. Sin embargo, su desventaja es que no asegura que sean reconocidas todas las barreras susceptibles de fallar, ni que los efectos de los riesgos/amenazas sean adecuadamente identificados. Jennex se apoya en los diagramas de barreras, los cuales muestran visualmente los ingredientes necesarios para un accidente. Posteriormente el análisis de barreras es usado para valorar la efectividad total del sistema de barreras y cada una de las barreras individualmente en prevenir el evento que provoca el accidente.

En cuanto a la defensa en profundidad, se trata de un concepto que utiliza múltiples mecanismos de compensación de control para prevenir o reducir una amenaza, y que usa una aproximación basada en capas para aumentar el nivel de esfuerzo requerido para dañar el sistema.

La metodología propuesta por el autor plantea por tanto, usar análisis de diagramas de barreras como un método gráfico de identificación y documentación de requisitos de seguridad. Esta aproximación además usa meta-notación para añadir detalles de seguridad a los existentes diagramas de desarrollo. También se entiende que el proceso sigue la aproximación de diseño integrado de seguridad en el ciclo de vida de desarrollo del software. Con lo que el objetivo del uso de diagramas de barreras en la fase de requisitos es que se identifiquen adecuadamente los requisitos de seguridad.

2.5 Modelado de amenazas como base para los requisitos de seguridad (propuesta de Myagmar, Lee, y Yurcik, 2005) [23]

En esta propuesta los autores parten de la siguiente pregunta, como cuestión importante que hay que hacerse en todo SI, es si ¿son necesarias las características de seguridad del sistema y satisfacen las necesidades de seguridad del mismo?

Ofrecen una visión del proceso de ingeniería de requisitos resumido a través de la (Figura 1. Proceso de ingeniería de requisitos de seguridad):

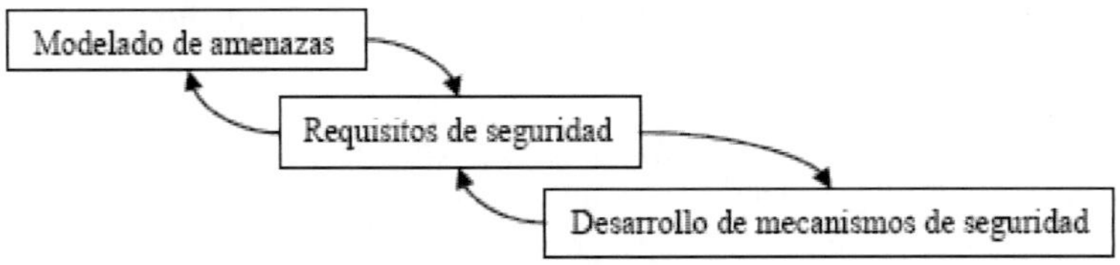

Figura 1. Proceso de ingeniería de requisitos de seguridad

De esta forma las amenazas son analizadas, y o bien se mitiga la amenaza o bien se acepta el riesgo asociada a ella. De tal modo que con una apropiada identificación de amenazas y una apropiada selección de medidas de salvaguarda se reduce la capacidad de los atacantes de hacer un mal uso / abusar del sistema.

El proceso de modelado de amenazas se suele requerir para sistemas de software complejos, soluciones personalizadas de aplicaciones y todos los otros casos en los que no se puede aplicar las listas estándar predefinidas de amenazas. Este proceso de modelado de amenazas planteado por los autores consta de tres pasos de alto nivel:

- Caracterización del sistema. Lo que supone la comprensión de todos los componentes y sus relaciones, definir escenarios de uso y identificar suposiciones y dependencias.
- Identificación de activos y puntos de acceso. Los analistas deben pensar como si fueran atacantes, determinando potenciales enemigos, sus motivaciones, sus objetivos y la información que disponen.
- Identificación de amenazas. Encontrar una lista de amenazas conocidas y vulnerabilidades encontradas en sistemas similares. Y revisar una lista de objetivos de ataque para cada activo. La salida de esta fase es un perfil de amenazas del sistema, describiendo todos los potenciales ataques y cada uno de los cuales necesita ser mitigado o aceptado, para lo cual una posible forma de acometerlo es usando de árboles de ataque.

En cuanto a la especificación de los requisitos de seguridad, éstos son frecuentemente especificados en términos de qué no debe ser permitido que pase. Un modelo de amenazas proporciona la mayor parte de la información necesaria para la elicitación de requisitos. Mediante la conversión de una declaración de amenaza en un requisito incluyendo "no debería" en la declaración, permite componer un conjunto inicial de requisitos de seguridad.

Por último, ya que se considera imposible garantizar el 100% de seguridad, los autores trabajan en conseguir el 100% de aceptación de riesgo. Para ello la gestión de riesgos que plantean consiste en: una valoración del riesgo, reducción del riesgo, y aceptación del riesgo. Para valorar el riesgo de las amenazas identificadas, éstas deben ser priorizadas según el daño que provoquen y su probabilidad de ocurrencia.

2.6 Requisitos de seguridad en SIREN y requisitos de seguridad para servicios web basados en SIREN (propuestas de Toval, et al. 2001 [27] **y Gutierrez, et al. 2005** [14])

En [27] Toval et al. definen un proceso de Ingeniería de Requisitos basado en la reutilización de los requisitos de seguridad y que es compatible con MAGERIT (Metodología de Análisis y GEstión de RIesgos del MinisTerio de Administraciones Públicas), el cual a su vez es compatible con el CCF (Common Criteria Framework) definido por el ISO 15408 (ISO/IEC, 1999). La reutilización de los requisitos de seguridad se lleva a cabo mediante dos niveles: A nivel de documentación mediante la definición de una estructura jerárquica de especificaciones de requisitos de seguridad; y a nivel de requisito de seguridad mediante su almacenamiento en un repositorio de requisitos reutilizables. Luego se aplica el método SIREN (SImple REuse of software requiremeNts) en la especificación de los requisitos de seguridad. SIREN define un modelo de proceso, unas directrices básicas, técnicas y herramientas. Las directrices de SIREN consisten de una jerarquía de documentos de especificación de requisitos conjuntamente con una plantilla para cada documento. En la siguiente figura (Figura 2. Jerarquía de documentación de Ingeniería de Requisitos definida en SIREN) se muestra dicha jerarquía.

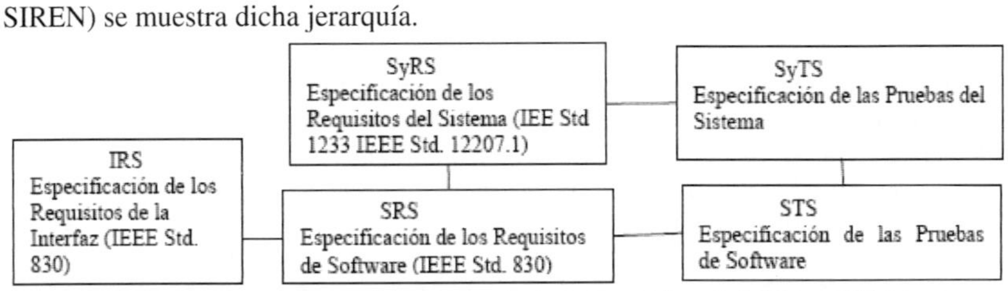

Figura 2. Jerarquía de documentación de Ingeniería de Requisitos definida en SIREN

El modelo del proceso definido es en espiral, y abarca las fases de elicitación de requisitos, análisis y negociación de requisitos, especificación de requisitos y validación. Además, se define un repositorio de requisitos clasificados por dominios y perfiles.

Adicionalmente, en [14] Gutiérrez et al. presentan un catálogo de plantillas de requisitos de seguridad para servicios web (WS) basados en el método de ingeniería de requisitos SIREN. Y centran sus esfuerzos en las plantillas de requisitos de seguridad para los siguientes subfactores: autenticación, autorización, confidencialidad, integridad y privacidad.

2.7 Ingeniería ágil de requisitos de seguridad (propuesta de Peeters, 2005)[24]

Para seguir siendo seguros los sistemas deben cambiar a la vez que lo hace su entorno, preferiblemente anticipándose a los cambios. Partiendo de esta premisas Peeters observa que las demandas de la ingeniería de seguridad encajan con la perspectiva de la agilidad. Por ello, Peeters propone extender prácticas ágiles para tratar con la seguridad con un espíritu informal, comunicativo y dirigido por la seguridad.

Las prácticas actuales de ingeniería ágil de requisitos se basan en las "historias de usuarios", que son breves e informales descripciones de requisitos escritas por los clientes del sistema. Al igual que se apoyan en la planificación, de modo que el desarrollo ágil es iterativo. Al final de cada iteración, los clientes del sistema verifican si el sistema satisface los requisitos capturados en las "historias de usuarios", mediante la realización por cada uno de ellos de unas pruebas de aceptación.

Para aumentar la agilidad de la ingeniería de requisitos Peeters plantea el uso de las "historias de abuso". Éstas identifican como los atacantes podrían abusar del sistema y hacer peligrar los activos de los interesados. De esta manera se facilita el establecimiento de los requisitos de seguridad. Y de la misma forma que las "historias de usuarios", son breves e informales, y son puntuadas y ordenadas según la percepción de amenaza sobre los activos de los clientes. Una correcta planificación por tanto, supondría considerar las "historias de usuarios" y las "historias de abuso" juntas, lo cual aseguraría un explícito y racional intercambio entre funcionalidad y seguridad.

2.8 Desarrollo de sistemas con seguridad crítica mediante extensión de los casos de uso (propuesta de Popp, et al. 2003) [25]

Esta propuesta proporciona una extensión al proceso convencional de los procesos desarrollados orientados a casos de uso [10, 15]. Este proceso consiste normalmente en 3 actividades en cuanto a la ingeniería de requisitos se refiere:

1. Tratan con los conceptos estáticos del dominio de una aplicación en un modelo de clases denominado Núcleo de la Aplicación. En este punto lo extienden modelando políticas de acceso y propiedades de seguridad basadas en UMLSec [17].
2. Identificación de los casos de uso y su manifestación en un Modelo de Casos de Uso, que son completados con la descripción textual mediante características que analizan las amenazas y las vulnerabilidades de la entrada y la salida. Además esbozan las políticas de seguridad que respondan a las anteriores amenazas. Al modelo resultante lo denominan Modelo de Casos de Uso de Seguridad
3. Integración de las dos vistas anteriores en un modelo orientado a objetos único, mediante, principalmente, la descripción de casos de uso en términos de flujos de mensajes entre los objetos. La extensión consiste en la integración del Modelo de Casos de Uso de Seguridad y el Núcleo de Aplicación refina la política de seguridad en términos de flujos de mensajes entre objetos

2.9 Requisitos de seguridad basado en el marco de trabajo i* (propuesta de Yu, 1997) [29]

El marco de trabajo *i**, es un marco de trabajo que soporta el modelado estratégico orientado a metas y a agentes así como la actividad de análisis de los requisitos, en resumen, ofrece una representación estructural de relaciones intencionales entre actores así como define una serie de conceptos estructurales como agentes o roles intencionales. Estos conceptos proporcionan un marco de trabajo que permite integrar fácilmente otras técnicas y conceptos para tratar la seguridad de los sistemas. La representación estructural definida en *i** muestra las relaciones de dependencia entre los actores lo cual hace que surjan los aspectos de la seguridad

En la (Figura 3. Proceso de requisitos i*) se muestra el proceso de elicitación y análisis de requisitos, funcionales definidos por *i** y cómo se integra éste con el proceso de elicitación y análisis de los requisitos de seguridad de [20].

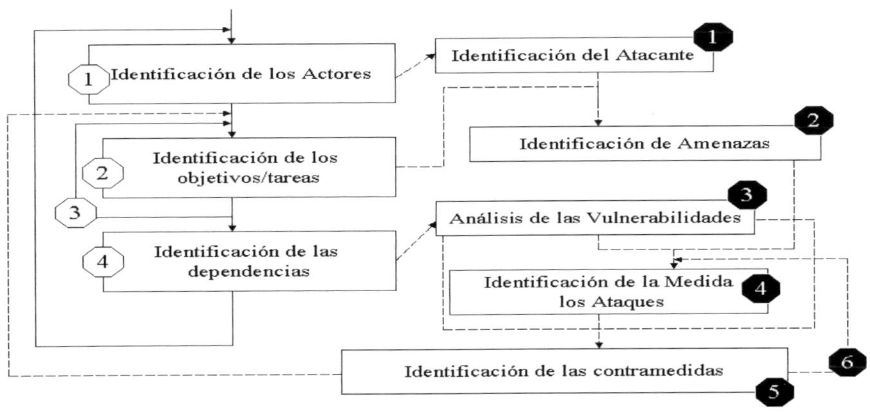

Figura 3. Proceso de requisitos i*

3. Comparación

En esta sección, con el objetivo de obtener una visión general de las diferentes propuestas expuestas anteriormente, se realizará una comparación de las mismas; para lo cual, proponemos un marco de análisis basado en los siguientes criterios:

- Grado de agilidad. Se refiere al grado agilidad de la metodología de desarrollo frente a las metodologías tradicionales planificadas. Es decir, si se trata de una propuesta de metodología más o menos pesada, o más o menos ágil. Para ello nos basaremos en las observaciones realizadas por Boehm y Turner [4, 5]. Quienes proponen un método basado en riesgos a través del cual tratan de mantener en equilibrio ambos métodos, aprovechando las ventajas de ambos (metodologías ágiles y las dirigidas por la planificación o tradicionales) y compensando sus desventajas.
- Soporte. Se refiere a aspectos como herramientas, procedimientos, guías, estándares y casos de estudio, que faciliten y ayuden a usar la propuesta.
- Grado de integración con los otros requisitos software. Se trata de cómo encaja el establecimiento de los requisitos de seguridad con el establecimiento de otros requisitos software (con los demás requisitos no funcionales y también con los funcionales) durante el desarrollo de un Sistema de Información. Para ello se tendrá en cuenta aspectos como el uso de técnicas similares ya existentes para el establecimiento de otros requisitos, como los diagramas UML, grado de paralelización y coordinación con la elicitación de otros requisitos, etc.

- Facilidad de uso. Se refiere a la facilidad con la que la técnica podría ser utilizada sin mucho conocimiento previo de la misma, y sin una formación especial. Para lo cual se tendrá en cuenta aspectos tales como el soporte de ayuda, el uso de técnicas similares ya existentes para otros requisitos, el uso de estándares ampliamente extendidos, etc.
- Contribuciones de la propuesta en cuanto a la seguridad. Aportación/es nuevas que dicha propuesta hace para mejorar el proceso de establecimiento de requisitos de seguridad.

Se calificará cada propuesta de forma cualitativa en la siguiente escala: alta, media-alta, media, media-baja, baja. De manera que para cada una de las propuestas hemos aplicado para cada criterio de comparación un método de ponderación lineal, mediante el cual hemos fijado un peso de manera directa para cada atributo y establecido unos intervalos aproximados para calificar cada criterio de la propuesta como alta, media-alta, media, media-baja, baja, en función de la puntuación aproximada obtenida. Por ejemplo, para el criterio de soporte de ayuda, el hecho de que la propuesta disponga de herramientas CARE (Computer-Aided Requirements Engineering) será el atributo de más peso a la hora de calificar el soporte ofrecido por la propuesta.

En la siguiente tabla (Tabla 1. Comparativa de propuestas) se muestra la comparación de las propuestas de los diferentes autores dentro del marco de análisis que proponemos.

Tabla 1. Comparativa de propuestas

Criterios / Propuestas	Grado de agilidad	Soporte de ayuda	Grado de integración con otros requisitos	Facilidad de uso	Contribuciones respecto a la seguridad
Bresciani, et al. 2004 [6]	Bajo	Medio (ST-Tool)	Media-Alta	Media	▪Desarrollo de sistemas software dirigido por los requisitos, orientada a agentes y metas
Breu, et al. 2004 [7] y Breu & Innerhofer–Oberperfler, 2005 [8]	Bajo	Medio (Herramienta que soporte UML)	Media	Media-Alta	▪"Aspectos de Seguridad". ▪Micro-proceso de análisis de seguridad

Firesmith, 2003 y 2004 [12, 13]	Medio	Medio-Alto (RequisitePro)	Media	Media-Alta	▪ Casos de uso de seguridad. ▪Y definición de requisitos de seguridad a partir de plantillas reutilizables
Jennex, 2005 [16]	Alto	Medio-Bajo	Media-Alta	Alta	▪Diagramas de barreras
Myagmar, Lee, y Yurcik 2005 [23]	Medio-Bajo	Medio	Media	Media-Alta	▪Modelado de amenazas como base para los requisitos de seguridad
Peeters, 2005 [24]	Alto	Medio-Bajo	Alta	Media-Alta	▪Historias de abuso
Popp, et al. 2003 [25]	Medio-Bajo	Alto (Poseidon + MDRLibrary)	Media-Alta	Media-Alta	▪UMLSec
Toval,, et al. 2001 [27] y Gutierrez, et al.2005 [14]	Bajo	Medio-Alto (RequisitePro + plugin)	Media	Media-Alta	▪Reutilización de requisitos de seguridad compatible con MAGERIT ▪Catálogo de requisitos de seguridad reutilizables para WS
Yu, 1997 [29]	Bajo	Medio-Bajo	Media-Alta	Media-Alta	▪Integración de requisitos funcionales y de seguridad

Como se observa en la tabla, y tras el análisis que realizamos, llegamos a la conclusión de que las anteriores propuestas presentan algunas debilidades:

- Como la dificultad de integrarlos con el desarrollo del SI, que provoca un creciente distanciamiento entre el desarrollo de SI y la implementación de la seguridad necesaria.
- La falta de soporte integral/completo del modelado de seguridad a nivel organizacional, conceptual y técnico.
- Estas propuestas nos son lo suficientemente específicas para el tratamiento sistemático e intuitivo de requisitos de seguridad de SI en las primeras fases de desa-

rrollo de software, ya que por ejemplo pocas propuestas apuestan por la reutilización de requisitos de seguridad, cuya utilización garantiza ciclos de desarrollo rápidos y basado en soluciones ya probadas, y ayudan a mejorar la calidad de dichos requisitos para los proyectos sucesivos.

- Y en su mayoría no tratan de integrar los Criterios Comunes (ISO/IEC 15408) en su proceso de establecimiento de requisitos de seguridad, siendo éstos el catálogo de requisitos estándar para la evaluación de sistemas donde la seguridad es crítica. Ni hacen mención de su conformidad o no con los estándares más relevantes de gestión de la seguridad como la norma ISO/IEC 17799.

En definitiva, las propuestas analizadas, satisfacen parcialmente los criterios necesarios para el establecimiento de requisitos de seguridad con garantías y no alcanzan el grado deseado de integración en el desarrollo de SI. Aunque, al mismo tiempo, cada una de estas metodologías aportan aspectos muy importantes relativos a la seguridad que pueden ser usados como base para nuevas metodologías o extensiones de las existentes. Destacándose de cada propuesta sus aportaciones más importantes respecto a la seguridad en la última columna de la Tabla 1.

4. Conclusiones

Hoy en día, en la llamada Sociedad de la Información, dada la criticidad creciente de los SI unido a los nuevos requisitos legales y gubernamentales, se hace necesario el desarrollo de enfoques cada vez más sofisticados para asegurar la seguridad de la información. Normalmente, la seguridad de la información se abordaba desde el punto de vista técnico en la fase de implementación, y aunque se trata de un aspecto importante, consideramos fundamental el tratamiento de la seguridad en todas las fases del desarrollo de SI, especialmente en el establecimiento de los requisitos de seguridad, ya que constituyen la base para la consecución de un SI robusto. Existen varias propuestas metodológicas interesantes al respecto, algunas de ellas han sido descritas y comparadas en este trabajo, aunque presentan algunas debilidades expuestas en la sección anterior. Sin embargo se considera también, que aportan aspectos muy importantes relativos a la seguridad que pueden ser usados para nuevas metodologías o procesos, o bien como extensión o mejora de las existentes.

Por tanto, consideramos que sería interesante obtener una forma sistemática e intuitiva para la elicitación y definición de requisitos de seguridad con garantías. Dicha técnica deberá permitir la integración de los requisitos de seguridad lo más posible con el desarrollo del SI, y permitir la reutilización de los requisitos de unos proyectos a otros. Además tendrá que ser válida para los nuevos SI basados en Internet y en especial para aquellos basados en la arquitectura SOA, apoyados en la tecnología de los Servicios Web. Para ello sería bueno que proporcionara herramientas de apoyo; así como que estuviera basada en estándares de normalización de la definición de requisitos, como pueda ser XML o mediante el uso de plantillas; al igual que el uso de estándares de modelado como UML. Y fuera conforme con los estándares de gestión de la seguridad como la ISO/IEC 17799 o COBIT (las cuales te dicen el qué, pero no el cómo en detalle), así como con la ISO/IEC 15408.

Finalmente, como trabajos futuros, trabajaremos hacia la obtención de un proceso de ingeniería de requisitos de seguridad para el desarrollo de SI seguros, y que tenga en cuenta especialmente las singularidades de los requisitos de seguridad de servicios web, los cuales últimamente han alcanzado una gran popularidad, y en los que la seguridad es un aspecto fundamental para su final adopción por toda la industria como tecnología de integración o '*middleware*'.

Agradecimientos

Este artículo ha sido desarrollado en el contexto de los proyectos CALIPO (TIC2003-07804-CO5-03) y RETISTIC (TIC2002-12487-E), de la Dirección General de Investigación del Ministerio de Ciencia y Tecnología y DIMENSIONS (PBC-05-012-2) de la Consejería de Ciencia y Tecnología de la Junta de Comunidades de Castilla- La Mancha y el FEDER.

Referencias Bibliográficas

1. Alberts, C.J., Behrens, S.G., Pethia, R.D., and Wilson, W.R., *OCTAVE Framework, Version 1.0*. 1999: Networked Systems Survivability Program. p. 84.
2. Barbacci, M.R., Ellison, R., Lattanze, A.J., Stafford, J.A., Weinstock, C.B., and Wood, W.G., *Quality Attribute Workshops (QWAs). Third Edition.*, in *Architecture Tradeoff Analysis Initiative*. 2003, Carnegie Mellon. Software Engineering Institute. p. 36.
3. Baskeville, R., *The development duality of information systems security*. Journal of Management Systems, 1992. **4**(1): p. 1-12.
4. Boehm, B. and Turner, R., *Observations on Balancing Discipline and Agility*. 2003: Agile Development Conference (ADC '03). p. 32.
5. Boehm, B. and Turner, R., *Balancing Agility and Discipline: Evaluating and Integrating Agile and Plan-Driven Methods*. 2004: ICSE'04. p. 718-719.
6. Bresciani, P., Giorgini, P., Giunchiglia, F., Mylopoulos, J., and Perini, A., *Tropos: Agent-Oriented Software Development Methodology*. 2004: Journal of Autonomous Agents and Multi-Agent System. p. 203-236.
7. Breu, R., Burger, K., Hafner, M., and Popp, G., *Towards a Systematic Development of Secure Systems*. 2004: WOSIS 2004.
8. Breu, R. and Innerhofer–Oberperfler, F., *Model based business driven IT security analysis*. 2005: SREIS 2005.
9. Cavusoglu, H., Mishra, B., and Raghunathan, S., *A Modelo for Evaluating IT Security Investments*. Commun. ACM, 2004. **47**(7): p. 87-92.
10. D'Souza, D.F. and Wills, A.C., *Objects, Components & Frameworks with UML: The Catalysis Approach*. 1998: Addison-Wesley Publishing Company.
11. Fernández-Medina, E., Moya, R., and Piattini Velthus, M., *Gestión de Requisitos de Seguridad*, in *Seguridad de las Tecnologías de la Información "La construcción de la confianza para una sociedad conectada"*, AENOR, Editor. 2003. p. pp 593-618.

12. Firesmith, D.G., *Security Use Cases*. 2003: Journal of Object Technology. p. 53-64.
13. Firesmith, D.G., *Specifying Reusable Security Requirements*. 2004: Journal of Object Technology. p. 61-75.
14. Gutiérrez, C., Moros, B., Toval, A., Fernández-Medina, E., and Piattini, M., *Security Requirements for Web Services based on SIREN*. Symposium on Requirements Engineering for Information Security (SREIS-2005), together with the 13th IEEE International Requirements Engineering Conference – RE'05, 2005.
15. Jacobson, I., Booch, G., and Rumbaugh, J., *The Unified Software Development Process*. 1999: Addison-Wesley Longman Inc.
16. Jennex, M.E., *Modeling security requirements for information systems development*. 2005: SREIS 2005.
17. Jürjens, J., *Secure Systems Development with UML*. 2005: Springer. 309.
18. Kim., H.-K., *Automatic Translation Form Requirements Model into Use Cases Modeling on UML*, C. Youn-Ky, Editor. 2005: ICCSA 2005.
19. Kotonya, G. and Sommerville, I., *Requirements Engineering Process and Techniques*. 1998.
20. Liu, L., Yu, E., and Mylopoulus, J., *Security and Privacy Requirements Analysis within Social Setting*. 2003: 11th IEEE International Requirements Engineering Conference.
21. McDermott, J. and Fox, C. *Using Abuse Case Models for Security Requirements Analysis*. in *Annual Computer Security Applications Conference*. 1999. Phoenix, Arizona.
22. Mouratidis, H., Giorgini, P., Manson, G., and Philp, I. *A Natural Extension of Tropos Methodology for Modelling Security*. in *Workshop on Agent-oriented methodologies, at OOPSLA 2002*. 2003. Seattle, WA, USA.
23. Myagmar, S., J. Lee, A., and Yurcik, W., *Threat Modeling as a Basis for Security Requirements*. 2005: SREIS 2005.
24. Peeters, J., *Agile Security Requirements Engineering*. 2005: SREIS 2005.
25. Popp, G., Jürjens, J., Wimmel, G., and Breu, R., *Security-Critical System Development with Extended Use Cases*. 2003: 10th Asia-Pacific Software Engineering Conference. p. 478-487.
26. Siponen, M. and Baskerville, R., *A new paradigm for adding security into IS development methods,*. 2001: 8th Annual Working Conference on Information Security Management andSmall Systems Security.
27. Toval, A., Nicolás, J., Moros, B., and García, F., *Requirements Reuse for Improving Information Systems Security: A Practitioner's Approach*. 2001: Requirements Engineering Journal. p. 205-219.
28. Walton, J.P., *Developing a Enterprise Information Security Policy*. 2002, ACM Press: Proceedings of the 30th annual ACM SIGUCCS conference on User services.
29. Yu, E., *Towards Modelling and Reasoning Support for Early-Phase Requirements Engineering*. 1997: 3rd IEEE International Symposium on Requirements Engineering (RE'97). p. 226-235.

Sesión 9:

Ingeniería de Requisitos y Arquitecturas

An Extensible Model for Representing and Tracing Architecture Based Design Processes

M. Luciana Roldán, Silvio Gonnet, Horacio Leone

CIDISI, Universidad Tecnológica Nacional
INGAR, Universidad Tecnológica Nacional, CONICET
Avellaneda 3657, 3000, Santa Fe, Argentina
{lroldan, sgonnet, hleone}@ceride.gov.ar

Abstract. Software Architecture Design is still considered as a challenging problem because it usually involves a complex process of exploration, evaluation, and composition of design alternatives. Increasingly, modelling languages, methods, and computer-aided tools are available to face these activities. However, they do not know how design is actually done. In fact, design knowledge exclusively rests in the mind of designers, and there is an urgent need to move it, as much as possible, to a computer-supported environment in order to capture this type of knowledge and make it reusable. This contribution addresses this objective by introducing a model for capturing how products under development are transformed along software architecture design processes. An operational perspective is considered where design decisions can be modelled by means of design operations. The situation calculus is used to formally express the existence of an object in a given state of a design process.

1 Introduction

Nowadays, it is vitally important for software production organizations to manage efficiently their development process with the intention of achieving a continuous improvement of design processes, capitalization of previous designs, and the use of experts' knowledge. That is significantly important at the early software architectures design stage, which requires accounting with the modelling languages [1, 2], methods [3], and computer-aided tools [4, 5]. Those methods and tools are basically focused on assisting a designer in generating a software architecture design to satisfy a set of requirements. During the Software Architecture Design Process (SADP), several different design products are generated (transformed and refined), which have different abstraction levels of the architecture being designed. However, most design knowledge still rests in the minds of experienced designers, and is lost as time goes by. Consequently, there is a need for tools able to capture and manage this process. By counting on such tools, both the tracking and tracing of the SADP and the analysis of its rationale would be possible. In this way, the expert's knowledge could be captured, thus providing the foundations for learning and training activities and for future reuse.

In order to develop a support environment with the aforementioned characteristics, this contribution introduces a model for capturing and tracing the products of SADP. Its goals are to make explicit the states of SADP and how they were obtained. The model is based on a generic Process Version Administration Model (PVAM) [6]. PVAM provides mechanisms for capturing and managing versions generated during the course of an engineering design project. It is summarized in the next section. After that, an extension of PVAM is described in Sections 3 and 4. The extension focuses on the products and operations of SADP. The proposed model is illustrated in Section 5 by designing a monitoring system for an industrial process. Finally, conclusions and future research guidelines are discussed.

2 An Integrated Model for Design Process Capture and Management

The proposed scheme considers the SADP as a sequence of activities that operate on the products of the design process, which are called *design objects*. Typical *design objects* are architectures of the software being designed, specifications and scenarios to be met. Naturally, these objects evolve as the SADP takes place, giving rise to several versions.

In order to maintain these versions, the previously proposed PVAM [6] is considered. The class diagram illustrated in Fig. 1 introduces its main concepts. PVAM represents a *design object* at two levels, the *repository* and the *versions' level* (Fig. 1). The *repository level* keeps a unique entity for each *design object* that has been created and/or modified due to model evolution during a design project. This object is regarded as a *versionable object* (o). On the other hand, the *versions' level* keeps the different versions of each *design object*, which are called *object versions* (v). The relationship between a *versionable object* o and one of its *object versions* v is represented by the *version* relationship. Therefore, a design object keeps a unique instance in the repository and all the versions it assumes belong to the versions' level.

At a given stage during the execution of a design project, the state assumed by the set of relevant design objects, from now on called *model version*, supplies a snapshot description of the state of the design process at that point. Each transformation operation applied to a *model version* incorporates the necessary information to trace a model evolution. This information is represented by *history* relationships between the *object versions* to which the *operation* is applied and the ones arising as the result of its execution (Fig. 1). This model was completely axiomatized using the situation calculus [7] and first order logic. PVAM is discussed in [6]. This contribution only presents the model extension needed to support the SADP.

A new model version m_n is generated when an activity a is executed. An activity a is materialised by a sequence of operations ϕ and the new model version m_n is the result of applying such sequence ϕ to the components of a previous model version m_p. This model evolution is posed as a history made up of discrete situations. The situation calculus is adopted for modelling such version generation process.

Therefore, the new model version m_n is achieved by performing the following evaluation: $apply(\phi, m_p) = m_n$.

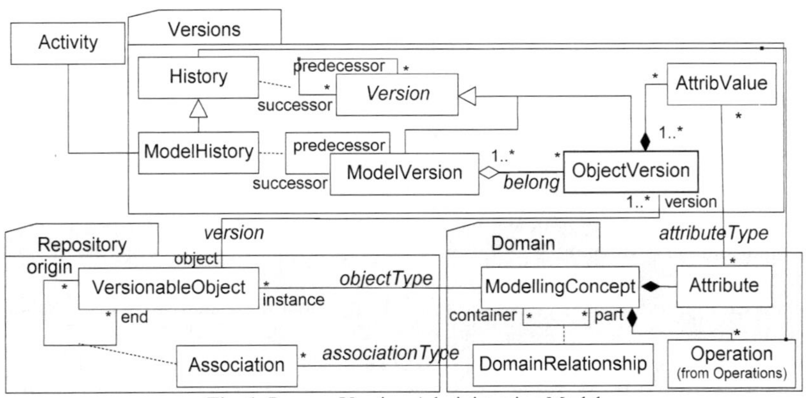

Fig. 1. Process Version Administration Model

The primitive operations that were proposed to represent the transformation of *model versions* are *add*, *delete*, and *modify*. By using the *add(v)* operation, an *object version* that did not exist in a previous *model version* can be incorporated into a successor. Conversely, the *delete(v)* operation eliminates an *object version* that existed in the previous *model version*. Also, if a *design object* has a version v_p, the $modify(v_p, v_s)$ operation creates a new *version* v_s of the existing *design object*, where v_s is a successor *version* of v_p. Thus, an *object version* v belongs to a *model version* that arises after applying the sequence of operations ϕ to *model version* m, if and only if one of the following conditions is met: i) v is added when the new *model version* is created by means of an *add* or *modify* operation (Expression 1); or ii) v already belonged to the previous *model version* m ($belong(v, m)$) and it is not deleted when ϕ is applied to it (Expression 2).

$$(\forall \phi, v, m)\ (add(v) \in \phi \vee (\exists v_p)\ modify(v_p, v)) \in \phi \Rightarrow added(v, apply(\phi, m)) \qquad (1)$$

$$(\forall \phi, v, m)\ (delete(v) \in \phi \vee (\exists v_s)\ modify(v, v_s) \in \phi) \Rightarrow deleted(v, apply(\phi, m)) \qquad (2)$$

From these definitions, and by using the format of successor state axioms proposed by [7], a formal specification of the cases in which an *object version* belongs to a *model version* is presented. In Expression 3, the predicate *belong(v, m)* is true when *object version* v belongs to model version m. From this expression, the *object versions* belonging to a *model version* can be determined. Then, it is possible to reconstruct a *model version* m_{i+1} by applying all operation sequences from the initial *model version* m_0.

$$(\forall \phi, v, m)\ belong(v, apply(\phi, m)) \Leftrightarrow$$
$$(belong(v, m) \vee added(v, apply(\phi, m))) \wedge (\neg deleted(v, apply(\phi, m))) \qquad (3)$$

3 Extending PVAM with an Operation Model

The primitive operations *add*, *delete*, and *modify* introduced in the previous section are not enough to capture and trace a SADP execution. Then, PVAM must be extended in terms of the suitable operations for this design domain. In order to identify the possible extensions, it is important to consider the large number of architecture description languages (ADLs). Each ADL embodies a particular approach to the specification and evolution of an architecture [2]. Therefore, a model to capture and trace SADPs must be enough flexible to enable the capture of particular operations carried out during a design process. To this end, PVAM is extended with an *operation* model where each relevant operation is specified in terms of the primitive operations. In addition operations previously defined in that domain can be used in their specification. The effects of these new operations are going to be expressed in terms of *added* and *deleted* predicates previously defined in Expressions 1 and 2.

Operations are associated to a *modelling concept* and are defined as an ordered set of operations (Fig. 2). Those operations can be *primitives* or *operations* defined at the domain where the operation is being defined. *Primitives* encapsulate the semantics defined by Expressions 1, 2 and 3. The execution of an *operation* generates one or more *results*, which can be a set of *versions*. Furthermore, *history* class is instantiated, linking the *predecessor* with the *successor versions*.

The operation definition is represented using the basic structure of the Abstract Syntax Kernel Metamodel for Expressions defined by the UML 2.0 OCL Specification [8]. To implement them, the well-known Command design pattern was used [9]. Therefore, a *command* abstract class is introduced in the *Operation* package illustrated in Fig. 2. An *operation* is defined as a *macro command* (*MacroCommand* class), a subclass of *command* that simply executes a sequence of commands, allowing string commands together. Therefore, when an operation is specified, it is necessary to define both the *arguments* and the *body* such operation will have. The commands that constitute its body are the other already defined commands, which are available for being used in the specification (primitives, loop, variable assignment, or other operations). Note that the *modelling concept* over which an operation is applied must be explicitly indicated.

Furthermore, there are other concrete classes that specialise the *command* class, and that can be part of a *macro command*. One of them is the *LoopCmd*, which represents a loop construct over a collection variable and has a body that is executed for each element in the collection. Another valid command is *VariableAssignment* that represents the assignment of a value to a variable of a given type.

As shown in Fig. 2, every *command* has one or more data typed *arguments*. *Arguments* are considered as a kind of *variable*. A *variable* can be also declared and used in the body of an *operation* and has a given type. The types described by the model are grouped by the abstract class *DataType*. *DataType* subclasses are *PrimitiveDataType*, *CollectionType*, and *ModellingConcept*. *PrimiteDataType* includes *Integer*, *Float*, *String* and *Boolean* types. *Collection* describes a list of elements of a particular given type that are ordered and have no duplicates and is parameterized with an element type. *ModellingConcept* is imported from *Domain*

Packet and enables specifying arguments that explicit the type of an expected object version to be added during the execution of an *add* primitive.

As regards *VariableAssignment*, it denotes the mapping between a *variable* and a *RunTimeValue*. This interface is not defined to specify operations. It is included to represent the run time values during the execution of an operation. *RunTimeValue* can be realized by different values like *literal*, *object version*, *modelling concept*, or *AttribValue* (value of an attribute of an object version, Fig. 1), depending on the variable type.

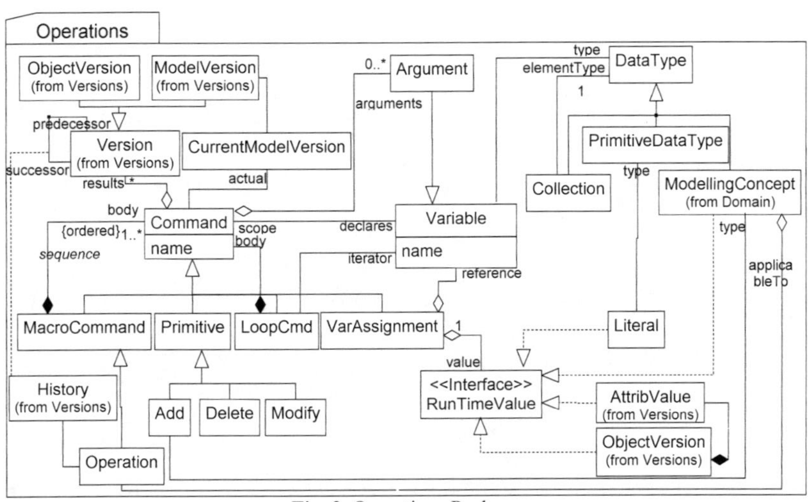

Fig. 2. Operations Package

4 Obtaining a Model for Capturing and Tracing Architecture Based Design Processes

With the aim of capturing the versions generated during a SADP, PVAM must be extended according to the particular design objects produced by that process. For this purpose, the Domain Package shown in Fig. 1 must be extended with concepts of the SADP domain. Furthermore, the different operations that are applied to the distinct design objects must be defined. This section defines such extension.

4.1 Products of SADP

As pointed out in the previous paragraph, it is necessary to have a model of the products of SADP. These products are taken from the Attribute-Driven Design Method (ADD) proposed at [3], and the architectural description language ACME [1]. The class diagram shown in Fig. 3 introduces these concepts and their relationships.

This model is implemented by the instantiation of the classes of *Domain package* (Fig. 1). The classes presented in Fig. 3 are going to be instances of *ModellingConcept* and their properties are going to be instances of *Attribute*. Finally, the relationships of Fig. 3 will be instantiated from *DomainRelationship* in *Domain package*.

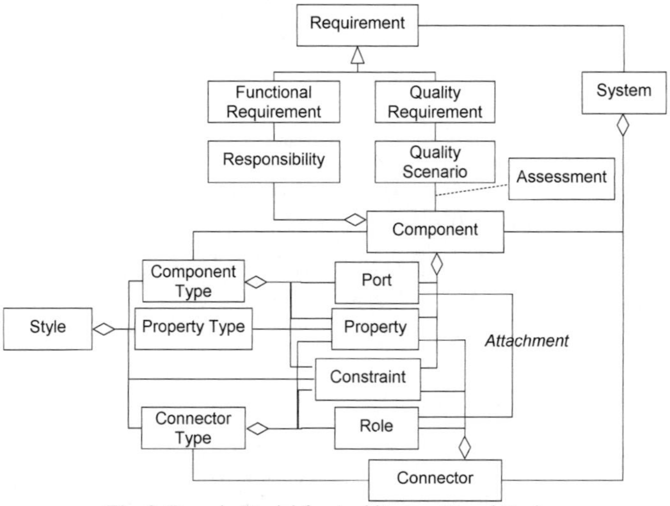

Fig. 3. Domain Model for Architecture Based Design

The ADD method is based on a recursive decomposition process where architectural patterns (or *styles*) are chosen at each stage to fulfil a set of *quality scenarios*. Then, *component* and *connector types* provided by the pattern are instantiated and functionality is allocated to them. The input to ADD is a set of requirements (*functional* and *quality requirements*). The *quality requirements* are expressed as a set of system specific *quality scenarios*, and the *functional requirements* are translated into a set of *responsibilities* [3]. Quality scenarios and responsibilities can be delegated to other components when the original component is refined. When the method iteration is finished, the designer verifies scenarios and set an *assessment*.

In ADD, the different model versions are represented by using various types of views. Only the component view is considered in the scope of this work in order to describe the architecture. Accordingly, ACME [1] has been chosen as the architectural description language. ACME defines a *component* as a computational element and data store of a system. A *component* may have multiple interfaces, each of which is termed *port*. The *connectors* represent interactions among *components* and have interfaces that are defined by a pair of *roles*. The *systems* comprise *components* and *connectors*, establishing *attachments* between *roles* and *ports*. In Fig. 3, the *attachment* concept is not considered as a *modelling concept* but as a relationship. Moreover, ACME proposes elements to document extra-structural properties of a system's architecture, as *Properties*. Furthermore, it is possible to attach *constrains* to design elements. With the aim of providing a more powerful language, ACME defines *component*, *connector*, and *properties type* building blocks. On the basis of these modelling concepts, it is possible to define *Families* or *Styles*. They are defined by a set of *property*, *component*, and *connector types* and a set of *constraints*.

4.2 Operations Specification

As it was outlined in Section 3, PVAM must be extended in terms of the suitable operations for the SADP domain, like the ones listed in Table 1. This operations range from the most basic to the most complex ones: i) *Basic*: operations that allow creating and deleting basic design objects (like *components* and *connectors*) (Fig. 4); ii) *Special*: more complex operations that involve object refinement or delegation (Fig. 5); iii) *Styles/Mechanisms application*: these operations generate a new set of design objects which have a configuration based on an architectural style; or even if they do not modify the model structure, they affect some design objects properties (Fig. 6).

Table 1. Possible Operations for the Software Architecture Design Domain

Operations

Basic Operations	
addComponent	deleteComponent
addConnector	deleteConnector
addFunctionalRequirement	deleteFunctionalRequirement
addPort	deletePort
addProperty	deleteProperty
addQualityRequirement	deleteQualityRequirement
addResponsibility	deleteResponsibility
addRole	deleteRole
addScenario	deleteScenario
addTypeComponent	deleteTypeComponent
addTypeConnector	deleteTypeConnector

Special Operations
refineComponent
refineResponsibility
delegateResponsibility
delegateScenario
verifyScenario

Styles/Mechanisms application
applyIntermediaryBlackboard
applyControlLoop
applyRuleEngine
applyClientServer
applyPoolOfConnections

Fig. 4 presents functional specifications for some of the basic operations defined in Table 1. These specifications are implemented as instances of the *Operation* model introduced in Fig. 2. The other operations are defined in a similar way, but they are not shown due to shortage of space. These operations are defined in terms of primitive operations as *add*(c), and non-primitive ones, as *addPort*(c, p), which is also defined in Fig. 4. For example, the *addComponent*(s, c, l_{Resps}, l_{Ports}) operation allows adding a component c to a system s. As seen in Fig. 4, this operation is carried out by a series of operations. First, a version of component c is added (*add(c)*). After that, a set of responsibilities (specified by list l_{Resp}) and ports (detailed by list l_{Ports}) are inserted. Finally, a relationship between the new component c and an existing system s is included. This last operation is performed by the *add* primitive operation (*add*(*rel*(s, c))).

Note that each of the aforementioned operations can be translated into a sequence of primitives operations *add, delete,* and/or *modify* that are applied to a previous model version, which results in a new model version. From this, it is possible to express these operations in terms of *added* and *deleted* predicates introduced in Expressions 1 and 2. For illustration purposes, let us consider again the *addComponent(s, c,* l_{Resps}, l_{Ports}*)* operation. If it is applied to a model version *m*, then a version of a component *c*, will belong to the successor model version (*apply(*ϕ*, m)*), as it is defined in Expression 4.

```
addComponent(s,c, lResps,lPorts)
  add(c)
  for each r in lResps
    addResponsibility(c,r)
  for each p in lPorts
    addPort(c, p)
  add(rel(s, c))

addPort(c, p)
  add(p)
  add(rel(c, p))
```

```
deleteComponent(s, c)
  lPorts = getPorts(c)
  for each p in lPorts
     deletePort(c, p)
  end for
  delete(rel(s,c))
  delete(c)

deletePort(c, p)
// port deletion implies
// deletion of connector
//attached to it
  deleteConnector(getConnector(
                     getRol(p)))
  delete(rel(c, p))
  delete(p)
```

Fig. 4. Specification of Basic Operations

$$(\forall\ \phi, s, c, l_{Resps}, l_{Ports}, m)\ addComponent(s, c, l_{Resps}, l_{Ports}) \in \phi \Rightarrow$$
$$added(c, apply(\phi, m)) \wedge added(rel(s,c), apply(\phi, m)) \wedge$$
$$((\forall\ r \in l_{Resps})\ added(r, apply(\phi, m)) \wedge added(rel(c,r), apply(\phi, m))) \wedge$$
$$((\forall\ p \in l_{Ports})\ added(p, apply(\phi, m)) \wedge added(rel(c,p), apply(\phi, m))) \qquad (4)$$

Similarly to Expression 4, the definition of new operations allows enlarging the set of operations. This can be done without modifying the successor state axiom (Expression 3).

The precondition for applying the *addComponent* operation is specified in Expression 5, where the *poss*(*op*, *m*) predicate expresses that an operation *op* is applicable to a given model version *m*.

$$(\forall\ s, c, l_{Resps}, l_{Ports}, m)\ poss(addComponent(s, c, l_{Resp}, l_{Ports}), m) \Leftrightarrow$$
$$belong(s, m) \wedge \neg\ belong(c, m) \wedge$$
$$(\forall\ r \in l_{Resps}) \neg\ belong(r, m) \wedge (\forall\ p \in l_{Ports}) \neg\ belong(p, m) \qquad (5)$$

Similarly to definition of basic operation, it is possible to define the special operations. Fig. 5 presents some examples. A functions with '?' symbol at the end indicates that it is an interactive function, thus, the user is asked about how to proceed. The *delegateResponsibility*(c_1, c_2) operation enables delegating a responsibility of component c_1 to component c_2. Thus, if a given responsibility is assigned to a component c_1 in a model version *m* and a *delegateResponsibility*(c_1, c_2)

operation is included in the sequence of operations applied to *m*, then the resulting model version shows that the responsibilities delegated to c_2 will not be assigned to c_1. An interactive function can be implemented as a special case of *VarAssignment* command. In a similar way, the operation *delegateScenario* proceeds. The *refineComponent*(c, l_{Comps}, l_{lPorts}, l_{lResps}, l_{Conns}, l_{lRoles}, l_{lAtts}) operation, another example of special operation (it is not include in Fig. 5), decomposes a component *c* into one or more components given by the list l_{Comps}. The ports and responsibilities of the new components are given by the lists l_{lPorts} and l_{lResps}, respectively. Furthermore, a set of connectors among the new components is added. These connectors are specified by l_{Conns} whose roles are given by the list l_{lRoles} and the attachments by the list l_{lAtts}.

```
delegateResponsibility(c1, c2)
lResps = getResponsibility(c1)
for each r in lResps
  if (delegate?(c2, r))
      delete(rel(c1, r))
      add(rel(c2, r))
  end if
 end for
```

```
delegateScenario(c1, c2)
  lScens = getScenario(c1)
  for each s in lScens
    if (delegate?(c2, s))
      delete(rel(c1, s))
      add(rel(c2, s))
    end if
  end for
```

Fig 5. Specification of Special Operations

```
applyControlLoop(c)
  s = getSystem(c)
  addComponent(s,{Diagnosis, TDiagnosis}, [P1,P6])
  addComponent(s,{PolicyManager, TPolicyManager}, [P2,P3])
  addComponent(s,{Reactor, TReactor}, [P4, P5])
  addConnector(s,{CDgnPMgr,TCDgnPMgr},[R1,R2],[P1,P2])
  addConnector(s,{CPMgrRct,TCPMgrRct},[R3,R4],[P3,P4])
  delegateScenario(c,Diagnosis)
  delegateScenario(c,PolicyManager)
  delegateScenario(c,Reactor)
  delegateResponsibility(c,Diagnosis)
  delegateResponsibility(c,PolicyManager)
  delegateResponsibility(c,Reactor)
  // Set mappings between previous connector and new components
  lp = getPorts(c)
  for each p in lp
    np = PortMap?(p) // Ask the user the port to map
    r = getRol(p)
    delete(rel(p, r))
    add(rel(np, r))
  end for
  deleteComponent(s, c)
```

Fig 6. Specification of applyControlLoop Operation

The operations that apply an architecture style refine a preexistent component with a new set of components and connectors that are instantiated from a preexisting style. They interact with the designer asking for the responsibilities and scenarios delegation, as well as connectors mapping between external components and refined components. An example of *applyStyle* operation is defined in Fig. 6. In this case, the *applyControlLoop* operation is specified. This style proceeds from the process control paradigm and defines the architecture to activate various monitoring policies when different events coming from sensors are produced [10]. The monitoring policies may in turn produce other events or actions in response to predefined situations. Note that this operation can be considered as a specialisation of *refineComponent* operation.

Here, the knowledge on how to proceed in the refinement is given by the control loop style and it is not given as argument. Therefore, a series of *addComponent* operations is performed. The *addComponent*(*s*, {*Diagnosis*, *TDiagnosis*}, [P_1,P_6]) operation indicates that a component and two ports must be created. The component is called *Diagnosis*, whose modelling concept is *TDiagnosis*, an instance of *TypeComponent* (see Fig. 3), and the ports are denominated P_1 and P_6.

5 Case Study: Monitoring System for an Industrial Process

The case study describes the design of a monitoring system for an industrial process (see Fig. 7). It is based on classical case studies included in other contributions [3, 4]. Monitoring activities are focused on the two core distillation columns: an extractive distillation column and a solvent stripping one, working together in a highly integrated manner. The system should monitor:

- control loops and temperature sensors, by continued acquisition of real-time process data, tracking set-point values, alarm conditions and outputs of valves, and comparing them with "normal" patterns behavior.
- process state, using real-time process data previously processed (e.g. averaged or integrated) in combination with expert knowledge in order to maintain process stability and performance
- flowrate sensors and validate material balances. This task should be carried out using cumulative values of flowrate data for sensor reconciliation and detection of solvent accumulation in the circuit.

In order to meet all these functional requirements, the system should be connected to input and output devices. Input devices allow the system to get the real time data from the process equipment and output devices are used by the system to inform the plant operator about process anomalies, like: solvent inventory buildup, sensor fault, abnormal process pattern, etc.

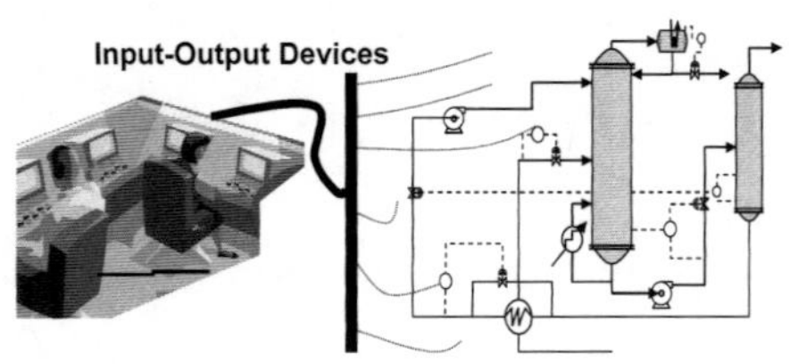

Fig 7. Monitoring System for an Industrial Process

The main functions considered in designing the monitoring system include: administration of users (process operator, plant supervisor, etc.) and permissions, configuration of input/output devices, priority-based event management, process diagnosis, specification of warning and process protective actions. In addition, all monitored information and process operator interactions should be recorded for future use. One of the key aspects of the system is its reactivity, which is how the system recognizes certain events and triggers corrective or warning messages. The model evolution for the proposed case is analyzed in the next sections. For reasons of space, some intermediate design versions will not be shown, and the associated rationale will not be detailed for all executed steps. Also, the last version obtained here can be further improved, applying additional operations. The goal of this case study is to show how the extended PVAM could support the SADP.

5.1 The First Model Version

The first model version resulting from the SADP is shown on Fig. 8. It is the result of applying a sequence of operations ϕ_1 to the initial model version. The initial model version is an empty one. The sequence ϕ_1 includes the *addSystem(MonitoringSystem)* operation, which adds a first object version of *MonitoringSystem* at the version level and a versionable object on repository. Also, a series of *addQualityRequirement* and *addFunctionalRequirement* operations are carried out when ϕ_1 is performed. These *functional* and *quality requirement*, are associated to *MonitoringSystem*. These are the quality scenarios to be considerated: i) a new type of sensor is attached, and the system has to get it without other modifications (*ScModif1*); ii) if an abnormal situation is detected by sensors, the system should start corrective or alarm actions in response to it in less than 1 second (*ScPerf1*); iii) a process operator should very easily configure 70% of system functionality (*ScModif2*); iv) the average time taken to provide a response to any kind of event should not be longer than 5 seconds (*ScPerf2*); v) new events can be defined, and they may change their priorities and carried information. These modifications should have minimal impact on the system, while the level of response of the system to events should be maintained (*ScPerfModif1*); vi) in order to incorporate personalization or deal with new devices, new configuration rules can be added, (*ScModif3*).

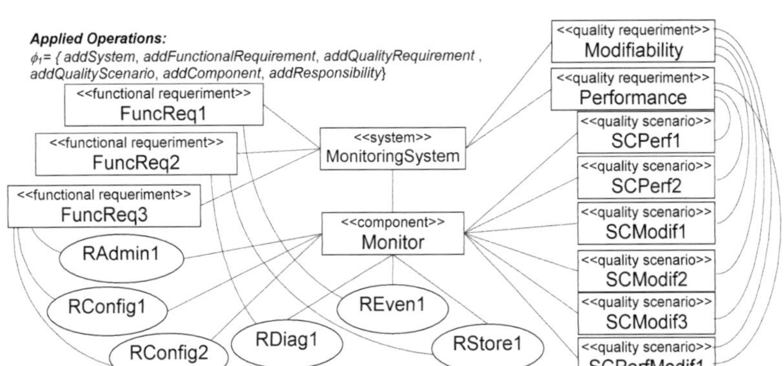

Fig. 8. A First Model Version resulting from the Software Architecture Design Process

Finally, the component *Monitor* is added by the *addComponent(MonitoringSystem, Monitor, {RAdmin1, RConfig1, REvent1, RDiag1, RConfig2, RStore1},{})* operation. The *responsibilities* are derived from the system *functional requirements* and *quality scenarios*. The *scenarios* are derived from the system *quality requirements*. The responsibilities associated to *Monitor* component are: Administration of users and permissions (*RAdmin1*); Input/Output devices configuration (*RConfig1*); Priority based event management (*REvent1*); Diagnostic (*RDiag1*); Warning and protective actions specification (*RConfig2*); Register and store every monitoring information for future uses (*RStore1*).

During the SADP these object versions can be modified, eliminated, refined (giving rise to new objects), delegated, etc., resulting in the various model versions.

5.2 An Intermediate Model Version i

In Fig. 9, we can observe the model version *i* where the main component *Monitor* belonging to a previous model version has been refined in four components: *Control&Diagnosis* (with responsibilities in priority based event management, protective actions execution, warning launch, input/output devices configuration); *UserInterface* (with responsibilities related to user interaction issues: set parameters values, show information, rule administration); *SensorActuatorLayer* (with responsibilities like sending out commands to actuators, receiving information from sensors); *Configuration*. The *responsibilities* are delegated to the new components, and *Monitor* component has been deleted.

From this model version, the designer can continue with the SADP, choosing refine *Control&Diagnosis* component by applying the *applyControlLoop* operation. This operation creates three new *components*: *Diagnosis*, *PolicyManager*, and *Reactor*. The *applyControlLoop* operation asks the necessary information for delegating responsibilities, and for reconnecting previous connections to the new configuration (see Fig. 6 for *applyControlLoop* specification).

Fig. 9 shows a partial view of the Version and Repository levels from which model version views can be inferred. This partial view is focus on the version of *Control&Diagnosis* evolution to a set of versions of components and connector due to *applyControlLoop* operation. This is traced by an instance of the history link (Fig. 1) which associates the previous versions with the successor versions.

Additionally, other operations were applied on the model version *i* to obtain the model version *i+1* that are not illustrated on Fig. 9 at version and repository levels. One of them arises due to the need of associating *PolicyManager* and *Configuration* components, so a new *connection* and their *roles* objects are added, applying *addConnector* operation. Using again operation *addConnector*, a new connection between *PolicyManager* and *SensorActuatorLayer* is added. It enables *PolicyManager* to receive information from and to send information to *SensorActuator* (see Fig. 9, *View of model version i+1*).

It is important to note that the proposed extension of PVAM enables applied operations on SADP´s products (Fig. 3) to be captured. For example, responsibilities are refined using *refineResponsibility* operation. The *RDiag1* responsibility (Fig. 9, *view of model version i*) was refined on the following responsibilities: i) listening notifications of situations coming from *SensorActuator* (*RDiag1.1*); ii) getting devices information (*RDiag1.2*); iii) probing device (*RDiag1.3*) (Fig. 9, *view of model version i + 1*).

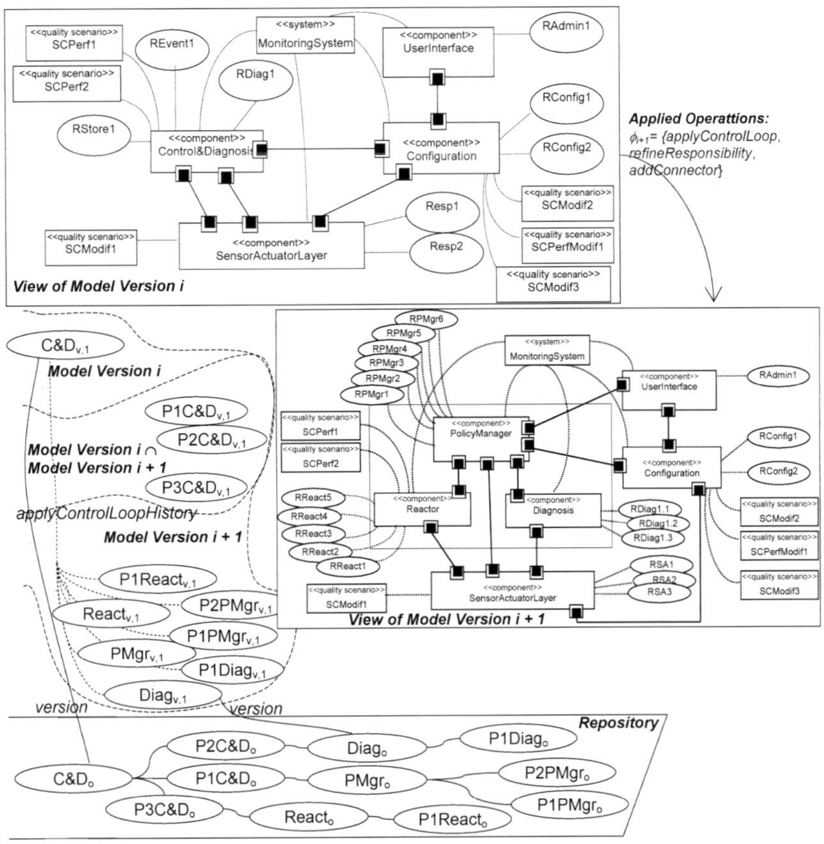

Fig. 9. Evolving the Products of the Software Architecture Design Process

6 Conclusions

The model proposed in this paper, an extension of PVAM, captures the operations that generate each design product during the SADP. Furthermore, it also offers an explicit mechanism to manage the different model versions generated during the SADP. Thus, it allows the tracing of the SADP and its resulting products, setting the grounds for learning and future reuse of the design process. This is a fundamental step towards the development of computational tools to support the SADP and to guide designers in the different activities of a design project.

Situation calculus, the formal background of the framework, let us represent the activities carried out during a SADP, and therefore, it enables the designer to get a better understanding of the information on how the various design objects (systems, components, connectors, functional requirements, quality requirements, quality scenarios, assessment, so on) have been obtained. Thus, the history of operations performed on versions of design objects can be kept. Also, this conceptual framework provides the foundations for the proposal of formal means for detecting potential conflicts.

The framework could incorporate extensions to the Domain package, integrated to the version administration model, defining others characteristics not included by ADD or ACME.

Furthermore, this contribution uses an operational perspective where design decisions can be modelled by means of design operations. This approach is employed in other contributions [3, 4]. The structure of the conceptual framework permits easily definition of specific design operations, like *applyControlLoop*, without modify the successor state axiom (Expression 3). Similarly, other design operations, like the ones defined by [3, 4], can be specified by instantiating the *Operation* model (Fig. 2).

Acknowledgments

This work has been supported by CONICET, Universidad Tecnológica Nacional and Agencia Nacional de Promoción Científica y Tecnológica (PICT 12628). Authors gratefully acknowledge help received from these institutions.

References

1. Garlan, D., Monroe, R. T., Wile, D.: Acme: Architectural Description of Component-Based Systems. Foundations of Component-Based Systems, Gary T. Leavens and Murali Sitaraman (eds.), Cambridge University Press (2000) 47-68
2. Medvidovic, N., Rosenblum, D., Redmiles, D., Robbins, J.: Modeling Software Architectures in the Unified Modeling Language, ACM Transaction on Software Engineering and Methodology, Vol. 11, N. 1, 2-57 (2002)
3. Bass, L., Clements, P., Kazman, R.: Software Architecture in Practice: Second Edition. Addison-Wesley (2003)
4. Diaz Pace, A.: A Planning-Based approach for the exploration of Quality-Driven design alternatives in Software Architectures. Tesis Doctoral, UNICEN, (2004)
5. Bachmann, F., Bass, L., Klein, M.: Preliminary Design of ArchE: A Software Architecture Design Assistant. Technical Report CMU/SEI-2003-TR-021 (2003)
6. Gonnet, S.: Un modelo integrado para la captura y administración del proceso de diseño. Tesis Doctoral, UNL, ISBN 987-43-9244-4 (2003)
7. Reiter, R.: Knowledge in Action: Logical Foundation for Describing and Implementing Dynamical Systems. The MIT Press (2001)
8. Object Management Group: OCL 2.0 Specification, 2005-06-06 (2005)
9. Gamma, E., Helm, R., Johnson, R., Vlissides, K.: Design Patterns. Elements of Reusable Object-Oriented Software, Addison-Wesley (1995)
10. Shaw, M.: Beyond Objects: A Software Design Paradigm Based on Process Control. Tech. Report CMU-CS-94-154, Carnegie Mellon University, Pittsburgh (1994)

Extensión de UML 2.0 para especificar Requisitos de Seguridad en Procesos de Negocios

Alfonso Rodríguez[1], Eduardo Fernández-Medina[2], Mario Piattini[2]

[1] Universidad del Bio Bio, Departamento de Auditoría e Informática,
La Castilla S/N, Chillán, Chile.
alfonso@ubiobio.cl
[2] Grupo ALARCOS
Departamento de Tecnologías y Sistemas de Información
Centro Mixto de Investigación y Desarrollo de Software UCLM-Soluziona
Universidad de Castilla-La Mancha
Paseo de la Universidad 4 – 13071, Ciudad Real, España.
{Eduardo.FdezMedina, Mario.Piattini}@uclm.es

Resumen. Los procesos de negocios tienen cada vez mayor importancia para las empresas ya que a través de ellos es posible obtener la flexibilidad que les permite optimizar y asegurar la calidad de sus productos y/o servicios. También la tienen para los desarrolladores de software debido a que es posible capturar desde allí los requisitos necesarios para el diseño y la creación del software. Paralelamente, las organizaciones se han abierto hacia sus clientes, internos y externos, lo que implica una mayor vulnerabilidad. A pesar de todo, la seguridad es un aspecto que ha sido escasamente tratado en el modelado de procesos de negocios. En este artículo proponemos una extensión que permite especificar requisitos de seguridad en el modelado de procesos de negocios a través de los diagramas de actividad de UML 2.0.

1 Introducción

Los procesos de negocios constituyen el centro de atención de paradigmas en el área de negocios y gestión tan importantes como la reingeniería de procesos de negocios [10] y la gestión de procesos de negocios [27]. Se definen como un conjunto de procedimientos o actividades que llevan a cabo, colectivamente, los objetivos o políticas del negocio [28]. Éstos se encuentran bastante difundidos ya que han resultado ser una buena respuesta a la complejidad del entorno, la velocidad con que se requieren nuevos productos y el creciente número de actores involucrados en las actividades cotidianas de una organización.

Por su parte, la introducción del comercio electrónico, con el consecuente uso intensivo de comunicaciones y tecnologías de información, propicia escenarios en que las empresas junto con ampliar sus negocios, también aumentan su vulnerabilidad. La consecuencia más inmediata es que, dado el creciente número de ataques sobre los sistemas, es altamente probable que tarde o temprano algún intruso tenga éxito [21]. Esta violación de la seguridad causa pérdidas en las organizaciones, por lo que es necesario proteger sus computadores y sus sistemas de la mejor forma posible. Esto no significa seguridad absoluta, sino un razonable alto nivel de seguridad en relación a las limitaciones que se tienen [29].

Aunque se reconoce la importancia de la seguridad, ésta ha sido a menudo descuidada en el modelado de procesos de negocios, ya que usualmente se concentran en el modelado del proceso propiamente dicho [1]. Esto se debe a que el experto en el dominio del proceso de negocios no es un especialista en seguridad [11]. Tampoco los ingenieros de requisitos están entrenados del todo en seguridad y los pocos que han sido entrenados, sólo tienen una idea general de los mecanismos de la arquitectura de seguridad, tales como claves de acceso y encriptación, en lugar de los requisitos reales de seguridad [8].

Si consideramos que una especificación de requisitos es un proceso de facilitación de la comunicación requerida entre los diferentes interesados [18] y que un proceso de negocios es el punto de partida para el desarrollo del software puesto que allí se definen los requisitos para el diseño y desarrollo [13], resulta más o menos evidente que conviene capturar, en ese punto, requisitos de seguridad. Por otra parte, existen estudios empíricos que muestran que es común que los usuarios finales sean capaces de expresar sus necesidades de seguridad en ese nivel [15]. Entonces el problema será abordado considerando *qué* requisitos de seguridad pueden ser expresados en el dominio del negocio y *cuál* es la manera en que pueden ser representados.

Para el modelado de proceso de negocios existen diversos lenguajes y notaciones siendo BPMN (Business Process Modeling Notation) y UML (Unified Modeling Language) los principales estándares [17]. UML 2.0 tiene, en los diagramas de actividad, su cambio más importante respecto de las versiones previas [25]. Esto puede resumirse en la redefinición de modelo de actividad en la nueva versión de UML para permitir un modelado intuitivo de los flujos y la integración de éstos con los modelos de acción de UML 1.5 [2].

Nuestro trabajo considera una extensión de UML 2.0 que permite incorporar los requisitos de seguridad desde la perspectiva de analista de negocios cuando éste especifica procesos de negocios utilizando diagramas de actividad. El uso de UML como lenguaje de modelado, robusto y ampliamente aceptado, permite garantizar el uso del estándar MOF (Meta Object Facility) y la definición de arquitecturas dirigidas por modelos (MDA, Model Driven Architecture).

Este artículo se encuentra organizado de la siguiente manera; en la sección 2 se presenta la forma en que se ha especificado la seguridad en el modelado de procesos de negocios, en la sección 3 se muestran los aspectos más importantes de los diagramas de actividad en UML 2.0. En la sección 4 se especifica una extensión de UML 2.0 que considera la representación de requisitos de seguridad en los diagramas de actividad y finalmente en la sección 5 se presenta un ejemplo que permite mostrar nuestra propuesta.

2 Especificación de seguridad en Procesos de negocios

A pesar de la importancia que supone la seguridad para los procesos de negocios, hemos podido detectar dos problemas. El primero de ellos está relacionado con el modelado propiamente dicho, el cual ha sido inadecuado, ya que generalmente quienes especifican los requisitos de seguridad son ingenieros de requisitos que han tendido, accidentalmente, a reemplazarlos por restricciones específicas de arquitectura [8]. Y en segundo lugar, y lo que en la práctica ha resultado ser lo más común, la seguridad ha sido integrada en forma tardía, a menudo durante la implementación real del proceso de manera ad-hoc [1], durante la fase de administración del sistema [14] o simplemente considerada como un servicio externo que será suministrado por un tercero [16]. Esto se explica, en parte, porque, a pesar de ser la seguridad un aspecto transversal que afecta tempranamente a los componentes de una aplicación, no es bien entendida y además hay carencia de herramientas que soporten la ingeniería de seguridad [14].

Una manera de modelar la seguridad que considera diversas perspectivas es la que se presenta en [11]. Ellos consideran las perspectivas: *Estática,* sobre la seguridad de la información procesada, *Funcional,* sobre los procesos del sistema, *Dinámica,* sobre los requisitos de seguridad desde el ciclo de vida de los objetos involucrados en el proceso de negocio, *Organizacional,* usada para relacionar las responsabilidades de los actores con los procesos de negocios y de *Procesos de Negocios*, la que corresponde a una visión integrada de todas las perspectivas con un alto grado de abstracción.

En cuanto a los requisitos, si bien los requisitos funcionales de seguridad tienden a variar entre aplicaciones de diverso tipo, no se puede decir lo mismo de los requisitos de seguridad, ya que cualquier aplicación en un alto nivel de abstracción tendrá la misma clase de valoración y potencialmente vulnerabilidad de sus activos [9]. De manera que, es posible establecer que los requisitos de seguridad, que se pueden especificar en un proceso de negocios, sean del mismo tipo para todas las organizaciones, debido a que en este nivel no se está pensando en la implementación.

Los trabajos que se relacionan con especificaciones de seguridad por parte de los expertos en el dominio del negocio son; *(i)* escasos [1][11][15], *(ii)* se orientan a la seguridad en la transacción [23], *(iii)* apuntan directamente a los sistemas de información en general [26] o *(iv)* están pensados para ingenieros de seguridad e ingenieros de software [16].

Los beneficios de representar tempranamente requisitos, en este caso de seguridad, repercuten favorablemente en la calidad del proceso de negocios, ya que le otorga mayor expresividad y mejora la calidad del software pues considera características que, de otro modo, tendrían que ser incorporadas en forma tardía, por lo que se ahorra en costes de mantenimiento y en el coste total del proyecto.

Para modelar requisitos de seguridad en procesos de negocios creemos que hay que tener presente dos aspectos importantes. Primero, quien modela el proceso es un experto en el dominio del negocio y que por lo tanto tiene una idea de seguridad exenta de tecnicismo y perturbaciones propias de quien está pensando en la implementación o en soluciones tecnológicas. Y segundo, que por la misma razón anterior, hay que considerar la parte de seguridad que esté más consensuada a nivel de usuarios no especialistas y cuyo significado y representación sea más o menos estándar. La representación de requisitos de seguridad usando BPMN, la notación propuesta por BPMI (Business Process Management Initiative), fue explorada en [22]. Se consideraron requisitos de seguridad que resultaran asimilables de manera sencilla por los analistas del negocio y que a su vez tuvieran un significado claro para los expertos en seguridad. Ahora, con los diagramas de actividad de UML 2.0, que permiten una mayor expresividad para los analistas de negocios o modeladores más cercanos al negocio, exploraremos la posibilidad de incorporar los requisitos de seguridad usando este lenguaje.

3 Diagramas de actividad en UML 2.0

Uno de los cambios más importante en la nueva versión de UML ha sido sobre los diagramas de actividad [25]. En las versiones previas a UML 2.0, en relación al modelado de actividades, se ha restringido la expresividad y confundido a los usuarios que no utilizan la orientación a objetos como enfoque para el modelado. Esta deficiencia de las versiones de UML 1.x ha sido considerada en la nueva versión de manera que es posible soportar el modelado de flujos a través de una amplia variedad de dominios [2]. Las actividades han sido rediseñadas para usar una semántica como la de las redes de Petri en vez de la máquinas de estado. Entre otros beneficios esto amplía el número de flujos que pueden ser modelados, especialmente los que tienen flujos paralelos [19].

UML 2.0 se divide en especificaciones estructurales y de comportamiento, con lo que permite el modelado de los aspectos estáticos y dinámicos de un sistema. Los modelos de comportamiento especifican cómo los aspectos estructurales de un sistema cambian en el tiempo. UML tiene tres modelos de comportamiento: actividades, máquinas de estado e interacciones. Las actividades se enfocan a representar secuencias, condiciones y entradas y salidas para invocar otros comportamientos; las máquinas de estado muestran cómo los eventos causan cambios en los estados de objetos e invocan otros comportamientos y los modelos de interacción describen los mensajes que pasan entre objetos que causan la inacción de otros comportamientos [3].

Los diagramas de actividad son los elementos de UML 2.0 que se usan para representar procesos de negocios y flujos de trabajos (workflows) [12][20]. Para ello, el modelamiento de las actividades pone énfasis en la secuencia y en las condiciones para la coordinación del comportamiento de bajo nivel tanto como de la propia clasificación de esos comportamientos. Esos son comúnmente llamados modelos de flujos de control y flujos de objetos. Una actividad especifica la coordinación de ejecución de una secuencia de unidades subordinadas cuyos elementos individuales son acciones. Cada acción puede ser ejecutada cero, una o más veces en cada ejecución de la actividad. Las acciones pueden ser ocurrencias de funciones primitivas como funciones matemáticas, invocaciones a comportamiento, como actividades, acciones de comunicación, como el envío de señales o manipulación de objetos como lectura o escritura de atributos o asociaciones [19].

La notación gráfica de una actividad, aunque opcional ya que puede ser reemplazada por una notación textual [19], es una combinación de nodos y conectores que permiten formar un flujo completo. Se consideran específicamente nodos de acción, control y objetos. Estos nodos son conectados por flujos de control y de objeto [2]. En la Figura 1 se muestra un proceso de negocios relacionado con el procesamiento de un orden de pago.

Un detalle completo de los símbolos utilizados para la notación gráfica puede encontrarse en [19] (pp: 402-406) y en [2][3][4][5][6][7].

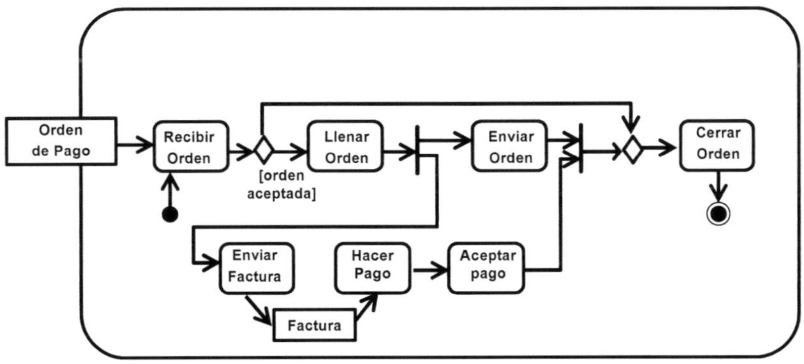

Figura 1: Proceso de negocios para el pago de una factura

4 Extensión de UML 2.0 para representar requisitos de seguridad

Las extensiones en UML 2.0 se hacen utilizando profiles. Este mecanismo permite extender los metamodelos existentes para adaptarlos con diferentes propósitos. Ello incluye la capacidad de ajustar el metamodelo a diferentes plataformas (por ejemplo: J2EE o .NET) o a distintos dominios (por ejemplo: tiempo real o modelado de proceso de negocios). Este mecanismo es consistente con Meta Object Facility de OMG [19].

Un Profile está compuesto por estereotipos, restricciones y valores etiquetados. El *estereotipo* es un elemento del modelo definido mediante su nombre y la clase base a la que pertenece, la que, normalmente, es una meta-clase de UML. Las *restricciones* se aplican al estereotipo con el objeto de indicar limitaciones. Por ejemplo, expresar pre o post condiciones, invariantes, etc. Las restricciones se pueden expresar en lenguaje natural, de programación o a través de OCL (Object Constraint Language). Los *valores etiquetados* son meta-atributos adicionales que se asignan al estereotipo y son especificados como el par nombre-valor.

Los trabajos relacionados con extensiones de UML 2.0 y procesos de negocios están referidos a aspectos propios del negocio, tales como; metas, clientes, tipos de procesos de negocio y productos o servicios [13], almacenes de datos (data warehouse) y su relación con las estructuras dinámicas de los procesos de negocios, indicando dónde y cómo los procesos de negocios usan un entorno de almacenes de datos [24] o agregan semántica a las actividades considerando aspectos organizaciones que permitan expresar ciertas restricciones de recursos cuando se lleva a cabo una actividad [12]. Todos ellos extienden UML con profiles agregando estereotipos al metamodelo.

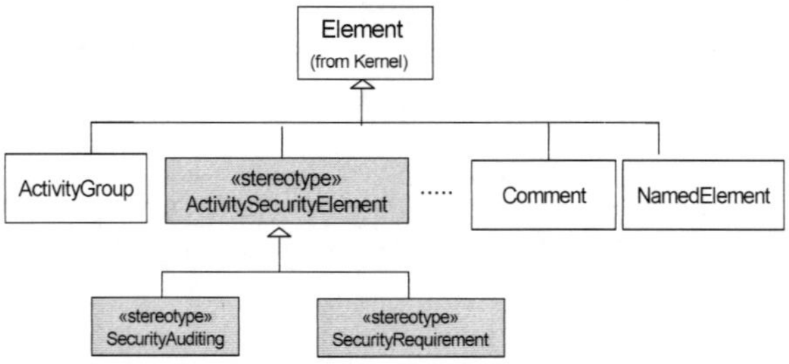

Figura 2: Estereotipo de elemento de seguridad.

Nuestra propuesta otorga, a los analistas del negocio, la posibilidad de expresar requisitos de seguridad cuando se construyen los diagramas de actividad que representan un determinado procesos de negocios. Posteriormente, estos requisitos serán transformados por los especialistas en seguridad en especificaciones que incluyan el detalle técnico necesario para su implementación. En este trabajo abordaremos sólo la primera parte. Para ello hemos extendido el metamodelo de UML 2.0 con un estereotipo que permita definir elementos de seguridad (ver Figura 2).

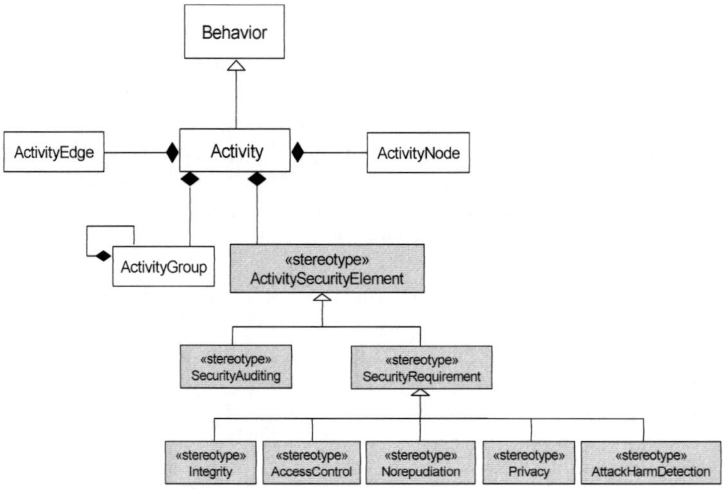

Figura 3: Relación de composición de los elementos de seguridad que pueden ser especificados para una actividad

Los elementos de seguridad serán usados sólo en los diagramas de actividad. El estereotipo «*ActivitySecurityElement*» corresponde a una clase abstracta creada para contener especificaciones de seguridad del tipo auditoría de seguridad y/o requisitos de seguridad. No tiene notación propia ya que será definida en las subclases.

El estereotipo «*ActivitySecurityElement*» tiene una relación de composición con la clase Activity (ver Figura 3). Ello permite relacionar los requisitos de seguridad con aquellos del diagrama de actividad especificados en la Tabla 1.

	Elementos diagrama de actividad UML 2.0						
Requisitos de seguridad	InterruptibleActivityRegion	ActivityPartition	Activity	Action	ObjectFlow	ControlFlow	DataStore
Integridad	✓	✓			✓		✓
Control de acceso	✓	✓	✓				
No repudio						✓	
Privacidad		✓					
Detección de ataques	✓	✓	✓	✓	✓		

Tabla 1: Requisitos de seguridad en los elementos del diagrama de actividad de UML 2.0

El estereotipo «*ActivitySecurityRequirement*» ha sido extendido con los estereotipos «*SecurityAuditing*» y «*SecurityRequirement*» (ver Tabla 2). Las especificaciones de «*SecurityAuditing*» son complementarias con las de «*SecurityRequirement*», esto es, podrán ser indicadas sólo si se ha indicado, para un mismo elemento del diagrama de actividad, alguno de los requisitos de seguridad que especializan el estereotipo «*SecurityRequirement*».

La descripción de cada estereotipo se muestra en las tablas 2 y 3. En cada una de ellas se indica el nombre de la clase (estereotipo), la clase base se la cual proviene, una descripción del significado de la clase, las restricciones, valores etiquetados y la notación.

Nombre	**ActivitySecurityElement**	
Clase Base	Element (from Kernel)	
Descripción	Es una clase abstracta que contiene especificaciones de auditoría y/o requisitos de seguridad	
Restricciones	No tiene	
Valores Etiquetados	No tiene	
Nombre	**SecurityAuditing**	**Notación** 
Clase Base	ActivitySecurityElement	
Descripción	Es un elemento relacionado con la especificación de seguridad en procesos de negocios en que se indica la necesidad de registrar los eventos relacionados con especificaciones de requisitos de seguridad con el propósito de ser auditados posteriormente.	
Restricciones	La especificación de este elemento sólo tiene sentido si se ha especificado al menos un SecurityRequirement. Puede complementarse con Comment	
Valores Etiquetados	No tiene	
Nombre	**SecurityRequirement**	**Notación** 
Clase Base	ActivitySecurityElement	
Descripción	Es un elemento que permite contener especificaciones de requisitos seguridad en procesos de negocios. Debe ser especializado para indicar claramente el tipo de seguridad requerida.	
Restricciones	Se debe especificar en alguna de sus especializaciones el tipo de seguridad requerida. Esa especificación debe estar conforme a las restricciones mostradas en la Tabla 1	
Valores Etiquetados	No tiene	

Tabla 2: Descripción de la clase «*ActivitySecurityElement*» y subclases

Los requisitos de seguridad derivados del estereotipo «*SecurityRequirement*» complementarán la notación propuesta agregándole letras que permitan identificar el tipo de requisito que se especifica. Cualquiera de los requisitos de seguridad derivados de «*SecurityRequirement*» puede ser especificado en forma complementaria, esto es, para un mismo elemento de un diagrama de actividad puede especificarse, por ejemplo, control de acceso y detección de ataques, teniendo en cuenta las restricciones mostradas en la Tabla 1. No se ha especificado valores etiquetados para los estereotipos derivados de «*SecurityRequirement*», no obstante, es posible agregar como comentarios (Comment) un nivel abstracto de representación de la criticidad de este requisito utilizando los conceptos alto/medio/bajo.

Nombre	**Integrity**	
Clase Base	SecurityRequirement	**Notación**
Descripción	Establece el grado en que los componentes (datos, hardware, personal y software) son protegidos de ser corrompidos en forma intencional y no autorizada.	
Restricciones	Sólo puede ser especificado en los elementos del diagrama en que se indica en la Tabla 1	
Nombre	**AccessControl**	
Clase Base	SecurityRequirement	**Notación**
Descripción	Establece la necesidad de definir y/o intensificar los mecanismos de control de acceso para restringir el acceso a determinados componentes en un diagrama de actividad.	
Restricciones	Sólo puede ser especificado en los elementos del diagrama en que se indica en la Tabla 1	
Nombre	**Norepudiation**	
Clase Base	SecurityRequirement	**Notación**
Descripción	Establece la necesidad de impedir la negación de cualquier aspecto de la interacción.	
Restricciones	Sólo puede ser especificado en los elementos del diagrama en que se indica en la Tabla 1	
Nombre	**Privacy**	
Clase Base	SecurityRequirement	**Notación**
Descripción	Indica el grado en que las partes no autorizadas están impedidos de obtener información sensible	
Restricciones	Sólo puede ser especificado en los elementos del diagrama en que se indica en la Tabla 1	
Nombre	**AttackHarmDetection**	
Clase Base	SecurityRequirement	**Notación**
Descripción	Indica el grado en que se detecta, registra y notifica el intento o éxito de ataques o daños	
Restricciones	Sólo puede ser especificado en los elementos del diagrama en que se indica en la Tabla 1	

Tabla 3: Subclases de *«SecurityRequirement»*

5 Ejemplo

La incorporación de requisitos de seguridad puede verse en la Figura 4. Se describe el proceso de negocios para el pago de una factura, similar al descrito en la Figura 1. Aquí junto con los requisitos de seguridad se han agrupado las acciones y decisiones relacionadas con el proceso en particiones (ActivityPartition). El analista de negocios ha especificado *No Repudio* sobre el flujo de control que traspasa el control desde la acción "Enviar Factura" hacia la acción "Hacer Pago" con la intención impedir la negación de recepción de la Factura. También se ha especificado *Integridad* sobre el almacén de datos "Factura" y *Control de Acceso* sobre la partición "Cliente". Adicionalmente se especificó *Auditoría de Seguridad*, con lo que se quiere decir que todos los requisitos de seguridad especificados sobre la partición "Cliente" deben quedar registrados para ser auditados posteriormente. También, se ha especificado *Detección de Ataques* sobre la acción "Cerrar Orden".

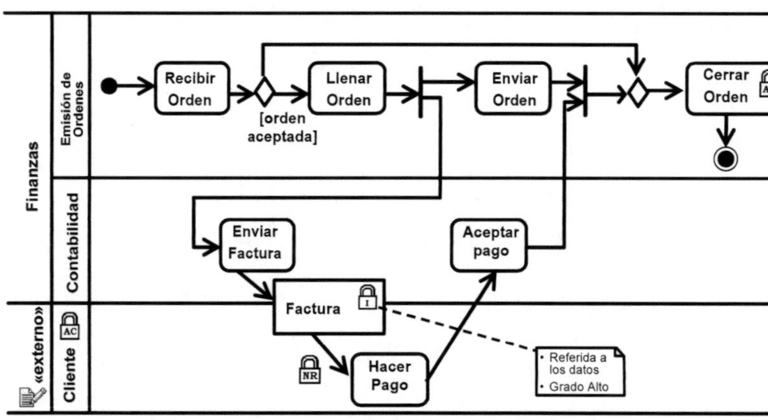

Figura 4: Descripción de proceso de negocios que incluye requisitos de seguridad en las particiones de actividad

6 Conclusiones

La estrecha relación que existe entre el desempeño de las empresas y la calidad de sus procesos de negocios hace que las primeras pongan mayor atención en la forma en que los procesos de negocios son modelados. Paralelamente se han ido mejorando los lenguajes de modelado permitiendo capturar con mayor precisión la esencia del negocio. Sin embargo, la seguridad es un aspecto del negocio que ha sido escasamente abordado en el modelado de procesos de negocios. Generalmente se ha privilegiado el proceso propiamente dicho y su implementación tecnológica. En nuestro trabajo hemos presentado una extensión de UML 2.0 que permite incorporar requisitos de seguridad en el modelado de procesos de negocios ampliando la capacidad expresiva de los diagramas de actividad. Los trabajos futuros se deben orientar a enriquecer la especificación de requisitos de seguridad, incorporándoles el punto de vista del experto en seguridad, para hacer posible la implementación.

Agradecimientos

Esta investigación es parte de los proyectos DIMENSIONS (PBC-05-012-1), parcialmente financiado por el FEDER y por la Consejería de Educación y Ciencia de la Junta de Comunidades de Castilla-La Mancha, CALIPO (TIC2003-07804-C05-03) y RETISTIC (TIC2002-12487-E) concedidos por la "Dirección General de Investigación del Ministerio de Ciencia y Tecnología" (España).

Referencias

1. Backes, M., Pfitzmann, B. and Waider, M.; *Security in Business Process Engineering*, International Conference on Business Process Management. Vol. 2678, LNCS. Eindhoven, The Netherlands. (2003). pp:168-183.
2. Bock, C.; *UML 2 Activity and Action Models*, Journal of Object Technology. Vol. 2 (4), July-August. (2003). pp:43-53.
3. Bock, C.; *UML 2 Activity and Action Models, Part 2: Actions*, Journal of Object Technology. Vol. 2 (5), September-October. (2003). pp:41-56.
4. Bock, C.; *UML 2 Activity and Action Models, Part 3: Control Nodes*, Journal of Object Technology. Vol. 2 (6), November-December. (2003). pp:7-23.
5. Bock, C.; *UML 2 Activity and Action Models, Part 4: Object Nodes*, Journal of Object Technology. Vol. 3 (1), January-February. (2004). pp:27-41.
6. Bock, C.; *UML 2 Activity and Action Models, Part 5: Partitions*, Journal of Object Technology. Vol. 3 (7), July-August. (2004). pp:37-56.
7. Bock, C.; *UML 2 Activity and Action Models, Part 6: Structured Activities*, Journal of Object Technology. Vol. 4 (4), May-June. (2005). pp:43-66.
8. Firesmith, D.; *Engineering Security Requirements*, Journal of Object Technology. Vol. 2 (1), January-February. (2003). pp:53-68.
9. Firesmith, D.; *Specifying Reusable Security Requirements*, Journal of Object Technology. Vol. 3 (1), January-February. (2004). pp:61-75.
10. Grant, D.; *A wider view of business process reengineering*, Communications of the ACM (CACM). Vol. 45 (2). (2002). pp:85-90.
11. Herrmann, G. and Pernul, G.; *Viewing Business Process Security from Different Perspectives*, 11th International Bled Electronic Commerce Conference "Electronic Commerce in the Information Society". Slovenia. (1998). pp:89-103.
12. Kalnins, A., Barzdins, J. and Celms, E.; *UML Business Modeling Profile*, Thirteenth International Conference on Information Systems Development, Advances in Theory, Practice and Education. Vilnius, Lithuania. (2004). pp:182-194.
13. List, B. and Korherr, B.; *A UML 2 Profile for Business Process Modelling*, Proceedings of the 1st International Workshop on Best Practices of UML (BP-UML 2005) at the 24th International Conference on Conceptual Modeling (ER 2005). Klagenfurt, Austria. (2005).

14. Lodderstedt, T., Basin, D. and Doser, J.; *SecureUML: A UML-Based Modeling Language for Model-Driven Security*, UML 2002 - The Unified Modeling Language, 5th International Conference. Vol. 2460. Dresden, Germany. (2002). pp:426-441.
15. Maña, A., Montenegro, J. A., Rudolph, C. and Vivas, J. L.; *A business process-driven approach to security engineering*, 14th. International Workshop on Database and Expert Systems Applications (DEXA). Prague, Czech Republic. (2003). pp:477-481.
16. Maña, A., Ray, D., Sánchez, F. and Yagüe, M. I.; *Integrando la Ingeniería de Seguridad en un Proceso de Ingeniería Software*, Actas de la VIII Reunión Española de Criptología y Seguridad de la Información, RECSI'04. Leganés, Madrid. España. (2004). pp:33-41.
17. Mega; *Business process Modeling and Standardization.* In http://www.bpmg.org/downloads/Articles/Article-MEGA-BusinessProcessModeling&StandardizationEN.pdf. (2004).
18. Nuseibeh, B. and Easterbrook, S. M.; *Requirements Engineering: A Roadmap*, ICSE 2000, 22nd International Conference on Software Engineering, Future of Software Engineering Track. Limerick Ireland. ACM. (2000). pp:35-46.
19. Object Management Group; *Unified Modeling Language: Superstructure*, version 2.0, formal/05-07-04. In http://www.omg.org/docs/formal/05-07-04.pdf. (2005).
20. Podeswa, H., *B.O.O.M.: Business Object-Oriented Modeling for Business Analysts*, Thomson Course Technology Incorporated, (2005). 401 p.
21. Quirchmayr, G.; *Survivability and Business Continuity Management*, ACSW Frontiers 2004 Workshops: The Australasian Information Security Workshop (AISW2004), The Australasian Workshop on Data Mining and Web Intelligence (DMWI2004), and The Australasian Workshop on Software Internationalisation (AWSI2004). Dunedin, New Zealand. (2004). pp:3-6.
22. Rodríguez, A., Fernández-Medina, E. and Piattini, M.; *Towards an integration of Security Requirements into Business Process Modeling*, Security In Information Systems, Proceedings of the Third International Workshop on Security In Information Systems, WOSIS 2005, In conjunction with ICEIS 2005. Miami, USA. (2005). pp:287-297.
23. Röhm, A. W., Herrmann, G. and Pernul, G.; *A Language for Modelling Secure Business Transactions*, Proceedings 15th. Annual Computer Security Applications Conference. Computer Society Press., Phoenix, Arizona. (1999). pp:22-31.
24. Stefanov, V., List, B. and Korherr, B.; *Extending UML 2 Activity Diagrams with Business Intelligence Objects*, Proceedings of the 7th International Conference on Data Warhousing and Knowledge Discovery (DaWaK2005). Copenhagen, Denmark. (2005).
25. Störrle, H.; *Semantics and Verification of Data Flow in UML 2.0 Activities*, Electronic Notes in Theoretical Computer Science. Vol. 127 (4). (2005). pp:35-52.
26. Tryfonas, T. and Kiountouzis, E. A.; *Perceptions of Security Contributing to the Implementation of Secure IS*, Security and Privacy in the Age of Uncertainty, IFIP TC11 18th International Conference on Information Security (SEC2003). Vol. 250. Athens, Greece. (2003). pp:313-324.
27. W.M.P. van der Aalst, Hofstede, A. H. M. t. and Weske, M.; *Business Process Management: A Survey*, International Conference on Business Process Management (BPM 2003). Volume 2678 (LNCS). Eindhoven, The Netherlands. (2003). pp:1-12.
28. WfMC, *Workflow Management Coalition: Terminology & Glossary.*, (1999). 65 p.
29. Zuccato, A.; *Holistic security requirement engineering for electronic commerce*, Computers & Security. Vol. 23 (1). (2004). pp:63-76.

This page intentionally left blank.

Avaliação da Qualidade de Documentos de Requisitos Orientado a Aspectos

Ricardo Argenton Ramos[1] , André Carvalho[1], Cleviton Monteiro[1], Carla Silva[1], *Jaelson Castro[1],[2], *Fernanda Alencar[3], Ricardo Afonso[4]

[1]Centro de Informática
Universidade Federal de Pernambuco – UFPE
Av. Prof. Luiz Freire s/n, Recife PE, Brasil
50732-970, +55 81 212618430
{rar2, allc, cvfm,ctlls, jbc}@cin.ufpe.br

[2]ITC- Istituto Trentino di Cultura
IRST -Instituto per la Ricerca Scientifica e Tecnologica,
Trento-Povo, Italy
jaelson@itc.it

[3]Departamento de Eletrônica e Sistemas Universidade Federal de Pernambuco – UFPE
Av. Prof. Luiz Freire s/n, Recife PE, Brasil
50732-970, +55 81 2126 8995
fmra@ufpe.br

[4]Grupo de Tecnologias da Informação em Saúde (TIS) Núcleo de Tele-Saúde – NUTES - Hospital das Clínicas, Av. Prof. Moraes Rego, s/n, Cidade Universitária, Recife-PE, Brasil
50.670-420, telefone: +55 81 2126-3903.
ricardo.afonso@nutes.ufpe.br

Resumo. Pesquisas promissoras na fase de requisitos utilizando a orientação a aspectos têm como propósito a utilização de técnicas que possibilitam separar e, posteriormente, compor os interesses que estão espalhados e entrelaçados no documento de requisitos. Novos fatores que surgem nesses documentos de requisito, tais como a separação de interesses, o tamanho e o acoplamento ainda não são avaliados qualitativamente, por falta de métricas. Este artigo apresenta um conjunto de métricas abstratas, que com o auxílio de diretrizes, podem ser instanciadas para medir um documento de requisitos orientado a aspectos que foi elaborado segundo qualquer abordagem. Além disso, é proposto um processo de medição.

Abstract. Recent proposals have looked at the requirements stage, using the aspect oriented programming, trying to separate and after to compose the concerns that are spread and tangled in the requirement document. New factors appear in these requirements documents, such as, crosscutting concerns, size and coupling are not qualitative evaluated, because there are not these metrics. This paper shows a set of abstract metrics that, with the help of guidelines, can be applied to measure an aspect oriented requirements document developed by any approach. Also a measurement process is proposed.

---

* Atualmente afastado da UFPE

1 Introdução

O uso inadequado de processos de desenvolvimento de software gera grandes custos nas fases de manutenção deste software em desenvolvimento. É do conhecimento geral [19], que o custo da correção de erros já na fase de projeto é cerca de três a seis vezes mais alto do que na fase de definição de requisitos. Todavia, esse custo aumenta ainda mais quando a correção de erros é realizada em fases mais avançadas no processo de desenvolvimento.

O desenvolvimento de software orientado a aspectos (Aspect Oriented Software Development AOSD) surge como uma opção para que engenheiros de software organizem melhor todas as fases de desenvolvimento, desde os documentos de requisitos até a implementação e testes de softwares [4, 11, 26]. Por ser uma linha de pesquisa ainda em evolução, a maioria dos esforços iniciais têm sido concentrados na fase da implementação como uma solução para aumentar a facilidade de entendimento e, conseqüentemente, facilitar a manutenção e evolução desse software. Por esse motivo, na fase de implementação, é possível encontrar tanto técnicas de modelagem [18] e reengenharia [20] como ferramentas [9] que minimizam os esforços de engenheiros de software que trabalham com o AOSD nessa fase.

Por outro lado, a utilização do conceito de separação de interesses [5] e orientação a aspectos [13], já na fase de requisitos, permite uma melhor organização do documento de requisitos. Nessa nova visão, os requisitos que entrecortam outros requisitos [22] e os que são voláteis (suscetíveis a mudanças) [31] são identificados e modularizados como aspectos. Em um primeiro momento os termos "interesses entrecortantes" (do inglês *crosscutting concerns*) foram utilizados para classificar requisitos não funcionais que entrecortavam outros requisitos (funcionais ou não). Dessa forma, somente poderia ser considerado um aspecto algum requisito não funcional. Em trabalhos recentes [31] o termo interesse é utilizado para classificar qualquer tipo de requisito (funcional ou não-funcional). Quando um desses interesses entrecorta outros interesses ou quando o interesse é volátil, esse é considerado um candidato a aspecto.

Contudo, apesar das prováveis facilidades que o AOSD sugere para a fase de requisitos, ainda não existe preocupação em se desenvolver trabalhos que avaliem qualitativamente um documento de requisitos orientado a aspectos. Santa´Ana e outros [25, 26] avaliam qualitativamente e quantitativamente os benefícios de implementações de padrões de projeto em sistemas orientados a aspectos e orientados a objetos. Não sendo avaliados, porém, os documentos de requisitos.

No contexto de métricas que auxiliem o engenheiro de software a avaliar a qualidade de documentos de requisitos orientados a aspectos, Ramos [21] elabora um conjunto de métricas para medir a qualidade dos aspectos especificados em uma abordagem orientada a casos de uso aspectuais. Nessa mesma linha, este artigo propõe um conjunto de métricas abstratas que podem ser instanciadas, com o auxilio de diretrizes em um documento de requisitos com aspectos, bem como um processo de medição. As métricas serão utilizadas em abordagens diferentes de engenharia de requisitos com aspectos. Para ilustrar é apresentado um estudo de caso.

Na Seção 2 estão sendo relatados alguns trabalhos na área da orientação a aspectos na fase de requisitos, na Seção 3 são apresentadas métricas para a avaliação da qualidade de aspectos em documentos de requisitos, na Seção 4 são apresentadas as métricas para avaliar documentos de requisitos orientados a aspectos, na Seção 5 é descrito como foi realizado o estudo de caso. As considerações finais são apresentadas na Seção 6.

2. Orientação a Aspectos na Fase de Requisitos

Czarnecki e Eisenecker [5] comentam que a necessidade de manipular um requisito importante de cada vez, durante o desenvolvimento de um sistema, é chamado de princípio da separação de interesses. Linguagens de programação geralmente fornecem construtores para organizar um sistema em unidades modulares que representam os interesses funcionais da aplicação. Essas unidades são expressas como objetos, módulos ou procedimentos. A maioria dos softwares consiste em um conjunto de interesses que se entrecortam em vários módulos diferentes. Como conseqüência da não modularização desses interesses, a implementação resulta em softwares de complexo entendimento e, conseqüentemente, de difícil manutenção [19, 29].

A separação destes interesses é de fundamental importância para que artefatos dos vários estágios do desenvolvimento do software sejam legíveis e sejam facilmente manuteníveis. Esse princípio estabelece que um problema deve ser decomposto em unidades menores, claramente separadas, de maneira que cada uma delas represente um único interesse. [3, 13, 14]

Com o objetivo de apresentar técnicas de programação capazes de cobrir a separação de interesses de um sistema, em código, foi estudado e implementado um novo paradigma de programação, a Programação Orientada a Aspectos POA [13]. A POA traz uma nova unidade modular chamada "aspecto", que encapsula comportamentos que interferem (entrecortam) em múltiplas classes. Trabalhos iniciais com POA foram desenvolvidos maciçamente para solucionar problemas que ocorrem em nível de código [7, 8, 13, 20]. Somente mais recentemente alguns pesquisadores começaram a trazer os benefícios da orientação a aspectos para as fases inicias do processo de desenvolvimento[2, 4, 22, 23, 28].

A Engenharia de Requisitos Orientada a Aspectos surgiu da necessidade de modelar certos requisitos que se encontram repetidos ou espalhados na especificação de requisitos, chamados requisitos aspectuais. As primeiras investigações realizadas foram sobre a relação entre atributos de qualidade e interesses que se encontram espalhados e repetidos na especificação de requisitos [17, 22]. Uma das primeiras abordagens que surgiram na área, propunha um modelo genérico para engenharia de requisitos orientada a aspectos, e foi chamada de AORE (*Aspect-Oriented Requirements Engineering*) [22]. O modelo trata propriedades não-funcionais como interesses do sistema e separa-os das propriedades funcionais, através de uma série de passos bem definidos.

Tendo como base, o modelo AORE, Rashid e outros [23] utilizam a técnica de pontos de vista para especificar requisitos e XML [32] para defini-los. Também usando XML, essa abordagem separa as regras de composição dos aspectos e dos pontos de vistas promovendo, assim, o reuso e a maior facilidade na identificação e no gerenciamento dos conflitos.

Araújo e outros [2] propõem o uso de aspectos concentrado na especificação de requisitos baseado em cenários. Nesse processo, primeiramente, os casos de uso são mapeados em um conjunto de cenários que, posteriormente, são separados em aspectuais e não-aspectuais. Os aspectuais são representados utilizando especificação de padrões de interações (*Interaction Patterns Specifications*) e os não-aspectuais como diagramas de casos de uso. No passo seguinte, cada cenário é traduzido para uma máquina de estados correspondente e combinados para formação de um conjunto de máquinas de estados que representam os requisitos de modo geral

Ainda no foco de trabalhos sobre requisitos orientados a aspectos, Silva e outros [27] propõem o uso de modelo de metas *V-graph* para modelar aspectos e requisitos. A proposta possui basicamente três fases: Separação, Composição e Visualização. A separação consiste na modelagem dos requisitos identificando algumas restrições. A composição funciona de forma semelhante ao combinador (*weaver*) das linguagens de programação orientadas a aspectos, interpretando as restrições transversais e gerando um modelo único com todas as informações. A última fase trata da geração de diferentes visões do modelo integrado. Assim, o modelo garante aos desenvolvedores uma ampla visualização das influências exercidas pelos requisitos em toda a estrutura do sistema.

Utilizando como base o processo de desenvolvimento unificado [12], Sousa [28] realiza uma adaptação desse processo para o desenvolvimento orientado a aspectos, onde o principal foco desta pesquisa é o desenvolvimento guiado por casos de uso [11], possibilitando a separação de interesses transversais nas fases de requisitos, análise e projeto utilizando fundamentos da orientação a aspectos. Nesse processo as unidades bases (que podem ser afetadas por aspectos) correspondem às unidades de decomposição comumente utilizadas em cada um dos fluxo de atividades do processo unificado, por exemplo: casos de uso no fluxo de requisitos; classes de análise no fluxo de análise; e classes de projeto no fluxo de projeto. Sendo que os possíveis pontos de junção referem-se a elementos nessas unidades que representam pontos de execução: no fluxo de requisitos pode-se especificá-los em função dos eventos (ou passos) nos cenários de um caso de uso; no de análise, em termos de mensagens trocadas entre objetos de análise; e no de projeto, em termos de operações de classes.

Partindo do princípio de que aspectos são encapsulados nas mesmas unidades de decomposição existentes em cada um dos fluxos considerados, Sousa [28] cria um estereotipo especial para cada fase, como por exemplo, caso de uso aspectual (Figura 1), classe de análise aspectual, para indicar que o comportamento do aspecto deverá ser inserido em alguma parte das unidades que ele afeta. O termo *crosscuts* refere-se ao relacionamento entre uma unidade aspectual e uma unidade afetada por ela. Uma tabela denominada de tabela de composição armazena para cada aspecto identificado e em cada fluxo, informações relativas à composição entre um aspecto e a(s) unidade(s) que ele afeta.

A Fig.1 apresenta o exemplo de um diagrama (parcial) de casos de uso elaborado pela abordagem de Sousa[28], nesse diagrama é possível observar alguns casos de uso aspectuais (representados por losangos) que especificam o interesse de segurança. O relacionamento que indica que um caso de uso aspectual entrecorta um caso de uso (normal) é nomeado como "<<*crosscuts*>>" e é representado por uma seta com linhas tracejadas.

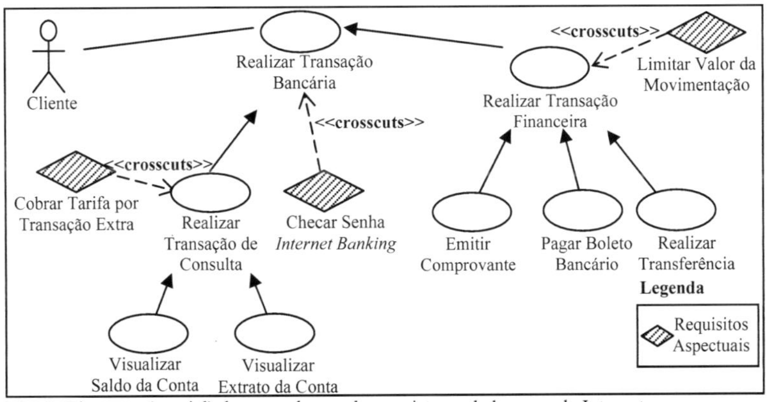

Fig. 1. Diagrama (parcial) de casos de uso de um sistema de banco pela Internet.

A principal contribuição das propostas de se usar aspectos nas fases inicias do processo de desenvolvimento é a ajuda na identificação de conflitos entre os requisitos, para que medidas sejam tomadas o quanto antes, onde o custo é muito menor do que em fases posteriores. Além, de promover uma melhor legibilidade e manutenibilidade dos artefatos produzidos nos vários estágios do desenvolvimento. [22]

A Seção seguinte apresenta alguns trabalhos que utilizam métricas para avaliar a qualidade na fase de requisitos.

3. Metodologias e Métricas para Avaliação da Qualidade de Requisitos

A comunidade de engenharia de software vem adaptando padrões existentes como a ISO 9126 [10] para que desta maneira se permita fornecer suporte para que haja conformidade e assim possibilitando elaborar métricas para medir a qualidade de um produto de software [19, 29]. A medição de um software é importante para garantir a qualidade do produto, avaliar a produtividade das pessoas que o produzem e formar uma linha base para estimativas. Portanto são muitas as vantagens de se poder medir a qualidade e corrigir seus erros, inconsistências e saber sua completitude, porém quanto mais cedo nas fases de desenvolvimento do software for descoberto os erros, menos custoso é o seu processo de correção [19]. Por esse motivo a medição da qualidade de um produto de software na fase de requisitos tem sido uma área bastante promissora.

Tabela 1. Atividades que asseguram a qualidade em documentos de requisitos.

Atividade	Objetivo Principal
Análise	Identifica conflitos em requisitos.
Verificação	Detecta defeitos em requisitos.
Validação	Certifica que os requisitos são consistentes com as intenções dos clientes e usuários.

As atividades que asseguram a qualidade em documentos de requisitos são divididas em três, como sumarizadas na Tabela 1 [6].

A medição quantitativa dos requisitos de um sistema é utilizada como meio de medir o tamanho do produto de software, por derivação, esforço, tempo e custo necessário para implementá-lo. Uma técnica bastante utilizada para esse fim é a analise de pontos de função, que foi introduzida por Allan Albrecht [1]. A proposta de Albrecht é que o software deveria ter o seu tamanho medido a partir das funções implementadas para o usuário, examinadas sob a ótica do usuário. [1]

A maioria dos métodos utilizados para avaliação de qualidade (métricas) de artefatos de software não levam em consideração o princípio da engenharia de software de que o custo para modificar um requisito na fase de manutenção chega a ser cinqüenta vezes maior do que na fase de definição de requisitos [19, 29]. Portanto, a medição da qualidade na fase de requisitos é uma estratégia importante para reduzir os custos de manutenção [19, 29]. Além de trazer esses benefícios, a obtenção de métricas na fase de requisitos possibilita também o respaldo de estudos estatísticos que viabilizem a melhoria do processo de engenharia de requisitos e do software em si.

Durán [6] propõe uma ferramenta denominada REM (*REquirements Manager* - Gerenciador de Requisitos), que dá apoio a verificação de requisitos que estão armazenados em XML [32]. Em seu trabalho são elaboradas heurísticas que tratam de alguns problemas recorrentes em documentos de requisitos, tais como: ambigüidade, completitude, rastreabilidade. A ferramenta REM também dá apoio a verificação de casos de uso, desta maneira foram elaboradas algumas métricas para verificar a qualidade em casos de uso.

As métricas elaboradas no trabalho de Durán [6] medem fatores de complexidade em caso de uso como o número de passos de um caso de uso, passos condicionais, exceções e o número de vezes que um caso de uso é incluído ou estendido em outros casos de uso.

Algumas métricas como a relatada anteriormente apenas fornecem mecanismos para se medir o tamanho, ou a complexidade, não fornecendo mecanismos para indicar se esse ou aquele valor obtido está bom ou ruim. Porém, existem métricas que auxiliam o engenheiro de software a fazer uma avaliação dando um escore final para um determinado fator que foi medido, como é o caso da metodologia apresentada por Reis [24].

Reis [24] elabora uma metodologia denominada REQE (*Requirements Engineering Quality valuation*), essa metodologia propõe a avaliação da qualidade de aplicações web na fase de requisitos através da medição de atributos de qualidade, tendo assim como benefício à possibilidade de descobrir erros de uma forma antecipada. A aplicação da metodologia REQE consiste em cinco fases: i) Representação das características, ii) Subcaracterísticas e atributos de qualidades, iii) Especificação descritiva da árvore de característica, subcaracterísticas e atributos de qualidade, iv) Associação de pesos aos nós, Associação de escores aos atributos de qualidade e v) Cálculo geral.

Com a utilização de pesos e escores, a metodologia de Reis [24] produz um número (resultado do cálculo geral), que é utilizados de parâmetro para que o engenheiro compare com outros valores e assim consiga avaliar a completitude do sistema que foi avaliado.

Na Seção seguinte são apresentadas as métricas elaboradas para se avaliar a qualidade de documentos de requisitos orientados a aspectos.

4. Métricas para Avaliar Documentos de Requisitos Orientados a Aspectos

A medição de software se ocupa em obter um valor numérico para alguns atributos de um produto ou um processo de software. Comparando esses valores uns com outros e com os padrões que se aplicam em uma organização, é possível tirar conclusões sobre a qualidade do software ou dos processos de software [29].

As métricas apresentadas nesse artigo são consideradas quantitativas (preditivas). Essas métricas são associadas a um produto de software (neste caso o documento de requisitos). Alguns exemplos desse tipo de métricas são: a medida da complexidade ciclomática de um módulo, o comprimento médio de identificadores em um programa, número de atributos e operações associadas com objetos em um projeto entre outras.

Um conjunto de atributos e alguns fatores são sugeridos por [29], para a elaboração de um conjunto de métricas, essas devem ser:

- Simples e computáveis: Deve ser relativamente fácil aprender como originar as métricas e seu cálculo não deve exigir esforço ou tempo exagerado.
- Empíricas e intuitivamente persuasivas: A métrica deve satisfazer as noções intuitivas do engenheiro sobre o atributo do produto que está sendo considerado.
- Consistentes e objetivas: a métrica deve produzir sempre resultados que não são ambíguos. Um terceirizado deve poder originar o mesmo valor para a métrica usando a mesma informação sobre o software.
- Consistentes no uso de unidades e dimensões: O cálculo matemático da métrica deve usar medidas que não levam a combinações de unidades bizarras. Por exemplo, multiplicar pessoas na equipe de projeto por variáveis da linguagem de programação do programa resulta numa mistura suspeita de unidades que não são intuitivamente convincentes.
- Independente da linguagem de programação: Métricas devem ser baseadas no modelo de análise, modelo de projeto e na estrutura propriamente dita do programa. Elas não devem estar dependentes das excentricidades da sintaxe ou da semântica de linguagens de programação.
- Mecanismo efetivo para realimentação de alta qualidade: Isto é, a métrica deve fornecer ao engenheiro de software informações que pode levar a um produto final de alta qualidade.

As métricas apresentadas nesse artigo focam na medição de documentos de requisitos orientados a aspectos em termos de separação de interesses, acoplamento e tamanho. Essas métricas são abstratas e devem ser instanciadas de acordo com a metodologia seguida no documento de requisitos, por exemplo, na metodologia apresentada por Sousa [28], os aspectos são especificados por casos de uso. Portando as métricas devem ser instanciadas para medir os módulos (casos de uso) dessa metodologia. Diretrizes que ajudam o engenheiro de software a instanciar as métricas abstratas para um sistema específico são dadas, Fig. 2.

Diretrizes

1. identificar qual a estrutura (módulo de decomposição) utilizada para especificar um aspecto ou interesse;
   1.1. na estrutura, identificar como esta é composta, se existem passos, sub estruturas, exceções, desvios ou condições;
2. identificar como é o mecanismo de combinação entre os módulos que se entrecortam;
   2.1. no mecanismo, identificar como este é composto, se existem passos, sub mecanismos, estruturas, exceções, desvios ou condições;
3. identificar outros relacionamentos que podem haver entre as estruturas;
   3.1. no relacionamento, identificar o seu tipo.

Fig. 2 - Diretrizes para Instanciação de Métricas Abstratas.

As métricas são divididas em três subconjuntos de métricas (Fig. 3): i) separação de interesses (M1); ii) tamanho (M2); e, iii) acoplamento (M3).

M1 - Separação de interesses:
Número de módulos que especificam um determinado interesse;
Número de passos que compõem esses módulos

M2 - Tamanho:
Número de passos nas descrições de cada módulo independente;
Número de passos condicionais de cada módulo independente;
Número de exceções de cada módulo independente.

M3 - Acoplamento:
Número de módulos que são incluídos ou estendidos em outros módulos;
Número de módulos que são entrecortados por um determinado módulo.

Legenda:
Módulo: qualquer estrutura que encapsula uma funcionalidade (ou parte dela), por exemplo: um caso de uso, um agente, um papel, uma classe, um caso de uso aspectual, um aspecto entre outros.
Interesse: representa funcionalidade e restrições de um sistema, podendo ser tanto um requisito funcional como um não-funcional, por exemplo: segurança, persistência, interface, tratamento de erros, cadastro de cliente, emissão de pedidos entre outros.
Aspecto: uma estrutura que encapsula um interesse (ou parte deste).
Entrecorta: é o relacionamento de um aspecto com um módulo, pelo fato de um aspecto especificar um interesse (ou parte deste) que será inserido no módulo.

Fig. 3 – Métricas Abstratas.

O primeiro conjunto de métricas M1, verifica o quão separado está um determinado interesse, ou seja, em quantos módulos estão especificados um determinado interesse e quantos passos foram necessários para descrever esse interesse. Esse primeiro tipo de métrica terá um valor para cada interesse, por exemplo: "Utilizando as métricas de separação de interesses foi possível verificar que o interesse de Segurança foi modularizado por 7 (sete) casos de uso aspectuais e descrito em 78 (setenta e oito) passos".

O segundo conjunto de métricas são relacionadas ao tamanho de cada módulo, indicando fatores como o número de passos, passos condicionais e exceções. Essas métricas terão um valor único para cada módulo, por exemplo: "Utilizando as métricas de tamanho foi possível verificar que o caso de uso aspectual Limitar Valor da Movimentação contém 2 (dois) passos e 0 (zero) exceções e passos condicionais".

O terceiro conjunto de métricas relacionadas com o acoplamento verifica a quantidade de relacionamentos tanto de entrecorte quanto de extensão e inclusão existentes em cada módulo.

Baseando-se nos processos de medição descritos em [19, 29], foi elaborado um processo que pode ser uma alternativa de como realizar a aplicação do conjunto de métricas abstratas em um documento de requisitos orientado a aspectos, Figura 4. São basicamente três etapas:

1 - Instanciação das métricas abstratas: tem como entrada as métricas abstratas, as diretrizes e um documento de requisitos orientado a aspectos. A saída dessa primeira etapa é um conjunto de métricas instanciadas para medir o documento de requisitos.

2 - Aplicação das métricas: tem como entrada o documento de requisitos e as métricas já instanciadas para esse documento. A saída dessa etapa é um conjunto de dados coletados a partir da aplicação das métricas.

3 - Análise dos dados coletados: tem como entrada o resultado dos dados obtidos a partir da aplicação das métricas e outros dados que podem ser desde estatísticas obtidas de outras aplicações de métricas como a própria experiência do engenheiro de software. A saída dessa ultima fase serão dados que auxiliarão o engenheiro de software na tomada de decisões e possíveis alterações no documento de requisitos avaliado.

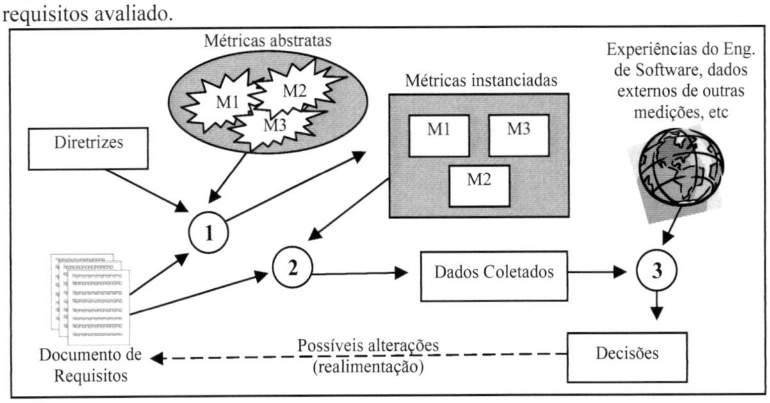

Fig. 4 - Um processo de utilização das métricas abstratas.

A Seção seguinte apresenta um estudo de caso em que as diretrizes auxiliam a instanciar as métricas abstratas para que seja realizada a medição de documento de requisitos orientado a aspectos.

5. Estudo de Caso

Existem duas técnicas básicas para avaliar uma abordagem: experimentos e estudos de caso. A realização de experimentos provê uma maneira de avaliação baseada em comparação direta, permitindo a pesquisadores investigar qual o impacto da tecnologia no processo de maneira detalhada [30]. Já a realização de estudos de caso está mais preocupada em avaliar os benefícios de uma abordagem de forma a verificar se as mudanças no processo proporcionam o resultado desejado [15]. A técnica escolhida para ser utilizada neste trabalho foi o estudo de caso, por se pretender avaliar o comportamento das métricas em um documento de requisitos orientado a aspectos.

O documento de requisitos orientados a aspectos que foi utilizado no estudo de caso trata de um sistema bancário via web, denominado Internet Banking (tem as funções básicas para realizar transações financeiras e bancárias). Esse documento foi elaborado utilizando a abordagem de Sousa [28], que foi especificado utilizando tabelas, para detalhar os relacionamentos de entrecorte, e casos de uso que contêm uma nova unidade modular que Sousa chamou de caso de uso aspectual. Esse trabalho é melhor detalhado na Seção 2.

Para ter alguma garantia que a aplicação das métricas foi efetuada corretamente, o engenheiro de software deverá estabelecer os objetivos da medição antes que a coleta de dados tenha início, definindo cada métrica de modo não ambíguo [19].

O estudo de caso foi realizado seguindo o processo de medição mostrado na Figura 4, porém a última etapa, de Análise dos dados coletados, não é relatada nesse artigo, assim este estudo ficou dividido em duas etapas que são apresentadas nas subseções seguintes.

5.1 Instanciação das Métricas Abstratas

Seguindo as diretrizes apresentadas na Seção anterior, Fig. 2, foram encontrados os seguintes itens mensuráveis no documento de requisitos:

1 - As unidades modulares utilizadas são: casos de uso e casos de uso aspectuais.

1.1 - Cada caso de uso (também os aspectuais) são compostos por passos.

2 - Os mecanismos de composição são especificados por tabelas.

2.1 - Cada tabela contém linhas que identificam os casos de uso afetados por um determinado caso de uso aspectual.

3 - Os relacionamentos existentes entre os casos de uso são os mesmos existentes em um diagrama de caso de uso habitual com a adição do relacionamento dos casos de uso aspectuais.

3.1 - Os relacionamentos podem ser de extensão (*extend*), inclusão (*include*) e entrecortes (*crosscuts*).

Após identificar os itens que compõem a abordagem utilizada no documento de requisitos, o engenheiro de software deve instanciar os itens mensuráveis de acordo com as métricas abstratas, Figura 3. A seguir é mostrado como ficou os três conjuntos de métricas após a instanciação.

M1 - Separação de interesses:

M1a - Número de casos de uso (aspectual ou não) que modelam um determinado interesse;

M1b - Número de passos nas descrições dos casos de uso (aspectual ou não) que descrevem um determinado interesse.

M2 - Tamanho:

M2a - Número de passos nas descrições de cada caso de uso (aspectual ou não);

M2b - Número de passos condicionais de cada caso de uso (aspectual ou não);

M2c - Número de exceções de cada caso de uso (aspectual ou não).

M3 - Acoplamento:

M3a - Número de casos de uso (aspectual ou não) que são incluídos ou estendidos em um determinado caso de uso aspectual;

M3b - Número de casos de uso (aspectual ou não) que são entrecortados por um determinado caso de uso aspectual.

5.2. Aplicação das Métricas

Após instanciar as métricas, o engenheiro deverá realizar a coleta dos dados a partir da medição dos itens especificados por cada métrica. No caso desse estudo os dados foram coletados manualmente, percorrendo todo o documento de requisitos. Ou seja, para cada métrica foi percorrido o documento por completo e contabilizado (somado todas as ocorrências) o item que estava sendo especificado na métrica.

Para coletar dados com a aplicação da métrica M1a, que tem a finalidade de medir o grau de separação de um Interesse, deve-se primeiramente selecionar um interesse (no caso do sistema de Internet Banking existe um interesse todo modularizado e especificado por aspectos), por exemplo, o interesse de Segurança. Deve-se localizar no documento de requisitos todos os casos de uso aspectuais que implementam esse interesse, neste caso foram encontrados os casos de uso aspectuais: Gravar informações Transação, Cobrar Tarifa por Transação Extra, Checar Senha Internet Banking, Checar Dados Pessoais do Cliente, Registrar CPMF, Limitar Valor da Movimentação (Tabela 2), Oferecer Bonificação. Ou seja, o valor obtido com a aplicação da métrica M1a é 7 (sete).

A Tabela 2, mostra o caso de uso aspectual "Limitar Valor da Movimentação"e seus 2 (dois) passos, para a aplicação da métrica M1b deverão ser contados todos os passos de todos os casos de uso encontrados para o interesse de Segurança. Para a métrica M1b o valor obtido é 78 (setenta e oito), ou seja, essa é soma de todos passos dos casos de uso aspectuais que especificam o interesse de Segurança.

Tabela 2. Especificação do caso de uso aspectual Limitar Valor de Movimentação.

OPERACIONALIZACAO #03: Limitar valor de movimentação	
INFORMAÇÕES CARACTERÍSTICAS	
Objetivo	Verificar limite do valor de transações financeiras para diminuir riscos de fraudes.
Pré-condições	Valor da transação é dado como entrada.
Ator Primário	Cliente do banco, titular da conta.
CENÁRIO PRINCIPAL DE SUCESSO	
Passo	Ação
1	O sistema verifica se o valor da transação supera limite.
2	O sistema retorna o resultado da verificação

Neste estudo de caso, optou-se por coletar somente dados referentes aos módulos (casos de uso) aspectuais. Portanto, primeiramente foi selecionado um caso de uso e se mediu o item desejado. Por exemplo, para o caso de uso aspectual

"Limitar Valor da Movimentação", Tabela 2, o valor da métrica M2a é 2 (dois), o valor da M2b é 0 (zero) e da métrica M2c é 0 (zero).

Tabela 3- Tabela de composição Limitar Valor de Movimentação.

REQUISITO ASPECTUAL: AR #07 LIMITAR VALOR DE MOVIMENTAÇÃO				
Caso de uso Afetado	Condição (Opcional)	Regra de Composição	Ponto de Junção	Informações Adicionais
UC #04 Realizar transferência	-	Wrap	3	Se limiteOk então execute(pto junção) Senão exibe(msgErro)
UC #05 Pagar boleto bancário	-	Wrap	4	Se limiteOk então execute(pto junção) Senão exibe(msgErro)
UC #06 Emitir comprovante	-	Wrap	3	Se limiteOk então execute(pto junção) Senão exibe(msgErro)

Selecionando o mesmo caso de uso aspectual "Limitar Valor da Movimentação", Tabela 2, e aplicando a métrica M3a obtém-se o valor 0 (zero). A coleta dos dados da aplicação da métrica M3b é basicamente obtido pela observação das Tabelas de composição, por exemplo a tabela "Limitar Valor de Movimentação", Tabela 3, pode-se obter a informação que o caso de uso aspectual "Limitar Valor de Movimentação" entrecorta os casos de uso: realizar transferência, pagar boleto bancário e emitir boleto bancário, ou seja, o valor da M3b para o caso de aspectual "Limitar Valor de Movimentação" é 3 (três). Esses relacionamentos de entrecorte podem ser também observados no diagrama de casos de uso, Fig. 1.

Após a aplicação das métricas os dados coletados deverão ser analisados e interpretados para ganhar profundidade na visão de qualidade do software e os resultados dessa interpretação poderá levar a modificações do documento de requisitos.

Utilizando como base os fatores de qualidade que podem ser medidos (diretamente) segundo McCall [16], as métricas apresentadas nesse estudo de caso auxiliarão o engenheiro a avaliar o documento de requisitos segundo os fatores de:

- Utilização: Esforço necessário para entender, operar, interpretar e aprender um documento.
- Mantenabilidade: O esforço necessário para localizar e consertar um erro.
- Flexibilidade: O esforço necessário para modificar um documento.
- Reutilização: Quanto um documento (ou parte dele) pode ser reusado em outros projetos, sistemas, aplicações, etc. Relativo ao empacotamento e escopo das funções que o sistema realiza

A Seção seguinte relata algumas considerações feitas sobre as métricas e o estudo de caso apresentado.

6. Considerações Finais

Este artigo apresentou um conjunto de métricas abstratas, que com o auxílio de diretrizes, podem ser instanciadas para medir um documento de requisitos orientado a aspectos em relação a separação de interesses, tamanho e acoplamento, sendo que esse documento pode ter sido elaborado por uma abordagem qualquer.

As métricas apresentadas auxiliam o engenheiro de software a elaborar uma base de conhecimento em relação ao interesse medido. Essa base de conhecimento deverá auxiliar decisões em projetos futuros que foram implementados utilizando os conceitos do desenvolvimento orientado a aspectos. Com a aplicação das métricas em vários documentos de requisitos será possível inferir qual seria um bom grau de separação de um determinado interesse.

Com a utilização de métricas abstratas, a aplicação dessas pode ser feita em qualquer tipo de documento de requisitos orientados a aspectos, independente da abordagem que foi seguida para sua criação. Isso facilita a adoção das métricas, pois, como a orientação a aspectos está em um estágio inicial, principalmente na fase de requisitos, a todo momento estão surgindo novas abordagens de como elaborar um documento de requisitos orientado a aspectos, além das várias já existentes.

Engenheiros de software devem adaptar as métricas ao ambiente de seu projeto de software, inserindo padronizações, como por exemplo, somente medir módulos aspectuais, ou então coletar os dados por módulos. Técnicas estatísticas válidas devem ser aplicadas para se estabelecer relações, como por exemplo o nível de complexidade. Cálculos que melhor expressem os dados coletados devem ser definidos, como por exemplo mostrar a média de uma determinada métrica.

As métricas apresentadas nesse artigo são o ponto de partida para se garantir a qualidade de documentos de requisitos especificados com base na orientação a aspectos. Porém deve-se levar em conta outros fatores para que haja sucesso em uma atividade métrica, como a condução da coleta dos dados e sua análise. Outro ponto que se deve estar ciente é que essa atividade de medição esta intimamente ligada ao apoio gerencial. Financiamento, treinamento e promoção devem ser considerados, se um programa de medição técnica deve ser estabelecido e sustentado.

Como trabalhos futuros novas avaliações deverão ser realizadas em outros documentos de requisitos orientados a aspectos elaborados por outras metodologias, para que deste modo seja possível validar a aplicabilidade das métricas abstratas.

Novas diretrizes deverão ser elaboradas para permitirem instanciar as métricas para qualquer fase do desenvolvimento de software e não somente na fase de requisitos.

Uma ferramenta que implemente as métricas e faça a coleta dos dados de forma, no mínimo semi-automática deverá ser elabora, para que assim agilize o processo de aplicação das métricas.

Agradecimentos

Este trabalho contou com o apoio de vários projetos de pesquisa (CNPq 304982/2002-4, CAPES BEX 1775/2005-7, CAPES BEX 3003/05-1 e CAPES/ GRICES 129/05).

Referências Bibliográficas

1. Albrecht, P. F. et al. "Reliability test system" IEEE trans. on Pas., Vol. Pas-98, No.6 , p. 2047-2054. Nov./Dec.1979.
2. Araújo, J.; Whittle, J.; Kim, D. "Modeling and Composing Scenario-Based Requirements with Aspects". In: The 12th Requirements Engineering Conference , Kyoto, Japan, September 2004.
3. Aksit, M.; Tekinerdogan, B. and Bergmans, L. "The Six Concerns for Separation of Concerns", In: Workshop on Advanced Separation of Concerns, Budapest, Hungary, June 18-22, 2001.
4. Brito, I. and Moreira, A. "Towards a Composition Process for Aspect-Oriented Requirements". In: Aspect-Oriented Requirements Engineering and Architecture Design, - Boston, USA, 2003.

5. Czarnecki, K.; Eisenecker, U. Generative Programming: Methods, Tools, and Applications. Addison-Wesley, 2000.
6. Durán, A.; Cortés, A. R.; Corchuelo, R.; Toro, M. "Supporting Requirements Verification Using XSLT ".Requirements Engineering Conference - RE 2002 – Essen, Alemanha, Setembro 2002.
7. Elrad, T., Filman, R. and Bader, A. "Aspect-Oriented Programming: Introduction", Communications of the ACM, v.44 n.10, p.29-32, Oct. 2001.
8. Elrad, T.; Aksit, M.; Kiczales, G.; Lieberherr, K. and Ossher, H. "Discussing Aspects of AOP". Communications of the ACM, 44(10):33–38, October 2001.
9. Hannemann, J.; Kiczales, G. "Overcoming the Prevalent Decomposition in Legacy Code". In: Workshop on Advanced Separation of Concerns, Toronto, Canada, Maio 2001.
10. ISO 9126, "Tecnologia da Informação – Qualidade de Produto – Parte 1: Modelo de Qualidade", International Standard ISO/IEC 9126, International Standard Organization, Junho, 2001.
11. Jacobson, I; Chriterson, M; Jonsson, P. and Overgaard, G. "Object-Oriented Software Engineering: A Use Case Driven Approach". Addison Wesley, 1992.
12. Jacobson, I.; Booch, G.; and Rumbaugh, J. "The Unified Software Development Process", Addison-Wesley, 1999.
13. Kiczales, G.; Lamping, J.; Mendhekar, A. RG: A Case-Study for Aspect-Oriented Programming. In: SPL97. Palo Alto Research Center, Technical Report, 1997.
14. Kiczales, G.; Hilsdale, E.; Hugunin, J.; Kersten, M.; Palm, J. and Griswold, W. "An Overview of AspectJ". In: 15th European Conference on Object-Oriented Programming, Berlin, Heidelberg, Springer Verlag, 2001.
15. Kitchenham, B.; Pickard, L. and Pfleeger, S. "Case Studies for Method and Tool Evaluation" . IEEE, 1994.
16. McCall, J.; Richards, P.; Walters, G. "Factors in software quality", Technical Report, Vols. 1--3, Rome Air Development Center, United States Air Force, Hanscom AFB, Springfield, VA. 1977.
17. Moreira, A.; Araújo, J. and Brito, I. "Crosscutting Quality Attributes for Requirements Engineering", SEKE 2002, ACM Press, Italy, July, 2002.
18. Pawlak, R., Duchien, L., Florin G., Legong-Aubry, F., Seinturier, L, Martelli, L. A UML Notation for Aspect-Oriented Software Design. In: Workshop of Aspect Oriented Modeling with UML of Proceedings of Aspect Oriented Software Development Conference , Enschede, Abril, 2002.
19. Pressman, R. Engenharia de Software. Makron Books, 5ª edição, 2002.
20. Ramos, R. A.; Penteado, R.; Masiero, P. C.; - "Um Processo de Reestruturação de Código Baseado em Aspectos" - SBES'2004 - Brasília/DF. Outubro, 2004.
21. Ramos, R. A, Castro, J. F. B. "Avaliação de uma Metodologia de Medição da Qualidade em um Documento de Requisitos Orientado a Aspectos". In: WER, Porto- Portugal, 2005.
22. Rashid, A.; Sawyer, P.; Moreira, A. and Araújo, J. "Early Aspects. A Model for Aspect-Oriented Requirements Engineering". Conference on Requirements Engineering, Essen, Germany, 2002.
23. Rashid, A.; Moreira, A. and Araújo, J. "Modularisation and Composition of Aspectual Requirements". In: 2nd International Conference on Aspect-Oriented Software Development, 2003.
24. Reis, T., P., C. "Uma Metodologia para Medição da Qualidade de Aplicações Web na Fase de Requisitos". Dissertação – Programa de Pós-Graduação em Ciência da Computação, UFPE, Recife – Pernambuco, 2004, 163f.
25. Sant'Anna, C.; Garcia, A.; Chavez, C.; Lucena C.; Staa A. On Reuse and Maintenance of Aspect-Oriented Software: An Assessment Framework. In: SBES'2003, Manaus/Amazonas. Outubro, 2003.
26. Sant'Anna, C.; Garcia, A.; Chavez, C.; Lucena C.; Staa A. "Design Patterns as Aspects: A Quantitative Assessment". In: SBES'2004, Brasilia - DF, 2004.
27. Silva, L.; Leite, J. "Uma linguagem de modelagem de requisitos orientada a aspectos", Proceedings of the Requirement Engineering Workshop at CAiSE 2005, Porto-Portugal, 2005.
28. Sousa, G. "Uma Abordagem Direcionada a Casos de Uso para o Desenvolvimento de Software Orientado a Aspectos". Dissertação – Programa de Pós-Graduação em Ciência da Computação, UFPE, Recife – Pernambuco, maio 2004, 180f.
29. Summerville, I. "Engenharia de Software". Addison- Wesley, 2003.
30. Travassos, G.; Gurov, D. and Amaral, E. "Introdução à Engenharia de Software Experimental". Relatório Técnico, RT-ES-590/02, Rio de Janeiro, 2002.
31. Whitte, J.; Araújo, J. "Scenario modelling with aspects". In: IEE Proceedings online no. 20040921, Vol. 151, No. 4, Agosto 2004.
32. W3C. Extensible Markup Language (XML) 1.0 (Second Edition). W3C Recommendation. Outubro 2000.

Sesión 10:

Medición y Evaluación 2

Análisis de Medidas en la Etapa de Elicitación de Requerimientos

M. Elena Centeno[1], Alejandro Oliveros[2]

[1]Departamento de Informática, Departamento de Matemática, Facultad de Ingeniería, UNPSJB
malena@ing.unp.edu.ar

[2]Departamento de Computación, Facultad de Ingeniería, UBA- Magister de Ingeniería de Software, Facultad de Informática, UNLP
oliveros@fibertel.com.ar

Resumen. En este trabajo se presenta una propuesta de aplicación de mediciones a la entidad símbolo del Léxico Extendido del Lenguaje (LEL), entre sus atributos interesa evaluar el tamaño. A partir de establecer como unidad de medida del tamaño de un texto expresado en Lenguaje Natural (LN) a la Palabra Normalizada (PN) [4], se propone un conjunto de mediciones que se aplican a los símbolos que componen el LEL. Existen medidas elementales que se obtienen al considerar la posibilidad de medir el tamaño de un texto, pero debido a las características del LN no son independientes del estilo del autor y por lo tanto no aseguran que las medidas sean un parámetro que permita comparar distintos LEL. Sin embargo, se espera que las mediciones aplicadas exclusivamente a las palabras normalizadas, obtenidas luego de aplicar el proceso de normalización al texto, estarán libres de las particularidades del redactor del LEL. Se consideran Medidas Directas y Medidas Indirectas.

1 Introducción

Realizar mediciones en las etapas tempranas del desarrollo del software permite el ahorro de recursos al detectar situaciones que pueden llegar a cancelar un proyecto si no se resuelven a tiempo. En este trabajo se propone un conjunto de mediciones para aplicar a cada símbolo del Léxico Extendido del Lenguaje (LEL) [15].

A continuación se establece el significado de algunos de los términos usados en este contexto. Una *entidad* es un objeto o un evento del mundo real y un *atributo* es una característica o propiedad de una entidad que permite diferenciarlas [7]. Se entiende por *medición* al proceso o conjunto de técnicas a aplicar a una entidad que permiten establecer una correspondencia entre el mundo empírico y el mundo formal y se denomina *medida* a la magnitud o símbolo de una escala asignado a un atributo luego del proceso de medición [7].

Según las normas ISO/IEC 9126 [11] (previamente establecidas en ISO/IEC 14598), las *Medidas Directas* surgen de la evaluación de un solo atributo, mientras que las *Medidas Indirectas* relacionan las medidas de los atributos para evidenciar características de las entidades.

Las mediciones propuestas se aplican a ocho casos de estudio elaborados por profesionales informáticos y estudiantes de grado y posgrado de carreras de informática.

Se buscaron casos elaborados por diferentes grupos, que tuvieran distintas cantidad de símbolos y que trataran temas diversos, se llega a los siguientes LEL: Recepción del Hotel [3], Pasaporte [14], LEL & Escenarios [7], Meeting Scheduler (Agenda) [10], Plan de Ahorro [17], Estación de Servicio [6], Banco de Sangre [9] y C.E.R.E.T. [1].

En lo que sigue se incluye en la sección 2 una breve descripción del concepto de LEL y cómo derivar los Escenarios a partir de él, en las secciones 3 y 4 se explican y ejemplifican las Medidas Directas y las Medidas Indirectas, en las últimas secciones se formulan las conclusiones y se plantean los pasos a seguir en futuras investigaciones.

2 El enfoque de LEL y Escenarios

Nombre1 / Nombre2 / ......
• Noción Explica el significado del símbolo en el contexto en estudio
• Impacto Define la incidencia del símbolo en los otros componentes del sistema

Fig. 1. Plantilla utilizada para definir un símbolo del LEL

Los Escenarios generados a partir del LEL [15], han probado ser satisfactorios para elicitar el conocimiento del UdD (Universo del Discurso) necesario para elaborar el documento de requisitos.

El LEL se presenta como un diccionario que contiene las definiciones de los términos de uso común y están expresados en LN. A diferencia de un diccionario convencional, cada entrada define un símbolo siguiendo un esquema prefijado que se presenta en la Figura 1.

3 Medidas Directas

Se establecen dos categorías de Medidas Directas: las *Medidas Inmediatas* que se aplican a todas las palabras que componen la definición de un símbolo sin tener en cuenta ninguna restricción y las *Medidas Normalizadas* que se aplican sólo al subconjunto de las Palabras Normalizadas [4] que componen una definición.

3.1 Medidas Inmediatas

La primer idea que surge cuando se plantea medir el tamaño de un documento escrito en LN es contar la cantidad de elementos constitutivos del texto que pueden ser palabras, párrafos, oraciones, líneas, espacios, signos de puntuación. Estas mediciones no contemplan ninguna restricción, son inmediatas e intuitivas y están fuertemente sesgadas por las particularidades intelectuales del autor.

Al evaluar el tamaño de un símbolo del LEL se han establecido algunas reglas para calcular la cantidad de palabras usadas en la definición: no se consideran las palabras que forman parte de la plantilla (*Noción*, *Impacto* ni el/los nombres del símbolo) y se incluyen todas las ocurrencias de una misma palabra. Dado un símbolo x del LEL, esta medida se indica con CP(x) y se denomina *cantidad de palabras*.

Otras medidas de tamaño de un símbolo del LEL son la *cantidad de oraciones* que se usaron para definirlo que se indicará como CO(x) y la *cantidad de símbolos* del LEL que intervienen en la definición de un símbolo x cualquiera incluyendo las repeticiones que pudiera haber y que se indicará como CS(x).

Haciendo una analogía con el diseño estructurado [18] se denomina *Fan In* de un símbolo x a la cantidad de símbolos que intervienen en su definición sin considerar las repeticiones y se indicará como FI(x). El *Fan Out* de un símbolo x es la cantidad de veces que x es usado en la definición de otros símbolos sin tener en cuenta las repeticiones y se indica con FO(x).

Para calcular el *Fan Out* y el *Fan In* de un símbolo del LEL, se completa una matriz de adyacencia (no ponderada) donde las filas y columnas corresponden a los nombres de los símbolos del LEL escritos en el mismo orden. Si el símbolo S_i utiliza en su definición al símbolo S_j, entonces en la intersección de la fila i con la columna j se escribirá un 1, caso contrario, habrá un 0.

Sea L un LEL formado por n símbolos S_k y F la *matriz de adyacencia* de dimensión n x n y sea F_{ij} = cantidad de veces que S_i usa a S_j entonces:
Fan Out del símbolo que está en la columna j será (sumando filas)

$$FO(S_j) = \sum_{i=1}^{n} F_{ij}$$

Fan In del símbolo que está en la fila i será (sumando columnas) $FI(S_i) = \sum_{j=1}^{n} F_{ij}$

Se espera que la diagonal principal de la matriz de adyacencia contenga valores 0 únicamente ya que no se considera una buena práctica usar en una definición la misma palabra que se está definiendo.

Las *Medidas Inmediatas* se obtuvieron para cada uno de los ocho casos de estudio y se calcularon los valores medios para establecer una base de comparación de este atributo para cada uno de los LEL bajo estudio. Los resultados se reproducen en la Tabla 1.

Tabla 1. Valores obtenidos para las Medidas Inmediatas

		En promedio por símbolo			
LEL	Cantidad de símbolos	Cantidad de Palabras (CP)	Cantidad de Oraciones (CO)	Cantidad de Símbolos (CS)	Fan In (FI)[1]
Agenda	34	56,50	5,94	9,53	8,09
Banco Sangre	55	44,89	4,49	6,20	4,53
C.E.R.E.T	28	55,39	4,93	7,46	5,36
Estación Servicio	90	57,58	4,30	4,32	3,49
Hotel	39	67,80	5,74	8,49	6,20
LEL & Esc.	78	62,42	5,35	8,49	5,90
Pasaporte	37	60,84	5,65	7,54	4,86
Plan de Ahorro	38	41,39	3,53	7,58	4,95
Amplitud%		**38,95**		**54,67**	

Este análisis estadístico permite destacar que la variación entre el mayor (67,80) y el menor (41,39) valor registrados para los ocho casos de estudio de CP promedio por símbolo es del 38,95%. Para la CS se observa una amplitud (calculada en base al mayor valor 9,53 y el menor 4,32) del 54,67%, este alto valor indica la existencia de estilos de redacción muy diferentes. Se podría pensar que esta medida sugiere, en algún grado, una medida de calidad del LEL.

El mayor valor consignado para la CS promedio corresponde al LEL Agenda (9,53) [10] que también es el que tiene la menor cantidad de símbolos (34), mientras que el LEL Estación de Servicio [6] tiene el menor promedio de símbolos por entrada (4,32) y la mayor cantidad de entradas (90). Este hecho podría sugerir la existencia de algún tipo de relación entre la cantidad de símbolos de un LEL y la cantidad promedio de símbolos por símbolo. Se ha investigado el grado de correlación lineal de estas dos mediciones para todos los casos de estudio y se ha obtenido un valor para el coeficiente de determinación $r^2 = 0,3513$. Un coeficiente de determinación $r^2 = 1$ indica que el modelo propuesto, en este caso lineal, describe perfectamente la relación entre los valores analizados [13]. Por lo tanto el valor 0,3513, indica que no existe afinidad entre estas medidas.

3.2 Medidas Normalizadas

Se ha establecido [4], [5] el concepto de *Palabra Normalizada* (PN) como unidad de medida del tamaño del LEL. La PN permite abstraerse de las singularidades de los estilos de redacción propios de cada individuo o grupo y medir sobre bases equitativas los diferentes LEL para compararlos. La PN es aquélla palabra que resulta imprescindible en una definición para transmitir un concepto. Tomando en cuenta sólo las palabras normalizadas, se ha podido crear un conjunto de definiciones que establecen las características de las medidas concebidas para evaluar el tamaño del LEL y de cada uno de sus símbolos. Al conjunto de medidas obtenidas se lo denomina *Medidas Normalizadas*.

[1] Los valores medios para el FO y el FI de un LEL dado resultan ser iguales.

El procedimiento de obtención de *palabras normalizadas* consiste en aplicar un conjunto de reglas a cada una de las palabras que contiene un texto escrito en LN, entonces una palabra se considera *Normalizada* si luego de aplicarle las reglas de normalización, no ha sido eliminada.

Las palabras normalizadas pertenecen a las categorías lingüísticas sustantivos, adjetivos, adverbios y verbos. Esto se asocia con la importancia de estas clases de palabras en cualquier texto.

Se analiza el símbolo *Agencia* perteneciente al LEL Recepción del Hotel [3] (Figura 2), las palabras subrayadas son a su vez símbolos del LEL.

Agencia / Agencia de viajes	
Noción	
u =	*"Es una organización externa e independiente del Hotel"*
w =	*"Administra las ventas de servicios turísticos al pasajero"*
Impacto	
y =	*"Puede hacer una solicitud de reserva o una cancelación de reserva para el pasajero"*
z =	*"Puede hacer un voucher para el pasajero"*

Fig. 2. Símbolo Agencia

Las oraciones de la entrada se representan con *u, w, y* y *z* la CP de cada una es 8, 8, 14 y 7, respectivamente. Por lo tanto, CP(Agencia) = 37. Después de aplicarle las transformaciones indicadas por las reglas propuestas se obtienen solo las palabras imprescindibles para transmitir el concepto a que hace referencia el símbolo.

Para la oración *u* las palabras normalizadas son: *organización, externa, independiente* y *Hotel*. En la oración *w* resultaron ser: *administra, ventas, servicios turísticos* y *pasajero*. En esta oración hay un conjunto de palabras que luego del proceso de normalización se consideran una palabra pues definen un concepto único: *servicios turísticos*. En la oración *y* las palabras normalizadas son: *puede, solicitud, cancelación* y *pasajero* y en la oración *z puede, voucher* y *pasajero*.

La suma de los resultados obtenidos al aplicar las Reglas de Normalización a cada oración de una entrada x es la *cantidad de palabras normalizadas* y se indica como CPN(x). En el caso del símbolo *Agencia* es igual a 15.

Para evitar una doble contabilidad durante el proceso de medición las palabras normalizadas se cuentan siguiendo un orden fijo, primero los símbolos del LEL, luego los verbos, a continuación los sustantivos y finalmente las otras palabras normalizadas Por ejemplo, si un símbolo del LEL contiene en su nombre algún verbo, éste no se cuenta como un verbo normalizado o si una frase verbal incluye un sustantivo, éste no se cuenta entre la cantidad de sustantivos de ese símbolo.

A pesar de ser la CPN una medida más estricta que la CP, no escapa a la influencia del estilo de redacción, esto se observa en el siguiente ejemplo. Al definir el símbolo lista de precios del LEL Recepción del Hotel [3] en el Impacto se utiliza la siguiente oración:

O1 = "Es usada por la administración para obtener la tarifa de una habitación"
que podría haber sido redactada como:
O2 = "La administración usa la lista de precios para obtener la tarifa de una habitación"

o bien como:
O3 = "La usa la administración para obtener la tarifa de una habitación"

Las tres oraciones expresan la misma idea, pero fueron redactadas con un estilo levemente diferente. La CPN(O1) = 5, la CPN(O2) = 7 y la CPN(O3) = 6. En las oraciones O1 y O3 se hace referencia a la lista de precios pero sin mencionarla específicamente. Pudo observarse que en general, las oraciones que componen una entrada del LEL son simples, contienen, un solo verbo y en muchos casos, ningún verbo normalizado.

3.3 Clases de Palabras Normalizadas

Las palabras normalizadas según su función en la estructura de la oración [12], se clasifican en símbolos del propio LEL, verbos, sustantivos y otras palabras normalizadas que no se incluyen en los grupos mencionados.

Algunos verbos no se consideran palabras normalizadas, por ejemplo el verbo ser. Existen locuciones verbales o verbos compuestos que están formados varias palabras y luego del proceso de normalización se contabilizan como una única palabra, de allí que tenga sentido definir la *cantidad de verbos normalizados* que contiene una entrada x que se indica con CVN(x).

En trabajos anteriores [4] y [5] los sustantivos se incluían en la categoría de Otras Palabras Normalizadas. Ahora se ha decidido evaluarlos en forma separada porque al ser descriptores de objetos del UdD tienen un importante peso semántico. Muchas veces forman parte de locuciones verbales o de símbolos del LEL, en cuyo caso no se cuentan como sustantivos pues se cometería el error de contarlos más de una vez. También ocurre que varios sustantivos forman la denominación de un único objeto, en ese caso se contarán como una sola palabra normalizada. Al conjunto de los sustantivos se les llama *cantidad de sustantivos normalizados* y se indica con CSN(x).

Las palabras normalizadas que no son verbos, sustantivos o símbolos se incluyen en la *cantidad de otras palabras normalizadas* y se indica COPN(x). Este valor presenta las mayores fluctuaciones y es el que mejor refleja el estilo del ingeniero de requerimientos para definir cada símbolo. Un valor bajo significa que las entradas están expresadas en forma simple y directa, caso contrario indica una mayor riqueza descriptiva.

En la Tabla 2 se presentan los valores obtenidos para las PN del símbolo *Agencia*

Tabla 2. Valores obtenidos para el símbolo *Agencia*

Total palabras (CP)	Oraciones (CO)	Palabras (CPN)	Símbolos (CS)	Verbos (CVN)	Sustantivos (CSN)	Otras Palabras (COPN)
37	4	15	6	3	5	1

3.4 Obtención de Medidas Normalizadas del LEL

En la Tabla 3 se consignan los valores medios obtenidos para las Medidas Normalizadas de cada caso de estudio, se sombrearon los valores extremos de cada medida.

En la fila rotulada Amplitud1% se consigna el resultado de calcular la amplitud porcentual entre las mediciones extremas obtenidas para los casos de estudio. Todos los valores son superiores al 30% y esta cantidad se considera elevada teniendo en cuenta las magnitudes involucradas. En la fila siguiente, rotulada Amplitud2%, se realiza el mismo cálculo, pero esta vez se descartan las medidas extremas y se consideran las medidas extremas siguientes, así se consiguen valores aceptables para la CPN (17,71%) y para la CS (26,97%), no ocurre lo mismo con las otras medidas. Entonces, se podría inferir que sólo las medidas CPN y CS exhiben un comportamiento homogéneo para todos los casos de estudio, entonces sería válido calcular, sin incluir las mediciones extremas, el promedio de PN y el promedio de CS. Se obtienen valores de 24,19 y de 7,63 respectivamente.

Tabla 3. Valores promedio de las Medidas Normalizadas

LEL	Palabras (CPN)	Símbolos (CS)	Verbos (CVN)	Sustantivos (CSN)	Otras Palabras (COPN)
Agenda	22,85	9,53	5,94	4,15	3,24
Banco de Sangre	22,07	6,20	3,40	6,24	6,24
C.E.R.E.T.	24,11	7,46	5,29	7,5	3,86
Est. de Servicio	22,70	4,32	4,77	7,81	5,80
Hotel	26,59	8,49	5,82	8,67	3,62
LEL & Esc.	26,82	8,49	5,65	5,73	6,95
Pasaporte	28,51	7,54	5,92	9,43	5,62
Plan de Ahorro	19,71	7,58	3,74	3,84	4,55
Amplitud1 %	**30,87**	**54,67**	**42,76**	**57,90**	**53,38**
Amplitud2 %	**17,71**	**26,97**	**36,82**	**52,13**	**41,99**

3.5 Análisis comparativo de los símbolos del LEL

El análisis de los valores medios de los casos de estudio presentados en la Tabla 3 permite comparar los símbolos del LEL. En el LEL Pasaporte [15] los símbolos contienen, término medio, la mayor cantidad de palabras normalizadas (28,51) y la mayor cantidad de sustantivos (9,43) en su definición. Por estos dos hechos, se podría decir que en este LEL se privilegió la descripción detallada de cada símbolo. En contraposición, el LEL Plan de Ahorro [17] presenta los valores más bajos para estas dos mismas medidas (19,71 y 3,84 respectivamente), la conclusión sería, entonces que la descripción de los símbolos es breve y concisa. Otro indicador corresponde al LEL Agenda [10] que tiene la cantidad media de Otras Palabras Normalizadas más bajo del conjunto (3,24) y el valor más alto de símbolos (9,53) y de verbos (5,94), nuevamente este hecho indicaría un estilo de redacción propio de este grupo que maximizó la aplicación del principio de circularidad [15] en desmedro del uso de otras palabras ajenas al lenguaje de la aplicación. El LEL Estación de Servicio [6] tiene el valor más bajo del conjunto para la cantidad de símbolos (4,32) y un valor relativamente alto para la cantidad de sustantivos (7,81), este valor indicaría que en este LEL no se aplicó el principio de vocabulario mínimo [15]

La CVN presenta un valor muy bajo (3,40), en comparación a los otros casos, para el LEL Banco de Sangre [9], esto sería un indicador del uso de oraciones simples, con uno o ningún verbo normalizado propio del lenguaje técnico.

A partir de estas mediciones se pueden realizar observaciones sobre el estilo o particularidades de cada LEL, se pueden comparar en relación con otros LEL pero no parecen ser de utilidad para realizar generalizaciones sobre cualquier LEL.

4 Medidas Indirectas

Las *Medidas Indirectas* son el resultado de combinar medidas obtenidas anteriormente para poner de manifiesto alguna propiedad o característica del sistema bajo análisis. Se proponen cuatro medidas: Coeficiente de Redundancia, Coeficiente de Simplicidad, Factor OI y Tasa de Uso.

4.1 Coeficiente de Redundancia

Es un indicador de la cantidad de palabras normalizadas en relación con las palabras superfluas o innecesarias que contiene la definición de un símbolo x por estar expresado en LN. Se indica con COER y se calcula como el cociente entre la *cantidad de palabras normalizadas* y la *cantidad de palabras*, esto es: COER(x) = CPN(x)/CP(x). En la definición de cualquier símbolo siempre se encuentran palabras que no son normalizadas, entonces se plantea la hipótesis de que el COER(x) es siempre menor estricto que 1. No debería ser 0 ya que esto indicaría la ausencia de PN en la definición, por lo tanto se espera que sea estrictamente mayor que 0.

4.2 Coeficiente de Simplicidad

El carácter central del verbo en una oración determina su correlación con el número de cláusulas de un discurso que será igual al número de verbos [12]. El *Coeficiente de Simplicidad* (COES) es un indicador de la estructura de las oraciones utilizadas para definir un símbolo. Se calcula como el cociente entre la *cantidad de verbos normalizadas* y la *cantidad de oraciones* en la definición del símbolo: COES(x) = CVN(x) / CO(x). Según sea su valor se tendrá que existen oraciones con más de un verbo normalizado (COES(x) >1), con un verbo normalizado (COES(x) =1) o sin verbos normalizados (COES(x) <1). Puede suceder que la definición de un símbolo incluya tres oraciones, una de ellas utilice dos verbos normalizados, otra un verbo normalizado y la otra ninguno, entonces el COES(x) = (2 + 1 + 0) / 3 = 1. Este resultado se interpretaría como que cada oración posee un verbo y en realidad esto no es así, entonces este coeficiente no se debe interpretar como un indicador absoluto de la estructura de la oración sino simplemente como un llamado de atención en los casos en que el valor se aleje notoriamente de 1.

Es deseable un COES igual a 1 porque indica que la oración tiene un solo verbo. Son oraciones simples que es lo que se busca para tener una definición clara. Sin embargo, hay excepciones:

a) se ejecutan varias acciones sobre el mismo sujeto, entonces la oración tiene varios verbos y esto evita la repetición del sujeto en distintas oraciones.
b) una misma acción se puede realizar sobre varios sujetos distintos, así se construye una oración que si bien no es simple, cumple con la premisa de usar un verbo por oración.

4.3 Factor OI

La relación que existe entre las veces que un símbolo es usado para definir otros símbolos y la cantidad de símbolos que usa en su definición sugiere una medida del papel que juega ese símbolo en el LEL. El *Factor OI* se indica como FOI(x) = FO(x) / FI(x) para el símbolo x del LEL. Un FOI(x) > 1 indica que el símbolo x es más usado en el LEL que la cantidad de símbolos que utiliza en su propia definición, si fuera < 1 indicaría que el símbolo x es poco usado para definir otros símbolos en relación a la cantidad de símbolos que utiliza en su definición. El caso en el que sea = 1 indica una cantidad de veces igual entre los símbolos que usa y en los que es usado.

4.4 Tasa de Uso

Una medida del símbolo en relación al conjunto es la relación entre las veces que un símbolo x se utiliza para definir otros símbolos y la cantidad total de símbolos del LEL. La *Tasa de Uso* (TU) del símbolo x del LEL L se calcula como TU(x) = FO(x) / CSL(L), siendo CSL(L) la cantidad de símbolos de L. Valores "altos" de TU(x) indican entradas del LEL que son muy usadas en la definición de otras entradas. No se puede determinar a priori qué valores son altos, esto sólo se podrá hacer dentro del contexto de cada LEL.

4.5 Análisis de Medidas Indirectas

Los valores obtenidos para estos coeficientes se consignan en la Tabla 4. En la última fila están los valores correspondientes a la amplitud entre observaciones extremas de la media para cada medida. Las magnitudes correspondientes al COES (29,91%), el FOI (38,41%) y al TU (83,33%) no permiten realizar generalizaciones sobre su valor para cualquier LEL. En cambio la amplitud exhibida por el COER (20,45%) es mucho menor entonces se podría considerar que el valor promedio de los valores obtenidos 0,44 es representativo para esta medida.

Un valor de COER(x) = 0,44 significa que un 44% de las palabras utilizadas para describir un símbolo del LEL son palabras normalizadas que incluyen verbos, sustantivos, otros símbolos del LEL y otras palabras normalizadas.

Con el objeto de determinar los valores dentro de los cuales se podría encontrar cada una de estas medidas, se calculó el rango que corresponde a ± 1 DV [2] a partir de la Media y los rangos obtenidos son los que figuran en la columna encabezada por la palabra Rango en la Tabla 4. Además se determinó el porcentaje de entradas que realmente se encuentran en ese rango y se especifica en la columna encabezada con %.

Tabla 4. Medidas Indirectas

LEL	Coef. Redundancia (COER)			Coef. Simplicidad (COES)			Factor OI (FOI)			Tasa de Uso (TU)		
	Media	Rango	%	Media	Rango	%	Media	Rango	%	Media	Rango	%
Agenda	0,42	0,47; 0,37	71	0,98	1,19; 0,77	71	1,22	2,21; 0,23	74	0,24	0,43; 0,04	82
Bco. Sangre	0,49	0,55; 0,44	69	0,75	1,10; 0,39	76	1,00	2,32; 0,00	89	0,08	0,19; 0,00	91
C.E.R.E.T.	0,44	0,53; 0,35	68	1,05	1,39; 0,71	64	1,51	3,63; 0	86	0,10	0,18; 0,02	82
Est. Servicio	0,39	0,44; 0,34	74	1,07	1,48; 0,66	70	1,00	2,06; 0,00	96	0,04	0,08; 0,00	89
Hotel	0,41	0,48; 0,34	77	1,01	1,29; 0,72	69	1,33	3,35; 0,00	90	0,16	0,32; 0,00	92
LEL & Esc.	0,44	0,51; 0,36	76	1,05	1,41; 0,69	73	1,06	1,98; 0,14	90	0,08	0,16; 0,01	91
Pasaporte	0,45	0,51; 0,39	70	1,04	1,35; 0,72	76	1,02	1,94; 0,11	68	0,13	0,29; 0,00	89
Plan Ahorro	0,48	0,54; 0,41	66	1,05	1,50; 0,60	68	0,93	1,91; 0,00	87	0,13	0,30; 0,00	87
Amplitud %	**20,45**			**29,91**			**38,41**			**83,33**		

Si la distribución fuera normal, al menos el 68% de las observaciones debería estar entre ± 1 DV. En todos estos casos de estudio, los porcentajes de cantidad de observaciones en el rango son mayores o iguales al 68%, excepto para el COES del LEL C.E.R.E.T. (64%) [1] y para el COER del LEL Plan de Ahorro (66%) [17] que son menores.

Si bien ocho casos de estudio es un número reducido para establecer conclusiones, a partir de los valores obtenidos se pueden sugerir algunas hipótesis. Por ejemplo, dado que la amplitud entre las medidas de la Media para el COER es un valor relativamente bajo (20,45%) y que la mayoría de los LEL, excepto el Plan de Ahorro [17], tiene un alto porcentaje de observaciones en ese rango, se podría aceptar el rango surgido al aplicar la ecuación Media ± 1 DV como válido, entonces podría decirse que el COER para un LEL cualquiera debe encontrarse en el rango [0,50; 0,38] (que es un promedio de los rangos calculados), esto significa que la CPN de los símbolos de un LEL dado debería estar entre el 38 y el 50% del total de palabras utilizadas para definir un símbolo. De ser válida esta hipótesis se podría disponer de un estimador temprano de la CPN de un LEL, esto es de su tamaño, como función de la CP que es una medida fácil de obtener.

En el caso del COES, si no se considera el valor de la media para el LEL Banco de Sangre [9] que tiene un valor muy bajo (0,75) respecto a los valores obtenidos para el resto de las medidas Indirectas para el COER, se obtiene una amplitud del 8,41% contra el 29,91% que se obtiene si se lo considera. El LEL Banco de Sangre [9] utiliza muchos verbos en infinitivo que cumplen en la oración la función de sustantivo por lo tanto no se consideran verbos normalizados. Entonces, estableciendo el criterio de calidad que dice que una oración no debería contener más de un verbo normalizado (esto COES (x) =1), se podría considerar como bien construidos los LEL cuyos símbolos tienen los valores del COES en el rango [1,37; 0,69].

Tanto el FOI como el TU, especialmente éste último, presentan magnitudes de la amplitud entre las medidas de la Media muy altas, 38,41% y 83,33% respectivamente.

La magnitud de estos valores no permite considerar estas medidas como indicadores de características del LEL.

5 Conclusiones

En la Figura 3 se esquematizan las relaciones que guardan entre ellas las medidas presentadas en este trabajo.

Basándose en los valores obtenidos para todos los casos de estudio se propone caracterizar al LEL en función de algunas de las medidas propuestas.

Las *Medidas Inmediatas* presentan valores que, dada su poca similitud entre los diferentes símbolos, no permiten inferir características para cualquier LEL.

Las *Medidas Normalizadas* presentan valores con extremos tan alejados que no permitirían, en primera instancia alguna generalización sobre ellos. Sin embargo (Tabla 3) para la Media de las diferentes clases de palabras normalizadas (símbolos, verbos, sustantivos y otras palabras) para cada caso de estudio, si se eliminan los casos extremos, se obtienen porcentajes de variación aceptables para las medidas CPN y CP. Entonces se podría generalizar diciendo que se espera que un LEL dado tenga aproximadamente un promedio por símbolo de 24,19 PN y de 7,63 símbolos.

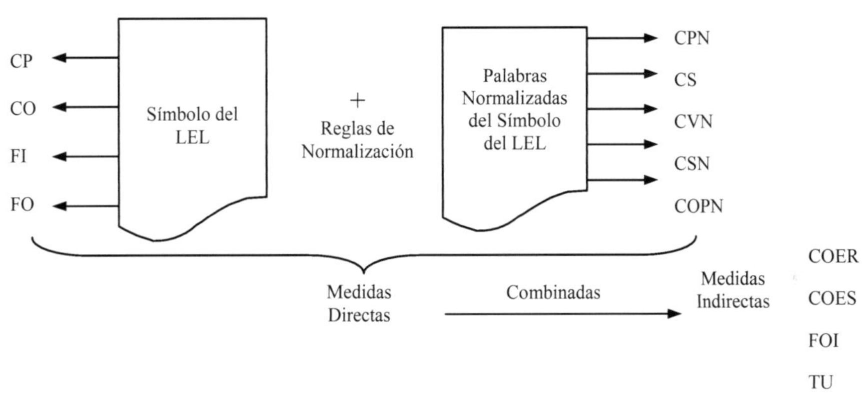

Fig. 3. Esquema de relación entre las Medidas Directas y las Medidas Indirectas

A partir de los valores obtenidos en la Tabla 3 para el porcentaje de cada tipo de palabra normalizada respecto del total de palabras normalizadas no se puede llegar a una generalización para cualquier LEL, ya que las amplitudes registradas entre los valores para cada caso de estudio es muy grande, mayor del 30%. Al calcular el porcentaje de PN respecto a las palabras usadas en las definiciones, se obtiene una amplitud del 20% entre los valores registrados, considerando esta magnitud aceptable, se podría inferir que para un LEL dado, aproximadamente el 44% de sus palabras son normalizadas.

Combinando los valores del 44% para la cantidad de palabras normalizadas y asumiendo que cada .símbolo del LEL tiene, término medio 24,19 palabras normalizadas se llega a que cada símbolo del LEL, tendrá término medio 46,66 palabras.

Para las *Medidas Indirectas* se encuentra que los Coeficientes de Redundancia (COER), Simplicidad (COES), el Factor OI (FOI) y la Tasa de Uso (TU) se calcularon para cada símbolo de cada uno de los casos de estudio (Tabla 4). Se tiene así que los símbolos presentan un COER promedio de 0,44 esto significa que la proporción entre la cantidad de palabras normalizadas y la cantidad de palabras involucradas en la definición de un símbolo es de 2:5. El valor promedio del COES es de 1 lo cual indica que la relación entre la cantidad de oraciones y los verbos que componen un símbolo es 1:1, es decir se usan oraciones sencillas. La medida FOI, por su parte relaciona la cantidad de veces que un símbolo se usa para definir otros símbolos y los símbolos que usa en su propia definición. Este indicador permite clasificar los símbolos en complejo, importante, clave o simple. Los valores obtenidos tienen entre el mayor y el menor registrado una amplitud del 38,41%, se considera un rango lo suficientemente amplio como para no pensar que pueda caracterizar a un LEL dado. Finalmente la medida TU relaciona el Fan Out de un símbolo con el total de símbolos definidos para el LEL, presenta valores promedio con una amplitud del 83,33% entonces, tampoco se lo podría considerar un indicador que permita caracterizar a cualquier LEL.

Algunas de las medidas obtenidas pueden ser consideradas indicadores de calidad del símbolo del LEL, como por ejemplo la cantidad de símbolos (CS) cuya magnitud es un indicador del uso de los principios de vocabulario mínimo y de circularidad [15] o el COER que relaciona la cantidad de palabras normalizadas (CPN) de un símbolo con la cantidad de palabras (CP) del mismo símbolo e indica la magnitud de palabras innecesarias usadas en la definición.

6 Trabajos Futuros

Todas las mediciones propuestas deben ser aplicadas a un mayor número de casos de estudio para ampliar las conclusiones. Esta es la actividad prioritaria.

Se desarrollará una herramienta semiautomática que soporte (asista) el proceso de medición que no podría ser totalmente automático pues involucra al lenguaje natural.

La estadística ofrece una amplia gama de mediciones que no han sido exploradas aún y sobre todo resulta importante utilizar las herramientas de validación estadística disponibles.

Durante el proceso de análisis de los LEL, se ha visto la necesidad de elaborar pautas para la construcción de LEL's medibles. Esto no significa quitarle la espontaneidad que necesita como método de elicitación de requerimientos, sino simplemente acotar ciertos usos del lenguaje.

Sería deseable establecer un modelo de calidad para el símbolo del LEL en función de algunas de las medidas propuestas.

Teniendo en cuenta la estrecha relación entre el LEL y los Escenarios derivados de él se investigará la extensión de este enfoque a los Escenarios para luego relacionarlos en función de las medidas obtenidas. Actualmente se dispone de medidas de funcionalidad de escenarios, por lo que se investigará la relación con ellas.

También se debe especificar el proceso al menos para disponerlo en un nivel de definición que permita compartirlo.

Referencias

1. Ballesteros, C., Minetti, G., Salto, C. "SISTEMA DE ALUMNOS, Centro Regional de Educación Tecnológica, (C.E.R.E.T.)", Trabajo práctico para la Maestría en Ing. de Software, Cátedra de Tópicos I, Universidad Nacional de La Plata, diciembre 1997
2. Berenson, Mark; Levine, David; "Estadística básica en administración", Prentice-Hall Hispanoamericana, S.A., 1996
3. Bertolami, Mabel; Centeno, M. Elena; "LEL y Escenarios de la recepción del Hotel", Caso de estudio desarrollado en el marco del Magister en Ingeniería del Software, UNLP, 2001.
4. Centeno, M. Elena; "Estimación del tamaño de los artefactos producidos en la elicitación de requerimientos", Tesis para el Magister en Ingeniería de Software, Facultad de Informática, U. N. L. P., 2004
5. Centeno, M. Elena; Oliveros, A.,"Medida del tamaño en la etapa de elicitación de requerimientos", Proceedings of the VII Workshop on Requirements Engineering, UNICEN, Tandil , Argentina, 2004
6. Esteban, N., Heidanowski, A., "LEL y Escenarios de una Estación de Servicio", desarrollado para el curso de Tópicos I del Magíster en Ingeniería de Software, UNLP, Argentina, 1998, revisión de la versión original por Bertolami, M. 2004.
7. Fenton, Norman E., Pfleeger, Shari L. "*Software Metrics: A Rigorous & Practical Approach*", International Thomson Computer Press, London, UK. 1996
8. García, Omar F., Gentile, Claudio G., "Análisis de requisitos al LEL (Léxico Extendido del Lenguaje) y a los Escenarios, con la metodología que se basa en el uso de LEL y escenarios", Página en Internet, http://usuarios.arnet.com.ar/ogarcia/
9. Gil, G. D., Arias Figueroa, D., "Lel y Escenarios del Instituto de Hemoterapia de la Pcia. De Buenos Aires", CIUNSa - Consejo de Investigación de la Universidad de Salta, 1999.
10. Hadad, G., Kaplan G., Leite, J.C.S.P., Oliveros, A. "Léxico Extendido del Lenguaje y Escenarios del Meeting Scheduler" Technical Report #13, Dto. Investigación Universidad de Belgrano, Buenos Aires, 1998
11. ISO / IEC 9126-1 - FCD 9126-1.2 Information Technology - Software product quality - Part 1: Quality model.
12. Lagunilla, Marina Fernández, Rebollo, A. Anula, "Sintaxis y cognición. Introducción al conocimiento, el procesamiento y los déficit sintácticos", Editorial Síntesis, S. A.,1995.
13. Levin, Richard; Rubin, David; "Estadística para administradores", Prentice-Hall Hispanoamericana, S.A., 1996
14. Leite, J.C.S.P., Oliveros, A., Rossi, G., Balaguer, F., Hadad, G., V., Kaplan, Maiorana, G., "Léxico extendido del lenguaje y escenarios del sistema nacional para la obtención de pasaportes", Documento de Trabajo Nro. 3, Universidad de Belgrano, Departamento de Investigación, 1996
15. Leite, J.C.S.P., Rossi, G., Balaguer, F., Maiorana, V., Kaplan, G., Hadad, G., Oliveros, A., "Enhancing a Requirement Baseline with Scenarios", in Proceedings of the Third IEEE International Symposium on Requirements Engineering, IEEE Computer Society Press, Los Alamitos, 1997
16. Microsoft Excel 2000 Planilla de Cálculo

17. Mauco, V., Ridao, M., del Fresno, M., Rivero, L., Doorn, J., "Proyecto Sistema Planes de Ahorro", Facultad de Ciencias Exactas, UNICEN, 1977
18. Yourdon, E., Constantine,L.L., "Structured Design. Fundamentals of a Discipline of Computer Program and System Design", Prentice-Hall, 1979

Métricas para la Evaluación de Modelos de Proceso de Negocio

Elvira Rolón[1], Francisco Ruiz[2], Félix García[2], Mario Piattini[2]

[1]Universidad Autónoma de Tamaulipas-FIANS
Centro Universitario Tampico-Madero
89336 Tampico, Tams. México
erolon@proyectos.inf-cr.uclm.es
[2]Universidad de Castilla-La Mancha
Paseo de la Universidad No. 4
13071 Ciudad Real, España.
{francisco.ruizg, felix.garcia,
mario.piattini}@uclm.es

Resumen. En este trabajo se presenta un conjunto de métricas que han sido definidas con el objetivo de evaluar la complejidad estructural de los modelos de procesos de negocio en un nivel conceptual. Además se presenta el material para realizar una familia de experimentos con el fin de validar empíricamente las métricas propuestas. Con una evaluación temprana de los modelos de procesos de negocio creemos que se puede proporcionar soporte a la gestión de procesos de negocio al facilitar las tareas de mantenimiento de los mismos. Esta propuesta está basada en la notación estándar para el modelado de procesos de negocio BPMN (Business Process Modeling Notation) y en la adaptación y extensión del marco FMESP (Framework for the Modeling and Evaluation of Software Processes).

1 Introducción

La globalización y el incremento de la competencia en la última década han forzado a las organizaciones a mejorar y a centrarse en sus procesos de negocio, lo que ha producido también el planteamiento de nuevas propuestas dirigidas al estudio y modelado de procesos de negocio [19], así como a estudios para evaluar la calidad de las técnicas de modelado [6,7].

Un medio para lograr la mejora de los procesos de negocio es la utilización de los BPMS (Business Process Management Systems) que en la actualidad son ampliamente conocidos por el mercado de negocios y la comunidad científica como una herramienta o sistema software que proporciona el soporte necesario de cualquier proceso de negocio para la integración de sistemas, automatización de actividades rutinarias, control de todas las fases del proceso, despliegue transparente de procesos, así como para proporcionar visibilidad y control de extremo a extremo [16].

Sin embargo, aunque los BPMS están dirigidos a lograr una adecuada Gestión de los Procesos de Negocio (Business Process Management, BPM), sólo representan una parte del soporte global de lo que constituye BPM como un todo. BPM es el soporte a los procesos de negocio mediante el uso de técnicas, métodos y sistemas software, que involucra al personal, organizaciones, aplicaciones, documentos y otras fuentes de in-formación para diseñar, promulgar, controlar y analizar los procesos operativos [18].

Una de las principales actividades que se lleva a cabo en las fases tempranas de los proyectos de gestión de procesos de negocio es la del diseño del proceso, la que a su vez está estrechamente relacionada con el modelado del proceso [21]. El concepto central en el modelado de procesos de negocio es el proceso mismo, ya que representa el medio a través del cual se muestra tanto el funcionamiento, como otros aspectos importantes del negocio [5].

Por ello, los procesos de negocio al ser un conjunto completo y dinámicamente coordinado de actividades colaborativas y transaccionales para distribuir valor a los clientes [15], constituyen el medio a través del cual las organizaciones buscan lograr su principal objetivo de producir bienes o servicios para satisfacer las demandas de los clientes. Adicionalmente, un entorno de mercado competitivo y en constante cambio ha incrementado en las organizaciones la necesidad de analizar, evaluar, medir y mejorar sus procesos de negocio.

Nosotros creemos que con un adecuado análisis y evaluación de los procesos de negocio en su etapa de modelado, se podrían facilitar las tareas de mantenimiento de los mismos con lo que también se estaría dando soporte a la gestión de procesos de negocio. Para lograr tal objetivo, nos hemos centrado en el nivel conceptual de los modelos de procesos de negocio para su evaluación y medición, debido a que hasta ahora la comunidad investigadora se ha enfocado principalmente en la evaluación de los modelos de procesos de negocio desde el punto de vista de la ejecución del proceso y de los resultados obtenidos, incluyendo aspectos como tiempo del ciclo del proceso y los costos del proceso [8].

Este artículo está organizado de la siguiente manera. En la sección 2 se definen las métricas propuestas para la evaluación de modelos de procesos de negocio en un nivel conceptual y a continuación en la sección 3 se describe e ilustra el material que se ha preparado para llevar a cabo una familia de experimentos con el fin de validar empíricamente las métricas propuestas. En la sección 4 se presentan algunos trabajos relacionados al tema de la medición de procesos de negocio, en donde se contrastan objetivos. Finalmente se presentan las conclusiones y los trabajos futuros.

2 Definición de métricas para modelos de procesos de negocio

Nuestro interés radica en la evaluación de los procesos de negocio a partir del modelo que los representa en un nivel conceptual, para ello nos hemos basado en la notación BPMN (Business Process Modeling Notation) [1], por ser la notación estándar más reciente y específica para el modelado de procesos de negocio. BPMN proporciona una notación gráfica para expresar procesos de negocio mediante un Diagrama de Procesos de Negocio (DPN) que está compuesto de dos categorías básicas de elementos, con los cuales es posible desarrollar desde modelos de procesos simples hasta modelos complejos o de alto nivel.

Además, nuestro trabajo esta basado en la propuesta de FMESP (Framework for the Modeling and Evaluation of Software Processes) [4] en el cual se definen un conjunto de métricas para evaluar los modelos de procesos software en dos niveles: i) a nivel de modelo para evaluar la complejidad estructural del modelo en su totalidad; ii) a nivel de los elementos fundamentales del modelo, para evaluar la complejidad concreta de elementos tales como *actividades*, *roles* o *productos de trabajo*. El objetivo de la definición y validación de métricas en FMESP fue el de determinar un conjunto de indicadores que fueran útiles para la mantenibilidad de los modelos de proceso software mediante la evaluación de la complejidad estructural de los mismos.

Para lograr nuestro objetivo se ha retomado la idea de FMESP adaptándola y extendiéndola a modelos de procesos de negocio (MPNs) representados con BPMN. Asimismo, se ha definido un conjunto de métricas para modelos representados con BPMN que han sido agrupadas en dos categorías: métricas base y métricas derivadas.

Las métricas base consisten principalmente en contar los elementos significativos del modelo de proceso de negocio y han sido definidas un total de 43 métricas base en función de los principales elementos que componen el metamodelo de BPMN, las cuales están distribuidas acorde a las cuatro categorías de elementos quedando de la siguiente manera: 37 métricas base corresponden a la categoría de *Objetos de Flujo,* 2 a la categoría de *Objetos de Conexión* , 2 a la categoría de *Carriles* y 2 métricas a la categoría de *Artefactos*.

Las primeras 37 métricas base correspondientes a la categoría de *Objetos de flujo*, están agrupadas en función del elemento común al que corresponden. De esta manera se han definido 23 métricas para el elemento *Evento*, 9 para el elemento *Actividad* y 5 para las *Decisiones*. A continuación, en la Tabla 1 se muestran las métricas base correspondientes al elemento *Evento.*

Tabla 1. Métricas base definidas para el elemento Evento.

Elemento Central	Nombre Métrica	Definición
Eventos de Inicio	NSNE	Número de Eventos de Inicio simple
	NSTE	Número de eventos de Inicio de Tiempo
	NSMsE	Número de Eventos de Inicio de Mensaje
	NSRE	Número de Eventos de Inicio de Regla
	NSLE	Número de Eventos de Inicio de Vínculo
	NSMuE	Número de Eventos de Inicio Múltiple
Eventos Intermedios	NINE	Número de Eventos Intermedios simples
	NITE	Núm. de Eventos Intermedios de Tiempo
	NIMsE	Núm. de Eventos Intermedios de Mensaje
	NIEE	Número de Eventos Intermedios de Error
	NICaE	Número de Eventos Intermedios de Cancelación
	NICoE	Núm. de Eventos Intermedios de Compensación
	NIRE	Número de Eventos Intermedios de Regla
	NILE	Núm. de Eventos Intermedios de Vínculo
	NIMuE	Núm. de Eventos Intermedios Múltiples
Eventos Finales	NENE	Número de Eventos Finales Simples
	NEMsE	Número de Eventos Finales de Mensaje
	NEEE	Número de Eventos Finales de Error
	NECaE	Núm. de Eventos Finales de Cancelación
	NECoE	Núm. de Eventos Finales de Compensación
	NELE	Número de Eventos Finales de Vínculo
	NEMuE	Número de Eventos Finales Múltiples
	NETE	Núm. de Eventos Finales de Terminación.

Un modelo de proceso de negocio representado con BPMN, puede tener diversos disparadores de eventos con los cuales es posible identificar el inicio o el final del flujo de secuencia del proceso, así como a los elementos que modifican al flujo en algún punto intermedio del mismo. Las métricas base mostradas en la Tabla 1 fueron definidas en función de cada uno de los distintos tipos de eventos que puede contener un Diagrama de Procesos de Negocio.

Dentro de la misma categoría de *Objetos de flujo*, está el elemento "Actividad" que puede ser de dos clases: actividades atómicas (tareas) o actividades compuestas (Sub-procesos). Las métricas base definidas en función del elemento actividad en sus dos modalidades se muestran en la Tabla 2.

Tabla 2. Métricas base definidas para el elemento Actividad

Elemento Central	Nombre Métrica	Definición
Tareas	**NT**	Número de Tareas
	NTL	Número de Tareas de Bucle
	NTMI	Número de Tareas de Instancia Múltiple
	NTC	Número de Tareas de Compensación
Sub-Procesos Colapsados	**NCS**	Número de Sub-Procesos Colapsados
	NCSL	Número de Sub-Procesos Colapsados de Bucle
	NCSMI	Número de Sub-Procesos Colapsados de Instancia Múltiple
	NCSC	Número de Sub-Procesos Colapsados de Compensación
	NCSA	Número de Sub-Procesos Colapsados Ad-Hoc

Las últimas cinco métricas base definidas dentro de la categoría de *Objetos de flujo* corresponden al elemento "Nodos de Decisión/Unión" y se muestran en la Tabla 3.

Tabla 3. Métricas base definidas para el elemento Nodos de Decisión

Elemento Central	Nombre Métrica	Definición
Decisión Exclusiva Basada en Datos (XOR)	**NEDDB**	Número de Decisión/Unión Exclusiva Basada en Datos
Decisión Exclusiva Basada en Eventos (XOR)	**NEDEB**	Número de Decisión/Unión Exclusiva Basada en Eventos
Inclusiva (OR)	**NID**	Número de Decisión/Unión Inclusiva
Compleja	**NCD**	Número de Decisión/Unión Compleja
Paralela (AND)	**NPF**	Número de Bifurcaciones/uniones Paralelas

Las métricas base definidas en la Tabla 3, permiten conocer el número de Nodos que generan bifurcaciones o uniones del flujo de secuencia en un punto específico del proceso. Las métricas base definidas en función de las tres categorías restantes, que son: Objetos de Conexión, Carriles y Artefactos se muestran en la Tabla 4.

La obtención de las métricas se ha realizado de manera manual y para la definición y validación de las métricas propuestas, se esta siguiendo el método de trabajo elaborado por el Grupo Alarcos en proyectos de medición [14].

Tabla 4. Métricas base para los Objetos de Conexión, Carriles y Artefactos

Elemento Central	Nombre Métrica	Definición
Flujo de Secuencia	NSF	Número de Flujos de Secuencia en el Proceso
Flujo de Mensaje	NMF	Número de Flujos de Mensaje entre participantes en el Proceso
Participantes	NP	Número de Participantes en el Proceso
Carriles	NL	Número de Carriles en el Proceso
Objetos de Datos (Entradas)	NDOIn	Número de Objetos de Datos de entrada a actividades en el Proceso
Objetos de Datos (salidas)	NDOOut	Número de Objetos de Datos de Salida de actividades en el proceso.

Con las métricas base, es posible conocer el número de elementos significativos que componen el diagrama de proceso de negocio. Ahora bien, a partir de las métricas base mostradas anteriormente se ha definido un conjunto de métricas derivadas, las cuales permiten conocer las proporciones existentes entre los diferentes elementos del modelo, así como otras propiedades del mismo. El conjunto de métricas derivadas definidas en función de las métricas base se muestra a continuación en la Tabla 5.

Tabla 5. Métricas derivadas definidas en función de las métricas base.

Métrica	Definición	Fórmula
TNSE	Número Total de Eventos de Inicio Del Modelo	TNSE = NSNE+NSTE+NSMsE +NSRE+NSLE+NSMuE
TNIE	Número Total de Eventos Intermedios Del modelo	TNIE = NINE+NITE+NIMsE+NIEE +NICaE+NICoE+NIRE+NILE+NIMuE
TNEE	Número Total de Eventos Finales Del Modelo	TNEE = NENE+NEMsE+NEEE+ NECaE+NECoE+NELE+NEMuE+NETE
TNT	Número Total de Tareas del Modelo	TNT = NT+NTL+NTMI+NTC
TNCS	Número Total de Sub-Procesos Colapsados Del Modelo	TNCS = NCS+NCSL+NCSMI +NCSC+NCSA
TNE	Número Total de Eventos del Modelo	TNE = TNSE + TNIE + TNEE
TNG	Número Total de Decisiones/Uniones del Modelo	TNG = NEDDB+NEDEB+NID +NCD+NPF
TNDO	Número Total de Objetos de Datos en el Modelo	TNDO = NDOIn + NDOOut
CLA	Nivel de Conectividad entre Actividades	$CLA = \frac{TNT}{NSF}$
CLP	Nivel de Conectividad entre Participantes	$CLP = \frac{NMF}{NP}$
PDOPIn	Proporción de Objetos de Datos como productos de entrada y el total de Objetos de Datos	$PDOPIn = \frac{NDOIn}{TNDO}$
PDOPOut	Proporción de Objetos de Datos como productos de salida y el total de Objetos de Datos.	$PDOPOut = \frac{NDOOut}{TNDO}$
PDOTOut	Proporción de Objetos de Datos Producto resultante de las Actividades del Modelo	$PDOTOut = \frac{NDOOut}{TNT}$
PLT	Proporción de Participantes y/o carriles y las actividades del Modelo	$PLT = \frac{NL}{TNT}$

Con la definición de las métricas base y derivadas, es posible evaluar la complejidad estructural de los modelos de proceso de negocio expresados con BPMN.

De esta manera, al analizar estructuralmente el modelo también es posible evaluar su calidad. Lindland *et al.* [11] definen tres criterios de calidad para modelos conceptuales: calidad semántica, calidad sintáctica y calidad pragmática; y mediante la evaluación propuesta de los modelos de procesos de negocio sería posible evaluar la calidad sintáctica de los mismos, es decir la referente al análisis de aspectos puramente estructurales del modelo.

Adicionalmente, para la mejora de los procesos de negocio se están considerando las características de usabilidad y mantenibilidad del modelo de calidad del software establecido en el estándar ISO 9126 [9], al considerar que dicho modelo es aplicable a los modelos de proceso de negocio y siendo estas características las más relacionadas con nuestro objetivo.

Para obtener resultados fehacientes y saber si las métricas propuestas para la evaluación de modelos de procesos de negocio son útiles en casos reales, es necesario efectuar una validación empírica de las mismas. Para tal efecto y basándonos en el trabajo realizado por Canfora *et al.* [3] se está desarrollando una familia de experimentos con el propósito de evaluar aspectos de calidad de modelos conceptuales de procesos de negocio expresados con BPMN. En la siguiente sección se describen aspectos relacionados a lo antes mencionado.

3 Material experimental para validación de las métricas

Considerando que nuestro objetivo está centrado en la evaluación de modelos de procesos de negocio (MPNs) a partir del modelo que los representa, y a fin de validar las métricas propuestas, se está desarrollando una familia de experimentos. A continuación se describe la planificación para llevar a cabo dicha familia de experimentos.

3.1 Participantes

Los participantes deberán tener algún conocimiento en el modelado de software (UML, bases de datos, etc.) e idealmente también deberán estar familiarizados con el modelado de procesos de negocio. Inicialmente se les dará una conferencia introductoria acerca del modelado de procesos de negocio y del metamodelo BPMN. Asimismo se desarrollará una sesión de entrenamiento para proporcionar a los participantes el conocimiento necesario para hacer las tareas requeridas en el experimento. Sin embargo, los sujetos no serán conscientes de los aspectos que intentamos estudiar.

3.2 Material

El material preparado consiste en una selección de diez modelos de procesos de negocio expresados con BPMN, que presentan entre sí diferentes dimensiones y características estructurales, por lo que presentan distintos grados de complejidad. Además, para cada uno de dichos modelos se han elaborado dos cuestionarios: el primero de ellos consta de una serie de preguntas relacionadas a la entendibilidad del modelo; y en el segundo se propone una serie modificaciones a realizar en el modelo. Al final de cada cuestionario se incluye una cuestión para que los sujetos evalúen de forma subjetiva la complejidad de los modelos de procesos presentados.

De esta manera, el material ha quedado dividido en dos grupos (X y Y): el grupo X consta de diez modelos de procesos de negocio, de los cuales cinco llevan un cuestionario relativo a la entendibilidad del modelo y los otros cinco un cuestionario relativo a la modificabilidad. El grupo Y está integrado por los mismos diez modelos del primer conjunto, pero con cuestionarios inversos, es decir, ahora a los primeros cinco modelos les corresponde un cuestionario respecto a la modificabilidad y a los cinco modelos restantes les corresponde un cuestionario sobre la entendibilidad del modelo.

3.3 Tarea Experimental

Cada sujeto recibirá un material compuesto de diez modelos de procesos de negocio (cinco de ellos con preguntas referentes a la entendibilidad y cinco con peticiones de modificación). Dependiendo del grupo de modelos (grupo X ó Y) los sujetos tendrán que hacer una de las siguientes tareas: responder "sí" o "no" a cinco cuestiones acerca del modelo o llevar a cabo cuatro modificaciones consistentes en adicionar y/o eliminar tareas, objetos de datos, roles o dependencias entre estos elementos.

Las tareas de cada tipo de desarrollo (entendibilidad o modificabilidad) deberán ser similares en cuanto al grado de complejidad, y este es un aspecto fundamental que se ha tenido en cuenta en la preparación del material. Por esta razón, la única variación en el esfuerzo para realizar las tareas del mismo tipo deberá ser la complejidad de cada modelo. Antes de empezar a realizar las tareas requeridas en cada modelo, se les pedirá a los sujetos que escriban la hora de inicio, y al término de las tareas solicitadas también deberán escribir la hora de finalización. Finalmente, los sujetos darán una valoración subjetiva de la complejidad total del modelo de acuerdo a su opinión.

3.4 Variables Dependientes, Variables Independientes e Hipótesis.

Las variables independientes corresponden a las métricas propuestas, a decir de las métricas base y las métricas derivadas ya descritas. Las variables dependientes son las relativas a la entendibilidad y modificabilidad de los modelos de proceso de negocio, que serán medidas a través de los tiempos para los aspectos de entendibilidad y modificabilidad, así como a través de los aciertos a las cuestiones relacionadas a las tareas de entendimiento, de los aciertos en las modificaciones en las tareas de modificación y la valoración subjetiva respecto a la complejidad.

Las hipótesis planteadas acorde al objetivo de nuestra investigación son las siguientes:

Hipótesis nula, H_{0u}: No hay una correlación significativa entre las métricas de complejidad estructural y el tiempo de entendibilidad.

Hipótesis alternativa, H_{1u}: Hay una correlación significativa entre las métricas de complejidad estructural y el tiempo de entendibilidad.

Hipótesis nula H_{0m}: No hay una correlación significativa entre las métricas de complejidad estructural y el tiempo de modificabilidad.
Hipótesis alternativa, H_{1m}: Hay una correlación significativa entre las métricas de complejidad estructural y el tiempo de modificabilidad.

3.5 Ejemplo del material experimental y de la aplicación de métricas

Para ilustrar el material antes mencionado, a continuación se presentan dos ejemplos de modelos de proceso de negocio representados con BPMN y posteriormente sus respectivos cuestionarios, los cuales forman parte del material preparado para realizar la familia de experimentos.

En la Figura 1, se presenta un modelo de proceso de negocio que resulta sencillo en cuanto a su dimensión, ya que está compuesto de pocas actividades y eventos, correspondientes a una sola entidad. Este modelo de proceso representa de manera resumida el trámite que se lleva a cabo en una oficina de Tráfico para obtener la licencia de conducir.

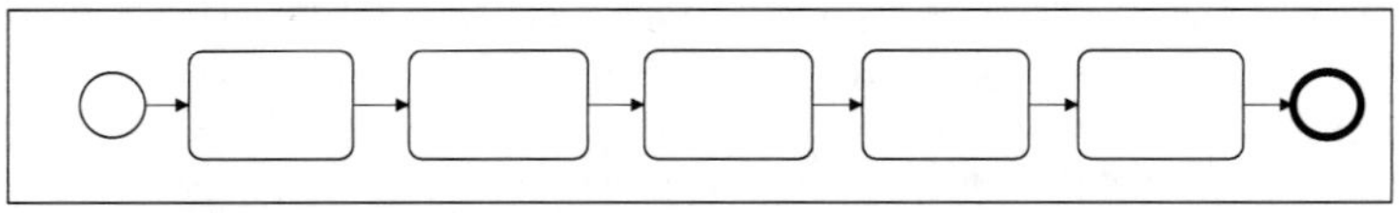

Figura 1. Proceso del trámite para obtención de licencia de conducir.

Un segundo ejemplo de modelo de proceso de negocio representado con BPMN se muestra en la Figura 2. Este modelo, que ha sido tomado de [2], corresponde al proceso expandido del posicionamiento de un pedido, en el que intervienen dos entidades, las cuales interactúan entre sí a efectos de llevar a cabo dicho proceso. El flujo de secuencia de este proceso resulta más complejo que el mostrado en la Figura 1, ya que incluye mayor cantidad de actividades, eventos y participantes.

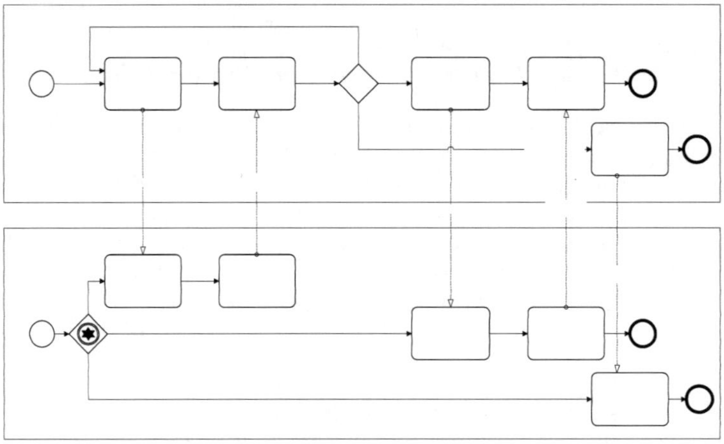

Figura 2. Proceso del posicionamiento de un pedido

Como se puede observar en la Figura 2, en este modelo se incluyen nuevos elementos, como son los nodos de decisión y los flujos de mensaje. Aunque los ejemplos seleccionados presentan algunas diferencias, siguen siendo de menor complejidad con respecto a otros modelos de procesos que forman parte del material experimental, que resultan ser más grandes y por tanto mucho más complejos al estar compuestos por un mayor número de elementos significativos.

La intención al elegir modelos de diversas dimensiones, es la de determinar la influencia de la complejidad del modelo en distintos usuarios como pueden ser los analistas de negocios y los ingenieros de software, en quienes particularmente está enfocado el objetivo de nuestro estudio.

La diferencia estructural de los modelos mostrados en las Figuras 1 y 2 también se puede apreciar al calcular los valores de las métricas definidas en este trabajo, de las cuales por motivos de espacio sólo se muestran en la Tabla 6 las métricas derivadas ya que nos permiten obtener una idea muy representativa de la complejidad estructural de ambos modelos.

Tabla 6. Valores de métricas derivadas de los ejemplos del material experimental.

Métrica	Modelo 1	Modelo 2
TNSE	1	2
TNIE	0	0
TNEE	1	4
TNT	5	10
TNCS	0	0
TNE	2	6
TNG	0	2
TNDO	0	0
CLA	0.833	0.625
CLP	0	2.5
PDOPIn	0	0
PDOPOut	0	0
PDOTOut	0	0
PLT	0	0.2

Los cuestionarios que se han preparado para cada uno de los modelos con el objetivo de evaluar la complejidad y entendibilidad de los mismos, tanto en su interpretación como en la influencia que puede representar la notación BPMN en la modificabilidad de los modelos, están estructurados de la siguiente manera:

1. En el primer cuestionario (grupo X) se hacen preguntas relacionadas a la entendibilidad del modelo, es decir al aspecto semántico de la representación gráfica del proceso relacionado al significado intrínseco del modelo.
2. En el segundo cuestionario (grupo Y) se propone una serie de modificaciones a realizar en el modelo original que han sido especialmente pensadas, a fin de evaluar la influencia que representa la notación BPMN en la modificabilidad de los modelos.

En cada cuestionario se incluye una pregunta referente a la valoración subjetiva del grado de complejidad del modelo de proceso presentado.

A continuación, en las Tablas 7 y 8 se muestran los cuestionarios para los grupos X y Y correspondientes al modelo de proceso de negocio (MPN) de la Figura 1.

Tabla 7. Cuestionario del Grupo X para el MPN del Trámite de licencia de conducir.

Cuestionario del Grupo X
Modelo 1: Trámite de licencia de conducir

Tareas a realizar:

Anotar la hora de inicio (indique hh:mm:ss): ____________

1) **Contestar las siguientes preguntas:**

____ 1) ¿Se puede llevar a cabo la actividad **Cobrar tasas correspondientes** sin realizar previamente la actividad **Revisar documentos**?

____ 2) ¿Sería la *licencia de conducir* un producto de salida de la actividad **Hacer fotografía y recabar firmas**?

____ 3) ¿El proceso finaliza una vez que se lleva a cabo la actividad de **Hacer fotografía y recabar firma**?

____ 4) ¿Podría llevarse a cabo el proceso si el solicitante no presenta los *documentos* requeridos?

____ 5) ¿Los documentos revisados serían un producto de entrada a la actividad de **Cobrar las tasas correspondientes**?

2) **Según su criterio valore la COMPLEJIDAD del Modelo de Proceso de Negocio.**

Muy Simple	Algo Simple	Normal	Algo Complejo	Muy Complejo

Anotar la hora de finalización (indique hh:mm:ss): ___________

Tabla 8. Cuestionario del Grupo Y para el MPN del Trámite de licencia de conducir.

Cuestionario del Grupo Y
Modelo 1: Trámite de licencia de conducir

Tareas a realizar:

Anotar la hora de inicio (indique hh:mm:ss): _____________

1) **Realizar las modificaciones necesarias para satisfacer los siguientes requisitos:**

1. Se desea reflejar que el proceso corresponde a las actividades llevadas a cabo por la entidad participante *Oficina de Tráfico*.
2. Se desea incluir el objeto de datos "*Documentos revisados*" que sea producto de salida de la actividad **Revisar documentos** y producto de entrada a la actividad **Cobrar tasas correspondientes**.
3. Se desea incluir el objeto de datos "*Licencia de Conducir*" que sea producto de salida de la actividad **Hacer fotografía y recabar firma**; y producto de entrada a la actividad **Entregar licencia de conducir**.
4. Se desea que la actividad **Hacer fotografía y recabar firma** se muestre como dos tareas separadas, por lo que se debe eliminar dicha tarea e incluir dos nuevas: la actividad **Hacer fotografía** y la actividad **Recabar firma.**

2) **Según su criterio valore la COMPLEJIDAD del Modelo de Proceso de Negocio.**

Muy Simple	Algo Simple	Normal	Algo Complejo	Muy Complejo

Anotar la hora de finalización (indique hh:mm:ss): ___________

Los cuestionarios correspondientes al modelo de proceso de la Figura 2 tanto del grupo X como del grupo Y, se muestran a continuación en las tablas 9 y 10.

Tabla 9. Cuestionario del grupo X para el MPN del posicionamiento de un pedido.

Cuestionario del Grupo X
Modelo 2: Posicionamiento de un pedido.

Tareas a realizar
Anotar la hora de inicio (indique hh:mm:ss): ____________

1) Contestar las siguientes preguntas:

____ 1. ¿Puede el *Proveedor* decidir que hacer al **Recibir Respuesta del Pedido**?

____ 2. ¿Al llevar acabo la actividad **Enviar Cancelación** del pedido se termina el proceso?

____ 3. ¿Puede el proveedor **Modificar el Pedido** antes de llevar a cabo la actividad **Enviar Respuesta del Pedido**?

____ 4. ¿Pueden llevarse a cabo en forma paralela o simultánea las actividades opcionales posteriores a la ejecución de la actividad **Recibir Respuesta del Pedido**?

____ 5. ¿Pudo el cliente haber **Modificado el Pedido** antes de realizar nuevamente la actividad **Enviar Pedido**?

2) Según su criterio valore la COMPLEJIDAD del Modelo de Proceso de Negocio.

Muy Simple	Algo Simple	Normal	Algo Complejo	Muy Complejo

Anotar la hora de finalización (indique hh:mm:ss): ____________

Tabla 10. Cuestionario del grupo Y para el MPN del posicionamiento de un pedido.

Cuestionario del Grupo Y
Modelo 2: Posicionamiento de un pedido

Tareas a realizar:
Anotar la hora de inicio (indique hh:mm:ss): ____________

1) Realizar las modificaciones necesarias para satisfacer los siguientes requisitos:

1. Se desea que el comprador al realizar la actividad **Recibir Respuesta del Pedido**, sólo pueda tener opción a dos actividades, **Cancelar el Pedido** ó **Confirmar el Pedido.**
2. Se desea que el Proveedor después de ejecutar la actividad **Enviar Respuesta de Cancelación** y antes de indicar el fin del proceso, realice una nueva tarea de **Registrar en Archivo de Pedidos Cancelados.**
3. Se desea incluir la nueva tarea de **Revisar Inventario** que sea posterior a la actividad **Recibir Pedido** y precedente a la actividad **Enviar Respuesta del Pedido.**
4. Se desea incluir la nueva tarea **Enviar Pedido al Almacén** que sea posterior a la actividad **Recibir Confirmación del Pedido** y precedente al evento final del proceso.

2) Según su criterio valore la COMPLEJIDAD del Modelo de Proceso de Negocio.

Muy Simple	Algo Simple	Normal	Algo Complejo	Muy Complejo

Anotar la hora de finalización (indique hh:mm:ss): ____________

Es importante mencionar que la notación BPMN ha sido diseñada con la intención de abarcar diversos públicos, ya que uno de sus objetivos centrales es la de proporcionar una notación que sea fácilmente entendible por todos los usuarios de negocios [22]. Una de las funciones del modelo de procesos de negocio es la de comunicar el objetivo de la compañía a todos los participantes en el negocio (empleados, clientes, proveedores, etc.) y en la construcción del modelo del proceso intervienen diversos roles [12], tales como el analista de negocios, el analista de sistemas, el diseñador y/o desarrollador de software y el modelador de datos.

Por lo anterior, la familia de experimentos se llevará a cabo con una población integrada por expertos en análisis de negocios y en ingeniería de software, lo que nos permitirá comparar los resultados de ambos tipos de perfiles, y algo aún más importante, nos permitirá validar las métricas propuestas.

Los procesos de negocio al ser de naturaleza compleja deben ser documentados, entendidos y controlados, y una de sus características es que pueden ser evaluados y medidos. De esta manera se proporciona la base necesaria para efectuar una adecuada gestión de los procesos y en su caso para llevar a cabo una reingeniería de procesos de negocio en la organización.

Nuestro trabajo está centrado en la evaluación de los modelos de proceso de negocio en un nivel conceptual, y con ello se pretende dar soporte a la gestión de procesos de negocio facilitando la evaluación temprana de ciertas propiedades de calidad de los modelos de procesos. Adicionalmente, se facilita la evolución de los modelos de procesos de negocio proporcionando información objetiva acerca de la mantenibilidad de dichos modelos en aquellas compañías que evalúan la mejora de sus procesos para su adaptación a entornos de mercado en constante cambio.

4 Trabajos relacionados

Poco se puede encontrar en la literatura relacionada con la medición y evaluación de los procesos de negocio (PN), al menos en un nivel conceptual como es nuestro tema de estudio. La mayoría de la investigación en este campo se ha centrado en otros aspectos tales como la evaluación de los resultados obtenidos, los tiempos de ejecución, los costos del proceso, etc., es decir se analiza a un nivel de ejecución del proceso. Sin embargo resulta interesante y benéfico analizar dichas propuestas.

La medición y control de los PN son temas que han sido abarcados en estudios como el de Powell *et al.* [13] en el que pretenden identificar mecanismos de control para PN que son efectivos en diferentes tipos de entornos. Por su parte, Tjaden *et.al.* [17], definen tres métricas para medir la efectividad estructural de los PN a las cuales llamó: de complejidad, integración y dinamismo, basándose en la idea de que para ser capaces de predecir la actuación antes de que un nuevo proceso sea implementado la gerencia necesita métricas estructurales que analicen propiedades más estáticas de los procesos de negocio.

Otra propuesta es presentada por Vitolins [20], en donde propone una nueva metodología para definir medidas de PN en base a un metamodelo de medición de procesos de negocio. En [10], se presenta una recopilación de métricas de complejidad de modelos de procesos de negocio encontradas en la literatura, las cuales fueron comparadas a un conjunto de criterios.

Otras líneas se enfocan a la evaluación de la calidad de las diversas técnicas utilizadas para el modelado de PN, como en [6, 7], donde se propone un marco para su descripción y evaluación, el cual dividen en dos partes: en la manera de modelar y en la manera de trabajar de una técnica de modelado. El objetivo de su estudio era el de proporcionar un conjunto de propiedades bien definidas, así como de una serie de procedimientos para hacer una medición objetiva de las mismas.

5 Conclusiones y trabajo futuro

En este trabajo se ha presentado un marco refinado y adaptado para la evaluación de modelos conceptuales de procesos de negocio representados con BPMN. El marco está basado en la filosofía de FMESP e incluye la definición de métricas base y métricas derivadas para evaluar la complejidad estructural de los modelos de PN.

Además, se han presentado ejemplos del material utilizado para el desarrollo de una familia de experimentos, con el fin de validar las métricas propuestas, así como para evaluar aspectos de calidad de los modelos de procesos de negocio en un nivel conceptual.

Consideramos que las métricas a nivel de modelo pueden ser útiles a la hora de seleccionar modelos que presenten mayor facilidad de mantenimiento de entre diversas alternativas. De esta manera se proporcionaría soporte a la gestión de procesos de negocio mediante la evaluación de una de sus etapas que es la definición y modelado de procesos, lo que a su vez generaría importantes beneficios para las organizaciones.

Los beneficios obtenidos al contar con modelos de mejor mantenimiento pueden ser: garantizar el entendimiento, difusión y evolución de los procesos sin que se afecte su correcta ejecución, así como reducir el esfuerzo necesario para cambiar los modelos con la consecuente reducción de mantenimiento futuro.

En cuanto al trabajo futuro, se tiene programado efectuar un primer experimento en el cual participará un grupo de personas relacionadas al área de ingeniería del software, lo que permitirá obtener resultados sobre la valoración de las métricas propuestas, desde el punto del vista del analista de sistemas. Posteriormente se pretende efectuar una réplica del experimento con gente relacionada al área de negocios y así poder contrastar resultados, ahora desde el punto de vista del analista de negocios.

Agradecimientos

Este trabajo ha sido parcialmente financiado por los proyectos ENIGMAS (Junta de Comunidades de Castilla-La Mancha, Consejería de Educación y Ciencia, referencia PBI-05-058) y MAS (Ministerio de Ciencia y Tecnología, referencia TIC 2003-02737-C02-02)

Referencias

1. BPMI, Business Process Modeling Notation, Business Process Management Initiative, Specification Version 1.0, (2004).
2. BPMN, Working Group. Business Process Management Initiative, Fecha de acceso: Mayo-2005, Fecha última actualización: Marzo-2005. www.bpmn.org/exampleIndex.htm
3. Canfora, G., García, F., Piattini, M., Ruiz, F. y Visaggio, C.A., A Family of Experiments to Validate Metrics for Software Process Models. Journal of Systems and Software, 77(2): (2005), 113-129.
4. García, F., Ruiz, F., Piattini, M., Canfora, G. y Visaggio, C.A., Framework for the Modeling and Evaluation of Software Processes. Journal of Systems Architecture, (aceptado para aparecer), (2006).
5. Gordijn, J., Akkermans, H. y van Vliet, H. Business Modelling is not Process Modelling. Conceptual Modeling for E-Business and The Web (ECOMO 2000). (Salt Lake City, USA, 2000) LNCS 1921. Springer-Verlag. 40-51
6. Hommes, B.J. y van Reijswoud V, The Quality of Business Process Modelling Techniques: The application of a framework for understanding the quality of UML, IFIP (1999).
7. Hommes, B.-J. y van Reijswoud, V. Assessing the Quality of Business Process Modelling Techniques. In Proceedings of the 33rd Hawaii International Conference on Systems Sciences, (Maui, Hawaii, USA, 2000) IEEE, 1007-1016
8. IBM, Modeling Business Measures, IBM WBI Workbench, (2003).
9. ISO/IEC, FCD9126-1.2, Information Technology-Software Product Quality-Part 1: Quality Model, (1998)
10. Latva-Koivisto, A. M. Finding a complexity measure for business process models. Systems Analysis Laboratory, Helsinky University of Technology, Reporte de investigación (2001).
11. Lindland, O.I., Sindre, G. y Solvnerg, A., Understanding Quality in Conceptual Modeling. Software IEEE, Vol. II(Issue 2), (1994). 42-49.
12. Popkin-Software, Enterprise Modeling: Aligning Business and Information Technology, White Paper, (1999).
13. Powell, S.G., Schwaninger, M. y Trimble, C., Measurement and control of business processes. System Dynamics Review, Vol. 17, No. 1, (Spring 2001): 63-61
14. Serrano, M., Piattini, M., Calero, C., Genero, M. y Miranda, D. Un Método para la Definición de Métricas de Software. MIFISIS, (Madrid, 2002) 65-74
15. Smith, H. y Fingar, P., Business Process Management: The Third Wave. USA: Meghan-Kiffer Press, (2003).
16. Smith, H., Neal, D., Ferrara, L. y Hayden, F., The Emergence of Business Process Management, CSC´s Research Services, (2002).
17. Tjaden, G.S., Narasimhan, S., y Mitra, S. Business Process Structural Analysis", Georgia Tech Center for Enterprise Systems, (1999).
18. van der Aalst, W.M.P., ter Hofstede, A.H.M. y Weske, M. Business Process Management: A Survey. In International Conference on Business Process Management. (Eindhoven, The Netherlands, 2003) Springer-Verlag. 1-12
19. Vasconcelos, A., Caetano, A., Neves, J., Sinogas, P., Mendes, R. y Tribolet, J. A Framework for Modeling Strategy, Business Process and Informations Systems. In Enterprise Distributed Object Computing Conference (EDOC´01). (Seattle Washington, USA. 2001) IEEE Computer Society, 69-80.
20. Vitolins, V. Business Process Measures. Proceedings of BALTIC DB&IS, (Riga, Latvia 2004) 186-197.
21. Weske, M., van der Aalst, W.M.P. y Verbeek, H.M.W., Advances in Business Process Management. Data & Knowledge Engineering, Vol. 50(Issue 1), (2004), 1-8
22. White, S.A., Introduction to BPMN, I. Corporation, Editor. (2004). www.bpmn.org

Evaluation Approaches for Software Architectural Documents: a Systematic Review

Rafael Ferreira Barcelos, Guilherme H. Travassos

{barcelos,ght}@cos.ufrj.br

Universidade Federal do Rio de Janeiro – COPPE/Sistemas
Caixa Postal 68.511 – CEP 21.941-972 – Rio de Janeiro – RJ – Brasil

Abstract. Due to the importance of software architectural documents, its review became a fundamental activity for the success of software projects and for the software quality improvement. Software architecture evaluation is a subject that has been intensively studied by diverse research groups. However there is a lack of formal reviews aiming at identifying the existence of software evaluation approaches. The bibliographical reviews that have been accomplished can not be audited or repeated, making them entirely dependent upon the researchers for the obtained results, which could introduce bias on the research results. To prevent these limitations, this paper describes a systematic review aiming at the identification of existing architectural evaluation approaches. Based on the result of this review, we summarize the main characteristics, advantages and limitations of the identified evaluation approaches and propose the requirements for a checklist based software architectural documents evaluation approach.

1. Introduction

As the complexity and size of software applications grow, it has been more and more difficult to define at the firsts stages of the software development process a computational solution to attend to the specified requirements.

In this context, software architecture has been used as a tool for this kind of activity, since it assists in the definition and visualization of the computational solution at a high abstraction level [1].

Software architecture is the structure, or set of structures, which comprises software elements, the externally visible properties of those elements, and the relationships among them [2]. This structure is an artifact from a software development process and is represented by a document composed by one or more models, which represent different perspectives about how the system will be structured, and information sets that facilitate the understanding of the proposed computational solution. It is defined based on the software requirements. Among the different types of requirements, the quality requirements are the most important for the specification of an architecture since it exerts considerable influence over it structure [2].

The representation that describes the architecture, known as architectural document, is extremely important for the stakeholders because of the advantages provided to diverse aspects of software development. Garlan [3], for instance, reports the use of architectural document as a tool to facilitate the understanding of the proposed solution and to communicate this solution to the stakeholders.

Therefore, due to the importance of architectural documents, its review became a fundamental activity for the success of software project and for the software quality improvement. This claim is fortified by some facts such as (1) the review of an artifact prevents defects propagation to the subsequently created software artifacts and (2) the defects correction is less expensive if performed during the first stages of the software development process [4], like at the architecture specification phase that usually is performed in the beginning of the software development process.

Software architecture evaluation is a subject that has been intensively studied in diverse research groups, like SEI's Product Line Systems Program [5, 6]. The review of an architectural document is extremely important and desired by the stakeholders because it may avoid the use of a defective document on the creation of subsequently artifacts [7]. An architectural evaluation consists in characterizing and evaluating architectural documents by means of systematic methods or procedures [8]. During this evaluation, it is verified if the information described on the architectural documents are consistent and if the represented architecture attends to the software requirements.

However, what could be considered regarding software architectural documents review? Is it possible to identify the existence of architectural evaluation approaches and characterize how such approaches could be accomplished?

This work intends to characterize how software architecture and architectural documents have been evaluated aiming at its quality improvement. The bibliographical reviews that have been previously conducted [5, 7-9] do not describe neither the searched scope nor the criteria used to select the evaluation approaches. Consequently, these reviews couldn't be audited or repeated, making them entirely dependent upon the researchers for the obtained results, which could introduce bias on the research results [10].

To prevent those reviews limitations, this paper describes a systematic review [11] aiming at collecting, on some of the Software Engineering main sources [12, 13], studies about software architectural documents evaluation that allow the identification of existing architectural evaluation approaches. Based on the result of this systematic review, it is possible to summarize knowledge and to identify indications related to the main characteristics, advantages and limitations of the existing evaluation approaches. Besides, some perspectives for future research concerned with the inspection of software architectural documents are discussed.

This paper has been structured in more five sections besides this introduction. In section 2 and 3, the concepts related to systematic review and how it was conducted aiming at identifying architectural evaluation approaches are described. In section 4, an analysis regarding the identified evaluation approaches is done. This analysis points out some advantages and limitations on their use. In section 5, our proposal for a software architectural documents evaluation approach is described. And section 6 presents conclusions.

2. Systematic review basic concepts

During the study of a new knowledge area, researchers usually conduct a bibliographical review to identify publications related to a specific subject. However, this kind of review doesn't use a systematic approach and doesn't offer any kind of support to avoid bias during the selection of the publications that will be analyzed. A way to systematize the identification and analysis of publications, and primary studies in general, is using systematic reviews [14].

A systematic review is a means of identifying, evaluating and interpreting all available research relevant to a particular research question, topic area, or phenomenon of interest. [14]. This approach is based on a specific sequence of activities that have to be accomplished, according to a research protocol previously defined.

The studies identified by a systematic review are classified as primary studies and the systematic review is a form of secondary study, since it depends on the primary studies results to be conducted. In the context of this work, the primary studies are scientific publications.

Kitchenham [14] describes diverse reasons for conducting a systematic review. We conducted one to summarize knowledge and identify indications related to the architectural evaluation approaches and consequently to be able to investigate the advantages and limitations of these approaches.

The information related to the conduction of this systematic review was analyzed and registered in a systematic review protocol, allowing its audit or repetition independently. An example can be found on [11, 14].

During the conduction of this systematic review the following process was used [11]:

- **Review planning**: During this step, the research's purpose has to be specified by means of defining what will be searched, the information sources where the search will be executed have to be identified and the criteria used to select the studies that will be analyzed have to be defined. At the end of this step, a version of the protocol has to be created and the feasibility of the review has to be evaluated.
- **Review execution**: During this step, the studies related to the research goals and that satisfy the selection criteria are identified. This identification is executed on the selected information sources, using the search strings that have been created based on the keywords defined on the protocol.
- **Result analysis:** During this step, the identified studies are analyzed for the answers to the research questions. In the context of this work, the research questions aiming to identify software architectural evaluation approaches.

3. Conducting a systematic review to identify architectural evaluation approaches

The systematic review that was conducted aiming at identifying architectural evaluation approaches was based on the concepts described in [11].

The objective of this study was defined as follows:

Table 1 – Objective of the study defined using the GQM method [15]

Analyze the software architectural evaluation approaches **For the purpose of** characterize **With respect to** the software inspection technique characteristics **From the point of view of** software artifacts inspectors **In the context of** the primary studies that describe these approaches

On the following sections, the main information related to the conduction of this systematic review was described. A more detailed description can be found at [16].

Review planning

During the planning of this systematic review, diverse decisions were made related to the scope and the purpose of this search. This information was registered on a protocol. On Table 2, the main information is described.

Table 2 – Our systematic review protocol main information, according to the template described in [11].

Research question focus: To identify and characterize approaches used to evaluate architectural documents;
Question: How is software architecture or an architectural document evaluated? Which are the approaches and what is the context that they are executed?
Context: These evaluation approaches have to be executed on software development projects that (1) have a requirement specification document, (2) have activities to project its architecture and (3) evaluate its architecture by using evaluation approaches.
Keywords: "software architecture", "software modularity", "architectural model", "high level design", "high level model", "evaluate", "assurance", "review", "inspection", "verification";
Sources selection criteria: The sources have to (1) make available a search engine allowing the conduction of the search on the web and (2) be evaluated by Qualis Capes[1] [17] higher than international level "C";
Source List: IEEE portal (IEEE Xplore) [13], ACM portal [18], SEI's technical report website [12], Technical books (Documenting Software Architecture [19], Evaluating Software Architecture [5] and Software Architecture in Practice, Second Edition [2]).
Inclusion and exclusion criteria: The publications have to be available and describe architectural evaluation approaches;

Review execution and obtained results

Two main steps compose the execution of a systematic review. The first one consists on the identification of scientific publications related to software architecture evaluations. This identification is done by searching in the sources' search engine for approaches, using the keywords defined on the protocol and organized according to specific search strings (Table 3).

[1] Qualis Capes: Brazilian system used to rank scientific periodic and proceedings. The grade range from C to A, being level C the lowest but still good.

Table 3 – IEEE Xplore´s search string example created with keywords defined on the protocol

(software <and> <not> (hardware, synthesize, circuit) <and> architecture <phrase> (<or> (evaluate, assurance, review, inspection, verification))) <in> metadata

After the identification, each publication had its abstract and introduction analyzed and, based on the inclusion and exclusion criteria, they were selected or not to a more thorough analysis.

During the first step, we had some problems with the ACM search engine [18]. These problems were related to inconsistencies observed when searches were executed on its engine, which made impossible to obtain the same results when the search was repeated. So, due to the sake of repeatability, we eliminated this source and the publications identified by its search engine.

This systematic review was conducted through December 2004. During this review, 80 scientific studies were identified and after its analysis, only 54 described at least one evaluation approach. Based on these studies, 20 software architectures evaluation approaches were identified.

During the identification of these approaches, we observed similarities on their evaluation technique. So, for the sake of space, we described these methods grouped by its evaluation technique.

The different kinds of evaluation technique that can be applied to architectural evaluation are [20]:

- **Questioning techniques:** These techniques can be used to investigate all software process artifact at any condition [5]. This group is characterized by the use of scenarios and checklists to accomplish this investigation.
- **Measuring techniques**: These techniques result in quantitative results. Rather than provide ways to generate the questions that will be asked about the software architecture, these techniques provide answers to questions an evaluation team might already have about particular qualities of the architecture. However, these techniques need a complete artifact to be measured during the evaluation. This kind of technique is composed mainly by simulation and prototypes approaches.
- **Hybrid techniques**: These techniques use simultaneously measuring and questioning techniques. This approach is used when some measuring techniques can be used to answer questions made by the questioning methods. [5].

3.1.1 Methods based on questioning techniques

Among the 20 identified evaluation methods, 11 use questioning techniques to evaluate software architectural documents. The most common questioning technique among them is scenario based execution, since scenarios allows the representation of the characteristics to be analyzed in an easy and complete way [20].

The method that stands out on this group against the others is SAAM [6], since it is used as the basis to create a great number of other evaluation methods.

SAAM (Software Architecture Analysis Method) evaluates the architecture by the analysis of how the changeability, variability and functional requirements have been attended. The main inputs of SAAM are the problem description, requirements documents and architectural representations.

This method can be used either for a single quality evaluation or for comparison of multiple ones. In the case of a single SA analysis, its main activities are (1) Scenario development based on the stakeholder's point of view, (2) Mapping the scenarios onto the architecture's structural decomposition and (3) Discrepancies identification based on the mapping results. Table 4 describes the main characteristics of questioning based methods, which are classified according to their publication date.

Table 4 – Main characteristics of questioning based methods

Evaluation Method	*Main characteristics*	*Ref.*
SAR	SAR (Software Review Architecture) evaluates an architecture by the perspective of evolution and confiability atributes. It uses checklists based on the system's characteristics and on criteria defined by the stakeholders. However, because the checklist depends on the system's characteristics, a new cheklist has to be created for each new evaluation candidate.	[21]
SAAM	SAAM (Software Architecture Analysis Method) evaluate the architecture's suitability to the modificability, variability and functional requirements. It is the base of a great number of evaluation methods.	[6]
SAAMER	SAAMER (Software Architecture Analysis Method for Evolution and Reusability) is a SAAM extension and was defined aiming at evaluating an architecture through the perspective of evolution and reusability attributes.	[9]
PASA	PASA (Performance Assesment of Software Architecture) evaluates mainly the suitability to the performance requirements.	[8]
ALPSM	ALPSM (Architecture-Level Prediction of Software Maintenance) evaluate the maintanibily of an architeture using a set of scenarios defined based on the desired adaptations and improvevements.	[7]
ESSAMI	ESSAMI (Extending SAAM by Integration in the Domain) is a combination of analytical and reuse concepts achieved by integrating SAAM in domain-specific and reuse-based development processes. The main differences introduced by ESSAMI knowledge domain reuse by using analysis templates.	[9]
SAAF	SAAF (Software Architecture Analysis of Flexibility) is very similar to SAAM, besides it supports the identification and use of high complexity scenarios during the evaluation.	[7]
ARID	ARID (Active Reviews for Intermediate Designs) performs suitability analysis of intermediate architectural artifacts. It combines the active review's philosophy with scenario based evaluation methos, like SAAM.	[5]
ALMA	ALMA (Architecture-Level Modificability Analysis) evaluates architectures using modificability scenarios. These method consists of the ALPSM and SAAF union, creating an unified architecture-level analysis method that focuses on modifiability, distinguishes multiple analysis goals, has explicit assumptions and provides repeatable techniques for performing the steps.	[7]
4+1	This method is used on architectural documents based on the 4+1 architectural representation [22]. By means of questioning, this method evaluates the coherence between the architectural visions and also the architectural decision made to attend to the requirements.	**4+1**
ASAAM	ASAAM (Aspectual Software Architecture Analysis Method) is complementary to SAAM and uses aspects and refactoring concepts to evaluate the quality of an architecture.	[23]

3.1.2 Methods based on measuring techniques

The identified evaluation methods that are based on measuring techniques use mainly simulation and metrics to analyse the architecture. Table 5 summarizes the main characteristics of the selected methods, which are classified according to their publication date.

Table 5 - Main characteristics of measuring based methods

Evaluation Method	*Main characteristics*	*Ref.*
SAEM	SAEM (Software Architecture Evaluation Model) uses quality metrics to evaluate an architecture ant its representation. One of the main characteristics of this method is the use of GQM [15] to organize the metrics.	[9]
Model Checking based method	This method combines simulation and complex evaluation techniques, like model checking, to evaluate the releability of an architecture. This method is one of the fewer that is suported by a tool (ARCADE - Architecture Analysis Dynamic Environment).	[24]
Simulation using RAPIDE	This method uses simulation to evaluate the performance of an architecture. To be evaluated, the architecture has to be represented by an ADL (Architecture Description Language) called RAPIDE.	[25]
OASE	OASE is used to experimentally evaluate the stability of an architecture. This method uses mainly metrics to summarize the software evolution pattern between diferents software product releases.	[8]
ArchOptions	ArchOptions evaluates the stability of an architecture by using some insights about possible modifications and informations about the architecture behavior in relation to these modiications.	[8]

3.1.3 Methods based on hybrid techniques

Among the methods based on hybrid techniques, ATAM is the most popular. ATAM (Architecture Tradeoff Analysis Method) [26] is an evolution of SAAM. Its purpose is to assess the consequences of architectural decisions in light of quality attribute requirements. So, it provides insights into how quality goals interact and trade off against each other.

To achieve these goals, ATAM uses both scenario based analysis and theoretical model of each considered quality attribute to evaluate the software architecture. The artifacts used as input to this method are the architectural document, the business goals and scenarios describing stakeholders' perspectives.

Table 6 - Main characteristics of hybrid based methods

Evaluation Method	*Main characteristics*	*Ref.*
SBAR	SBAR (Scenario-Based Architecture Reengineering) is an architectural reengineering method that can use diferent evaluation techniques, depending on the system characteristiques, to evaluate the achitecture and identify if the reengenering proccess can finish.	[7]
ATAM	ATAM (Architecture Tradeoff Analysis Method) is an evolution of SAAM. It provides insights into how quality goals interact and trade off against each other. It uses both scenario based analysis and theoretical model of each considered quality attribute to evaluate an architecture	[26]
CBAM	CBAM (Cost Benefit Analysis Method) is an ATAM extension that does an economic modeling of the software by evaluaintg its architecture. So, it adds a monetary dimension to ATAM as an additional attribute to be traded off, allowing to model the costs and benefits of architectural design decisions and to provide means of optimising such decisions.	[8]
AD	This method is used to evaluate the performance of embedded systems. It uses scenarios and simulations techiniques specifics to embedded domain to evaluate software architecture.	[27]

Table 6 summarizes the main characteristics of the methods based on hybrid techniques, which are classified according to their publication date.

4. Obtained results analysis

After the identification and characterization of the evaluation methods, we accomplished two analyses: a general analysis about the scientific studies that describes the evaluation methods and another analysis about the characteristics of these methods. These analyses were accomplished to allow the comprehension about how the methods evaluate software architectural documents.

Analysis of the selected publications

During the analysis of the selected publications, we noted that the collected information weren't enough for the characterization of some methods. This happened because the selected publications weren't the one that originated the methods. So, to allow the characterization, we had to locate when possible those publications.

However, during the analysis of the selected publications, some features have been observed.

The first one is the lack of experimental studies. We looked for this kind of study because they allow a more thorough comprehension of the method and its application.

The studies accomplished with these methods are basically proof of concepts that aimed at to show its application and the quality improvement that the method could bring to the architectural documents [6, 28]. However, none of the selected publications describe how these studies were done or describe a comparison, for example, between the described method and an *ad-hoc* approach that also aimed at the evaluation of software architectures documents.

The second feature is the existence of bibliographical reviews that also aimed to identify architectural evaluation approaches [5, 7-9]. These reviews neither describe the inclusion and exclusion criteria used to select the approaches nor the sources used on the search, preventing the repetition of the review. However, two stands out because they define a framework to characterize the selected methods [7, 9].

Another characteristic of some of these reviews is that they were conducted aiming at the identification of motivations to justify their own evaluation approach. So, when a review is executed with these purposes, for example [8], usually all the selected approaches present a specific limitation that is treated by the new proposed method. The obtained results of this kind of review can be biased, since the researches may identify only methods that have the limitations that their approach deals with.

The third observed feature is the number of architectural evaluation methods that the systematic review was able to identify when compared to the other reviews. This systematic review identified 20 methods whereas the others ad-hoc reviews [5, 7-9] identified, on average, 8 methods.

Analysis of the identified software architecture evaluation methods

The main goal of the identified methods is the improvement of software architecture quality by the analysis of the document that describes it.

Since experimental studies have demonstrated that the use of inspections techniques also improves the software artifact quality [29, 30], we used a set of characteristics present on inspections based approaches to characterize the identified evaluation methods aiming at their better understanding.

Based on these characteristics, the following ones have been extracted from the methods: the kind of evaluation technique, its evaluation process, inputs and outputs artifacts, the type of identified defects, the moment that it is executed, studies accomplished to evaluate the method and tools to support its use. A more detailed description of this characterization can be found in [16].

After the characterization and analysis of each method, four issues regarding these approaches have been identified (Table 7)[2]: some methods are too subjective, some have high execution costs, some doesn't allow simultaneously evaluate the attendance to several quality requirements and some of them have a limited application context.

Table 7 – Mapping the limitations to the identified evaluations methods

Evaluation Method	*High Subjectivity*	*High execution costs*	*Restrict number of quality requirements*	*Limited application context*
SAR			X	X
SAAM	X	X		
SAAMER	X	X	X	
PASA	X	X	X	
SBAR	X			
ALPSM	X		X	
ESAAMI	X	X	X	
SAAF	X	X	X	
ATAM	X	X		
ARID	X			
Model Checking based method		X	X	X
4+1		X		X
CBAM	X	X		
ALMA	X	X	X	
Simulation using RAPIDE		X	X	X
OASE		X	X	
ArchOptions		X	X	
ASAAM	X	X		
AD		X	X	X

These limitations were identified after an analysis of the information collected during the methods characterization. Therefore, the subjectivity of some methods was based on the kind of its evaluation technique. The execution costs was identified based on the activities presented on the evaluation process, the non-evaluation of the architecture by the attendance to multi-quality characteristics was identified based on

[2] The obtained information related to the method SAEM were not enough to characterize it, so we didn't include it on Table 6.

the types of defects identified by each method. The application on a limited context was identified based on the input artifacts required by each method.

In the context of this work, the subjectivity of an evaluation method consists on the lack of a deterministic approach or an exact and complete definition of the architectural artifacts analyzed during an evaluation method.

The methods defined as subjective are methods that mainly use scenario-based technique for evaluate architectural documents. This subjectivity occurs due to the incapacity of the stakeholders on identify and generate all possible scenarios that could be used during the evaluation. So, the definition of the selected scenarios set used during the evaluation depends on the subjectivity and creativity of the stakeholders [9]. Also, during the scenarios specification, problems related to bias can arise if the stakeholder unconsciously defines scenarios that don't completely evaluate the architecture due to his/her familiarization with this artifact, for instance.

The execution cost of an evaluation method is defined by the number of stakeholders needed to take part of the evaluation process and by the complexity of the techniques used during this evaluation, like simulations and formal methods, which require specialists. Due to this, an evaluation method could require a great amount of time, human resources and monetary resources to be executed.

The methods that present high execution costs are related to the fact that they were developed to be used in academic or in large projects, which have high resources availability. So, because of the need of this high availability, only a small number of companies apply the methods in the right way [31].

Another deficiency observed is that these methodologies evaluate the architectures against a restrict number of qualities attributes. Dobrica and Niemela [9] suggest that the evaluation has to be done against several attributes, allowing a better understanding of the week points and the strengths of the complex systems actually developed.

Therefore, some approaches [32], knowing its limitation related to the number of quality attributes evaluated, execute several evaluation methods simultaneously aiming at a more complete analysis, increasing the evaluation costs.

The fourth identified problem is the main one present in Software Architecture field, which is related to the immaturity of this knowledge field. It is related to the lack of consensus in the community on the basics concepts and on how architectures have to represented [19, 33]. The software architectural evaluation methods, for example, are based on their own and specific documentation architecture approaches, what makes it difficult to apply in different project or contexts.

5. Proposal for an inspection based approach

The results obtained by the systematic review have identified limitations related to the use of architectural evaluations approaches that make difficult to apply them in industrial environments [31]. Several approaches based on checklist have already been defined aiming at the defects identification in software architecture models. However, the questionings asked by these checklists are either domain specific [34, 35], what makes it hard to apply in a different context from the one where the checklists were projected, or are solution specific [21], what requires the creation of a new checklist for each new evaluation.

Based on this context, some improvements should be done regarding the checklists to make them effective and scalable to fit in industrial software projects. Our hypotheses is that a more general checklist based inspection approach, if used to identify defects on architectural documents related to the attendance of the software specified requirements, could minimize the limitations described previously.

The suggestion of keeping the checklist based evaluation technique is justified by its properties when compared to the others available evaluation techniques:

- An ad-hoc inspection offers neither support nor a formal and systematic process for the realization of the inspection. Additionally, the results obtained depend on the inspector's expertise, skill, competence and experience [36].
- Reading technique is a procedure that aims to guide the inspectors to understand a software artifact and, as consequence, to identify discrepancies [29]. Evaluation approaches based on this technique [29, 30] have shown be more efficient in detecting defects when compared to others inspection techniques, as checklist for example. However, to use this technique, the artifact has to be represented in a specific and standardized way that can't be achieved with software architectures yet.

So, the checklist based software architectural documents evaluation approach should be created with the following characteristics:

- The questioning items shall use concepts from the architectural construction activities, taking into account mainly how the suitability of the architectural models to the desired software quality characteristics can be done. The results of this analysis can avoid subjectivity in the choice of what will be evaluated.
- The items shall be grouped by the type of requirements that they evaluate. The existence of these items groups allows the evaluation of the suitability for the desired quality requirements.
- The evaluation of an architecture using the proposed approach shall be executed without the need of elaborated activities, such as the scenarios specification, allowing low investments.
- The questioning items shall evaluate the information on architectural documents which makes it independent of the architectural representation approach used, making possible to apply this method on different contexts and projects.

6. Conclusions and next steps

The conduction of a systematic review, mainly its planning step, when used as a tool on a bibliographical review allows a more complete specification about what has to be searched on technical sources, facilitating the search and improving the researcher's focus during the read and analysis of the publications.

As result of this work, some indications related to the use of systematic review in Software Engineering can be identified. One of these indications are the advantages obtained on using systematic review as a tool to accomplish bibliographical review, due to the number of identified evaluation approaches when compared to the ad-hoc reviews.

Therefore, the main contribution of this work for the software architectural evaluation area is a more complete identification of evaluation methods and its characterization. Based on this characterization, that wasn't entirely described here due to space limitations, it was possible to identify the advantages and limitations of these methods.

Besides, the obtained results motivated the proposal of a software evaluation approach. This inspection approach is being composed by a configurable checklist that evaluates the suitability of the architecture model, described by means of an architectural document, regarding the specified quality requirements [37] (Table 8).

This checklist has been defined based on the hypothesis that (1) knowledge used by the software architect to construct software architectures and that was used to define de questioning items and (2) configuration of the checklist according to the characteristics that have to be evaluated, allow the identification of defects on architectural documents and minimize the limitations presented on the current evaluation approaches.

Table 8 – An evaluating item from the proposed checklist

Consistency evaluating item	
Item description	After the analysis of all graphical diagrams, have you found an architectural element without relationships, isolated from the others?
Expected answer	No
Type of defect	Extraneous information or Incorrect fact
Item purpose	To identifiy architectural elements that has no purpose on the software architecture
Example	

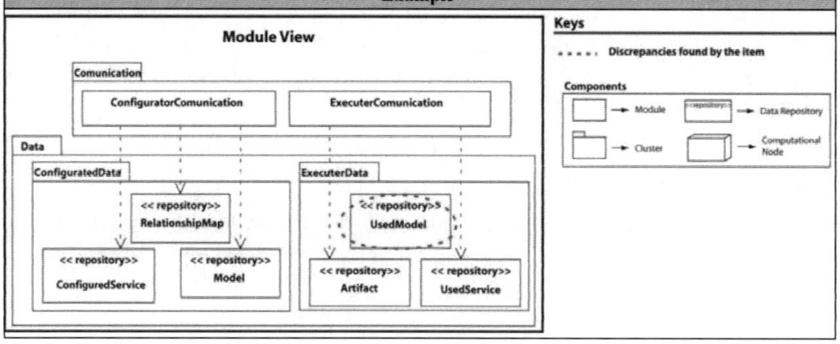

This checklist based approach is going to be evaluated by two experimental studies. The first one is a pilot study that will be conducted aiming at evaluating the feasibility of such evaluation approach. The second, we have planed a case study that will be conducted to evaluate the application of the approach to evaluate software architectural documents elaborated on real industrial projects.

Acknowledgment

The authors acknowledge FAPEAM and CNPq – eSEE Project (4732135/2005-0) for the financial support for this work. Thanks to Arilo Claudio Dias Neto for his comments and suggestions regarding this text.

References

1. Garlan, D. and M. Shaw. An Introduction to Software Architecture. in Advances in Software Engineering and Knowledge Engineering. 1993: World Scientific Publishing Company.
2. Bass, L., P. Clements, and R. Kazman, Software Architecture in Practice, Second Edition. 2003: Addison Wesley.
3. Garlan, D. Software architecture: a roadmap. in Proceedings of The Conference on The Future of Software Engineering. 2000: ACM Press.
4. Boehm, B.W., Software Engineering Economics, ed. E. Cliffs. 1981: Prentice-Hall.
5. Clements, P., R. Kazman, and M. Klein, Evaluating Software Architectures: Methods and Case Studies. 2002: Addison-Wesley.
6. Kazman, R., L. Bass, G. Abowd, and M. Webb. SAAM: a method for analyzing the properties of software architectures. in Proceedings of the International conference on Software Engineering (ICSE). 1994.
7. Babar, M.A., L. Zhu, and R. Jeffery. A framework for classifying and comparing software architecture evaluation methods. in Proceedings of the Australian Software Engineering Conference. 2004.
8. Bahsoon, R. and W. Emmerich. Evaluating software architectures: development, stability, and evolution. in Book of Abstracts of the ACS/IEEE International Conference on Computer Systems and Applications. 2003.
9. Dobrica, L. and E. Niemela, A survey on software architecture analysis methods. IEEE Transactions on Software Engineering, 2002. 28(7): p. 638-653.
10. Mafra, S.N. and G.H. Travassos. Software reading techniques: a systematic review. in Proceedings of the SBES. 2005. (in Portuguese)
11. Biolchini, J., P.G. Mian, A.C.C. Natali, and G.H. Travassos, Systematic Review in Software Engineering. 2005, COPPE / UFRJ.
12. Sei. SEI Reports. [cited 2004 December] Available from: http://www.sei.cmu.edu/publications/index.html
13. IEEE. IEEE Xplore. [cited 2004 December] Available from: http://ieeexplore.ieee.org/Xplore/guesthome.jsp
14. Kitchenham, B., Procedures for Performing Systematic Reviews. 2004, Keele University: Australia.
15. Basili, V., G. Caldieira, and H. Rombach, Goal Question Metrics Paradigm, in Encyclopedia of Software Engineering, J.J. Marciniak, Editor. 1994, Wiley.
16. Barcelos, R.F. and G.H. Travassos, Software Architecture: Identifying the approaches that evaluate its quality. 2004 (in Portuguese)
17. Capes. Qualis Capes - Brazilian system to rank scientific periodic and proceedings. [cited 2004 December] Available from: http://qualis.capes.gov.br/ (in Portuguese)
18. Acm. Association for Computing Machinery (ACM) Digital Library. [cited 2004 December] Available from: http://portal.acm.org/dl.cfm
19. Clements, P., F. Bachmann, L. Bass, D. Garlan, J. Ivers, R. Little, R. Nord, and J. Stafford, Documenting Software Architectures. SEI Series in Software Engineering. 2004: Addison-Wesley.

20.Abowd, G., L. Bass, P. Clements, R. Kazman, L. Northrop, and A. Zaremski, Recommended Best Industrial Practice for Software Architecture Evaluation. 1997, SEI, Carnegie Mellon University.
21.Erickson, R.L., N.D. Griffeth, M.Y. Lai, and S.Y. Wang. Software architecture review for telecommunications software improvement. in IEEE International Conference on Communications. 1993.
22.Kruchten, P. Architectural Blueprints - The "4+1" View Model of Software Architecture. in IEEE Software. 1995.
23.Tekinerdogan, B. ASAAM: aspectual software architecture analysis method. in Proceedings of the Fourth Working IEEE/IFIP Conference on Software Architecture. 2004.
24.Barber, K.S., T. Graser, and J. Holt. Providing early feedback in the development cycle through automated application of model checking to software architectures. in 16th Annual International Conference on Automated Software Engineering. 2001.
25.Perez, M., A. Griman, and F. Losavio. Simulation-based architectural evaluation for collaborative systems. in Proceedings of the 22nd International Conference of the Chilean Computer Science Society. 2002.
26.Kazman, R., M. Klein, and P. Clements, ATAM: Method for Architecture Evaluation. 2000, CMU/SEI.
27.Purhonen, A. Performance optimization of embedded software architecture - a case study. in Proceedings of the Working IEEE/IFIP Conference on Software Architecture (WICSA). 2004.
28.Lee, J.E., K. Choi, and N.D. Dutt. Evaluating memory architectures for media applications on coarse-grained reconfigurable architectures. in Proceedings of the IEEE International Conference on Application-Specific Systems. 2003.
29.Shull, F., I. Rus, and V. Basili, How perspective-based reading can improve requirements inspections. IEEE Computer, 2000. 33(7): p. 73-79.
30.Conradi, R., P. Mohagheghi, and T. Arif. Object-Oriented Reading Techniques for Inspection of UML Models - An Industrial Experiment. in Proceedings of the European Conference on Object-Oriented Programming. 2003.
31.Lattanze, A.J., The Architecture Centric Development Method. 2005, Carnegie Mellon University.
32.Bengtsson, P., N. Lassing, J. Bosch, and H. van Vliet, Architecture-Level Modifiability Analysis (ALMA). Journal of Systems and Software, 2004. 69(1-2): p. 129-147.
33.Buschmann, F., R. Meunier, H. Rohnert, P. Sommerlad, and M. Stal, Pattern-Oriented Software Architecture: A System of Patterns. 1996: Jon Wiley and Sons.
34.Aeronautics, N. and S. Administration, Software Formal Inspection Guidebook. 1993, NASA.
35.Hollocker, C.P., Software Reviews and Audits Handbook. 1990, New York: John Wiley \& Sons, Inc.
36.Chen, T.Y., P.L. Poon, and S.F. Tang. Towards a Problem-Driven Approach to Perspective-Based Reading. in Proceedings of the 7th IEEE International Symposium on High Assurance Systems Engineering (HASE'02). 2002.
37.Barcelos, R.F. and G.H. Travassos. Towards software architectural documents evaluation using quality attributes based checklist. in Proceedings of WTES - SBES. 2005. MG, Brazil. (in Portuguese)

Sesión 11

Medición y Evaluación 3 y Procesos

Teste de Desempenho em Aplicações SIG Web

Arturo H. Torres-Zenteno[1], Eliane Martins[1], Ricardo da S. Torres[1], María J. Escalona Cuaresma[2]

[1] Instituto de Computação – Universidade Estadual de Campinas (UNICAMP)
Caixa Postal 6176, 13084-971 – Campinas – SP – Brasil.
{arturo.zenteno,eliane,rtorres}@ic.unicamp.br
[2] Departamento de Linguagens e Sistemas Informáticos – Universidade de Sevilha
Av. Reina Mercedes s/n. 401012 – Sevilha – Espanha.
mjescalona@us.es

Resumo. Este artigo propõe um modelo de processo de teste de desempenho para aplicações SIG Web. O modelo considera os casos de uso mais críticos ou de maior risco quanto ao desempenho de um sistema para a criação de cenários de testes. Além disso, prevê a utilização de ferramentas livres para automatização de etapas do processo de avaliação. O modelo foi aplicado ao projeto WebMaps, que é uma aplicação SIG Web cuja finalidade é auxiliar seus usuários no planejamento agrícola a partir de regiões de interesse. Os resultados preliminares obtidos indicam que os testes foram úteis na identificação de problemas da arquitetura preliminar do sistema.

1 Introdução

Um Sistema de Informação Geográfica (SIG) é um software voltado para o gerenciamento de dados geo-referenciados. Os SIG's são sistemas automatizados usados para armazenar, analisar e manipular dados geográficos, ou seja, dados que representam objetos e fenômenos em que a localização geográfica é uma característica inerente e indispensável para analisá-los [1, 2].

Neste contexto, um SIG Web é um sistema que provê diferentes serviços SIG de análise e visualização de dados espaciais através da Web [3]. O desenvolvimento de sistemas deste tipo é complexo e deve considerar requisitos pouco encontrados em aplicações tradicionais: por exemplo, o grande volume de dados gerenciado (convencionais e geo-referenciados), a diversidade de usuários no ambiente Web e processamento concorrente de requisições. Neste cenário, um dos meios utilizados para se garantir a qualidade destes sistemas é a realização de testes [4] ao longo do processo de desenvolvimento.

O propósito deste artigo é propor um modelo de processo de teste para aplicações SIG Web a partir dos casos de uso mais críticos ou de maior risco quanto ao desempenho. A realização de testes de desempenho é fundamental para assegurar que estas aplicações sejam adequadas quando da sua implantação e uso.

O processo proposto de teste de desempenho lida com as características inerentes das aplicações SIG Web, grande volume de dados e carga de usuários simultâneos, fornecendo um conjunto de atividades de teste bem detalhadas. Estas atividades são integradas em um processo robusto, onde o ponto de partida é identificação dos casos de uso críticos que precisam ser testados. Para isso se supõe que os requisitos do sistema foram corretamente especificados.

O modelo de processo de teste de desempenho foi aplicado na avaliação do sistema WebMaps, que é uma aplicação SIG Web cuja finalidade é auxiliar seus usuários no planejamento agrícola a partir de regiões de interesse. Estes testes foram feitos de acordo com cenários reais construídos baseando-se em estatísticas de uso reais no Sistema de Monitoramento Agrometereológico [5]. Os resultados preliminares obtidos indicam que os testes foram úteis na identificação de problemas da arquitetura preliminar do WebMaps antes da sua implantação.

O artigo inicia com uma descrição geral dos testes de desempenho, assim como, a sua identificação dentro de um processo de desenvolvimento (seção 2). Em seguida, a seção 3 detalha os tipos de testes de desempenho em aplicações Web, mostrando alguns processos de teste existentes. Estas abordagens servem como base para a especificação da proposta do processo de teste de desempenho para aplicações SIG Web (seção 4). A seção 5 apresenta um caso de estudo onde o processo de teste de desempenho proposto é usado na avaliação de um SIG Web real. Por fim, a seção 6 apresenta as conclusões e trabalhos futuros.

2 Testes de desempenho

A realização de testes tem como finalidade assegurar a qualidade do sistema, sendo seu objetivo principal encontrar erros. Os testes também servem para se obter medidas de requisitos não funcionais do software, tais como confiabilidade ou desempenho, usando-se técnicas estatísticas apropriadas [6].

Entre os diferentes tipos de testes de sistema existentes [7], destacam-se os testes de desempenho. A Fig. 1 mostra uma adaptação do modelo "V", indicando as diferentes fases do desenvolvimento de sistemas associadas com os tipos de teste existentes [8]. Embora este modelo de testes seja discutível [8], ele será utilizado neste artigo para fim didático.

A realização de testes tem por objetivo determinar se o desempenho do sistema integrado é adequado, de acordo com os requisitos do sistema. Testes de desempenho podem ser realizados ao longo do desenvolvimento, mas somente quando todos os componentes são finalmente integrados é que se pode ter uma medida real do seu desempenho [9]. Note que, na Fig. 1, o teste de desempenho se encontra dentro dos testes de sistema, associados à fase de Detalhamento de Requisitos.

Molinari [10] mostra a relação entre risco de teste versus requisito de qualidade em aplicações Web, ou seja, quais os requisitos de qualidade que mais comprometem o correto funcionamento destes sistemas caso não sejam corretamente testados. Segundo Molinari, o desempenho é o requisito de qualidade que deveria ter mais cuidado em aplicações Web. Esta importância é ainda mais crítica em aplicações SIG Web tendo em vista o grande volume de dados gerenciados.

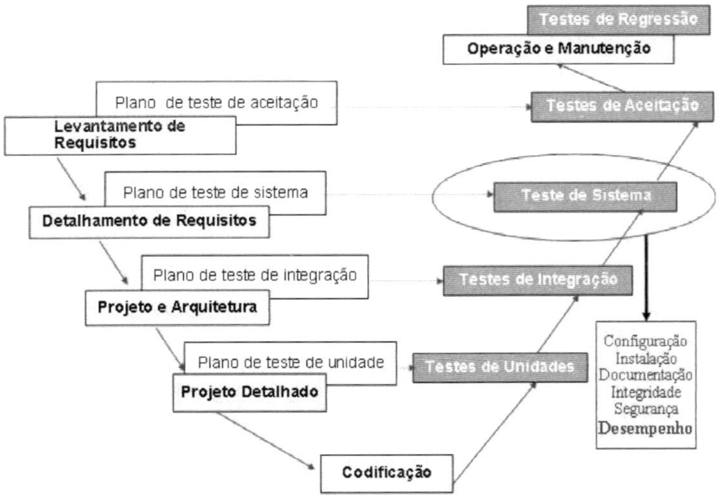

Fig. 1. Fases no processo de desenvolvimento vs Tipos de teste (modelo V).

3 Processos de Teste de Desempenho em Aplicações Web

Como parte dos testes de desempenho tem os testes de carga (testam o desempenho do sistema levando-se em conta uma carga de usuários simultâneos reais), testes de estresse (testam o desempenho do sistema considerando o número máximo de usuários simultâneos que pode suportar) e os testes de volume (testam a quantidade de dados que o sistema pode gerenciar) [9]. A seguir é descrito os processos de teste de cada um deles.

3.1 Processo de Teste de Carga / Estresse

Vários processos de teste de desempenho para aplicações web vêm sendo propostos recentemente [10, 11, 12, 13]. A Fig. 2 mostra dois destes processos de teste de desempenho: o de Molinari [10] que apresenta o processo em 5 fases (a); e o de Menascé [13] que possui 7 fases (b). Estes processos são aplicáveis tanto para teste de carga como estresse.

Molinari inicia o processo com o planejamento de teste de carga / estresse (Fase 1), cujo objetivo principal é identificar e projetar quais funcionalidades poderiam ser testadas no sistema. Já na Fase 2, se procede a especificação e criação de usuários virtuais. Uma vez criados os usuários virtuais, um cenário de teste (Fase 3) correspondente a esta quantidade de usuários é especificado. O cenário é executado na Fase 4. Por fim, a Fase 5 compreende a análise do sistema testado.

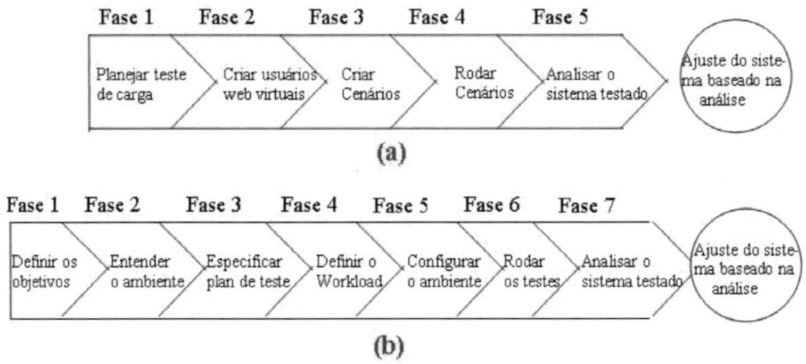

Fig. 2. Processo de teste de desempenho em aplicações Web. (a) Processo proposto por Molinari [10] e (b) processo proposto por Menascé [13].

Menascé apresenta fases mais abrangentes. Para ele o processo se inicia com uma fase de definição de objetivos do teste de desempenho (Fase 1). Logo na Fase 2 estuda-se o ambiente, ou seja, a infraestrutura (servidores, serviços web), software (sistemas operacionais, middleware e aplicações), as conexões de rede e os protocolos de rede presentes no sistema. A Fase 3 é a mesma da Fase 1 de Molinari. A Fase 4, definição do *Workload*, é equivalente à fase de criação de cenários e à fase de criação de usuários virtuais de Molinari. Depois, na Fase 6, as ferramentas de teste são instaladas e configuradas. Nas Fases 7 e 8, os testes são executados e o sistema é analisado, respectivamente. Tanto o processo de Molinari quanto o de Menascé é finalizado com o ajuste do sistema, a partir da análise dos resultados dos testes de desempenho.

3.2 Processo de Teste de Volume

O teste de volume avalia a quantidade de dados gerenciados em um sistema Web. O objetivo deste teste é determinar a capacidade do sistema em lidar com o volume de dados especificado nos seus requisitos. Em geral, este tipo de teste usa grandes quantidades de dados, o que permite determinar os limites em que o sistema falha. Além disso, costumam ser utilizados na identicação da carga máxima ou volume de dados que o sistema pode gerenciar em um dado período de tempo.

A pesquisa realizada até o momento não identificou nenhum processo de teste de volume bem definido que pudesse ser utilizados na avaliação de aplicações web.

4 Processo proposto de Teste de Desempenho em Aplicações SIG Web

Esta seção apresenta uma proposta de processo de teste de desempenho em aplicações SIG Web. Primeiramente, as especificações dos processos de teste de carga / estresse e de volume são apresentados de maneira isolada (seções 4.1 e 4.2). Em seguida, suas atividades são integradas em um processo único (seção 4.3).

4.1 Processo proposto de Teste de Carga / Estresse

Esta proposta consiste, basicamente, na adaptação dos processos de teste de carga / estresse em aplicações Web vistos na seção 3.1. A Fig. 3(a) mostra que no processo de Molinari se considerou uma inversão da ordem das fases 2 e 3. Esta inversão justifica-se pela importância da criação de cenários para a especificação da quantidade de usuários virtuais que deverão ser criados. Esta inversão permite, portanto, criar diferentes cenários para um mesmo teste de carga / estresse, considerando, por exemplo, diferentes quantidades de usuários virtuais.

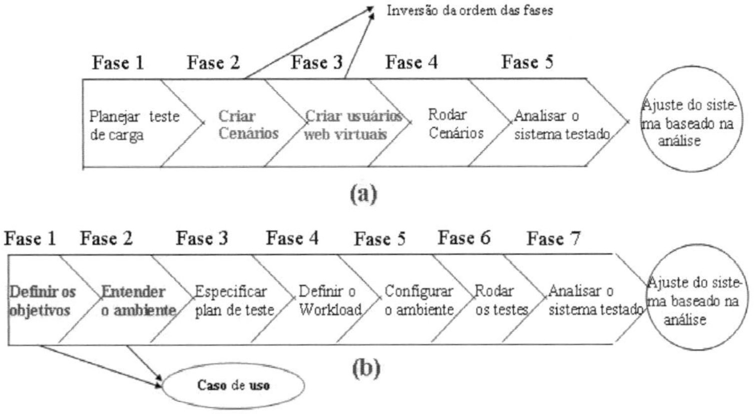

Fig. 3. (a) Adaptação apartir do processo proposto por Molinari [10]
(b) Adaptação do processo proposto por Menascé [13].

A Fig. 3(b) mostra que, no processo de Menascé, as fases 1 e 2 foram consideradas importantes. Estas fases foram agrupadas e consideradas equivalentes à definição dos casos de uso de maior risco.

A etapa de definição de casos de uso foi incorporada ao processo de Molinari modificado (veja seção 4.3).

4.2 Processo proposto de Teste de Volume

Este trabalho apresenta um processo de teste de volume, ilustrado na Fig. 4. Este processo se inicia com uma fase de planejamento, cujo objetivo principal é identificar a finalidade do teste (Fase 1). Já na Fase 2 identificam-se os cenários de volume, ou seja, cenários que envolvem armazenamento de informação em dispositivos de armazenamento primários (unidades de disco rígido), secundários (CD, DVD), em banco de dados ou em algum outro tipo de armazenamento. Estes cenários são criados na Fase 3. A Fase 4 corresponde ao cálculo do volume de dados que o sistema gerencia para cada cenário de teste. Finalmente, na Fase 5, o sistema testado é analisado levando-se em conta os resultados do teste realizado e, caso necessário, modificado.

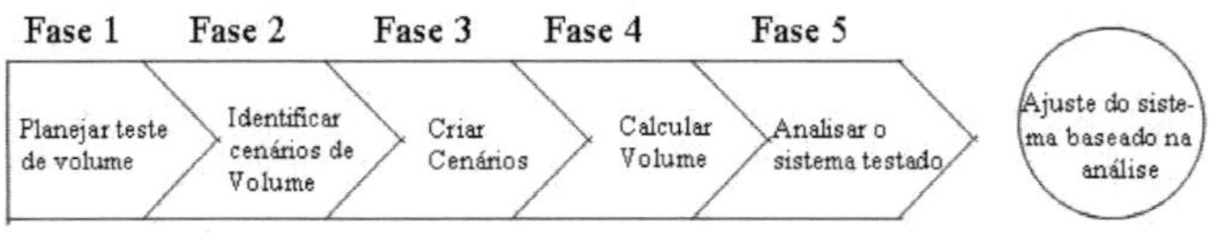

Fig. 4. Processo proposto de teste de volume.

4.3 Processo proposto de Teste de Desempenho

Este trabalhão propõe um processo que integra os testes de carga, estresse e volume na avaliação do desempenho de um sistema SIG Web. A Fig. 5 mostra o modelo proposto, usando a notação UML do diagrama de atividades [14]. Atividades são mostradas através de elipses enquanto setas indicam a ordem nas quais as atividades devem ser realizadas. As setas pontilhadas significam que a relação entre duas atividades não é obrigatória. O processo se inicia com uma fase de planejamento em um nível superior (Fase 0), onde se identifica os casos de uso que serão testados. Como dito anteriormente, a identificação de casos de uso críticos e de grande risco é vital para a realização de um bom teste de desempenho.

O teste de desempenho pode conter um ou mais testes de carga, estresse e volume. Tanto para os testes de carga como para os testes de estresse se considerou as modificações descritas na seção 4.1. Na parte A da Fig. 5, essas adaptações são apresentadas.

O processo começa com uma fase de planejamento do teste de carga ou estresse seguido da fase de criação de cenários. É importante notar que no planejamento dos testes da Fase 1 podem ser definidos um ou mais cenários. Uma vez criados o(s) cenário(s) correspondentes a um teste de carga ou estresse criam-se os usuários web virtuais. Na Fase 4 são executados o(s) cenário(s), enquanto que na última fase (Fase 5), o sistema testado é analisado.

A parte B da Fig. 5 mostra o processo proposto para a realização de testes de volume descrito na seção 4.2. Além disso, mostra como os cenários de teste de volume podem se baseiar nos cenários de teste de carga ou estresse caso tenham sido criados. Os testes de volume se iniciam na Fase 1 (planejamento), onde se define o objetivo do teste. Logo na Fase 2 identificam-se o(s) cenário(s) de volume. Esta identificação considera os cenários criados no proceso paralelo de carga ou estresse, ou seja, aqueles cenários que envolvem interação com banco(s) de dados ou com algum tipo de armazenamento de informação. Uma vez identificados, os cenários são criados (Fase 3). Um teste de volume pode conter um ou mais cenários e para cada cenário se determina o volume de dados que suporta (Fase 4). Na Fase 5, estes dados são usados na análise do sistema quanto ao volume de dados permitido. Nesta fase pode-se fazer também uma projeção do volume de dados ao longo do tempo dependendo do planejamento na Fase 1.

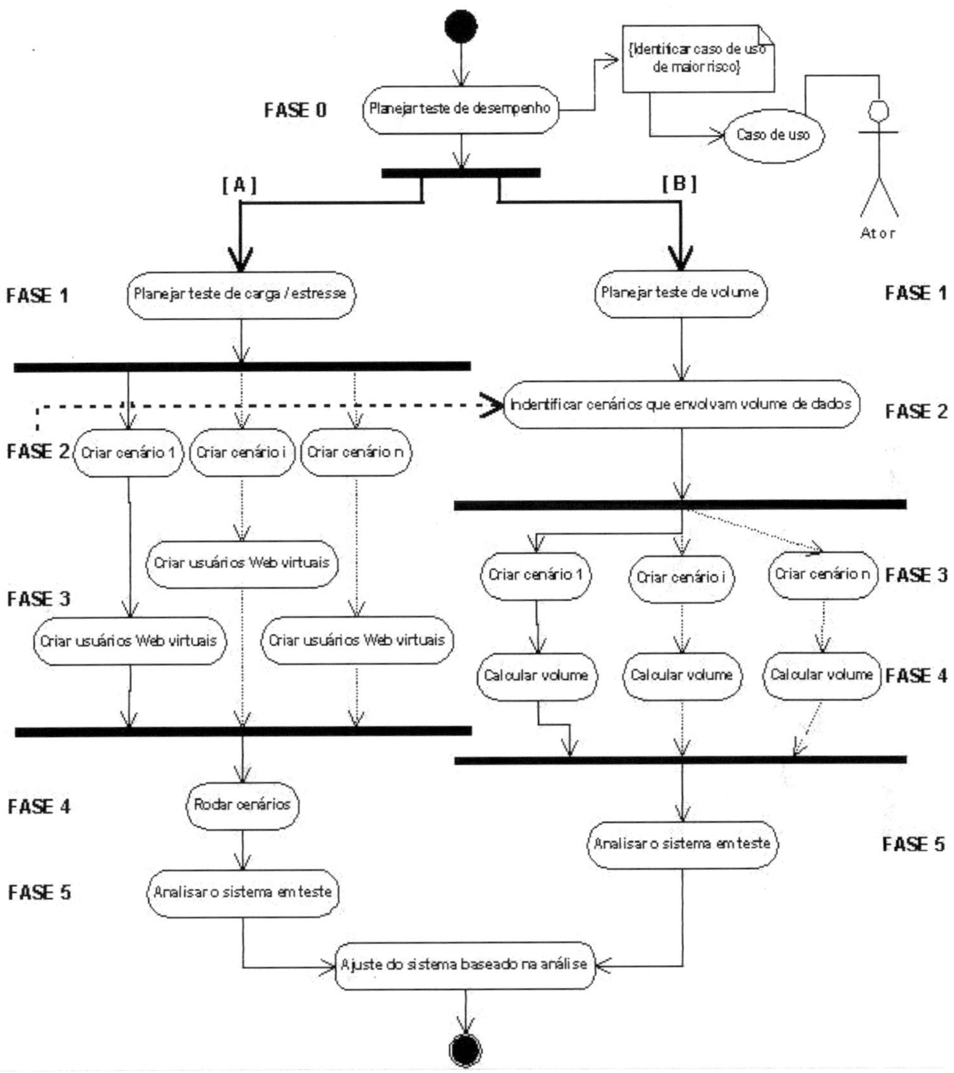

Fig. 5. Processo proposto de teste de desempenho para aplicações SIG Web.

A última atividade do processo de teste de desempenho é o ajuste do sistema. Este ajuste requer a colaboração de todos os membros da equipe de testes na análise dos problemas encontrados e na proposta de soluções.

5 Estudo de caso

O processo de teste de desempenho proposto foi usado na avaliação do sistema WebMaps, a partir de em um caso de uso crítico. Esta seção descreve este SIG web, bem como apresenta os resultados preliminares obtidos.

5.1 WebMaps

O WebMaps é um projeto em andamento no Instituto de Computação da Unicamp que tem como objetivo permitir o monitoramento e planejamento de safras agrícolas no Brasil. Este sistema integra, em rede, dados heterogêneos de diversas fontes e alguns serviços que gerenciam estes dados. Assim, pretende-se estabelecer uma plataforma base para a formulação, implementação e avaliação de políticas integradas de planejamento agrícola.

A Fig. 6 mostra o modelo de casos de uso do WebMaps, onde se especifica os requisitos funcionais do sistema. De maneira geral, o sistema deve permitir cadastros e consultas tanto aos seus usuários cadastrados quanto aos não cadastrados.

A versão atual do sistema permite que usuários cadastrem propriedades agrícolas e suas divisões (talhões) indicando as coordenadas geográficas junto com a informação de produtos cultivados. Além disso, permite a realização de consultas referentes à evolução dos plantios ao longo do tempo. Para tanto, o sistema gera para os usuários curvas NDVI (do inglês *Normalized Difference Vegetation Index*) [15], que são curvas que mostram os índices de vegetação por diferença normalizada, ou seja, a quantidade de vegetação em um dado local em um período determinado. Estes índices são obtidos a partir do processamento de imagens de satélite obtidas periodicamente. No momento, o WebMaps trabalha com imagens do tipo MODIS de todo o território brasileiro referentes a 4 anos (2001 até 2004) fornecidas pela NASA [16]. Cada imagem ocupa 109,6 MB e uma nova imagem foi obtida a cada 15 dias.

O processamento das imagens de satélite para geração de curvas NDVI é lento. Sendo assim, optou-se pelo uso de recortes (máscaras) das imagens, relativas a cada propriedade cadastrada, para diminuir o tempo de processamento.

A Fig. 7 apresenta a arquitetura do sistema WebMaps. Ela é composta de uma camada Cliente e uma de Servidor. A parte do Cliente é o navegador que mostra as páginas processadas pela camada servidora. O Servidor é dividido em três grandes módulos, implementados usando Java e a linguangem C: a) módulo responsável pelo cadastro de usuários e propriedades; b) módulo responsável pela realização de consultas; e c) repositórios de dados (Postgresql e disco rígido (HD)).

Do lado do servidor, emcontram-se páginas JSP's, bem como o módulo "Código em C" cuja tarefa é processar as imagens de satélite gerando as máscaras que servem para montar a curva NDVI de interesse para o usuário quando requisitado. A interação entre o código na linguagem C e o código Java é feito mediante o JNI (Java Native Interface). Em [17], Czajkowski apresenta os benefícios do uso de interfaces com códigos nativos no desenvolvimento de aplicações.

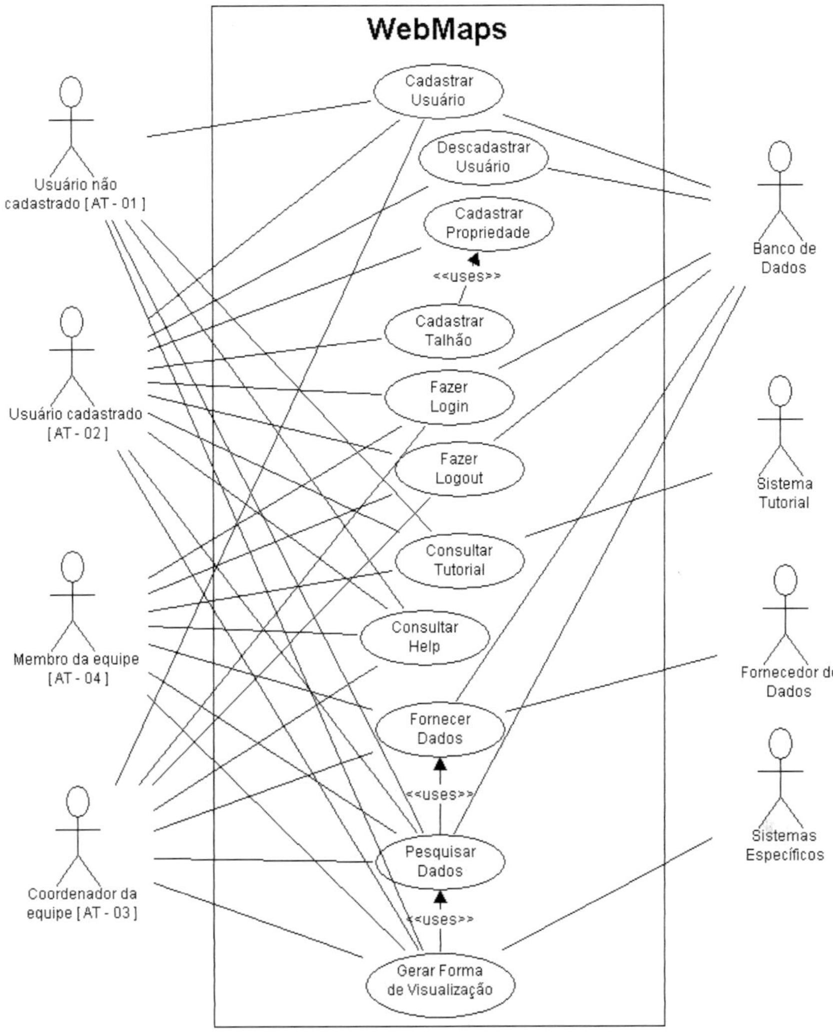

Fig. 6. Modelo de casos de uso do sistema WebMaps.

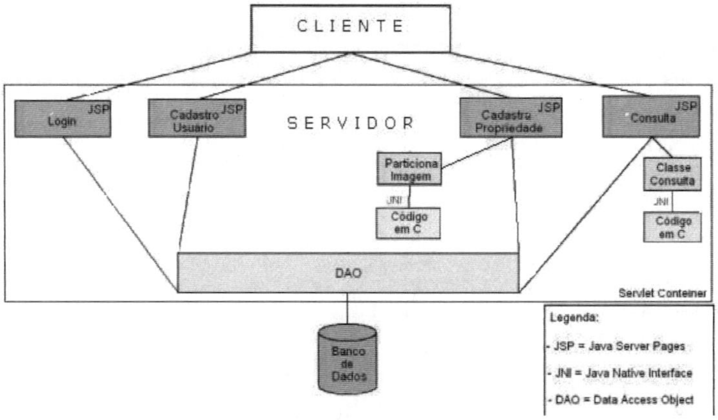

Fig. 7. Arquitetura do sistema WebMaps.

5.2 Aplicação da proposta

A primeira tarefa é identificar o caso de uso de maior risco no sistema. Neste caso, o módulo que requer maior processamento no sistema WebMaps é o módulo de cadastro de propriedade, já que é responsável pelos recortes das imagens de satélite.

A Tabela 1 mostra a especificação deste caso de uso com o padrão de requisitos funcionais do NDT (Navigational Development Techniques) [18].

Tabela 1. RF – 01: Requisito funcional de cadastro de propriedade.

RF – 01	Cadastrar propriedade	
Objetivos Associados	OBJ – 01: Fornecer dados e informações de uma determinada região geográfica. OBJ – 02: Trabalhar com dados geo-refenciados.	
Descrição	O cadastro de uma propriedade no sistema WebMaps deve seguir as especificações descritas nos itens subsequentes.	
Atores	**Ator do caso de uso**	**Ator do sistema**
	Usuário cadastrado	AT – 02
Seqüência normal	**Passo**	**Ação**
	1	O usuário solicita a realização de um cadastro de uma propriedade.
	2	O sistema mostra a tela de cadastro de propriedade.
	3	O usuário introduz o nome da sua propriedade.
	4	O usuário introduz as coordenadas geográficas da sua propriedade.
	5	O usuário introduz o tipo de acesso de sua propriedade (público / privado).

	6	O usuário pede ao sistema cadastrar sua propriedade.
	7	O sistema faz o cadastro da propriedade.
Pós-condição	São feitos os recortes das imagens de satélite e é gerada a máscara correspondente a esta propriedade.	
Exceções	**Passo**	**Ação**
	3	É opcional que o usuário introduza uma descrição de sua propriedade.
	5	Caso o usuário escolha um tipo de acceso privado para sua propriedade, há ainda a possibilidade de permitir acesso para usuários cadastrados específicos.

A Tabela 2 ilustra a aplicação da proposta de testes de desempenho para o sistema WebMaps, considerando o caso de uso mais crítico para o WebMaps: o cadastro da propriedade.

Este exemplo aplica cada uma das fases mostradas do processo de teste de desempenho para aplicações SIG Web apresentadas na seção 4.3. Vale ressaltar a relação existente entre o cenário 1 do processo de carga A e o cenário 1 do processo de volume. Esta relação é importante porque a boa especificação do cenário 1 no processo de carga (ou estresse) falicita a identificação e posterior especificação do seu correspondente cenário no processo de teste de volume.

A Fase 2, para o processo de teste de carga ou estresse, precisa de dados reais para a especificação correta dos cenários de teste. Estes testes foram feitos de acordo com cenários reais construídos baseando-se em estatísticas de uso reais no Sistema de Monitoramento Agrometereológico, Agritempo [4]. Este sistema, um dos mais utilizados pelos usuários-alvo do WebMaps, obteve no máximo 200 usuários reais conetados simultâneamente.

Tabela 2. Exemplo de aplicação da proposta.

TESTE DE DESEMPENHO				
Fase 0	Testar o sistema com o objetivo de avaliar o desempenho do caso de uso: cadastro de propriedade.			
TESTE DE CARGA [A]			**TESTE DE VOLUME [B]**	
Fase 1	Testar o sistema simulando os usuários entrando na página principal da aplicação e entrando na página de cadastro de propriedade.		**Fase 1**	Fazer o teste de volume do módulo de cadastro de propriedades.
Fase 2	**Cenário 1:** Uma carga de 200 usuários virtuais a cada 10 segundos até 1000 usuários na página de cadastro de propriedades.	**Cenário 2:** Uma carga de 300 usuários virtuais a cada 10 segundos até 3000 usuários na página principal da aplicação.	**Fase 2**	O cenário 1 do teste de carga é identificado como o cenário de volume, já que envolve o armazenamento de informação tanto no banco de dados quando no HD (disco rígido).

Fase 3	Criação de usuários virtuais apoiada pelo JMeter.	Criação de usuários virtuais apoiada pelo JMeter	**Fase 3**	**Cenário1:** *relacionado ao Cenário 1 do processo [A]* Quantidade de armazenamento de informação para 200 usuários cadastrando uma propriedade.
Fase 4	Para rodar os cenários se fez uso do JMeter.		**Fase 4**	Cálculo de volume para um usário: Criação de 92 recortes ~ 1 Mb. Para 200 usuários ~200 Mb.
Fase 5	Análise do sistema, aqui, se analisa as curvas obtidas no JMeter.		**Fase 5**	Análise do sistema, aqui, por exemplo, se pode fazer uma projeção do comportamento do sistema para o volume de dados esperado ao longo do tempo.

A Fase 4 do processo de carga poder ser feito de duas formas: manual ou automática. A forma manual é complexa do ponto de vista de gerenciamento, pois se precisa de um coordenador. No entanto, a forma automática é mais efetiva para a criação de usuários virtuais. Esta automatização pode ser apoiada por ferramentas livres de teste, algumas delas estão especificadas em [19]. Os experimentos aqui reportados utilizaram a ferramenta JMeter [20, 21]. As fases 4, 5 e 6 são discutidas na seção seguinte.

5.3 Resultados obtidos

O servidor do WebMaps considerado nos experimentos é um computador Intel(R) Pentium(R) 4 CPU 2.40GHz, 1Gb de memoria RAM e com sistema operacional Linux, distribução SUSE Linux.
A Fig. 8 mostra uma tela da ferramenta JMeter versão 2.1 [20] usada na Fase 3 e 4 do cenário 1 do processo de carga A considerando o caso de uso descrito na seção anterior. Esta ferramenta apresenta de maneira gráfica o tempo de resposta do sistema sobre os cenários montados na Tabela 1.

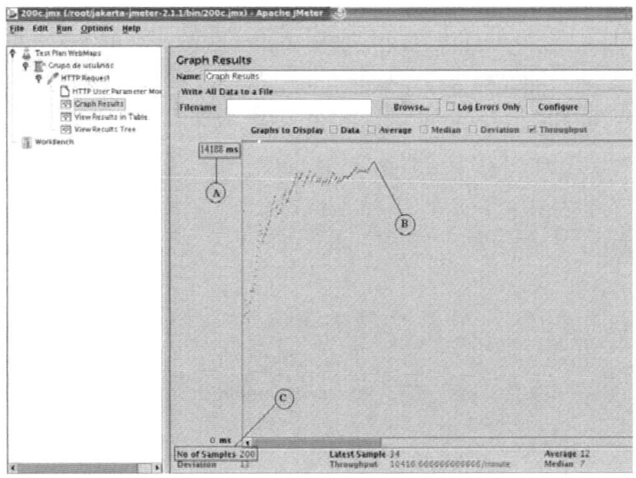

Fig. 8. Interface de resultados no Apache JMeter.

O sistema foi testado com uma quantidade de 200 usuários virtuais simultâneos (ver círculo C) cadastrando uma propriedade que gerava uma máscara de tamanho médio de 131 kb. O círculo A indica o eixo correspondente ao tempo de resposta do sistema, enquanto o círculo B indica o tempo de resposta do último usuário virtual. Segundo os resultados obtidos, o tempo médio de resposta do sistema foi de 14s. Este resultado, segundo Menascé [13], seria crítico, levando-se em conta que 95% das consultas dos usuários são abortadas caso o tempo de resposta de suas transações exceda em 6 segundos.

Também foram realizados testes de estresse. Verificou-se que o servidor WebMaps aborta quando (na média) 267 usuários estão cadastrando uma propriedade simultaneamente.

Assim, estes resultados foram muito úteis, já que forneceram indicativos para revisão da arquitetura do sistema WebMaps. Uma possibilidade de ajuste que ven senndo considerada consiste na melhoria da infra-estrutura de processamento, com, por exemplo, o uso de clusters e/ou a não realização de processamento on-line. Considera-se ainda a possibilidade de revisão do modelo de banco de dados do sistema de modo a evitar a gravação em disco de grande quantidade de imagens.

5 Conclusões

Este artigo apresentou trabalho em andamento que visa a definição de um processo para realização de testes de desempenho em SIG's Web. O processo proposto inclui a realização de testes de carga, estresse e volume, a partir de casos de uso.

O processo de realização de testes de desempenho proposto é parcialmente validado através de experimentos envolvendo o SIG Web WebMaps, atualmente em desenvolvimento no Instituto de Computação da Unicamp. O conjunto de testes realizado permitiu a identificação de problemas de desempenho no sistema que resultaram na revisão da sua arquitetura.

Trabalhos em andamento incluem a adaptação do processo de testes de desempenho proposto visando à elaboração de uma metodologia genérica para realização de testes em SIG web. Esta metodologia genérica incluirá, além dos testes de desempenho, testes de usabilidade, testes funcionais, dentre outros.

Referências

1. Aronoff S.: Geographic Information Systems. WDL Publications, Canada (1989)
2. Bull G.: Ecosystem Modelling with GIS. Environmental Management. (1994) 18(3):345-349.–438
3. Do-Hyun Kim; Min-Soo Kim: Web GIS service component based on open environment. Geoscience and Remote Sensing Symposium, 2002. IGARSS '02. 2002 IEEE InternationalVolume 6, 24-28 June (2002) Page(s):3346 - 3348 vol.6
4. Filipak Machado C. A.: A importância dos testes no desenvolvimento de sistemas. Compañia de Informática do Paraná, CELEPAR (2003)
5. Agritempo, http://www.agritempo.gov.br, última visita: novembro (2005)
6. Martins, E.: Apostila sobre Testes de Software. Instituto de Computação, UNICAMP, Campinas, Brasil (2005)
7. Myers, Glendord J.: The Art of Software Testing. Jhon Wiley & Sons, Inc, Canada (1979)
8. Marick, B.: New Models for Test Development. Reliable Software Technologies.Testing Foundations. (1999)
9. Pressman, Roger S.: Software Engineering: A practioner's approach. MacGraw Hill (2001)
10. Molinari, L.:Testes de Software: Produzindo Sistemas Melhores e Confiáveis. Editora Érica Ltda, São Paulo (2003)
11. Miller E.: WebSite Loading and Capacity Analysis. Software Research, Inc. San Francisco, USA (2000)
12. Subraya, B.M.; Subrahmanya, S.V.: Object driven performance testing of Web applications. Quality Software, 2000. Proceedings. First Asia-Pacific Conference on 30-31 (2000) Page(s):17 - 26
13. Menascé Daniel A. and Almeida Virgilio A. F.: Capacity Planning for Web Services: Metrics, Models, and Methods. Prentice Hall (2002)
14. UML : Unified Modeling Language, http://www.uml.org/, última visita: novembro (2005)
15.CPTEC, http://satelite.cptec.inpe.br/htmldocs/ndvi/ndvi_fram.htm, última visita: novembro (2005)
16.Modis, Moderate Resolution Imaging Spectroradiometer, http://modis.gsfc.nasa.gov/, última visita: novembro (2005)
17.Czajkowski, G.; Daynes, L.; Wolczko, M.: Automated and portable native code isolation. Software Reliability Engineering, 2001. ISSRE 2001. Proceedings. 12th International Symposium on 27-30 Nov. (2001) Page(s):298 - 307
18.Escalona M. J.: Modelos y técnicas para la especificación y el análisis de la navegación en sistemas software. Tese doutoral. Escuela Técnica Superior de Ingeniería Informática. Universidad de Sevilla, Octubre (2004)
19.Pillat F. R., Ferreira L., Dias A. P.: Ferramentas para automatização de testes, http://dinf.unicruz.edu.br/~pillatt/2004_urcamp.pdf, última visita: novembro (2004)
20. Apache JMeter, http://jakarta.apache.org/jmeter/, última visita: novembro (2005)
21. Gutiérrez J.J., Pineda R., Villadiego D., Escalona M.J., Mejías M. : Pruebas funcionales y pruebas de carga sobre aplicaciones Web. Proceedings of Mundo Internet 2005. Vol. II. (2005) pp.208-219 Madrid, Spain

Una Estrategia para elevar la competitividad de las industrias de software PYMES[1]

Raquel Anaya[1], Luís Fernando Londoño[2], Julio Ariel Hurtado[3]

[1] Universidad EAFIT, Departamento Informática y Sistemas. Medellín, Colombia
ranaya@eafit.edu.co,
[2] Avansoft s.a, Grupo I+D, Medellín, Colombia
lflondono@avansoft.com
[3] Universidad del Cauca, Departamento de Sistemas. Popayán, Colombia
jhurtado@unicauca.edu.co

Resumen. El desarrollo de software es un renglón prometedor de la economía en los países latinoamericanos. Existe una necesidad generalizada de plantear estrategias que permitan elevar el nivel de competitividad de las empresas de software. Una de las estrategias que se considera mas adecuada es la definición de un modelo de tipo vertical que facilite la adopción e implantación de referentes internacionales como CMMI-SW (considerado un modelo de tipo horizontal). La flexibilidad, la arquitectura, el alcance, el apalancamiento y la evolución del modelo son características que deben ser consideradas para la definición de un modelo de tipo vertical. El modelo representa una estrategia de implementación de procesos fundamentada en el enfoque de línea base de proceso en el que los activos de proceso se configuran de manera flexible de acuerdo a las condiciones de la empresa de software y teniendo en cuenta las características particulares de cada proyecto

1 Introducción

El proceso software es el conjunto de procedimientos, métodos, equipos y herramientas que están a disposición de las personas con el propósito de concebir, desarrollar, instalar y mantener un producto software [1]. Con el ánimo de convertir el desarrollo de software en un proceso de ingeniería que pueda ser estimado, medido, evaluado y mejorado de manera repetitiva y controlada, el proceso software se ha convertido en uno de los elementos centrales de estudio en el campo de la Ingeniería de Software, que adquiere diversas connotaciones y niveles de detalle.

De acuerdo a SWEBOK [2] el proceso software se puede ver en dos niveles: (a) Actividades técnicas y gerenciales dentro del ciclo de vida del desarrollo que son

[1] Este trabajo ha sido soportado por la Universidad Eafit, la Universidad del Cauca y la empresa Avansoft s.a. y cuenta con el apoyo del proyecto COMPETISOFT (Proyecto CYTED 3789).

realizadas durante la adquisición, desarrollo, soporte y mantenimiento del software. (b) La concepción del proceso a nivel meta el cual es concerniente con la definición, implementación, aseguramiento, medición, gestión y cambio de los procesos del ciclo de vida en si mismos.

Propuestas como CMM, BOOTSTRAP, ISO/IEC TR 15504 (SPICE) son modelos de procesos orientados a la actividad del desarrollo de software, los cuales plantean un proceso de mejoramiento progresivo orientado hacia la madurez y capacidad de los procesos de una organización [4]. CMMI-SW [2] [5], desarrollado como una evolución de CMM[3], se ha posicionado como el principal referente internacional de calidad exigido por las compañías que contratan software a nivel mundial.

Un modelo de procesos pueden caracterizarse desde su origen (formal ó empírico) y desde su nivel de detalle (descriptivo o prescriptivo); un modelo es descriptivo cuando sólo se ocupa de *qué hacer* o puede ser prescriptivo cuando detalla el *cómo hacerlo*. La mayoría de los modelos mencionados caen en la categoría de ser empíricos descriptivos [4]. Para propósitos del presente estudio, caracterizaremos los modelos de procesos de software en dos grupos: (a) Modelos como CMMI-SW, que definen un conjunto de prácticas agrupadas en áreas de procesos que están encaminadas a cumplir unas metas, sin precisar la manera de llevar a cabo dichas prácticas, serán denominados *modelos horizontales*. Modelos como Métrica 3 [7], que además de proveer una visión general, precisa cursos específicos de acción para cumplir las metas establecidas, serán denominadas *modelos verticales*.

De otra parte, el desplazamiento de la actividad de desarrollo de software hacia compañías especializadas, crea una nueva actividad económica alrededor de la industria del software que hoy en día se considera promisoria a nivel latinoamericano [6]. No obstante, los estudios actuales coinciden en afirmar que las empresas latinoamericanas están en desventaja frente a los niveles de competitividad exigidos a nivel internacional [6] [7]. Esta realidad de las empresas de software es un problema que interesa a los gobiernos y a diversos organismos a nivel descentralizado de todos los países.

Modelos como Moprosoft [8], mps BR [9] y SIMEP-SW[4] [10] surgen como iniciativas nacionales y han sido definidos con el propósito de articularlos a la cultura y realidad del contexto sin los altos costos que implica la adopción de modelos internacionales referidos anteriormente. Algunas empresas de software, por su parte, definen modelos de procesos a la medida que van evolucionando para ajustarse a sus requerimientos particulares [11].

---

[2] *Capability Maturity Model Integration- Software*

[3] *Capability Maturity Model*

[4] El proyecto SIMEP-SW (Sistema Integral de mejoramiento de los procesos de desarrollo de software en Colombia) es financiado por la Universidad del Cauca, Colciencias y SITIS Ltda. bajo el contrato 421 de 2003 Colciencias-Unicauca.

El objetivo de este artículo es justificar una estrategia que podría seguir un país latinoamericano con el propósito de emprender esfuerzos colectivos para elevar la competitividad de las empresas de software pequeñas y medianas. En la sección 2 se analizan algunas de las alternativas existentes y se opta por la estrategia de definición de un modelo de tipo vertical. En la sección 3 se definen los criterios que deberían caracterizar el modelo. La sección 4 sintetiza los requerimientos básicos de dicho modelo y se hace una presentación conceptual del mismo. La sección 5 establece una comparación inicial del modelo propuesto frente a algunas iniciativas desarrolladas en Latinoamérica y, finalmente, en la sección 6 se presentan las conclusiones y trabajos actuales y futuros en los que se enmarca esta propuesta

2 Alternativas de mejoramiento de las empresas de software

En esta sección se describen tres de las posibles alternativas que, de forma colectiva, se pueden emprender para apoyar el desarrollo de la industria de software a nivel latinoamericano.

2.1 Primera Alternativa. Adoptar directamente CMMI-SW como modelo de calidad

Es evidente que la adopción de un modelo de calidad como CMMI-SW es una de las estrategias ideales para el mejoramiento de la práctica de desarrollo en las empresas de software. Las compañías que logren adoptar e implantar de forma consciente este modelo, lograran los niveles de competitividad exigidos a nivel mundial. Sin embargo, la adopción de esta alternativa como estrategia a nivel país presenta las siguientes dificultades:

Generalidad de los modelos. Como ya mencionamos, CMMI es un modelo de tipo horizontal que define el *qué hacer* pero no el *cómo hacerlo,* lo que significa que se requieren altos esfuerzo de adopción por parte de las empresas de software, especialmente de aquellas medianas y pequeñas, para lograr articularlo a su práctica diaria.

Altos costos de asesoría y certificación. Esta es una de las mayores causas que hace que la pretensión de adopción de dichos modelos se limite a las grandes compañías de software. Se requiere soporte de personal altamente calificado y de procesos de evaluación con entidades foráneas a costos muy elevados [13] [14]. Existen iniciativas interesantes en países como Colombia que emprenden el proceso de adopción de CMMI-SW como un programa de gobierno logrando de esta manera una distribución de los altos costos que deroga un proceso de este tipo. Sin embargo, estas acciones solo favorecen a empresas que tienen cierto nivel de madurez en procesos de desarrollo de software, dejando fuera del alcance de las empresas incipientes ó con muy pocas prácticas enfocadas hacia la calidad.

Brecha cultural. Existe un riesgo cultural importante que debe ser considerado cuando se trata de importar y adoptar, modelos definidos en países con otros problemas y contextos. Este riesgo se torna más crítico cuando el proceso de adopción del modelo se impone como una decisión gerencial sin contar con la motivación y participación activa de todos los involucrados.

2.2 Segunda Alternativa. Definir un modelo de calidad propio que se convierta en estándar a nivel país

Este es el camino que han seguido países como México, en donde MoProsoft fue definido en un esfuerzo colectivo Universidad-Gobierno con el propósito de tener un modelo nacional que permitiera elevar la capacidad de las organizaciones para ofrecer servicios con calidad y alcanzar niveles internacionales de competitividad. Las experiencias de adopción de este modelo han demostrado que efectivamente por ser un modelo simplificado que se adapta a la cultura del país requiere un menor esfuerzo de adopción [15]. No obstante, la adopción de esta alternativa conlleva las siguientes dificultades:

Generalidad del modelo. A pesar de ser un modelo adaptado a una realidad nacional, éste se percibe como un modelo de tipo horizontal puesto que no precisa métodos, técnicas y guías de acción específicas. Esto implica que se deja al esfuerzo de cada compañía la definición de las acciones concretas a seguir.

Imposición como norma nacional. El hecho de que sea un modelo "exigible" a nivel de gobierno, puede significar que algunas empresas de software consideren un doble esfuerzo el tener que certificarse en un modelo nacional que no es reconocido internacionalmente y a la vez emprender los procesos de adopción y evaluación de CMMI-SW que le permitan figurar en el mercado mundial.

2.3 Tercera alternativa. Definición de un modelo que guíe la adopción de CMMI-SW

Esta tercera alternativa está orientada a definir un modelo de tipo vertical que facilite la implementación progresiva de CMMI-SW. Este modelo debería ser definido en cada país como un esfuerzo unificado de la academia, centros de investigación y gobierno con la participación de algunas industrias de software que estén interesadas en apalancar con su experiencia una iniciativa nacional de este tipo. Se esperaría que un modelo de este tipo tome como referente de partida los niveles, prácticas y metas definidas en CMMI-SW y apropie características importantes de modelos existentes. Su característica fundamental está centrada en proponer cursos de acción alternativos y flexibles de implementación de dichas prácticas, que faciliten la adopción por parte de las empresas de software y, de forma especial, a aquellas incipientes en el uso de prácticas y procesos.

3. Características del modelo de procesos propuesto

Como apoyo a esta tercera alternativa, se ha definido un conjunto de características deseables de modelo de procesos propuesto; dichas características surgen a partir del estudio de algunos de los modelos de procesos existentes (Moprosoft[8] , Métrica 3[12] y un modelo propio de una empresa de software[11]).

3.1 Flexibilidad

La flexibilización permite definir el grado de adaptación y evolución del modelo ante cambios en las condiciones de contexto. Esta es una de las características consideradas fundamentales a la hora de proponer un modelo del proceso software. La flexibilidad puede ser entendida en dos sentidos: (a) ser flexible en el sentido de que el modelo define lineamientos, metas y prácticas generales sin entrar a precisar la manera como dichas prácticas pueden ser implementadas. (d) ser flexible en el sentido en que el modelo propone guías de acción concretas que hacen ejecutables las metas y prácticas, sin que esto implique un curso obligatorio de acciones. La flexibilidad estará fundamentada en definición de reglas y heurísticas que guiarán la definición del plan del proyecto de acuerdo a las condiciones del contexto.

3.2 Arquitectura

Por medio de este factor se analiza la estructura tanto general como detallada del modelo. El modelo de procesos software es un producto que debe ser entendido y analizado por los diversos roles implicados en el proceso de desarrollo. Es por lo tanto importante que provea facilidades para ser entendido y analizado desde diferentes perspectivas y a diferentes niveles de detalle.

3.3 Alcance del modelo

Este factor considera el cubrimiento que hace el modelo de las diversas áreas de proceso involucradas. Teniendo en cuenta que el modelo estará orientado hacia empresas de software, cuya cadena de valor esta concentrada en las actividades propias de desarrollo del producto, es importante que el modelo apoye de manera primaria los procesos de ingeniería y que a la vez precise los procesos de apoyo y soporte a dicha cadena de valor, en sus diferentes frentes de trabajo: la calidad, la organización, la medición y la gestión del conocimiento. Se enfatiza la medición y la gestión de conocimiento como elementos independientes que se articulan en todas las actividades del proceso y se reconocen como elementos claves a la hora de garantizar un proceso de mejoramiento a largo plazo [16] [17].

3.4 Apalancamiento del modelo

Los modelos de procesos software generalmente están acompañados de propuestas (también de tipo descriptivo) orientadas a analizar el estado actual del proceso en una organización y a determinar su nivel de madurez (SPA[5]) y a establecer un plan sistemático de mejoramiento a partir del diagnóstico inicial (SPI[6]) [4]. El apalancamiento es definido en este trabajo como el conjunto de principios, actividades y guías que contribuyen al establecimiento del proceso ajustado a las condiciones de la organización, siguiendo propuestas como IDEAL [18].

En este factor se desea hacer especial énfasis a las disciplinas o estrategias explícitas del modelo orientadas hacia el recurso humano, con el objetivo de que sea articulado en un contexto particular. Buena parte del éxito de adopción de un modelo de procesos en una compañía, depende de la manera como los lineamientos y prácticas son aceptados y asimilados por las personas involucradas [19]. En este factor se analizan elementos como entrenamiento, consideraciones sociales y psicológicas para la adopción del modelo, guías de evaluación y herramientas de apoyo en la realización de las diferentes tareas.

3.5 Evolución

Como cualquier otro modelo, el modelo vertical debe soportar la evolución en el tiempo. La evolución de un modelo vertical como el que se propone tiene consideraciones particulares. La evolución de los procesos particulares y del mismo modelo vertical debe ser cuidadosamente controlada, con el fin de garantizar su mantenibilidad y su concepción integrada. La evolución tiene una particularidad importante, no sólo en el tiempo sino en el espacio (conjunto de procesos), por tanto se requiere visualizar la evolución tanto de los procesos particulares, del modelo vertical que los soporta y sus influencias mutuas.

---

[5] *Software Process Assessment*

[6] *Software Process Improvement*

4. Requisitos del modelo de procesos vertical

En esta sección se sintetizan los requisitos de alto nivel del modelo que se propone; dichos requisitos se encuentran agrupados de acuerdo a las categorías que fueron presentadas en la sección anterior. Para algunos de los requisitos se define la estrategia básica como se piensa abordar tomando como referentes iniciales los trabajos relevantes en el área y el conocimiento y la experiencia de empresas de software y grupo de investigación que han trabajado el tema.

Categoría	Descripción	Estrategia básica
Flexibilidad	R1.1 El modelo debe tener como característica fundamental la flexibilidad. R1.2 El modelo debe establecer los criterios de caracterización de un proyecto y la definición de heurísticas que ayuden a la definición de la línea base del proceso para cada proyecto. R1.3 El modelo debe presentar, a manera de activos de proceso, diversas técnicas que pueden ser utilizadas. R1.4 El modelo debe garantizar una evolución permanente proveyendo los mecanismos para actualización de activos de procesos o definición de nuevos activos. R1.5 El modelo debe poder ser implementado de manera escalonada, teniendo en cuenta el nivel de madurez actual de la compañía.	Establecer varios niveles de definición de proceso (Línea Base, Organización y proyecto) para garantizar integración, interoperabilidad y evolución. Desarrollo de una ontología del proceso software. Tomar como punto de partida el gestor metodológico definido en Métrica 3. Adecuar activos de procesos de marcos metodológicos actuales como el Proceso Unificado y las metodologías ágiles.
Arquitectura	R2.1 El modelo debe multidimensional permitiendo ser visualizado desde diferentes vistas (según proceso, según roles, según prácticas que apoya, etc.) R2.2 El modelo de partir de la categorización de áreas de proceso definidas por CMMI-SW	Definir varios niveles de definición de proceso (Línea Base, Organización y proyecto) para garantizar integración, interoperabilidad y evolución Partir de la visión multidimensional definida en el modelo de Avansoft
Alcance	R3.1 El modelo debe identificar claramente procesos de ingeniería, de apoyo y de gestión R3.2 Debe ser característica importante del modelo la medición como elemento de (a) control en el mejoramiento del proceso (b) veri-	Identificación y estudio de tipos de empresas. Determinación de necesidades comunes y variables. Incluir de un modelo de medi-

	ficación de que el producto de software cumple con unas características de calidad establecidas R3.3 El modelo debe establecer guías de adopción de herramientas *Open Source* que apoyen diversos frentes del proceso R3.4 El modelo debe articular la gestión de conocimiento como una de las prácticas transversales que capitalizan la experiencia de los desarrolladores	ción.
Apalancamiento	R4.1 El modelo debe estar acompañado de guías de mejoramiento R4.2 El modelo debe estar acompañado de recursos de formación en las teorías fundamentales de ingeniería de software en las que se soporta cada práctica R4.3 El modelo debe estar acompañado de un modelo de evaluación que permita diagnosticar el estado de las empresas de software en diferentes puntos del tiempo R4.3 El modelo debe definir estrategias para el desarrollo de competencias y habilidades de los desarrolladores R4.4 Como resultado de un esfuerzo colectivo el modelo debe estar disponible en un sitio web como referente de consulta público	Tomar el proceso de mejora de Agile-SPI como modelo de referencia para la guía de mejoramiento. Tomar el modelo SWEBOK como referente de la estructura del conocimiento. Partir del modelo de evaluación desarrollado en el marco del proyecto SIMEP-SW. Partir de las experiencias de algunas de las empresas de software en la construcción de la intranet del modelo de procesos. Tomar resultados de investigación de universidades. Definir la estructura del repositorio de procesos y establecer mecanismos de alimentación de éstos de manera colectiva. . El marco de trabajo para la definición de procesos FrameworkPDS de Agile SPI puede ser tomado como punto de partida.
Evolución	R6.1. El modelo debe evolucionar como un conjunto: el modelo vertical y los procesos. R6.2. Garantizar la trazabilidad de los activos de proceso en cada nivel de definición y entre niveles de definición.	Seguir la estrategia de línea de producto de software para obtener y expresar el modelo. La ontología de procesos debe incluir los conceptos adecuados a cada nivel, así como las relaciones intranivel e internivel entre estos conceptos para garantizar la

	R6.7. Integrar la evolución con los programas de mejora implementados sobre el nivel de modelo vertical y sobre el nivel de proceso.	trazabilidad. Extensión de la guía de mejora de Agile SPI para la mejora de proceso multinivel.

4.1 Vista conceptual del modelo

Para dotar el modelo de la flexibilidad, dinámica y precisión que se desea se propone orientar su definición siguiendo los enfoques desarrollo alrededor de familias de productos que propone SPL[7] [20] orientadas, esta vez, hacia el desarrollo de familias de procesos. El modelo establece tres niveles de abstracción diferentes (figura 1). En el nivel superior se define la línea base del proceso y los activos de proceso que puede ser reutilizados; en el segundo nivel la línea base del proceso se instancia para definir o articular los procesos de la organización de acuerdo orientación propia de la empresa de software, su cultura y objetivos de negocio y el tercer nivel, representa los procesos ejecutables en un proyecto particular, los cuales son configurados de acuerdo a las condiciones particulares del problema, los recursos disponibles y las restricciones impuestas por el cliente.

La definición de los procesos organizacionales y del proyecto a partir de un conjunto de activos de procesos reutilizables y flexibles, en el marco de una línea base de proceso, permitiría que las empresas y agremiaciones de Software dispongan de una infraestructura suficiente y ajustable al tipo de proceso que la empresa requiera, con el fin de alcanzar las capacidades en diferentes áreas del CMMI-SW.

5. El modelo frente a algunas iniciativas desarrolladas en Latinoamérica

Algunos países de Latinoamérica se han preocupado por la calidad de los procesos de desarrollo de software para su industria, prueba de esto es el modelo MoProSoft de México [8], el modelo MR mps de Brasil [9] y el modelo SIMEP-SW [10] de la Universidad del Cauca de Colombia.

[7] *Software Product Line*

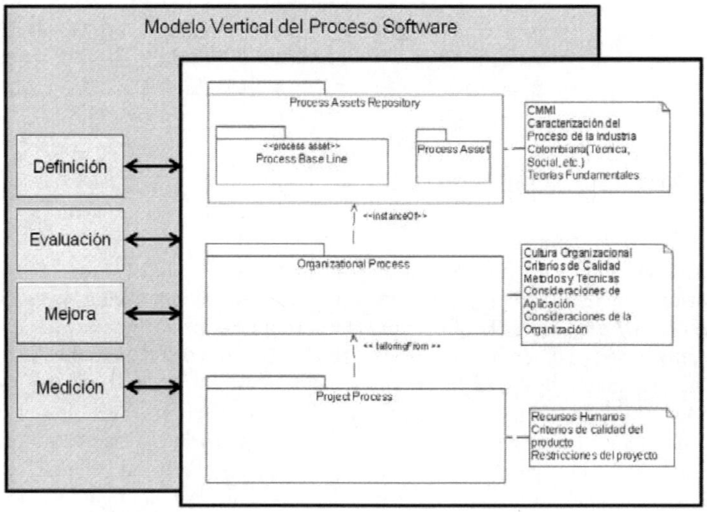

Figura 1. Vista conceptual del modelo propuesto

En el caso de México, se ha desarrollado el modelo MoProSoft - Modelo de Procesos para la Industria de Software en México, el cual tiene como propósito fomentar la estandarización de su operación a través de la incorporación de las mejores prácticas en gestión e ingeniería de software. A pesar de que la propuesta de procesos que propone MoProSoft lo caracterizan como un modelo fácil de adoptar, se sigue considerando como un modelo de tipo horizontal en el sentido en que no especifica los mecanismos para implementación de la prácticas.

En el caso de Brasil, se esta desarrollando el proyecto mps Br cuyo objetivo principal es definir e implementar un modelo para la mejora de procesos de software orientado hacia de micro, pequeñas y medianas empresas de forma que estas obtengan un nivel de madurez 2 o 3, a un costo accesible. Para resolver este problema el proyecto mps Br, desarrollo dos modelos: un Modelo de Referencia para la mejora del proceso del software – MR mps y un Modelo de Negocio para la mejora del proceso del software – MN mps. El Modelo de Negocio para la mejora del proceso del software, define los elementos e interacciones involucrados para la certificación de la empresa a través de la implementación de MR de dos maneras: personalizada para una empresa o conjunta entre un grupo de empresas, logrando así costos más accesibles para las empresas micro, pequeñas ó medianas.

El proyecto SIMEP-SW, desarrollado en Colombia, basa su estrategia de mejora en proporcionar a la organización un proceso ágil que guía a un programa de mejora de procesos, el cual debe contar con los elementos básicos para hacer posible que una micro, pequeña o mediana empresa pueda adelantar esfuerzos de mejora acorde a sus necesidades. Para esto cuenta con un modelo de calidad liviano, un modelo de evaluación liviano y un marco de referencia para la definición de procesos, que recibe el nombre de agile-SPI [10].

Métrica 3 [12] es una propuesta gubernamental del Ministerio de Administraciones Publicas de España. Aunque dicho modelo no ha tenido una evolución activa[8], conviene resaltarlo en este trabajo por ser uno de los modelos que describe cursos de acción concretos que apoyan las diversas actividades del desarrollo y por lo tanto se puede caracterizar como un modelo de tipo vertical. El enfoque prescriptivo del modelo debe ser matizado con mecanismos de flexibilidad con que los métodos, técnicas y cursos de acción deben articularse para facilitar su aplicación en diversos contextos y su evolución ante nuevas aproximaciones.

Existen modelos de procesos definidos al interior de las empresas de software los cuales, si bien no cuentan con la generalidad de los modelos anteriores, son modelos de tipo vertical que poseen cursos de acción que tienen resultados demostrables. Por ejemplo [11] es un modelo construido en el área I+D de una empresa de software que surge desde la ingeniería misma, con énfasis en el uso de modelos y herramientas de apoyo y la articulación de un sistema de métricas que permiten diagnosticar el estado de la práctica del desarrollo con respecto a las metas establecidas a nivel de la organización.

El modelo vertical propuesto en este trabajo esta basado en CMMI, y define una línea base de procesos repetible para una agremiación de industrias de software. La estrategia vertical que sigue este modelo es una base de implementación de procesos (SPE [9]) más que una base de especificación y por lo tanto puede verse como un aporte que se articula a los modelos horizontales internacionales, regionales, nacionales o locales.

6. Conclusiones y trabajos futuros

Este trabajo ha analizado diferentes alternativas que los países latinoamericanos podrían seguir con el propósito de elevar la competitividad de las empresas de software. Se ha propuesto, como la alternativa más adecuada, la definición de modelos de tipo vertical que faciliten la adopción progresiva y flexible de CMMI-SW teniendo en cuenta las condiciones particulares de cada empresa de software.

A partir de estudios de modelos de procesos existentes, este trabajo ha definido un conjunto de características básicas de un modelo de tipo vertical: flexibilidad, arquitectura, alcance y apalancamiento. La motivación fundamental del modelo es servir

---

[8] En enero del 2000 se liberó el borrador de la versión 3

[9] *Software Process Establishment*

como base de implementación de procesos que apoyen a las empresas de software a mejorar su competitividad. El modelo tiene como propósito servir de guía para la adopción de CMMI-SW integrando de manera flexible, a manera de activos de procesos, guías y prácticas que han resultado exitosas.

Este trabajo se enmarca dentro del proyecto COMPETISOFT; este proyecto fue aprobado por CYTED para el período 2006-2008. El proyecto tiene por objetivo "*Incrementar el nivel de competitividad de las PyMES Iberoamericanas productoras de software mediante la creación y difusión de un marco metodológico reconocido en toda Ibero América*" [21]. En este proyecto participan grupos de investigación de buena parte de países iberoamericanos (Brasil, Colombia, México, Argentina, Venezuela, España y Portugal). La concepción del modelo de procesos vertical presentado en este trabajo pretende ser un primer aporte para la caracterización de dicho marco metodológico.

Una premisa básica de la propuesta es lograr la complementariedad del modelo con trabajos y propuestas ya existentes que se perciben con un enfoque más horizontal. Aunque el enfoque vertical debe ser acotado a una industria más especifica, la ganancia en la definición, evaluación y mejora es considerable. Ejemplos de agremiaciones que podrían dar uso al modelo vertical serían parques tecnológicos de software, incubadoras de empresas de software, agremiaciones industriales de empresas de software, universidades y redes de investigación y desarrollo en ingeniería de software. El modelo no sólo permitiría que las empresas agilizaran sus procesos de definición, evaluación, medición y mejora de sus procesos, sino que la información condensada de un conjunto de proyectos reportando su desempeño en un repositorio global, serviría de observatorio del proceso de software de este grupo de entidades, permitiendo (1) Vitalizar problemáticas recurrentes (2) Evaluar y mejorar procesos organizacionales y (3) Evolucionar la línea base de procesos de software.

Se trata de una iniciativa ambiciosa que obligatoriamente requiere la articulación de esfuerzos de diversos grupos (academia, centros de investigación, empresas de software, gobierno) tanto en el entorno nacional como a nivel iberoamericano. El compromiso que tienen los centros de especialización e investigación para apoyar este proceso es evidente. Un trabajo de este tipo permitiría formar expertos que con sentido crítico evalúen las propuestas de calidad que ofrecen los modelos internacionales y apropien y propongan soluciones que se adecuen a las necesidades del contexto y a las capacidades de las empresas de software nacionales.

Reconocimientos

Agradecemos los valiosos aportes realizados por los miembros del grupo de investigación de Ingeniería de Software de la Universidad Eafit (docentes, estudiantes de postgrado, personal de industria) para consolidar esta propuesta del modelo.

Referencias

1. ISO/IEC 15504. Software Process Assessment - Part 2: A reference model for processes and process capability. International Organization for Standardization. 1998.
2. Guide to the Software Engineering Body of Knowledge. IEEE Computer Society. 2004.
3. Pressman, Roger. Ingeniería del Software: Un enfoque Práctico, 6ª Edición. McGraw Hill. 2005.
4. Wang, Yingxu; King, Gram. Software Engineering Processes. Principles and Applications. CRC Press, 2000
5. Crisis, Mary, et.al. CMMI. Guidelines for Process Integration and Product Improvement. Addison Wesley 2003.
6. Mayer & Bunge Informática LTDA. Panorama de la Industria del Software en Latinoamérica. Brasil. 2004.
7. Luis E. Valdes, Situación Actual de la Informática en Colombia. Informe del CATI. Bogotá, Abril 2004)
8. OKTAVA. H. "Modelo de Procesos para la Industria de Software MoProSoft" Versión 1.1. México 2003.
9. Kival C. Weber, et Al. Modelo de Referência para Melhoria de Processo de Software: uma abordagem brasileira. CLEI 2004.
10. Hurtado J. y otros. SIMEP-SW- Sistema Integral de Mejoramiento de los Procesos de Desarrollo Software en Colombia. Colciencias. 2003.
11. Avansoft. www.avansoft.com
12. Consejo Superior de Informática, Ministerio de Administraciones Públicas MAP. MÉTRICA versión 3. 2001,
13. Batista J. Figueiredo A. SPI in very small team: a case with CMM. Software Process Improvement and Practice 5 (4), 243-250. 2000.
14. Hareton L. and Terence Y. A Process Framework for Small Projects. Software Process Improvement and Practice 6, 67-83. 2001.
15. Software.net.mx. http://www.software.net.mx/desarrolladores/directorios/asociaciones/amcis/MoProSoft.htm. Fecha de consulta: 13/11/2005.
16. McGarry, J.; Card, D.; Jones, C.; Layman, B.; Clark, E.; Dean, J.; Hall, F.: *Practical Software Measurement - Objective Information for Decision Makers.* Addison Wesley Publ., 2002
17. T. Dingsøyr and R. Conradi. A Survey of Case Studies of the Use of Knowledge Management in Software Engineering. International Journal of Software Engineering and Knowledge Engineering, no. 4, vol. 12, pp. 391 - 414, 2002.
18. SEI. The IDEAL model. http://www.sei.cmu.edu/ideal/ideal.html. Fecha de acceso: 20/11/2005
19. Tomayko, J.; Hazzan Orit. Human Aspects of Software Engineering. Electrical and Computer Engineering Series, 2004

20. Gomaa, H. Designing Software Product Lines with UML: From Use Cases to Pattern-based Software Architectures. Addison-Wesley, 2004.
21. Documento propuesta proyecto CYTED número 3789. Grupo RITOS

El Problema de la Duplicidad de Movimientos de Datos en un Procedimiento de Medición[1]

Nelly Condori-Fernández, Silvia Abrahão, Oscar Pastor

Departamento de Sistemas Informáticos y Computación
Universidad Politécnica de Valencia, Camino de Vera s/n, 46022, Valencia.
{nelly, sabrahao, opastor}@dsic.upv.es

Resumen. COSMIC-FFP es un método estándar cuyo principio de medición está basado en la cantidad de movimientos de datos. Un movimiento de dato es la unidad elemental de este método y puede ser de cuatro tipos: entrada, lectura, escritura y salida. En este trabajo se discute el problema de la duplicidad de movimientos de datos que puede originarse al aplicar un procedimiento de medición, el cual ha sido instanciado del metamodelo de COSMIC-FFP. La identificación correcta de estos movimientos es importante para asegurar la fiabilidad de los resultados.

1. Introducción

Hoy en día, muchas organizaciones de la industria del software reconocen la importancia de contar con un buen proceso de desarrollo para evitar fallos como la insuficiencia de recursos ya sea en forma de tiempo, dinero, tecnología y personal. Además, en la actualidad CMM (*Capability Maturity Model*) es el modelo con mayor aceptación para entender y mejorar la eficacia del proceso de desarrollo del software. Este modelo se organiza básicamente en cinco niveles de madurez, donde cada nivel representa una etapa evolutiva de madurez organizacional [1]. El *nivel 2 está justamente relacionado con la buena administración de proyectos*. Por consiguiente, la medición de tamaño funcional desempeña un rol importante a este nivel por su contribución en la estimación de indicadores para la administración de proyectos. Este hecho ha permitido que los métodos de medición estén ganando mayor aceptación en la industria del software.

Actualmente, existe una gran variedad de métodos de medición de tamaño funcional tales como IFPUG FPA [2], MARK II FPA [3], NESMA [4], COSMIC-FFP [5]. El carácter genérico de estos métodos ocasiona la necesidad de ser instanciados para contextos de desarrollo más específicos. Así, el vocabulario de términos generales y básicos en metrología define un procedimiento de medición como un *"conjunto de operaciones usadas en una medición particular de acuerdo a un método de medición dado"* [6]. El presente artículo, por un lado, describe el proceso de un procedimiento de medición llamado RmFFP, el cual ha sido definido

[1] Este trabajo está subvencionado por el proyecto DESTINO con ref. TIN2004-03534 del Ministerio de Ciencia y Tecnología.

conforme al estándar COSMIC-FFP para el método de desarrollo OO-Method, un método de producción automática de software basado en la transformación de modelos [7].

Por otro lado, teniendo en cuenta que el principio de medición de COSMIC-FFP[2] que considera como componente básico al tipo de movimiento de dato; este trabajo, también aborda el problema de la duplicidad de los movimientos de datos, aspecto importante a considerar dentro del proceso de medición para contribuir a la fiabilidad de las estimaciones. De este modo, la calidad de los resultados obtenidos en un proceso de medición influirá en la calidad de la gestión de proyectos. Sin embargo, a pesar de que varias propuestas han surgido (Azzouz [8], Bevo[9] y Habela[10]) teniendo en cuenta el método COSMIC-FFP,, la mayoría de ellas no identifican todos los conceptos existentes en el metamodelo de COSMIC-FFP en sus respectivas primitivas. Además, la propuesta de Habela es la única que cuestiona la redundancia en los flujos de datos, pero no plantea una solución a este problema.

El presente artículo está organizado de la siguiente manera: en la sección 2, se introduce brevemente el Modelo de Requisitos de OO-Method. En la sección 3, se describe el proceso del procedimiento de medición RmFFP. En la sección 4 describimos el problema de la duplicidad de movimientos de datos y presentamos un conjunto de reglas las cuales son ilustradas mediante ejemplos. En la sección 5 describimos la aplicación de RmFFP con un caso de estudio. Finalmente, en la sección 6, presentamos conclusiones y trabajos futuros.

2.- El Modelo de Requisitos de OO-Method

El Modelo de Requisitos provee un conjunto de técnicas complementarias entre si, que permiten capturar las propiedades funcionales en una etapa temprana del proceso de producción de OO-Method (Vea Figura 1) [7]. Estas técnicas son: la Misión del Sistema, el Árbol de Refinamiento de Funciones, el Modelo de Casos de Uso y el Proceso de Análisis de Requisitos [12].

La *Misión del Sistema* describe el propósito del sistema. A través de la definición de su misión es posible determinar con precisión qué hará y qué no hará el sistema.

El *Árbol de Refinamiento de Funciones* representa la descomposición jerárquica de las funciones de un sistema. Este árbol resultante, es una organización de interacciones externas que no dice nada acerca de la composición interna del sistema. Sin embargo, es un insumo muy útil para la construcción del Modelo de Casos de Uso con un nivel de abstracción adecuado.

El *Modelo de Casos de Uso* permite modelar los requisitos funcionales del sistema desde la perspectiva del usuario. Si los casos de uso tienen una correspondencia directa con los nodos hoja del Árbol de Refinamiento de Funciones (función elemental), se consideran como primarios, estos representan las funciones más importantes del sistema. Por lo contrario, los casos de uso secundarios surgen con la finalidad de descomponer la complejidad de los casos de uso primarios mediante

[2] *"El tamaño funcional es directamente proporcional al número de sus movimientos de datos"* [8]

relaciones de EXTEND e INCLUDE. A partir de los casos de uso especificados, los diagramas de secuencia son construidos de manera semiautomática (Vea Figura 1).

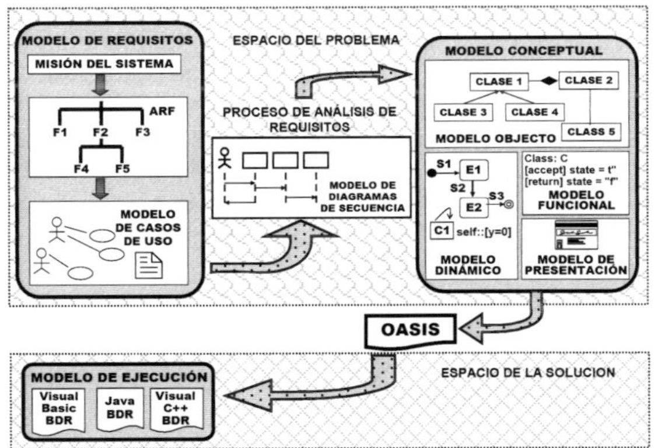

Figura. 1. Proceso de Producción de Software OO-Method

Para esto, un marco llamado Metamorfosis, basado en un enfoque lingüístico, permite la transformación de un modelo de casos de uso a un modelo de diagramas de secuencia [13]. De este modo, un mismo nivel de detalle para los diagramas de secuencia sería asegurado. Actualmente, la herramienta RETO[3] que da soporte al Modelo de Requisitos de OO-Method no incluye aún la implementación de Metamorfosis.

La notación de estos diagramas es provista por UML con algunas extensiones que se han incorporado en los mensajes para identificar elementos del Modelo Conceptual OO-Method. De esta manera, se distingue básicamente cuatro tipos mensajes en los diagramas de secuencia:

- *Mensajes de Señal:* Su estereotipo es <<signal>>, representan interacción entre el actor y el sistema. La única propiedad que discrimina este tipo de mensajes es la dirección del mensaje que puede tener dos tipos de valores: Input y Output.
- *Mensajes de Servicio:* Los mensajes estereotipados con la etiqueta <<service>>, representan la modificación de estado de la clase receptora del mensaje cuando ocurre una interacción. El tipo de cambio puede ser de tres tipos: New, Destroy y Update.
- *Mensajes de Consulta:* Son estereotipados con la etiqueta <<query>> y representan consultas sobre el estado de un objeto, cuyo resultado es un valor calculado; o consultas sobre una población de la clase receptora, cuyo resultado es un listado de objetos.
- *Mensajes de Conexión:* Los mensajes con el estereotipo <<connect>> se utilizan para establecer una relación estructural entre los objetos participantes en la interacción.

Estos mensajes adicionalmente, pueden ser etiquetados con alguna condición que si es satisfecha se permite la interacción. La sintaxis para esta condición es: *[Bolean-expresión] message-name*.

[3] http://reto.dsic.upv.es/reto/

Por otro lado, una relación INCLUDE permite que un escenario base ejecute una inclusión explícita de un escenario incluido. Esta relación es representada en un diagrama de secuencia base a través de la llamada de un mensaje con la sintaxis: *[condición] INCLUDE nombreEscenarioIncluido*. En cuanto a la relación EXTEND, sólo es conocida por el escenario que extiende por lo que, en el diagrama de secuencia del escenario base, no se hace ninguna referencia a la misma.

La iteración de un conjunto de mensajes es representado gráficamente por una caja etiquetada con la expresión de iteración, el cual es denominado como "Bloque".
La estructura general de un diagrama de secuencia es como se presenta en la Figura 2. Básicamente, tiene dos dimensiones: la dimensión vertical representa el tiempo y la horizontal representa las diferentes clases del sistema. Una de las propiedades de estas clases, son las restricciones de integridad que definen condiciones al conjunto de posibles estados en los que puede encontrarse un objeto a lo largo de su existencia.

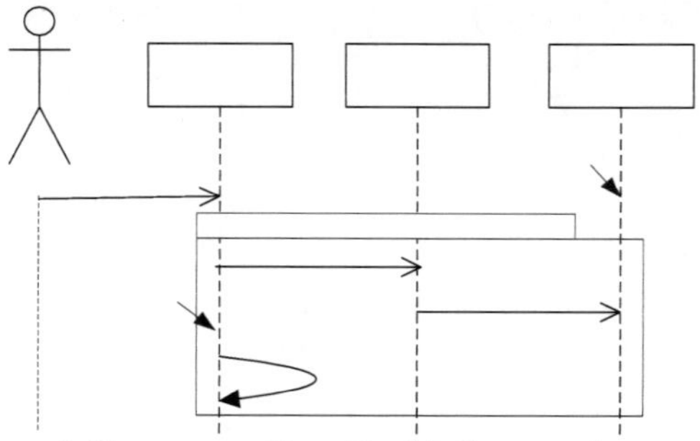

Figura. 2. Estructura y Notación del diagrama de secuencia

A continuación, presentamos el proceso de un procedimiento de medición, el cual considera conceptos del Modelo de Requisitos de OO-Method [12] y del Método estándar COSMIC-FFP [8].

3.- RmFFP: Un procedimiento de medición de tamaño funcional

RmFFP es un procedimiento de medición diseñado sobre la base del método COSMIC-FFP, el cual ha sido aprobado por la ISO/IEC 19761 [5].
Tal como se muestra en la Figura 3, el proceso de medición comienza con la definición del ***contexto de medición***, que incluye la identificación del propósito, el alcance y el punto de vista de la medición.

El *propósito de RmFFP* es estimar el tamaño funcional de sistemas orientado a objetos a partir de la especificación de los requisitos funcionales. El *alcance de medición* indica la funcionalidad a ser incluida en una medición particular; esta funcionalidad es especificada a través de un conjunto de técnicas que forman parte del Modelo de Requisitos. El *punto de vista de medición* determina el nivel de detalle que puede ser enfocado en un objeto de interés. RmFFP considera al modelo de requisitos como un objeto de interés en el proceso de medición cuyo punto de vista es la del usuario final.

*** Formatting Issue - Best Available Paper/Graphic ***

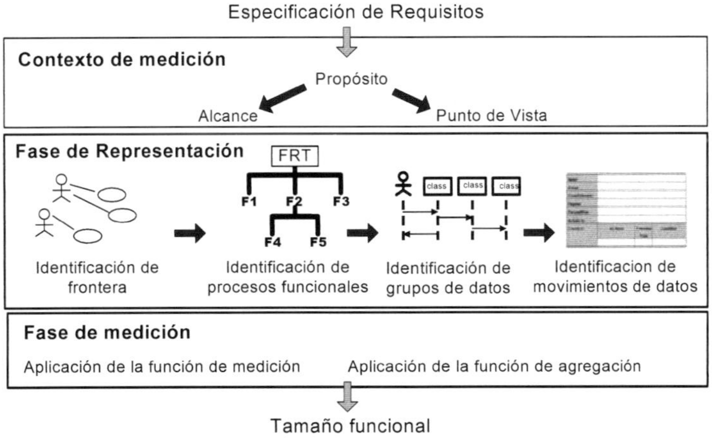

Figura. 3. Proceso de medición de RmFFP

El siguiente paso del proceso de medición de RmFFP es la representación de los conceptos principales de COSMIC-FFP en las primitivas del Modelo de Requisitos de OO-Method. Para hacer esto, tal como se muestra en la Figura 3, la ***fase de representación*** incluye un conjunto de pasos, tales como:

- La *identificación de la frontera* que es llevada a cabo en los diagramas de casos de uso. La frontera es definida como la interfaz que existe entre el software a ser medido y sus usuarios.
- La *identificación de los procesos funcionales* que es llevada a cabo sobre el árbol de refinamiento de funciones y el modelo de casos de uso. Un proceso funcional, es definido como un conjunto único, cohesivo y ejecutable de movimientos de datos. Los procesos funcionales están dentro de la frontera identificada.
- La *identificación de los grupos de datos* que es llevado a cabo en los diagramas de secuencia mediante las clases y actores implicados. Al conjunto de atributos distintos, no vacíos y no redundantes se denominan grupos de datos.
- La *identificación de los movimientos de datos* que es crucial porque el tamaño funcional es reflejado en su cantidad. Un movimiento de dato, mueve uno o más atributos de datos que pertenecen a un único grupo de dato. Se distingue principalmente cuatro tipos de movimiento de datos: entrada, lectura, escritura y salida. Estos movimientos son identificados en los respectivos tipos de mensajes de los diagramas de secuencia y la especificación de casos de uso.

Para facilitar la representación de los conceptos abstractos y genéricos de COSMIC-FFP, un conjunto de reglas de representación han sido definidas, las cuales han sido explicadas con mayor detalle en [14]. La Tabla 1 muestra la relación entre COSMIC-FFP y el Modelo de Requisitos de OO-Method y el número de reglas definidas para esta fase.

Tabla 1. Fase de representación: COSMIC-FFP y OO-Method

Conceptos COSMIC-FFP		Primitivas de OO-Method
Usuarios		(Regla 1) Actores
Frontera		(Regla 2) Diagrama de casos de uso
Procesos Funcionales		(Regla 3) Casos de Uso Primarios (Regla 4) Casos de uso Secundarios
Grupos de datos		(Regla 5) Clases (Regla 6) Actores
Atributos de datos		(Regla 7) Atributos de Clases
Movimientos de Datos	Entrada	(Regla 8) Mensaje Signal con valor Input
	Lectura	(Regla 9) Mensaje Query (Regla 10) Condición de Mensaje (Regla 11) Precondición de Caso de Uso (Regla 12) Condición de relación EXTEND (Regla 13) Restricción de integridad
	Escritura	(Regla 14) Mensaje Service con propiedad New o Destroy o Update (Regla 15) Mensaje Connect
	Salida	(Regla 16) Mensaje Signal con valor Output

Una vez identificado los movimientos de datos, teniendo en cuenta los grupos de datos afectados en cada proceso funcional, procedemos con la ***fase de medición***. Esta fase tiene como propósito producir un valor cuantitativo que represente el tamaño funcional de una especificación de requisitos de OO-Method. Para esto, la fase de medición incluye dos pasos:

- La *aplicación de la función de medición*, el cual consiste en asignar a cada movimiento de dato un valor numérico de 1 Cfsu *(Cosmic functional size unit).*

Tabla 2. Fase de Medición: COSMIC-FFP y OO-Method

COSMIC-FFP	Fase de Medición en RmFFP	
Función de medición	$f(x) = 1cfsu \quad \forall x \in P / P = \{entrada, salida, lectura, escritura\}$	
Función de agregación a nivel de proceso funcional	Regla 21:	$Size(CU) = \sum_{i=1}^{n} f(movimientos\_datos_i)$
	Reglas 22 y 23:	$Size(CUB_1) = \sum_{i=1}^{n} Size(CUS_i) + Size_p(CUB)$ *CUB = Caso de Uso Base* *CUS = Caso de Uso Secundario*
Función de agregación a nivel de capa	Regla 24:	$Size(Capa_1) = \sum_{i=1}^{n} Size(CUP_i)$ *CUP = Caso de Uso Primario*

- La *aplicación de las funciones de agregación,* las cuales pueden ser a nivel de proceso funcional y a nivel de capa[4]. Para el nivel de procesos funcionales, tres reglas han sido definidas, tal como se muestra en la Tabla 2. Las Reglas 22 y 23 corresponden a las relaciones entre casos de uso, INCLUDE y EXTEND respectivamente. Para el nivel de capa, se considera en la agregación únicamente a los casos de uso primarios para la representación del tamaño funcional del sistema. Cabe indicar que la medición de la especificación de requisitos es llevada a cabo a un mismo nivel de abstracción funcional, por esta razón es que consideramos una sola capa.

Este conjunto de reglas definidas para las fases de representación y de medición han sido verificadas mediante su aplicación a varios casos de estudio. Como resultado de esta verificación se identificó la necesidad de definir de manera explicita un conjunto de reglas que evitaran la duplicidad de movimientos de datos, a continuación explicamos cada una de estas reglas adicionales.

4.- Duplicidad de movimientos de datos

El término "de-duplication" se define en el manual de COSMIC-FFP como *el proceso de eliminar copias duplicadas de un listado* [8]. A partir de esta definición y teniendo en cuenta el concepto de movimiento de dato, identificamos un conjunto de reglas complementarias para la fase de representación.

La finalidad de esta definición es mejorar la repetibilidad y reproducibilidad de los resultados de medición. Ambos atributos de calidad son definidos en la ISO 14143-3 [15], así un *procedimiento de medición es repetible* si los resultados de mediciones sucesivas realizadas bajo las mismas condiciones son similares. En cambio, un *procedimiento de medición es reproducible* si los resultados de mediciones realizadas bajo diferentes condiciones son similares. Sin embargo, este conjunto de reglas no pretende asegurar la repetibilidad y reproducibilidad de RmFFP puesto que existen otros factores que deben ser considerados para lograr la fiabilidad de un procedimiento de medición, tales como: la experiencia en el uso del procedimiento de medición, la claridad de la guía de la medición, el nivel de detalle con que puede ser construido los diagramas de secuencia, etc.

No obstante, el conocimiento sobre las primitivas del modelo de requisitos sí influye en la correcta aplicación de las reglas. De este modo, en esta sección identificamos ciertas primitivas que pueden originar diferentes interpretaciones en los sujetos al momento de aplicar RmFFP y por ende originar a la identificación de *pseudos-movimientos de datos.*

A continuación presentamos el conjunto de reglas que eviten la duplicidad de movimientos de datos, el cual será explicado mediante ejemplos para cada caso identificado.

---

[4] Una capa es un conjunto de procesos funcionales que se ejecutan en un mismo nivel de abstracción [8].

CASO 1: Mensajes que involucran un mismo grupo de dato

Suponiendo que una consulta de datos es requerida, pero el analista decide especificarlo mediante dos consultas parciales con el fin de recuperar diferentes subconjuntos de atributos del mismo grupo de dato. Para propósitos de tamaño sólo se consideraría un movimiento de dato de tipo lectura.
En la Figura 4, se ilustra dos diagramas de secuencia con mensajes que tienen el mismo estereotipo y que involucran un mismo grupo de dato (clase 1). Para este caso a pesar de identificar dos movimientos de datos tipo lectura, se detectaría duplicidad de movimientos de datos, por lo tanto para evitar esta redundancia proponemos la siguiente regla:

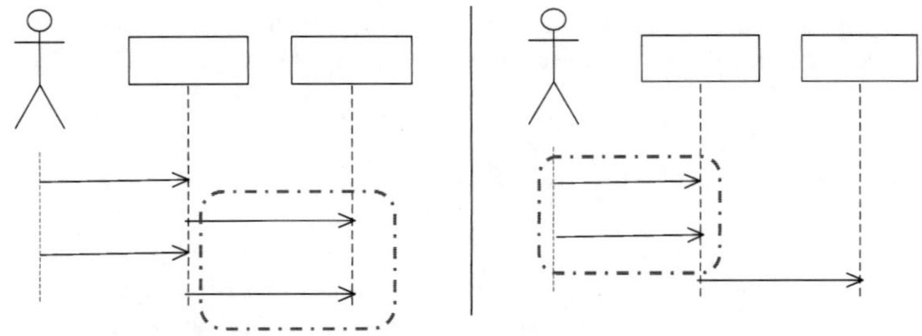

Figura. 4. Ejemplo de duplicidad de movimientos de datos

Regla 17: "Los n-mensajes del mismo tipo relacionados con el mismo objeto de la clase receptora y un mismo origen son identificados como un único movimiento de dato".

CASO 2: Mensajes de error, confirmación y advertencia

Suponiendo que en la especificación de un caso de uso: *"retirar dinero de un cajero"* especificamos un mensaje de confirmación de usuario, un mensaje de advertencia si el usuario no seleccionó la cantidad de dinero a retirar, así como un mensaje de error si el usuario ingresó mal su clave de identificación. Para este caso, los tres mensajes generados son considerados como ocurrencias separadas del mismo tipo, es decir se consideraría sólo como un movimiento de dato de tipo salida. La regla a considerar sería:

Regla 18: "Los mensajes de error, confirmación y advertencia de un mismo proceso funcional son identificados una sola vez como un movimiento de dato tipo SALIDA".

CASO 3: Iteración de mensajes

Suponiendo que un administrador de campo de golf necesita registrar un número de hoyos. Para esto, una consulta será necesaria para averiguar si existe el hoyo, si no existe se creará una instancia de la clase hoyo, esto se hará de manera repetitiva hasta

*** Formatting Issue - Best Available Paper/Graphic ***

que el número de hoyos sea igual a diez, esta condición de iteración es representada en un bloque tal como se ilustra en la Figura 5.

En este caso los dos movimientos de datos identificados dentro del bloque serán considerados una sola vez y no diez veces, debido a que identificamos tipos de movimientos y no ocurrencias. De este modo, la regla a considerar sería:

Regla 19: "El conjunto de movimientos de datos identificados en un bloque del diagrama de secuencia debe ser considerado una sola vez".

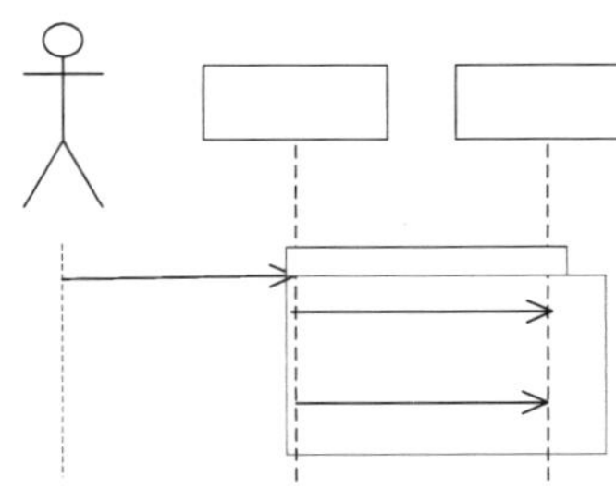

Figura. 5. Ejemplo de ocurrencia de movimientos de datos

CASO 4: Relaciones INCLUDE en un bloque

Supóngase que se necesita realizar varios pedidos solicitados por diferentes clientes, y que para esto especificamos el caso de uso *"realización de un pedido"* (A) que incluye otro caso de uso *"información de cliente"* (B). La Figura 6 ilustra de manera genérica la inclusión del caso de uso B especificada dentro de un bloque. Al lado derecho, se observa que para determinar el tamaño del caso de uso A se considera una sola vez el tamaño funcional de B a pesar de ser invocado varias veces mientras se cumpla la condición del bloque. Por lo tanto, esta regla, considerada como un caso particular del caso 3, se describe a continuación:

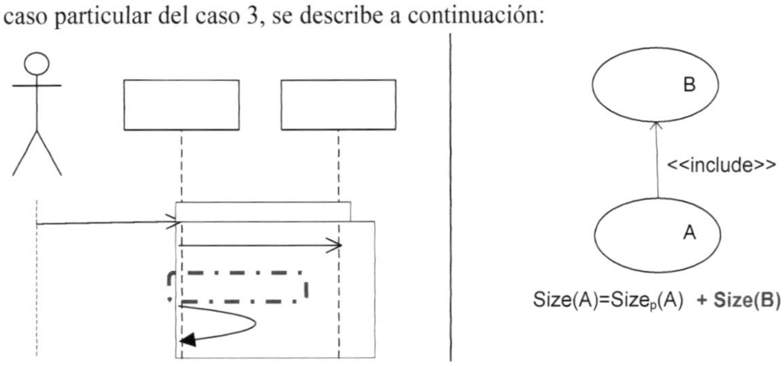

Figura. 6. Ejemplo de ocurrencia de movimientos de datos, relación INCLUDE

Regla 20: "Las relaciones INCLUDE especificadas dentro de un bloque del diagrama de secuencia deben ser consideradas una sola vez".

RmFFP junto con este conjunto de reglas adicionales ha sido aplicado en tres casos de estudio: un Sistema de Alquiler de Vehículos, un Sistema de Gestión de Servicios de Mantenimiento de un Hospital, y un Sistema de Gestión de Golf. En la siguiente sección explicamos el proceso de esta aplicación en un caso de estudio ilustrativo.

5.- Aplicación de RmFFP

La aplicación de RmFFP fue llevada a cabo siguiendo tres pasos del modelo de proceso de medición [16]: la *documentación del software,* mediante la especificación de los requisitos funcionales a través del conjunto de técnicas del Modelo de Requisitos OO-Method. La *construcción del modelo del software a medir,* mediante la aplicación de las respectivas reglas de representación (Tabla 1) y las reglas de duplicidad definidas. La *aplicación de las reglas de asignación numérica,* mediante la aplicación de las funciones de medición y agregación definidas (Tabla 2).

Con el propósito de ilustrar esta aplicación, se ha visto por conveniente considerar el módulo de un Sistema de Gestión de Servicios de Mantenimiento (SGSM), cuya actividad principal es la gestión de averías que se producen en cualquier área de un hospital.

5.1 Documentación del software

Los requisitos funcionales del SGSM son especificados usando el Modelo de Requisitos de OO-Method. Tal como se observa en la Figura 1, el modelo inicia con la definición de la *misión del sistema,* el cual para el SGSM es *"gestionar de manera automática las averías que se producen en un hospital*". Luego, el Árbol de Refinamiento de Funciones (ARF) es construido mediante la descomposición de la funcionalidad del sistema (Vea Figura 7).

Figura. 7. Árbol de Refinamiento de Funciones

A partir de las funciones elementales identificadas se derivan los respectivos casos de uso y los actores del sistema son identificados. La Figura 8 representa el diagrama de casos de uso para el sub-grupo funcional *"Gestión de Material".* Luego, cada caso de uso es representado por uno o más diagramas de secuencia. Estos diagramas serán presentados con mayor detalle en la siguiente sección.

*** Formatting Issue - Best Available Paper/Graphic ***

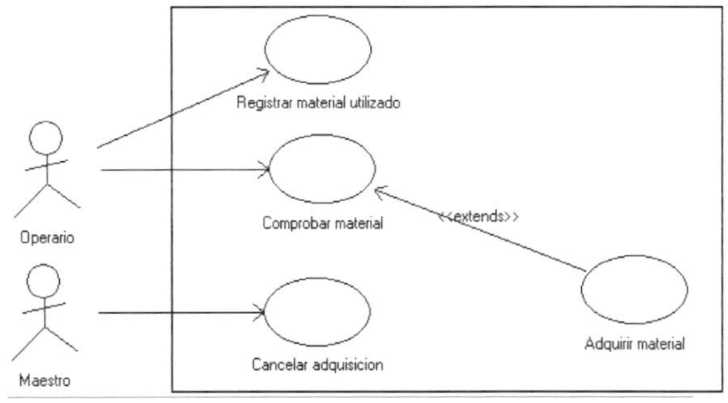

Figura. 8. Diagrama de casos de uso de Gestión de Material

5.2 Construcción del modelo del software

La construcción del modelo de software para RmFFP es entendida como la instanciación del metamodelo de COSMIC-FFP en un entorno especifico llamado OO-Method.

Tal como se observa en la Figura 3, antes de construir este modelo (fase de representación), primero identificamos el ***contexto de la medición***, el cual es determinado mediante la identificación del propósito, el alcance y el punto de vista de medición. El *propósito de la medición* será estimar el tamaño funcional de gestionar los materiales necesarios del SGSM. El *alcance de la medición* incluye toda la funcionalidad especificada a ser considerada en el proceso de medición. Teniendo en cuenta nuestro propósito, consideraremos únicamente al sub-grupo funcional *Gestión de Material* como alcance de la medición, la cual será llevada a cabo bajo el *punto de vista* del usuario final.

Una vez identificado qué es lo que se va a medir, iniciamos la ***fase de representación*** por medio de la identificación de la frontera, de los procesos funcionales, de los grupos de datos y de los movimientos de datos (Vea Figura 3). Para cada paso aplicaremos las reglas correspondientes de la Tabla 1.

Identificación de la frontera. Aplicando la Regla 1, los actores *Operario y Maestro* son identificados como usuarios. Por consiguiente, aplicando la Regla 2, la frontera está entre los usuarios identificados y todos los casos de uso representados en el diagrama de casos de uso (Figura 8).

Identificación de los procesos funcionales. Aplicando la Regla 3, los casos de uso primarios *"Registrar material utilizado", "Comprobar material" y "Cancelar adquisición" como proceso funcional.* El caso de uso secundario *"Adquirir Material"* también es identificado como proceso funcional.

Identificación de los grupos de datos. Aplicando la Regla 5, las clases representadas en todos los diagramas de secuencia de cada caso de uso del sistema, son identificadas como grupos de datos: *"Avería", "Material", "Orden de Trabajo", "Pedido" y "Línea de Pedido".* Aplicando la Regla 6, los actores *"Operario"* y *"Maestro"* son también identificados como grupos de datos.

Identificación de los movimientos de datos. Para cada proceso funcional identificado anteriormente se procede a identificar los diferentes movimientos de datos involucrados. Para ilustrar la aplicación de las respectivas reglas se ha considerado el proceso funcional *"Adquirir material",* el cual es representado en el siguiente diagrama de secuencia (Figura 9).

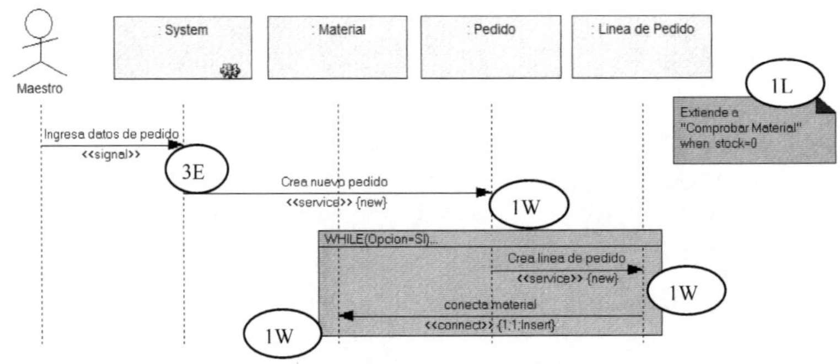

Figura. 9. Adquirir material

Aplicando la Regla 8, el mensaje "Ingresa datos de pedido" implica atributos de los grupos de datos *"Pedido", "Línea de Pedido" y "Material"* este mensaje será identificado como un movimiento de dato tipo ENTRADA por cada grupo de dato involucrado.

Aplicando la Regla 14, el mensaje *"Crea nuevo pedido"* con el estereotipo <<service>>{new} es identificado como un movimiento de dato de tipo ESCRITURA.

Aplicando la Regla 14, el mensaje *"Crea línea de pedido"* con el estereotipo <<service>>{new} es identificado como un movimiento de dato de tipo ESCRITURA.

Aplicando la Regla 15, el mensaje *"Conecta material"* con el estereotipo <<connect>> es identificado como un movimiento de dato de tipo ESCRITURA.

Aplicando la Regla 12, se identifica un movimiento tipo LECTURA por la condición EXTEND.

Como los movimientos de datos identificados en los mensajes *"Crea línea de pedido" y "Conecta material"* serán ejecutados de manera iterativa mientras se cumpla la condición del bloque; aplicamos la regla de duplicidad correspondiente (Regla 19). Por lo tanto, estos dos movimientos de datos identificados dentro del bloque serán considerados una sola vez para la siguiente fase.

5.3 Aplicación de las reglas de asignación numérica

La ***fase de medición*** toma como entrada al conjunto de movimientos de datos identificados en los procesos funcionales. Para su cuantificación aplicamos la *función de medición* que consiste en asignar el valor de 1 unidad *Cfsu* para cualquier tipo de movimiento (entrada, salida, lectura, escritura). Luego, aplicamos las reglas correspondientes a la fase de medición (Tabla 2).

Aplicando la regla 21 para el proceso funcional *"Adquirir material"* se tiene:

$$Size(Adquirir\_material) = \sum f(entrada) + \sum f(lectura) + \sum f(escritura) + \sum f(salida)$$

$$Size(Adquirir\_material) = 3 + 1 + 3 + 0$$

$$Size(Adquirir\_material) = 7\ Cfsu$$

Como el caso de uso *"Adquirir Material"* extiende al caso de uso *"Comprobar Material"*, aplicamos la Regla 23 mediante la siguiente ecuación general:

$$Size(CUB_1) = \sum_{i=1}^{n} Size(CUS_i) + Size_p(CUB)$$

Donde: *"Comprobar Material" es* el caso de uso base y *"Adquirir Material"* es el caso de uso secundario.

$Size_p\ (CUB)$ significa el tamaño parcial del caso de uso base, el cual es también obtenido aplicando la Regla 21.

Por lo tanto, el tamaño funcional del caso de uso *Comprobar Material* es de 16 Cfsu:

$$Size(Comprobar\_Material) = Size(Adquirir\_Material) + Size_p(Comprobar\_Material)$$

$$Size\ (Comprobar\_Material) = 7\ Cfsu + 9\ Cfsu$$

$$Size\ (Comprobar\_Material) = 16\ Cfsu$$

Nótese que damos por supuesto la satisfacción de la condición de la relación EXTEND.

De manera similar la medición de los casos de uso *"Registrar material"* y *"Cancelar adquisición"* es llevada a cabo. Finalmente, aplicando la Regla 24, estimamos el tamaño funcional de *30 Cfsu* para el módulo definido en el alcance de la medición: *"Gestión de Material"*.

6.- Conclusiones y Trabajos futuros

El procedimiento de medición RmFFP ha sido diseñado para el Modelo de Requisitos de OO-Method. El paso de eliminación de duplicidad de movimientos de datos ha sido añadido una vez que dichos movimientos de datos han sido identificados. De esta manera, aseguramos que la fase de medición, mediante la aplicación de la función de medición, sea más consistente al excluir de la cuantificación del tamaño funcional aquellos movimientos de datos duplicados. El conjunto de reglas adicionales han sido definidas teniendo en cuenta conceptos básicos del manual de medición de COSMIC-FFP para ser instanciados en casos particulares del modelo de requisitos de OO-Method. Es importante resaltar que la calidad de una especificación de requisitos es un factor a considerar para efectos de exactitud más no de fiabilidad.

Como trabajo futuro inmediato se pretende aplicar el procedimiento de medición con profesionales de la industria, lo que ayudará a mejorar el análisis de la fiabilidad de RmFFP. Además, actualmente se está automatizando el procedimiento de medición RmFFP, mediante la implementación de un módulo de medición que será incorporado a la herramienta de Gestión de Requisitos RETO-UPV.

*** Formatting Issue - Best Available Paper/Graphic ***

Referencias

[1] M. Paulk, B. Curtis, M. Chrissis, V. Weber, "Capability Maturity Model for Software, Version 1.1", Technical report CMU/SEI-93-TR-024, Febrero 1993.

[2] IFPUG, "Function Point Counting Practices Manual, Release 4.1", International Function Point Users Group, Westerville, Ohio, USA 1999.

[3] UKSMA, "MKII Function Point Analysis Counting Practices Manual. Version 1.3.1", United Kingdom Software Metrics Association 1998.

[4] NESMA, 1997. Definitions and Counting Guidelines for the Application of Function Point Analysis.

[5] ISO, "ISO/IEC 19762 Software Engineering, COSMIC-FFP, A functional size measurement method," International Standards Organization, 2002.

[6] ISO, 1993. International Vocabulary of Basic and General Terms in Metrology, International Organization for Standardization, Switzerland.

[7] O. Pastor, J. Gomez, E. Insfran, and V. Pelechano: The OO-Method approach for information systems modeling: from object-oriented conceptual modeling to automated programming. Information Systems 26 (2001) 507-534.

[8] Azzouz S., Abran A., "A Proposed Measurement Role in the Rational Unified Process and its Implementation with ISO 19761: COSMIC-FFP" in Software Measurement European Forum, Rome, Italy, 2004.

[9] Bévo V., Lévesque G., and Abran A., Application de la méthode FFP à partir d'une spécification selon la notation UML: compte rendu des premiers essais d'application et questions, Workshop Soft. Measurement, pp. 230-242, 1999.

[10] Habela P., Glowacki E., Serafinski T., Adapting Use Case Model for COSMIC-FFP based Measurement, in the 15th International Workshop on Software Measurement, Montreal, Canada, Shaker-Verlag, 2005.

[11] COSMIC-FFP Measurement Manual version 2.2, Common Software Measurement International Consortium, January 2003.

[12] E. Insfrán "A Requirements Engineering Approach for Object-Oriented Conceptual Modeling", PhD Thesis, Valencia Polytechnic University, 2003.

[13] I. Diaz, L. Moreno, O. Pastor, A. Matteo. Interaction Transformation Patterns Based on Semantic Roles, International Conference on Applications of Natural Language to Information Systems, Alicante-Spain, 2005.

[14] N. Condori-Fernández, S. Abrahão, O. Pastor, Towards a Functional Size Measure for Object-Oriented Systems from Requirements Specifications Abstract Functional Size Measurement. IEEE Quality Software International Conference 2004, Braunschweig, Alemania, pp. 94-101.

[15] ISO, "ISO/IEC 14143-3 - Information technology - Software measurement - Functional size measurement-Part 3: Verification of functional size measurement methods", 2003.

[16] Jacquet J. P. and Abran A., 1997. From Software Metrics to Software Measurement Methods: A Process Model, 3rd Int. Standard Symposium and Forum on Software Engineering Standards Walnut Creek, USA.

Sesión Poster

Uma Ferramenta Integrada de Apoio a Estimativas de Tamanho e Esforço em um Ambiente de Desenvolvimento de Software

Lucas de Oliveira Arantes, Victorio Albani de Carvalho, Ricardo de A. Falbo

Departamento de Informática – Universidade Federal do Espírito Santo, Vitória - ES - Brasil
lucasdeoliveira@gmail.com, victorioalbani@yahoo.com.br, falbo@inf.ufes.br

Abstract. Estimation requires experience and access to good historical information. Given software estimation complexity, project managers need tools to support them in doing this task. Ideally, these tools should allow applying different approaches for estimating. This paper presents EstimaODE, a tool that offers functionalities for estimating size and effort. EstimaODE is integrated to a software engineering environment and uses its knowledge management infrastructure, including a framework for similarity computing.

1 Introdução

A realização de estimativas não é uma tarefa fácil. Para se chegar a boas estimativas, é aconselhável que o engenheiro de software possua experiência, utilize diferentes abordagens para realizar estimativas e pondere complexidade e riscos [1].

O tamanho do produto de software tem sido apontado como um ponto de partida para a realização de estimativas [2]. Tomando por base estimativas de tamanho, é possível chegar a estimativas de esforço e, a partir dessas, fica mais fácil estimar recursos, tempo e custo. Tendo em vista a importância das estimativas de tamanho e esforço, é desejável que os gerentes de projeto tenham à disposição ferramentas para apoiá-los, preferencialmente permitindo aplicar diferentes abordagens, de modo que eles possam confrontar valores e chegar a um valor adequado.

Este artigo apresenta, sucintamente, EstimaODE, a ferramenta de apoio à realização de estimativas do ambiente de desenvolvimento de software ODE [3].

2 Estimativas em ODE

ODE (*Ontology-based software Development Environment*) [3] é um Ambiente de Desenvolvimento de Software Centrado em Processo, que possui várias ferramentas, dentre elas: de apoio à definição de processos de software, de apoio à gerência de riscos e de apoio à gerência de recursos humanos. Além disso, ODE oferece serviços de gerência de conhecimento que podem ser utilizados pelas suas diversas ferramentas. A infra-estrutura de gerência de conhecimento de ODE provê uma estrutura flexível e poderosa para caracterizar itens de software e calcular similaridade entre eles, desenvolvida utilizando técnicas de raciocínio baseado em casos.

Uma primeira versão parcial do ambiente foi implantada em uma organização de software no final de outubro de 2004, por meio de uma parceria universidade-empresa, visando apontar oportunidades de melhoria nas diversas ferramentas do ambiente, tomando por base situações reais dessa organização.

Dentre as ferramentas de ODE, está EstimaODE, uma ferramenta de apoio a estimativas. Na primeira versão de ODE implantada na empresa parceira, o apoio à realização de estimativas restringia-se a uma ferramenta de apoio à Análise de Pontos de Função (APF). Contudo, já se encontrava em desenvolvimento uma segunda ferramenta de apoio à Análise de Pontos de Casos de Uso (APCU). Dentre as oportunidades de melhoria (OM) apontadas na primeira avaliação entregue no final de dezembro de 2004, duas delas apontavam a área de estimativas, a saber:

OM1. Uma vez que a organização tinha pouca experiência no uso da técnica de APF, problemas foram detectados no sentido de se obter um indicativo sobre a real precisão das estimativas.

OM2. Na versão disponibilizada, toda vez que se desejava fazer uma recontagem de PFs, os dados da última contagem não eram considerados, sendo essa tarefa considerada uma nova contagem. Assim, ficava difícil gerar um histórico de evolução das contagens de pontos de função, de forma a avaliar os erros de estimativa a partir das características de cada projeto.

Considerando OM1, a solução adotada considerou o uso de dados de projetos passados para fornecer um indicativo de precisão. Uma vez que a organização tinha uma base de dados de projetos com informações a cerca do esforço despendido em projetos anteriores, a estratégia consistiu em usar a ferramenta para realizar a contagem de PFs desses projetos. A partir do número de PFs encontrado, comparado a dados reais de esforço, chegou-se a um fator de produtividade (PF / homens-hora) para a organização. Usando esse fator de produtividade, passou-se a trabalhar com estimativas de esforço (homens-hora), que é uma grandeza com a qual os gerentes de projeto estão mais habituados a trabalhar e, portanto, mais fácil de se avaliar a precisão das estimativas obtidas. Além disso, foi apontada como uma boa abordagem que esse fator de produtividade passasse a ser calculado pela ferramenta, tomando por base projetos similares e não todos os projetos da organização.

Para tratar OM2, foi necessário reestruturar a ferramenta, de modo que fosse possível registrar o histórico da evolução das estimativas. Tomando por base essa reestruturação, foi definida uma estrutura geral para representar estimativas diversas, integrando diversas formas de estimativas em uma única ferramenta, denominada, então, EstimaODE. Essa nova estrutura foi desenvolvida e foram incorporadas estimativas com base em dados históricos por decomposição do processo e aplicando a técnica de APCU.

Para que EstimaODE pudesse satisfazer os requisitos colocados, foram considerados dois pontos principais em sua arquitetura: (i) a possibilidade de tratar diferentes abordagens de estimativas com uniformidade e (ii) permitir o registro de evolução de cada uma das estimativas existentes.

Foi desenvolvida, então, uma infra-estrutura em que diferentes tipos de estimativas, organizados pela natureza da estimativa sendo realizada (atualmente, de esforço e tamanho), ou pelo escopo da estimativa (atualmente, para o projeto como um todo, para um módulo do projeto ou para atividades específicas), são abrigados como especializações da classe `Estimativa`, como mostra a figura 1. As classes `ExecucaoProjeto`, `ExecucaoModulo` e `ExecucaoAtividade` isolam informações sobre a execução e as estimativas das respectivas classes de controle de ODE, `Projeto`, `Modulo` e `Atividade`. Isso é importante, uma vez que essas classes são muito utilizadas por diversas ferramentas do ambiente e, portanto, idealmente, devem ser mantidas o mais simples possível.

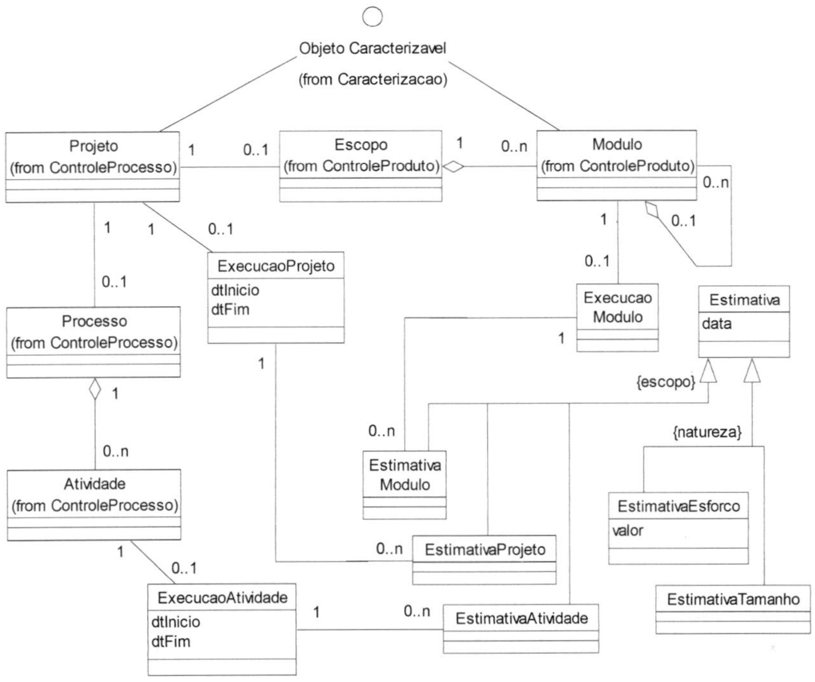

Fig. 1. A infra-estrutura para tratar estimativas de EstimaODE.

Essa infra-estrutura pode ser facilmente estendida incorporando-se abordagens de estimativas como especializações de seus tipos em diferentes níveis. Por exemplo, é possível introduzir o tratamento de estimativas de naturezas ainda não consideradas, tais como tempo e custo, como subclasses de `Estimativa` na hierarquia de naturezas. Analogamente, é possível introduzir o tratamento de tipos de estimativas com escopo ainda não considerado, tal como iteração, em que as estimativas são feitas para cada iteração em um processo de software iterativo, como subclasses de `Estimativa` na hierarquia de escopo. Finalmente, podem ser tratadas formas específicas de se realizar algum tipo de estimativa, como subclasses do tipo específico. Por exemplo, estimativas de Pontos de Função e de Pontos de Caso de Uso são tratadas como especializações de `EstimativaTamanho`. Dessa forma, estimativas, mesmo sendo de diferentes abordagens, são tratadas de maneira uniforme no contexto do ambiente. Isso traz vantagens, uma vez que a criação, a recuperação e a comparação das estimativas são facilitadas.

A infra-estrutura proposta permite, ainda, que um mesmo elemento de escopo (atualmente projeto, módulo e atividade) seja estimado segundo diversas abordagens, buscando valores mais precisos, ou estimado várias vezes segundo a mesma abordagem, traçando uma evolução dos valores previstos ao longo do tempo. Manter um histórico dos valores estimados no decorrer dos projetos é de grande importância para que se possa avaliar o nível de acerto desses valores, comparando-os aos dados reais obtidos ao final do projeto.

3 Conclusões

Efetuar estimativas não é uma tarefa fácil e requer apoio. Idealmente, esse apoio deve ser provido de forma automatizada, utilizando dados históricos de projetos similares, e, sobretudo, permitindo o uso de diferentes abordagens.

Neste artigo, foi brevemente apresentada a ferramenta EstimaODE. Em sua versão atual, EstimaODE contempla três formas de estimativas: (i) utilizando decomposição do processo de software e dados de projetos similares passados, (ii) utilizando Análise de Pontos de Pontos de Função e (iii) utilizando Análise de Pontos de Casos de Uso.

Por estar integrada a um ambiente de desenvolvimento de software (ODE), EstimaODE se beneficia de suas estruturas de controle de processos de software e gerência de conhecimento, evitando que muito trabalho tenha de ser refeito para se usar a ferramenta de estimativas. Além disso, EstimaODE foi projetada para ser facilmente estendida para contemplar outras formas de estimativa.

Agradecimentos

Este trabalho foi realizado com o apoio do CNPq e da CAPES, entidades do Governo Brasileiro dedicadas ao desenvolvimento científico e tecnológico, da FAPES, Fundação de Apoio à Ciência e Tecnologia do Espírito Santo, e das empresas VixTeam e Projeta, parceiras do projeto.

Referências

1. Pressman, R. S., Software Engineering: A Practitioner's Approach, Mc Graw Hill, 6th edition, 2005.
2. Fiorini, S. T., Staa, A., Baptista, R. M., Engenharia de Software com CMM, Brasport, 1998.
3. Falbo, R. A., Natali, A. C. C., Mian, P.G., Bertollo, G., Ruy, F.B., "ODE: Ontology-based software Development Environment", In: Memórias de IX Congreso Argentino de Ciencias de la Computación, p. 1124-1135, La Plata, Argentina, 2003.

Modelado de Procesos de Negocio Basados en Servicios Web*

Valeria de Castro, Marcos López Sanz, Esperanza Marcos

Grupo de Investigación Kybele
Universidad Rey Juan Carlos
Madrid (España)
valeria.decastro@urjc.es, mlsanz@escet.urjc.es, esperanza.marcos@urjc.es

Resumen. Los servicios Web proveen un marco basado en estándares que permite la interacción de aplicaciones a través de la Web. En los últimos años se ha incrementado la atención, tanto en los servicios Web como en los beneficios que estos aportan a la hora de construir aplicaciones. Actualmente, existen varios lenguajes que permiten realizar la composición de servicios Web. Sin embargo, una debilidad de estos lenguajes, es su dificultad para ser utilizados por los analistas, quienes realizan el modelado de alto nivel de los procesos de negocio. En este artículo ilustramos un método para el modelado de procesos de negocio basados en servicios Web.

1. Introducción

En los últimos años, las nuevas propuestas tecnológicas para la Web, tales como XML, Servicios Web, automatización de procesos de negocios, B2B, etc.; han favorecido el surgimiento de un nuevo paradigma para el desarrollo de aplicaciones conocido como Computación Orientada a Servicios (SOC - *Service Oriented Computing*) [7]. SOC utiliza servicios como elementos para el desarrollo de aplicaciones, basándose para ello en una arquitectura orientada a servicios (SOA - *Service Oriented Architecture*).

Los Servicios Web proveen un marco para la realización basada en estándares del paradigma SOC [4]. Los servicios Web definen mecanismos estandarizados para describir, publicar/localizar e interactuar con aplicaciones en línea [3]. Pero más allá de la idea básica de "describir, publicar, interactuar" es necesario contar con mecanismos para la composición de servicios. Por este motivo en los últimos años han surgido numerosas especificaciones en este área, tales como: XLANG [10], WSFL (*Web Services Flow Languaje*) [9], BPEL4WS (*Business Process Execution Language for Web Services*) [2] que combina las características de los dos primeros y que se ha convertido en el lenguaje estándar más aceptado para la composición de servicios Web.

* Este trabajo se ha llevado a cabo dentro de los proyectos: GOLD (TIN2005-00010), financiado por la Subdirección General de Proyectos de Investigación del Ministerio de Ciencia y Tecnología y URJC (PPR-2004-15) financiado por la Universidad Rey Juan Carlos.

Ahora bien, aunque el diseño e implementación de un servicio Web parece una tarea bastante simple, no se puede decir lo mismo de la implementación de los procesos de negocios. Los lenguajes para la implementación de procesos de negocios, tienen bastantes limitaciones a la hora de ser utilizados en etapas tempranas del proceso de desarrollo de software [8]. Esto sucede principalmente, por el hecho de que no es "trivial" pasar del modelado de proceso de negocios de alto nivel, realizado generalmente por los analistas de negocios, a un lenguaje de composición que implemente dichos procesos de negocios a través de Servicios Web.

En este trabajo se ilustra, a través de un ejemplo, un método para el modelado de procesos de negocios basados en Servicios Web. El método se extiende desde el modelado de los *"servicios"* que deberán ser ofrecidos a los usuarios, para lo que se tendrán en cuenta los requisitos del sistema capturados a través del modelo de negocio; hasta la implementación de los servicios del sistema, mediante procesos de negocios.

El resto del artículo se organiza de la siguiente forma: en la Sección 2 se resume el proceso para el modelado de procesos de negocios. En la Sección 3 se ilustra el método a través de un sistema para la gestión y procesamiento de imágenes médicas tomado como caso de estudio. La Sección 4 presenta las principales conclusiones, como también lecciones aprendidas a través del caso de estudio.

2. El método

El método para el modelado de procesos de negocios basados que se ilustra en este trabajo define un proceso (vea figura 1), nuevos conceptos, modelos y transformaciones entre los modelos [5].

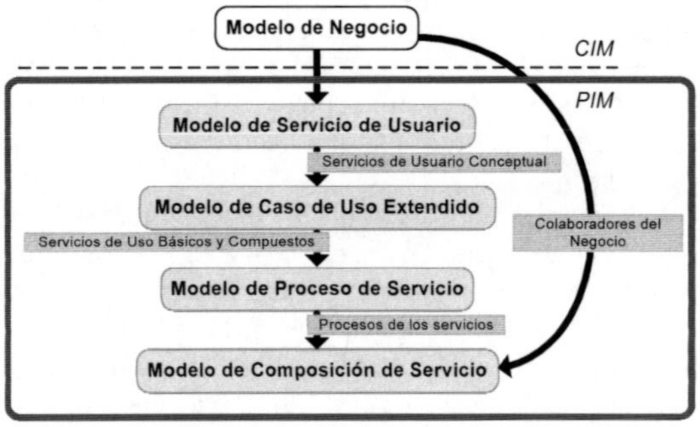

Fig. 1. Proceso de modelado de procesos de negocios

Como puede verse en la figura 1 el proceso toma como entrada el modelado de negocios, realizado por los analistas, y permite obtener a través de la transformación entre modelos un modelo de composición de servicios en el que se describe un proceso de negocio y a partir del cual es posible realizar la transformación a la tecnología de servicios Web. Los modelos propuestos por el método, remarcado en la figura 1, son representados a través de diagramas UML [6]. Dichos modelos se ilustran en la siguiente sección a través de un caso de estudio.

3. Sistema GesIMED

GESiMED, es un SIW para la gestión y procesamiento de imágenes médicas a través de la Web que se está desarrollando actualmente por los grupos Kybele y GTEBIM de la Universidad Rey Juan Carlos [1] [†].

La figura 2 muestra el ***modelo de servicios de usuarios*** para el sistema GesIMED. En este modelo se representan, como casos de usos estereotipados con *<<CUS>>*, los servicios que el sistema ofrece a los usuarios.

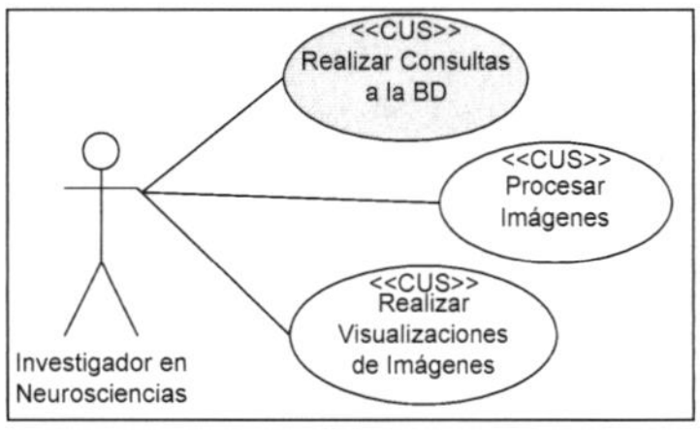

Fig. 2. Modelo de Servicio de Usuario

El ***modelo de caso de uso extendido*** permite modelar aquellas funcionalidades que son requeridas por el sistema para llevar a cabo un servicio. Así, por ejemplo, el servicio 'Realizar consultas a la BD' se descompone en varias funcionalidades: identificarse en el sistema, realizar la consulta, ver los resultados de la consulta y, opcionalmente, descargarse las imágenes obtenidas como resultado.

El ***modelo de proceso de servicio*** representa a través de un diagrama de actividad, el flujo para la ejecución de un servicio. Las actividades de dicho modelo son obtenidas a partir de las funcionalidades identificadas en el modelo anterior.

Este proceso también se ilustra en el ***modelo de composición de servicios***, pero de una manera más detallada. En este modelo se identifican los distintos *"colaboradores del negocio"*, es decir entidades que llevan a cabo ciertas operaciones necesarias para la ejecución de cada servicio.

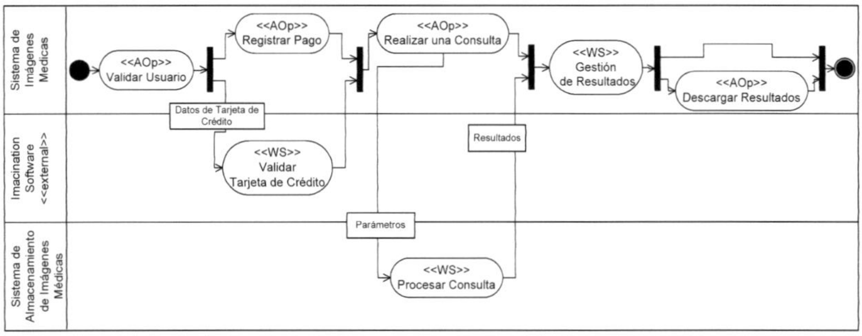

Fig. 3. Modelo de Composición de Servicios para el servicio 'Realizar Consultas a la BD'

[†] Agradecemos a *Juan Antonio Hernández Tamames* del grupo GTEBIM y a *César Javier acuña* del Grupo Kybele por su colaboración en el sistema GESiMED.

Las operaciones identificadas en este modelo (estereotipada con <<*AOp*>>) son obtenidas a partir de las actividades de modelo anterior. El estereotipo <<*WS*>> identifica aquellas operaciones que pueden ser implementadas como Servicios Web.

4. Conclusiones

En este artículo se ha ilustrado a través de un caso de estudio, un método para el modelado de proceso de negocios. Por razones de espacio, no es posible incluir todos los modelos del caso. Una descripción más detallada del método puede verse en [5].

Para la implementación de los procesos de negocios obtenidos para cada uno de los servicios ofrecidos por el sistema GesIMED, se ha utilizado la herramienta que ofrece Oracle para el desarrollo de sistemas con BPEL: *Oracle BPEL Development Tool.* Para lo que fue necesario el desarrollo de los servicios Web que formaban parte de los procesos.

A través del caso de estudio presentado en este trabajo, se han detectado importantes limitaciones del lenguaje BPEL a la hora de realizar la implementación de procesos de negocios. Por ejemplo, la necesidad de recibir como parámetro de entrada para la ejecución del proceso BPEL todos los parámetros necesarios para la ejecución de los distintos servicios Web que forman parte del proceso. Esto sucede porque no es posible definir interfaces para los servicios Web que forman parte del mismo.

Referencias

1. Acuña, C., Marcos, E., de Castro, V., and Hernández J.A. A Web Information System for Medical Image Management. 5th International Symposium on Biological and Medical Data Analysis. LNCS 3337. Springer-Verlag. pp. 49-59, 2004.
2. Andrews, T., Curbera, F., Dholakia, H., Goland, Y., Klein, J., Leiman, F., Liu, K., Roller, D., Smith, D., Thatte, S., Trickovik, I., Weerewarana, S., Business Process Execution Language for Web Services, 2003.
3. Curbera, F., Duftler, M., Khalaf, R., Nagy, W., Mukhi, N. y Weerawarana, S., Unraveling the Web services web: an introduction to SOAP, WSDL, and UDDI. Internet Computing, IEEE. 6(2): 86-93, 2002.
4. Curbera, F., Khalaf, R., Mukhi, N., Tai, S., Weerawarana, S, The next step in Web services. Communication of ACM 46(10), pp. 29-34, 2003.
5. De Castro, V., Marcos, E., López Sanz., M., A Model Driven Method for Service Composition Modeling: A Case Study. Int. Journal of Web Engineering and Technology. Pendiente de publicación.
6. OMG. OMG Unified Modeling Language Specification. Version 1.5. http://www.omg.org/technology/documents/formal/uml.htm, 2003.
7. Papazoglou, M.P., Georgakopoulos, D., Serviced-Oriented Computing, Communications of ACM, Vol. 46, No. 10, pp. 25-28, 2003.
8. Verner, L., BPM The Promise and the Challenge. Queue of ACM, Vol. 2 (4), pp. 82-91, 2004.
9. Web Services Flow Language (WSFL 1.0). Recuperado de: http://www-306.ibm.com/software/solutions/webservices/pdf/WSFL.pdf
10. XLANG. Web Services for Business Process Design. Recuperado de: http://www.gotdotnet.com/team/xml_wsspecs/xlang-c/default.htm, 2004.

Uma Abordagem Baseada em Responsabilidades Aplicada ao Processo de Desenvolvimento de *Frameworks*

Simone Nasser Matos[1,2], Clovis Torres Fernandes[2]

[1] Universidade Tecnológica Federal do Paraná, Coordenação de Informática,
84016210 Ponta Grossa, Brasil
simone@pg.cefetpr.br
http://www.pg.cefetpr.br/
[2] Instituto Tecnológico de Aeronáutica,
12228901 São Paulo, Brasil
clovis@ita.com.br
http://www.ita.br

Abstract: Developing *frameworks* in order to create applications is not a trivial task. These *frameworks* generally are produced by experts because they have deep knowledge the of application domain and a large experience on software design. Several methodologies which present positive and negative points are available to facilitate their development. Some negative points can be mentioned: not foreseeing the activities segmentation to be executed by the development team, emphasis in understanding the classes structures of concrete examples without the accomplishment of a more detailed domain analysis, among others. Therefore, this article proposes a new way of contributing to their creation process to ease those difficulties, aiming at the increase of the reuse for other applications.

Key-words: *Frameworks*, Methodologies, Responsibility.

1 Introdução

O processo de desenvolvimento de *frameworks* corresponde a uma evolução iterativa de sua estrutura de classes, que envolve atividades como modelagem de cenários, levantamento de estados de objetos, identificação de classes, entre outras.

Por isso, na literatura são encontradas diversas abordagens que auxiliam em seu processo de desenvolvimento. Dentre elas pode-se citar as seguintes: Projeto Dirigido por Exemplo [4], Baseada em Captura de Requisitos [5], Projeto Dirigido por Pontos de Flexibilidade [7], Baseada no Desenvolvimento, Uso e Manutenção [3], Baseada em Aspectos [6] [2] e a Baseada em Linguagem de Padrões de Braga e Masiero [1].

Durante a análise dessas abordagens constatou-se que as mesmas apresentam alguns pontos positivos e negativos. Dentre os pontos positivos pode-se citar os seguintes: definição dos passos do processo, sendo algumas mais voltadas a análise de casos concretos, enquanto outras dão maior ênfase na identificação dos pontos de flexibilidade; distribuição de diagramas a serem utilizados em cada fase; estabelecimento do uso de padrões de projeto e metapadrões [7].

Com relação aos pontos negativos que podem ser melhorados tem-se os seguintes: como modelar de forma que as atividades possam ser divididas entre a equipe de desenvolvimento; permitindo dessa forma a segregação das atividades; como reusar o projeto arquitetural dos exemplos concretos na criação da arquitetura do *framework*; como determinar os pontos de flexibilidade e de estabilidade a partir dos requisitos e não da estrutura de classes.

Por isso, neste artigo apresenta-se uma abordagem baseada em responsabilidades [8] para o desenvolvimento de *frameworks*, de forma a contribuir para o aumento do reuso, procurando sanar os pontos que não são enfatizados pelas metodologia analisadas, bem como contemplar seus pontos positivos.

Este artigo tem a seguinte organização. A motivação para se propor uma nova abordagem, aplicada ao desenvolvimento de *frameworks* é relatada na Seção 1. A nova abordagem com suas respectivas fases são apresentadas na Seção 2. Na última Seção descrevem-se as conclusões finais deste trabalho.

2 Abordagem Baseada em Responsabilidades Aplicada ao Processo de Desenvolvimento de *Frameworks*

As fases da abordagem proposta são descritas a seguir:

- Definir o Domínio: define qual o domínio que se pretende desenvolver o *framework*. Por exemplo, o domínio de Jogos de Corrida.
- Projetar *Framework* da Aplicação: permite realizar a generalização de casos concretos, buscando os elementos que recebem nomes diferentes, mas são a mesma coisa, com o objetivo de definir os pontos de flexibilidade e os de estabilidade para o desenvolvimento do *framework*.
- Implementar o *Framework*: traduz-se a especificação das classes para a linguagem escolhida, de acordo com a especificação da fase anterior.
- Instanciar o *Framework*: cada classe ou grupo de classes constituintes do *framework* será instanciado, com a finalidade de se gerar a aplicação para um ou mais exemplos concretos.
- Validar o *Framework*: esta etapa é utilizada para validar o *framework*, confrontando o que foi desenvolvido com o que foi especificado.

É importante ressaltar que a fase *Projetar Framework da Aplicação* é formada por duas subfases: *Compreender Exemplos Concretos* e *Definir Framework Base e de Aplicação*. Portanto, a ênfase deste trabalho será nessa fase, procurando descrever de forma sucinta seu funcionamento.

A abordagem propõe que o desenvolvedor inicie sua análise pela subfase *Compreender Exemplos Concretos*, que tem como finalidade modelar e entender os exemplos concretos do domínio, permitindo a criação do modelo de classes[1] e de requisitos[2] para cada exemplo que está sendo analisado.

---

[1] Conjunto de classes interagindo e colaborando entre si.

[2] É composto por um ou mais diagrama de caso de uso, bem como sua descrição textual separada por responsabilidades.

Esta subfase é realizada de forma iterativa, de maneira que, ao final, o desenvolvedor consiga gerar um conjunto de classes ditas satisfatórias para todos os seus subsistemas do exemplo selecionado.

A partir do momento que forem gerados o modelo de classes e de requisitos para o primeiro exemplo escolhido, o desenvolvedor deverá retornar a segunda atividade, *Escolher um Exemplo Concreto*. Nesse momento, seleciona-se um outro exemplo que já havia sido levantado na primeira atividade. Repete-se o processo até que se encontre um conjunto de classes e um modelo de requisitos ditos satisfatórios para ele. Isso será repetido para os *n* exemplos selecionados.

É importante ressaltar que a atividade de *Escolher um Subsistema do Exemplo* deve selecionar o mesmo tipo ou subsistemas correlatos para os *n* exemplos, de acordo com a iteração atual.

Também cabe salientar que a subfase de *Compreender Exemplos Concretos* permite a segmentação das atividades, pois cada subsistema pode estar sendo modelado por uma pessoa ou um grupo, concomitantemente, sendo esta composta por várias atividades que não serão explicadas neste trabalho.

A segunda subfase, *Definir Framework Base e de Aplicação*, permite a elaboração da modelagem do *framework*. É essencial que o desenvolvedor tenha o conhecimento do modelo de requisitos e do modelo de classes de cada exemplo.

Nessa subfase, a arquitetura do *framework* que será gerada tem como ponto de partida para sua elaboração a arquitetura definida para cada exemplo concreto, sendo aqui realizado o reuso arquitetural. Define-se também os pontos de flexibilidade e de estabilidade que formaram o *framework* base e de aplicação. Para facilitar sua identificação utiliza-se o modelo de requisitos gerado para cada exemplo analisado e não se analisa as estruturas de classes, facilitando desta forma seu levantamento.

O produto final desta subfase é o modelo do *framework* base e de aplicação, que serve como entrada para a fase de *Implementar Framework*. Esta fase também poderá ser executada de forma iterativa. As atividades da subfase *Definir Framework Base e de Aplicação* estão ilustradas na Figura 1.

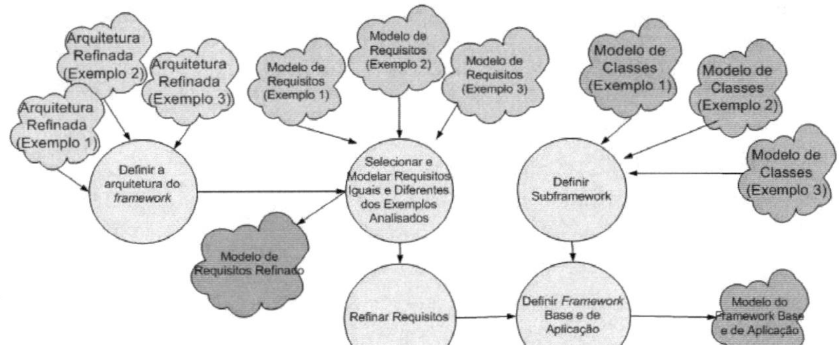

Fig. 1. Atividades da subfase *Definir Framework Base e de Aplicação.*

Através desta abordagem, pretende-se amenizar os pontos negativos relacionados com outras abordagens, melhorando os seguintes aspectos: *a análise mais detalhada*, sendo alcançada através da fase de *Projetar Framework da Aplicação*, o que implica maior compreensão do domínio e na diminuição do retrabalho; *o reuso arquitetural*, pois as abordagens da literatura realizam o projeto arquitetural somente na fase de projeto, sendo que na nova proposta a arquitetura é elaborada no início, fase *Definir ou Adaptar Arquitetura do Exemplo*, o que pode contribuir para o reuso durante a elaboração da arquitetura do *framework*; *a segmentação das atividades*, pois os subsistemas podem ser gerados por uma pessoa ou um grupo concomitantemente, sendo que isso é obtido através da fase de *Escolher Subsistema do Exemplo*; *a definição dos pontos de estabilidade e de flexibilidade* a partir do modelo de requisitos onde são verificados quais os pontos que devem ser mantidos estáveis ou flexíveis.

5 Conclusões

Framework são difíceis de desenvolver, contudo eles custam mais para confeccionar e requerem melhores programadores do que o desenvolvimento de uma aplicação normal. Estas são algumas das razões pela qual o desenvolvedor deverá conhecer abordagens destinadas ao seu processo de desenvolvimento.

Neste artigo forneceu-se uma abordagem baseada em responsabilidades que pode ser aplicada ao seu processo, permitindo a segmentação das atividades; reuso do modelo de requisitos e de arquitetura a partir da fase de análise, fases definidas de forma clara, utilização de padrões de projeto e metapadrões e estabelecimento em cada fase dos diagramas a serem confeccionados.

Referências

1. Braga, R. T. V.; Masiero, P. C. A process for *framework* construction based on a pattern language. In: Proceedings of the 26th Annual International Computer Software and Applications Conference (COMPSAC), IEEE Computer Society, Oxford-England (2002) 615-620.
2. Camargo, V. V, Masieiro, P. C. *Framework* Orientados a Aspectos. 19th Brazilian Symposium on Software Engineering (SBES). October 3-7. Federal University of Uberlândia (2005) 200-215.
3. Fayad, M. Schmidt, D. Johnson, R. Building Application *Frameworks* – Object-Oriented Foundations of *Framework* Design. Wiley (1999) 688.
4. Johnson, R. E. How to design *frameworks*. In: Object-Oriented Programming Systems, Languages and Aplications Conference – OOPSLA, Washington Proceedings (1993).
5. Landin, N. Niklasson, A. Development of Object-Oriented *Frameworks*. Department of Communication System. Lund Institute of Technology. Lund University. Lund, Sweden, PhD Thesis (1995).
6. Netinant, P. & Constantinides, T. Elrad, T. & Fayad, M. E. Aspect-Oriented *Frameworks*: The Design of Adpatable Operating Systems. OOPSLA 2000 Companion Minneapolis, Minnesota. In ACM 2000 1-58113-307-3 (2000).
7. Pree, W. Design Patterns for Object-Oriented Software Development. Addison-Wesley, Reading, Mass (1995).
8. Wirfs-Brock, R, Mckean., A. Object Design: Roles, Responsabilities, and Collaborations. Addison Wesley. (2003).

Integración Dinámica de Funcionalidad Basada en el Contexto de los Componentes de la Aplicación

Andrés Nieto, Luciano Mengoni, Liliana Nuño Silva

LIFIA, UNLP - Departamento de Informática, 50 y 115,
1900 La Plata, Argentina
{anieto, lmengoni, lilica}@sol.info.unlp.edu.ar

Abstract. En este artículo presentamos un mecanismo flexible para integrar, de manera dinámica, funcionalidad volátil dentro de una aplicación hipermedia. La motivación de este trabajo surge a partir de evitar la modificación de componentes existentes en el momento de la integración de nuevos requerimientos. Planteamos cómo estos requerimientos se pueden incorporar sobre aquellos componentes cuyo contexto, en el momento de la integración, se adapte a lo que requiere el diseñador sin necesidad de hacer modificaciones. Mediante un ejemplo mostramos las ventajas de integrar funcionalidad de la manera propuesta, comparándola con la manera tradicional. Presentamos al Servicio V como la nueva funcionalidad a agregar mediante las afinidades, que describen el contexto de los componentes existentes a los cuáles se ligan estos servicios.

1. Introducción

La integración de nuevos requerimientos a una aplicación web suele ser muy costoso. Se requiere de un proceso de ingeniería complejo para poder agregar un requerimiento dentro del sistema que ya está funcionando. Además debemos modificar módulos que ya están testeados y funcionando de manera estable. Esto último nos puede llevar a introducir errores en el módulo en cuestión, o en otros módulos relacionados.

Estos problemas se duplican en el caso de que estemos integrando una funcionalidad de prueba, por ejemplo cuando su consolidación depende de la aceptación de los usuarios del sistema; o cuando se trata de una funcionalidad temporal. En ambas situaciones estamos frente a un punto crítico al modificar el componente de la aplicación. Sería deseable que, cuando el componente agregado deja de ser parte del sistema, el costo de volver el sistema al estado previo sea nulo.

Suponemos el diseño de una aplicación web como lo plantean algunos métodos de diseños actuales tales como OOHDM[1] ó OOWS[2]; donde primero diseñamos un modelo conceptual, utilizando primitivas similares a las de UML[3], con la definición de clases que representan el corazón de la aplicación. Luego definimos el modelo navigacional, donde especificamos las características de navegación de nuestro sistema. Y por último el modelado de la interfase de usuario (aunque solo abordaremos los dos primeros modelos). Para hacer concreta nuestra discusión, nuestras ideas se basarán en el contexto de OOHDM.

El objetivo de este artículo es proponer una manera de introducir funcionalidad volátil dentro de una aplicación sin modificar sus componentes, mediante el concepto de afinidades. En la siguiente sección mostramos un ejemplo de motivación, luego presentamos la solución al problema que proponemos.

2. Motivación

Aquí presentamos un ejemplo donde podemos ver el tipo de funcionalidad volátil a la que nos estamos refiriendo. Situándonos en la pagina web del último CD del grupo musical Rolling Stones, dentro del sitio comercial Amazon[4] (Figura 1), podemos ver la información referente al CD, y agregado a esta, hay un hipervínculo que nos lleva a una página donde podemos comprar una entrada para un recital del grupo.

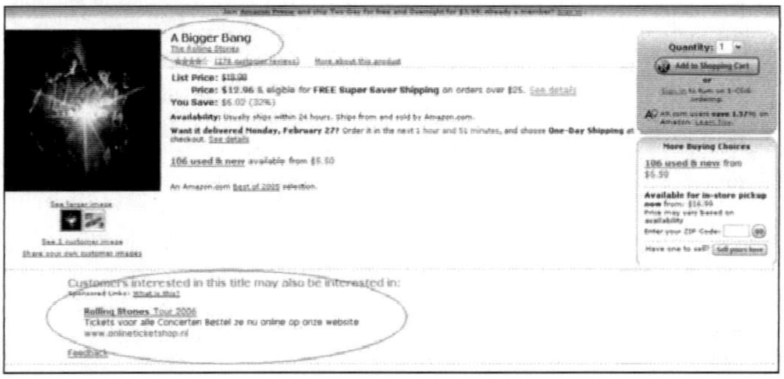

Fig. 1. Página web de "A Bigger Bang" con el vínculo a la funcionalidad de venta de entradas.

A priori no sabemos cuánto tiempo va a durar esa información en el nodo, por diferentes causas:

- Puede que lo esté recargando de información.
- Quizás no resulte de demasiado interés para los usuarios que naveguen por el mismo.
- Luego que el grupo termine la gira, no tiene sentido seguir teniendo dicha funcionalidad en el nodo.

Podemos decir que esta funcionalidad no es intrínseca al nodo, ya que antes de que el grupo realizara la gira, el nodo ya existía. Por otro lado, existen diversos factores, mencionados anteriormente, que determinan que esta funcionalidad se torna temporal o volátil. Por esta razón en un momento u otro debemos eliminarla del sistema, lo que nos llevará a modificar el esquema navigacional o conceptual de la aplicación.

Estas cuestiones nos llevan a lidiar con problemas tales como tener que modificar clases y objetos navegacionales que estaban funcionando correctamente en la aplicación, o no poder asignar funcionalidad a nivel de instancia (La compra de entradas solo concierne a CD's del grupo o de grupos relacionados, no a todos los CD's).

3. Integración de Funcionalidad Volátil en la Aplicación

En nuestro esquema de diseño consideramos dos capas: una capa de sistema base (aquí se diseña el modelo conceptual y navigacional de la aplicación) y la capa de servicios (aquí integramos la funcionalidad volátil). Además consideramos la existencia de una capa intermedia o capa de conexión, que se encarga del proceso de ligado de la funcionalidad volátil de los nodos en la capa de sistema base.

El modelado que se realiza en la capa de servicios es similar al realizado en la capa de modelo base. Cada vez que definimos una nueva funcionalidad volátil, de ahora en más *Servicio V*, describimos un modelo conceptual y uno navigacional. Además determinamos un nodo de partida y su forma de integración, que son elementos relevantes al momento de integrar la nueva funcionalidad con los nodos elegidos del sistema base. La capa de conexión consiste de un conjunto de clases que colaboran en la definición de Servicios V y en el ligado de estos con el sistema base.

El punto de partida de nuestra idea fue inspirado en la noción de servicios descripta en IUHM[5], donde se tratan los servicios como objetos relevantes de diseño. Podemos ver a un Servicio V como un Command[6] y un Decorator[6] a la vez. Es un Command porque encapsula el comportamiento en una clase y no en un método, y es un Decorator porque permite agregar nuevas características de manera no intrusiva.

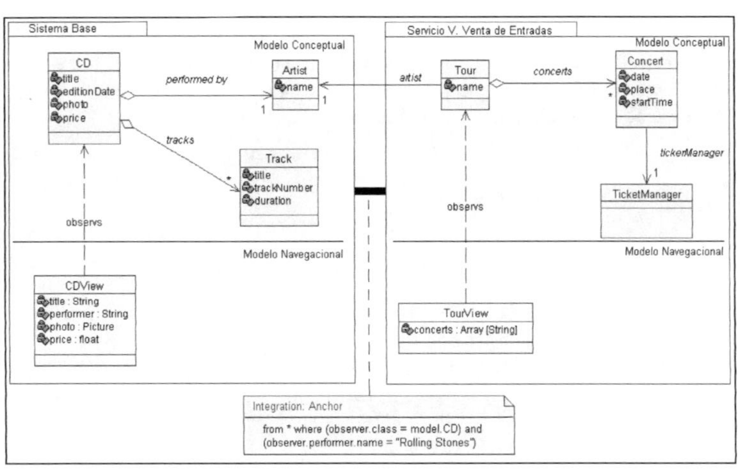

Fig. 2. Modelo que representa el diseño del sistema base y del servicio V denominado "Venta de Entradas", en conjunto con la conexión y la afinidad del servicio

Cada servicio V lleva especificado cuales serán los nodos del modelo conceptual que enriquecerá. A esta especificación la llamamos *afinidad.* La afinidad de un servicio depende de los *surroundings* de los nodos del modelo navigacional del sistema base. El *surrounding* de un nodo comprende las relaciones existentes entre éste y los demás nodos del modelo navigacional, y a su vez las relaciones que mantiene el objeto conceptual que éste nodo observa, con otros objetos del modelo conceptual. La afinidad de un servicio se refiere al tipo de surroundings que deben tener los nodos que quieran utilizar ese servicio. La afinidad de un servicio la expresamos utilizando un lenguaje de consulta similar al definido en [7].

En el ejemplo abordado en la sección anterior, nos interesaba que solo los nodos que modelan un CD de Rolling Stones tuvieran acceso al servicio que nos provee la venta de entradas para un recital. Nótese que no es deseable que el servicio esté disponible para otros CD's, ya que por ejemplo otros usuarios que frecuentan música clásica, quizás no se interesarían en un recital de los Rolling Stones. En la figura 2 podemos observar un posible modelo del sistema base y del servicio V que representa la venta de entradas para un recital.

4. Conclusiones y Trabajo Futuro

En este artículo presentamos un enfoque de cómo resolver la aparición de funcionalidad volátil dentro de una aplicación web. Discutimos que el hecho de incorporar este tipo de funcionalidad al sistema, puede afectar al mantenimiento de nuestra aplicación. Propusimos un mecanismo de diseño que involucra la separación en tres capas de la aplicación y definimos una forma flexible de incorporar funcionalidad volátil dentro del sistema existente, sin tener que modificar las clases del mismo.

En este momento estamos culminando el desarrollo de un framework construido sobre la base de Apache Struts[8], que soporta la especificación e implementación directa de un modelo navegacional de una aplicación web, y además brinda soporte para el agregado de funcionalidad dinámica en la aplicación.

5. Referencias

1. Gustavo Rossi, Daniel Schwabe, Fernando Lyardet.: Web Application Models are more than Conceptual, ER (Workshops) 1999: 239-253
2. Ricardo Quintero, Vicente Pelechano, Joan Fons, Oscar Pastor: Aplicación de MDA al Desarrollo de Aplicaciones Web en OOWS. JISBD 2003: 379-388
3. Unified Modeling Language, http://www-306.ibm.com/software/rational/uml/
4. Amazon.com, http://www.amazon.com
5. Marc Nanard, Jocelyne Nanard, Peter King: IUHM: A Hypermedia-based Model for Integrating Open Services, Data and Metadata, Hypertext 2003: 128-137
6. Gamma, R. Helm, R. Johnson and J. Vlissides: "Design Patterns: Elements of reusable object oriented software", Addison Wesley, 1995
7. W. Kim, "Advanced Database systems", ACM Press, 1994.
8. Apache Struts, http://struts.apache.org

Detección y Resolución de Conflictos entre Aspectos basado en un Sistema Experto de Reglas.

Sandra I. Casas[1] J. Baltasar García Perez-Schofield[2] Claudia A. Marcos[3]

[1]Unidad Académica Río Gallegos, Universidad Nacional de la Patagonia Austral, Argentina, lis@uarg.unpa.edu.ar
[2]Departamento de Informática, Universidad deVigo, España, jbgarcia@uvigo.es
[3]Instituto de Sistemas de Tandil, Universidad Nacional del Centro, Argentina cmarcos@exa.unicen.edu.ar

Abstract. La ocurrencia de conflictos entre aspectos es una consecuencia de la descomposición de los sistemas software en el desarrollo orientado a aspectos. Dicho fenómeno es independiente a las herramientas y requiere una especial atención y tratamiento ya que la activación de ciertos conflictos puede provocar comportamientos no deseados. El presente trabajo plantea un enfoque basado en un sistema experto de reglas para resolver el problema de conflictos entre aspectos en forma integral y simultánea.

1 Introducción

La programación orientada a aspectos [1] (POA) es un nuevo paradigma para el desarrollo de sistemas software que proporciona mecanismos y abstracciones para la implementación de las propiedades no funcionales (logging, seguridad, persistencia, concurrencia, registro de actividades, etc.), de manera separada y aislada.

Un nuevo tópico es considerado como área de investigación y problemática del paradigma a resolver, *"el fenómeno de los conflictos entre aspectos"*, también denominados como *"interacciones"* [2] o *"interferencias"* [3]. Un conflicto puede ocurrir cuando dos o más aspectos compiten por su activación [4]. En ciertas ocasiones estas interacciones, pueden tener por resultado un comportamiento no deseado.

En la mayoría de las herramientas POA, la identificación y resolución de conflictos es una tarea absolutamente manual y como se ha observado [5]. La mayoría de éstas ofrece como resolución un mecanismo que consiste en la fijación de orden, prioridad o precedencia, para lo cual los lenguajes proporcionan alguna semántica especial. Por ejemplo, AspectJ proporciona la cláusula "declare precedence" para ordenar la ejecución de los avisos de los aspectos que provocan el conflicto; de manera similar ocurre con AspectC++, DJ Aspect y AOP/ST.

Los trabajos y contribuciones se han alineados principalmente en las siguientes direcciones: (a) tratamiento parcial del problema de conflictos entre aspectos, ya que apuntan únicamente al análisis y detección del conflicto [6] [7] [8]; (b) una cantidad importante de los trabajos son específicos para AspectJ; (c) las propuestas que tienden a ser más generales aún ofrecen escasa capacidad y creatividad en cuanto a la resolución.

El presente trabajo presenta una propuesta de solución al problema de conflictos entre aspectos, basada en un sistema experto de reglas.

2. Gestión de Conflictos mediante un Sistema Experto de Reglas

Un sistema experto es una estrategia que permitirá detectar y resolver conflictos de forma automática y en forma simultánea. La resolución de cada conflicto depende exclusivamente de la semántica de la aplicación, y en este sentido el desarrollador de la aplicación se constituye en "el experto", que especifica reglas de resolución para cada conflicto. El objetivo principal es que a partir del conjunto de reglas definidas por el experto, el resto del proceso (detección y aplicación de las reglas) se efectúe en forma automática y transparente. En un sistema experto de reglas, la siguiente expresión permitirá no solo determinar la existencia de un determinado conflicto, sino además aplicar un método para resolverlo que será incluido en el proceso de tejido.

SI *<existe conflicto X >*
ENTONCES *<aplicar resolución Y >*

De esta forma, si todas las asociaciones entre aspectos y clases son mapeadas en la base de conocimientos del sistema experto, pueden ser utilizadas en una regla tanto para la detección como para la resolución del conflicto que plantean. Por ejemplo, la siguiente regla R1 expresada en CLIPS, verificará la existencia de dos asociaciones distintas (Asp1 y Asp2) relacionadas al mismo punto de unión (Clase 1 metodoA):

```
R1: (and (asociación (Asp1 call-before Clase1 metodoA))
         (asociación (Asp2 call-before Clase1 metodoA)))
=>
  S1
```

Resolución Amplia de Conflictos

Una estrategia "amplia" de resolución de conflictos significa que existen múltiples y variados métodos para solucionar un conflicto. Se puede aplicar una categoría de resolución básica o combinada. A continuación se explican brevemente las categorías.

» Categorías de Resolución básicas:

Orden: se establece un orden de ejecución para los aspectos integrantes del conflicto.
Opcional: se establecen condiciones para que se ejecuten opcionalmente los aspectos integrantes del conflicto.
Exclusión: se establece la exclusión (eliminación) de la ejecución de algunos de los aspectos integrantes del conflicto.
Anulación: se establece la anulación (eliminación) de la ejecución de todos los aspectos integrantes del conflicto.

Por ejemplo, la regla R3 especifica que si existe un conflicto entre los aspectos A1 y A3, sobre el punto de unión clase Clase1 y método MetX, la acción que se ejecutará es opcional, depende de la evaluación de una condición. En este caso si la condición es verdadera se ejecutará el aspecto A3, caso contrario se ejecutará el aspecto A1.

```
R3: (and (asociación ( A1 call-before Clase1 MetX ))
         (asociación ( A3 call-before Clase1 MetX )))
```

```
=> If (condicion)
     A3
   Else
     A1
```

» *Combinación de categorías básicas*
Cuando el conflicto involucra más de dos asociaciones, puede ser necesario resolver el conflicto aplicando más de una categoría de resolución básica. De esta forma, nuevas categorías se definen a partir de la combinación de las básicas, y así se brindan mayores posibilidades de resolución. Por ejemplo, la regla R1, aplica como acción la combinación de las categorías de Exclusión y Orden.

```
R1: (and (asociación ( A1  pa1 call-before Clase1 MetX ))
         (asociación ( A2  pa2 call-before Clase1 MetX ))
         (asociación ( A3  pa3 call-before Clase1 MetX )))
 => Excluir (A1)
    Ordenar (A2, A3)
```

3 Diseño Arquitectónico Preliminar

Se ha diseñado una herramienta de desarrollo de sistemas orientados a aspectos que extienda al lenguaje Java basada en la definición de tres módulos de software. A continuación se describe brevemente cada módulo de la arquitectura.

3.1 Development Module (Módulo de Desarrollo)

El objetivo principal de este módulo es capturar toda la información que se requiere como entrada para el desarrollo de un sistema software: clases, interfaces, aspectos, asociaciones y reglas. El componente Units Manager gestiona la codificación de las unidades funcionales (clases e interfaces) y no funcionales (aspectos) de una aplicación. El componente Association Manager gestiona las relaciones de asociación[1] entre unidades funcionales y no funcionales. El componente Rules Manager gestiona la especificación de las reglas para la detección y resolución de conflictos de manera fácil y sencilla. Las reglas generadas válidas son almacenadas en la base de conocimiento para efectuar el proceso de resolución de conflictos en tiempo de compilación.

3.2 Compiler Module (Módulo de Compilación)

El propósito de este módulo es realizar una serie de procesos necesarios que preparen al sistema software desarrollado para su ejecución. Los componentes principales de este módulo son: Aspect Manager, Conflict Manager y Class Compiler El componente Aspect Manager genera automáticamente la base de hechos de asociaciones (base de conocimiento) y transformar los aspectos en clases y preparar el código fuente en lenguaje Java para que el componente Class Compiler efectúe luego la compilación. El componente Conflict Manager es en si mismo el sistema experto de reglas cuyo objetivo es detectar y resolver los conflictos. Una vez que la

[1] Una asociación es una entidad que relaciona a un elemento de un aspecto (especie de método) con un elemento de una clase (punto de unión). Así, una asociación define con exactitud un punto de corte.

base de conocimientos esta generada, puede lanzarse la ejecución del motor de inferencia. Como resultado algunas reglas se "dispararán" produciendo como acción asociada, la resolución de determinados conflictos. La resolución de los conflictos implica la "modificación" de la estructura de las asociaciones.

3.3 Execution Module (Módulo de Ejecución)

Este módulo es el responsable de ejecutar la aplicación desarrollada. Antes de la ejecución, las clases del sistema software se cargan en demanda, para la posterior interpretación de la JVM. Un ClassLoader personalizado permitirá detectar previamente a las clases que son afectadas por alguna asociación y en consecuencia requieren ser tejidas. En estos casos, se derivará el control al componente Aspect Weaver para que efectúe las transformaciones (tejido) necesarias.

5 Conclusiones

Este trabajo propone una solución al problema de conflictos entre aspectos que satisface los siguientes objetivos: i) aborda las dos dimensiones del problema de conflictos entre aspectos, la detección y resolución de los conflictos. Se propone un mecanismo que de manera automática detecta los conflictos entre aspectos y de manera semi-automática los resuelve; ii) es un enfoque amplio y flexible en cuanto a los métodos de resolución que propone, en contraposición al limitado y restringido enfoque convencionalmente soportado de orden. El trabajo actual y futuro esta centrado en la implementación de la herramienta que de soporte al enfoque propuesto en este artículo.

El presente trabajo fue parcialmente financiado por la Universidad Nacional de la Patagonia Austral, Santa Cruz, Argentina.

Referencias

1. Kiczales G., Lamping J., Mendhekar A., Maeda C., Lopes C., Loingtier J., Irwin J: Aspect-Oriented Programming. In Proceedings of ECOOP (1.997).
2. Duoence R., Fradet P. and Südholt M.: "Detection and Resolution of Aspect Interactions", TR N°4435, INRIA, ISSN 0249-6399, Francia (2.002).
3. ROOTS: LogicAJ – A Uniformly Generic and Interference-Aware Aspect Language. http://roots.iai.uni-bonn.de/researh/logicaj/ , (2.005).
4. Pryor J., Diaz Pace A., Campo M.: Reflection on Separation of Concerns. RITA. Vol.9. Num.1 (2.002).
5. Casas S., Reinaga H., Sierpe L., Vanoli V., Saldivia C., Prior J.: Clasificación y Resolución de Conflictos entre Aspectos. VII WICC – Argentina (2.005).
6. Storzer M., Krinkle J.: Interference Analisys for AspectJ. FOAL USA (2.003).
7. Tessier F., Badri M., Badri L.: A Model-Based Detection of Conflicts Between Crosscutting Concern: Towards a Formal Approach. WAOSD 04, China (2.004).
8. Monga M., Beltagui F., Blair L.: Investigating Feature Interactions by Exploiting Aspect Oriented Programming. TR N.comp-002-2.003, Lancaster University, Inglaterra (2.003).

Experiencia en el desarrollo de una aplicación de contabilidad de código abierto usando XP

Iván Prieto, Luca Cernuzzi, Oscar Parra

DEI - Universidad Católica "Nuestra Señora de la Asunción", Asunción, Paraguay
ivan_prieto_c@yahoo.com, lcernzz@uca.edu.py, oparra@gmail.com

Abstract. *Extreme Programming* (XP) es una de las llamadas metodologías ágiles que más interés ha generado en el ámbito industrial y académico. En este caso de estudio se analiza proceso de definición, implementación e integración de una aplicación de contabilidad multiplataforma de código abierto, evaluándolo con las técnicas del análisis *post mortem* y el proyecto NAME (*Network for Agile Methodologies Experience*). Finalmente, se citan algunas ventajas y problemas encontrados en su aplicación, debido sobre todo al minimalismo utilizado en su proceso de diseño y documentación.

1 Introducción

La necesidad de enfoques flexibles, normalmente denominados evolucionarios o incrementales, ha sido ampliamente reconocida en la ingeniería del software para abordar muchos de los proyectos actuales que cuentan con un entorno cambiante, y en donde se exige reducir drásticamente los tiempos de desarrollo manteniendo una alta calidad. En este contexto, los métodos y metodologías ágiles (ver el manifiesto ágil [1]), por estar especialmente orientadas para proyectos pequeños, ofrecen oportunidades prometedoras, aportando una elevada simplificación, sin renunciar a las prácticas esenciales para asegurar la calidad del producto. Posiblemente uno de los más interesantes ejemplos de métodos ágiles es *eXtreme Programming* (XP) [2].

Por otro lado, para alcanzar una cierta confianza en la eficiencia de los procesos es fundamental contar con evaluaciones de las metodologías. Sin embargo, considerando su surgimiento relativamente reciente, las propuestas de evaluación de metodologías ágiles son aún escasas y esto ha motivado uno de los objetivos del proyecto *Network for Agile Methodologies Experience* - NAME [3] inherente a la necesidad de validar los métodos ágiles utilizando técnicas de evaluación conforme al enfoque ágil.

Para el efecto, en este trabajo se presenta un caso de estudio centrado en el desarrollo de una aplicación de contabilidad de código abierto utilizando la metodología XP y al que se aplica la técnica de revisión *post mortem* [4] para analizar las ventajas y problemáticas en el uso de dicha metodología.

El resto del trabajo se estructura de la siguiente forma: en la sección 2 se presenta el caso de estudio y su proceso de implementación; en la sección 3 se presenta su evaluación utilizando los instrumentos propuestos en el análisis *post mortem* y el proyecto NAME; y en la sección 4 las conclusiones.

2 CONTAPY: un caso de estudio usando XP

CONTAPY [5] es una aplicación básica de contabilidad de código abierto multiplataforma que intenta fomentar el uso de aplicaciones de código abierto tanto a los usuarios, brindando herramientas orientadas a las PYMES (pequeñas y medianas empresas), así como a los desarrolladores en el uso de entornos de programación integrados y libres en la construcción de herramientas multiplataforma. Para la construcción de esta aplicación, se siguieron los lineamientos definidos en la metodología de desarrollo XP [2].

En primer lugar, se definió el equipo de desarrollo. Fueron seleccionados como cliente un contador y como programadores a dos estudiantes de último año de Ingeniería Informática.

A continuación, se definió la herramienta de desarrollo de la aplicación. Como uno de los objetivos del proyecto era elegir herramientas multiplataforma y compatibles con los que estos programadores utilizan regularmente, se seleccionó *MONO* [6], un *framework* de desarrollo libre compatible con *.NET*, y el lenguaje elegido fue *C#*. Como base de datos transaccional se adoptó *PostgreSQL* [7].

En tercer lugar se definieron las historias de usuario. Se esbozaron los casos de uso del sistema y los requisitos funcionales y no funcionales de la aplicación, generándose un total de 18 historias con todas las funcionalidades que podrían ser interesantes para esta aplicación. Para cada uno de estos requisitos, el cliente (en consulta con el grupo de desarrolladores) definió una prioridad o valor de negocio. Así también, los desarrolladores definieron estimaciones del esfuerzo necesario para realizar cada una de las historias y las relaciones entre ellas.

Finalmente se especificó el plan de entregas, donde a partir de las prioridades, el esfuerzo necesario y las relaciones entre las historias a implementar, se definió la versión 1 del sistema consistente en 10 historias de usuario, repartidas en 3 iteraciones, para un total de 350 horas/hombre según el cálculo del esfuerzo necesario realizado en la etapa anterior.

Al concluir cada iteración, se realizaron pruebas integradas con el cliente y se tomaron datos objetivos como el tamaño, funcionalidades, defectos y costo del proyecto para ir midiendo los grados de avance.

3 Evaluación de la experiencia

En particular, el propósito de esta evaluación fue analizar el proceso de definición, implementación e integración de la aplicación CONTAPY.

Para el efecto se utilizaron los instrumentos introducidos por el proyecto NAME [3] y el análisis *post mortem* [4] que consisten en: una encuesta (dirigida al grupo de desarrollo); datos objetivos (el tamaño del proyecto, el costo y la calidad del desarrollo); reunión indagatoria; día de historia del proyecto.

A continuación se presentan los resultados del análisis *post mortem* que considera todos los aspectos del proyecto, incluyendo productos, procesos y recursos, y está orientada a identificar las áreas de mejora para el futuro.

Los resultados de la encuesta se muestran en la tabla 1 y se describen a continuación.

Tabla 1. Resultados de la encuesta

RESPUESTAS / CATEGORÍAS	MUY BUENO 76-100%	BUENO 51-75%	ACEPTABLE 26-50%	MALO 0-25%
Soporte y metas del equipo	67%	25%	8%	0%
Expectativas y comunicaciones	58%	42%	0%	0%
Resolución de problemas	67%	11%	22%	0%
Acceso a la información	67%	33%	0%	0%
Especificaciones del producto	67%	33%	0%	0%
Prácticas de ingeniería	33%	42%	0%	25%
Panorama	0%	67%	33%	0%

SOPORTE Y METAS: Los usuarios conocían las metas, pero se reportaron dificultades para estimar el esfuerzo necesario, debido sobre todo al desconocimiento de la herramienta y la falta de documentación sobre la misma.
EXPECTATIVAS Y COMUNICACIONES: El producto cumplió con las expectativas y la programación a pares apoyó el proceso de desarrollo.
RESOLUCIÓN DE PROBLEMAS: Los problemas surgidos fueron rápidamente resueltos gracias a la comunicación oral. La falta de prototipos y un diseño inicial afectó negativamente en la fase de implementación.
ACCESO A LA INFORMACIÓN: El uso de las guías de desarrollo, las historias de usuario y los planes de entrega impactaron positivamente en el transcurso del desarrollo del producto.
ESPECIFICACIONES DEL PRODUCTO: No se hizo un diseño inicial completo (no previsto en XP). Diseño y revisiones fueron realizados por las personas adecuadas.
PRÁCTICAS DE INGENIERÍA: Aunque el proceso de desarrollo fue considerado eficaz, se notó que la falta de un diseño inicial afectó adversamente al proceso de construcción de la aplicación.
PANORAMA: Los encuestados opinaron que se hicieron compromisos correctos entre características, calidad y recursos, pero que podrían haber mejorado contando con un diseño inicial más completo.

Los resultados de los datos objetivos del proyectos se muestran en la tabla 2.

Tabla 2. Datos objetivos obtenidos. Se muestran con (*) aquellos acumulados desde el inicio del proyecto

	ITERACIÓN 1	ITERACIÓN 2	ITERACIÓN 3	TOTAL
Historias por iteración	3	2	4	9
Esfuerzo por iteración	88 hs	96 hs	150 hs	334 hs
Relaciones entre las historias	Fuerte	Fuerte	Medio	-
Metáforas	1	3	4	4
Casos de prueba	8	0	0	8
Cantidad de clases (*)	2	5	6	6
Cantidad de métodos y triggers (*)	21	73	98	98
Contado de defectos	1	4	3	8
Cantidad de iteraciones al SVN	1	1	1	3

En la reunión indagatoria se discutieron con el grupo de desarrollo las ventajas y desventajas encontradas durante el proceso de desarrollo complementando la encuesta y las medidas objetivas tomadas. Entre las ventajas, se alabaron: la programación a pares (sobre todo en la etapa de descubrimiento de la herramienta de programación), el uso de historias de usuario, la valoración de cada una de ellas, la simplicidad de las soluciones adoptadas y la frecuente comunicación verbal. Como aspectos negativos se citaron: la falta de diseño inicial que afectó negativamente al desarrollo del producto y, que las pruebas automáticas no es muy adecuado en aplicaciones GUI o donde las relaciones entre clases son débiles.

En la historia del proyecto se discutió el principal problema encontrado en el desarrollo del sistema que fue la falta de un diseño inicial. Este hecho ocasionó que ciertas historias que fueron consideradas en el plan de entregas, al no ser tomadas en cuenta en un diseño inicial completo, llegado el momento no podían ser implementadas.

4 Conclusiones

En nuestra experiencia, el uso de XP presenta varias características positivas como ser: fluida y directa relación con el cliente en forma verbal, lo que ayuda a la rápida resolución de dudas; simplicidad y control de características relevantes mediante un análisis de costo-beneficio en cada etapa; mejoramiento de la curva de aprendizaje de nuevas herramientas mediante la programación a pares; y uso de herramientas automáticas para el apoyo a la programación, documentación y control del proyecto.

Por otro lado, algunas dificultades encontradas y que consideramos se puedan generalizar son: la falta de diseño inicial que posibilita un riesgo muy alto en la definición de una versión del sistema; y la práctica de pruebas unitarias parece más adecuada para programas con poca interacción con usuarios. Por estos motivos, consideramos que es altamente recomendable un diseño inicial completo, previendo todas las relaciones entre las historias a nivel de cada versión de manera a tratar de maximizar las características, la calidad y los recursos involucrados en el proyecto.

Referencias

1. Manifiesto Ágil, disponible en: www.agilemanifesto.org
2. Beck K.. Extreme Programming Explained: Embrace Change. Addison-Wesley,1999.
3. Red Europea del VI programa marco NAME (Network of Agile Methods Experience), disponible en: http://name.case.unibz.it
4. B. Collier, T. DeMarco, and P. Feary, "A Defined Process for Project Postmortem Review," IEEE Software, July 1996.
5. CONTAPY: disponible en: http://www.linux.org.py/contapy/
6. Mono Proyect, disponible en: http://www.mono-project.com/
7. PostgreSQL, disponible en: http://www.postgresql.org/

Geração da Modelagem de Sistemas Multi-Agentes a Partir de Cenários

Leonardo Santos, Ulf Bergmann, and Ricardo Choren

Seção de Engenharia de Computação e Telemática (SE/8) – IME,
Pça General Tibúrcio 80, Rio de Janeiro/RJ, 22290-270, Brazil
{lima, ulf, choren}@de9.ime.eb.br

Abstract. Este artigo apresenta um conjunto de diretrizes, que utiliza o Léxico Ampliado de Linguagem e cenários, para gerar os artefatos de modelagem de um Sistema Multi-Agentes (SMA). O conjunto de heurísticas proposto guia a construção da modelagem de SMA, permitindo um rastreamento inicial dos elementos presentes nos modelos. Nosso trabalho está focado na geração dos diagramas estruturais de ANote (objetivos, ambiente e agentes). Finalmente, ilustramos o uso das diretrizes propostas por meio de um simples exemplo de SMA (meeting scheduler)

1 Introdução

Com o crescente interesse na área de Orientação a Agentes, diversas metodologias de especificação de sistemas multi-agentes (SMA) foram desenvolvidas [1][6]. Entretanto, em muitos poucos trabalhos há uma preocupação explícita em como tratar os requisitos para gerar a modelagem de um SMA. Para lidar com este problema, este artigo apresenta um conjunto de diretrizes que se baseiam no Léxico Ampliado de Linguagem (LAL) [3] e em cenários [4] como fontes de informação para a geração da modelagem de SMA. Seu objetivo é diminuir a lacuna entre o levantamento de requisitos e a fase de análise orientada a agentes, procurando identificar como os requisitos podem guiar a construção dos artefatos de modelagem de SMA.

2 Diretrizes Para Geração de Artefatos de Modelagem para SMA

O método proposto de geração de artefatos de modelagem de SMA é composto por um conjunto de 12 diretrizes e utiliza como fonte de informação o LAL e um conjunto de cenários. Estas diretrizes permitem a geração dos três diagramas que compõem o pacote estrutural da linguagem de modelagem ANote [2]: os diagramas de objetivos, ambiente e agentes. Para ilustrar a aplicação das diretrizes, utilizou-se o Meeting Scheduler [5]. Para este sistema foi desenvolvido um LAL com 33 termos e, a partir dele, foi desenvolvido um conjunto de 16 cenários, com um cenário integrador.

2.1 Diagrama de Objetivos

Para de gerar o diagrama de objetivos de Anote, devem-se seguir as seguintes diretrizes: Extrair Objetivos dos Cenários; Identificar os Macro-objetivos; Verificar Hierarquias entre Objetivos e Refinar Objetivos. Em *Extrair Objetivos dos Cenários*, deve-se listar o nome de todos os cenários acompanhados dos objetivos. O objetivo deve ser o verbo principal da oração que descreve objetivo do cenário e deve estar no infinitivo. Em *Identificar os Macro-objetivos*, devem-se verificar quais são os cenários, representantes de hierarquias, que o cenário integrador referencia. Para cada um destes cenários, devem-se destacar os objetivos extraídos com a regra anterior. E com estas informações elabora-se o diagrama de objetivos inicial.

Em *Verificar Hierarquias entre Objetivos*, para cada cenário representante de uma hierarquia devem-se verificar quais são os demais cenários referenciados por ele. Os relacionamentos existentes entre os cenários devem ser levados para o diagrama de objetivos. Finalmente, em *Refinar Objetivos*, devem-se analisar todos os cenários, buscando por aqueles que, em seus episódios, apresentem mais de um ator que participe ativamente, dado que estes atores podem ter objetivos individuais e devem agir colaborativamente para atingir um objetivo maior: o objetivo atrelado ao cenário. A figura 1 apresenta o diagrama de objetivos (visão parcial) obtido com a aplicação das diretrizes apresentadas.

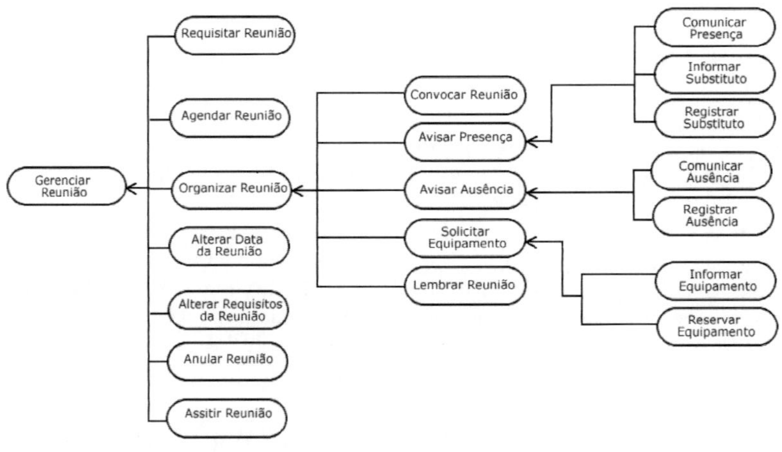

Fig. 1. Diagrama de objetivos para o Meeting Scheduler

2.2 Digrama de Ambiente

Para de gerar o diagrama de ambiente de Anote, devem-se seguir as seguintes diretrizes: Destacar os Recursos; Incluir Atores; Eliminar Redundâncias e Identificar Relacionamentos Entre Recursos. Em *Destacar os Recursos*, devem-se percorrer os cenários, sempre respeitando as hierarquias, buscando pelos recursos descritos em cada um deles. Com isso, elabora-se uma lista com todos os recursos. Em *Incluir Atores*, devem ser incluídos os atores dos cenários na lista anterior. A inclusão dos atores se faz necessária, pois é neste ponto que se garante que as informações relativas aos atores serão consideradas na modelagem do SMA.

Em *Eliminar Redundâncias*, deve-se proceder à eliminação dos termos que representam a mesma informação além de se descartar os termos que o desenvolvedor não deseja utilizar na solução do problema. Finalmente, em *Identificar Relacionamentos Entre Recursos*, devem-se analisar os episódios de todos os cenários, buscando-se por sentenças que mostrem alguma relação entre estes elementos. O LAL deve ser utilizado como fonte complementar de informação. A figura 2 apresenta o diagrama de ambiente obtido com a aplicação das diretrizes apresentadas.

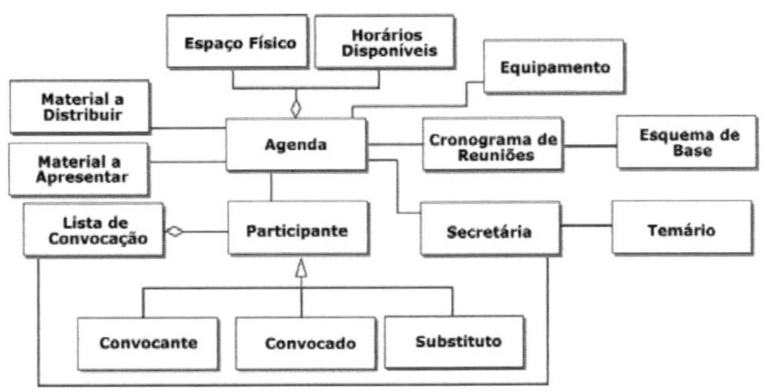

Fig. 2. Diagrama de ambiente para o Meeting Scheduler

2.3 Digrama de Agentes

Para de gerar o diagrama de agentes de Anote, devem-se seguir as seguintes diretrizes: Relacionar Recursos com Objetivos Funcionais; Identificar Atores Primários; Definir Agentes, e; Identificar Colaborações entre Agentes. Em *Relacionar Recursos com Objetivos Funcionais*, devem-se analisar as descrições dos episódios relacionados a cada um dos objetivos funcionais, indicando se o recurso é produzido, alterado ou apenas utilizado nestes episódios. Em *Identificar Atores Primários*, devem-se listar os atores primários em cada um dos cenários atrelados aos objetivos funcionais.

Em *Definir Agentes*, procede-se a delegação dos objetivos a um dado conjunto de agentes. Para tanto, deve-se executar dois passos: (i) agrupar em um mesmo subconjunto os objetivos que têm os mesmos atores primários; (ii) agrupar os objetivos que possuem um dado conjunto de recursos em comum. Finalmente, em *Identificar Colaborações entre Agentes*, devem-se analisar os recursos utilizados em cada um dos objetivos. Quando um dado recurso é utilizado ou alterado por um objetivo delegado a um dado agente e este recurso é produzido ou alterado por outro objetivo delegado a um agente diferente, há o estabelecimento de uma colaboração entre os agentes. A figura 3 apresenta o diagrama de agentes obtido com a aplicação das diretrizes apresentadas.

Ao final da elaboração dos diagramas deve ser feita a revisão de todos eles com o objetivo de encontrar informações inconsistentes e refinar os mesmo. Por exemplo, um problema que pode ocorrer diz respeito à consideração de um dado ator, inicialmente, sendo um recurso do sistema e mais tarde opta-se pela inclusão dele como um agente. Nesta situação, o ator deve ser retirado do diagrama de ambiente.

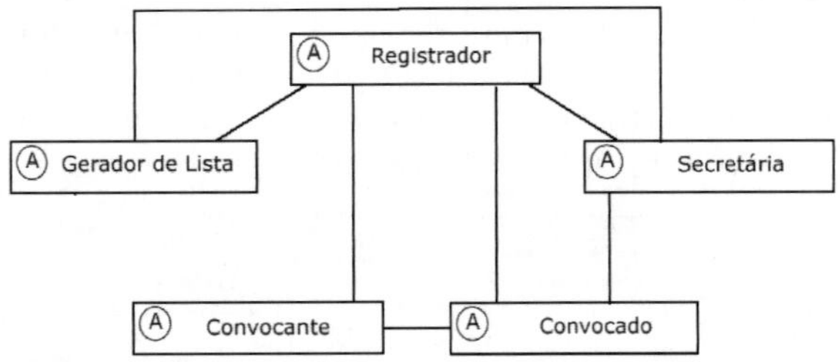

Fig. 3. Diagrama de agentes para o Meeting Scheduler

3 Conclusão

Neste artigo foi proposta a utilização do LAL e dos cenários para o levantamento dos requisitos para SMA e apresentado a um conjunto de diretrizes para a geração de artefatos de modelagem de SMA. Estas diretrizes permitem a elaboração dos três diagramas estruturais de ANote. O objetivo deste método é eliminar a lacuna existente entre os requisitos e os modelos de SMA, uma vez que sua execução permite uma passagem dos requisitos para a especificação sem saltos.

References

1. Cernuzzi, L., Cossentino, M., Zambonelli, F.: Process Models for Agent-based Development. Engineering Applications of Artificial Intelligence 18, n.2 (2005) 205-222
2. Choren, R., Lucena, C.: Modeling Multi-agent Systems with ANote. Journal on Software and Systems Modeling 4, n.2 (2005) 199-208
3. Kaplan, G., Hadad, G., Doorn, J., Leite, J.C.S.P: Inspección del Lexico Extendido del Lenguaje. In: Proceedings of WER00 (2000) 70-91
4. Leite, J.C.S.P., Hadad, G.D.S., Doorn, J.H., Kaplan, G.N.: A Scenario Construction Process. Engineering Journal 5, n.1 (2000) 38-61
5. van Lamsweerde, A., Darimont, R., Massonet, P.: The Meeting Scheduler System– Preliminary Definition. Internal Report, University of Louvain, Belgium (1993)
6. Wooldridge, M., Ciancarini, P.: Agent-Oriented Software Engineering: The State of the Art. In: Proceedings of AOSE 2000 (2000) 1-28

User Centred Requirements for improving an Intensive Care Unit Information System

Mónica Sara Santos [1], João Falcão e Cunha [2], Altamiro da Costa Pereira [3]

[1] Faculdade de Engenharia da Universidade do Porto / Escola Superior de Tecnologia da Saúde do Instituto Politécnico do Porto, Porto, Portugal
mss@estsp.ipp.pt

[2] Faculdade de Engenharia da Universidade do Porto, Porto, Portugal
jfcunha@fe.up.pt

[3] Faculdade de Medicina da Universidade do Porto, Porto, Portugal
altamiro@med.up.pt

Abstract. The Intensive Care Units (ICUs) of several Portuguese hospitals have been using the *intensive.care* information system (ICS) for the past three years. This system was developed under specification of Medical Doctors (MDs) from ICUs. As the main focus of the initial project was on adding functionality to the system, little attention was given to non-functional requirements such as usability.

This paper describes the current ICS and the results of preliminary interviews with its main stakeholders to determine high-level functional and non-functional evolution requirements. The objective of the overall study is to propose usability requirements for such system, in particular from MDs and nurses, its main users. A prototype of an improved user interface will be evaluated to support the development of the next version of the system.

The interviews with a key developer and several MDs resulted so far in the conclusion that ICS is a very helpful tool but requires improvements in several modules, such as *Patient Entrance* and *Patient Evolution*. However, more advanced modules, such as *Infections Management*, will also require some adaptations of work processes in ICUs, in order to benefit from the full support that ICS can provide.

1 Introduction

The ICU application used in four major hospitals in the North of Portugal is called *intensive.care* (ICS) and is being developed at the Biostatistics and Medical Informatics Service (SBIM) from the Medicine School of Universidade do Porto (FMUP) [1].

The main functions of ICS are to register patients' data from the moment they enter the ICU until they leave. ICS's modules vary in complexity as there are some basic ones, such as the patients' admission and discharge notes, and others that are more complex, such as the infections' or complications' management.

ICS works with large amounts of data and amongst its stakeholders are the ICU patients, people that are critically ill, and the ICU MDs for whom time is extremely valuable. So there is the need for very high quality data, good system performance and lack of errors.

ICS has never had a Human Computer Interaction (HCI) development plan and has not been developed having usability as a main concern. Therefore ICS has some notorious usability problems and its users feel there are many things about it that could be improved. Moreover, there are some modules of ICS that have never been used, in particular because of their HCI problems.

Meetings with several ICS users, reported in the next sections, indicate that it is a successful application, but still with numerous problems. The current study aims at identifying modules that most need improvements and at defining overall requirements. There is a plan of implementing ICS in other ICUs, so usability problems need to be addressed. A formal HCI evaluation is being conducted in order to propose an improvement plan for ICS.

The next section presents the methodology of the study, section 3 presents the preliminary results of the interviews with key stakeholders, in particular general system requirements, and the final sections the proposed future work and conclusions.

2 Methodology

An HCI study and evaluation is being conducted in order to produce an HCI evolution plan for ICS. This evolution plan is based on a set of usability requirements that will be specified and evaluated with the help of a prototype. Well-known HCI techniques are being used.

The current project started with the study of ICS and of the ICU information management problem. This was made to gain some knowledge about the system and the way it interacts with its users' needs. There were some meetings with the development team, including the current project manager and the first project manager of ICS.

Some interviews were held with users in order to collect information about the most problematic issues about ICS. These were semi-structured interviews, having only few questions intended to obtain an overview of the current usage of ICS and its users' satisfaction, so a study focus could be established [2]. There were three interviews to key users of ICS in three different hospitals.

After compiling the results of the interviews, there was a qualitative study to set the main module from ICS where the HCI evaluation would be centred.

When the focus area was established, the second set of interviews took place. They happened in two hospitals with experts in infection in ICU. Since the evaluators have no medical background, these interviews aimed to understand the basis of infection, its implications and its management.

ICS's users are mainly MDs and it is very difficult to have meetings with them, as they have such tight and unpredictable schedules. This happens because they work at ICUs and deal with critically ill patients that might need attention at any time [3].

There was a visit to one of the ICUs, which was intended to provide an overview of the environment and the existing machines in such units [4].

3 Analysis of Stakeholders' Interview Results

After understanding the overall ICS characteristics, the study concentrated on understanding the evolution requirements of the main user stakeholders. In order to do so three MDs involved with the system in different hospitals have been interviewed. In these interviews, some information about the users' global opinion about the system and its functionality was gathered.

The interviewed users are MDs specialized in intensive care, who are the key users of ICS in their unit. It is very interesting to have users from different ICUs because these units do not all have the same work methods. Given that, these users' usage of ICS is not exactly equal from an ICU to another.

After the first set of interviews there were some coinciding responses about parts of ICS that should be improved. In a general way its users enjoy working with ICS and feel the application eases their everyday work, but when it comes to complex tasks, such as infections and complications, users have some resistance in switching from the traditional paper reports to the electronic version of ICS. This happens mainly because of the difficulty to map the procedures in ICS exactly as they are made on paper. Also, for some of the most complex tasks there is the need for adjustment in work methods, in order to make ICS a simple and standard system.

Patients' admission and release data, and prognostic scoring indicators are referred to as being easy to register, navigate and use. When it comes to more intricate tasks, such as registering and managing of infections, complications, diagnosis, procedures and surgery, the users say they find it difficult to use the system.

In a general way, most of the previously referred to complex tasks are available and being used in all ICS, even though they need improvements. However the infection module is being used in only one of the hospitals, and the complications module is not being used at all. In all cases, users believe the complex modules should be improved because they are difficult to use, and yet very important.

Requirements related to the usability of ICS's modules will be further specified, as some ICU tasks are difficult to perform in ICS, and therefore do not have the acceptance they could have otherwise. Requirements related to mobility might be included too, as usually there are few computer terminals within the ICS and a terminal in each MD's office. It might be interesting to have a mobility study to determine whether it would be reasonable to have mobile devices to register patients' data.

4 Future Work

The next step in this study is to do a heuristic evaluation of the most relevant ICS modules to find out the most obvious HCI problems. This evaluation will provide the basis to a first set of much more specific user centred requirements [5].

Afterwards, there will be some field observations where several users will be followed while they perform their everyday tasks in the ICU they belong to. This task will require careful preparation due to the place where ICS works, and involve the permission from the Ethical Committee of the hospitals involved.

After that, a new set of interviews will be performed to deepen the knowledge about ICS's usability problems. A larger number of stakeholders will be interviewed.

When the previous steps are fully documented, a focus group will be conducted, that will gather several MDs from different ICUs. This is expected to be one of the main contributors to the final requirements specification for the evolution of ICS [6].

In the final stage of the evaluation, some prototyping will be made to support the requirements specification and validation by ICS's main stakeholders [7] [6].

5 Conclusions

ICS is a product that meets the majority of the ICU needs, but its users feel it has some unresolved usability problems and expect them to be solved. There is a clear objective to expand ICS to other ICUs in Portugal, but usability problems need to be eliminated. The main usability problems in ICS are related to the way complex ICU activities are implemented. They are described as being complex by themselves and difficult to work with in ICS.

A formal HCI evaluation is being conducted with the objective of finding ICS's usability problems. After the evaluation is finished, there will be new requirements for the system evolution that concern HCI improvements for ICS.

After these requirements are implemented in the system, ICS is expected to be a much more effective and pleasant application to work with, and therefore, a much more successful product.

References

1. Pereira, A.d.C. and T. Fonseca, *intensive.care Reference Manual*, SBIM, Editor. 2005.
2. Ghiglione, R. and B. Matalon, *O Inquérito – Teoria e prática*. Third Edition ed. 1997: Celta.
3. Gosbee, J. and E. Ritchie, *Human-Computer Interaction and Medical Software Development*. Interactions (ACM), 1997. **nr. 4**(4): p. pag. 13-18.
4. Santos, M.S., J.F. Cunha, and A.C. Pereira, *Internal Report, submitted to the 11th International Workshop on Design, Specification, and Verification of Interactive Systems, DSV-IS 2006*. 2006, Gavin Doherty, Ann Blandford (organizers): Dublin, Ireland.
5. Nielsen, J., *Usability Engineering*. 1993: Morgan Kaufman.
6. Preece, J., Y. Rogers, and H. Sharp, *Interaction Design – beyond human-computer interaction*. 2002: John Wiley & Sons, Inc.
7. Rudd, J., K. Stern, and S. Isensee, *Low vs. high-fidelity prototyping debate*. interactions, 1996. **3**(1): p. 76-85.
8. Nielsen, J. *How to Conduct a Heuristic Evaluation (http://www.useit.com/ Feb 2006)*. [Web Site] 2006 [cited Feb 2006]; Available from: http://www.useit.com/papers/heuristic/heuristic_evaluation.html.

INDICE DE AUTORES

A

Abrahão, Silvia, Universidad Politécnica de Valencia (España)
Afonso, Ricardo, Grupo de Tecnologias da Informação em Saúde (Brasil)
Albani de Carvalho, Victorio, Universidade Federal do Espírito Santo (Brasil)
Alentar, Fernanda, Universidade Federal de Pernambuco (Brazil)
Anaya, Raquel, Universidad EAFIT (Colombia)
Andrade Brito, Regiane, Universidade Federal de Pernambuco (Brasil)
Andriano, Natalia, GSG (Argentina)
Arango I., Fernando, Universidad Nacional de Colombia (Colombia)
Argenton Ramos, Ricardo, Universidade Federal de Pernambuco (Brasil)

B

Balzarini, Mónica, Universidad Nacional de Córdoba (Argentina)
Bergmann, Ulf, Seção de Engenharia de Computação e Telemática (Brazil)
Bidart F., Catherine, Empresas TUXPAN (Chile)
Brogi, Antonio, University of Pisa (Italy)

C

Camps, Rafael, Universitat Politècnica de Catalunya (Spain)
Carvalho, André, Universidade Federal de Pernambuco (Brasil)
Casallas, Rubby, Universidad de los Andes (Colombia)
Casas, Sandra I., Universidad Nacional de la Patagonia Austral (Argentina)
Castro, Jaelson, Universidade Federal de Pernambuco (Brazil)
Cechich, Alejandra, Universidad Nacional del Comahue (Argentina)
Celma, Matilde, Universidad politécnica de Valencia (España)
Centeno, Elena, Universidad Nacional de La Patagonia San Juan Bosco (Argentina)
Cernuzzi, Luca, Universidad Católica "Nuestra Señora de la Asunción" (Paraguay)
Cetina, Carlos, Universidad Politécnica de Valencia (Spain)
Chiotti, Omar, Universidad Tecnológica Nacional (Argentina)
Choren, Ricardo, Seção de Engenharia de Computação e Telemática (Brazil)
Condori-Fernández, Nelly, Universidad Politécnica de Valencia (España)
Covella, Guillermo, Universidad Nacional de La Pampa (Argentina)
Cuadra, Dolores, Universidad Carlos-III (Spain)

D

Da Costa Pereira, Altamiro, Universidade do Porto (Portugal)
Da S. Torres, Ricardo, Universidade Estadual de Campinas (Brasil)
De Almeida Falbo, Ricardo, Universidade Federal do Espírito Santo (Brasil)
De Oliveira Arantes, Lucas, Universidade Federal do Espírito Santo (Brasil)
Dias Belchior, Arnaldo, Universidade de Fortaleza (Brasil)
Díaz, Miguel, Universidad Nacional del Centro (Argentina)

E

Escalona Cuaresma, María J., Universidade de Sevilha (Espanha)
España, Sergio, Inés Pederiva, Universidad Politécnica de Valencia (España)
Falcão e Cunha, João, Universidade do Porto (Portugal)
Fernández-Medina, Eduardo, Universidad de Castilla-La Mancha (España)
Ferreira Barcelos, Rafael, Universidade Federal do Rio de Janeiro (Brasil)

Fontoura, Lisandra M., Universidade Federal do Rio Grande do Sul (Brasil)

G

Galvão Martins, Luiz Eduardo, Universidade Metodista de Piracicaba (Brasil)
García Perez-Schofield, J. Baltasar, Universidad deVigo (España)
García, Félix, Universidad de Castilla-La Mancha (España)
García, Rafael, Universidad de los Andes (Colombia)
Gonnet, Silvio, Universidad Tecnológica Nacional (Argentina)

H

Haak, Betina, Universidad Nacional del Centro (Argentina)
Hartmann, Júlio, Universidade Federal do Rio Grande do Sul (Brasil)
Hurtado, Julio Ariel, Universidad del Cauca (Colombia)

J

Jaramillo, Aldrin Fredy, Universidad de Antioquia (Colombia)
Jiménez C., Jorge, Empresas TUXPAN (Chile)

K

Katrib, Miguel, Universidad de La Habana (Cuba)

L

Lencastre, Maria, Universidade Federal de Pernambuco (Brasil)
Leone, Horacio, Universidad Tecnológica Nacional (Argentina)
Lins de Vasconcelos, Alexandre, Serviço Federal de Processamento de Dados (Brasil)
Londoño, Luís Fernando, Avansoft S.A. (Colombia)
López Sanz, Marcos, Universidad Rey Juan Carlos (España)
Louvadino Junior, Dério, Universidade Metodista de Piracicaba (Brasil)

M

Marcos, Claudia A., Universidad Nacional del Centro (Argentina)
Marcos, Esperanza, Universidad Rey Juan Carlos (España)
Martins, Eliane, Universidade Estadual de Campinas (Brasil)
Medeiros Jr., Raul A., Universidade de Fortaleza (Brasil)
Mellado, Daniel, Ministerio de Trabajo y Asuntos Sociales (España)
Mengoni, Luciano, LIFIA, UNLP (Argentina)
Monteiro, Cleviton, Universidade Federal de Pernambuco (Brasil)
Muñoz, Javier, Universidad Politécnica de Valencia (Spain)

N

Nardo, Julio Cesar, Universidade Federal do Espírito Santo (Brasil)
Nasser Matos, Simone, Universidade Tecnológica Federal do Paraná (Brasil)
Nieto, Andrés, LIFIA, UNLP (Argentina)
Nuño Silva, Liliana, LIFIA, UNLP (Argentina)

O

Ochoa, Sergio F., Universidad de Chile (Chile)
Oliveros, Alejandro, Universidad de Buenos Aires (Argentina)
Olsina, Luis, Universidad Nacional de La Pampa (Argentina)
Ormeño, Emilio G., Universidad Nacional de San Juan (Argentina)

P

Panach, José Ignacio, Universidad Politécnica de Valencia (España)
Parra, Oscar, Universidad Católica "Nuestra Señora de la Asunción" (Paraguay)
Pastor, Óscar, Universidad Politécnica de Valencia (España)
Pastrana, José L., Universidad de Málaga (España)
Pedroza, Flavio, Federal University of Pernambuco (Brazil)
Pelechado, Vicente, Universidad Politécnica de Valencia (Spain)
Piattini, Mario, Universidad de Castilla-La Mancha (España)
Pimentel, Ernesto, Universidad de Málaga (España)
Popescu, Razvan, University of Pisa (Italy)
Porfírio M. Farias, Pedro, Universidade de Fortaleza (Brasil)
Prieto, Iván, Universidad Católica "Nuestra Señora de la Asunción" (Paraguay)
Prior, Jane, Universidad Nacional del Centro (Argentina)

R

Ramos, Ricardo, Universidade Federal de Pernambuco (Brazil)
Rocha, Camilo, Escuela Colombiana de Ingeniería (Colombia)
Rodríguez Alfonso, Universidad del Bio Bio (Chile)
Rodríguez Mier, Mario, Microsoft (Argentina)
Roldán, M. Luciana, Universidad Tecnológica Nacional (Argentina)
Rolón, Elvira, Universidad Autónoma de Tamaulipas (México)
Ruiz , Francisco, Universidad de Castilla-La Mancha (España)

S

Salomone, Enrique, Universidad Tecnológica Nacional (Argentina)
Santos, Leonardo, Seção de Engenharia de Computação e Telemática (Brazil)
Santos, Mónica S., Universidade do Porto / Instituto Politécnico do Porto (Portugal)
Serral, Estefanía, Universidad Politécnica de Valencia (Spain)
Silva, Carla, Universidade Federal de Pernambuco (Brasil)

T

Tom Price, Roberto, Universidade Federal do Rio Grande do Sul (Brasil)
Torres Fernández, Clovis, Universidade Tecnológica Federal do Paraná (Brasil)
Torres-Zenteno, Arturo H., Universidade Estadual de Campinas (Brasil)
Travassos, Guilherme H., Universidade Federal do Rio de Janeiro (Brasil)

V

Valeria de Castro, Universidad Rey Juan Carlos (España)
Vela, Belén, Universidad Rey Juan Carlos (España)
Villarreal, Pablo David, Universidad Tecnológica Nacional (Argentina)

Z

Zapata J., Carlos Mario, Universidad Nacional de Colombia (Colombia)
Zepeda, Leopoldo, Universidad politécnica de Valencia (España)

CIbSE - IberoAmerican Conference on Software Engineering
c/o Luca Cernuzzi
Universidad Católica "Nuestra Seóra de la Asunción",
Campus Universitario, Asunción
Barrio Santa Ana, C.C.1683, C.P. 1364
Asunción - Paraguay

ISBN 978-1-5108-4100-0
9 781510 841000

CURRAN ASSOCIATES INC.
proceedings.com

12th International Conference on Strategic Management and Its Support by Information Systems 2017

Ostrava, Czech Republic
25 – 26 May 2017